The SAGE Handbook of
Persuasion

Second Edition

We dedicate this book to Michael Pfau: a scholar, a colleague, and a friend.

The SAGE Handbook of
Persuasion
Second Edition

Developments in Theory and Practice

Edited by

James Price Dillard
Pennsylvania State University

Lijiang Shen
University of Georgia

Los Angeles | London | New Delhi
Singapore | Washington DC

HM
1196
.P47
2013

SAGE

Los Angeles | London | New Delhi
Singapore | Washington DC

FOR INFORMATION:

SAGE Publications, Inc.
2455 Teller Road
Thousand Oaks, California 91320
E-mail: order@sagepub.com

SAGE Publications Ltd.
1 Oliver's Yard
55 City Road
London EC1Y 1SP
United Kingdom

SAGE Publications India Pvt. Ltd.
B 1/I 1 Mohan Cooperative Industrial Area
Mathura Road, New Delhi 110 044
India

SAGE Publications Asia-Pacific Pte. Ltd.
3 Church Street
#10-04 Samsung Hub
Singapore 049483

Acquisitions Editor: Matthew Byrnie
Editorial Assistant: Stephanie Palermini
Production Editor: Laura Stewart
Copy Editor: Amy Freitag
Typesetter: C&M Digitals (P) Ltd.
Proofreader: Jennifer Gritt
Indexer: Wendy Allex
Cover Designer: Candice Harman
Marketing Manager: Liz Thornton
Permissions Editor: Karen Ehrmann

Printed in the United States of America

Library of Congress Cataloging-in-Publication Data

The SAGE handbook of persuasion : developments in theory and practice / edited by James Price Dillard, Lijiang Shen. — 2nd ed.

p. cm.
Includes bibliographical references and index.

ISBN 978-1-4129-8313-6 (cloth)

1. Persuasion (Psychology)—Social aspects.
2. Persuasion (Rhetoric) I. Dillard, James Price.
II. Shen, Lijiang. III. Title: Handbook of persuasion.

HM1196.P47
2013 153.8′52—dc23   2012017340

This book is printed on acid-free paper.

SFI Certified Sourcing
www.sfiprogram.org
SFI-00453

12 13 14 15 16 10 9 8 7 6 5 4 3 2 1

Contents

PART I

Fundamental Issues

CHAPTER 1

Persuasion in
the Rhetorical Tradition

J. Michael Hogan

The study of persuasion can be traced back to ancient Greece, the birthplace of both rhetoric and democracy. As Dillard and Pfau (2002) noted in the first edition of *The Persuasion Handbook*, Aristotle "provided the first comprehensive theory of rhetorical discourse" (p. ix) in the fifth century BCE, and persuasion was central to that theory. Yet persuasion has not always been at the center of rhetorical theory. During the Enlightenment, the scope of rhetoric broadened to include aesthetic and psychological concerns, rendering persuasion secondary to considerations of "taste" and "sympathy." More recently, narrative and dramatistic theories of rhetoric have emphasized identity or "identification" over persuasion, and some rhetorical scholars have even denounced persuasion as a mechanism of "control and domination" (Foss & Griffin, 1995, p. 2). Still, persuasion has remained a dominant theme in the rhetorical tradition, with two broad concerns distinguishing the rhetorical perspective from more scientific or empirical approaches to persuasion: a focus on the *political* or *civic* contexts of persuasion, and an overriding emphasis on *ethical* concerns.

In this chapter, I survey the rhetorical tradition with a view toward illuminating some of the differing, even competing, perspectives on persuasion over the long history of rhetorical studies. In the process I highlight two cultural imperatives that help to account for the emphasis on politics and ethics in the Western rhetorical tradition: (1) the need to educate for citizenship, and (2) an ongoing debate over the rules or norms of democratic deliberation. In the rhetorical tradition, these two imperatives link the study of rhetoric to democratic theory, inspiring normative conceptions of persuasion that emphasize the *responsibilities* that go along with the *right* of free speech in a democracy. By surveying how rhetorical theorists historically have distinguished responsible or legitimate free speech from propaganda and demagoguery, I illuminate the intimate connections between rhetorical theories of persuasion and democracy itself.

I begin by revisiting the classical/humanistic roots of the rhetorical tradition, from the sophists of ancient Greece to the Roman rhetoricians, Cicero and Quintilian. I then sketch the history of rhetorical theory through modern times, including the attack on rhetoric in the early modern period and the impact of the belletristic and elocutionary movements on rhetorical theory. Finally, I consider more recent developments in rhetorical theory, including the influence of Burkean "dramatism," the rise of social movement studies, and the "postmodern" challenge to the rhetorical tradition. As we shall see, many of these more recent developments have been cast as alternatives to the classical/humanistic tradition of persuasion (indeed, some have challenged the very idea of a "rhetorical tradition"). Yet despite these various challenges, the classical tradition's emphasis on the ethics of civic persuasion remains strong in contemporary rhetorical theory and criticism.

In the second section of the chapter, I reflect on the distinctive contributions of the American tradition of rhetoric and public address to the theory and practice of persuasion. Surveying the linkages between America's great experiment in democracy and evolving attitudes toward rhetoric and persuasion, I begin by recalling how the founders' constitutional design reflected a vision of a deliberative democracy grounded in neoclassical rhetorical theory. I then trace how the American rhetorical tradition evolved during the so-called golden age of American oratory, as Jacksonian democracy brought a more populist rhetorical style to American politics and the debate over slavery tested the limits of civic persuasion. I next consider the revival of the American rhetorical tradition during the Progressive Era, as new media, changing demographics, and a culture of professionalization revolutionized the way Americans talked about politics and gave rise to a new "science" of mass persuasion. Finally, I reflect on the impact of new electronic media and the relationship between television and the decline of civic discourse in the closing decades of the 20th century. I conclude with some brief reflections on the contemporary crisis of democracy in America and the efforts of a new, interdisciplinary deliberative democracy movement to revive the public sphere.

The Concept of Persuasion in Rhetorical Theory

The story of rhetoric's roots in ancient Greece has been told many times—and for a variety of purposes. For generations, that story was used to justify speech programs in American colleges and universities. At the height of the Cold War, for example, W. Norwood Brigance, one of the pioneers of the American speech discipline, invoked rhetoric's ancient roots to argue that the teaching of speech was one of the distinguishing marks of a free society. Democracy and the "system of speechmaking were born together," Brigance (1961) wrote, and since ancient times "we have never had a successful democracy unless a large part, a very large part, of its citizens were effective, intelligent, and responsible speakers." According to Brigance, there were only two kinds of people in the modern world: "Those who in disagreements and crises want to *shoot* it out, and those who have learned to *talk* it out." Brigance concluded that if America hoped to remain a "government by talk," it needed leaders who knew how to talk "effectively, intelligently, and responsibly," as well as citizens trained to "listen and judge" (pp. 4–5).

Since Brigance's day, revisionist scholars have told and "retold" rhetoric's story to advance a variety of agendas. In *Rereading the Sophists*, for example, Jarratt (1991) reconsidered the Greek sophists from a feminist perspective and concluded that they were more progressive in their thinking about "social needs" (p. 28) than most of the more prominent figures in the classical tradition. In Jarratt's rereading of the tradition, the sophists provided an alternative to patriarchal rhetoric by privileging "imaginative reconstructions" over "empirical data" (p. 13) and by broadening the purview of rhetoric beyond canonical texts. The sophists also modeled a more collaborative and democratic model of rhetorical education, according to Jarratt—one more consistent with today's best research on critical pedagogy and "social cognition" (p. 92).

The sophists were no doubt important to the rhetorical tradition. But so, too, were Plato, Aristotle, and the great Roman rhetoricians, Cicero and Quintilian. It is important to recognize that no single paradigm defines the classical rhetorical tradition. Rather, that tradition consists of ongoing debates over the philosophical status of rhetoric, the best methods of rhetorical education, and the aims, scope, power, and ethics of rhetoric—indeed, over the very definition of "rhetoric" itself. Yet even as we recognize the rhetorical tradition itself as a dynamic and ongoing set of controversies, we can identify two emphases in the classical tradition that have distinguished the rhetorical perspective ever since: (1) an emphasis on the role of persuasion in *politics* and *civic* life, and (2) an overriding concern with the *moral character* of the speaker and the *ethics* of persuasion.

The Ancient Tradition

The sophists were the original professors of rhetoric in Greece, and they initiated a long tradition of teaching speech and persuasion as education for citizenship. As Hunt (1965) noted, the original sophists were professional teachers who helped meet the need for rhetorical and civic training in Athens, and the term "sophist" initially referred to "any man . . . thought to be learned" (p. 71). Over time, however, the sophists acquired a negative reputation as arrogant and boastful—a reputation that echoed down through the centuries because of a famous dialogue written by their best-known critic, the philosopher Plato. In the *Gorgias*, Plato accused the sophists of teaching students to flatter or pander to their audiences, and Plato's criticisms so impressed succeeding generations that the sophists came to stand for a whole range of human flaws: the "false pretense of knowledge, overweening conceit, fallacious argument, cultivation of style for its own sake, demagoguery, corruption of youth . . . , and, in general, a ready substitution of appearance for reality" (Hunt, 1965, p. 69).

In the master narrative of the rhetorical tradition, Plato's student, Aristotle, rescued rhetoric's reputation by devising an "amoral" or "morally neutral" theory focused purely on *techné*, or the mechanics of persuasive speaking. Leaving ethical questions to the philosophers, Aristotle defined rhetoric as the faculty of "discovering in the particular case . . . the available means of persuasion" (Cooper, 1932, p. 7), and he recognized that this power "could be used either for good or ill" (Kennedy, 1991, p. ix). While Aristotle refrained from grand moral pronouncements, however, he did infuse his rhetorical theory with a strong *ethical* or *normative* component. Emphasizing moral character as a key element in persuasion and celebrating reasoned argument over appeals to the emotions, Aristotle's rhetoric was hardly morally neutral about what constituted responsible persuasion in civic life. Moreover, his vision of civic persuasion demanded broad learning in philosophy, history, literature, and human psychology. For Aristotle, rhetoric was not only a *moral* but also an *architectonic* art, encompassing all realms of humanistic and scientific understanding.

Similarly, Isocrates, one of the later sophists, responded to Plato's attack on rhetoric by rejecting both the empty and commercialized speech of his fellow sophists *and* the abstract philosophizing of Plato and the Socratics. Rather than mere *techné*, Isocrates viewed rhetoric as a means for educating students to "think and speak noble, virtuous ideas" and to "implement them in civic policy" (Kennedy, 1991, p. 11). For Isocrates, the ultimate goal of a rhetorical education was not to prepare students for personal success, but to train them for public service and "inspire the political life of [the] nation with a higher moral creed" (Jaeger, 1965, p. 108). The ethical and civic spirit of the Greek rhetoricians was even stronger in the writings of the Roman rhetoricians, Cicero and Quintilian. Bringing a more pragmatic, pedagogical emphasis to the study of rhetoric, the Romans added little to the Greeks' repertoire of persuasive techniques. In systematizing rhetorical instruction and grounding it in a theory of civic republicanism, however, they painted a portrait of the ideal citizen in a free republic and upheld a high moral standard: the "common good." For the Romans, the ideal orator was not merely one with "exceptional gifts of speech," but also a "good man" with "all the excellences of character" (Butler, 1969, pp. 9–11). They considered the principles of moral conduct an integral part of the rhetorical art, not something to be left to the ethicists or philosophers.

Cicero's chief contribution to the theory of civic rhetoric was his emphasis on the practical or functional aspects of the art, which he elucidated from the perspective of a practicing orator. As the "most eminent orator of Roman civilization" (Baldwin, 1924, p. 43), Cicero aspired to restore the art of rhetoric to its exalted status in Greek civilization, and he was "influenced and guided" in this effort "by the doctrines of Isocrates," whom he regarded as the "father of eloquence" (Thonssen & Baird, 1948, p. 81). Like Isocrates, Cicero painted a portrait of the ideal orator as an engaged citizen of high moral character and broad learning, one devoted not to his own selfish interests but to the "common good." In the first book of his most important work, *De Oratore*, Cicero lamented the scarcity of great orators in his own day and blamed that problem on the "incredible vastness and difficulty of the subject" (Sutton & Rackham, 1983, p. 13). In addition to "knowledge of very many matters," Cicero's ideal orator mastered the psychology of the human emotions, stocked his memory with "the complete history of the past," and commanded a "store of precedents" grounded in both "statute law and our national law" (p. 15). Then he had to deliver all that knowledge effectively, with the voice, facial expressions, physical gestures, and the movement of the body all carefully regulated. For Cicero, true eloquence demanded training "in all the liberal arts" (p. 55), as well as mastery of the "moral science" of "human life and conduct" (pp. 50–51).

Like Cicero, Quintilian was concerned about the paucity of great orators in the Roman republic. At a time when politics and public morals in Rome had declined to a "savage low" (Murphy, 1965, p. xiii), he aspired to nothing short of a cultural revolution through rhetorical education. Quintilian's monumental four-volume work, *Institutio Oratoria* (Butler, 1969), was the "most ambitious single treatise on education" produced by the ancient world (Murphy, 1965, p. xi), and it set out a program for educating the citizen-orator from cradle to grave. More than just a handbook of rhetoric, Quintilian's *Institutio* placed at least as much emphasis on developing moral character as oratorical skills. For Quintilian, it was not enough that young men grew up to be effective orators; they also needed to be broadly educated and morally principled, capable of "analysis, reflection, and then powerful action in public affairs" (Murphy, 1965, p. xx). In the "dissolute society of his time," Quintilian's emphasis on "moral principle as a factor in education" made a most "profound impression" (Murphy, 1965, p. viii), and his portrait of the ideal citizen has been passed down through the ages in a phrase familiar to every student of classical rhetoric: the "good man speaking well."

Much of the modern scholarship on the classical/humanist tradition has emphasized the differences among these various "schools" of rhetoric in the ancient world. Yet a common thread ran through all of classical rhetoric: the need to educate for citizenship. Concerned with the practical and ethical requirements of civic life, the ancient rhetoricians aspired to equip young people with the skills and knowledge they would need to be citizens in a free society. All recognized the need for rules of civic persuasion, and they all imagined some ideal orator—a speaker who embodied civic virtue and a commitment to the "common good." As Garsten (2006) has concluded, the ancient rhetorical tradition constituted a "politics of persuasion" where both leaders and ordinary citizens possessed "a certain moral compass" that served as a check on demagoguery and allowed for "responsible judgment" in civic affairs (p. 146). It was a tradition that, as we shall see later, had great appeal to America's founders.

The Modern Era

Over the centuries, there have been a number of challenges to the classical tradition, including alternatives to its emphasis on persuasion in civic life. In this section, I provide a brief overview of the philosophical critique of the classical rhetorical tradition that emerged in the early modern era. I then take a closer look at the alternative paradigm that emerged across the 18th and 19th centuries—a period that Golden and Corbett (1968) have called one of the "most prolific eras in rhetorical history" (p. 7). During this time, British and American rhetoricians shifted the emphasis in rhetorical theory from persuasion to the aesthetic, literary, and performative dimensions of discourse, and they dramatically broadened the scope of rhetoric to include written and literary forms.

The beginnings of what Garsten (2006) has characterized as the early modern "attack on rhetoric" (p. 10) can be traced to the rise of political and religious fanaticism in the sixteenth and seventeenth centuries. Fearing the effects of demoguery on public opinion, philosophers such as Hobbes, Rousseau, and Kant searched for some unitary and authoritative source of public judgment to replace the everyday opinions of ordinary citizens, in effect "asking citizens to distance themselves from their private judgments and to judge from a sovereign, unitary, public standpoint instead" (p. 11). Hobbes alternative was expressed in a "rhetoric of representation"; for Rousseau and Kant the alternatives were a "rhetoric of prophetic nationalism" (seeking to "instill in citizens a prerational, quasi-religious sense of sympathetic identification with their fellow citizens") and a "rhetoric of public reason" (calling on ordinary citizens to defer to philosophers who had achieved a higher level of "enlightenment"). According to Garsten, all of these "rhetorics against rhetoric" undermined "the classical humanist tradition" by downplaying the role of persuasion and individual judgment in politics. They also contributed to an "aestheticization" of rhetoric that

transformed it into "a literary enterprise rather than a political one" (pp. 11–12).

This "aestheticization of rhetoric" was most obvious in the belletristic movement of the late 18th century. Led by Hugh Blair and George Campbell, this movement combined the study of rhetoric and "polite arts" (including poetry, drama, and even biography and history) into a common discipline, with an emphasis on taste, style, culture, and critical analysis. In his enormously influential *Lectures on Rhetoric and Belles Lettres* (1965), for example, Blair devoted only 10 of his 47 lectures to eloquence and public speaking, while he committed four lectures to "taste," four to "language," fifteen to "style," and thirteen to the "critical examination of the most distinguished *species of composition,* both in prose and verse" (Vol. 1, p. xi). For Blair and other belletristic writers, there was no real distinction between oral and written rhetoric, nor did they draw firm distinctions between expository, literary, and persuasive genres of discourse. Moreover, they believed that the same principles might guide both rhetorical practitioners and critics of public discourse.

The belletristic rhetorics represented the first real alternative to the classical tradition, as they radically expanded the scope of the discipline and elevated the importance of concepts that had been neglected by the classical rhetoricians, such as taste, style, sympathy, and sublimity. The belletristic movement also reflected some larger intellectual trends at the time, including "a pervasive enthusiasm for the newly developing empirical method, a commitment to rationalism, a curiosity to understand human nature and man's relationship to God, a preoccupation with the origin and use of language, and an appreciation of the potentialities of persuasion as a force in a democracy and in a Christian society" (Golden & Corbett, 1968, p. 7). In contrast to the classical tradition, the belletristic rhetoricians paid little attention to the canon of *invention* (Blair's *Lectures,* for example, had no separate chapters on argumentation, reasoning, or evidence). They also emphasized emotion over reason, distinguishing between "conviction" and "persuasion" and associating the latter with the human passions. In all of these senses, then, there was clearly something "new" about these so-called "new rhetorics." Not only were they more "scientific," but also much broader in scope, embracing expository and literary forms of discourse as well as civic persuasion.

Not all modern rhetoricians shared the belletristic rhetoricians' interest in "style" and "taste"—their "aestheticization" of rhetoric. Some, like John Ward (1759), remained slavishly devoted to the classical tradition, writing monumental yet wholly unoriginal restatements of classical doctrines (Golden & Corbett, 1968, p. 7). Others responded to complaints about the decline of oratory by writing detailed handbooks on vocal and nonverbal delivery, including elaborate taxonomies of facial expressions and gestures. These modern elaborations on the canon of delivery became so popular as to constitute yet another major trend in the history of rhetoric: the "Elocutionary Movement" (Cohen, 1994, pp. 1–12). Yet by conceding concern with the substantive content of discourse to other disciplines, the Elocutionary Movement only contributed further to the marginalization of rhetoric.

In sum, the classical tradition was never supplanted entirely by the modern or "new rhetorics" of the 18th and 19th centuries. The ancients still had their champions, and the elocutionists at least preserved the study of speech as a distinctive discipline—albeit one focused narrowly on the performative dimensions of rhetoric. Most of the "modern" rhetoricians continued to acknowledge their debt to the ancients, and most still embraced the ancient view of the purposes of rhetorical education. Reflecting the spirit of Quintilian, for example, Hugh Blair argued that the goal of rhetorical pedagogy should be to prepare well-rounded, liberally educated, and morally virtuous citizens. Nevertheless, neither Blair nor any of the other modern rhetoricians treated civic discourse as the primary focus of rhetoric. Even those who did focus on argumentation and persuasion, like Richard Whately, seemed "strangely aloof" from the world of politics, making "few references to contemporary economic and political problems" (Whately, 1963, p. xii).

Not surprisingly, many of these trends became even more pronounced in the 20th century, including the blurring of the distinction between written and oral discourse, the broadening of the scope of rhetoric, and the treatment of persuasion as but one of many purposes or "ends" of rhetoric. In addition, the study of rhetoric would continue to become more interdisciplinary, as rhetorical theorists explored the connections between rhetoric and literature, religion, history, philosophy, and psychology. In the next section, I describe just a few of the most influential paradigms of contemporary rhetorical theory that accelerated these trends: Burke's "dramatism," Perlman's "new rhetoric," and the social movement and postmodern perspectives on rhetorical theory and criticism.

Persuasion in Contemporary Rhetorical Theory

Few would deny Kenneth Burke's status as the most influential rhetorical theorist of the twentieth century. Long recognized as a literary scholar, the significance of Burke's contributions to rhetoric were first illuminated by Nichols (1952), who distinguished between the "old rhetoric," with its emphasis on "deliberative design" (p. 136), and Burke's "new rhetoric" with its broader perspective on symbolic inducement. According to Nichols, the key difference between the old and the new rhetorics could be summed up by contrasting two words: whereas the key term in the old rhetoric was *persuasion*, Burke's new rhetoric emphasized *identification*, which could refer to a "deliberative device," a "means" of persuasion, an "end" of rhetoric, or even "unconscious" processes of the human mind (p. 136). For Burke, as Day (1960) later observed, identification was a "strategy," but one that encompassed "the whole area of language usage for the purpose of inducement to action or attitude" (p. 271). In other words, as Zappen (2009) argues, Burke's "concept of rhetoric as identification" broadened "the traditional view of rhetoric as persuasion" to include virtually any means of "inducing cooperation and building communities" (p. 279).

Burke's "new rhetoric" appeared at a time of growing dissatisfaction with the constraints of the classical paradigm, and it inspired a variety of new theoretical and critical alternatives over the next half century: the narrative paradigm, fantasy theme analysis, genre studies, social movement studies, and even psychological and visual "turns" in rhetorical theory and criticism. Burke's theorizing changed the way rhetoricians thought about standards of judgment and the concept of "rhetorical effect," and it encouraged new ways of thinking about "audience"—not just as the objects of persuasion, but as active participants in the construction or constitution of meaning and identity (Charland, 1987). This *constitutive* approach represented a fundamentally different way of thinking about the purposes and functions of all sorts of symbolic action, from traditional platform speeches, to visual and nonverbal cues, to music, art, and architecture, to the rhetorics of religion and science. In the Burkean spirit, all human activity was, at some level, "rhetorical," for human beings were the "symbol-using animal[s]" (Burke, 1966, p. 3). Rhetoric, for Burke, encompassed not just persuasion but the broad range of symbolic actions that constituted the drama of human life.

The liberating effect of Burke's "dramatism" was perhaps most evident in the rhetorical study of social movements. Traditionally, rhetorical scholars were inclined to condemn radical speech as unreasonable or ineffective. "Since the time of Aristotle," as Scott and Smith (1969) observed, academic rhetorics had functioned as "instruments of established society, presupposing the 'goods' of order, civility, reason, decorum, and civil or theocratic law" (p. 7). In the 1960s and 1970s, however, rhetorical scholars sought alternatives that might make better sense out of the rhetoric of social movements. Burkean theory provided one such alternative. Focusing on the identity-building functions of movement rhetoric, Burkean theory suggested how rhetorical strategies that might seem counterproductive, irrational, or even coercive by traditional standards might serve to foster group cohesion or dramatize shared grievances. Burke, in other words, opened critics' eyes to the constitutive or "ego-functions" of protest rhetoric (Gregg, 1971, 71–91).

The study of social movement rhetoric thus redefined the "rules" of public discourse, introducing new standards that acknowledged and even celebrated the role of radical speech in a democracy. In 1968, for example, McEdwards proclaimed the "jolting, combative, and passionate" (p. 37) rhetoric of the agitator "a necessary drivewheel of a dynamic democracy" (p. 36) and celebrated both Wendell Phillips and Malcolm X as agents of positive social change. Similarly, Burgess (1968) justified the confrontational, even threatening rhetoric of Black Power activists as their "only strategic choice" and explained that "behind all the sound and fury" was an effort to "force upon the culture a moral decision" (p. 123). A few years later, Windt (1972) even proclaimed the obscene diatribes of the Yippies an expression of their sincere "moral commitments" and a necessary response to circumstances—at least as they perceived them (p. 3). In their efforts to better understand or even justify the "rhetoric of confrontation" (Scott & Smith, 1969), rhetorical scholars argued that civility and decorum too often served as "masks for the preservation of injustice," and they turned to Burkean theories of identity and dramatism to help fashion a rhetorical theory more "suitable to our age" (p. 8).

Feminist rhetorical scholars likewise have developed alternatives to the traditional paradigm. In her pioneering work on the rhetoric of women's liberation, for example, Karlyn Kohrs Campbell (1973) explained that "feminist advocacy" wavered "between . . . the persuasive and the non-persuasive" and called for theoretical perspectives that focused not on "public issues" but on "personal exigences and private, concrete experience" (p. 85). Other feminist theorists have renounced persuasion altogether, insisting that the conscious intent to change others is anathema to feminist thought. "Embedded in efforts to change others," Foss and Griffin (1995) declared, "is a desire for control and domination, for the act of changing another establishes the power of the change agent over that other" (p. 3). Foss and Griffin's alternative, the "invitational" approach, instead invites listeners "to enter the rhetor's world and to see it as the rhetor does" (p. 5). Contrasting the invitational with the persuasive, Bone, Griffin, and Scholz (2008) explain that while "the ontological orientation" of persuasive rhetoric is "the desire to move another rhetor toward accepting a particular position," invitational rhetoric aims instead to "understand the perspectives" of others and to foster "dialogue" that not only allows for "mutual understanding but also self-determination" (p. 446).

The postmodern turn in rhetorical theory might be seen as the ultimate rejection of persuasion-centered theories. Skeptical about the very possibility for human communication and understanding in the "postmodern age," these scholars generally reject traditional notions of human agency and shared meaning. They argue that "the subject of the rhetorical act cannot be regarded as the unified, coherent, autonomous, transcendent subject of liberal humanism," but rather must be viewed as "multiple and conflicted, composed of numerous subject formations or positions" (Berlin, 1992, p. 20). In addition, postmodernists view language not as a "transparent medium" or a "simple signaling device," but rather as a "pluralistic and complex system of signifying practices" that *construct* rather than reflect or simply communicate about external realities (Berlin, 1992, pp. 18–19). For postmodernists, it simply makes no sense to talk about a speaker using language to persuade a group of listeners, as rhetoric traditionally has emphasized. Indeed, some postmodernists reject the idea of a rhetorical tradition itself, insisting that all histories and traditions are "necessarily partial" and work "on behalf of some interests to

the disadvantage of other interests" (Walzer & Beard, 2009, p. 16).

Of course, not all 20th-century rhetorical theorists have rejected the classical tradition's emphasis on persuasion, civic discourse, and the ethics of speech. Most notably, Chaim Perleman and Lucie Olbrechts-Tyteca, in their influential *New Rhetoric* (1969), drew heavily on the classical tradition to develop a theory of practical or "non-formal reasoning" designed to "inform value choices and action" in law, politics, and everyday life (Frank & Bolduc, 2010, p. 145). Although Perelman and Olbrechts-Tyteca went well beyond the ancients' emphasis on persuasive *speaking*, their concept of a "universal audience" reflected the same concern for the moral or ethical foundations of rhetoric (Ray, 1978), and they ultimately sought to answer the same basic questions as the Greek and Roman rhetoricians: How do we distinguish "good" from "bad" arguments? What separates "reasonable" attempts to persuade from propaganda or demagoguery? What sorts of standards or "rules" of speech and debate should prevail in a free society? And how might we best educate citizens to be responsible, effective participants in the civic dialogue?

As we continue to grapple with these questions, it is useful to follow the example of Perlman and Olbrechts-Tyteca, who looked beyond the writings of rhetorical theorists and philosophers to consider how the ethical and pragmatic standards of public discourse are actually manifested in practice. In the second half of this chapter, I do just that by surveying the history and traditions of American public address in an effort to show how the "rules" governing civic persuasion have been tested and revised over the course of our nation's history.

The American Tradition of Rhetoric and Public Address

The American rhetorical tradition is a dynamic tradition marked by a series of transformative "moments"—moments when the "rules" of public discourse changed. Those moments begin, of course, with the American Revolution itself, when America's founders created a government "of the people," despite strong fears of the power of demagogues to manipulate public opinion. A half century later, the democratization of American politics brought about a more "populist" style of political speech, yet even the so-called golden age of American oratory ultimately degenerated into demagoguery and war. After a prolonged period of political and cultural malaise, the Progressive Era brought another renaissance of rhetoric and public address, along with a revolution in the science and technologies of mass persuasion. Yet that era too ended in war and cultural decline. Through the remainder of the 20th century, political developments, new technologies, and cultural trends continued to change the character and rules of civic persuasion in America. Today, however, we still face the same rhetorical challenge that democracies have always faced: how to promote democratic deliberations that lead to sound collective decisions.

The Founders' Vision of Deliberative Democracy

The central paradox of America's constitutional tradition lies in a persistent tension between our commitment to popular sovereignty and fears that "the people" might be too easily distracted or manipulated to govern themselves. America's founders infused the concept of popular sovereignty with extraordinary meaning, creating the first government in history that derived all of its power "directly or indirectly from the great body of the people" (Rossiter, 1961, p. 241). At the same time, however, they worried that the people might too easily be led astray by "the wiles of parasites and sycophants, by the snares of the ambitious, the avaricious, [or] the desperate" (Rossiter, 1961, p. 432). This tension was evident in what Rossiter (1961) described as the "split personality" of the *Federalist* papers (p. xv): the seemingly mixed feelings about a government "of

the people" in that famous series of articles advocating ratification of the new Constitution.

This split personality is also evident in the Constitution itself, most notably in its provisions for a bicameral legislative branch. On the one hand, the House of Representatives was to have "a common interest," a "dependence on," even an "intimate sympathy" with "the people." It was to provide a "true picture of the people, possess a knowledge of their circumstances and their wants, sympathize in all their distresses, and [be] disposed to seek their true interest" (Wood, 1969, p. 515). The Senate, on the other hand, was to be more insulated from the people—a "defense to the people against their own temporary errors and delusions" (Rossiter, 1961, p. 384). Especially in foreign affairs, Alexander Hamilton (1974) argued, it was important to protect policy-making from the "prejudices," the "intemperate passions," and the "fluctuations" of the popular will (Vol. 2, p. 301). As James Madison explained in *Federalist* 63, there were "particular moments in public affairs" when the people, "stimulated by some irregular passion," would demand measures which they themselves would "afterwards be the most ready to lament and condemn." At such times, the Senate (a "temperate and respectable body") was "to suspend the blow mediated by the people against themselves," until "reason, justice, and truth" could "regain their authority over the public mind" (Rossiter, 1961, p. 384).

The founders' attitudes toward persuasion and demagoguery reflected their neoclassical rhetorical training. As Kraig (2003) has observed, the founders lived in a "rhetorical world" where a classical rhetorical education was considered necessary for civic leadership and where "statesmen were expected to be orators" (p. 3). At the time of the Revolution, historian Wood (1974) has noted, classical rhetoric "lay at the heart of [a] . . . liberal education," and the ability to deliver an eloquent and persuasive speech was "regarded as a necessary mark of a gentleman and an indispensible skill for a statesman, especially for a statesman in a republic" (p. 70). At the same time, the founders shared the ancients' fear of deceptive or manipulative speech, and they regarded demagoguery—speech that flattered or aroused the masses—as "the peculiar vice to which democracies were susceptible" (Tulis, 1987, p. 28). Thus, they built buffers against demagoguery and public passion into the Constitution itself. Still, they still worried that, without leaders of the highest moral character, their great experiment in democracy would fail.

The neoclassical tradition remained dominant in American politics and education throughout the early republic. As the first Boylston Chair of Rhetoric and Oratory at Harvard, for example, John Quincy Adams (1810) fashioned himself an "American Cicero" (Portolano, 2009, pp. 13–51), teaching a brand of neoclassical rhetoric specifically designed for the American political context. With a heavy emphasis on the ethical responsibilities of the orator-statesman, Adams approached rhetoric as a "system of deliberative invention and social engagement," and he had a distinctively republican "vision for the use of the art of rhetoric in moral leadership" (Portolano, 2009, pp. x–xi). Adams was familiar with Blair and other modern rhetoricians, yet he drew his teachings almost entirely from the ancients, transplanting Cicero's ideal of "statecraft and leadership, the *orator perfectus*, to American soil" (Portolano, 2009, p. 5). Drawing upon "Christian ethical touchstones," Adams' rhetoric had a certain "religious quality" that distinguished it from the classical tradition (Portolono, 2009, pp. 26–27), but he emphasized the same rhetorical and civic virtues: broad liberal learning, a commitment to reason, and a devotion to service and the public good.

Over the first half of the 19th century, political and cultural developments began to chip away at the neoclassical tradition in American politics and culture. Raising new challenges to the founders' vision, uprisings like the Whiskey Rebellion resurrected fears of demagoguery, and the rise of Jacksonian democracy in the 1830s brought populist "rabble-rousing" to the mainstream of American politics. The "rules" of civic discourse would continue to evolve through the 1840s and the 1850s, but the question of slavery would ultimately test the limits of democratic persuasion. For a time, the nation managed to defer the issue through a series of historic compromises, but Lincoln ultimately proved right: the nation could not endure "permanently half slave and half free" (Reid & Klumpp, 2005, p. 399). By 1860, the debate over slavery had degenerated into a toxic rhetorical mixture of conspiracy theories and ultimatums, and the issue would finally have to be settled not through persuasion but by force of arms.

The Golden Age of Oratory and the Limits of Persuasion

Between ratification of the Constitution and the election of Abraham Lincoln in 1860, new styles of public address gained favor, reflecting changing political circumstances and an expanding democratic public. Jacksonian democracy brought a more populist style to American politics, while the years leading up to the Civil War—the so-called golden age of American oratory—produced a series of great speeches and debates on the two most intractable issues in U.S. history: slavery and union. The golden age is remembered for high eloquence, dramatic debates on the floor of Congress, and universal admiration for the great orators of the day (especially the Great Triumvarite of Webster, Clay, and Calhoun). At the same time, however, it was marred by propaganda and demagoguery on both sides of the slavery issue. For some, the golden age remains a nostalgic memory, a time of "grandiloquence" when "virtuosos" like Webster demonstrated their "prudence and erudition" from the public platform and people flocked to hear serious oratory on the Chautauqua and Lyceum circuits (Duffy & Leeman, 2005, pp. xi–xxv). Yet culminating in the bloodiest war in U.S. history, the golden age also might be seen as a case study in the *limits* of persuasion.

Slavery was not the first issue to threaten the founders' "great experiment" in democracy.

In 1798, the Federalist Party of Washington and Adams passed the Alien and Sedition Acts, which (among other things) made it a crime to make "false, scandalous, and malicious" statements about the government. In effect, the new legislation criminalized political opposition, creating a political backlash that helped elect Thomas Jefferson president in 1800. Some doubted that the Federalists would peacefully relinquish power, while others urged Jefferson to turn the Sedition law against its authors. Instead, Jefferson delivered perhaps the most magnanimous inaugural address in history, labeling the bitter election a mere "contest of opinion" and announcing that all Americans would, *of course*, now "unite in common efforts for the common good." "We are all republicans—we are all federalists," Jefferson intoned. "If there be any among us who would wish to dissolve this Union or to change its republican form, let them stand undisturbed as monuments of the safety with which error of opinion may be tolerated where reason is left free to combat it" (Reid & Klumpp, 2005, p. 205).

Other threats to the founders' vision were more subtle but even more far-reaching in their implications and effects. When a trend toward presidential candidates appealing directly to the people culminated in the election of Andrew Jackson in 1828, some worried that the founders' worst fears had been realized; demagoguery and mob rule would now be the order of the day. Criticizing President Jackson's bank veto message in 1832, for example, Daniel Webster complained of the president's "reprehensible means for influencing public opinion," and he accused him of appealing to "every prejudice" and "every passion" to persuade the public to a "mistaken view of their own interests" (Kraig, 2003, p. 11). However, it was Webster's own party, the Whigs, who pioneered the use of slogans, songs, parades, and rabble-rousing stump speeches in presidential campaigns. Ten years earlier, Webster had delivered what many still regard as "the most eloquent speech ever delivered in Congress" (Nevins, 1947, p. 288): his first reply to Hayne during the Webster-Hayne debate. By 1840, however, Webster found himself defending the populist hoopla of William Henry Harrison's Log Cabin campaign: "It is our duty to spare no pains to circulate information, and to spread the truth far and wide" (Kraig, 2003, p. 12).

Still, Webster continued to draw the line between such mainstream populism and the propaganda and demagoguery on *both* sides of the slavery debate. With radical abolitionists and pro-slavery zealots questioning the motives and character of their political opponents, Webster took to the floor of the Senate to warn metaphorically of the dangers posed by demonization, conspiracy theories, and other forms of radical speech. In both the North and the "stormy South," he warned during debate over the Compromise of 1850, the "strong agitations" threatened to "let loose" the "imprisoned winds" of passion and throw "the whole sea into commotion," tossing its "billows to the skies" and disclosing "its profoundest depths." Reminding the Senate of its "own dignity and its own high responsibilities," Webster argued that the country looked to the senators "for wise, moderate, patriotic, and healing counsels," and he urged his colleagues to think of the "good of the whole, and the preservation of all": "I speak to-day for the preservation of the Union. . . . I speak to-day, out of a solicitous and anxious heart, for the restoration . . . of that quiet and that harmony which make the blessings of this Union so rich, and so dear to us all" (Reid & Klumpp, 2005, pp. 387–388).

Webster's plea went unheeded, of course, and so "the war came"—as Lincoln passively recalled in his Second Inaugural Address (Reid & Klumpp, 2005, p. 461). Everyone knew that slavery was "somehow the cause of the war" (p. 460), as Lincoln noted, but the more direct and proximate cause was the widening rhetorical divide between extremists on both sides of the slavery issue. While abolitionists in the North warned of a Great Slave Power Conspiracy, Fire-Eaters in the South pledged to fight to the death to defend their way of life. Thus, the debate over slavery breached the limits of reason, compromise, and democratic persuasion. Both sides had grown intransigent; there was nothing left to debate.

During the Civil War, Lincoln refrained from the sort of populist rabble-rousing that fueled the hostilities in both the North and the South. Lincoln reflected the populist impulses of the day, but his was a backwoods populism—a "middling style" that was "at times refined but at other times crude" (Cmiel, 1990, pp. 12–13). Lincoln used words like "howdy" and "hornswoggled," but he also *reasoned* with his audiences, engaging them on complex issues and employing archaic language, biblical imagery, and rhythmic cadences in service of lofty ideals. Eschewing the angry, vengeful populism of many of his contemporaries, Lincoln's wartime speeches soared with the eloquence of great literary works, and today we still celebrate them as examples of "the democratic sublime" (Cmiel, 1990, p. 118). Lincoln's speeches often fell on deaf ears, but they live on today as our touchstones of democratic eloquence.

As mass democracy took hold in the Antebellum Era, populist rhetoric thus appeared "in various guises," from the "rank demagoguery" of radicals on both sides of the slavery debate to the "kind of humble nobility" modeled by Lincoln (Cmiel, 1990, p. 12). During the war, of course, rhetoric gave way to the force of arms, and that eclipse of the deliberative public sphere left a rhetorical legacy of degraded and impoverished public talk. Through the trials of Reconstruction and the excesses of the Gilded Age, little of rhetorical note took place, save for the impeachment of Andrew Johnson, a president known as an "obstinate demagogue" inclined toward drunken harangues (Browne, 2008, p. 209). With the dawn of the Progressive Era, however, came another rhetorical renaissance, along with a revolution in the science and technology of mass persuasion.

The Rhetorical Renaissance of the Progressive Era

The Progressive Era is, in a sense, a political fiction. Sparked by the spread of agrarian populism

in the 1890s, this era of supposedly "progressive" reform actually produced even more virulent forms of racial apartheid in the South, as well as foreign policies that were neither forward-looking nor liberal-minded. *Rhetorically*, however, the Progressive Era ushered in new ways of *talking* about politics and social reform, and it eventually gave rise to a new "science" of mass persuasion that revolutionized American politics. Progressives often disagreed over specific policies, and they had very different ideas about what "progress" meant. Yet by inventing new ways of speaking and new forums for democratic deliberation, they revitalized the public sphere and returned *ethics* and *civic responsibility* to the core of the nation's rhetorical tradition.

For many progressives, the essential problem of the age was not poverty, nor government corruption, nor even the industrial monopolies, but rather what John Dewey (1991) would later call "the problem of the public": the need for improvements in "the methods and conditions of debate, discussion, and persuasion" (p. 208). In an increasingly complex world, Progressives feared that powerful special interests had supplanted the voice of the people, and they embraced a variety of "practical measures to increase the quantity, quality, and inclusiveness of public deliberation" (Levine, 2000, p. xiii). Progressives launched a "social centers" movement that opened school buildings to town meetings and debates, and they founded many of the civic and voluntary associations that still exist today. Progressives staged community forums in settlement houses, and they revived the Chautauqua Movement to educate farmers and other rural folk. In small Midwestern cities, they appointed Civic Secretaries to organize public meetings and debates, and they invented school newspapers and student governments to teach young people about politics. Meanwhile, debate and forensics clubs flourished in colleges and universities, and the University of Wisconsin even established a Department of Debating and Public Discussion to promote off-campus public debates on the income tax, woman suffrage, and other issues (Hogan, 2010, p. 439).

The result was what Robert Kraig (2003) has dubbed the "second oratorical renaissance"—an era in which oratory "that advanced issues and ideas became a more important part of the political landscape than it had been for a generation" (p. 99). In political campaigns, on the lecture circuit, and in a variety of crusades led by reform-minded politicians, oratory and debate once again became central to American political and social life. Again there were great debates in Congress, and during this time, the presidency became "a mighty platform for oratorical leadership" (Kraig, 2003, p. 1). Most important, ordinary citizens once again became involved in civic life, in the process learning "the necessary skills of a democratic public: how to listen, how to argue, and how to deliberate" (Mattson, 1998, p. 45). The Progressive Era, in short, was most rhetorical of times.

Yet some of the central terms of the Progressive Era—organization, efficiency, rationality, expertise, and science—also contained the seeds of a very different view of persuasion in a democracy. This view, rarely expressed early in the era but clearly manifested after World War I, was more distrustful of ordinary citizens—and of democracy itself. Convinced that many citizens lacked sufficient virtue and knowledge to discern the "public good," some even pushed for literacy tests and tougher voter registration rules in the name of "good government"—that is, as "progressive" reforms. This view of democracy—the view that an enlightened public opinion had to be directed or even manufactured from above—did not emerge out of some reactionary backlash against progressive reform. Rather, it was implicit in the writings of some of the leading progressive thinkers, including the young Walter Lippmann. In his 1914 book *Drift and Mastery*, for example, Lippmann (1961) proclaimed the "scientific spirit" the "discipline of democracy" (p. 151), and he argued for government guided by experts rather than public opinion—an anti-democratic sentiment that would reach full flower during World War I.

President Wilson's Committee on Public Information (CPI), of course, was the most obvious manifestation of this anti-democratic impulse.

Headed by progressive journalist George Creel, the CPI saturated the popular media with pro-war rhetoric, in the process pioneering many of the modern techniques for manipulating mass opinion. With its "calculated appeal to emotion," the CPI aroused public opinion to "white hot" intensity (Vaughn, 1980, pp. 235–236), and in the process, it radically changed prevailing understandings of mass persuasion and public opinion. Instead of a rational and freely deliberating body, the CPI encouraged a new view of the public as "a passive object to be manipulated by mass propaganda" (Mattson, 1998, p. 115). After the war, Edward Bernays and other veterans of the CPI would carry that view into civilian life, arguing that "efforts comparable to those applied by the CPI . . . could be applied with equal facility to peacetime pursuits" (Cutlip, 1994, p. 168). The result was a whole new industry of "scientific" propaganda, advertising, and public relations. The rhetorical renaissance of the Progressive Era had given way to a new age of "scientific" persuasion and "opinion management."

Amusing Ourselves in the Age of Television

The emergence of a new "science" of mass persuasion in the 1920s was followed by one communication "revolution" after another. First radio, and then television vastly expanded the reach and impact of mass media, and with each new technology came optimistic predictions of a democratic revival. Like most new technologies, for example, television was at one time hailed as a magical new tool of civic deliberation—a technology that could inform and inspire the citizenry with news and "public interest" programming and even provide a way for citizens to "talk back" to their leaders. Instead, of course, it quickly became a "vast wasteland," in the famous words of former FCC Chairman Newton N. Minow (2009, p. 347)—a landscape dominated by mindless entertainment with little serious attention to news and public affairs.

Neil Postman's critique of television exposed the fallacy underlying the early optimism about television's democratic possibilities. In *Amusing Ourselves to Death* (1985), Postman argued that the problem was not that there was too much "junk" on the tube; rather, it was that television, *as a medium*, was inherently incapable of hosting serious discussion and debate. According to Postman, television was "at its most trivial" and "most dangerous" when its aspirations were high—that is, when it pretended to be "a carrier of important cultural conversations" (p. 16). On television, any attempt at "serious" speech was destined to fail, for "sustained, complex talk" simply did not "play well on television" (p. 92). As a visual medium, television was better suited to conveying images than arguments, and it implied a different epistemology—and a different "philosophy of rhetoric"—than print. Under the "governance of television," the "generally coherent, serious and rational" discourse of the print culture inevitably became "shriveled and absurd," reducing public deliberation to "dangerous nonsense" (pp. 16–17).

Rhetorical scholars have elaborated on Postman's critique by illuminating *how* television has truncated and trivialized our public discourse. Noting that "dramatic, digestive, [and] visual moments" have largely supplanted "memorable words" in our political consciousness, Jamieson (1988) argues that television redefined "eloquence" itself by elevating a more intimate, even "effeminate" style of speech over the "manly" and rational oratory of the golden age. "Unmoored from our own great literature and from the lessons of history" (p. 241), Jamieson argued, we now deem "eloquent" those speakers who are adept at relating personal stories or dramatic vignettes. Rather than marshaling arguments and evidence, today's most celebrated speakers talk in sound bites and anecdotes, wearing their emotions on their sleeves and exploiting the intimacy of television with personal stories. Ronald Reagan paved the way for this transition to a more emotional and "intimate" style of public discourse, as Jamieson noted. Since Reagan, however, this style

has become the norm, depriving citizens of the substantive discourse they need to form sound political judgments.

Put simply, television has "dumbed down" American politics. And the result, as Al Gore argued in his campus best-seller, *The Assault on Reason* (2007), is clearly evident in our political discourse. As Gore wrote, it "simply is no longer possible to ignore the strangeness of our public discourse" (p. 3). The proliferation of "superficial, emotional, and manipulative appeals" (p. 104)—not just on television but throughout our public sphere—points to a "systematic decay of the public forum" (p. 10), and that bodes ill for the future of our democracy. Robert D. Putnam (2000) agrees, pointing to evidence that fewer and fewer Americans are participating in the "everyday deliberations that constitute grassroots democracy" (p. 43) and labeling the decline of civic engagement and public deliberation in America a "tremendous civic plague" (Putnam, 1997, p. 35). Fortunately, this "plague" has not gone unnoticed by scholars, educators, philanthropists, and others concerned with the health and vitality of our democracy. In the conclusion to this chapter, I will touch on some of the ways the deliberative democracy movement is fighting back, and I will suggest how scholars of rhetoric and persuasion might be part of that effort.

Conclusion: Rhetoric, Persuasion, and the Revival of American Civic Culture

The study of persuasion has a long and illustrious history in the rhetorical tradition. Born of the need to educate for citizenship, rhetoric traditionally has been concerned with the techniques and ethics of *civic* persuasion—with an emphasis on the *responsibilities* that accompany the *right* of free speech in a democracy. Today we have a pressing need to revive the spirit of that classical tradition, particularly its emphasis on the responsibilities of citizenship and the ethics of speech. As more and more citizens have become spectators rather than participants in civic life (National Commission on Civic Renewal, 1998), our public discourse has been hijacked by professionally managed advocacy groups employing appeals shaped by polling and focus groups. Special interests now take precedence over the "common good." In other words, we now live in a "diminished democracy," as Harvard political scientist Theda Skocpol (2003) has argued, with ordinary citizens squeezed out of the public sphere by partisan ideologues and professional propagandists.

How can we fight back? We can begin by reminding our students and fellow citizens of the critical role that speech, argumentation, and persuasion play in the politics and policy-making processes of our democracy. We also can revive the classical tradition's emphasis on the habits and skills of engaged citizenship, teaching our students what it means to be a good citizen and an ethical communicator. Additionally, we can continue to write about the rights and responsibilities of free speech in America, and we can contribute to ongoing scholarly conversations about hate speech, fear appeals, and other techniques routinely employed by demagogues and propagandists. Finally, we can recapture the *public* spirit of both the classical tradition and the land-grant movement of the 19th century, recommitting ourselves to educating for citizenship and promoting what Garsten (2006) has called a healthy "politics of persuasion" (p. 14).

A healthy politics of persuasion is one in which ideas are tested in public discourse. In a healthy politics of persuasion, reasoned argument prevails over appeals to fears or prejudices, and diverse perspectives and opinions are encouraged and respected. In a healthy politics of persuasion, public advocates aspire neither to manipulate nor to pander to public opinion, and those who refuse to deliberate in good faith are relegated to the fringes. In a healthy politics of persuasion, citizens are educated to listen carefully, think critically, and communicate responsibly. In a healthy politics of persuasion, citizens have a sense of civic duty, but they also *choose* to participate because they know their voice matters.

A healthy politics of persuasion is not just a relic of the ancient rhetorical tradition. It is also the vision of today's "deliberative democracy movement"—a loose coalition of scholars and practitioners aspiring to a "deliberative renaissance" not just in the U.S. but around the world (Gastil & Keith, 2005, pp. 14–18). Bridging disciplinary divides, the deliberative democracy movement has inspired an explosion of scholarship over the past two decades, including theoretical reflections on democratic deliberation (e.g., Bohman, 1996), historical studies of particular eras (e.g., Mattson, 1998), and studies of deliberation in specific contexts, like school boards (Tracy, 2010) and town hall meetings (Zimmerman, 1989). Deliberative democracy scholars have championed "deliberative polling" (Fishkin, 1991) and "deliberative elections" (Gastil, 2000), and Ackerman and Fishkin (2004) have even proposed a new national holiday—Deliberation Day—for citizens to come together to discuss "the choices facing the nation" (p. 3). Within the deliberative democracy movement, there is considerable enthusiasm for a return to "a more local, popular democracy, reminiscent of the New England town meeting" (Keith, 2002, p. 219), and there is at least "cautious optimism" about the potential for new technologies to promote engaged citizenship and more robust deliberation (Anderson, 2003). In the final analysis, however, a healthy deliberative democracy—a healthy "politics of persuasion"—rests on the same foundation that it always has: an educated citizenry with the habits and skills of engaged citizenship.

For the deliberative democracy movement, the democratic crisis in America is both a challenge and an opportunity. The challenge lies in reviving the spirit of the classical rhetorical tradition—particularly its emphasis on the *ethics* of speech and the *responsibilities* of citizenship— in a culturally diverse and technologically advanced society. The opportunity lies in the collaborative possibilities; not only has the deliberative democracy movement brought together humanistic and scientific scholars in communication studies, but it also has inspired collaborations between communication scholars and historians, philosophers, political scientists, legal scholars, and information technologists. Civic literacy, which Milner (2002) defines as the knowledge and skills citizens need "to make sense of their political world" (p. 1), is not within the domain of any one discipline, nor is the broader mission of the deliberative democracy movement. Rebuilding our deliberative democracy requires contributions from across the academy, and it should be part of the mission of every college and university, particularly public and land-grant institutions. As the great 19th-century philosopher William James (1982) said, the "civic genius" of a people is demonstrated "day by day" in their speaking, writing, voting, and "good temper," in their refusal to tolerate corruption or be persuaded by the demagoguery of "rabid partisans or empty quacks" (p. 73). With all due respect to Stanley Fish (2008) and others who urge us to avoid all things political, we have an obligation to help our fellow citizens reclaim their democracy. Students of rhetoric and persuasion have an important—indeed, a crucial—role to play in that effort.

References

Ackerman, B., & Fishkin, J. S. (2004). *Deliberation day.* New Haven, CT: Yale University Press.

Adams, J. Q. (1810). *Lectures on rhetoric and oratory, delivered to the classes of senior and junior sophisters in Harvard University* (Vols. 1–2). Cambridge, MA: Hilliard and Metcalf.

Anderson, D. M. (2003). Cautious optimism about online politics and citizenship. In D. M. Anderson & M. Cornfield (Eds.), *The civic web* (pp. 19–34). Lanham, MD: Rowman & Littlefield.

Baldwin, C. S. (1924). *Ancient rhetoric and poetic.* New York, NY: Macmillan.

Berlin, J. (1992). Poststructuralism, cultural studies, and the composition classroom: Postmodern theory in practice. *Rhetoric Review, 11,* 16–33.

Blair, H. (1965). *Lectures on rhetoric and belles letters* (Vols. 1–2) H. F. Harding (Ed.), Carbondale: Southern Illinois University Press. (Original work published 1783)

Bohman, J. F. (1996). *Public deliberation: Pluralism, complexity, and democracy.* Cambridge, MA: MIT Press.

Bone, J. E., Griffin, C. L., & Scholz, T. M. L. (2008). Beyond traditional conceptualizations of rhetoric: Invitational rhetoric and a move toward civility. *Western Journal of Communication, 72,* 434–462.

Brigance, W. N. (1961). *Speech: Its techniques and disciplines in a free society* (2nd ed.). New York, NY: Appleton-Century-Crofts.

Browne, S. H. (2008). Andrew Johnson and the politics of character. In M. J. Medhurst (Ed.), *Before the rhetorical presidency* (pp. 194–212). College Station: Texas A&M University Press.

Burgess, P. G. (1968). The rhetoric of black power: A moral demand? *Quarterly Journal of Speech, 54,* 122–133.

Burke, K. (1966). *Language as symbolic action: Essays on life, literature, and method.* Berkeley: University of California Press.

Butler, H. E. (Ed.). (1969). *The Institutio Oratoria of Quintilian* (Vols. 1–4). Cambridge: Harvard University Press (Loeb Classical Library).

Campbell, K. K. (1973). The rhetoric of women's liberation: An oxymoron. *Quarterly Journal of Speech, 50,* 74–86.

Charland, M. (1987). Constitutive rhetoric: The case of the People Quebecois. *Quarterly Journal of Speech, 73,* 133–150.

Cmiel, K. (1990). *Democratic eloquence: The fight over popular speech in nineteenth-century America.* New York, NY: William Morrow.

Cohen, H. (1994). *The history of speech communication: The emergence of a discipline, 1914–1945.* Annandale, VA: Speech Communication Association.

Cooper, L. (Ed.). (1932). *The rhetoric of Aristotle.* New York, NY: Appleton-Century-Crofts.

Cutlip, S. M. (1994). *The unseen power: Public relations, a history.* Hillsdale, NJ: Lawrence Erlbaum.

Day, D. G. (1960). Persuasion and the concept of identification. *Quarterly Journal of Speech, 46,* 270–273.

Dewey, J. (1991). *The public and its problems.* Athens, OH: Swallow Press. (Original work published 1927)

Dillard, J. P., & Pfau, M. (Eds.). (2002). *The persuasion handbook: Developments in theory and practice.* Thousand Oaks, CA: Sage.

Duffy, B. K., & Leeman, R. W. (Eds.). (2005). *American voices: An encyclopedia of contemporary oratory.* Westport, CT: Greenwood Press.

Fish, S. (2008). *Save the world on your own time.* New York, NY: Oxford University Press.

Fishkin, J. S. (1991). *Democracy and deliberation: New directions for democratic reform.* New Haven, CT: Yale University Press.

Foss, S. K., & Griffin, C. L. (1995). Beyond persuasion: A proposal for an invitational rhetoric. *Communication Monographs, 62,* 2–18.

Frank, D. A., & Bolduc, M. (2010). Lucie Olbrechts-Tyteca's new rhetoric. *Quarterly Journal of Speech, 96,* 141–163.

Garsten, B. (2006). *Saving persuasion: A defense of rhetoric and judgment.* Cambridge, MA: Harvard University Press.

Gastil, J. (2000). *By popular demand: Revitalizing representative democracy through deliberative elections.* Berkeley: University of California Press.

Gastil, J., & Keith, W. M. (2005). A nation that (sometimes) likes to talk: A brief history of public deliberation in the United States. In J. Gastil & P. Levine (Eds.), *The deliberative democracy handbook.* San Francisco, CA: Jossey-Bass.

Golden, J. & Corbett, P. J. (Eds.). (1968). *The rhetoric of Blair, Campbell, and Whately.* New York, NY: Holt, Rinehart, and Winston.

Gore, A. (2007). *The assault on reason.* New York, NY: Penguin Press.

Gregg, R. B. (1971). The ego-function of the rhetoric of protest. *Philosophy and Rhetoric, 4,* 71–91.

Hamilton, A. (1974). On the powers of the Senate. In J. Elliot (Ed.), *The debates in the several state conventions on the adoption of the federal Constitution* (Vols. 1–5). New York, NY: Burt Franklin Reprints. (Original work published 1888)

Hogan, J. M. (2010). Public address and the revival of American civic culture. In S. J. Parry-Giles and J. M. Hogan (Eds.), *The handbook of rhetoric and public address* (pp. 442–447). Malden, MA: Blackwell.

Hunt, E. L. (1965). On the sophists. In J. Schwartz & J. A. Rycenga (Eds.), *The province of rhetoric* (pp. 69–84). New York, NY: Ronald Press.

Jaeger, W. (1965). The rhetoric of Isocrates and its cultural ideal. In J. Schwartz & J. A. Rycenga (Eds.), *The province of rhetoric* (pp. 84–111). New York, NY: Ronald Press.

James, W. (1982). Robert Gould Shaw: Oration by Professor William James. In *Essays in religion and morality (The works of Henry James).* Cambridge, MA: Harvard University Press.

Jamieson, K. H. (1988). *Eloquence in an electronic age: The transformation of political speechmaking.* New York, NY: Oxford University Press.

Jarratt, S. C. (1991). *Rereading the sophists: Classical rhetoric refigured.* Carbondale: Southern Illinois University Press.

Keith, W. (2002). Introduction: Cultural resources for deliberative democracy. *Rhetoric and Public Affairs, 5,* 219–221.

Kennedy, G. A. (Ed.). (1991). *Aristotle on rhetoric: A theory of civic discourse.* New York, NY: Oxford University Press.

Kraig, R. A. (2003). The second oratorical renaissance. In J. M. Hogan (Ed.), *Rhetoric and reform in the progressive era* (pp. 1–48). East Lansing: Michigan State University Press.

Levine, P. (2000). *The new progressive era: Toward a fair and deliberative democracy.* Lanham, MD: Rowman and Littlefield.

Lippmann, W. (1961). *Drift and mastery.* Englewood Cliffs, NJ: Prentice-Hall. (Original work published 1914)

Mattson, K. (1998). *Creating a democratic public: The struggle for urban participatory democracy during the progressive era.* University Park: Pennsylvania State University Press.

McEdwards, M. (1968). Agitative rhetoric: Its nature and effect. *Western Speech, 32,* 36–43.

Milner, H. (2002). *Civic literacy: How informed citizens make democracy work.* Hanover, NH: University Press of New England.

Minow, N. N. (2009). Television in the public interest. In S. E. Lucas & M. J. Medhurst (Eds.), *Words of a century: The top 100 American speeches, 1900–1999.* New York, NY: Oxford University Press. (Original speech delivered 1961)

Murphy, J. J. (Ed.). (1965). *On the early education of the citizen-orator: Institutio oratoria.* Indianapolis: Bobbs-Merril.

National Commission on Civic Renewal. (1998). *A nation of spectators: How civic disengagement weakens America and what we can do about it.* College Park: National Commission on Civic Renewal, University of Maryland.

Nevins, A. (1947). *Fruits of Manifest Destiny, 1847–1852.* New York, NY: Charles Scribner's Sons.

Nichols, M. H. (1952). Kenneth Burke and the 'new rhetoric.' *Quarterly Journal of Speech, 38*, 133–144.

Perelman, C., & Olbrechhts-Tyteca, L. (1969). *The new rhetoric: A treatise on argumentation.* Notre Dame, IN: University of Notre Dame Press.

Portolano, M. (2009). *The passionate empiricist: The eloquence of John Quincy Adams in the service of science.* Albany: State University of New York Press.

Postman, N. (1985). *Amusing ourselves to death: Public discourse in the age of show business.* New York, NY: Penguin Books.

Putnam, R. D. (2000). *Bowling alone: The collapse and revival of American community.* New York, NY: Simon & Schuster.

Putnam, R. D. (1997). The decline of civil society: How come? So what?" *Optimum: The Journal of Public Sector Management, 27*, 27–37.

Ray, J. W. (1978). Perelman's universal audience. *The Quarterly Journal of Speech, 64*, 361–375.

Reid, R. F., & Klumpp, J. F. (2005). *American rhetorical discourse* (3rd ed.). Long Grove, IL: Waveland Press.

Rossiter, C. (Ed.). (1961). *The federalist papers.* New York, NY: New American Library.

Scott, R. L., & Smith, D. K. (1969). The rhetoric of confrontation. *Quarterly Journal of Speech, 55*, 1–8.

Skocpol, T. (2003). *Diminished democracy: From membership to management in American civic life.* Norman: University of Oklahoma Press.

Sutton, E. W., & Rackham, H. (Eds.). (1983). *Cicero in twenty-eight volumes: De oratore.* (Vol. 3). Cambridge, MA: Harvard University Press (Loeb Classical Library).

Thonssen, L., & Baird, A. C. (1948). *Speech criticism: The development of standards for rhetorical appraisal.* New York, NY: Ronald Press.

Tracy, K. (2010). *Challenges of ordinary democracy: A case study in deliberation and dissent.* University Park: Pennsylvania State University Press.

Tulis, J. K. (1987). *The rhetorical presidency.* Princeton, NJ: Princeton University Press.

Vaughn, S. (1980). *Holding fast the inner lines: Democracy, nationalism, and the Committee on Public Information.* Chapel Hill: University of North Carolina Press.

Walzer, A. E., & Beard, D. (2009). Historiography and the study of rhetoric. In A. A. Lunsford (Ed.), *The SAGE handbook of rhetorical studies* (pp. 13–33). Thousand Oaks, CA: Sage.

Ward, J. (1759). *A system of oratory.* London: J. Ward.

Whately, R. (1963). *Elements of rhetoric: Comprising an analysis of the laws of moral evidence and of persuasion, with rules for argumentative composition and elocution* (D. Ehninger, Ed.). Carbondale: Southern Illinois University Press. (Original work published 1828)

Windt, T. O., Jr. (1972). The diatribe: Last resort for protest. *Quarterly Journal of Speech, 58*, 1–14.

Wood, G. S. (1969). *The creation of the American republic, 1776–1787.* New York, NY: W. W. Norton.

Wood, G. S. (1974). The democratization of the American mind. In *Leadership in the American Revolution.* Washington: Library of Congress.

Zappen, J. P. (2009). Kenneth Burke on dialectical-rhetorical transcendence. *Philosophy and Rhetoric, 42*, 279–301.

Zimmerman, J. (1989). *The New England town hall meeting: Democracy in action.* Westport, CT: Praeger.

CHAPTER 2

The Effects of Message Features

Content, Structure, and Style

Lijiang Shen and Elisabeth Bigsby

Consider a generic model of the persuasion process. Affective, cognitive, and behavioral processes mediate the relationship between the message-related variables (source, message, recipient, and context) and the desired outcome variables (attitude, intention, and behavior; Petty & Wegener, 1998). Although communication scholars are interested in the mediating processes of persuasion, as reflected in the chapters on theories and models in this handbook, the study of message features distinguishes *communication* research in persuasion from that in other disciplines such as psychology. The study of message features refers to aspects of communication itself; and as pointed out by Dillard and Pfau (2002), "questions concerning how messages might be designed to produce the greatest suasory impact lies at the very center of persuasion research" (p. xvi; see also Miller & Burgoon, 1978). In this chapter, we strive to present a review of research findings regarding the effects of message features on persuasion with a discussion of both practical and theoretical implications.

Persuasive messages are often broken into parts for study and analysis with researchers examining the persuasive influence of specific message features. Message construction also encourages this type of conceptualization and often addresses one message component at a time. From a campaign design perspective for example, decisions on the message topic or theme are made prior to any work on arguments or visuals. The topic, theme, or story being told (including plot and characters) is the *content* of the message (Lang, 2000; Stephenson & Palmgreen, 2001). Essentially, what the message is about. Closely aligned with the content is the presentation or *structure* of the message's arguments. The number of arguments the message contains, the order of the arguments, and whether or not points of opposition are acknowledged and/or addressed. The final major message component, *style*, generally includes language use like word choices and figure of speech. In mediated messages, style also refers to features like edits, music, and pacing (Geiger & Reeves, 1993; Lang, 2000; Morgan, Palmgreen, Stephenson, Hoyle, &

Lorch, 2003). Each message feature influences the persuasion process in unique ways. The following sections will outline important research in this area, with an emphasis on reviewing meta-analytic studies when possible, and attempt to provide an overview of how message features may work together to influence persuasion.

Message Content

Inherent in the theme of a message is the supporting evidence and whether or not opposing viewpoints will be acknowledged. For example, the theme of a political campaign advertisement is often built on the underlying goal of the message: support for our candidate or attacking an opponent. The following section focuses on the results of meta-analyses on the effects of two content-related features that have received substantial attention in persuasion research, type of evidence and message sidedness.

Type of Evidence

All persuasive messages advocate a particular position with the goal of getting the receivers to think or behave a particular way. The advocacy, therefore, more or less states a claim that the source expects the receivers to accept as true (e.g., indoor tanning damages your skin), or actions for them to enact (e.g., you should not tan indoors). Toulmin (1969) argues a claim should be backed by data to make an argument strong. Data is therefore the basis for persuasion and consists of evidence such as factual information and the reasoning behind the claim. Data are linked to the claim by a warrant, which legitimizes the claim by demonstrating that the data are relevant. This model of argument suggests that the strength, as well as type of evidence presented to support the message advocacy, may directly impact message effectiveness (see also Reinard, 1998; Reynolds & Reynolds, 2002).

In general there are four types of evidence. *Statistical evidence* presents statistics such as frequencies and percentages to support the claim. For example, "More than 1 million skin cancer cases are diagnosed annually in the U.S.", or "Between 40–50% of Americans who live to age 65 will at least once have basal cell carcinoma (BCC) or squamous cell carcinoma (SCC)." *Testimonial evidence* uses a person's personal experience, eye-witness account, or personal opinion to support the claim (including expert testimony). For example, "It was hard, but I quit smoking so you can do it, too." *Anecdotal evidence* is evidence that is based on a person's observations of the world. It is a personal interpretation of or opinion toward a target and is often subjective in nature. *Analogical evidence* use analogies to support a claim, comparing one idea/situation to another. Analogies are mainly useful when dealing with a topic that is novel.

Neither anecdotal nor analogical evidence are as widely used or studied as statistical and testimonial evidence, likely because the latter are considered strong types of evidence. A meta-analysis examining the effectiveness of testimonial evidence provides support for this claim. The average effect size was $r = .23$, $k = 16$, $N = 2,800$ for studies with group interactions, and $r = .25$, $k = 14$, $N = 1,920$ for studies without group interactions (Reinard, 1998). However, Allen and Preiss (1997) conducted a meta-analysis comparing the persuasive impact of testimonial and statistical evidence and their results suggested that statistical evidence is more pervasive than testimonial evidence ($r = .10$, $k = 15$, $N = 1,760$), with homogenous effect sizes. Hornikx (2005) hypothesized that the inconsistent findings may be a result of the differences in evidence types and their conceptualizations and operationalizations. In a comparison of studies, Hornikx tentatively claimed anecdotal evidence to be the least effective; however, a formal statistical analysis of the data was not conducted. Hornikx was focused on describing the methodological differences between the studies, and instead provided a count of the number of studies that found certain results. For example, studies that found (1) statistical evidence to be more persuasive than anecdotal evidence ($k = 6$), (2) anecdotal evidence to be more persuasive than statistical evidence ($k = 1$), and (3) no significant difference between statistical and anecdotal evidence ($k = 5$; Hornikx, 2005).

Message Sidedness

In addition to having a strong argument, the context of the argument presentation is important to the persuasion process. That is, whether or not the message will reference the opposition. Messages that only include arguments that support the position of the persuader are *one-sided messages*. A one-sided message does not make statements about the opposition's view or even acknowledge the existence of an opposing point of view. *Two-sided messages* include both supportive arguments and an acknowledgement or mention of the opposition's arguments. A two-sided message can be *non-refutational*, that is, it does not provide counter-arguments against the opposing view; or can be *refutational* and provide counter-arguments to demonstrate the superiority of their own arguments and advocacy over the opponents'.

Clearly, the question of which is more effective, one- or two-sided messages, has gained much attention in persuasion research. In fact, three meta-analyses, which report inconsistent conclusions, have been published on this topic (Allen, 1991; 1998; O'Keefe, 1999). Allen (1991) found a slight advantage for two-sided messages ($r = .04$, $k = 26$, $N = 7,547$) regarding persuasive effectiveness. With more data (primary studies), Allen (1998) confirmed the conclusion of his previous study: $r = .03$, $k = 70$, $N = 10,580$. On the contrary, O'Keefe (1999) found no difference between one- and two-sided messages regarding their overall persuasive effect ($r = -.00$, $k = 107$, $N = 20,111$). Although it appears that as more and more recent studies were included, the difference in effectiveness disappears, a closer examination of these meta-analyses reveals a

new picture, an understanding of instances when a one-sided message will be more persuasive than a two-sided message and vice versa. Ultimately, there was more consensus than inconsistency between Allen and O'Keefe's analyses when potential moderators are considered.

Potential Moderators

Type of two-sided message (i.e., refutational vs. non-refutational) has been found to be a significant moderator. Allen (1991) found that one-sided messages were actually more effective than two-sided messages when they are non-refutational ($r = -.06$, $k = 6$, $N = 1,819$); while the pattern is reversed when the two-sided messages are refutational ($r = .08$, $k = 19$, $N = 5,624$). Again, this finding is confirmed in the 1998 piece. One-sided messages were more effective than non-refutational two-sided messages ($r = -.09$, $k = 26$, $N = 3,159$); and the pattern is reversed when the two-sided messages are refutational ($r = .07$, $k = 43$, $N = 7,317$). With more data, O'Keefe's (1999) findings were very similar. One-sided messages were again found to be more persuasive than non-refutational two-sided messages ($r = -.05$, $k = 65$), but less persuasive than refutational two-sided messages ($r = .08$, $k = 42$). This shows that the inconsistency in overall conclusion was due to the fact that O'Keefe's analysis included more studies that compared one-sided and non-refutational two-sided messages, which privileged one-sided messages (65 in O'Keefe, 1999, vs. 26 in Allen, 1998), and canceled out the advantage of refutational two-sided messages over one-sided messages.

It is generally believed that refutational two-sided messages are more effective because the representation of opposing statements reduces counter-arguing by the recipients. Instead of trying to think of the opposition's arguments to combat the message advocacy, they are presented in the message. This in turn may lead to more positive cognitive responses than would occur in non-refutational messages (McGuire, 1985).

Audience Favorability

Allen (1991, 1998) and O'Keefe (1999) both found audience favorability to be a significant moderator. Allen (1991) found that one- and two-sided messages did not differ in their persuasiveness when the audience's pre-existing attitude was favorable, that is, toward the message advocacy ($r = .00$, $k = 8$, $N = 2,952$); while two-sided messages were more effective when the audience's pre-existing attitude was unfavorable ($r = .08$, $k = 9$, $N = 1,195$). Allen (1998) suggested the interaction between type of two-sided message and audience favorability could be a moderator because the sample was heterogeneous. However, because of the small number of studies available, a formal test of this potential moderator was impossible. On the other hand, while O'Keefe (1999) also found audience favorability appeared to have some influence on the persuasion process, his conclusion was not exactly consistent with that of Allen (1991). O'Keefe found one-sided messages were significantly more effective than two-sided messages when the audience had an initial attitude toward the topic, whether it was initially favorable ($r = -.14$, $k = 10$) or unfavorable ($r = -.11$, $k = 9$). There was no such difference between one- and two-sided messages when the audience was initially neutral ($r = -.02$, $k = 36$).

Advertisement Versus Non-advertisement

One key difference between Allen (1998) and O'Keefe (1999) was the number and types of primary studies included in the meta-analysis. More advertising research was included in O'Keefe's study, which appears to be a moderator as well. O'Keefe found that whether the message was an advertisement or non-advertisement did not make a difference in the effectiveness of one- vs. two-sided messages ($r = .00$, $k = 35$ for advertising messages, and $r = -.00$, $k = 72$ for non-advertising messages). However, when combined with type of two-sided message, whether or not

the message was an advertisement did appear to have some influence. For non-advertising messages, there was a pattern in which refutational two-sided messages were more effective than one-sided messages ($r = .08$, $k = 33$), which in turn were more effective than non-refutational two-sided messages ($r = -.07$, $k = 39$). This pattern did not hold when only advertisements were examined; there was no significant difference in persuasion between two-sided messages of either kind and one-sided messages.

O'Keefe (1999) also assessed the impact of one- and two-sided messages on credibility. Overall, there was a significant advantage in perceived credibility for two-sided messages ($r = .09$, $k = 56$, $N = 6,937$). However, this advantage was only significant for advertising messages ($r = .15$) and not for non-advertising messages ($r = .04$). O'Keefe suggested credibility may be jointly influenced by topic and type of two-sided message, but there was not sufficient data to test that possibility.

Including only studies that used advertisements, Eisend (2006) conducted a meta-analysis examining differences between one- and two-sided messages based on message structure, the persuader (marketer), and audience variables. Unlike O'Keefe, Eisend found two-sided advertisements were more effective than one-sided advertisements ($r = .07$, $k = 217$); although the effect size was small. Two-sided messages also significantly increased source credibility ($r = .22$, $k = 32$, $N = 1,554$), perceived novelty ($r = .35$, $k = 4$, $N = 185$), and positive cognitive responses ($r = .09$, $k = 10$, $N = 465$); they decreased negative cognitive responses ($r = -.18$, $k = 13$, $N = 615$) and resulted in more favorable attitudes toward the message ($r = -.05$, $k = 56$, $N = 3,305$) and the brand ($r = .12$, $k = 65$, $N = 3,152$). Several moderators, conducted with two-sided messages only in regression models, were found to significantly impact one or more of the outcome variables.

For example, greater amounts of negative information presented increased favorable attitudes toward the brand (unstandardized regression coefficient $B = .47$, $k = 40$, $p < .05$), and increased purchase intention ($B = .63$, $k = 22$, $p < .001$), but it also increased negative attitudes toward the advertisement ($B = -.39$, $p < .001$). When negative information was placed first, source credibility ($B = -.64$, $k = 32$, $p < .001$) and favorable attitude toward the brand ($B = -.12$, $k = 48$, $p < .001$) decreased. When negative information was placed last, favorable attitude toward the brand increased ($B = .15$, $k = 40$, $p < .001$). Eisend's results suggest that negative information should be included at the end of an advertisement; but this may not be true with other types of messages (i.e., health and political).

O'Keefe's (1999) meta-analysis included more advertising studies ($n = 35$) than Eisend's (2006) meta-analysis ($n = 29$), and between the two authors, only 13 articles overlapped. The analyses for the most part also examined different outcome variables, so it seems likely the differences between the meta-analyses account for some of the differences among their results. One result, however, was consistent between them. Both found two-sided advertisements to be more credible than one-sided advertisements.

Message Structure

Message structure concerns primarily with how either the data or the claim are presented in persuasive communication. Two features related to message structure have received some attention in the persuasion literature: (1) climax versus anticlimax order of arguments and (2) conclusion explicitness.

Climax Versus Anticlimax

In a climax structure, the most important arguments of a persuasive message are presented at the end of the message; while in an anticlimax structure, the most important arguments are presented first. Regarding overall persuasive effectiveness, there seems to be little difference between the two structures (Gilkinson, Paulson, & Sikkink, 1954; Gulley & Berlo, 1956; Sikkink, 1956; Sponberg, 1946). Available studies on climax versus anticlimax structure seem to be dated; and no systematic review is available. The lack of interest in this topic has probably been due to a lack of significant differences; and the lack of systematic review is probably due to a small number of studies. Available studies also tend to be in a public speaking setting, rather than in mediated persuasion. O'Keefe (2002) observed that it might be more advantageous to present a message in an anticlimax structure when time is limited and the message will likely be interrupted or stopped, for example, appellate oral arguments in U.S. courts or (televised) debate between political candidates. Such benefits, however, might be nonexistent in mediated persuasive messages, especially when the message is presented in a modality with high level of referability (i.e., the receiver is able to play back or read the message multiple times if they want to).

Conclusion Explicitness

Conclusion explicitness, however, has received substantially more attention in the literature, with two meta-analytic studies on the topic (Cruz, 1998; O'Keefe, 1997). Conceptually, researchers have disagreed over which conclusion, explicit or implicit, is more effective in terms of persuasion. Three explanations have been proposed to argue that messages with implicit conclusions should be more persuasive than those with explicit conclusions. First, Hovland and Mandell (1952) argued that messages are more persuasive when the conclusion is omitted and receivers are able to draw their own conclusions. The second explanation is rooted in the theory of psychological reactance (Brehm, 1966; Brehm & Brehm, 1981) and suggests that messages with explicit conclusions show clear intention to persuade and may be perceived as more threatening to an individual's freedom.

Hence, messages with explicit conclusions are more likely to activate psychological reactance, which reduces their persuasive impact. The third explanation suggests that explicit conclusions in persuasive messages reduce source credibility because an explicit message source may appear to have a vested interest in persuading the audience, and is therefore perceived as less trustworthy. On the other hand, an implicit message source may appear to be less biased and more objective, and therefore perceived as more trustworthy.

However, others disagree regarding the impact of conclusion explicitness on source credibility; and consequently disagree about the persuasiveness of implicit conclusion messages. Results from two meta-analyses showed that in fact the opposite was true. O'Keefe (1997) found that messages with explicit conclusions were more persuasive than those with implicit conclusions ($r = .12$, $k = 14$, $N = 2,649$), as did Cruz (1998; $r = .05$, $k = 7$, $N = 1,675$). It should be noted that there were eight studies included in O'Keefe that were not in Cruz, while Cruz had one study that was not included in O'Keefe. One explanation for the relative effectiveness of messages with explicit conclusions is related to source credibility, essentially reversing the argument made in favor of implicit conclusions. Hovland and Mandell (1952) argued that an explicit conclusion would increase source credibility because the source of an implicit message may be seen as having something to conceal; while the source of an explicit message may be seen as frank and forthright.

Potential Moderators

Researchers also have proposed conditions when messages with explicit conclusions would be more persuasive. First, when receivers are unable (due to lack of intelligence or prior knowledge) to comprehend an implicit conclusion, according to McGuire's (1968, 1989) information processing model, they will not be persuaded. In other words, ability could be a moderator of the relative effectiveness of explicit versus implicit

messages. Less intelligent receivers require an explicit conclusion for understanding (to be persuaded), whereas more intelligent receivers can comprehend implicit conclusions. Another potential moderator is involvement (Kardes, 1988; Sawyer & Howard, 1991; Tubbs, 1968). These scholars argue that individuals with high levels of involvement tend to reach the correct conclusions spontaneously after hearing an implicit message, and more frequently so than would individuals with low levels of involvement. Such self-generated conclusions then lead to more persuasion. The third potential moderator is the recipient's pre-existing/initial position (Fine, 1957; Weiss & Steenbock, 1965). Weiss and Steenbock argued that individuals would resist a persuasive message with an explicit conclusion, but accept an implicit message, if the message advocacy is inconsistent with their pre-existing position. On the other hand, when the conclusion is consistent with the recipients' pre-existing position, individuals would be more receptive to explicit messages.

O'Keefe (1997) tested two potential moderators: intelligence and initial position. Neither was found to be significant. Cruz (1998) attempted to assess the role of all three potential moderators, but also lacked significant results. He found source credibility does not moderate the association between conclusion type and persuasion; nor does it mediate the relationship between conclusion drawing and persuasion. Initial position was not found to be a significant moderator either, and there were too few studies that looked at the potential role of involvement to draw any conclusions. In the same article, Cruz also reported an empirical study he conducted to test these three moderators. The results were consistent with both his and O'Keefe's meta-analyses: Involvement was not a significant moderator and conclusion drawing was not associated with source credibility. However, Cruz did find the impact of conclusion drawing on persuasion was mediated by comprehension and perceived position of the source.

Message Style

Persuasive messages can vary in the ways information is presented linguistically (McQuarrie & Mick, 1999), although the information might be the same or equivalent. Some examples of message styles include: the use of hyperbole (Colston & Keller, 1998) and visual hyperbole (Callister & Stern, 2007), coherence markers (Kamalski, Lentz, Sanders, & Zwaan, 2008), phonetic symbolism (Lowrey & Shrum, 2007; Yorkston & Menon, 2004), powerful versus powerless language (Lakoff, 1975; O'Barr, 1982), metaphor (Sopory & Dillard, 2002), and message framing (O'Keefe & Jensen, 2006). The research reviewed in this chapter focuses on the effects of such stylistic features that are intrinsic to the messages, rather than the corresponding psychological responses (O'Keefe, 2003; Tao & Bucy, 2007) that might mediate such effects. The persuasive impacts of three message style features are examined: powerful versus powerless language, metaphor, and message framing. A brief overview of recent work on coherence markers in text-based persuasion is also included.

Powerful Versus Powerless Language

Based on Lakoff's (1975) model of women's language, O'Barr (1982) and associates started investigating the effects of powerful and powerless language. Powerless language is characterized with frequent use of specific linguistic features that indicate lower social power/status of the speaker such as hedges, hesitation forms, polite forms, and questioning intonations. Language that does not demonstrate frequent use of such features is considered powerful language. The majority of the research on powerful versus powerless language focuses on applied contexts, such as the courtroom, although the messages are not necessarily delivered as speeches (e.g., Areni & Sparks, 2005; Hosman & Siltanen, 2006). Source credibility is oftentimes an outcome variable of interest in addition to attitude change.

To date, there has been one meta-analytic study on the impact of powerful/powerless language on source credibility and persuasion (Burrell & Koper, 1998). Burrell and Koper found that powerful language is significantly more persuasive than powerless language ($r = .23$, $k = 5$, $N = 413$. In addition, powerful language also enhances source credibility ($r = .21$, $k = 14$, $N = 1,299$). The effect sizes appeared to be homogenous in both cases, but the obvious limitation is that there were a small number of studies reviewed.

Additional evidence comes from more recent studies that replicated and extended the results from the Burrell and Koper (1998) meta-analysis. The impact of powerful language on source credibility was replicated by Hosman and Siltanen (2006), and Areni and Sparks (2005) replicated the impact of powerful language on persuasion. In addition, Areni and Sparks (2005) found evidence that when presented in video format, powerful/powerless language functions as a peripheral cue: Powerful language led to more positive source-related thoughts than powerless language. On the other hand, when presented in print format, powerless linguistic features (i.e., hedges, hesitation forms, polite forms, and questioning intonations) might direct the receivers' attention toward the message source and results in more source-related cognitive response (but of negative valence). The (relative) ineffectiveness of powerless language may be attributed to the negative perception of the source and the resulting biasing influence.

Metaphor

As a figure of speech, metaphor is traditionally defined as a comparison between two (dissimilar) objects (e.g., "A is B."), such that the comparison results in aspects that normally apply to one object would be transferred to the other (Sopory & Dillard, 2002). The object whose meaning is transferred (B in this particular example) is called the base, and the object that receives the meaning that it is otherwise not associated with (A in this example) is the target. Sopory and Dillard argued that, despite being distinctive linguistic devices, simile, analogy, and personification can be treated as equivalent to metaphor when it comes to persuasive effects because they all involve transferring a certain meaning from the base to the target.

Scholars believe that metaphor has a powerful impact on persuasion and can structure, transform, and create knowledge; evoke emotions; and change attitudes (Aristotle, 1952; Lakoff & Turner, 1989; MacCormac, 1985). Six different explanations have been provided for the persuasive impact of metaphor. The first explanation, *pleasure or relief*, is rooted in the assumption that metaphors are semantic anomalies, and the impact of a metaphor comes from how it is comprehended. Both pleasure and relief approaches argue that the perception that there is an "error" in the metaphorical message leads to negative tension, although the reasoning of these approaches is slightly different. The pleasure approach suggests that resolving the true meaning for the metaphor and finding the novel similarities between the base and the target is a pleasurable experience. On the other hand, the relief approach posits that comprehending the metaphor dissipates the negative tension, thus experiencing relief. Pleasure and relief are both rewarding and reinforce the metaphorical meaning, which results in the persuasive impact.

The second explanation lies in *source credibility*. This explanation argues that communicators who use metaphors are perceived to be more credible than ones who do not. Aristotle (1952) argued that the use of metaphor is a sign of genius. Bowers and Osborn (1966) suggested that by using metaphor, the communicator points out previously unknown similarities between the target and the base, which is a source of interest and pleasure to the receiver; hence, source credibility is enhanced.

The third explanation assumes that any persuasive message is going to encounter considerable resistance in the form of counter-arguments. This view argues that the comprehension of a metaphor requires a great deal of cognitive capacity, thus fewer cognitive resources are available for counter-arguments. Persuasion is then increased by *reducing counter-arguments*.

The fourth explanation, *resource matching*, also concerns cognitive capacity in message processing. Similar to the reduced counter-arguments explanation, this view proposes that comprehending a metaphor requires cognitive elaboration, hence higher demand for cognitive capacity. In addition, this explanation acknowledges that there is limited cognitive capacity. When there is a match between the resources required to comprehend the metaphor and the resources available, maximum elaboration is possible and persuasion is enhanced. On the other hand, when there is too little or too much cognitive resource (i.e., a mismatch), persuasion is inhibited. When resources are insufficient, the metaphor is not comprehended; hence, less persuasion. When resources are too abundant, there will either be more counter-arguments or more irrelevant thoughts that dilute the persuasive impact of the metaphor.

The fifth explanation, *stimulated elaboration*, is attributed to two theories. The structure-mapping theory (Gentner, 1983, 1989; Whaley & Wagner, 2000) proposes that understanding metaphors stimulates cognitive elaboration by focusing on a similar relational structure between the target and the base, rather than simple inferences. The increased semantic connections then produce greater message elaboration. The salience-imbalance theory (Ortony, 1979) proposes that the common features of the target and base are assembled into the ground when a metaphor is comprehended. The evaluation associated with these common features is also part of the ground. In other words, both the ground-relevant attributes and their associated evaluations are integrated in the message elaboration. Therefore, more valenced thoughts would be generated, which leads to more persuasion. With different assumptions and rationale, both theories argue that metaphors facilitate persuasion by enhancing the number of favorable cognitive responses to the persuasive message.

The sixth explanation, *superior organization*, is also based on the structure-mapping theory (Gentner, 1983, 1989). This view proposes that a metaphor helps to structure and organize the arguments in a persuasive message (see Mio, 1996). When a metaphor activates a great number of semantic associations, the arguments are connected more coherently. In addition, a metaphor also increases the salience of these arguments. Better coherence and salience facilitates the comprehension of the arguments, leading to more persuasion (McGuire, 1985).

The meta-analysis by Sopory and Dillard (2002) assessed the overall persuasive effectiveness of metaphor and tested some of the explanations. They found that compared to literal messages, metaphor is significantly more persuasive ($r = .07$, $k = 38$, $N = 3,945$). The data did not allow for a test of the pleasure or relief explanation since no mediating variable was measured; and the same was more or less true for the resource matching explanation. The advantage of novel metaphors ($r = .12$) over old metaphors ($r = .01$) implies that source credibility could be an explanation; however, there was no significant effect of metaphor on perceived competence or character aspects of source credibility. The use of metaphor did enhance the perceived dynamism of the source ($r = .06$), meaning that it is less likely that source credibility could have explained the effect of metaphor on persuasion, as the theoretical explanation lies in the aspects of competence and character in source credibility. There was also no evidence for the reduced counterargument or the stimulated elaboration explanation. One potential reason, however, could be due to the small number of studies that looked at message elaboration (i.e., number of thoughts of agreements and/or disagreements).

One explanation, the superior organization explanation, did receive consistent support. The results from the meta-analysis showed that: (1) Persuasive messages are more persuasive with a single metaphor ($r = .31$) than with more than one metaphor ($r = .11$); (2) metaphors are also most persuasive when non-extended ($r = .42$) than extended ($r = .18$); and (3) metaphors are more persuasive when placed in the introduction position of a message ($r = .25$) than when introduced later in the message ($r = -.05$; Sopory & Dillard, 2002). Combined, these results show that superior organization seems to be the best explanation for the persuasive impact of metaphors.

Message Framing

Another stylistic feature that has received substantial attention in the literature is message framing. Message framing refers to the persuasive strategy either to highlight benefits and rewards from compliance with the message advocacy (i.e., the gain frame), or to emphasize the costs and punishments associated with noncompliance (i.e., the loss frame). There are several explanations for the relative effectiveness of gain versus loss frame.

One explanation in favor of the loss frame is based on the premise that the loss frame leads to higher levels of message elaboration, hence better persuasion. The most frequently mentioned perspective in support of this claim is the negativity bias, which proposes that individuals assign greater weight to negatively valenced information than positively valenced information, even when they are equivalent in intensity (Rozin & Royzman, 2001). The second explanation is rooted in the elaboration likelihood model (ELM, Petty & Cacioppo, 1986). This explanation considers the inherent valence associated with the two frames as peripheral cues (e.g., Maheswaran & Meyers-Levy, 1990; Rothman, Salovey, Antone, Keough, & Martin, 1993), which affect subsequent message processing. This logic suggests that the loss frame would be processed more carefully because it is more attention grabbing and/or it is more likely to violate individuals' expectancies. The third explanation lies in the fear appeal literature. Conceptually and operationally, the loss frame and the threat-to-health component of a fear appeal message share certain common characteristics (O'Keefe & Jensen, 2008). Other research shows that fear can increase message processing (e.g., Das, de Wit, & Stroebe, 2003; Hale, Lemieux, & Mongeau, 1995; Slater, Karan, Rouner, & Walters, 2002). Lazarus's (1991) cognitive-motivational-relational theory also suggests that the function of fear is to protect the individual from risks. Thus, fear motivates individuals to seek and process information that offers protection from and/or reduction of risks involved in the message (Das et al., 2003; Nabi, 2003).

There are also a few explanations in favor of the gain frame. The first explanation lies in affect and persuasion. There has been evidence that the gain frame leads to stronger positive affect and the loss frame stronger negative affect (e.g., Millar & Millar, 2000; Schneider et al., 2001; Shen & Dillard, 2007). In turn, this positive affect might facilitate persuasion (Hullett, 2005). The second explanation involves psychological reactance (Reinhart, Marshall, Feeley, & Tutzauer, 2007). The loss frame might be perceived as more threatening to an individual's freedom for two reasons: (1) by depicting negative consequences, the language used in the loss frame might be perceived as more intense; and (2) due to the fact that the loss frame arouses stronger negative emotions, it tends to be perceived as more manipulative (e.g., Witte, 1994). Therefore, the loss frame tends to arouse stronger psychological reactance, which potentially makes the gain frame more persuasive.

O'Keefe and Jensen have conducted a series of meta-analyses examining the relative effectiveness of gain versus loss frame and potential moderators (2006, 2007, 2009) and the impact of message framing on message processing (2008). These meta-analyses showed that the two message frames do not differ in their overall persuasive impact ($r = .02$, k = 164, $N = 50{,}780$); the effect size was not statistically different from zero (95% confidence interval: $-.01–.04$; O'Keefe & Jensen, 2006). Surprisingly, the gain frame leads to slightly but significantly greater message elaboration than the loss frame ($r = .06$, k = 42, $N = 6{,}378$; O'Keefe & Jensen, 2008). Scholars have suggested that main effects conclusions regarding depth of message processing tend to be overly simple, and that

moderators should be considered. There has been evidence that behavioral inhibition/activation systems (BIS/BAS) might be moderators. Specifically, BIS-oriented individuals process the loss frame in more depth, while BAS-oriented individuals process the gain frame in a more effortful manner (e.g., Shen & Dillard, 2009).

Rothman and colleagues (Rothman, Bartels, Wlaschin, & Salovey, 2006; Rothman & Salovey, 1997; Salovey, Schneider, & Apanovitch, 2002) argue that when the targeted behavior is perceived as risky and uncertain (i.e., detection behavior), the loss frame is more effective; while the gain frame will be more effective when the targeted behavior is viewed as safe and certain (i.e., prevention behavior). O'Keefe and Jensen also tested these potential moderators in their meta-analysis series. Type of behavior did not emerge as a significant moderator for the persuasive effect (O'Keefe & Jensen, 2006), nor for the impact on message elaboration (O'Keefe & Jensen, 2008). When examined within each type of behavior, the gain frame was found to be more persuasive than the loss frame for encouraging disease prevention behaviors ($r = .03$, k = .93, $N = 21{,}656$); however, this effect can be attributed to the studies included that examined the topic of dental hygiene behaviors. Brushing and flossing are behaviors generally thought of positively; most individuals believe these are useful preventative behaviors and are widely socially acceptable. There was no significant difference between the effectiveness of the two frames for any other prevention behaviors (O'Keefe & Jensen, 2007). In addition, the gain frame leads to greater message elaboration than the loss frame within the topic of disease prevention behavior ($r = .08$; O'Keefe & Jensen, 2008).

Similarly, the loss frame was found to be more persuasive than the gain frame when advocating disease detection behaviors ($r = -.04$, k = 53, $N = 9{,}145$). Again, this effect can be attributed to the included studies on the topic of breast cancer self-exams, another widely accepted health behavior. There was no message framing effect for any other type of disease detection behaviors

(O'Keefe & Jensen, 2009). Within disease detection behavior, there was also no difference between the two frames regarding their impact on message elaboration (O'Keefe & Jensen, 2008).

Despite the presence of attractive explanatory mechanisms (e.g., the negativity bias), together these results suggest that there is no overall difference in persuasiveness between gain-framed and loss-framed messages. Rothman and Updegraff (2010) suggest that we need to turn to both mediating and moderating variables to better our understanding of message framing effects. One possible explanation for the null effect is that the mechanism in favor of the loss frame and the one in favor of the gain frame (e.g., psychological reactance) could be at work at the same time and end up canceling each other out. To better understand and investigate message framing, both mediating mechanisms need to be operationalized and accounted for in empirical studies simultaneously, rather than just assumed, or only one of them should be included.

In their responses to O'Keefe and Jensen (2007), Latimer, Salovey, and Rothman (2007) called for more research on potential moderators, particularly motivational variables. That call was echoed in Rothman and Updegraff (2010). Rothman and Updegraff proposed that there are two general perspectives regarding moderators of message framing effects: (1) individuals' *construal* of targeted health behavior (e.g., detection vs. prevention, Rothman et al., 2006; Salovey et al., 2002), and (2) individuals' dispositional sensitivity to outcomes presented in gain/loss (e.g., Mann, Sherman, & Updegraff, 2004; Shen & Dillard, 2007; Yan, Dillard, & Shen, 2010). So far, these studies have offered some evidence for these mediating and moderating variables, but there has yet to be systematic/meta-analytic reviews regarding the role and impact of these factors.

Textual Messages and Style

Although no meta-analyses are currently available, recent and interesting research has been conducted on the persuasive impact of coherence markers in written messages. Coherence markers like connectives (because, therefore, so) and lexical cue phrases (as a result, for that reason) are grammatical tools that allow the author to make an explicit connection between the cause and result or evidence and conclusion. It has been argued this more complex sentence structure actually makes reading easier for the audience because they do not need to make an implicit connection (Sanders & Spooren, 2007).

Not all coherence markers have the same effect on persuasive communication; however, and recent work has explored some of these differences. Coherence markers of subjective relationships may cause a forewarning effect (signaling the audience that the message is persuasive) and result in message resistance. Coherence markers of objective relationships, however, may not. Whether a relationship is subjective or objective is determined by the word or phrase choice and, occasionally, the structure of the sentence. Subjective causality occurs when the persuader presents arguments to demonstrate her or his conclusion; objective causality occurs when the persuader is simply reporting a causal relationship that already exists. Take the following sentences as examples: (1) Crest is the best brand of toothpaste because it is the brand my mom bought; (2) I ran out of toothpaste this morning, so I need to stop at the store on my way home. The first sentence demonstrates subjective causality; it equates my mom's taste with quality and serves as an argument for why Crest is the best brand of toothpaste. The second sentence demonstrates objective causality; it explains why I am stopping at the store.

Controlling for previous knowledge, Kamalski and colleagues (Kamalski et al., 2008), found that sentences with objective markers were more persuasive than sentences with subjective markers within topic. However, the text with no markers and the version that contained both objective and subjective markers were not significantly different from the objective-only or subjective-only text versions. It is important to note, though, that the comparison sentences were not equivalent and the manipulations were complex; each version of text was two pages long and contained 25 different manipulations of text. Ultimately, additional research is needed to determine potential moderators. For example, text-based persuasion is a context when the education level, or more specifically reading ability, of the audience could be extremely important.

Message Features and Persuasion

In this chapter, we reviewed existing research on the effects of some major message features on persuasion outcomes, including content (type of evidence and one- vs. two-sided messages), structure (climax vs. anti-climax structure and explicit vs. implicit conclusion), and style (powerful vs. powerless language, metaphor, message framing, and coherence markers). Overall, available meta-analyses show that these message features have significant effects on persuasion. Dillard and Pfau (2002) argued that studies on the impact of message features are at the heart of persuasion research. Conceptually speaking, persuasion research on message features is uniquely communicative and distinguishes such research from those in the psychology tradition. It does not mean, however, that we can study message effects without considering the psychological mechanisms that underlie such effects. Burleson (1992) argued that if we are to take communication research seriously, we need to study both. This review of the literature suggests that communication scholars are indeed doing that. Researchers have proposed mediating variables that explain effects of message features, and have been testing moderators in meta-analytic studies as well.

Practically speaking, findings regarding the effectiveness of message features have direct implications and should provide clear guidelines for message design and production. Arguably, all persuasion theories must consider message features

and have implications for message design and production to be good theories. This is what brings truth-value to Kurt Lewin's (1951, p. 169) famous quote "there is nothing so practical as a good theory."

In his chapter in the first edition, Hosman (2002) suggested that in persuasion studies, message features can be analyzed at a micro and linguistic level: phonology, syntax, lexicon, and text/narrative. The literature reviewed in this chapter analyzes message features at a rather macro level: content, structure, and style. This difference demonstrates that there are different approaches to the study of message features in persuasion; and that the meaning of message features is not necessarily objective in nature. McQuarrie and Mick (1999) suggested that interpretation of message features can be (1) based on the presence/absence of features (i.e., more objective); (2) based on receiver response, which emphasizes the receivers' perception and interpretation of the message features; and (3) text-interpretative meaning that draws on semiotic, rhetorical, and literary theories. Similarly, O'Keefe (2003) observed that in the literature, message features are either defined in an effect-based approach or in terms of intrinsic features (see also Tao & Bucy, 2007).

For both theoretical and practical purposes, message feature definitions based on effects should be avoided in favor of definitions based on intrinsic features (O'Keefe, 2003). On one hand, variations in message effects variables are caused by the intrinsic features of the message. Implicitly or explicitly, these message effects variables are the mediators of the message features–persuasion outcomes relationship. On the other hand, effects-based definitions offer little when it comes to guidance for message design and production. O'Keefe (2003) argued that failure to recognize the difference between the two types of definitions and oversight of the relationships among these two types of variables and persuasion outcomes would thwart progress in understanding of the effects of message features on persuasion, and understanding of the persuasion process in general. We strive to echo his position and the call for more and better conceptualized and operationalized research on message features and persuasion, with emphasis not just on effects, but on the mediating mechanisms and potential moderators as well. Only in this approach can we further our understanding of the effects of message features on persuasion, test and extend persuasion theories, and at the same time, provide guidance for message design and production for the practice of persuasion.

References

Allen, M. (1991). Meta-analysis comparing the persuasiveness of one-sided and two-sided messages. *Western Journal of Communication, 55,* 390–404.

Allen, M. (1998). Comparing the persuasive effectiveness of one- and two-sided messages. In M. Allen & R. W. Preiss (Eds.), *Persuasion: Advances through meta-analysis* (pp. 87–98). Cresskill, MJ: Hampton Press.

Allen, M., & Preiss, R. W. (1997). Comparing the persuasiveness of narrative and statistical evidence using meta-analysis. *Communication Research Reports, 4,* 125–131.

Areni, C. S., & Sparks, J. R. (2005). Language power and persuasion. *Psychology & Marketing, 22,* 507–525.

Aristotle. (1952). Poetics. (I. Bywater, Trans.). In W. D. Ross (Ed.), *The works of Aristotle: Rhetorica, de rhetorica ad Alexandrum, poetica.* Oxford, UK: Clarendon Press.

Bowers, J. W., & Osborn, M. M. (1966). Attitudinal effects of selected types of concluding metaphors in persuasive speeches. *Speech Monographs, 33,* 147–155.

Brehm, J. W. (1966). *A theory of psychological reactance.* New York, NY: Academic Press.

Brehm, S. S., & Brehm, J. W. (1981). *Psychological reactance: A theory of freedom and control.* New York, NY: Academic Press.

Burleson, B. R. (1992). Taking communication seriously. *Communication Monographs, 59,* 79–86.

Burrell, N. A., & Koper, R. J. (1998). The efficacy of powerful/powerless language on attitude and source credibility. In M. Allen & R. W. Preiss (Eds.), *Persuasion: Advances through meta-analysis* (pp. 203–215). Cresskill, MJ: Hampton Press.

Callister, M. A., & Stern, L. A. (2007). The role of visual hyperbole in advertising effectiveness. *Journal of Current Issues and Research in Advertising, 29,* 1–14.

Colston, H. L., & Keller, S. B. (1998). You'll never believe this: Irony and hyperbole in expressing surprise. *Journal of Psycholinguistic Research, 27,* 499–513.

Cruz, M. (1998). Explicit and implicit conclusions in persuasive messages. In M. Allen, & R. W. Preiss (Eds.), *Persuasion: Advances through meta-analysis* (pp. 217–230). Cresskill, MJ: Hampton Press.

Das, E., de Wit, J., & Stroebe, W. (2003). Fear appeals motivates acceptance of action recommendations: Evidence for a positive bias in the processing of persuasive messages. *Personality and Social Psychology Bulletin, 29,* 650–664.

Dillard, J.P., & Pfau, M. (2002). Introduction. In J. P. Dillard & M. Pfau (Eds.), *The persuasion handbook: Developments in theory and practice* (pp. ix–xx). Thousand Oaks, CA: Sage.

Eisend, M. (2006). Two-sided advertising: A meta-analysis. *International Journal of Research in Marketing, 23,* 187–198.

Fine, B. (1957). Conclusion-drawing, communicator credibility, and anxiety as factors in opinion change. *Journal of Abnormal and Social Psychology, 54,* 369–374.

Geiger, S., & Reeves, B. (1993). The effects of scene changes and semantic relatedness on attention to television. *Communication Research, 20,* 155–175.

Gentner, D. (1983). Structure-mapping: A theoretical framework for analogy. *Cognitive Science, 7,* 155–170.

Gentner, D. (1989). The mechanisms of analogical learning. In S. Vosniadou & A. Ortony (Eds.), *Similarity and analogical reasoning* (pp. 199–241). Cambridge, UK: Cambridge University Press.

Gilkinson, H., Paulson, S. F., & Sikkink, D. E. (1954). Effects of order and authority in an argumentative speech. *Quarterly Journal of Speech, 40,* 183–192.

Gulley, H. E., & Berlo, D. K. (1956). Effect of intercellular and intracellular speech structure on attitude change and learning. *Speech Monographs, 23,* 288–297.

Hale, J. L., Lemieux, R., & Mongeau, P. A. (1995). Cognitive processing of fear-arousing message content. *Communication Research, 22,* 459–474.

Hornikx, J. (2005). A review of experimental research on the relative persuasiveness of anecdotal, statistical, causal, and expert evidence. *Studies in Communication Sciences, 5,* 205–216.

Hosman, L. A. (2002). Language and persuasion. In J. P. Dillard & M. Pfau (Eds.). *The handbook of persuasion: Developments in theory and practice* (pp. 371–390). Thousand Oaks, CA: Sage.

Hosman, L. A., & Siltanen, S. A. (2006). Powerful and powerless language forms: Their consequences for impression formation, attributions of control of self and control of others, cognitive responses, and message memory. *Journal of Language and Social Psychology, 25,* 33–46.

Hovland, C., & Mandell, V. (1952). An experimental comparison of conclusion-drawing by the communicator and by the audience. *Journal of Abnormal and Social Psychology, 47,* 581–588.

Hullett, C. R. (2005). The impact of mood on persuasion: A meta-analysis. *Communication Research, 32,* 423–442.

Kamalski, J., Lentz, L., Sanders, T., & Zwaan, R. A. (2008). The forewarning effect of coherence markers in persuasive discourse: Evidence from persuasion and processing. *Discourse Processes, 45,* 545–579.

Kardes, F. (1988). Spontaneous inference processes in advertising: The effects of conclusion omission and involvement on persuasion. *Journal of Consumer Research, 15,* 225–233.

Lakoff, R. (1975). *Language and woman's place.* New York, NY: Harper and Row.

Lakoff, G., & Turner, M. (1989). *More than cool reason: A field guide to poetic metaphor.* Chicago: University of Chicago Press.

Lang, A. (2000). The limited capacity model of mediated message processing. *Journal of Communication, 50,* 46–70.

Latimer, A. E., Salovey, P., & Rothman, A. J. (2007). The effectiveness of gain-framed messages for encouraging disease prevention behavior: Is all hope lost? *Journal of Health Communication, 12,* 645–649.

Lazarus, R. S. (1991). *Emotion and adaptation.* New York, NY: Oxford University Press.

Lewin, K. (1951). *Field theory in social science; selected theoretical papers* (D. Cartwright, Ed., pp. 188–237). New York, NY: Harper and Row.

Lowrey, T. M., & Shrum, L. J. (2007). Phonetic symbolism and brand name preference. *Journal of Consumer Research, 34,* 406–414.

MacCormac, E. (1985). *A cognitive theory of metaphor.* Cambridge, MA: MIT Press.

Maheswaran, D., & Meyers-Levy, J. (1990). The influence of message framing and issue involvement. *Journal of Marketing Research, 27,* 361–367.

Mann, T., Sherman, D., & Updegraff, J. (2004). Dispositional motivations and message framing: A test of the congruency hypothesis in college students. *Health Psychology, 23,* 330–334.

McGuire, W. J. (1968). Personality and attitude change: An information processing theory. In A. G. Greenwald, T. C. Brock, and T. M. Ostrom (Eds.), *Psychological foundations of attitudes* (pp. 171–196). San Diego, CA: Academic Press.

McGuire, W. J. (1985). Attitudes and attitude change. In G. Lindzey & E. Aronson (Eds.), *Handbook of social psychology* (3rd ed., Vol. 2, pp. 233–346). New York, NY: Random House.

McGuire, W. J. (1989). Theoretical foundations of campaigns. In R. E. Rice & C. K. Atkin (Eds.), *Public communication campaigns* (2nd ed., pp. 43–65). Newbury Park, CA: Sage.

McQuarrie, E. F., & Mick, D. G. (1999). Visual rhetoric in advertising: Text-interpretive, experimental, and reader-response analyses. *Journal of Consumer Research, 26,* 37–54.

Millar, M. G. & Millar, K. (2000). Promoting safe driving behavior: The influence of message framing and issue involvement. *Journal of Applied Social Psychology, 30,* 853–866.

Miller, G. R., & Burgoon, M. (1978). Persuasion research: Review and commentary. In B. D. Ruben (Ed.), *Communication yearbook* (Vol. 2, pp. 29–47). New Brunswick, NJ: Transaction Books.

Mio, J. S. (1996). Metaphor, politics, and persuasion. In J. S. Mio & A. N. Katz (Eds.), *Metaphor: Implications and applications* (pp. 127–146). Mahwah, NJ: Lawrence Erlbaum.

Morgan, S. E., Palmgreen, P., Stephenson, M. T., Hoyle, R. H., & Lorch, E. P. (2003). Associations between message features and subjective evaluations of the sensation value of antidrug public service announcements. *Journal of Communication, 53,* 512–526.

Nabi, R. L. (2003). Exploring the framing effects of emotion: Do discrete emotions differentially influence information accessibility, information seeking, and policy preference? *Communication Research, 30,* 224–247.

O'Barr, W. (1982). *Linguistic evidence: Language, power, and strategy in the courtroom.* New York, NY: Academic Press.

O'Keefe, D. J. (1997). Standpoint explicitness and persuasive effect: A meta-analytic review of the effects of varying conclusion articulation in persuasive messages. *Argumentation and Advocacy, 34,* 1–12.

O'Keefe, D. J. (1999). How to handle opposing arguments in persuasive messages: A meta-analytic review of effects of one-sided and two-sided messages. In M. E. Roloff (Ed.), *Communication yearbook 22* (pp. 209–249). Thousand Oaks, CA: Sage.

O'Keefe, D. J. (2002). *Persuasion: Theory and research* (2nd ed.). Thousand Oaks, CA: Sage.

O'Keefe, D. J. (2003). Message properties, mediating states, and manipulation checks: Claims, evidence, and data analysis in experimental persuasive message effects research. *Communication Theory, 13,* 251–274.

O'Keefe, D. J., & Jensen, J. D. (2006). The advantages of compliance or the disadvantages of noncompliance? A meta-analytic review of the relative persuasive effectiveness of gain-framed and loss-framed messages. In C. S. Beck (Ed.), *Communication yearbook 30* (pp. 1–44). Mahwah, NJ: Lawrence Erlbaum.

O'Keefe, D. J., & Jensen, J. D. (2007). The relative persuasiveness of gain-framed and loss-framed messages for encouraging disease prevention behaviors: A meta-analytic review. *Journal of Health Communication, 12,* 623–644.

O'Keefe, D. J., & Jensen, J. D. (2008). Do loss-framed persuasive messages engender greater message processing than do gain-framed messages? A meta-analytic view. *Communication Studies, 59,* 51–67.

O'Keefe, D. J., & Jensen, J. D. (2009). The relative persuasiveness of gain-framed and loss-framed messages for encouraging disease detection behaviors: A meta-analytic review. *Journal of Communication, 59,* 296–316.

Ortony, A. (1979). Beyond literal similarity. *Psychological Review, 86,* 161–180.

Petty, R. E., & Cacioppo, J. T. (1986). The elaboration likelihood model of persuasion. In L. Berkowitz (Ed.), *Advances in experimental social psychology* (Vol. 19, pp. 123–205). New York, NY: Academic Press.

Petty, R. E., & Wegener, D. T. (1998). Attitude change: Multiple roles for persuasion variables. In D. T. Gilbert, S. T. Fiske, & G. Lindzey (Eds.), *The handbook of social psychology* (4th ed., pp. 323–390). Boston: McGraw-Hill.

Reinard, J. C. (1998). The persuasive effects of testimonial assertion evidence. In M. Allen, & R. W. Preiss (Eds.), *Persuasion: Advances through meta-analysis* (pp. 69–86). Cresskill, MJ: Hampton Press.

Reinhart, A. M., Marshall, H. M., Feeley, T. H., & Tutzauer, F. (2007). The persuasive effects of message framing on organ donation: The mediating role of psychological reactance. *Communication Monographs, 74,* 229–255.

Reynolds, R. A., & Reynolds, J. L. (2002). Evidence. In J. P. Dillard & M. Pfau (Eds.). *The handbook of persuasion: Developments in theory and practice* (pp. 427–444). Thousand Oaks, CA: Sage.

Rothman, A. J., Bartels, R. D., Wlaschin, J., & Salovey, P. (2006). The strategic use of gain- and loss-framed messages to promote healthy behavior: How theory can inform practice. *Journal of Communication, 56,* S202–S220.

Rothman, A. J., & Salovey, P. (1997). Shaping perceptions to motivate healthy behavior: The role of message framing. *Psychological Bulletin, 121,* 3–19.

Rothman, A. J., Salovey, P., Antone, C., Keough, K., & Martin, C. D. (1993). The influence of message framing on intentions to perform health behaviors. *Journal of Experimental Social Psychology, 29,* 408–433.

Rothman, A. J., & Updegraff, J. A. (2010). Specifying when and how gain- and loss-framed messages motivate healthy behavior: An integrated approach. In G. Keren (Ed.), *Perspectives on framing* (pp. 257–277). New York, NY: Psychology Press.

Rozin, P., & Royzman, E. B. (2001). Negativity bias, negativity dominance, and contagion. *Personality and Social Psychology Review, 5,* 296–320.

Salovey, P., Schneider, T. R., & Apanovitch, A. M. (2002). Message framing in the prevention and early detection of illness. In J. P. Dillard & M. Pfau, (Eds.), *The persuasion handbook: Developments in theory and practice* (pp. 391–406). Thousand Oaks, CA: Sage.

Sanders, T., & Spooren, W. (2007). Discourse and text structure. In H. Cuyckens & D. Geeraerts (Eds.), *Handbook of cognitive linguistics* (pp. 1414–1446). Oxford, UK: Oxford University Press.

Sawyer, A., & Howard, D. (1991). Effects of omitting conclusions in advertisement to involved and uninvolved audiences. *Journal of Marketing Research, 28*, 467–474.

Schneider, T. R., Salovey, P., Apanovitch, A. M., Pizarro, J., McCarthy, D. Zullo, J. & Rothman, A. (2001). The effect of message framing and ethnic targeting on mammography use among low-income women. *Health Psychology, 20*, 256–266.

Shen, L., & Dillard, J. P. (2007). The influence of BIS/BAS and message framing on the processing of persuasive health messages. *Communication Research, 34*, 433–467.

Shen, L., & Dillard, J. P. (2009). Message frames interact with motivational systems to determine depth of message processing. *Health Communication, 24*, 504–514.

Sikkink, D. (1956). An experimental study of the effects on the listener of anti-climax order and authority in an argumentative speech. *Southern Speech Journal, 22*, 73–78.

Slater, M. D., Karan, D. N., Rouner, D., & Walters, D. (2002). Effects of threatening visuals and announcer differences on responses to televised alcohol warnings. *Journal of Applied Communication Research, 30*, 27–49.

Sopory, P. & Dillard, J. P. (2002). The persuasive effects of metaphor: A meta-analysis. *Human Communication Research, 28*, 382–419.

Sponberg, H. (1946). A study of the relative effectiveness of climax and anti-climax order in an argumentative speech. *Speech Monographs, 1*, 35–44.

Stephenson, M. T., & Palmgreen, P. (2001). Sensation seeking, perceived message sensation value, personal involvement, and processing of anti-marijuana PSAs. *Communication Monographs, 68*, 49–71.

Tao, C., & Bucy, E. P. (2007). Conceptualizing media stimuli in experimental research: Psychological versus attribute-based definitions. *Human Communication Research, 33*, 397–426.

Toulmin, S. (1969). *The uses of argument.* Cambridge, UK: Cambridge University Press.

Tubbs, S. (1968). Explicit versus implicit conclusions and audience commitment. *Speech Monographs, 35*, 14–19.

Weiss, W., & Steenbock, S. (1965). The influence on communication effectiveness of explicitly urging action and policy consequences. *Journal of Experimental Social Psychology, 1*, 396–406.

Whaley, B. B., & Wagner, L. S. (2000). Rebuttal analogy in persuasive messages: Communicator likability and cognitive responses. *Journal of Language and Social Psychology, 19*, 66–84.

Witte, K. (1994). Fear control and danger control: A test of the extended parallel process model (EPPM). *Communication Monographs, 61*, 113–134.

Yan, C., Dillard, J. P., & Shen, F. (2010). The effects of mood, message framing, and behavioral advocacy on persuasion. *Journal of Communication, 60*, 344–363.

Yorkston, E., & Menon, G. (2004). A sound idea: Phonetic effects of brand names on consumer judgments. *Journal of Consumer Research, 31*, 43–51.

CHAPTER 3

Media Influence as Persuasion

R. Lance Holbert and John M. Tchernev

For almost a century, mass communication researchers have wrestled with questions of how, why, when, and where media produce effects. These issues, which span a broad range of areas including health communication, political communication, and commercial advertising, can all be viewed as questions of persuasion. Lasswell's (1927) own early studies of media focused on "the management of collective attitudes by the manipulation of significant symbols" (p. 627). This description coincides with Dillard's (2010) more recent definition of persuasion as the following: "the use of symbols (sometimes accompanied by images) by one social actor for the purpose of changing or maintaining another social actor's opinion or behavior" (p. 203). The two traditions of research, one on media and one on persuasion, focus on many of the same questions and underlying processes.

The purpose of this chapter is to illuminate those similarities as well as highlight points of potential synergy between the two. Our argument for the study of media influence as persuasion unfolds in two stages. First, we offer a systematic overview of a series of empirical studies that focus on (1) media and (2) the generation of persuasion-based outcomes. To structure this review, we juxtapose two classic persuasion typologies, then locate instances of media research in each resulting cell. Second, we provide an overview of how a handful of mass communication's most frequently utilized theories can be viewed as frameworks for the study of persuasion processes and outcomes. The various elements of this chapter stem from a single overarching argument that the study of media effects has always been linked to assessments of persuasion. This realization can provide tangible benefits for how the field approaches future studies of media influence, and these benefits are outlined in the closing portions of this chapter. The study of media influence is multifaceted and difficult to grasp as a single entity (see Nabi & Oliver, 2009). However, linking the study of media influence with persuasion allows for connections to be made between seemingly disparate lines of research in a manner that allows for the field's empirical work to be "interpretable, cumulative, and socially significant" (Bennett & Iyengar, 2008, p. 709).

A Typology of Persuasion and Media Influence

There are several different ways to approach developing more formal linkages between media effects and persuasion. One possibility would be to utilize a single persuasion theory (e.g., cognitive dissonance theory, social judgment theory, elaboration likelihood model) and describe any one study of media influence through this particular theoretical lens. However, the use of a lone theory would be far too limiting when attempting to explain all that comprises the study of media effects research. No one theory of persuasion can serve as a grand theory of media influence. Instead, it is essential to step back from a theory-specific approach and focus on two broader aims: properly bounding persuasion and acknowledging the inherent complexity of producing a media effect. We turn to the work of Miller (1980/2002) to address the bounds of persuasion and to McGuire (1989) for how best to approach media influence.

Miller (1980/2002) stresses that persuasion encompasses three different processes: Response shaping, response reinforcement, and response change. *Response shaping* focuses on the initial formation of how someone reacts to an object, while *response reinforcement* speaks to a strengthening of a preexisting reaction toward an object (this type of response is not purely evaluative and can include generating resistance to influence as well; Szabo & Pfau, 2002). *Response change* in its purest form is identified as a shift in the valence (positive/negative) of someone's reaction to an object. Discussions of media effects in relation to persuasion often form around an artificial boundary constraint of defining persuasion as being about response change only (Chaffee & Hochheimer, 1985; Holbert, Garrett, & Gleason, 2010). Defining persuasion as being about response change only represents a disservice to the concept. Any discussion of media effects that focuses solely on response change implicitly adopts a limited effects paradigm (see Bennett &

Iyengar, 2008). But, when persuasion is seen also to include response shaping and response reinforcement, it becomes clear that media influence and all its complexities can be understood as persuasion.

In addition, any discussion of mass communication influence must take into account the full range of factors that are at work in the production of a media effect. McGuire (1989) argues that five factors play a role in the production of a media effect: Message, source, recipient, channel, and context. It is easy to fall prey to focusing only on message influence in relation to persuasion, but media effects scholarship examines much more than just this single communication input. Any one media message functions alongside the source of that message, a broad range of recipient characteristics (e.g., demographics, needs, traits), the context within which the message is provided, and the channel through which it is offered (e.g., television, radio, newspaper) in the production of an effect. All five communication inputs are necessary for a thorough account.

We developed a 15-part typology to show that all varieties of persuasion in relation to the communication input variables of message, source, recipient, channel, and context are evident in the mass communication literature. The 3×5 typology focuses on (1) Miller's original conceptualization of persuasion as being about the shaping, reinforcing and/or changing of responses to attitude objects and (2) McGuire's (1989) five communication inputs. In offering this organizational structure, we strive to present a systematic assessment of the state of existing media research in relation to persuasion so that readers can better envision how seemingly distinct pieces of media effects scholarship form a more coherent whole.

Peer-reviewed journal articles were selected to represent each of the 15 areas of the typology (see Table 3.1). The study of media can be thought of as a broad tent, one that is large enough to cover both media and persuasion. Subsequent chapters of this handbook deal with political campaigns (see chapter 16 in this volume), health campaigns (see see chapter 17 in this volume), advertising (see see chapter 19 in this volume), and entertainment-oriented messages (i.e., narrative; see chapter 13 in this volume). It is appropriate to discuss these areas of study in persuasion terms, and so too is it proper to state that these areas are resolutely focused on the study of media influence. As a result, we have sought to represent of all of these media research areas within our typology, extracting works from outlets that typically publish pieces in the areas of commercial strategic communication, health communication, and political communication, as well as more general works in mass communication.

The presentation of the typology will focus on the five communication inputs in the following order: source, message, channel, recipient, and context. The presentation of Miller's three categories of persuasion is nested within each communication input and offered in the following order: formation, reinforcement, and change. We focus on only those works published since 2000 in order to show that the mix of Miller's and

McGuire's works remains a vibrant part of current mass communication research. But, it is important to note that there are numerous examples of works from earlier decades that could be slotted into any area of the typology.

Source

Formation

Karmarkar and Tormala (2010) examined attitude formation by asking participants to read a review of a fictional Italian restaurant, which was attributed to an expert source versus a source with markedly lower expertise. The source either expressed certainty or uncertainty in the review. The researchers demonstrated that both source expertise and source certainty significantly and directly impacted participants' attitudes and behavioral intentions toward the fictional restaurant. Additionally, readers formed the most favorable attitudes when the low-expertise source expressed a great deal of certainty, and when the high-expertise source expressed uncertainty.

Table 3.1 Miller-by-McGuire Typology

	Formation	**Reinforcement**	**Change**
Source	Karmarker & Tormala, 2010, *Journal of Consumer Research*	Gunther & Liebhart, 2006, *Journal of Communication*	Bailenson, Garland, Iyengar, & Lee, 2006, *Political Psychology*
Message	Putrevu, 2010, *Journal of Advertising*	Barker & Knight, 2000, *Public Opinion Quarterly*	Slater, Rouner, & Long, 2006, *Journal of Communication*
Channel	Sundar, 2000, *Journalism and Mass Communication Quarterly*	Pfau, Holbert, Zubric, Pasha, & Lin, 2000, *Media Psychology*	Overby & Barth, 2009, *Mass Communication and Society*
Recipient	Stephenson & Palmgreen, 2001, *Communication Monographs*	Holbert & Hansen, 2006, *Human Communication Research*	Chang, 2009, *Health Communication*
Context	Lee, Scheufele, & Lowenstein, 2005, *Science Communication*	Nathanson, 2001, *Communication Research*	McCluskey, Stein, Boyle, & McLeod, 2009, *Mass Communication and Society*

Subjects had no prior attitudes toward the attitude object (i.e., the restaurant). As a result, this media effect derived from a source manipulation reflects response formation.

Reinforcement

The hostile media phenomenon is a tendency for strong partisans on either side of an issue to view relatively balanced news coverage as biased *against* their point of view (Vallone, Ross, & Lepper, 1985). In studying this type of media effect, Gunther and Liebhart (2006) presented the same message to all participants, but manipulated the attribution of the message to either a professional journalist or a college student. When the article was attributed to a journalist, partisans on both sides perceived the article as strongly biased toward the other side. This divergent outcome derived from this source manipulation is an example of how a specific act of media engagement can produce a reinforcement of one's responses toward specific attitude objects. Partisans reinforced their own positions by distancing themselves from a news piece written by the journalist as source in particular.

Change

Bailenson, Garland, Iyengar, and Yee (2006) focused their attention on digital transformations of facial similarity between politicians and potential voters. The ratio of candidate-to-voter facial image meshing was varied between conditions (low similarity, 100% candidate facial image; high similarity, 60% candidate/40% voter). This study focused on only a male candidate, but a mix of male and female respondents. The increased morphing of the male political candidate with male voter facial images resulted in male subjects responding more favorably to the political candidate, as measured by a feeling thermometer, attractiveness, and voting intention. However, females went from ranking the political candidate relatively high on all three of these categories when similarity was low (i.e.,

male candidate's image was not morphed) to responding to the candidate much more unfavorably in the high candidate-voter morphing condition. Males shifted upward in their response toward the political candidate as a result of enhanced candidate-voter facial morphing, while females moved in the opposite direction. This study reveals how the manipulation of a single source element (i.e., facial similarity) can generate opposing response change reactions in audience members.

Message

Formation

Putrevu (2010) conducted a series of experiments examining the effects of advertising style on attitude formation. The experiments looked at the attitudes that participants formed toward a fictional airline, attitudes toward the advertisements, and behavioral intentions. The baseline persuasion message was manipulated to create four versions: an attribute-framed message and a goal-framed message, with positive and negative versions of each. The study found that when the advertisement used an attribute-framed approach, the positive message led to significantly more positive attitudes toward the brand. However, when a goal-framed message was used, the negative version of the message was more effective than the positive one.

Reinforcement

Barker and Knight (2000) looked at the effects of political talk radio on listener attitudes. Using an analysis of topics that were frequently mentioned on Rush Limbaugh's radio show and cross-sectional survey data from the 1995 American National Election Survey, Barker and Knight found that even after controlling for a host of demographic and prior ideology variables, the frequency that topics were mentioned on Limbaugh's show predicted stronger listener agreement with Limbaugh on those topics. The researchers found that listening to this content led to significantly more conservative attitudes beyond any overall shifts in opinion in the general public, particularly for topics that were discussed frequently via this outlet. These effects reflect how media messages can generate response reinforcement.

Change

Slater, Rouner, and Long (2006) studied the influence of two television dramas on viewer attitudes. The topics of the television narratives were two controversial and well-known public issues: the death penalty and the legal rights of same-sex couples. With regards to the same-sex drama, viewers' post-viewing attitudes did not differ significantly from the control group, but for the episode regarding the death penalty, post-viewing attitude measures indicated that the television show did in fact lead to attitude change (i.e., more favorable views of the death penalty). The death penalty drama also led to increased behavioral intentions to support the death penalty, and appeared to achieve these effects by weakening the link between prior ideology and subsequent attitudes toward the death penalty. The fact that the death penalty drama led to significant attitude shift demonstrates that in some cases narrative messages can be effective persuasive devices in producing response change (see chapter 13 by Busselle and Bilandzic in this volume).

Channel

Formation

Sundar (2000) manipulated the format in which news content was presented on a website in order to gauge the impact of various channels of information delivery on memory and attitudes toward the news stories. Participants saw one of five possible versions of a news website: text only, text stories with pictures, text stories with audio, text stories with pictures and audio, or text stories with pictures, audio, and video.

Attitudes toward the website (evaluations of design and coherence) were significantly lower when the stories were presented with text, pictures, and audio together. Evaluations of the website were most favorable in the "text with pictures" condition and the "text with pictures, audio, and video" condition. With regard to news quality, attitudes were the most favorable in the text with pictures condition, and were the least favorable in the conditions with more channels: "text with pictures and audio" and "text with pictures, audio, and video." Thus, there was a clear influence of the mix of channel presentation on a range of attitude objects with which the subjects had no prior interaction (e.g., news website, specific articles).

Reinforcement

Pfau, Holbert, Zubric, Pasha, and Lin (2000) focused their research on the influence of channel (print versus video) on the ability to confer *resistance* to unwanted persuasion (i.e., inoculation). This study found a direct and statistically significant effect of the channel manipulation on post-inoculation stimulus attitudes. As stated by Pfau et al., "compared to print, video inoculation treatments elicited an immediate impact, triggering resistance to attitudes at Phase 2" (2000, p. 23). Those subjects who held a specific attitude toward the topic of the message were better able to maintain that attitude at Time 2 as a result of coming into contact with the inoculation message via video rather than via a purely text-based message. There was a greater likelihood of being able to generate a reinforcement of a preexisting attitude through the use of video than through the use of text only. As a result, channel had a direct effect on response reinforcement.

Change

Overby and Barth (2009) used data from a three-wave panel survey of voters in Arkansas and Missouri to analyze political behavior concerning

U.S. Senate races. The researchers were examining the phenomenon known as "media malaise," which posits that a large amount of exposure to political ads, particularly negative ads, can lead to negative attitudes toward the American political system. The researchers found that, even after controlling for prior attitudes, radio and television had significant effects on attitudes toward our political system, but in different ways. Greater exposure to campaign ads on television led to significantly lower evaluations of the quality of election campaigns. Radio ad exposure and political e-mail exposure did not significantly affect evaluations of campaign quality. With regard to participant satisfaction with how democracy works in the United States, television and radio ads worked in opposite directions. Greater exposure to radio ads led to significantly *more favorable* evaluations of U.S. democracy, while greater exposure to TV ads led to significantly *less favorable* evaluations.

Recipient

Formation

Mass media scholars often focus their attention on how various individual-difference variables serve to form a response to a persuasive message as an object, and how then reactions to the message itself (e.g., perceived liking) generates a persuasive outcome (e.g., Nan, 2008). Stephenson and Palmgreen (2001) revealed that those individuals who were identified as high sensation seekers[1] had an automatic and positive response to antidrug public service media messages that were classified as being high in sensation value (e.g., quick cuts, strobe lighting, deep base beats). The recipient characteristic of sensation seeking influenced how certain audience members responded to the antidrug messages. The Stephenson and Palmgreen (2001) study is an example of how an individual-difference recipient characteristic allows for the formation of a response to a specific message,

and the indirect effects of the individual-difference variable on traditional persuasion outcomes are generated through reactions to the message itself as an object.

Reinforcement

Holbert and Hansen (2006) conducted a study on affective ambivalence (i.e., the internal consistency of affective responses to then-President George W. Bush) in reaction to the viewing of the controversial Michael Moore film, *Fahrenheit 9-11*. Subjects were randomly placed into either the stimulus condition (i.e., viewing the film in its entirety) or the control condition (i.e., no media material offered). These researchers reported a statistically significant two-way interaction of message condition (film, no film) by political party identification (Democrat, Republican, Independent), with a steep reduction in affective ambivalence toward President Bush for Democrats who viewed the film. Democrats already possessed relatively low levels of affective ambivalence toward Bush as attitude object prior to viewing the film, but this group developed even more internally consistent affective reactions toward Bush after having viewed the film (as hypothesized). The role of political party identification as a receiver characteristic played a key role in creating response reinforcement (i.e., increase in internal consistency of affective responses) to an attitude object through media exposure.

Change

Chang (2009) conducted an experiment examining attitudes toward smoking among high school students in Taiwan. Participants were asked to read print advertisements containing antismoking messages that focused on either the health impacts or psychological motives (e.g., tension relief) for smoking. The researcher found that among participants who were smokers, the health-oriented messages led to attitude change, reducing positive attitudes towards smoking, while motives-oriented based messages were less effective. Surprisingly, for nonsmokers, the motives-oriented messages had a boomerang effect and actually led to more positive attitudes toward smoking. Thus, the recipient characteristic of being a smoker or nonsmoker impacted the outcome of attitude change.

Context

Formation

The area of science communication is on the rise (e.g., Nisbet & Scheufele, 2009). There is much discussion in this area concerning a general "deficit model" when it comes to reaching out to a public to discuss science issues (see Sturgis & Allum, 2004). The general public has little to no awareness, knowledge, or attitude toward a wide variety of science-related matters, and many of these topics are exceedingly complex and often involve long-term, indirect outcomes that are not tangible for those with little understanding. One contextual factor often focused on in this line of research is "opinion climate"—one element of opinion climate would be a general trust in science. Generalized trust levels in science and scientists influence more specific attitudes toward new science issues (e.g., biotechnology) brought to public light through media (Priest, Bonfadelli, & Rusanen, 2003). Lee, Scheufele, and Lewenstein (2005) found the contextual factor of opinion climate (e.g., trust in business leaders) to affect the formation of public attitudes toward the risks associated with specific and emerging science-related issues (e.g., nanotechnology). The general public at large had no well-defined attitudes toward these science-related issues (i.e., reflective of the deficit model). However, when presented with these issues (most often times through news reports), initial attitudes were shaped by the macrolevel contextual factors of trust in science and actors (e.g., scientists, business leaders) who are influential in how these science- or science

technology-related matters play themselves out in the public arena.

Reinforcement

The context in which children watch television (e.g., alone or with others) can have a significant impact on their interpretations of television content and its subsequent impact. Nathanson (2001) found that the children in her sample watched violent and aggressive content far more with peers than with parents, and that rates of peer coviewing and peer discussion of this type of content were strongly correlated with positive attitudes and greater acceptance of this content. It has clearly been shown that those who are already aggressive gravitate toward aggressive content (Bandura, 1986), and the work of Nathanson indicates that the contextual factor of viewing aggressive content with one's peers will serve to reinforce positive attitudes toward this content.

Change

Classic media research on the Knowledge Gap Hypothesis is another area of mass communication research that takes into account context (Tichenor, Donohue, & Olien, 1980). For instance, communities that are more diverse tend to allow for more positive presentations of social protest given the wider variance of opinion at the macrosocial level, while communities that are less pluralistic will be less receptive to social protests taking place within their limited geographic area. This lower level of palatability will be reflected in more negative news coverage of social protests in these communities as well. A recent study by McCluskey, Stein, Boyle, and McLeod (2009) found that newspapers in less pluralistic communities (1) provided less coverage of protests and (2) covered protests in ways that were more critical of those social movements. This was especially true when the social protests were directed at local government. It is clear though various experimental works that varied news coverage of social protests can produce response change in how media audience members view not only the protesters and the stances they are taking on various issues, but also the police who are responding to/seeking to control the movements (see McLeod, 1995; McLeod & Detenber, 1999). However, a broader point being made by this area of research is that these types of response change outcomes will only become evident in communities that are pluralistic.

Summary

The studies summarized represent how the study of mass communication influence, undertaken across a wide range of subfields, can be linked to a full range of persuasion outcomes. We have offered a series of works that deal with response formation, reinforcement, and change. In addition, it was revealed through these works that persuasion in its many facets has been addressed by mass communication scholarship. As a result, there is a clear case to be made that the study of media influence is well matched with the study of persuasion.

Persuasion Components in Mass Communication Theories

The previous section provided a systematic overview of individual empirical works across a wide range of mass communication-related areas that demonstrate media effects as persuasion. However, the treatment of the study of media as being in line with the study of persuasion can and should be addressed at a broader theoretical level as well. Bryant and Miron (2004) cast a wide net in terms of what they included as mass communication *theory* when providing an overview of the current state of theory building in the field. They identified 26 major media-oriented theories that were referenced across a sample of journals

affiliated with distinct national/international scholarly associations. A handful clearly rise above the others in terms of the frequency with which they are referenced: agenda setting (McCombs & Shaw, 1972), cultivation (e.g., Gerbner, Gross, Morgan, & Signorielli, 1980), social learning (e.g., Bandura, 1973), McLuhan's study of media form influence (e.g., McLuhan, 1964), and the diffusion of innovations (e.g., Rogers & Shoemaker, 1971). As we demonstrate, there are processes of influence within each of these theories that are representative of our understanding of persuasion.

Agenda Setting

Agenda setting as a theory of news media influence represented a shift away from the more marketing-oriented model of campaign influence that was a driving force behind the work of Lazarsfeld and colleagues (e.g., Lazarsfeld, Berelson, & Gaudet, 1944). McCombs and Shaw (1972) steered the attention of political communication scholarship away from the latter stages of the hierarchy of effects (i.e., attitudes and behaviors) and the high bar of defining only "change" (i.e., Miller's response change as defined as a shift in valence) as an "effect." Instead, an argument was put forward by McCombs and Shaw, and backed by strong empirical evidence, that media can have strong influence on the earlier stages of the hierarchy of effects (i.e., awareness and salience).

Intricately connected to the process of salience transfer (from the media to the public) detailed in agenda setting theory is the subsequent process of political media priming effects (see McCombs, 2004).[2] This transfer effect has been studied at both the individual and aggregate levels (see Acapulco typology; McCombs et al., 2011). Priming is first and foremost about evaluation—what objects do people focus on when evaluating political actors and/or where they stand on particular issues? (see Scheufele, 2000). The process of salience transfer that is at the heart of agenda setting establishes the specific elements deemed to be most important within the public. If news media outlets are constantly talking about the state of the economy and jobs, then the public will be thinking about the state of the economy and jobs. In terms of priming, it would then be the case that the economy and job creation would be salient in people's minds when they are asked to evaluate how well President Obama is doing as President of the United States (e.g., stating their attitude toward Obama on a public opinion survey). The issues of the economy and job creation, as a result of being placed prominently within the news media's agenda, will be used disproportionately by citizens when it comes time to judge President Obama's job performance.

It is clear from this summary of the processes of influence detailed in agenda setting and priming that a process of persuasion unfolds, leading up to citizens forming attitudes and opinions toward political actors. The notion of treating agenda setting theory as detailing a process of persuasion is legitimized further when expanding our discussion to include not just the first level of agenda setting (i.e., salience transfer of *objects*), but also the second level of agenda setting theory (i.e., salience transfer of *attributes*; see Ghanem, 1997). Returning to the example of President Obama, specific attributes that are constantly raised in news media about our current president include his racial/ethnic profile, his being an intellectual, a family man, and the sense of calm/reason he brings to most decision-making functions. All of these attributes, made salient through the 24-7 news cycle, work to aid in the shaping of our attitudes toward our current president and whether we plan to vote for him in the 2012 general presidential election. As a result, the salience transfer process outlined in agenda setting theory can and should be viewed as part of broader persuasive processes evident in media.

Cultivation

Gerbner's cultivation theory reinforced the notion that media had the potential to produce moderate to large effects on individuals and society, especially over the long term (Shanahan & Morgan, 1999). Cultivation researchers argue that television, in particular, "cultivate[s] stable and common conceptions of reality" and it does so because "viewers are born into [a] symbolic world and cannot avoid exposure to its recurrent patterns" (Gerbner, Gross, Morgan, Signorielli, & Shanahan, 2002, p. 45). The "symbolic world" of television presents society in a manner that does not match reality. Our constant contact with televised messages shapes how we come to see the role of violence in a social world (e.g., Gerbner & Gross, 1976), determines specific sex roles (e.g., Signorielli, 1989), and establishes our views on the environment (e.g., Shanahan & McComas, 1999). The symbolic world offered by television stems from the industrialized mass production of messages by the few for consumption by the many, and the basic influences described by Gerbner and colleagues can very much be seen as a parallel to Miller's basic notion of response-shaping persuasion effects. Television through a process defined as "mainstreaming" leads individuals to react in similar ways to objects in the real world based on how the world is presented to us through television as a storyteller.

Cultivation as a theory of media influence also includes discussion of what can best be defined as response-reinforcement processes. A key process described by cultivation scholarship is "mainstreaming" (Gerbner, Gross, Morgan, & Signorielli, 1980). Mainstreaming is defined by Gerbner et al. (2002) as a process by which media generates "a relative commonality of outlooks and values" through heavy exposure. The medium of television consistently offers a symbolic representation of the world that is violent, sexist, and lacking in a healthy respect for the environment (once again, to name just a few elements that have been explored extensively by cultivation scholars). The mainstreaming effect is a classic reinforcement effect—the consistency and universality of television's symbolic representation of the world creates macrosocial uniformity of worldviews by continually reinforcing mainstream views.

Finally, the cognitive processes undertaken by audience members that lead to cultivation outcomes further show that cultivation theory can be viewed as a persuasion theory. Shrum and colleagues (e.g., Shrum, 1995, 1996, 1997; Shrum & O'Guinn, 1993) argue that television's influence stems from the audience engaging the medium via traditional heuristic processing. If audience members were to engage in more effortful, systematic processing of television messages, then the social judgments that match the symbolic world of television would not be seen as strongly in audience members. Not only did Gerbner and the early cultivation scholars discuss the role of the systematic manipulation of symbols in the formation of audience attitudes, but they also described core processes of influence (e.g., mainstreaming) that match well with our basic conceptualizations of certain aspects of persuasion (e.g., response reinforcement). Furthermore, the basic cognitive processes underlying cultivation are direct parallels to the paths of influence that are central to persuasion theories such as the elaboration likelihood model (ELM) and the heuristic-systematic model (HSM; cf., O'Keefe, chapter 9 of this volume). It is clear that much of what has been outlined to date in the area of cultivation research can be seen as describing persuasion-based processes and outcomes.

Social Learning

Of the five mass communication theories under consideration, the most explicitly persuasive in orientation is Bandura's social learning theory (see Bandura, 2001). The basic argument put forward by Bandura is that individuals are social learners: We learn how to act through our observations of others. Bandura (1986) details a four-stage process for how social learning unfolds over time. First, an individual pays attention to another person (either through unmediated or mediated contact). The second stage is defined as "retention processes," and one way in which

retention is enhanced is through repeated viewing of the behavior (Smith et al., 2006). Media, especially a visually oriented medium like television, allow for a tremendous amount of repeated viewing of specific acts, and in a manner that affords undivided attention to be given if the viewer chooses to do so. For example, a child may come into contact with a cartoon where one character acts out in an aggressive manner toward another character and is rewarded for these actions. The child is intrigued by the action-outcome pairing, pays more attention to this message, and consumes subsequent airings of the same program where similar cause-and-effect scenarios play themselves out in various storylines. This media example can be thought of as a classic response-shaping activity, and, as a result, producing a persuasive outcome.

It is important that the full social learning process does not end with the repeated viewing and retention. The latter two stages of social learning play themselves out in nonmediated environments. Third, there is the production process. The production processes involve guided enactment, the monitoring of social feedback of those enactments, and the manufacturing of creative adjustments to a modeled behavior to make it more appropriate for various situations. Finally, there are motivational processes, which involve the individual making determinations regarding the utility of adopting various modeled behaviors relative to the achievement of his or her goals. Those modeled behaviors that produce sufficient utility will be retained, while those that are unfruitful will be discarded. These nonmediated activities can produce response-change or response-reinforcement. If the actions learned through media, and being mimicked in real life, are producing positive outcomes, then the initial response shaping will be reinforced. If the actions taken on by the media audience member do not produce desirable outcomes, then the response is likely to change. In short, the first two stages of social learning theory speak to response-shaping processes, while the latter two stages detail how and why there can be response-reinforcement or response-change. No matter what process of social learning unfolds, all of these activities are representative of persuasive acts that take shape over time and that were initiated by the consumption of media messages.

McLuhan

McLuhan's (1978) work is fixated most squarely on form/channel. McLuhan argued that "it is the medium that shapes and controls the scale and form of human association and action" (McLuhan & Carson, 2003, pp. 230–231). By "association," McLuhan was speaking to the notion of what concepts we link together in our minds to form meaning (akin to associative networks in the mind), and by "action" he was speaking of the human behaviors generated by the associative networks. So, McLuhan was focused most squarely on that area of the hierarchy of effects where persuasion scholars often reside (i.e., attitudes and behaviors). It is clear that McLuhan did not believe in the notion of "media effects" as short-term, direct outcomes of media content consumption. Nonetheless, there are clear empirical principles and value that can be extracted from his work (see Holbert, 2004).

Meyrowitz (1998) describes three classifications of media research: media as conduit, media as language, and media as environment. Media-as-environment scholars argue that each medium represents a unique way of viewing the world based on its inherent strengths and limitations. No one way of presenting the world is any better or worse, just different from other ways. A major area of study for this line of research is at the macrosocial level, which focuses on when there are shifts in dominant forms of communication within a culture. McLuhan's work, epitomized by classic adages like "the medium is the message," is representative of a media-as-environment approach to mass communication influence, and there is a clear case to be made that this take on the study of media can be viewed as the study of persuasion and persuasive outcomes.

Building on earlier work by Chesebro (1984) on media epistemologies, Chesebro and Bertelsen (1996) make an argument that "communication technologies invite responses, particularly critical evaluations of the symbols and cognitive systems human beings are to live with, by, and through on a daily basis" (p. 176). The classic study of persuasion focuses on someone's manipulation of symbols to shape the attitudes and behaviors of others, but what McLuhan, Meyrowitz, Chesebro, and other media-as-environment scholars emphasize is that media technologies establish boundaries within which human beings as communicators must function in their attempts to influence others. More specifically, the inherent characteristics of one medium relative to other media forms tend to lead to human beings forming specific patterns of responses to symbolic systems. This process is representative of the technological determinism that is pervasive in the work of McLuhan and others who share his perspectives on media influence (Carey, 1981). Regardless of your assessment of the validity of these claims, the argument being offered is that the form/channel of communication, in particular one medium of mass communication versus another, shapes how we approach and gain meaning of the symbols we come into contact with on a daily basis.

The theorizing of McLuhan at the more microlevels, in particular his discussion of the use of different senses in relation to different media, offers the best means by which to test form influence in an empirical manner (Holbert, 2004). McLuhan (1975) argued that there was an environmental residue to any piece of information that landed in the brain—all pieces of information that landed in the brain were tagged by the sense used to extract that piece of information from an environment we engaged (real or mediated). These sensory tags were one criterion by which various pieces of information could be linked in the mind. So, our mental models are constructed not just around symbolic meaning, but also retain an environmental residue of sensory input. The more we take in pieces of information with similar tags (e.g., the sensorial tags associated with television as dominant medium of electronic age), the more humans would begin to see and interpret the world in line with what television offers us in terms of a unique environment and a symbolic manipulation of that environment. If such media-as-environment tags were to remain part of the information stored in our memories, then there would be a direct medium/channel influence that shapes how we approach various attitude objects, how our responses toward those objects are reinforced over time, and also when there would be any shifting/alteration in the valence of our responses to these objects.

Diffusion of Innovations

In making a case for diffusion of innovation theory as persuasion, it is important to first outline what can be defined as an innovation. An innovation can be just about anything that is perceived as new. This new object can be as tangible as a technological advancement or as abstract as a theory. As a result of the focus being on an innovation (i.e., that which is new), then it is most appropriate to approach this theory from the perspective of it describing response shaping activities. Of particular interest to the study of any innovation's diffusion is the S-curve (Rai, Ravichandran, & Samaddar, 1998), the pattern and rate by which any one innovation becomes diffuse within a society. The S-curves for some innovations have been rather steep, signaling a rather quick process by which the innovation made its way to the masses (e.g., the microwave). However, the diffusion of other innovations can be tracked along a curve that is much more horizontal (e.g., clothes washer). Why is it that some innovations become diffuse rather quickly, while others take longer to reach the late majority and laggard groups?

Rogers and colleagues identified a few characteristics that influence the speed and degree to which any one innovation becomes diffuse: Does

the innovation represent a relative advantage (i.e., is it a better mouse trap)? Is the innovation compatible with existing lifestyles and worldviews? How simple is the innovation (i.e., tangible, easy to use, parsimonious)? Is there a trial period? How big are the risks (e.g., financial, social) associated with adoption? Are there directly observable results? (Pashupati & Kendrick, 2010). Innovations that enjoy a relative advantage, function in line with existing values, are simple to understand or use, allow for a trial period, are less risky, and have directly observable results are those that are adopted at a quicker pace. However, rarely does any single innovation retain all the qualities needed to ensure immediate adoption. In fact, it is often the case that an innovation ranks high on some of these criteria, but relatively low on others. This is where persuasive acts come into play in determining the nature of the S-curve. Any innovation is most likely competing with other innovations, and it is a competitive process by which one innovation attempts to become diffuse relative to competing products, ideas, or theories. It is within this competitive environment that communication becomes essential and persuasive outcomes are produced. Promoters of a given innovation will see to make salient specific attributes that would lead to higher levels of adoption in the shortest period of time, while opponents of the same innovation will emphasize those attributes that will stunt widespread adoption. It is important to remember that the diffusion of any innovation is a social effort and an outcome of many communicative acts that are competitive. This competitive communication process is reflective of persuasion.

Future Research

The study of media influence is complex and multifaceted. A broad array of theories have been put forward to detail certain aspects of how mass communication produces effects in a wide range of contexts (e.g., politics, health, advertising, popular culture). It is often difficult, if not impossible, to gain a handle on how various empirical works on media effects, much less theoretically grounded lines of research, work together to form a coherent whole that would allow for media researchers to present to the broader public a concise summary of how, when, where, and why media have an impact on various aspects of their lives. In short, this field of study lacks organizational power. Diversity clearly has its strengths (Page, 2007), but the field would be well served to bring a broad range of research into a framework that forms a more coherent whole. This chapter has made an argument that linking the study of media effects to persuasion allows for greater organizational power to emerge. Additional theoretical argumentation should build off of the foundation offered in this work, focusing on how the broad principles of persuasion theory can serve as a means by which to bring together seemingly disparate areas of media research. There is a real need to establish a unified identity in the field of mass communication research, and persuasion may serve as a vehicle through which a shared identity for media effects research could be established.

At its most basic level, an endeavor of this kind would require researchers to properly define the scope of what can and should be labeled as a media effect. Adopting a properly bounded persuasion-oriented lens for the study of media influence (i.e., embracing the notion of an effect being representative of response formation, response reinforcement, and/or response change) would at the very least serve to guard against researchers falling into the trap of artificially constraining the concept of a "media effect" to being representative of change only (e.g., Bennett & Iyengar, 2008). Some theories of media influence are closely wedded to a media effects tradition, while other theorists (e.g., McLuhan, Gerbner) have argued explicitly against treating their subject matter as paralleling to anything so mundane as a "media effect." Nevertheless, several mass communication theories, as detailed in this chapter, are speaking to matters of response

formation, response reinforcement, and/or response change. In addition, the cumulative insights provided by various lines of research that have utilized these theories represent the full range of communication inputs highlighted by McGuire (albeit to varying degrees). Future research building off of the myriad of rich theoretical mass communication traditions offered in this chapter would be well served to better understand how any new inquiry reflects the study of response formation, reinforcement, or change. Making light of this most immediate connection to persuasion would allow any single empirical media effects work to be connected to a much broader set of insights already offered within the field.

Mass communication inquiry can utilize persuasion theory at two levels. The most basic level reflects thinking about effects-based research from the standpoint of Miller and McGuire. As already stressed, there needs to be better recognition of Miller's definition of persuasion being about formation, reinforcement, and change, and a corresponding reassessment of what constitutes an "effect." In addition, looking at any one media effect from the standpoint of McGuire's five communication input variables (i.e., message, source, recipient, channel, and context) can reveal gaps in what we know about any one type of media phenomenon. All of these input variables are at work at some level in the production of media influence, but not all have been addressed in the study of any one type of effect.

The more advanced level is representative of seeking to create more formal links between theories of persuasion and theories of media influence. The work of Shrum (1995, 1996, 1997) is a solid example of the potential benefits derived from linking persuasion-based theories (e.g., HSM) with a traditional mass communication theory (e.g., cultivation) to provide new insights as to why media are having impacts on individuals and societies. Bringing persuasion theory into the fold of existing mass communication theories could serve to enrich several lines of inquiry in all contexts within which media are analyzed. The arguments and linkages offered in this chapter should serve as nothing more than a jumping off point from which more substantive theoretical connections can be formed that would allow for new knowledge about communication to be generated.

Conclusion

The goal of this chapter is to establish more formal links between the studies of media influence and persuasion. First, a typology was constructed that reflected an appropriate bounding of both areas of influence. Persuasion is defined as encompassing response formation, response reinforcement, and response change (Miller, 1980/2002); and a media effect consists of five communication inputs: message, source, recipient, channel, and context (McGuire, 1989). Various pieces of media effects scholarship were then slotted into the 3 (Miller) × 5 (McGuire) matrix to show that there is an exhaustive list of media effects works that address all response-communication input combinations. Stepping beyond the individual study level, five mass communication theories are presented in relation to the study of persuasion. Not only do various elements of persuasion become evident in single empirical works detailing a variety of media effects, but the basic tenets of persuasion-based processes of communication influence can be found in media's most important theories. No grand theory of media influence as persuasion is offered in this work, but what is being stressed is that seeking to form closer connections between persuasion and media effects scholarship can bring greater organizational power to our understanding of media influence. In addition, extracting persuasion elements from the study of media influence may aid in the advancement of core persuasion theories. It is our hope that the connections forged in this chapter will serve as a starting point for more fruitful discussions on how the studies of persuasion and media influence can reciprocate in a manner that allows for knowledge advancement on some of our most basic and important communicative processes.

Notes

1. Sensation Seeking is defined as a biologically based personality trait that reflects a willingness to take risks in order to experience physiological arousal (Stephenson, Hoyle, Palmgreen, & Slater, 2003).

2. The term "priming" as employed by political communication scholarship is distinct from how it is utilized in more classic psychological work (Roskos-Ewoldsen, Roskos-Ewoldsen, & Carpentier, 2002). The priming effects described in political communication media effects scholarship play themselves out over a longer period of time than what is outlined in psychology and deal most squarely with what aspects of a particular object are utilized by an individual when evaluating the object.

References

Bailenson, J. N., Garland, P., Iyengar, S., & Yee, N. (2006). Transformed facial similarity as a political cue: A preliminary investigation. *Political Psychology, 27*, 373–386.

Bandura, A. (1973). *Aggression: A social learning analysis.* Upper Saddle River, NJ: Prentice Hall.

Bandura, A. (1978). Social learning theory of aggression. *Journal of Communication, 28*, 12–29.

Bandura, A. (1986). *Social foundations of thought and action: A social cognitive theory.* Upper Saddle River, NJ: Prentice Hall.

Bandura, A. (2001). Social cognitive theory of mass communication. *Media Psychology, 3*, 265–299.

Barker, D., & Knight, K. (2000). Political talk radio and public opinion. *Public Opinion Quarterly, 64*, 149–170.

Bennett, W. L., & Iyengar, S. (2008). A new era of minimal effects? The changing foundations of political communication. *Journal of Communication, 58*, 707–731.

Bryant, J., & Miron, D. (2004). Theory and research in mass communication. *Journal of Communication, 54*, 662–704.

Carey, J. (1981). McLuhan and Mumford: The roots of modern media analysis. *Journal of Communications, 31*, 162–178.

Chaffee, S. H., & Hochheimer, J. L. (1985). The beginnings of political communication research in the United States: Origins of the "limited effects" model. In M. Gurevitch & M. R. Levy (Eds.), *Mass communication review yearbook* (Vol. 5, pp. 75–104). Beverly Hills, CA: Sage.

Chaiken, S., & Stangor, C. (1987). Attitudes and attitude change. *Annual Review of Psychology, 38*, 575–630.

Chang, C. (2009). Psychological motives versus health concerns: Predicting smoking attitudes and promoting antismoking attitudes. *Health Communication, 24*, 1–11.

Chesebro, J. W. (1984). The media reality: Epistemological functions of media in cultural systems. *Critical Studies in Mass Communication, 1*, 111–130.

Chesebro, J. W., & Bertelsen, D. A. (1996). *Analyzing media: Communication technologies as symbolic and cognitive systems.* New York, NY: Guilford Press.

Desmond, A., & Moore, J. (1991). *Darwin.* New York, NY: W. W. Norton.

Dillard, J. P. (2010). Persuasion. In C. R. Berger, M. E. Roloff, & D. R. Roskos-Ewoldsen (Eds.), *The handbook of communication science* (2nd ed., pp. 203–218). Los Angeles, CA: SAGE.

Dillard, J. P., & Pfau, M. (2002). *The persuasion handbook: Developments in theory and practice.* Thousand Oaks, CA: Sage.

Gerbner, G., & Gross, L. (1976). Living with television: The violence profile. *Journal of Communication, 26*, 173–199.

Gerbner, G., Gross, L., Morgan, M., & Signorielli, N. (1980). The "mainstreaming" of America: Violence profile No. 11. *Journal of Communication, 30*, 10–29.

Gerbner, G., Gross, L., Morgan, M., Signorielli, N., & Shanahan, J. (2002). Growing up with television: Cultivation processes. In J. Bryant & D. Zillmann (Eds.), *Media effects: Advances in theory and research* (2nd ed., pp. 43–68). Mahwah, NJ: Lawrence Erlbaum.

Ghanem, S. (1997). Filling in the tapestry: The second level of agenda setting. In M. McCombs, D. L. Shaw, & D. Weaver (Eds.), *Communication and democracy: Exploring the intellectual frontiers in agenda-setting theory* (pp. 3–14). Mahwah, NJ: Lawrence Erlbaum.

Griffin, R. J., Neuwirth, K., Giese, J., & Dunwoody, S. (2002). Linking the heuristic-systematic model and depth of processing. *Communication Research, 29*, 705–732.

Gunther, A. C., & Liebhart, J. L. (2006). Broad reach or biased source? Decomposing the hostile media effect. *Journal of Communication, 56*, 449–466.

Hayes, A. F. (2007). Exploring the forms of self-censorship: On the spiral of silence and the use of opinion expression avoidance strategies. *Journal of Communication, 57*, 785–802.

Holbert, R. L. (2004). An embodied approach to the study of media forms: Introducing a social scientific component to medium theory. *Explorations in Media Ecology, 3*, 101–120.

Holbert, R. L., Garrett, R. K., & Gleason, L. S. (2010). A new era of minimal effects? A response to Bennett and Iyengar. *Journal of Communication, 60*, 15–34.

Holbert, R. L., & Hansen, G. J. (2006). *Fahrenheit 9-11,* Need for closure and the priming of affective ambivalence: An assessment of intra-affective structures by party identification. *Human Communication Research, 32*, 109–129.

Karmarkar, U. R., & Tormala, Z. L. (2009). Believe me: I have no idea what I'm talking about: The effects of source certainty on consumer involvement and persuasion. *Journal of Consumer Research, 36*(6), 1033–1049.

Lasswell, H. D. (1927). The theory of political propaganda. *The American Political Science Review, 21*, 627–631.

Lazarsfeld, P. F., Berelson, B., & Gaudet, H. (1944). *The people's choice: How the voter makes up his mind in a presidential campaign.* New York, NY: Duell, Sloan, and Pearce.

Lee, C. J., Scheufele, D. A., & Lowenstein, B. V. (2005). Public attitudes toward emerging technologies: Examining the interactive effects of cognitions and affect on public attitudes toward nanotechnology. *Science Communication, 27*, 240–267.

Matthes, J., Rios Morrison, K., & Schemer, C. (2010). A spiral of silence for some: Attitude certainty and the expression of political minority opinions. *Communication Research, 37*, 774–800.

McCluskey, M., Stein, S. E., Boyle, M. P., & McLeod, D. M. (2009). Community structure and social protest: Influences of newspaper coverage. *Mass Communication and Society, 12*, 353–371.

McCombs, M. E. (2004). *Setting the agenda: The mass media and public opinion.* Cambridge, UK: Polity.

McCombs, M. E., Ghanem, S., Lennon, F. R., Blood, R. W., Chen, Y., & Ban, H. (2011). International applications of agenda setting theory's Acapulco typology. In E. P. Bucy & R. L. Holbert (Eds.), *The sourcebook of political communication research* (pp. 383–394). New York, NY: Routledge.

McCombs, M. E., & Shaw, D. L. (1972). The agenda-setting function of mass media. *Public Opinion Quarterly, 36,* 176–187.

McGuire, W. J. (1989). Theoretical foundations of campaigns. In R. E. Rice & C. K. Atkin (Eds.), *Public communication campaigns* (2nd ed., pp. 43–65). Newbury Park, CA: Sage.

McLeod, D. M. (1995). Communicating deviance: The effects of television news coverage of social protest. *Journal of Broadcasting and Electronic Media, 39,* 4–19.

McLeod, D. M., & Detenber, B. H. (1999). Framing effects of television news coverage of social protest. *Journal of Communication, 49,* 3–23.

McLuhan, M. (1964). *Understanding media: The extension of man.* New York, NY: Mentor. McLuhan, M. (1975). Misunderstanding the media's laws. *Technology and Culture, 16,* 263.

McLuhan, M. (1978). The brain and the media: The "Western" hemisphere. *Journal of Communication, 28,* 54–60.

McLuhan, M., & Carson, D. (2003). *The book of probes.* Corte Madera, CA: Gingko Press.

Mery, F., & Kawecki, T. J. (2002). Experimental evolution of learning ability in fruit flies. *Proceedings of the National Academy of Sciences of the United States, 99,* 14274–14279.

Meyrowitz, J. (1998). Multiple media literacies. *Journal of Communication, 48,* 96–108.

Miller, G. R. (2002). On being persuaded: Some basic distinctions. In J. P. Dillard & M. Pfau (Eds.), *The persuasion handbook: Developments in theory and practice* (pp. 3–16). Thousand Oaks, CA: Sage. (Original work published 1980)

Nabi, R. L., & Oliver, M. B. (2009). *The SAGE handbook of media processes and effects.* Thousand Oaks, CA: Sage.

Nan, X. (2008). The influence of liking for a public service announcement on issue attitude. *Communication Research, 35,* 503–528.

Nathanson, A. I. (2001). Parents versus peers: Exploring the significance of peer mediation of antisocial television. *Communication Research, 28,* 251–274.

Neuman, W. R., & Guggenheim, L. (2011). The evolution of media effects theory: A six-stage model of cumulative research. *Communication Theory, 21,* 169–196.

Nisbet, M. C., & Scheufele, D. A. (2009). What's next for science communication? Promising directions and lingering distractions. *American Journal of Botany, 96,* 1767–1778.

Noelle-Neumann, E. (1974). The spiral of silence: A theory of public opinion. *Journal of Communication, 24,* 43–51.

Overby, L., & Barth, J. (2009). The media, the medium, and malaise: Assessing the effects of campaign media exposure with panel data. *Mass Communication and Society, 12*(3), 271–290.

Page, S. E. (2007). *The difference: How the power of diversity creates better groups, forms, schools, and societies.* Princeton, NJ: Princeton University Press.

Pashupati, K., & Kendrick, A. (2010). Advertising practitioner perceptions of HDTV advertising: A diffusion of innovations perspective. *The International Journal of Media Management, 10,* 158–178.

Petty, R. E., & Cacioppo, J. T. (1986). *Communication and persuasion: Central and peripheral routes to attitude change.* New York, NY: Springer-Verlag.

Pfau, M., Holbert, R. L., Zubric, S. J., Pasha, N. H., & Lin, W. (2000). Role and influence of communication modality in the process of resistance to persuasion. *Media Psychology, 2*(1), 1–33.

Priest, S. H., Bonfadelli, H., & Rusanen, M. (2003). The "trust gap" hypothesis: Predicting support for biotechnology across national cultures as a function of trust in actors. *Risk Analysis, 23,* 751–766.

Putrevu, S. (2010). An examination of consumer responses toward attribute- and goal-framed messages. *Journal of Advertising, 39,* 5–24.

Rai, A., Ravichandran, T., & Samaddar, S. (1998). How to anticipate the Internet's global diffusion. *Communications of the ACM, 41,* 97–106.

Rogers, E. M., & Shoemaker, F. F. (1971). *Communication of innovations: A cross-cultural approach.* New York, NY: Free Press.

Roskos-Ewoldsen, D. R., Roskos-Ewoldsen, B., & Carpentier, F. R. (2002). Media priming: A synthesis. In J. Bryant and D. Zillmann (Eds.), *Media effects: Advances in theory and research* (pp. 97–120). Mahwah, NJ: Lawrence Erlbaum.

Scheufele, D. A. (2000). Agenda-setting, priming, and framing revisited: Another look at cognitive effects of political communication. *Mass Communication and Society, 3,* 297–316.

Schroeder, L. M. (2005). Cultivation and the elaboration likelihood model: The learning and construction of availability heuristic models. *Communication Studies, 56,* 227–242.

Shanahan, J., & McComas, K. (1999). *Nature stories.* Cresskill, NJ: Hampton Press.

Shanahan, J., & Morgan, M. (1999). *Television and its viewers: Cultivation theory and research.* Cambridge, UK: Cambridge University Press.

Shrum, L. J. (1995). Assessing the social influence of television: A social cognition perspective on cultivation effects. *Communication Research, 22,* 402–429.

Shrum, L. J. (1996). Psychological processes underlying cultivation effects: Further tests of construct accessibility. *Human Communication Research, 22,* 482–509.

Shrum, L. J. (1997). The role of source confusion in cultivation effects may depend on processing strategy: A comment to Mares (1996). *Human Communication Research, 24,* 349–358.

Shrum, L. J., & O'Guinn, T. C. (1993). Processes and effects in the construction of social reality: Construct accessibility as an explanatory variable. *Communication Research, 20,* 436–471.

Signorielli, N. (1989). Television and conceptions about sex roles: Maintaining conventionality and the status quo. *Sex Roles, 21,* 337–356.

Slater, M., Rouner, D., & Long, M. (2006). Television dramas and support for controversial public policies: Effects and mechanisms. *Journal of Communication, 56,* 235–252.

Smith, S. W., Smith, S. L., Pieper, K. M., Yoo, J. H., Ferris, A. L., Downs, E., et al. (2006). Altruism and American television: Examining the amount of, and context surrounding, acts of helping and sharing. *Journal of Communication, 56,* 707–727.

Stephenson, M. T., Hoyle, R. H., Palmgreen, P., & Slater, M. D. (2003). Brief measures of sensation seeking for screening and large-scale surveys. *Drug and Alcohol Dependence, 72,* 279–286.

Stephenson, M. T., & Palmgreen, P. (2001). Sensation seeking, perceived message sensation value, personal involvement, and processing of anti-marijuana PSAs. *Communication Monographs, 68,* 49–71.

Sturgis, P., & Allum, N. (2004). Science in society: Re-evaluating the deficit model of public attitudes. *Public Understanding of Science, 13,* 55–74.

Sundar, S. S. (2000). Multimedia effects on processing and perception of online news: A study of picture, audio, and video downloads. *Journalism and Mass Communication Quarterly, 77,* 480–499.

Szabo, E. A., & Pfau, M. (2002). Nuances in inoculation: Theory and applications. In J. P. Dillard & M. Pfau (Eds.), *The persuasion handbook: Developments in theory and practice* (pp. 233–258). Thousand Oaks, CA: Sage.

Tichenor, P. J., Donohue, G. A., & Olien, C. N. (1980). *Community conflict and the press.* Beverly Hills, CA: Sage.

Vallone, R. P., Ross, L., & Lepper, M. R. (1985). The hostile media phenomenon. *Journal of Personality and Social Psychology, 49*(3), 577–585.

Verhey, S. D. (2005). The effect of engaging prior learning on student attitudes toward creationism and evolution. *BioScience, 55,* 996–1003.

CHAPTER 4

Outcomes of Persuasion

Behavioral, Cognitive, and Social

Nancy Rhodes and David R. Ewoldsen

Imagine a situation in which your doctor is attempting to influence your behavior—she wants you to have a colonoscopy as routine screening procedure. She tells you that it is a time-consuming procedure that requires general anesthesia and an uncomfortable preparation the night before, but that it is the best procedure to find early forms of colon cancer. Although you had no initial opinion about the test, you find yourself thinking about how much you dislike medical "procedures" and how doctors always seem to underestimate the discomfort of such things. In spite of that, you sense that your doctor really wants you to get the test, so you tell her that you will call and schedule the test the following day. When the next day arrives, however, your car doesn't start and you are late for work and you totally forget about making the appointment. Later that week, you are having lunch with a group of friends. When a friend mentions that her cousin was recently diagnosed with end-stage colon cancer, you remember your conversation with your doctor and you listen carefully. Your friend talks about the likelihood that an earlier colonoscopy could have caught the disease at a more treatable stage. In the

course of the conversation you find out that most of your friends have already had a colonoscopy, and they urge you to get yours done. When you get back to work that afternoon, you call and schedule an appointment for your colonoscopy.

Many elements of persuasion are illustrated in this vignette. First, the persuasive argument made by your doctor got you to begin thinking about the costs and benefits of the procedure. The thoughts generated, which linked to your own experiences with medical tests were the initial outcomes of the persuasive process. These thoughts, and the statements you made in response to those thoughts, then became further inputs to your processing of the dilemma at hand. Although you initially had an *intention* to call to make the appointment, the challenges of daily life interceded. Finally, it was when you had a chance to talk with friends about a related case, and when you learned that there is a supportive norm within your friendship group, that you finally engaged in behavior and made the call.

It is important to consider the nature of the persuasion process when discussing the outcomes of persuasion. As previously noted, the outcomes traditionally studied in lab experiments focusing on persuasion are attitudes, behavioral intention, and to a lesser extent, behavior. Simply put, persuasion endeavors to change attitudes, which has often been assumed would result in behavior change. Research in persuasion has a long history in the social sciences, perhaps because what appears simple on the face (that attitudes guide behavior) turns out to be far more complex and interesting when examined more deeply (Prislin & Crano, 2008; Zanna & Fazio, 1982). Allport (1935) argued that:

> Attitudes determine for each individual what he [or she] will see and hear, what he [or she] will think and what he [or she] will do. To borrow a phrase from William James, they "engender meaning upon the world"; they draw lines about and segregate an otherwise chaotic environment; they are our methods for finding our way about in an ambiguous universe. (p. 806)

We argue in this chapter that attitudes do all that, and that the interplay of attitudes and behavior gives fascinating insight into how people make sense of, and behave sensibly in, this chaotic world.

Behavior as an Outcome of Persuasion

Behavior as an outcome of persuasion is the gold standard because it is often the main point of a persuasive attempt. However, it can be very difficult to measure actual behavior, because researchers are not always present when the behavior of interest is performed (e.g., voting behavior). Even when it is possible to measure actual behavior, it can be very costly in terms of time and financial resources. Additionally, it is sometimes unethical to measure actual behavior (e.g., drug use, underage drinking, or smoking).

Rather than examining actual behavior, researchers rely on participants' self-reports of behavior in the vast majority of studies in persuasion. However, relying on self-reports of behavior is problematic because we can never be sure that participants' reports are accurate. Participants' memories could be faulty, they may want to portray themselves in a positive light, and the nature of the persuasion study may telegraph the "correct" answer. For all of these reasons, self-reports of behavior may not be reliable and research should be conducted validating the self-report measures that are used. The difficulties in observing actual behavior and in measuring reported behavior reliably has had a number of consequences. Researchers have begun to rely on a number of proxies, or stand-ins, for actual behavior measurement. Some of these are described in the following.

Proxies for Behavior

Aggregated Behavior

An intriguing line of research by Fishbein and Ajzen (1974) focused on the specificity with which we measure both attitudes and behavior (see also Ajzen & Fishbein, 2005). Their contention was that attitudes are measured in very general terms in traditional work on attitudes and persuasion. For example, if the study is concerned with a government policy, the policy is explained and then participants indicate whether they are in favor of the policy or not. In political persuasion, attitudes toward candidates are measured by participants indicating how favorably they feel toward the candidate. In marketing research, the participants' overall judgment of a product may be measured. Yet, the behavioral measure tends to be something very specific, such as whether the participant voted for the candidate in the election or whether the respondent purchased the product in question at his or her last trip to the store.

Ajzen and Fishbein noted that when people make aggregated judgments of an attitude object, they are taking into account the range of beliefs they have about that object in different contexts.

Confining behavioral measures to a single place and time disadvantages the attempt to correlate attitudes and behaviors because there may be vagaries in the specific situation that affect the behavior. However, by examining the pattern of behavior over time, one would obtain a more reliable measure of the individual's propensity to engage in the behavior. For example, in the case of whether attitudes direct TV watching behavior, a person with a favorable attitude toward one of the late-night comic hosts might or might not have watched the show in the previous evening for a number of reasons—they may have been out with friends, they may have had to catch up on work, they may have fallen asleep early. However, by measuring viewing behavior over, say, a one-month period, it is likely that those having a positive attitude toward the program will tune in more frequently than those having a negative attitude.

Behavioral Intention and Behavioral Willingness

Another way in which Fishbein and Ajzen (1975) dealt with the lack of predictive validity of attitudes was to espouse the use of measures of behavioral intention (see also Ajzen & Fishbein, 2005). In their model, behavioral intention is a strong predictor of actual behavior. The key for Fishbein and Ajzen is that the measure of behavioral intention must be anchored to a specific time and place. Thus, asking someone if they intend to watch Conan O'Brian on a specific night will give a closer approximation to the actual behavior that night than if they were asked if they intend to watch Conan O'Brian in some vaguely defined future.

Measures of behavioral intention are prevalent in health communication research. In part, this is because it is unethical to present opportunities for research participants to engage in health risk behaviors in the lab. Thus, studies in which anti-smoking messages are presented will ask about specific intentions to smoke in the future instead of offering participants a cigarette

to determine if the anti-smoking message was successful. For example, participants might be asked questions such as "Do you think you will smoke a cigarette sometime today?" or "Do you think you will smoke a cigarette sometime in the coming week?" Measures such as these have been used as proxies for behavior with good success. In studies where follow-up surveys have been conducted, the ability of the behavior intention measure to predict actual behavior is reasonably strong, for example, resulting in an average correlation of .5 in one meta-analysis (Albarracín, Johnson, Fishbein, & Mullerleile, 2001). To be sure, behavioral intention falls short of being a perfect measure of behavior, but it does provide an index of propensity to behave.

One of the criticisms of measuring behavioral intentions is that it assumes that a person's behavior is the result of deliberative decision-making (Fazio, 1990; Roskos-Ewoldsen, & Fazio, 1997). However, there are many varieties of behavior and it is important to understand how different behaviors influence the relationship between attitudes and behavior (Jaccard & Blanton, 2005). Certainly, people often deliberate carefully about a decision before forming an intention to engage in some behavior. For example, people may carefully deliberate about important decisions, such as buying a car or deciding what college to attend. However, much of people's everyday social behavior is more spontaneous in nature (Fazio, 1990; Gerrard, Gibbons, Vande Lune, Pexa, & Gano, 2002; Gerrard, Gibbons, Houlihan, Stock, & Pomery, 2008). For example, people rarely carefully consider all of the available information about all the different choices in a vending machine before making a selection.

Fazio's Motivation and Opportunities as DEterminants (MODE) model attempts to capture this difference between deliberative and more spontaneous behavior (Fazio, 1990; Olson & Fazio, 2009). According to the model, there are two factors that can influence whether a judgment or behavior is spontaneous or deliberative in nature: motivation and opportunity. Motivation can influence the judgment when individuals have a reason to more carefully scrutinize the attitude object. Some motivations that might lead to more careful scrutiny of an attitude object include desire to make accurate judgments, the need to belong, and motivation to avoid appearing prejudiced (Olson & Fazio, 2009). Opportunity refers to an individual's actual ability to make a deliberative judgment at a given time. Factors such as time and available cognitive resources can influence a person's opportunity to make deliberative judgments (Olson & Fazio, 2009). According to the MODE model, when people are highly motivated and they have sufficient opportunity to carefully consider the available information, they are more likely to make decisions in a deliberative fashion. However, when motivation or opportunity is low, people are more likely to engage in a spontaneous manner.

Spontaneous decisions are characterized by the consideration of information that is *accessible*, that is, quickly activated from memory (Fazio, 1990; Gerrard et al., 2008; Roskos-Ewoldsen, 1997; Olson & Fazio, 2009). Consider the adolescent who, in surveys, reports that peer pressure has no influence on his or her behavior. Yet when asked by a best friend at a party if he or she wants to try a cigarette, this same adolescent takes a few puffs. Behavioral willingness refers to a person's willingness to engage in risky behavior in circumstances that promote that behavior such as the friend asking if you want a cigarette. Consequently, behavioral willingness is an outcome measure that represents a teen's likelihood of spontaneously engaging in smoking behavior if an opportunity presents itself (Gerrard et al., 2002; Gerrard et al., 2008; Rhodes & Ewoldsen, 2009) and is an indicator of spontaneous decision making.

Self-Reports of Behavior

Although we said earlier that it is difficult to trust respondents' reports of their own behavior, self-reports are often used as outcome variables in persuasion research. The use of such self-reports is subject to criticism because of the issues previously described, but it is also true that sometimes respondents' own reports are the best information it is possible to obtain. To address this problem, work in various behavioral domains has focused on constructing reliable indices for behavior. For example, cigarette smoking behavior is frequently measured with a set of items developed for the behavioral risk factor surveillance system, which has been shown to have good reliability and validity.

To some extent, the necessity for accurate measures of actual behavior depends on the goals of the research being conducted. From the perspective of researchers interested in how individuals process and react to persuasive appeals, showing that message characteristics have predicted effects on these types of indices is usually sufficient for the purposes of testing their hypotheses. For researchers in the field, however, more precise measures are often required to evaluate the effectiveness of a health-related intervention.

Attitudes as Outcomes

One approach to the problem of measuring behavior reliably is to ignore the problems associated with measuring behavior and simply study the effects of persuasive messages on attitudes. Researchers in this stream have largely been content to leave the question of behavior to other scholars and focus on the processes through with attitude change occurs. Huge advances in theory about the effects of persuasive messages have occurred, including Petty and Cacioppo's (1986) elaboration likelihood model and Chaiken's heuristic-systematic model (Chaiken, Liberman, & Eagly, 1989), which have advanced thinking about how dual processes of decision making relate to persuasive attempts.

A great deal of research along these lines has been conducted to test predictions of dual process models. Consistent with these models, studies such as these have generally found that strong arguments are persuasive when participants are motivated and able to carefully think about the argument claims. Attitude formation or change that is based on a careful consideration of the arguments tends to be more durable and more predictive of behavior than attitudes that are formed or changed on the basis of persuasive elements that are peripheral to the message claims, such as the attractiveness of the spokesperson (Andrews & Shimp, 1990). There are numerous sources that address these approaches to the study of attitudes and persuasion (Albarracín, Johnson, & Zanna, 2005; Crano & Prislin, 2008), including other chapters in this volume. We focus the bulk of our review of the recent work on accessible and implicit attitudes because this is a burgeoning area of research with important theoretical and methodological contributions.

Accessible or Implicit Attitudes

Recent work has focused on spontaneously or implicitly activated attitudes. As discussed earlier, work on accessible and implicit attitudes is an outgrowth of the cognitive revolution in social science research and particularly in social psychology that began in the 1970s. This perspective is consistent with dual process approaches, and focuses directly on the role of spontaneous or automatic processing of attitudinally relevant constructs. Accessible attitudes are those attitudes that are readily available in memory. An example of an accessible attitude is one's attitude toward a cockroach. Most people do not need to search their memory long to find their attitude toward this object when they see it crawling on their kitchen floor: the evaluation is retrieved extremely quickly, and appropriate action is initiated. What is important is that these implicit and accessible attitudes are activated automatically and without controlled thought, and thus they can affect behavior at times when motivation to process information carefully is low.

Attitude Accessibility

Attitude accessibility involves the ease with which an attitude is activated from memory

(Fazio, 1986; Roskos-Ewoldsen, 1997). Within the attitude accessibility framework, attitudes are defined as associations between objects and evaluations of those objects stored in memory (Fazio, 1986, 1989). Based on the idea of memory as a semantic network, the mental representation of the attitude object is stored as a node in this network. Similarly, the evaluation of this object is also represented as a node in the network. To the extent that an evaluation is strongly associated with the object, the evaluation will be highly accessible: that is, when the node for the attitude object is activated, the strength of the association will ensure that the node containing the evaluation of the object is also activated. In this way, judgments can be made rapidly and without extensive reflection (Fazio, 1986).

In contrast, for attitudes that are not accessible, the associations between the object and the evaluation of that object are not as strong, or perhaps the object has no evaluation associated with it. In this case, the activation of the object does not spontaneously activate the evaluation of the object, and, it may take more time to activate the judgment. Many attitudes lie somewhere between these two extremes. Most people, when asked, can report their evaluation of a wide range of attitude objects. For any given person, some of these attitudes will be strong and very quickly retrieved, others may be relatively weak and slowly accessed.

Accessible attitudes are important predictors of various phenomenon of interest to communication scholars and psychologists (Dillard, 1993; Roskos-Ewoldsen, 1997). We continue Fazio's (1989) practice of discussing the *functions* that accessible attitudes serve for the individual because we feel it is important to focus on what the attitude does for the individual. To use Allport's words (1935; previously quoted), how does the accessible attitude influence how a person finds their way in an ambiguous universe?

Initially, accessible attitudes influence what attracts our attention, literally determining what we notice in our environment. Roskos-Ewoldsen and Fazio (1992) found that research participants were more likely to orient their attention to objects in a complex visual field when they had more accessible attitudes toward those objects. Likewise, people are more likely to attend to brands within an advertisement when they already have an accessible attitude toward that brand (Goodall & Ewoldsen, 2011). Similarly, research participants who had more accessible attitudes toward particular consumer products were more likely to find those products on a shelf and choose them from a group of many other products toward which their attitudes were less accessible (Fazio, Powell, & Williams, 1989). The implications are clear in a world full of information and visual clutter. We cannot act positively (or negatively) toward objects we do not "see." The orienting function of accessible attitudes will be the gateway to attitude-consistent behaviors in most cases.

Second, accessible attitudes offer us an efficient, though not always desirable, means of processing myriad pieces of information we encounter each day by motivating us to attend to and carefully consider some messages and by facilitating avoidance or biased processing of other messages (Fazio, Roskos-Ewoldsen, & Powell, 1994; Fazio & Towles-Schwen, 1999; Roskos-Ewoldsen, 1997). Accessible attitudes often signal for us which topics are important, thereby encouraging us to attend to and elaborate on persuasive messages related to the important topic or delivered by a favored message source (Fabrigar, Priester, Petty, & Wegener, 1998; Roskos-Ewoldsen, Bichsel, & Hoffman, 2002). For example, Fabrigar et al. (1998) found that people with more accessible attitudes toward vegetarianism were more likely to centrally process a message about vegetarianism. Roskos-Ewoldsen et al. (2002) extended this finding by demonstrating that the activation of an attitude toward other components of the message such as the source of the message could also increase central processing. People with more accessible positive attitudes toward the source of the message are more likely to centrally process a message attributed to that source, and the attitude toward the source does not bias the processing of the message. Rather, the accessible attitude toward the source of the message acts as a piece of information indicating the importance of the message, which motivates participants to more carefully process the message (see also Fabrigar et al., 1998; Roese & Olson, 1994).

Accessible attitudes can also encourage us to cognitively reinforce our existing attitudes and behaviors by motivating us to process information in a biased manner. Early scholars recognized that attitudes can function as lenses through which we view and interpret our world (Allport, 1935; Katz, 1960; Smith, Bruner, & White, 1956). More recent research has shown that accessible attitudes often color our judgments of messages and attitude objects in a manner that is consistent with our attitudes (Fazio, 1990; Fazio et al., 1994). For example, research participants with more accessible, positive attitudes toward smoking were more likely to perceive antismoking PSAs as biased (Rhodes, Roskos-Ewoldsen, Edison, & Bradford, 2008; Shen, Monahan, Rhodes, & Roskos-Ewoldsen, 2009). An important caveat to these studies is that accessible attitudes are more likely to bias processing when the information or situation is relatively ambiguous (Roskos-Ewoldsen, 1997).

Finally, perhaps the most important contribution of the conceptualization and study of attitude accessibility is the identification of consistently strong correlations between accessible attitudes and behavior (for general reviews, see Fazio, 1986, 1990; Fazio & Roskos-Ewoldsen, 2005) in the areas of health behaviors, voting behavior, consumer product choice, loyalty to retail stores, intended charitable contributions, exercise behaviors, choice of a game to play, and racist behaviors (Bassili, 1995; Kokkinaki, & Lunt, 1997; Posavac, Sanbonmatsu, & Fazio, 1997; Rhodes, Ewoldsen, Shen, Monahan, & Eno, 2011; Rhodes & Ewoldsen, 2009; Woodside & Trappey, 1996). It makes sense that attitudes are most likely to affect behavior when they are activated from memory at the moment the attitude object is initially observed.

Of course, attitudes that are more accessible from memory are more likely to be activated and to influence behaviors. Fazio (1986) proposed a process model of the attitude-behavior relationship that basically argues that accessible attitudes are more likely to be activated, and once activated, they will bias how information within the environment is perceived, which then influences a person's behavior. If you have a highly accessible negative attitude toward cockroaches and you see a cockroach, that attitude will be activated. The activated negative attitude will lead to the judgment that this is an aversive situation and you should act accordingly by either leaving the situation or doing something to remove the cockroach, such as stepping on it.

Consistent with the MODE model, accessible attitudes most often affect behavior in situations that allow or require spontaneous decisions (e.g., deciding which gas station to turn into when your tank is on empty), or in ambiguous social situations (Fazio, 1986, 1990). With situations that facilitate or require spontaneous behaviors, highly accessible attitudes will likely determine which evaluations or objects come to mind when a behavioral decision must be made. For example, when research participants were asked to which charity they would donate monetary compensation for research participation, they chose the charities for which their attitudes were most accessible, even though they had evaluated other charities just as or more favorably in a pretest (Posavac et al., 1997). However, in situations that require accurate decisions or a consideration of norms, we might reflect on the underpinnings or cognitive components of our attitude toward the behavior, social norms regarding the behavior, and the unique characteristics of the situation and then act accordingly (Ajzen, 1991; Fazio, 1990). Hence, our behavior might not be strongly correlated with our attitudes in more deliberative situations that give us the opportunity to reflect on those attitudes. However, even in situations that involve careful, deliberative decision making, accessible attitudes can influence decisions (Roskos-Ewoldsen, 1997; Roskos-Ewoldsen, Yu,

& Rhodes, 2004). Consistent with this, Roskos-Ewoldsen et al. (2004) found that women with more accessible attitudes toward breast self-exams were more likely to intend to perform breast self-exams in the future.

According to the transactive model of attitude accessibility, accessible attitudes tend to operate in a manner that maintains their accessibility through frequent activation and through elaboration. For example, because accessible attitudes orient our attention to objects in our environment, they are reactivated or rehearsed via the automatic judgment that occurs when one attends to a liked or disliked object (Roskos-Ewoldsen, 1997). Likewise, direct experience with an attitude object makes attitudes more accessible from memory, which can easily and consistently initiate the process from accessibility to attention to behavior that constitutes the remaining section of the transactive model (DeBono & Snyder, 1995; Fazio, 1986). For example, in a recent study, cigarette smokers showed more biased processing of antismoking messages than nonsmokers (Rhodes & Ewoldsen, 2009). In addition, as the smokers judged the antismoking ad to be more biased, they also indicated they were less likely to quit smoking. In other words, the antismoking ad created reactance in the smoker, which reinforced their desire to smoke. In this study, it is important to note that the *accessibility* of the smokers' attitudes mediated this process. It was smokers with more accessible attitudes that judged the antismoking ads as more biased and were less likely to want to quit smoking. The accessible prosmoking attitude operated as a defense mechanism for these smokers to protect their smoking behavior from threats such as antismoking ads, and their accessible attitudes also strengthened the behavioral response to continue smoking (Arpan, Rhodes, & Roskos-Ewoldsen, 2007).

Implicitly Measured Attitudes

There has been a surge of interest in the social sciences in the study of implicitly measured attitudes (e.g., Bassili & Brown, 2005; Petty, Fazio, &

Brinol, 2009; Wittenbrink & Schwarz, 2007). The designation of "implicit attitude" means that the attitude is measured without asking someone to explicitly indicate their attitude, in contrast to commonly used paper-and-pencil measures of attitudes (DeHouwer, 2006; Fazio & Olson, 2003). An example of an implicit measure of an attitude is the affective misattribution procedure (AMP; Payne, 2009), which involves presenting participants with a picture of a critical item (e.g., a bottle of beer), which is quickly followed by a picture of a Chinese ideograph. The participants' task is to indicate whether they like or dislike the ideograph, participants are never asked to indicate their attitude toward the critical item (the bottle of beer). Payne, Cheng, Govorun, and Steward (2005) demonstrated that participants' attitude toward the target (the beer) influenced how they responded to the ideograph. The attitude toward the target influenced responses to the target even when participants were explicitly told they should not allow that to occur. However, as DeHouwer (2006) has noted, none of the implicit measures can ensure that participants are not considering their attitudes toward the target item when they are responding. The critical point is that implicit measures either never make it explicit that people's attitudes toward a certain object is being measured or (as is the case with some research using the AMP) instruct participants to ignore their attitude toward the target item when responding.

In theory, implicit measures of attitudes may have advantages over explicit measures for topics where social desirability concerns may result in participants not wanting to express their true attitudes. A consistent finding in the literature is that explicit and implicit measures of attitudes, although moderately correlated overall, diverge when the attitude target is one where there are strong social motivations for reporting a particular attitude (Greenwald & Nosek, 2009). For example, implicitly measured attitudes have been used quite extensively in the study of racial attitudes because explicitly measured racial attitudes have been shown to be strongly influenced by

motivational factors (e.g., Amodio & Devine, 2009; Fazio, Jackson, Dunton, & Williams, 2005).

The extensive research on implicit measures of attitudes has resulted in some scholars arguing that there are two separate attitude systems—an explicit and an implicit system of attitudes (Greenwald & Nosek, 2009; Wilson, Lindsey, & Schooler, 2000). According to this dissociative view, attitudes that are measured implicitly are not strongly correlated with explicitly measured attitudes because the underlying attitudes measured by the different procedures represent distinct attitudes within two distinct cognitive systems. More specifically, implicitly measured attitudes are assumed to reflect a system of attitudes that operate outside of people's awareness, are automatically activated from memory (see earlier discussion on attitude accessibility), and are beyond people's control. In contrast, explicitly measured attitudes are hypothesized to reflect a more deliberative system that is available for people's introspection and can be controlled. Evidence for these distinct attitudes comes from research suggesting that the two different types of attitudes develop via different mechanisms. For example, research suggests that implicitly measured attitudes are more influenced by socialization, as well as associations with the self and culture, than are explicitly measured attitudes (Devos, 2008).

A more parsimonious explanation is found in the MODE model (Fazio & Olson, 2003; Olson & Fazio, 2009). When attitudes are measured with different methods, it is important to consider how motivation and opportunity might influence those measurements (Olson & Fazio, 2009). With self-report or explicit measures of attitudes, individuals are more aware of the content of the questions and are rarely placed under time constraints. Neither motivation nor opportunity to respond are constrained, which should result in more deliberative judgments of the attitude object, and motivational factors can influence the attitude that is reported. In contrast, with implicit measures of attitudes, individuals are typically asked to make rapid judgments of seemingly unrelated stimuli. Both opportunity and motivation to respond are limited, which results in more spontaneous judgments of the attitude object (Olson & Fazio, 2009). For most topics, explicitly measured attitudes are correlated with implicitly measured attitudes because respondents are not motivated to report an attitude that is different from the attitude that is activated from memory.

However, for socially sensitive topics such as prejudice, explicitly and implicitly measured attitudes often diverge. According to the MODE model, this divergence reflects individuals' motivation and opportunity. When responding to implicit measures of attitudes, prejudiced respondents are not motivated to change their response because they are unaware of what attitude is being measured. Further, they have no opportunity to control their response because most implicit measures of attitudes place participants under time pressure to respond. However, on explicit measures where it is clear the goal of the scale is to measure racial attitudes, individuals with racist attitudes are motivated to mask their true feelings so as not to appear prejudiced (Eno & Ewoldsen, 2010; Fazio, Jackson, Dunton, & Williams, 1995). In addition, they have the opportunity to control their response because explicit measures of attitudes typically allow participants unlimited time to complete the scale. Consequently, respondents will make more deliberative judgments and respond with a non-prejudiced attitude.

This discussion of explicitly and implicitly measured attitudes probably seems far removed from the central concern of this chapter—the outcomes of persuasion. Research on persuasion-based attitude changes has almost exclusively focused on explicit measures of attitudes, so why address implicitly measured attitudes in this chapter? We discuss this distinction because we believe this distinction will become increasingly important for persuasion scholars. Recent research suggests that implicitly measured attitudes can be changed through communication (Brinol, Petty, & McCaslin, 2009; Eno & Ewoldsen, 2010; Maio, Haddock, Watt, & Hewstone, 2009). For example, Eno and Ewoldsen (2010)

demonstrated that people's implicitly measured attitudes toward African Americans became less prejudiced after watching a movie that attacked racist attitudes toward African Americans. Perhaps more important, given the focus of this chapter on deliberative versus spontaneous processes as outcomes of persuasion, research very clearly demonstrates that, consistent with the MODE model, implicitly measured attitudes are more predictive of spontaneous behaviors and explicitly measured attitudes tend to be more predictive of deliberative behaviors (Devos, 2008; Fazio et al., 2005).

Norms as Outcomes

There are a number of reasons to consider the role of norms in persuasion contexts. First, norms are important in models of behavior maintenance and change (e.g., theory of reasoned action/theory of planned behavior/ integrative model, Ajzen, 1991; Fishbein & Yzer, 2003; process model, Fazio, 1986), thus considering their role both in the persuasion process and in the maintenance of behavior has theoretical value. More fully understanding these processes holds promise in a range of contexts. For example, a young teen who is offered a cigarette at a party may have to quickly determine the relative social costs and benefits of taking the cigarette or not. However, relatively little research has explored the psychological mechanisms underlying social influence (Cialdini, Kallgren, & Reno, 1991; Glynn, 1997). Indeed, recent efforts to change health risk behaviors through normative appeals has emphasized the importance of studying the processes through which norm appeals are (or are not) effective.

Deliberative Approaches: Social Norms Campaigns

An intriguing line of research that began in the context of trying to reduce episodes of binge drinking on college campuses focused on people's normative beliefs about engaging in a behavior. Early work in this stream observed that there tends to be an exaggerated norm for many risky behaviors young people might consider performing, and especially for drinking on college campuses (Miller, Monin, & Prentice, 2000; Prentice & Miller, 1993; Schroeder & Prentice, 1998), with the general finding that college students individually tend to be less accepting of alcohol use than they perceive their peers to be. It is important to note that those who see the norm as most accepting of alcohol use tend to drink the most (Borsari & Carey, 2003; Park, Smith, Klein, & Martell, 2011).

The consistency with which these findings have been found led to the logical extension that one way to reduce college drinking behavior is to inform college students of the actual norm, specifically, that the norm for drinking alcohol is less permissive than they believe it to be. On this assumption, many campuses began social norms campaigns, in which it is emphasized that the majority of students on campus do not engage in binge drinking. In spite of some initially promising results (Haines & Spear, 1996), these norms campaigns have produced mixed findings (e.g., Campo & Cameron, 2006), and have been heavily criticized (Wechsler et al., 2002). There are problems with both the implementation of these programs and the evaluation of them, which renders making judgments about their effectiveness problematic, however. Specifically, there is a great deal of ambiguity surrounding the concept of norms. Various researchers have discussed descriptive norms, injunctive norms, subjective norms, moral norms, and customs. Each of these ways of looking at norms has its strengths, but overall, the use of these diverse operational definitions makes it difficult to draw any firm conclusions about how norms affect behavior (Rimal & Real, 2003; Schultz, Nolan, Cialdini, Goldstein, & Griskevidius, 2007).

Additionally, it is unclear which norms are being targeted in the various campaigns, and whether one would expect a change in such norms to affect individual behavior. Specifically,

most of the campaigns have emphasized a campuswide descriptive norm (e.g., 80% of students at X University drink three or fewer drinks when they go out). It is unclear that students make decisions about drinking on the basis of a descriptive norm (how many other students drink) as opposed to an injunctive norm (what social costs and benefits accrue from drinking). It is likely that judgments about the norms for the campus subgroup that is central to one's identity are more likely to play a role in one's own behavior (Terry & Hogg, 2001). In particular, it is clear from much of the work on campus drinking patterns that certain subgroups of students are at significantly elevated risk (e.g., fraternities), and that those subgroups are characterized by both descriptive and injunctive norms that are strongly supportive of high levels of drinking (Phua, 2011). Certainly the publication of a campuswide norm showing less drinking would be unsuccessful for such groups. Further work to clarify how norms affect behavior will help to target norms' messages more effectively.

Spontaneous Approaches: Norm Accessibility and Implicit Norms

Work by Cialdini and colleagues on the focus theory of norms (Kallgren, Reno, & Cialdini, 2000) found that social norms can be a strong determinant of behaviors such as littering when the norm is salient in the situation (Cialdini et al., 1991; Reno, Cialdini, & Kallgren, 1993). In this research, the manipulations of norm salience temporarily increase the accessibility of the norm in memory. In several studies, the injunctive norm against littering was primed through a manipulation of the content of leaflets that were left on participants' windshields, which affected littering behavior. Cialdini and his colleagues (1990) interpret this finding by arguing that the priming manipulation increased the temporary accessibility of the injunctive norm against littering. As described in the section on accessible attitudes, a specific behavior is more likely to be driven by mental constructs that are activated, or made accessible, at the time the behavioral act is performed (Fazio, 1986, 1990; Kallgren et al., 2000). This idea has led to the examination of norm accessibility, or how quickly some can activate from memory his or her judgment of the social costs and benefits of engaging in a particular behavior (Rhodes & Ewoldsen, 2009).

The concept of norm accessibility also draws from social identity theory (and related literatures) that emphasize the extent to which membership in a specific group is central to the self-concept of the actor will determine how accessible the associated norm is for that behavior (Terry & Hogg, 2001). Research has shown that groups that are important to one's identity are more influential on individual attitudes and behaviors (Terry, Hogg, & White, 2000). Norms associated with important in-groups are likely to be chronically more accessible than those associated with less important groups, and thus are more likely to be activated and guide behavior. Thus, important in-groups may be associated with both chronically and temporarily accessible norms.

As in our discussion of attitude accessibility, norm accessibility appears to play an important role in spontaneous processes related to persuasion. The process model (Fazio, 1986) focuses on the role of attitude accessibility in predicting behavior. In the fully described model, accessible attitudes toward the object, *along with social norms*, influence how people perceive and define social situations (Fazio, 1986). How people define the situation influences how they act in that situation. Numerous studies have demonstrated that accessible attitudes influence how people perceive and interpret social information (e.g., Fazio et al., 1994; Roskos-Ewoldsen, Yu, & Rhodes, 2004). However, the influence of norms has only recently been explicitly tested within this model. This stream of research has found that accessible norms are predictive of behavior and intention to engage in behavior (Rhodes & Ewoldsen, 2009). In a sample of college students, Rhodes et al. (2008) showed participants four different antismoking public service announcements

(PSAs). Using cognitive response data, we found that smokers with accessible prosmoking subjective norms avoided processing antismoking messages and instead focused on heuristic cues to discount the message, suggesting that health risk behaviors that are supported by accessible norms may be particularly resistant to change.

Extensive research has demonstrated the important role that social norms play in influencing people's behavior. The lack of research specifying the cognitive and affective mechanisms underlying the influence of norms is unfortunate given the importance of norms in explaining social behavior. We propose that norm accessibility, that is, the ease of accessing normative information from memory, provides an explanatory mechanism for understanding the influences of norms on social behavior. Specifically, when people can easily bring to mind that there are important people in their lives who support health risk behaviors such as cigarette smoking, they are less likely to even think about a message opposing the behavior that is supported by that norm. This has important implications for health promotion campaigns: addressing health risk behaviors prior to the establishment of a supportive norm is the key to making that message heard by the audience. Additionally, as was recently found by Rhodes and colleagues, young teenagers who have accessible antirisk family norms engage in less risk behavior (Rhodes et al., 2011). This emphasizes the role of the family in teenagers' lives and suggests that parents of young teens should talk frequently with their teens about their desire that the teen avoid engaging in risky behavior.

A Dynamic View

The Role of Behavior, Attitudes, and Norms as Inputs to and Outcomes of Persuasion

One of the aspects of persuasion we would like to emphasize in this chapter is the recursive nature of the persuasive process. In many lab experiments, persuasion is represented as a one-shot, self-limited event in which a participant is exposed to a message, reacts to it, and then goes away. That is, they are representing the persuasion process as input → process → output. Starting with Roskos-Ewoldsen's (1997) transactive model, we think of persuasion as a far more dynamic process that occurs over time. As persuasive information on a topic is encountered in the environment, the thoughts generated in response, the accessibility of the attitude, norms, and associated constructs, and any resulting behavior all feed back into the system and are then part of the inputs the next time the topic is encountered (Nowak & Vallacher, 1998). Thus, in our view, even titling this chapter "Outcomes of Persuasion" is a misnomer, in the sense that anything that results from a single persuasive attempt can become a subsequent input on later attempts. It is in this way that beliefs, attitudes, norms, and habits are made more accessible and strengthened over time (Arpan et al., 2007).

Take, for example, the case of a new political candidate on the national scene. We hypothesize a dynamic process such that an individual might begin to hear people talking about the candidate at work. This talk among coworkers may begin to affect the person's judgment of the descriptive norm—that is, the person may begin to perceive that others in the social environment are in favor of this candidate. Thinking about the normative support for this candidate makes that norm more accessible and easier to activate in the future. Having an accessible norm is likely to attract this person's attention to future communication about this candidate, and the person may engage in behaviors such as turning the sound up on the TV when this candidate is featured on the news. Through self-perception processes (Bem, 1972), the behavior of turning up the TV further cues the individual that this is important, and that information becomes encoded along with the content of the arguments the candidate is making (Roese & Olson, 1994).

Perhaps this person attends a local rally for the candidate with a coworker. The individual may still not feel committed to the candidate, but goes to the rally because of the social benefits of accompanying a valued other to an event. Later, when trying to decide which candidate to vote for, all of these ancillary inputs (the social norm and behaviors) then are evaluated in addition to any policy statements or persuasive arguments the candidate has made. We see this as an ongoing process in which each time the individual thinks about, talks about, or engages in activity related to the candidate, it becomes a reinforcement to the developing attitude that this is a good candidate. In addition, as the social norms and attitudes develop across time, they also become more accessible from memory. Critically, as the norms and attitudes become more accessible, they will influence what messages a person is likely to attend to (Goodall & Ewoldsen, 2011; Roskos-Ewoldsen & Fazio, 1992), how those messages are likely to be processed (Fabrigar et al., 1998; Rhodes et al., 2008; Roskos-Ewoldsen et al., 2002), and whether that processing will be relatively objective or biased (Fazio et al., 1994; Rhodes et al., 2008). Once developed, attitudes and norms influence information processing such that subsequent message process is likely to reinforce and strengthen the attitudes and norms.

Future Directions

It is our view that future study in the outcomes of persuasion needs to look more broadly at these dynamic processes. Some of this work is already in progress; more needs to be done. Already, as we have mentioned, the work in implicitly measured attitudes and attitude accessibility is examining increases in accessibility as a function of persuasive communication (Brinol et al., 2009; Eno & Ewoldsen, 2010; Maio et al., 2009; Roskos-Ewoldsen et al., 2004). We believe this line of research is critically important: being able to increase the extent to which attitudes or norms are operating at an automatic level makes it more likely that they will have an impact on subsequent behavior. Accessible attitudes and norms have stronger effects on behavior than those that are less accessible.

Our work on the accessibility of injunctive norms and descriptive norms is important in this stream of research as well. Research aimed at increasing the accessibility of injunctive norms (for example, "my mom will ground me if I smoke a cigarette" or "my friends will laugh at me") and decreasing the accessibility of prorisk descriptive norms ("everyone does it") can lead to beneficial interventions in teen risk behavior, for example. Some of the work that needs to be done in this area is to better understand when and how injunctive and descriptive norms affect behavior. Recent work has begun to reduce some of the conceptual ambiguity that has been plaguing the work in norms (Jacobson, Mortensen, & Cialdini, 2010; Rimal & Real, 2003; Schultz et al., 2007). Although the early promise of social norm approaches to reducing heavy drinking by college students, for example, has proved to be over-blown (Wechsler et al., 2002), we are less pessimistic about the future of social norms approaches because we feel that more fully understanding how norms function will lead to more effective interventions.

Finally, we think it is important for future research to consider the distinction between spontaneous and deliberative decision processes and behavior. Hopefully, this chapter has demonstrated that the measures that are used to ascertain the effectiveness of a persuasive message need to match the type of process that is hypothesized to occur. If the goal of a persuasive message is to change people's everyday behavior, and the available research suggests that this behavior is likely to be spontaneous rather than deliberative, then it is important that researchers use implicit or reaction time measures of attitudes (Arpan et al., 2007; Petty, Fazio, & Brinol, 2009; Wittenbrink & Schwarz, 2007) because these measures are more predictive of spontaneous behaviors.

Conclusion

This chapter has summarized some of the research findings related to the outcomes of persuasion. Behavior, as the ultimate goal of many persuasive attempts, may be difficult to observe directly, and we discussed proxies to the measurement of behavior. By far, the most popular proxy has been attitudes. We summarized work on both spontaneous and deliberative attitudes as outcomes, and we touched on the newly emerging research and theory on norms as outcomes of persuasion. Across this research, we have highlighted the important differences between spontaneous and deliberative outcomes. Persuasion will continue to be one of the most important areas of study within the social sciences. But this research is informative only to the extent that we adequately understand the likely outcomes of these processes, and the dynamic nature of these processes.

References

Ajzen, I. (1991). The theory of planned behavior. *Organizational Behavior and Human Decision Processes, 50,* 179–211.

Ajzen, I., & Fishbein, M. (2005). The influence of attitudes on behavior. In D. Albarracín, B. T. Johnson, & M. P. Zanna (Eds.), *The handbook of attitudes* (pp. 173–221). Mahwah, NJ: Erlbaum.

Albarracín, D., Johnson, B. T., Fishbein, M., & Muellerleile, P. A. (2001). Theories of reasoned action and planned behavior as models of condom use: A meta-analysis. *Psychological Bulletin, 127*(1), 142–161.

Albarracín, D., Johnson, B. T., & Zanna, M. P. (2005). *The handbook of attitudes.* Mahwah, NJ: Erlbaum.

Allport, G. W. (1935). Attitudes. In C. A. Murchison (Ed.), *Handbook of social psychology* (Vol. 2, pp. 798–844). Worchester, MA: Clark University Press.

Amodio, D., & Devine, P. G. (2009). On the interpersonal functions of implicit stereotyping and evaluative race bias: Insights from social neuroscience. In R. E. Petty, R. H. Fazio, & P. Briñol (Eds.), *Attitudes: Insights from the new implicit measures* (pp. 193–226). New York, NY: Psychology Press.

Andrews, J., & Shimp, T. A. (1990). Effects of involvement, argument strength, and source characteristics on central and peripheral processing of advertising. *Psychology and Marketing, 7*(3), 195–214. doi:10.1002/mar.4220070305

Arpan, L., Rhodes, N., & Roskos-Ewoldsen, D. R. (2007). Accessibility, persuasion, and behavior. In D. R. Rosks-Ewoldsen & J. L. Monahan (Eds.), *Communication and social cognition: Theories and methods.* Mahwah, NJ: Erlbaum.

Bassili, J. N. (1995). Response latency and the accessibility of voting intentions: What contributes to accessibility and how it affects vote choice. *Personality and Social Psychology Bulletin, 21,* 686–695.

Bassili, J. N., & Brown, R. D. (2005). Implicit and explicit attitudes: Research, challenges, and theory. In D. Albarracín, B. T. Johnson, & M. P. Zanna (Eds.), *The handbook of attitudes* (pp. 543–574). Mahwah, NJ: Erlbaum.

Bem, D. J. (1972). Self-perception theory. In L. Berkowitz (Ed.), *Advances in experimental social psychology* (Vol. 6, pp. 1–62). New York, NY: Academic Press.

Borsari, B., & Carey, K. B. (2003). Descriptive and injunctive norms in college drinking: A meta-analytic integration. *Journal of Studies on Alcohol, 64,* 331–341.

Brinol, P., Petty, R. E., & McCaslin, M. J. (2009). Changing attitudes on implicit vs. explicit measures: What is the difference? In R. E. Petty, R. H. Fazio, & P. Briñol (Eds.), *Attitudes: Insights from the new implicit measures* (pp. 285–326). New York, NY: Psychology Press.

Campo, S., & Cameron, K. A. (2006). Differential effects of exposure to social norms campaigns: A cause for concern. *Health Communication, 19*(3), 209–219.

Chaiken, S., Liberman, A., & Eagly, A. H. (1989). Heuristic and systematic information processing within and beyond the persuasion context. In J. S. Uleman & J. A. Bargh (Eds.), *Unintended thought* (pp. 212–252). New York, NY: Guilford Press.

Cialdini, R. B., Kallgren, C. A., & Reno, R. R. (1991). A focus theory of normative conduct: A theoretical refinement and reevaluation of the role of norms in human conduct. In M. P. Zanna (Ed.), *The development of prosocial behavior* (pp. 339–359). New York, NY: Academic Press.

Cialdini, R. B., Reno, R. R., & Kallgren, C. A. (1990). A focus theory of normative conduct: Recycling the concept of norms to reduce littering in public places. *Journal of Personality and Social Psychology, 58,* 1015–1026.

Crano, W. D., & Prislin, R. (2008). *Attitudes and attitude change.* New York, NY: Psychology Press.

DeBono, K. G., & Snyder, M. (1995). Acting on one's attitudes: The role of a history of choosing situations. *Personality and Social Psychology Bulletin, 21,* 620–628.

DeHouwer, J. (2006). What are implicit measures and why are we using them? In R. W. Wiers & A. W. Stacy (Eds.), *Handbook of implicit cognition and addition* (pp. 11–28). Thousand Oaks, CA: Sage.

Devos, T. (2008). Implicit attitudes 101: Theoretical and empirical insights. In W. D. Crano, R. Prislin, (Eds.), *Attitudes and attitude change* (pp. 61–84). New York, NY: Psychology Press.

Dillard, J. P. (1993). Persuasion past and present: Attitudes aren't what they used to be. *Communication Monographs, 60,* 90–97.

Eno, C. A. & Ewoldsen, D. R. (2010). The influence of explicitly and implicitly measured prejudice on interpretations of and reactions to Black film. *Media Psychology, 13,* 1–30.

Fabrigar, L. R., Priester, J. R., Petty, R. E., & Wegener, D. T. (1998). The impact of attitude accessibility on elaboration of persuasive messages. *Personality and Social Psychology Bulletin, 24,* 339–352.

Fazio, R. H. (1986). How do attitudes guide behavior? In R. H. Sorrentino & E. T. Higgins (Eds.), *The handbook of motivation and cognition: Foundations of social behavior* (pp. 204–243). New York, NY: Guilford Press.

Fazio, R. H. (1989). On the power and functionality of attitudes: The role of attitude accessibility. In A. R. Pratkanis & S. J. Breckler (Eds.), *Attitude structure and function* (pp. 153–179). Hillsdale, NJ: Erlbaum.

Fazio, R. H. (1990). Multiple processes by which attitudes guide behavior: The MODE model as an integrative framework. In M. Zanna (Ed.), *Advances in experimental social psychology* (Vol. 23; pp. 75–109). Orlando, FL: Academic Press.

Fazio, R. H., Jackson, J. R., Dunton, B. C., & Williams, C. J. (1995). Variability in automatic activation as an unobtrusive measure of racial attitudes: A bona fide pipeline? *Journal of Personality and Social Psychology, 69,* 1013–1027.

Fazio, R., & Olson, M. (2003). Implicit measures in social cognition: Their meaning and use. *Annual Review of Psychology, 54,* 297–327.

Fazio, R. H., Powell, M. C., & Williams, C. J. (1989). The role of attitude accessibility in the attitude to behavior process. *Journal of Consumer Research, 16*(3), 280–288.

Fazio, R. H., & Roskos-Ewoldsen, D. R. (2005). Acting as we feel: When and how attitudes guide behavior. In T. C. Brock & M. C. Green (Eds.), *Persuasion: Psychological insights and perspectives* (2nd ed., pp. 41–62). Thousand Oaks, CA: Sage.

Fazio, R. H., Roskos-Ewoldsen, D. R., & Powell, M. C. (1994). Attitudes, perception, and attention. In P. M. Niedenthal & S. Kitayama (Eds.), *The heart's eye: Emotional influences in perception and attention* (pp. 197–216). Orlando, FL: Academic Press.

Fazio, R. H., & Towles-Schwen, T. (1999). The MODE model of attitude-behavior processes. In S. Chaiken & Y. Trope (Eds.), *Dual process theories in social psychology* (pp. 97–116). New York, NY: Guilford.

Fishbein, M., & Ajzen, I. (1974). Attitudes toward objects as predictors of single and multiple behavioral criteria. *Psychological Review, 81,* 59–74.

Fishbein, M., & Ajzen, I. (1975). *Belief, attitude, intention, and behavior.* Reading, MA: Addison-Wesley.

Fishbein, M., & Yzer, M. C. (2003). Using theory to design effective health behavior interventions. *Communication Theory, 13,* 164–176.

Gerrard, M., Gibbons, F. X., Houlihan, A. E., Stock, M. L., & Pomery, E. A. (2008). A dual-process approach to health risk decision making: The prototype willingness model. *Developmental Review, 28,* 29–61.

Gerrard, M., Gibbons, F. X., Vande Lune, L. S., Pexa, N. A., & Gano, M. L. (2002). Adolescents' substance-related risk perceptions: Antecedents, mediators and consequences. *Risk decision and policy, 7,* 175–191.

Glynn, C. J. (1997). Public opinion as a normative opinion process. In B. Burleson (Ed.), *Communication Yearbook 20* (pp.157–183). Beverly Hills, CA: Sage.

Goodall, C. E., & Ewoldsen, D. R. (2011). *Attitude accessibility and automatic orientation to products and brands in advertising.* Paper presented at the annual convention of the National Communication Association, New Orleans.

Greenwald, A. G., & Nosek, B. A. (2009). Attitudinal dissociation: What does it mean? In R. E. Petty, R. H. Fazio, & P. Briñol (Eds.), *Attitudes: Insights from the new implicit measures* (pp. 65–82). New York, NY: Psychology Press.

Haines, M., & Spear, S. F. (1996). Changing the perception of the norm: A strategy to decrease binge drinking among college students. *Journal of American College Health, 45*(3), 134–140.

Jaccard, J., & Blanton, H. (2005). The origins and structure of behavior: Conceptualizing behavior in attitude research. In D. Albarracín, B. T. Johnson, & M. P. Zanna (Eds.), *The handbook of attitudes* (pp. 125–171). Mahwah, NJ: Erlbaum.

Jacobson, R. P., Mortensen, C. R., & Cialdini, R. B. (2010). Bodies obliged and unbound: Differentiated response tendencies for injunctive and descriptive social norms. *Journal of Personality and Social Psychology.* doi: 10.1037/a0021470

Kallgren, C. A., Reno, R. R., & Cialdini, R. B. (2000). A focus theory of normative conduct: When norms do and do not affect behavior. *Personality and Social Psychology Bulletin, 26,* 1002–1012.

Katz, D. (1960). The functional approach to the study of attitudes. *Public Opinion Quarterly, 24,* 163–204.

Kokkinaki, F., & Lunt, P. (1997). The relationship between involvement, attitude accessibility, and attitude-behaviour consistency. *British Journal of Social Psychology, 36,* 497–509.

Maio, G. R., Haddock, G., Watt, S. E., & Hewstone, M. (2009). Implicit measures in applied contexts: An illustrative examination of antiracism advertising. In R. E. Petty, R. H. Fazio, & P. Briñol (Eds.), *Attitudes: Insights from the new implicit measures* (pp. 327–357). New York, NY: Psychology Press.

Miller, D. T., Monin, B., & Prentice, D. A. (2000). Pluralistic ignorance and inconsistency between private attitudes and public behaviors. In D. J. Terry, M. A. Hogg, D. J. Terry, M. A. Hogg (Eds.), *Attitudes, behavior, and social context: The role of norms and group membership* (pp. 95–113). Mahwah, NJ: Erlbaum.

Nowak, A., & Vallacher, R. R. (1998). *Dynamical social psychology.* New York, NY: Guilford Press.

Olson, M. A., & Fazio, R. H. (2009). Implicit and explicit measures of attitudes: The perspective of the MODE model. In R. E. Petty, R. H. Fazio, & P. Briñol (Eds.), *Attitudes: Insights from the new implicit measures* (pp. 19–63). New York, NY: Psychology Press.

Park, H., Smith, S. W., Klein, K. A., & Martell, D. (2011). College students' estimation and accuracy of other students' drinking and believability of advertisements featured in a social norms campaign. *Journal of Health Communication, 16*(5), 504–518.

Payne, B. K. (2009). Attitude misattribution: Implications for attitude measurement and the implicit-explicit relationship. In R. E. Petty, R. H. Fazio, & P. Briñol (Eds.), *Attitudes: Insights from the new implicit measures* (pp. 459–483). New York, NY: Psychology Press.

Payne, B. K., Cheng, C. M., Govorun, O., & Steward, B. (2005). An inkblot for attitudes: Affect misattribution as implicit measurement. *Journal of Personality and Social Psychology, 89,* 277–293.

Petty, R. E., & Cacioppo, J. T. (1986). *Communication and persuasion: Central and peripheral routes to attitude change.* New York, NY: Springer-Verlag.

Petty, R. E., Fazio, R. H., & Brinol, P. (2009). The new implicit measures: An overview. In R. E. Petty, R. H. Fazio, & P. Briñol (Eds.), *Attitudes: Insights from the new implicit measures* (pp. 3–18). New York, NY: Psychology Press.

Phua, J. (2011). The influence of peer norms and popularity on smoking and drinking behavior among college fraternity members: A social network analysis. *Social Influence, 6*(3), 153–168.

Posavac, S. S., Sanbonmatsu, D. M., & Fazio, R. H. (1997). Considering the best choice: Effects of the salience and accessibility of alternatives on attitude-decision consistency. *Journal of Personality and Social Psychology, 72,* 253–261.

Prentice, D. A., & Miller, D. T. (1993). Pluralistic ignorance and alcohol use on campus: Some consequences of misperceiving the social norm. *Journal of Personality and Social Psychology, 64*(2), 243–256. doi:10.1037/0022-3514.64.2.243

Prislin, R., & Crano, W. D. (2008). Attitudes and attitude change: The fourth peak. In W. D. Crano & R. Prislin, (Eds.), *Attitudes and attitude change* (pp. 3–15). New York, NY: Psychology Press.

Reno, R. R., Cialdini, R. B., & Kallgren, C. A. (1993). The transsituational influence of social norms. *Journal of Personality and Social Psychology, 64,* 104–112.

Rhodes, N., & Ewoldsen, D. R. (2009). Attitude and norm accessibility and cigarette smoking. *Journal of Applied Social Psychology, 39,* 2355–2372.

Rhodes, N., Ewoldsen, D. R., Shen, L., Monahan, J. L., & Eno, C. (2011). The accessibility of family and peer norms as predictors of young adolescent risk behavior. *Communication Research, 39*(3).

Rhodes, N., Roskos-Ewoldsen, D. R., Edison, A., & Bradford, B. (2008). Attitude and norm accessibility affect processing of anti-smoking messages. *Health Psychology, 27,* S224–S232.

Rimal, R. N., & Real, K. (2003). Understanding the influence of perceived norms on behaviors. *Communication Theory, 13*(2), 184–203.

Roese, N. J., & Olson, J. M. (1994). Attitude importance as a function of repeated attitude expression. *Journal of Experimental Social Psychology, 30,* 39–51.

Roskos-Ewoldsen, D. R. (1997). Attitude accessibility and persuasion: Review and a transactive model. In B. Burleson (Ed.), *Communication Yearbook 20* (pp. 185–225). Beverly Hills, CA: Sage.

Roskos-Ewoldsen, D. R., Bichsel, J., & Hoffman, K. (2002). The influence of accessibility of source likability on persuasion. *Journal of Experimental Social Psychology, 38,* 137–143.

Roskos-Ewoldsen, D. R., & Fazio, R. H. (1992). On the orienting value of attitudes: Attitude accessibility as a determinant of an object's attraction of visual attention. *Journal of Personality and Social Psychology, 63,* 198–211.

Roskos-Ewoldsen, D. R., & Fazio, R. H. (1997). The role of belief accessibility in attitude formation. *Southern Communication Journal, 62,* 107–116.

Roskos-Ewoldsen, D. R., Yu, H. J., & Rhodes, N. (2004). Fear appeal messages effect accessibility of attitudes toward the threat and adaptive behaviors. *Communication Monographs, 71,* 49–69.

Schroeder, C. M., & Prentice, D. A. (1998). Exposing pluralistic ignorance to reduce alcohol use among college students. *Journal of Applied Social Psychology, 28*(23), 2150–2180. doi:10.1111/j.1559-1816.1998.tb01365.x

Schultz, P., Nolan, J. M., Cialdini, R. B., Goldstein, N. J., & Griskevicius, V. (2007). The constructive, destructive, and reconstructive power of social norms. *Psychological Science, 18*(5), 429–434. doi:10.1111/j.1467-9280.2007.01917.x

Shen, L., Monahan, J. L., Rhodes, N., & Roskos-Ewoldsen, D. R. (2009). The impact of attitude accessibility and decision style on adolescents' biased processing of health-related PSAs. *Communication Research, 36,* 104–128.

Smith, M., Bruner, J. S., & White, R. W. (1956). *Opinions and personality.* Oxford, UK: Wiley.

Terry, D. J., & Hogg, M. A. (2001). Attitudes, behavior, and social context: The role of norms and group membership in social influence processes. In J. P. Forgas, K. D. Williams, J. P. Forgas, K. D. Williams (Eds.), *Social influence: Direct and indirect processes* (pp. 253–270). New York, NY: Psychology Press.

Terry, D. J., Hogg, M. A., & White, K. M. (2000). Attitude–behavior relations: Social identity and group membership. In D. J. Terry, M. A. Hogg, D. J. Terry, M. A. Hogg (Eds.), *Attitudes, behavior, and social context: The role of norms and group membership* (pp. 67–93). Mahwah, NJ: Erlbaum.

Wechsler, H., Kelley, K., Weitzman, E. R., Elissa, R., San Giovanni, J. P., & Seibring, M. (2002). What colleges are doing about student binge drinking: A survey of college administrators. *Journal of American College Health, 48,* 219–226.

Wilson, T. D., Lindsey, S., & Schooler, T. Y. (2000). A model of dual attitudes. *Psychological Review, 107,* 101–126.

Wittenbrink, B., & Schwarz, N. (2007). Introduction. In B. Wittenbrink & N. Schwarz (Eds.), *Implicit measures of attitudes* (pp. 1–13). New York, NY: Guilford Press.

Woodside, A. G., & Trappey, R. J. (1996). Customer portfolio analysis among competing retail stores. *Journal of Business Research, 35,* 189–200.

Zanna, M. P., & Fazio, R. H. (1982). The attitude-behavior relation: Moving toward a third generation of research. In M. P. Zanna, E. T. Higgins, & C. P. Herman (Eds.), *Consistency in social behavior: The Ontario Symposium* (Vol. 2, pp. 283–301). Hillsdale, NJ: Erlbaum.

CHAPTER 5

On Being Persuaded

Some Basic Distinctions

The late Gerald R. Miller

Avolume dealing with the process of persuasion should profit from a tentative answer to the question: What does it mean to be *persuaded*? The well-advised qualifier "tentative" underscores two limitations of the analysis offered in this chapter. First, as with most complex definitional issues, the author has no illusions that his answer will satisfy every reader—or, for that matter, any reader. After all, a lively debate has raged for centuries over the defining characteristics of the term *persuasion,* and it would be the height of naïveté or arrogance to assume that this brief analysis will lay to rest all outstanding definitional controversies. Second, at a more modest level, this chapter certainly does not address all of the questions raised in succeeding chapters of this volume. The authors of these chapters have attacked numerous theoretical and applied issues of persuasion from various vantage points; to subsume all the nuances of their remarks about the persuasive process is a formidable, if not impossible, task far exceeding the capabilities of this writer.

Notwithstanding these disclaimers, this chapter can assist readers in making sense out of many of the issues explored later by providing a general frame of reference for viewing the process of persuasion. Stated differently, the chapter seeks to establish broad definitional boundaries for the phase "being persuaded." Furthermore, in the process of staking out these boundaries, certain persistent issues will inevitably be identified, issues that heavily influence some of the positions taken in other chapters. Thus, this chapter anticipates rather than resolves subsequent scholarly debates.

EDITORS' NOTE: Readers of this chapter may be puzzled by Miller's reference to Chairman Brezhnev's "recent" appeal for Senate ratification of the SALT II treaty and to the "current" energy crisis, and they may be misled by his allusions to "the chapters in this volume." In fact, this contribution is a reprint of the opening chapter in M. Roloff and G. R. Miller's (1980) edited volume titled *Persuasion: New Directions in Theory and Research* (also published by Sage). While the examples may be slightly tarnished, Miller's ideas are as bright and instructive today as they were three decades ago.

Being Persuaded:
The Central Elements

Persuasive attempts fall short of blatant coercion; persuasion, as typically conceived of, is not *directly* coercive. Coercion takes the form of guns or economic sanctions, while persuasion relies on the power of verbal and nonverbal symbols. Frequently, of course, coercive acts are preceded by persuasive messages; seldom is a child's allowance suspended or an armed attack launched on a neighboring state without a period of message exchanges. These messages are aimed at persuading the child to study harder at school or at persuading the neighboring state to relinquish claim to a parcel of disputed territory. If persuasion proves inadequate to the task at hand, economic or military force may be employed to achieve the desired compliance.

From these examples, it follows that much persuasive discourse is *indirectly* coercive; that is, the persuasive effectiveness of messages often depends heavily on the credibility of threats and promises proffered by the communicator. If the child perceives that the threatening parent is, for some reason or another, unlikely to suspend the child's allowance, the parent's persuasive messages will have minimum impact on the child's study habits. Similarly, threats of armed attacks by nations with powerful defense establishments usually cause potential adversaries to take persuasive appeals quite seriously, while the same threats uttered by countries of limited military might are likely to be greeted with scorn or amusement. One can only speculate how the ensuing 1962 scenario might have differed had the government of Haiti, rather than that of the United States, called on the Soviet Union to dismantle its missiles in Cuba under threat of naval blockade and possible attack on the missile sites themselves.

Some students of persuasion have found it distasteful to ponder the indirectly coercive dimension of many persuasive exchanges, perhaps because the notion of *means control*—Kelman's (1961) term for describing a situation where the influence agent, or persuader, is successful because of his or her ability to dispense rewards or punishments—conflicts with the way persuasion ought to function in a democratic society. Simons (1974) captured the crux of this ideological opposition well:

> Although persuasion is often characterized as a weak sister in relation to its relatives within the influence family—note such expressions as "talk is cheap," "talk rather than substance," and "mere rhetoric"—it is nevertheless regarded by many as a more ethical method of influencing others. One generally shuns the coercive label like the plague, takes pains to deny that he is bribing others when he offers them inducements, and represents himself as a persuader—if possible, as someone using "rational persuasion." Persuasion is especially valued as an instrument of democracy. . . . Officials of government proudly proclaim that ours is indeed a system run by persuasion. . . . Inducements and constraints are said to have no place in ideally democratic forms of government; they are the coinage of the realm of corrupt governments or of totalitarian regimes. (pp. 174–175)

Simon went on to argue convincingly that in the rough-and-tumble world of everyday social conflict, as distinct from the polite confines of drawing room controversy, coercive potential determines the relative impact of most persuasive messages.

The prevalence of indirectly coercive elements in many persuasive transactions can also be detected by examining the symbolic weapons readily available to would-be persuaders. Marwell and Schmitt (1967) have generated a list of 16 strategies that can be used to gain compliance from others. Several of these strategies—among them *promise, threat,* and *aversive stimulation*—clearly derive their effectiveness from the persuader's ability to dispense rewards or mete out punishments to the intended persuadee(s). More subtlety dependent on coercive pressure are

strategies stressing the harmful social consequences of failure to comply with message recommendations as well as strategies underscoring
the social rewards resulting from compliance—
such as *moral appeal, altruism, esteem position,*
and *esteem negative.* To be sure, many people
would hesitate to equate blackballing with black-
jacking. Nevertheless, in a society where the pervasive importance of "being respected," "being
popular," and "being 'in'" extends to matters so
trivial as the name tag one sports on a pair of
denim jeans, it would be a mistake to underestimate the coercive potential of social approval
and disapproval, a fact readily grasped by those
who create the country's daily diet of media
advertisements and commercials.

The preceding discussion has alluded to a
second defining characteristic of the phrase
"being persuaded": Persuasion relies on symbolic transactions. Although a Mafia hireling in
a Hollywood production may remark menac-
ingly, "It looks like you need a little persuading," as he starts to work over a stubborn
merchant who has refused to purchase mob
protection, the scholarly endeavors of persuasion researchers—and, for that matter, the
ordinary language uses of the term *persuasion*—
have consistently centered on the manipulation
of symbols. In the domain of verbal utterances,
this distinction fosters little ambiguity because
language is inherently symbolic. When Chairman Brezhnev recently appealed for Senate
ratification of the SALT II treaty by linking its
adoption with "divine" approval, most observers probably would have agreed that he was
embarked on a persuasive campaign, albeit one
employing symbolic weapons not usually found
in Communist arsenals. In the nonverbal realm,
however, the distinction does not emerge as
crisply, and there is often room for disagreement as to whether a particular nonverbal act is
or is not symbolic. When Chairman Khruschev
banged his shoe on a United Nations table during his 1959 visit to the United States, some
observers might have interpreted his behavior
as symbolic and reflecting persuasive intent,
but others might have interpreted it as nothing
more than a manifestation of poor manners by
an uncouth visitor. Granted, the latter interpretation also involved a symbolic inference, but
not one directly linked to conscious persuasive
intent.

In view of the ambiguous status of some
nonverbal behaviors, the utility of restricting
the term *persuasion* to symbolic transactions
may seem questionable. Unfortunately, the
conceptual alternative is even more trouble-
some, for it would permit any act that sought
to modify another's behavior to qualify as an
instance of persuasion. Rather than falling
prey to the unmanageable generality fostered
by such definitional permissiveness and allowing the persuasive process to be conceived of so
broadly that it embraces nearly every instance
of social behavior, it seems wiser to struggle
with occasional uncertainty. In most instances,
language is an integral aspect of the persuasive
transaction, with nonverbal behavior coming
into play as an instrument for reinforcing the
meaning and/or credibility of verbal messages.
Because the goal of this chapter is to identify
the central definitional elements of the phrase
"being persuaded" rather than to fix its precise
outer boundaries, imposition of a symbolic
criterion is consistent with the prevailing theoretical and empirical concerns of persuasion
scholars.

On agreeing that individuals are persuaded by
symbolic means, the question can be raised as to
whether certain types of symbolic strategies
should be viewed as typifying the persuasion
process, with others being exempted. More specifically, some writers (such as Rowell, 1932a,
1932b; Woolbert, 1917) have explored the wisdom of distinguishing between convincing and
persuading—the so-called *conviction/persuasion
duality.* This duality holds that persuasion relies
primarily on symbolic strategies that trigger the
emotions of intended persuadees, while conviction
is accomplished primarily by using strategies
rooted in logical proof and that appeal to persuadees' reason and intellect. Stated in evaluative

terms, conviction derives its force from people's rationality, while persuasion caters to their irrationality.

While this distinction has unquestionably influenced some of the research carried out by contemporary persuasion researchers—for example, studies comparing the relative persuasiveness of logical and emotional appeals such as those conducted by Hartmann (1936), Matthews (1947), and Weiss (1960)—its utility seems dubious at best. Attempts to crisply conceptualize and operationalize distinctions between logical and emotional appeals have been fraught with difficulty (Becker, 1963). As a result of prior learning, nearly all ordinary language is laden with emotional overtones. Even the appeal to "be logical" itself carries strong normative force; indeed, Bettinghaus (1973, pp. 157–158) found that messages containing cues stressing the importance of logical thought were highly persuasive, even though the arguments presented were themselves illogical. Faced with these considerations, it seems more useful to conceive of persuasive discourse as an amalgam of logic and emotion while at the same time granting that particular messages may differ in the relative amount of each element. Furthermore, the motivation for distinguishing between conviction and persuasion rests largely on value concerns for the way influence ought to be accomplished; influence resulting from rational reasoned messages is ethically preferable to influence resulting from appeals to the emotions—appeals that, in the eyes of some writers (e.g., Diggs, 1964; Nilsen, 1966), "short-circuit" the reasoning processes. Although questions regarding the relative moral acceptability of various means and ends of persuasion are of vital import to all citizens of the democratic society (including persuasion researchers), conceptual distinctions that make for sound ethical analysis may sometimes make for unsound scientific practice. The conviction/persuasion duality strikes the author as such a conceptual animal. People are seldom, if ever, persuaded by "pure" logic or "pure" emotion; indeed, as the previous comments suggest, it is doubtful that these "pure"

cases exist in humanity's workaday persuasive commerce.

Thus, the phrase "being persuaded" applies to *situations where behavior has been modified by symbolic transactions (messages) that are sometimes, but not always, linked with coercive force (indirectly coercive) and that appeal to the reason and emotions of the person(s) being persuaded.* This definition still suffers from lack of specificity concerning the kinds of behavioral modification that can result from persuasive communication. Let us next turn our attention to this problem.

Being Persuaded: Three Behavioral Outcomes

In popular parlance, "being persuaded" is equated with instances of behavioral conversion; that is, individuals are persuaded when they have been induced to abandon one set of behaviors and to adopt another. Thus, the assertion, "I am going to try to persuade Gerry to quit smoking," translates into the following situation: (1) Gerry is presently engaged in smoking behaviors, and (2) I want to induce him to stop these behaviors and begin to perform nonsmoking behaviors. On the surface, the phrase "nonsmoking behaviors" may seem nonsensical, but as any reformed smoker will attest, the transition from smoking to not smoking involves acquisition of a whole new set of behavioral alternatives ranging from substituting gum or mints for cigarettes to sitting in the nonsmoking rather than the smoking sections of restaurants. Indeed, the success of attempts to persuade people to stop smoking may often hinge on inducing them to adopt certain of these new behaviors.

Despite the tendency to equate persuasion with behavioral conversion, it seems useful to distinguish among three different behavioral outcomes commonly served by the persuasion process. Although some overlapping must be granted (the three outcomes are not always mutually exclusive), the utility of the distinction rests on the fact that the outcome sought sometimes affects the relative importance of variables contained in the persuasive equation as well as the probably ease or difficulty with which persuaders may hope to accomplish their goals.

Being Persuaded as a Response-Shaping Process

Frequently, individuals possess no clearly established pattern of responses to specific environmental stimuli. In such instances, persuasion takes the form of shaping and conditioning particular response patterns to these stimuli. Such persuasive undertakings are particularly relevant when dealing with persons who have limited prior learning histories or with situations where radically new and novel stimuli have been introduced into the environment.

Although it may be fallacious to assert that the mind of a small child is a tabula rasa, it is indisputable that children initially lack a response repertory for dealing with most social, political, economic, and ethical matters. Much of what is commonly referred to as *socialization* consists of persuading the child to respond consistently (shaping responses) to stimuli associated with these matters. Thus, at a relatively early age, the child can be observed responding as a "good" Catholic (Lutheran, Presbyterian, Unitarian-Universalist, atheist, etc.) should respond, expressing rudimentary opinions about political candidates or programs, and manifesting a relatively consistent code of conduct and ethics in dealing with others. In these instances, parents, teachers, ministers, peers, and others collectively shape and condition the responses the child performs.

It should be emphasized that all instances of response-shaping are not commonly thought of as instances of being persuaded. This distinction, while admittedly nebulous and slippery, implies that persuasion is a species of the genus commonly labeled *learning*. For instance, it would sound strange to speak of children "being persuaded." It would sound strange to speak of children *being persuaded* to tie their shoes correctly; typically, we assert that they have *learned* to tie their shoes. On the other hand, should children refuse to attempt shoe-tieing behaviors, rebel against feeding themselves, and neglect to pick up clothing or toys, they are likely to be bombarded with messages by parents and teachers aimed at shaping these behaviors. If such messages produce the desired effect, the communicators are likely to claim they have persuaded the children to become more self-reliant or independent; if not, they will probably lament the failure of their persuasive mission and devise other strategies for coping with the problem. In short, the behaviors associated with "being persuaded" are usually directly linked with more abstract attitudes and values that are prized by society or some significant segment of it—or, as Doob (1947) phrased it, responses considered socially significant by the individual's society.

As indicated earlier, response-shaping is not limited to small children. When the first nuclear device exploded over Hiroshima, Japan, in 1945, humanity witnessed the advent of a radically new energy source whose effects were so awesome they could scarcely be compared with anything preceding them. Before that August day, no one, save perhaps a few sophisticated physicists and technologists, had acquired patterns of responding to concepts such as *nuclear warfare* and *nuclear power* because these concepts were literally unheard of by most persons. That considerable response-shaping has occurred during the interim from 1945 to 1980 is attested to by the currently raging controversy regarding the wisdom of developing nuclear power sources; members of the Clamshell Alliance have been persuaded that the dangers of nuclear power far outweigh its potential benefits, while officials of the Nuclear Regulatory Agency have been convinced that the contributions of nuclear energy can be realized without serious attendant risks for humankind.

It must be granted, of course, that such instances of response-shaping are often confounded by elements of people's prior learning histories. While citizens of 1945 had acquired no established patterns of responding to the concept of *nuclear warfare*, most of them had developed response repertoires vis-à-vis the concept of *warfare*. For those who already viewed warfare as ethically and politically irresponsible, nuclear weapons were yet a further argument for the abolition of armed conflict, a powerful new persuasive weapon in their pacific arsenal. Conversely, those who sought to defend the continued utility of war as an instrument of national policy were forced to reevaluate their strategic doctrines; post-World War II Realpolitik, as embodied in the messages of spokespersons like Henry Kissinger, spawned doctrinal concepts such as *limited war* and *strategic deterrence*. (As an aside, these concepts have not seemed to carry the same persuasive force as earlier ones; people who were motivated to enthusiastic efforts by the battle cry for "unconditional surrender" in World War II grew quickly disenchanted with the "limited war/ limited objectives" rhetoric of the Korean and Vietnam conflicts.)

In the case of the concept *nuclear power*, the confounding influences of prior learning, while more subtle, are nevertheless present. Arguing for greater concern with values than with attitudes in studying persuasion, Rokeach (1973) has contended that

> a person has as many values as he has learned beliefs concerning desirable modes of conduct and end-states of existence, and as many attitudes as direct or indirect encounters he has had with specific objects and situations. It is thus estimated that values number in the dozens, whereas attitudes number in the thousands. (p. 18; see also Rokeach, 1968)

Applying Rokeach's contention to this example, it follows that while individuals may have no established response patterns for the stimulus "nuclear power"—to use his terminology, they may have no present attitude about the issue—they are likely to have well-developed response repertories for terminal values (Rokeach, 1973) such as *family security* and *a comfortable life*. Inevitably, messages seeking to persuade these persons to adopt a particular response stance regarding nuclear power will be linked to these values. Thus, an anti-nuclear power spokesperson may assert, "The existence of nuclear power plants, such as Three Mile Island, poses a threat to the safety of your family," while an advocate of increased development of nuclear power facilities may contend, "Only by expanded use of nuclear power can you hope to retain the many comforts and conveniences you now enjoy." In both cases, success in shaping the responses of the intended persuadee hinges on the linkage of these responses to strongly held values; that is, the public will be persuaded to the extent it perceives that maintenance of an important value, or values, mandates adoption of a particular set of responses regarding the issue of nuclear power.

In spite of the limitations and complications just outlined, it remains useful to conceive of response-shaping and conditioning as one behavioral manifestation of "being persuaded." Traditionally, the persuasion literature has characterized this process as "attitude formation," reserving the term "attitude change" for attempts to replace one set of established behaviors with another. From a pragmatic vantage point, messages seeking to shape and condition responses may have a higher likelihood of success than do communications aiming to convert established behavioral patterns; in addition, the two goals may imply the use of differing persuasive strategies. Moreover, from a scientific perspective, the two outcomes may suggest different theoretical and empirical literatures; for example, learning theories thus far have been most frequently and profitably employed in the arena of response-shaping and conditioning. Thus, for persuasive practitioners and researchers alike, the distinction possesses potential utility.

Being Persuaded as a Response-Reinforcing Process

Rather than aiming at changes in attitudes and behaviors, much persuasive communication seeks to reinforce currently held convictions and to make them more resistant to change. Most Sunday sermons serve this function, as do keynote speeches at political conventions and presidential addresses at meetings of scholarly societies. In such cases, emphasis is on making the persuadees more devout Methodists, more active Democrats, or more committed psychologists, not on converting them to Unitarianism, the Socialist Workers Party, or romance languages. (Miller & Burgoon, 1973, p. 5)

The position espoused in the preceding quotation is certainly not earth-shaking, even though the popular tendency to view persuasion as a tool for bringing about conversion may cause people to overlook, or shortchange, this important behavioral outcome. The response-reinforcing function underscores the fact that "being persuaded" is seldom, if ever, a one-message proposition; instead, people are constantly *in the process of* being persuaded. If an individual clings to an attitude (and the behaviors associated with it) more strongly after exposure to a communication, then persuasion has occurred as surely as if the individual had shifted from one set of responses to another. Moreover, those beliefs and behaviors most resistant to change are likely to be grounded in a long history of confirming messages along with other positive reinforcers. One current theory of attitude formation and change holds that the strength of people's attitudes depends entirely on the number of incoming messages about the attitude issue they have processed (Saltiel & Woelfel, 1975).

There are strong grounds for believing that much persuasive communication in our society serves a response-reinforcing function. Although students of persuasion disagree about the extent to which the selective exposure principle (Festinger, 1957) dictates message choices (Freedman & Sears, 1965; Sears & Freedman, 1967), few, if any, would question people's affinity for supportive information (McGuire, 1969). Such an affinity, in turn, suggests that under conditions of voluntary exposure, the majority of individuals' persuasive transactions will involve messages that reinforce their existing response repertories. This possibility is further supported by early mass media research documenting the reinforcement function served by the media (e.g., Katz & Lazarsfeld, 1955).

If people do, in fact, relish hearing what they already believe, it may seem that the response-reinforcing function of persuasion is so simple as to require little concern. Distortion of information is not as likely to occur, and the initial credibility of the communicator should have less impact than in cases where persuasive intent centers on response-shaping or behavioral change—although even in the case of response reinforcement, the work of Osgood and his associates (Osgood, Suci, & Tannenbaum, 1957; Osgood & Tannenbaum, 1955) indicates that extremely low credibility may inhibit persuasive impact. Logical fallacies and evidential shortcomings are likely to be overlooked, while phenomena such as counterarguing (Brandt, 1976; Festinger & Maccoby, 1964; Osterhouse & Brock, 1970) will be largely absent. Unquestionably, message recipients are set to be persuaded; hence, would-be persuaders are assured of optimal conditions for plying their communicative wares.

Nevertheless, there are at least three good reasons for not losing sight of the response-reinforcing dimension of "being persuaded." For the practicing communicator, this dimension underscores the importance of keeping old persuasive friends as well as making new ones. In the heat of a political campaign or a fund-raising drive, it may be tempting to center efforts on potential converts at the expense of ignoring those whose prevailing response tendencies already coincide with the intent of the political candidate or the fund-raiser. Such a mistake can easily yield low vote counts or depleted treasuries. Turning to the interpersonal sphere, close relationships may be damaged, or even terminated, because the parties take each other for granted—in the terminology employed here, fail to send persuasive messages aimed at reinforcing mutually held positive attitudes and mutually performed positive behaviors. In short, failure to recognize that being persuaded is an ongoing process requiring periodic message attention can harm one's political aspirations, pocketbook, or romantic relationship.

The need for continued reinforcement of acquired responses also constitutes one possible explanation for the ephemerality of many persuasion research outcomes. The typical persuasion study involves a single message, presented to recipients under controlled laboratory conditions, with a measure of attitude or behavior change taken immediately afterward. On numerous occasions, researchers have observed immediate changes, only to discover that they have vanished when later follow-up measures were taken. Although a number of substantive and procedural reasons can be offered for the fleeting impact of the persuasive stimulus, one obvious explanation rests in the likelihood that the behaviors engendered by the message received no further reinforcement after the recipients departed from the research setting. Thus, the response-reinforcing dimension of being persuaded has implications for the way persuasion researchers design and interpret their studies.

Perhaps most important, however, is the fact that all response-reinforcing strategies and schedules are not destined to be equally effective. Research using cultural truisms (McGuire, 1964, 1969) has demonstrated the low resistance to change that results when behaviors and attitudes rest on a history of nearly 100% positive reinforcement; apparently, too much exclusively behavior-congruent information is not a good

thing. Although studies such as those of McGuire and of Burgoon and his associates (Burgoon & Chase, 1973; Burgoon & King, 1974) have been characterized as dealing with the problem of *inducing resistance to persuasion,* the conceptualization that has been offered here views this label as a misnomer. Research dealing with the response-reinforcing function of persuasion is research on *how* to persuade, albeit in a different sense from what the popular use implies, a position that has also recently been espoused by other writers (Burgoon, Cohen, Miller, & Montgomery, 1978). Including response reinforcement as one of the three behavioral outcomes subsumed under the phrase "being persuaded" not only calls attention to the continued need for research concerning the workings of the reinforcing process but also results in a tidier conceptualization than has previously existed.

Being Persuaded as a Response-Changing Process

As has been repeatedly noted, "being persuaded" is most typically thought of as a response-changing process; smokers are persuaded to become nonsmokers, automobile drivers are persuaded to walk or use public transportation, Christians are persuaded to become Moslems, and so on. Popular use equates "being persuaded" with "being changed." Moreover, definitions of persuasions found in most texts emphasize the notion of changing responses (Bettinghaus, 1973; Cronkhite, 1969), and even when other terms such as *modify* (Brembeck & Howell, 1952) and *influence* (Scheidel, 1967) are used, the lion's share of the text is devoted to analysis of persuasion as a response-changing process.

This view of persuasion is, of course, consistent with the ideological tenets of democratic societies. Problems of social and political change are problems of persuasion; the public must be induced to change current attitudes and behaviors to comport with the realities of new situations.

The current energy crisis provides a convenient illustration of the process at work. Eschewing more coercive steps such as rationing, those charged with managing America's energy resources have bombarded the public with messages urging behavioral changes calculated to conserve these resources: dialing down thermostats, driving at slower speeds (a message buttressed by the coercive power of speeding laws), and voluntarily sharing rides—to mention but a few. Naturally, patience and faith in persuasion are not boundless; nevertheless, the democratic ethic strongly mandates that attempts to change behavior symbolically should precede more coercive remedies.

If one departs from the realm of public policy issues to conceive also of persuasion as a process involving modification of people's relational behaviors, a step recently urged by this writer (Miller, 1978), the same change-centered orientation is readily apparent. For instance, the continuing popularity of Dale Carnegie-type courses rests primarily on the following claim: Our instruction will motivate you to change your manner of self-presentation (i.e., to alter established patterns of social behavior); this change, in turn, will cause others to change dramatically their patterns of responding to you (i.e., others will be persuaded by your changed behavior to relate to you in different ways). Similarly, the popularity of Zimbardo's (1977) shyness volume and the spate of books and courses that deal with assertiveness training attest to the pervasiveness of people's attempts to alter their ongoing social behaviors and, concomitantly, to persuade others to respond differently to them. Although these processes are typically treated under rubrics such as *interpersonal communication* and *interpersonal relations*, the conceptualization outlined here argues that they should be counted as instances of the response-changing dimension of "being persuaded."

The largely unchallenged hegemony of the response-changing conception of persuasion obviates the need for further discussion. Most prior research in persuasion deals with behavioral change; at best, it treats response-shaping and response reinforcement indirectly. What remains in order to complete this analysis of the phrase "being persuaded" is a brief consideration of the way persuasive effects have typically been characterized.

Although terms such as *response* and *behavior* have been employed herein to refer to the effects of persuasive communications, the concept of *attitude* has also been mentioned on several occasions. Its emergence is not surprising, for concern with attitude formation and change has consistently guided the efforts of persuasion researchers ever since Allport (1935) confidently proclaimed *attitude* to be the single most important concept in social psychology. Notwithstanding widespread faith in the utility of the attitude construct, certain of its conceptual aspects pose knotty problems for students of persuasion. If "being persuaded" is to be considered synonymous with "shaping, reinforcing, and changing attitudes," these problems eventually must be resolved.

In persuasion research, an attitude is an *intervening variable*; that is, it is an internal mediator that intrudes between presentation of a particular overt stimulus and observation of a particular overt response (Fishbein & Ajzen, 1975; Triandis, 1971). Oskamp (1977) captured the crux of the matter, stating, "In social science, the term [attitude] has come to mean 'a posture of the mind' rather than of the body" (p. 7).

Given its conceptual status, all statements about the construct of *attitude* (or *attitude formation* or *attitude change*) are, of necessity, inferential; no means exist for directly observing or measuring an attitude. If someone asserts, "Roloff has a positive attitude about research," it means that the speaker has probably observed one or more of the following behaviors: Roloff proclaiming the importance of research, Roloff gathering data, Roloff writing research reports, Roloff forgoing a recreational outing to analyze data at the computer center, Roloff investing substantial sums of money in journals containing research reports, and so on. What the person has *not* observed is Roloff's *attitude* toward research; instead, his "positive attitude" is an inference (in the terminology of one currently popular theoretical position, an *attribution*) based on observation of Roloff's research-related behaviors.

Although this point is patently obvious, its implications have often escaped persuasion researchers. Nowhere has the mischief perpetrated by this oversight been more evident than in the countless pages written about the misleadingly labeled *attitude-behavior* problem (Liska, 1975). The crux of this problem lies in the minimal relationship often observed between verbal indicators of an attitude (i.e., paper-and-pencil "attitude" scales) and other attitudinally related behaviors. While the issue centers on lack of correlation between two behavioral measures, persuasion researchers have fallen into the trap of reifying the paper-and-pencil verbal reports traditionally used as inferential measures of the attitude construct.

> Despite any rational justification for doing so, persuasion researchers have continued to equate responses to these scales with the intervening variable of attitude and to speak of other responses as behavior—hence, the roots of the so-called *attitude-behavior* problem. (Miller, 1980, p. 322)

Pointing out this basic conceptual confusion in no way suggests that the minimal relationships observed between verbal attitude reports and other attitudinally related behaviors are unimportant to persuasion researchers. Because they are convenient to administer and lend themselves to a variety of statistical operations, paper-and-pencil verbal reports have been, and are likely to continue to be, widely used to measure persuasive effects. Any useful, reasonably fully developed theory of persuasion must seek to identify the conditions that determine when verbal reports will be correlated with other types of attitudinal behavior. Still, the continuing emphasis on attitude as the primary dependent variable, along with the prevailing tendency to view verbal

reports as attitudes, may have done more to hinder this search than to help it.

Most writers also posit that attitudes are motivational or drive producing (Allport, 1935; Doob, 1947; Oskamp, 1977). Whether current methods of attitude measurement tap this drive-producing dimension is open to serious question. The motivational force of an attitude stems from the strength or intensity with which it is held. Most widely used attitude scales measure only the magnitude of the attitude's deviation from zero, in other words, the degree of positiveness or negativeness respondents assign to their positions. If pressed, many persuasion researchers would probably argue that extremely deviating responses—for example, *plus three* or *minus three* responses on a seven-interval, semantic differential-type scale—reflect more strongly held attitudes than do responses falling closer to the scale's midpoint. *There is no necessary relationship between the position of one's attitude about an issue and the strength with which the attitude is held; position and intensity may be viewed usefully as two relatively independent dimensions.* Undoubtedly, people frequently have middling plus three or minus three attitudes; they may, for example, say that killing harp seals is *very good* or *very bad* yet not feel strongly about the issue. Conversely, less sharply polarized viewpoints sometimes may be held with great intensity; after weighing the matter thoroughly, an individual may conclude that killing harp seals is *slightly good* or *slightly bad* and at the same time feel quite strongly about the issue. It should be noted that the drive-producing potential of the attitude is one potentially important determinant of the extent to which verbal responses will correlate with other attitudinally consistent behaviors; if a respondent consistently says that killing harp seals is *very bad* but the issue is relatively uninvolving, that person will be unlikely to engage in more demanding, higher threshold responses (Campbell, 1963) such as giving money to naturalist organizations that oppose harp seal harvests, circulating anti-harp seal harvest petitions, and journeying to the scene of the harvest to demonstrate against it. On the other hand, if the issue is very involving and the drive-producing potential of the attitude is therefore high, these related behaviors are more likely to occur.

In some preliminary work, several of us (Miller, 1967; Peretz, 1974) have sought to index the drive-producing potential of attitudinal stimuli by measuring the vigor of the respondent's behavior (Brown, 1961). Rather than marking responses to attitudinal stimuli on paper, respondents press the appropriate button and the vigor of the button press is recorded. Because respondents experiencing high drive states are expected to behave more vigorously, the magnitude of the button press is assumed to be directly related to the attitude's intensity. Although findings have been mixed as well as confounded with numerous technical problems encountered in developing the instrumentation, some encouraging results have been obtained. In one study, Michigan State University football players responded quite vigorously to highly involving items dealing with the abolition of football scholarships and the presumed academic inferiority of athletes while at the same time responding less vigorously (yet positively or negatively) to items judged on an a priori basis to be less involving.

If using attitude as a primary behavioral indicant of "being persuaded" poses perplexing problems, what can be done to remedy the situation? One approach lies in retaining the construct while at the same time seeking to refine it and add to its utility by building more comprehensive models of attitude change (Fishbein & Ajzen, 1975). A second possibility involves replacing attitude with some other intervening construct such as value (Rokeach, 1968, 1973). Finally, persuasion researchers can abandon their reliance on mediating processes and focus exclusively on behavioristic analyses of persuasive effects. Although this latter possibility has received limited attention, a recent controversial paper (Larson & Sanders, 1975) has questioned the utility of predispositional mediating constructs

and suggested that the function of persuasion might be viewed more fruitfully as the appropriate alignment of *behavior* in various social situations.

Regardless of the direction in which a researcher's preferences may point, it remains clear that "being persuaded" is a process grounded in behavioral data. No matter whether the goal is shaping, reinforcing, or changing responses, both practical and scientific successes hinge on careful observation and measurement of persuasive impact. Perhaps inferences to intervening variables, such as attitudes and values, will eventually prove indispensable to theoretical success, but these constructs are not essential ingredients of the conceptual analysis of "being persuaded" that has been offered in this chapter.

References

Allport, G. W. (1935). Attitudes. In C. M. Murchison (Ed.), *Handbook of social psychology* (pp. 798–844). Worcester, MA: Clark University Press.

Becker, S. L. (1963). Research on logical and emotional proof. *Southern Speech Journal, 28,* 198–207.

Bettinghaus, E. P. (1973). *Persuasive communication.* New York: Holt, Rinehart & Winston.

Brandt, D. R. (1976, May). Listener propensity to counterargue, distraction, and resistance to persuasion. Paper presented at the convention of the International Communication Association, Portland, OR.

Brembeck, W. L., & Howell, W. A. (1952). *Persuasion.* Englewood Cliffs, NJ: Prentice Hall.

Brown, J.S. (1961). *The motivation of behavior.* New York: McGraw-Hill.

Burgoon, M., & Chase, L. J. (1973). The effects of differential linguistic patterns in messages attempting to induce resistance to persuasion. *Speech Monographs, 40,* 1–7.

Burgoon, M., & King, L. B. (1974). The mediation of resistance to persuasion strategies by language variables and active-passive participation. *Human Communication Research, 1,* 30–41.

Burgoon, M., Cohen, M., Miller, M. D., & Montgomery, C. L. (1978). An empirical test of a model of resistance to persuasion. *Human Communication Research, 5,* 27–39.

Campbell, D. T. (1963). Social attitudes and other acquired behavioral dispositions. In S. Koch (Ed.), *Psychology: A study of a science* (Vol. 6, pp. 94–172). New York: McGraw-Hill.

Cronkhite, G. L. (1969). *Persuasion: Speech and behavioral change.* Indianapolis, IN: Bobbs-Merrill.

Diggs, B. J. (1964). Persuasion and ethics. *Quarterly Journal of Speech, 50,* 359–373.

Doob, L. W. (1947). The behavior of attitudes. *Psychological Review, 54,* 135–156.

Festinger, L. (1957). *A theory of cognitive dissonance.* Evanston, IL: Row, Peterson.

Festinger, L., & Maccoby, N. (1964). On resistance to persuasive communications. *Journal of Abnormal and Social Psychology, 68,* 359–366.

Fishbein, M., & Ajzen, I. (1975). *Belief, attitude, intention, and behavior: An introduction to theory and research.* Reading, MA: Addison-Wesley.

Freedman, J. L., & Sears, D. O. (1965). Selective exposure. In L. Berkowitz (Ed.), *Advances in experimental social psychology* (Vol. 2, pp. 57–97). New York: Academic Press.

Hartmann, G. W. (1936). A field experiment on the comparative effectiveness of "emotional" and "rational" political leaflets in determining election results. *Journal of Abnormal and Social Psychology, 31,* 99–114.

Katz, E., & Lazarsfeld, P. F. (1955). *Personal influence.* New York: Free Press.

Kelman, H. C. (1961). Processes of opinion change. *Public Opinion Quarterly, 25,* 57–78.

Larson, C., & Sanders, R. (1975). Faith, mystery, and data: An analysis of "scientific" studies of persuasion. *Quarterly Journal of Speech, 61,* 178–194.

Liska, A. E. (1975). *The consistency controversy: Readings on the impact of attitude on behavior.* Cambridge, MA: Schenkman.

Marwell, G., & Schmitt, D. R. (1967). Dimensions of compliance-gaining behavior: An empirical analysis. *Sociometry, 30,* 350–364.

Matthews, J. (1947). The effect of loaded language on audience comprehension of speeches. *Speech Monographs, 14,* 176–187.

McGuire, W. J. (1964). Inducing resistance to persuasion: Some contemporary approaches. In L. Berkowitz (Ed.), *Advances in experimental social psychology* (Vol. 1, pp. 191–229). New York: Academic Press.

McGuire, W. J. (1969). The nature of attitudes and attitude change. In G. Lindzey & E. Aronson (Eds.), *Handbook of social psychology* (Vol. 3, pp. 136–314). Reading, MA: Addison-Wesley.

Miller, G. R. (1967). A crucial problem in attitude research. *Quarterly Journal of Speech, 53,* 235–240.

Miller, G. R. (1980). Afterword. In D. P. Cushman & R. McPhee (Eds.), *Message-attitude-behavior relationship: Theory, methodology, and application* (pp. 319–327). New York: Academic Press.

Miller, G. R., & Burgoon, M. (1973). *New techniques of persuasion.* New York: Harper & Row.

Miller, G. R. (1978). Persuasion research: Review and commentary. In B. D. Ruben (Ed.), *Communication yearbook 2* (pp. 29–47). New Brunswick, NJ: Transaction Books.

Nilsen, T. R. (1966). *Ethics of speech communication.* Indianapolis, IN: Bobbs-Merrill.

Osgood, C. E., Suci, G. J., & Tannenbaum, P. H. (1957). *The measurement of meaning.* Urbana: University of Illinois Press.

Osgood, C. E., & Tannenbaum, P. H. (1955). The principle of congruity in the prediction of attitude change. *Psychological Review, 62,* 42–55.

Oskamp, S. (1977). *Attitudes and opinions.* Englewood Cliffs, NJ: Prentice Hall.

Osterhouse, R. A., & Brock, T. C. (1970). Distraction increases yielding to propaganda by inhibiting counter-arguing. *Journal of Personality and Social Psychology, 15,* 344–358.

Peretz, M. D. (1974). *Studies on the measurement of attitude intensity.* Unpublished master's thesis, Michigan State University.

Rokeach, M. (1968). *Beliefs, attitudes, and values.* San Francisco: Jossey-Bass.

Rokeach, M. (1973). *The nature of human values.* New York: Free Press.

Rowell, E. Z. (1932a). Prolegomena to argumentation: Part I. *Quarterly Journal of Speech, 18,* 1–13.

Rowell, E. Z. (1932b). Prolegomena to argumentation: Part II. *Quarterly Journal of Speech, 18,* 224–248.

Saltiel, J., & Woelfel, J. (1975). Inertia in cognitive processes: The role of accumulated information in attitude change. *Human Communication Research, 1,* 333–344.

Scheidel, T. M. (1967). *Persuasive speaking.* Glencoe, IL: Scott, Foresman.

Sears, D. O., & Freedman, J. L. (1967). Selective exposure to information: A critical review. *Public Opinion Quarterly, 31,* 194–213.

Simons, H. W. (1974). The carrot and stick as handmaidens of persuasion in conflict situations. In G. R. Miller & H. W. Simons (Eds.), *Perspectives on communication in social conflict.* Englewood Cliffs, NJ: Prentice Hall.

Triandis, H. C. (1971). *Attitude and attitude change.* New York: John Wiley.

Weiss, W. (1960). Emotional arousal and attitude change. *Psychological Reports, 6,* 267–280.

Woolbert, C. H. (1917). Conviction and persuasion: Some considerations of theory. *Quarterly Journal of Speech, 3,* 249–264.

Zimbardo, P. G. (1977). *Shyness: What it is and what to do about it.* Reading, MA: Addison-Wesley.

PART II

Theories, Perspectives, and Traditions

CHAPTER 6

Discrepancy Models of Belief Change

Edward L. Fink and Deborah A. Cai

In the context of attitude and belief change, *discrepancy* refers to the difference between a position advocated in a message (P_A) and the immediately prior premessage position of an individual (P_0); thus, message discrepancy (hereinafter *discrepancy*) = ($P_A - P_0$). Suppose for example that you were asked to contribute (perhaps with some justification) $100.00 ($P_A$) to your alma mater, and your immediately prior view regarding how much you would be willing to give your alma mater was $10.00 ($P_0$). In this case, the discrepancy of the message is $90.00.

The logic behind discrepancy studies is a simple one: It is assumed that discrepancy is a predictor of change in attitude or belief (and sometimes behavior). To be precise, an *attitude* is a response of the form or a conveyance of the idea that "I like [or dislike] *X*." An *evaluative belief* is a response of the form or conveyance of the idea "*X* is good [or bad]." A *nonevaluative belief* is a response of the form or a conveyance of the idea "*X* is *Y*," where *Y* is nonevaluative. These definitions are not meant to be restrictive but rather to differentiate possible foci of research (cf. Woelfel & Fink, 1980). However, the use of a standard terminology is complicated in part because different authors studying this phenomenon have used different terms. For simplicity in what follows, the discussion of discrepancy models as applied to attitudes also applies to beliefs, and belief is used as the generic term throughout.

AUTHOR' NOTE: Some of the ideas presented here are taken from Kaplowitz, S. A., & Fink, E. L. (1997). Message discrepancy and persuasion. In G. A. Barnett & F. J. Boster (Eds.), *Progress in communication sciences* (Vol. 13, pp. 75–106). Greenwich, CT: Ablex.

The authors acknowledge the work of our collaborators in the study of discrepancy models, and in particular Joseph Woelfel, Stan A. Kaplowitz, and Sungeun Chung. We thank Jeffrey C. Williams for description of discrepancy models from other sciences.

A *discrepancy model* is a model that relates the differences between values of a dependent variable to differences in the values of one or more independent variables. This chapter first describes the logic and role of discrepancy models in the sciences. Next, we examine the simplest belief change model regarding discrepancy, the linear discrepancy model. We indicate its assumptions and its implications for message repetition and message order, and explicate the meaning of its single parameter. Finally, we examine the theories and literature regarding discrepancy models of belief change and the evidence regarding the validity of the linear discrepancy model and its major tenets. This discussion includes an excursus in the form of a methodological wish list, recommending how research in this area may be improved.

Discrepancy Models in Scientific Theory

Discrepancy models play a central role in scientific theory: It is common for differences in one or more variables to predict differences in a dependent variable. Here are a few examples from physics.

Models

Bernoulli's Principle

Bernoulli's principle states that the difference in pressures of a fluid system at any two points in a flow is a function of the difference in the flow velocities squared and the difference in the vertical locations of the two points (Bar-Meir, 2011).

First Law of Thermodynamics

The First Law of Thermodynamics relates the differences in the internal energy of a system at equilibrium to the difference between the heat transfer and the work done (Knight, 2007).

Kinematics of a Particle With Constant Acceleration

The equations relating the three basic quantities of particle kinematics (position, velocity, and acceleration) are explained in terms of differences in time, differences in displacement, and velocity in acceleration (Knight, 2007).

Relevance of Physical Models

What is the relevance of these physical examples for human communication science? First, these examples show the successful application of a model (Lave & March, 1993); these examples are literally textbook cases. Second, these examples are parsimonious: The variables and relationships that are included fit within a framework that implicitly dismisses variables that are deemed irrelevant. Compare these examples with studies in the communication discipline that add a potpourri of variables, seemingly without limit (see Pacanowsky, 1976, for an example of a line of research that, although a caricature, fits into the "no variable need be excluded" category and appears all too realistic).

Third, the physics examples all specify the measurement rules—the metrics—that apply to all included variables; these metrics are balanced in the sense that the units on one side of the equation generate the same units as the other side. Thus, the units on both sides work out to be the same (created by what is referred to as *dimensional analysis*).

These examples are only a few that could be used to show the success of models based on discrepancy. In the following, we start with a simple discrepancy model, a model applied to beliefs, and then examine the extent to which theory and research have extended, modified, and complemented the simple ideas about discrepancy and belief change.

A Linear Model

The simplest form of change induced by discrepancy would be linear. If we define the relevant change induced by a message as the difference between the position adopted by the individual after message receipt (P_1) and the individual's premessage position (P_0), then belief change = ($P_1 - P_0$). The linear function relating change to discrepancy is

$$(P_1 - P_0) = \forall (P_A - P_0), \qquad (1)$$

where $\forall$ is a constant of proportionality. This model has several different names, including the *linear discrepancy model*, the *linear balance model*, the *distance-proportional model* (Anderson & Hovland, 1957), and the *proportional change model* (e.g., Danes, Hunter, & Woelfel, 1978); the model is also consistent with the logic of Anderson's (1974) *information integration theory*.

We may rewrite Equation 1 as follows:

$$P_1 = P_0 + \forall (P_A - P_0)$$
$$\therefore P_1 = P_0 + \forall P_A - \forall P_0$$
$$\therefore P_1 = (1 - \forall)P_0 + \forall P_A. \qquad (2)$$

Equation 2, which is mathematically equivalent to Equation 1, highlights another aspect of this model: Because $(1 - \forall)$ and $\forall$ sum to 1, we see that the new position (P_1) is the weighted sum of the initial position (P_0) and the position advocated in the message (P_A). This model can be directly applied to the receipt of more than one message, either simultaneously or sequentially; the latter case is addressed in the following.

Using the "contribution to alma mater" example, if the linear discrepancy model were correct and we arbitrarily set $\forall = \frac{1}{3}$ (the meaning of $\forall$ is discussed in detail two sections later in this chapter), then

$$(P_1 - P_0) = \forall (P_A - P_0)$$
$$(P_1 - 10) = \frac{1}{3}(100 - 10)$$
$$(P_1 - 10) = 30$$
$$P_1 = 10 + 30 = 40.$$

So, the new position adopted by the individual would be a contribution of $40.00.

Assumptions

This model has several assumptions. The first set of assumptions reflects general issues of attitude and belief change studies:

A.0. The subjects [i.e., individuals who are involved in the investigation] are capable of attending to and comprehending the messages.

A.1. The subjects' attitudes [and beliefs] and the relevant messages may be placed on a unidimensional [quantitative] continuum.

A.2. Each equation is static, and thus assumes that an equilibrium value for the dependent variable has been achieved prior to or simultaneously with [its measurement].

A.3. . . . parameters in the attitude [and belief] change models . . . are identical for all subjects given the same facilitating or inhibiting factors represented by the equivalent experimental conditions. (bracketed material added; Fink, Kaplowitz, & Bauer, 1983, n20, pp. 416–417)

Assumptions A.0, A.2, and A.3 are typical assumptions in experimental attitude and belief change research, although these assumptions are generally implicit. Assumption A.1 is particularly relevant to discrepancy models: Attitude or belief positions may be implicit in messages and in the message recipient, but the model requires that they be made explicit. If the information is not explicit, this assumption may be interpreted in two different ways: (1) All messages and positions can be quantified, even if they are not quantified explicitly in a message or by the message recipient. So, if you are asked to donate to your alma mater, you may respond as if your initial position (P_0) was $10.00, although you may not have been aware of that number, and a message like "Please donate to our alma mater" may be interpreted by you to mean "donate

$100.00." (2) An alternate interpretation is to suggest that the message position, the recipient's initial position, and the new position are qualitative (categorical); in that case, belief change would be better modeled by logistic regression, a catastrophe model (Flay, 1978; Latané & Nowak, 1994; van der Maas, Kolstein, & van der Plight, 2003), or a cellular automata model (Corman, 1996); due to space limitations, these models are not discussed further, but suffice it to say that the linear discrepancy model is incompatible with this second possibility.

Assumption A.2 means that the time interval between message receipt and P_i is long enough for the individual to integrate the message in his or her set of beliefs; the actual time interval has been estimated using a dynamic model, discussed next.

A different assumption concerns the range of values for $\forall$. Many authors, including, for example, Hunter, Levine, and Sayers (1976), assume that $0 < \forall < 1$ (Assumption A.4). This assumption means that (for $0 < \forall$) there can be no boomerang effect: A message cannot cause a person to change an attitude or belief in a direction opposite to that which was advocated. This assumption also means that (for $\forall < 1$) the person cannot adopt a position more discrepant than that which was advocated. In the following section, we examine the effect of various values of $\forall$ that disregard Assumption A.4.

Message Repetition

We can use the linear discrepancy model recursively. If the same message is given repeatedly with enough time for each message in the sequence to be integrated (Assumption A.2), one can take Equation 1 and change the 0 subscript to 1 and the 1 to 2, and we have

$$(P_2 - P_1) = \forall(P_A - P_1).$$

Or, in general,

$$(P_\tau - P_{\tau-1}) = \forall(P_A - P_{\tau-1}),$$

where τ is the number of repetitions. Note that we have another assumption here, namely (Assumption B.0) that the model, and more specifically the value of $\forall$, is unchanged by repetition.

Given assumptions A.1-A.3 and B.0, if $\forall = 0$ (which disregards A.4), the person's initial position is unchanged by repetition: If $P_0 = 0$ and $P_A = 100$, repetition of the message leaves all subsequent positions (P_1, P_2, etc.) = 0.

In Figures 6.1., 6.2., and 6.3., the effect of repetition is shown with other values of $\forall$. Figure 6.1. shows that if $0 < \forall \leq 1$, repetition causes the individual to move toward the position advocated (here, 100). With $0 < \forall < 1$, an individual's position approaches 1.00 asymptotically; with $\forall = 1$, the individual adopts the position advocated ($P_A = 100$) after the first message and remains at that value with additional repetitions of the message.

Figure 6.2. shows that when $\forall > 1.00$, the trajectory of belief positions oscillates due to message repetition. With $\forall = 1.50$, we see that the newly adopted positions oscillate with damping

Figure 6.1   Effect of Number of Repetitions on Belief Position, by Different Values of Alpha: 1.00, 0.75, 0.50, 0.25. $P_0 = 0$, $P_A = 100$

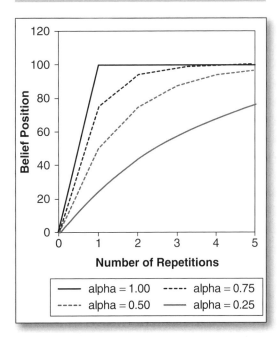

Figure 6.2 Effect of Number of Repetitions on Belief Position, by Different Values of Alpha: 2.00, 1.50. $P_0 = 0$, $P_A = 100$

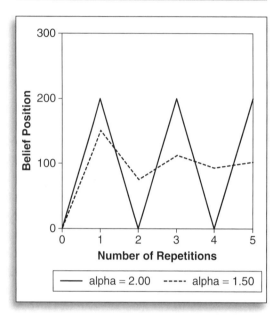

alpha = 2.00   ----- alpha = 1.50

Figure 6.3 Effect of Number of Repetitions on Belief Position, Alpha = -0.50. $P_0 = 0$, $P_A = 100$

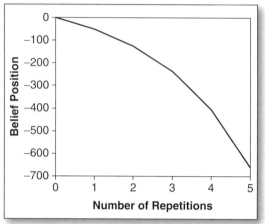

(the decrease in oscillation amplitude), alternately overshooting and undershooting the position advocated, with the absolute value of the difference from the position advocated getting smaller and smaller. With $\forall = 2.00$, message repetition causes the position adopted to alternate between a position of 200 (for an odd number of repetitions) and a new position of 0 (for an even number of repetitions). Not shown in Figure 6.2. is what happens if $\forall > 2.00$: In that case, the oscillations explode, increasingly moving away from the position advocated.

Figure 6.3. shows the effect of a negative value for $\forall$. In this case, repetition causes the positions adopted by the individual to move increasingly away from the position advocated, always in a negative direction.

What Is $\forall$?

The value $\forall$ has so far been mysterious. Clearly $\forall$ is the ratio of the change achieved by a message $(P_1 - P_0)$ to the change advocated by the message $(P_A - P_0)$: It is the slope of the line relating these two quantities. However, neither of these descriptions of $\forall$ relates it to the study of belief change.

Let's consider Berlo's (1960; see also Shannon & Weaver, 1949) four aspects of communication: source, message, channel, and receiver. Imagine a thought experiment (*Gedankenexperiment*) in which we hold the message, channel, and receiver constant, and vary only the source. In other words, we have two or more sources, and we have empirically determined the receiver's P_0 and the message's P_A. After giving the message and having the receiver integrate the message with other attitudes and beliefs (Assumption A.2), we measure P_1, which allows us to estimate $\forall$. We would expect that some sources are more effective than others, and that these more effective sources are associated with higher values of $\forall$, which is consistent with findings regarding source credibility (Aronson, Turner, & Carlsmith, 1963; Hovland & Weiss, 1951; Jaccard, 1981). In this case, $\forall$ is source credibility: Credibility means believability, so rather than say that properties of a source, as assessed by a scale, provide an operationalization of credibility, we can say that such measures may be indicators of credibility, but, in our hypothetical example, the value of $\forall$ *is* the source's level of credibility.

Our next thought experiment holds source, channel, and receiver constant, and varies the message. By the same logic as previously noted, in this case $\forall$ is message persuadability or message effectiveness. Continuing this logic, if we hold the source, the message, and the receiver constant, $\forall$ becomes channel effectiveness. Finally, if we hold the source, the message, and the channel constant, $\forall$ is receiver persuadability or, more derisively, gullibility.

Of course, in an actual investigation (1) we may never completely hold these factors constant, (2) these factors may interact in predicting belief change, and (3) there may be factors to consider other than or as a component of source, message, channel, and receiver. For example, greater ego involvement (a receiver characteristic) should reduce belief change (Freedman, 1964; Jaccard, 1981; Zimbardo, 1960), which should reduce $\forall$, whereas stronger arguments (a message characteristic) should increase $\forall$ (Petty & Cacioppo, 1986).

Another interpretation of $\forall$ is to consider it as the ratio of the weight of the message position (P_A) divided by the weight of the message position plus the weight that exists for the effects of prior messages (which becomes the weight of P_0). Because the coefficients for P_0 and P_A sum to 1 (see Equation 2), $(1 - \forall)$ reflects the ratio of the weight of the initial position (P_0) divided by the weight of the message position plus the weight of the initial position. Algebraically,

$$\forall = w_A/(w_A + w_0) \qquad (3)$$

and

$$(1 - \forall) = w_0/(w_A + w_0) \qquad (4)$$

so that

$$P_1 = [w_0/(w_A + w_0)]P_0 + [w_A/(w_A + w_0)]P_A \qquad (5)$$

(see Fink et al., 1983; Saltiel & Woelfel, 1975). By this interpretation, the greater the weight of the message position, the more belief change is

achieved. On the other hand, holding the weight of a new message position constant, the more massive ("weightier") a receiver's initial position, the less the belief change induced by a new message. The weight of the initial position can reflect the number of or involvement with prior messages while taking into account the processes of forgetting, which should reduce the weight, and activation, which may increase or restore the weight to a previous higher value.

Summarizing this discussion, the value of $\forall$ is composed of factors that inhibit (low values of $\forall$) or bolster (high values of $\forall$) belief change; in any given investigation, its composition reflects the factors that vary the most across the comparisons to be assessed. The linear model assumes that $\forall$ is a constant, and this assumption is investigated further.

Message Order

The linear discrepancy model makes specific predictions about the way that combinations of messages produce belief change. If we retain Assumption A.2, we can consider whether a message that is extremely discrepant followed by a message that is moderately discrepant is more or less effective than if the messages were in the opposite order.

In the following example, let $P_0 = 0$, $\forall = 0.50$, P_E (the position of an extremely discrepant message) = 100, and P_M (the position of a moderately discrepant message) = 40. The analysis of the two message orders looks like this:

The extreme message followed by the moderate message:	The moderate message followed by the extreme message:
$(P_1 - P_0) = \forall(P_E - P_0)$	$(P_1 - P_0) = \forall(P_M - P_0)$
$(P_1 - 0) = 0.50(100 - 0)$	$(P_1 - 0) = 0.50(40 - 0)$
$P_1 = 50$	$P_1 = 20$
$(P_2 - P_1) = \forall(P_M - P_1)$	$(P_2 - P_1) = \forall(P_E - P_1)$
$(P_2 - 50) = 0.50$	$(P_2 - 20) = 0.50$
$(40 - 50)$	$(100 - 20)$
$P_2 = 45$	$P_2 = 60$

We see that, with the assumptions that were made, the moderate message followed by the extreme message is more effective than the messages in the reverse order.

Summarizing this section, we see the linear discrepancy model makes clear predictions about several aspects of belief change: the effect due to a single message, the relation of communication factors (e.g., source, message, channel, receiver) to the model's single parameter ($\forall$), the effect of message repetition, and the effect of message order. The model has nonobvious implications; for example, the same equation, used to assess message repetition, generates incremental upward motion toward an asymptote, oscillatory motion that damps out, oscillatory motion that does not damp out, oscillatory motion that is unstable, and accelerating motion away from the position advocated. We now examine how various theories relate to this model.

Theories Regarding Discrepancy

Social Judgment Theory

M. Sherif and Hovland (1961; C. W. Sherif & Sherif, 1967; C. W. Sherif, Sherif, & Nebergall, 1965) created social judgment theory, which is based on the idea that beliefs are perceived, and therefore judged, the way that physical quantities are perceived and judged. The usual analogy (referred to as the contrast principle) considers how a hand first put in cold water, after adapting to that temperature, when put in lukewarm water feels hot, whereas a hand first put in hot water, after adapting to that temperature, when put in lukewarm water feels cold. In other words, the initial location (i.e., cold or hot water) acts as an anchor that leads to a misperception of how hot or cold the subsequent location (i.e., lukewarm water) is. C. W. Sherif et al. (1965) proposed that an individual's initial beliefs or attitudes determine how a position in a message is perceived. If the position in the message is close to the individual's initial position (i.e., it is

within the individual's *latitude of acceptance*), the message position is perceived to be closer than it actually is, and therefore the message seems not very discrepant (i.e., it is assimilated). If the position in the message is far from the individual's initial position (i.e., it is within the individual's *latitude of rejection*), the message position is perceived to be further than it actually is, and therefore the message seems very discrepant (i.e., it is contrasted). The less discrepant the message appears, the more change it induces. Therefore, messages within the latitude of acceptance are effective in bringing about belief or attitude change, whereas messages within the latitude of rejection are ineffective in bringing about such change. (C. W. Sherif et al. also posit a latitude of noncommitment, in which no distortion of the message position is perceived.)

The implication of the social judgment approach is that the relation of discrepancy and belief change should not be linear: A message that is as discrepant as possible but still within the individual's latitude of acceptance should be most persuasive. Messages within the latitude of acceptance would be expected to cause change similar to that expected by the linear discrepancy model, whereas messages in the latitude of rejection should bring about less change. Overall, the curve representing the relation of discrepancy to belief change should be an inverted-*U*, first increasing to the point of maximum change and then decreasing; see Figure 6.4. In the terminology of the linear discrepancy model, $\forall$ (the slope) is not a constant: At low levels of discrepancy it is positive, and then at high levels of discrepancy it becomes negative.

Social judgment theory complicates this simple picture by adding the effects of two other variables. First, source credibility is expected to interact with discrepancy: In general, the greater the credibility, the greater the belief change (a main effect), but more important, the extremum of the curve (here, the maximum, which is the highest point on the *y*-axis) should occur at higher values of discrepancy the more credible the source. (Note: The extremum is not an inflection point.)

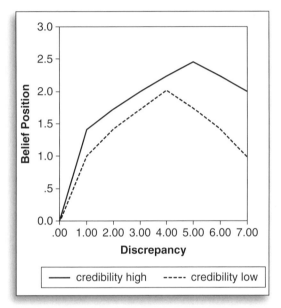

Figure 6.4 Hypothetical Relationship Between Discrepancy and Belief Change as Affected by Source Credibility, Consistent With the Social Judgment Approach and Cognitive Dissonance Theory. The Same Relationship Is Expected to Hold if Low Credibility Is Replaced With High Ego Involvement and High Source Credibility Is Replaced With Low Ego Involvement.

Second, ego involvement—the idea that the issue is personally important to the message recipient—is also expected to interact with discrepancy: The lower the involvement, the greater the persuasion (a main effect), and the extremum of the curve should occur at higher values of discrepancy the lower the involvement.

The logic for the effect of source credibility is straightforward: More credible sources should widen the latitude of acceptance and, as a result, induce more belief change. Greater ego involvement should result in "larger latitudes of rejection" because with high involvement "a person's own attitude acts as a stronger anchor" (Petty & Cacioppo, 1981, p. 107).

The evidence for the social judgment effects is not strong. For example, Eagly and Telaak (1972)

found that it is the width of the latitude of acceptance, rather than the discrepancy level of the message, that determined the amount of change induced by a message: the greater the width, the greater the change. A study by Miller (1965) showed that the latitude of rejection did not increase for those highly involved with the relevant message issue as compared to control group members who were highly involved with an unrelated issue. Both these studies' findings are inconsistent with social judgment theory (see also Petty & Cacioppo, 1981). Thus, the social judgment approach lacks sufficient evidence of its validity. Eagly and Chaiken (1993) summarized this view by stating that "existing research provides little, if any, convincing evidence that the perceptual processes of assimilation and contrast covary with attitude change, let alone *precede* attitude change as the theory maintains" (p. 380, emphasis in original).

Cognitive Dissonance Theory

Both Aronson et al. (1963) and Bochner and Insko (1966) proposed that the theory of cognitive dissonance (Festinger, 1957) was relevant to understanding the effect of discrepancy on attitude change. Aronson et al. proposed that a discrepant message, assumed to be counterattitudinal, is a cause of dissonance. Furthermore, they suggested that there should be more dissonance when the message source is credible.

Bochner and Insko stated that discrepancy causes dissonance that can be reduced in any of four ways: conformity to the communicator's [i.e., the source's] point of view, disparagement of the communicator, persuasion of the communicator that he is incorrect, and obtained social support. (p. 614)

Because laboratory studies are not amenable to the third or fourth of these ways of reducing dissonance, Bochner and Insko (1966) proposed that an individual must respond to a discrepant message by being persuaded, by disparaging the source, or by some combination of the two. (Notice that this conclusion is not a requirement of theory but rather of the research design.) They then suggested that at low levels of discrepancy, belief change occurs, and that at high levels of discrepancy, disparagement occurs. Thus, they predicted the same curvilinear relationship that was predicted by social judgment theory, with disparagement and belief change treated as functional alternatives in response to a discrepant message: They predicted (1) the relationship between discrepancy and belief change is curvilinear, and (2) the extremum of the curve occurs at higher values of discrepancy the more credible the source; see Figure 6.4.

Cognitive Elaboration: Counterarguing

It seems reasonable that messages that are more discrepant induce more counterarguments, both as thoughts and as vocal disparagement of the communicator and the communication. Brock (1967) found empirical support for this relationship when considering subvocal counterarguments. This finding suggests that discrepancy causes processing through the central rather than the peripheral route (Petty & Cacioppo, 1986). The central route involves greater elaboration, indicated by a greater number of thoughts, which may be pro-attitudinal, counterattitudinal, or both. Because discrepancy is counter to one's beliefs, when an individual has the ability and motivation to think about a message, greater discrepancy → greater elaboration → more counterarguments → reduced belief change. The reduced effectiveness of the more discrepant messages may also be associated with the greater scrutiny that these messages receive as well as their perceived weakness, because arguments in messages that are incompatible with prior beliefs are judged to be weaker than arguments in messages compatible with one's beliefs (Edwards & Smith, 1996).

Two additional studies examined the relation of discrepancy to cognitive elaboration (see Kaplowitz & Fink, 1997). Kaplowitz and Fink (1991) manipulated discrepancy, measured the individual's belief, measured other evaluations (including manipulation checks), and finally assessed cognitive elaboration; they found that discrepancy and its effects were not related to elaboration. In a later study (Kaplowitz & Fink, 1995), in which participants indicated their belief continuously and then reported their thoughts, discrepancy was significantly associated with elaboration in terms of the number of counterarguments but not in terms of the number of pro-belief thoughts. In this 1995 study, participants considered their position repeatedly before reporting their cognitive responses, whereas in the 1991 study other measures intervened between the belief measure and the elaboration measure. Thus, it appears that when participants are directed to consider their belief as it is being formed, discrepancy increases cognitive responses at least with regard to counterarguments. However, based on a comparison of the 1991 and 1995 studies, it appears that this elaboration *reduces* the effect of discrepancy on belief change, suggesting that discrepancy is more effective if it serves as a peripheral cue. Given the procedural differences between these two studies, more research on this issue is needed.

Assuming that discrepancy does increase elaboration, the elaboration likelihood model predicts the same outcome as social judgment theory and the theory of cognitive dissonance: The relation between discrepancy and belief change should be an inverted-U shaped curve, as shown in Figure 6.4. On the other hand, if discrepancy or belief position serves as a peripheral cue, a discrepant message may be rejected without any need for elaboration. Kaplowitz and Fink's (1991) study found a large effect of discrepancy on belief change, but that study found no evidence of a downturn in belief position or of cognitive elaboration associated with discrepancy.

Is the Relation Between Discrepancy and Belief Change Nonmonotonic?

Bochner and Insko Redux

Bochner and Insko (1966) conducted an experiment that tested the functional form of the relationship of discrepancy to belief change using daily hours of sleep as the topic. Through a pilot study, P_0, the participants' initial position, was found to be 7.89 hours. Bochner and Insko's dependent variables were belief position ("For maximum health and well being, how many hours of sleep per night do you think the average young adult should get?") and two measures of disparagement: disparagement of the source and of the message. They manipulated three variables: message discrepancy, with nine levels (messages advocating 8, 7, 6, 5, 4, 3, 2, 1, and 0 hours of sleep); source credibility, with two levels (high vs. moderate); and the order in which the dependent variables were measured (belief then disparagement vs. disparagement then belief).

Figure 6.5. shows Bochner and Insko's (1966) results, combining data for the two different orders, which did not differ in their effects. The figure shows that messages attributed to the source with greater credibility were not more persuasive over all levels of discrepancy: For intermediate levels of discrepancy, the messages from the moderately credible source were more persuasive.

More important, the figure and its analysis shed light on the functional form of the relationship between discrepancy and belief change. These results, however, have often been misstated because the statistical analysis of the data appears inconsistent with what is shown in the figure: The statistical analysis reveals that the relationship is linear for discrepancy induced by the high credibility source, whereas the relationship is curvilinear and nonmonotonic for the discrepancy induced by the moderately credible source.

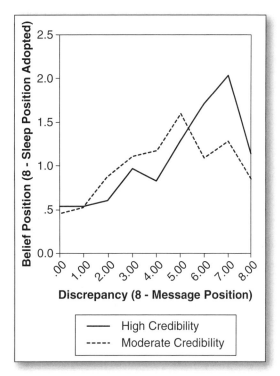

Figure 6.5   Bochner and Insko's (1966) Findings Relating Discrepancy to Belief Change

Although there were some significant findings regarding disparagement, it did not appear that disparagement acted simply as a functional alternative to belief change.

A Mathematical Integration: Laroche (1977)

Laroche (1977) created a mathematical model that incorporated source credibility, message discrepancy, and ego involvement in predicting belief change. Laroche's model requires that all variables are transformed to be between 0 and 1. Laroche's key equation is

$$y_{Eq} = D_p e^{-\gamma D_p}, \text{ with } 0 \leq D_p \leq 1.00,$$
$$0 \leq y \leq 1.00, \gamma \geq 0, \qquad (3)$$

where D_p is message discrepancy, $P_0 = 0$, and y_{Eq} = belief position at equilibrium. The parameter γ is a function of source credibility and noninvolvement.

The critical feature of Laroche's (1977) model is that, depending on the levels of credibility and noninvolvement, three different relations between discrepancy and belief position are possible: When $\gamma > 1.00$, there is a downturn in the graph (i.e., the relation is nonmonotonic); when $0 < \gamma < 1.00$, the curve is monotonic, decelerating with a positive slope; when $\gamma = 0$, the relation is linear. In other words, we can think of γ as a dial that changes the shape of the curve relating discrepancy to belief change. Greater credibility and greater noninvolvement reduce γ, thereby making the relation approach linearity. Using the results of prior studies, Laroche found that "γ was generally higher for low-credibility sources than for high-credibility sources and higher for conditions with high involvement than for those with low involvement" (Chung, Fink, & Kaplowitz, 2008, pp. 161–162).

Additional Evidence From Static Models

Aggregating Prior Studies

To investigate the functional form of the relationship between discrepancy and belief position, we can look at the average slope for different levels of discrepancy. Kaplowitz and Fink (1997) did just that, using their own prior research. In the works of Fink et al. (1983), Kaplowitz, Fink, Armstrong, and Bauer (1986), and Kaplowitz and Fink (1991), the relationship between discrepancy and belief position was a curve with a positive slope that decelerated; in other words, as discrepancy went up belief change went up, but the rate of change decreased. However, these differences in slope were relatively small. Furthermore, after reviewing other investigations, Kaplowitz and Fink (1997) concluded that there was little evidence for nonmonotonicity or boomerang effects

(see Kaplowitz & Fink, 1997, pp. 83–85; cf. McGuire, 1985, p. 276); they speculated that "strong supportive arguments may increase the effectiveness of an extremely discrepant message from a mildly credible source and thus inhibit nonmonotonicity" (p. 84).

Positional Versus Psychological Discrepancy

Laroche's key equation (Equation 3, presented earlier) has discrepancy in two places, as a coefficient and as an exponentiated value: $y_{Eq} = D_p e^{-\gamma D_p}$. Fink and colleagues (1983) created a variant of this model that incorporates two different aspects of discrepancy: *positional discrepancy*, which is the same as what was previously referred to as discrepancy, and *psychological discrepancy*, which is the "level of discrepancy between two positions as experienced by an individual" (Fink et al., 1983, p. 415). Using our notation, the model's key equation for the receipt of one message is:

$$P_I = [w_0 P_0 + w_A \Delta(\psi) P_A]/[w_0 + w_A \Delta(\psi)],$$

where w_0 is the weight of the initial position (P_0), w_A is the weight of the message position (P_A), and $\Delta(\psi)$ is a discounting function that reduces the weight of the message as psychological discrepancy increases (compare with Equation 5). More specifically,

$$\Delta(\psi) = e^{-\gamma\psi},$$

where $\gamma > 0$ and ψ is a positive monotonic transformation of measured psychological discrepancy. As psychological discrepancy increases, $\Delta(\psi)$ decreases, which reduces the impact of the message.

Psychological discrepancy reflects positional discrepancy as well as context effects. For example, holding positional discrepancy constant, the message environment can change a message's psychological discrepancy. Compare the following scenarios: (1) you are asked to give $100 to your alma mater; (2) you are asked to give $1,000 to your alma mater, and then, after a moment, you are asked to give $100. The request for $100 that follows the $1,000 request should seem less psychologically discrepant than the single $100 request, and therefore it should be more effective.

Fink et al. (1983), using what was termed the *psychological-discrepancy-discounting model*, showed that the greater the psychological discrepancy, the less the effectiveness of messages with the same positional discrepancy, and that psychological discrepancy can be manipulated by the combination of messages that are presented to the receiver. Not all the model's predictions were supported, but many were. For example, it was found that the "psychological discrepancy of the moderate message is less when the extreme message precedes the moderate message than vice versa," resulting in "greater attitude change in the former condition" (p. 429).

More critical to the present discussion, the psychological-discrepancy-discounting model allows for nonmonotonic effects, and this model was found to be statistically superior to the linear discrepancy model.

Evidence From Dynamic Models

The theories and studies previously reviewed have been used to assess questions of *statics*, which is the study of forces in equilibrium rather than the movement toward equilibrium. Another way to examine the process activated by discrepant messages is to examine the changes over time or the movement from one equilibrium to another, the *dynamics* (see Eiser, 1994, for a general statement on dynamics, and for material related to the dynamics discussed next, see Fink & Kaplowitz, 1993; Fink, Kaplowitz, & Hubbard, 2002; Kaplowitz & Fink, 1996).

Kaplowitz, Fink, and Bauer (1983)

Kaplowitz et al. (1983), using a between-participants design, manipulated discrepancy and

the amount of time respondents had to consider a message. The topic was the health service fee at the respondents' university, and the message advocated an increase in the fee. Participants, who were not in favor of a fee increase, were presented with a message that took no position on the fee, proposed a moderate increase in the fee, or proposed an extremely large increase in the fee.

Based on a dynamic model, the estimated equilibrium message effectiveness (i.e., change achieved divided by change advocated) was about 0 for the no position advocated message, whereas the moderately discrepant message was about 15% effective, and the extremely discrepant message was about 18% effective. Furthermore, it was estimated that the time to achieve 90% of the movement toward the equilibrium position was about 2 ¼ minutes. The trajectories were found to exhibit oscillation with a period of oscillation of about 13.5 seconds (s), and the amplitude of oscillation was greatest for the extremely discrepant message and much less and not that different for the no-position message and the moderately discrepant message.

The key findings of this study are that (1) greater discrepancy caused a greater change at equilibrium; (2) integrating a message takes time, and for these particular messages, it took well over two minutes; and (3) because of oscillations, the trajectories of messages with different discrepancies will likely cross prior to the achievement of equilibrium, which means that "if messages of different discrepancies cause oscillations which have different frequencies . . . one's conclusion as to which message was most effective may be determined by the time interval from message to measurement" (Kaplowitz et al., 1983, p. 247). If we do not control the time between a discrepant message and the belief measurement, we may misidentify the message that caused the greatest change at equilibrium.

Chung and Colleagues (2008)

Chung et al. (2008) gathered data by having participants, who were university students, respond via a computer mouse, indicating their view approximately every 77 milliseconds (ms). Each participant responded to two topics: criminal sentencing, a topic relatively low in ego-involvement for university students, and a tuition increase, a topic relatively high in ego-involvement for them. For both topics, message discrepancy (with 3 levels) and source credibility (with 2 levels) were manipulated, and eleven time points for each individual, spread out over each individual's trajectory, were analyzed. Participants were not limited in the time that they took to consider the message that they received. For the criminal-sentencing issue, participants took from 8.55 s to 146.92 s, with an average of 48.48 s; for the tuition issue, participants took from 3.93 s to 151.23 s, with an average of 48.46 s. The relationship of discrepancy and belief position was found to be monotonic and positive in three of the four combinations of topic by credibility; nonmonotonicity was found only in the condition with the low-credibility source and the low-involvement message.

These data allowed the simultaneous testing of both Laroche's model, which is static (i.e., it relates discrepancy to the equilibrium belief position), as well as the dynamic model from Kaplowitz et al. (1983; referred to in Chung et al., 2008, as the *single-push with friction model*). The dynamic single-push with friction model predicts that over-time (i.e., the x-axis is time, not discrepancy), belief trajectories are positive and decelerating, and that trajectories associated with different levels of source credibility and discrepancy do not cross each other. (The possibility of oscillation was not included in this model.)

An alternative model, a *push-with-pullback model*, was proposed to represent two different possible ways for counterarguing to have an effect: First, discrepancy is associated with subvocal counterarguments (Brock, 1967; see also Cook, 1969; Toy, 1982), which occur after the discrepant message has been considered. Second, the Spinozan procedure (Gilbert, Krull, & Malone, 1990) may suggest that the recipient of a discrepant message may first entertain it as true

before rejecting it. Both these processes—the generation of counterarguments and the rejection of discrepant information—should take time. Therefore, if counterarguing or the Spinozan procedure apply, we should find that after being presented with a discrepant message, (1) the early part of the over-time belief trajectory should move in the direction advocated by the message, and (2) then, when counterarguments have been generated sufficiently, the movement of one's belief should be in the opposite direction. Therefore, the push-with-pullback model proposes a nonmonotonic relationship between time and belief change, making the push-with-pullback model an alternative to the single-push with friction model.

Based on the analysis of the over-time data, no evidence of nonmonotonicity was found, which supports the single-push-with friction model rather than the push-with-pullback model. However, cognitive responses did play a role in some of the study's outcomes: There is evidence that in some conditions, the effects of source and of discrepancy increased over time, which may be due to cognitive responses.

Although the study by Chung and colleagues is complex, it analyzed the questions about discrepancy we posed earlier, and it provided a tentative answer about the shape of the discrepancy-belief change relation: With high involvement, the curve is monotonic; with low involvement and a high-credibility source, the curve is monotonic; and with low involvement and a low-credibility source, the curve is nonmonotonic. Furthermore, over-time data were not consistent with the idea that strong counterarguments create a downturn in the over-time movement to equilibrium.

Auxiliary Issues

Discrepancy or Disconfirmation?

At this point we note something that should be obvious, at least in retrospect: In almost all the investigations concerning discrepancy, and in all the ones included here, messages that were greatly discrepant were also greatly surprising. Consider Bochner and Insko's (1966) messages: Some of them argued for 4, 3, 2, 1, or even 0 hours of sleep per night as appropriate for the average young adult; these messages are clearly surprising. What's more, the level of surprise correlates with the level of discrepancy. In other words, these two variables were confounded, and for all we know it may have been the surprise value, rather than the level of discrepancy, that accounted for the results of the studies that have been reviewed here.

Kaplowitz and Fink (1991), discussed previously, labeled a message's surprise value as its *level of disconfirmation*; they conducted two experiments in which manipulated discrepancy and manipulated disconfirmation were orthogonal. The topic of both experiments was criminal sentencing. One dependent variable was the number of years of imprisonment respondents recommended for a convicted armed robber (P_1). The second dependent variable was the comparative evaluation of the robber: "How bad is Defendant X?" In Experiment 1, a third independent variable was focus of attention: Respondents were directed either to focus on the source (the judge) or the reasons given for the sentence. In Experiment 2, a third independent variable was the size of the sample of defendants (3 vs. 100) previously sentenced by the judge. These additional independent variables were associated with hypotheses designed to tease out the role of cognitive elaboration.

In both experiments, discrepancy was found to directly and positively affect P_1 (the person's position after the message) and not comparative evaluation, whereas disconfirmation was found to directly and negatively affect comparative evaluation and not directly affect (Experiment 1) or weakly and negatively affect (Experiment 2) P_1. The proportion of variance directly explained by discrepancy in predicting P_1 (about 30%) was much greater than the proportion of variance that disconfirmation directly explained in predicting

comparative evaluation (about 4%). Finally, the "effects of comparative evaluation on position [P_1] appear to require substantial cognitive elaboration" (Kaplowitz & Fink, 1991, p. 191), although the effects due to discrepancy did not. This study clearly shows that it is discrepancy rather than disconfirmation that accounts for the effects on belief position. However, a second process also occurs: Disconfirmation affects the evaluation of the focal object. Furthermore, disconfirmation's effect on comparative evaluation "appears to require thinking about one's expectancy regarding the source and about the disconfirmation of that expectancy" (p. 205).

Social and Psychological Factors Examined Over Time

The research that has been presented to this point has dealt principally with psychological processes: the perceptions, thoughts, and other cognitive activities related to processing discrepant messages. (We note that emotions, which may play a role, have not been the focus of our discussion.) But implicit social processes are clearly entwined with the psychological ones. For one thing, every study cited involved humans interacting with humans, even if the experimenter merely gave out questionnaires in a classroom; that human-to-human interaction undoubtedly has some effect. Second, recall the two responses that Bochner and Insko (1966) described as "unavailable": arguing with the message source against the position of the message and obtaining social support. In responding to messages outside of the lab, both of these behaviors are clearly social and generally available (see Smith & Fink, 2010).

To incorporate potential social processes, Kaplowitz et al. (1986) conducted an experiment using panel data at two points in time. The study replicated Fink and colleagues (1983) research, which gathered data immediately after respondents read the messages: The 1986 study used the same topic (a tuition increase) at the same university, and five of the experimental conditions appear in both the 1983 and 1986 studies. Kaplowitz et al. (1986) asked participants the same question, both immediately and four to eight days after the initial response, about the tuition increase that they (the participants) would propose. The second, later data gathering was disguised in several ways and seemed to be part of a different study. In addition, after the initial (time 1) data were collected, the participants were debriefed about the deception involved in that part of the study.

The time-1 results were essentially identical to Fink and colleagues' (1983) results: The rank order correlation of the means of the five conditions that were in common across these two studies was 1.00, and the Pearson correlation was .89. This replication was successful.

More important for our current discussion is what was found at time 2. There was a dramatic change in the relative effectiveness of the experimental conditions. The six time-1 conditions that had messages advocating a tuition increase of some amount (i.e., excluding a no-position control condition) were initially ordered (from most change to least change; E = extreme, M = moderate) E/E (i.e., two messages, the first and the second extremely discrepant), E/M, M/M, M/E, E, and M. At time 2, the messages formed two clusters: The most-change cluster consisted of messages in which the first or only message was M; the least-change cluster consisted of messages in which the first or only message was E. Note that the message that was most effective at time 1 became one of the least effective messages at time 2, and the message that was least effective at time 1 became one of the most effective at time 2.

Although the processes involved were not directly assessed, the data analysis allowed the authors to make a reasonable interpretation of what took place over time. Summarizing the relevant results (Kaplowitz et al., 1986, pp. 525–526):

- Forgetting affects the long-term effectiveness of messages.
- Recipients of the moderately discrepant message received more messages in the

days between time 1 and time 2. These messages could be external (from others) or internal (based on the recipient's cognitive elaboration); furthermore, these messages supported a belief position that was greater than P_0.

- Recipients of the extremely discrepant message received messages in the days between time 1 and time 2 that supported a belief position that was less than P_0.
- The more discrepant message "was *either* remembered better *or* produced fewer delayed messages" (italics in original; pp. 525–526). There is reason to believe that the former explanation was more plausible.

In other words, over time, forgetting, thinking, and social processes—such as arguing with the communicator's position and seeking social support—changed the initial response and changed it dramatically. This study clearly shows that a complete understanding of discrepancy of beliefs requires data over longer times—at least several days—to understand the interplay of the cognitive and social processes that may be at work.

Remaining Questions and Future Research

Discrepancy and Oscillation

The first study that examined oscillation of beliefs and discrepancy has already been discussed: the study by Kaplowitz and colleagues (1983), which used a between-participants design. Since that study, oscillation studies have used within-participant designs, relying on participants making decisions between belief alternatives, such as whom to recommend for college admission (McGreevy, 1996; Wang, 1993; this research has been reviewed in Fink et al., 2002).

The relevance of oscillation for modeling discrepancy is clear: If different discrepant messages induce oscillations of different amplitudes or phases, conclusions about their relative effectiveness have a good chance of being incorrect.

If the process has not yet reached equilibrium, results reflect the belief that exists at the moment of measurement. For example, Chung and Fink (2008, based on McGreevy's, 1996, data) examined the number of belief changes induced by univalent versus mixed-valence messages. Using a computer mouse, participants continuously reported their belief while reading a message (message-receipt phase; average time = 126.41 s), and after receipt of the message, they continuously reported their belief while making their decision (postmessage phase; average time = 59.22 s). During the postmessage phase, the mixed-valence message was found to cause more changes in belief than did the univalent message, and these temporary beliefs could be mistaken for equilibrium values.

Future research needs to examine the trajectories and impacts of discrepant messages on oscillation. The current models of over-time effects have been only partially successful in capturing the processes at work.

Cognitive Responses, Cognitive Dissonance, and Discrepancy

Cognitive Responses

Related to the analysis of discrepancy and oscillation is the role of cognitive responses. When a trajectory of beliefs indicates oscillation, are there accompanying thoughts that are associated with that change? Given the findings of Chung and Fink (2008), it seems likely that that thinking is associated with oscillation. To further examine this question, research needs to be conducted that interrupts a participant to find what, if any, thoughts are being considered while the participant is moving the computer mouse—indicating a change in belief position—in one direction or another. It may be that cognitive responses direct the movement toward a new belief position, but it is also possible that the position, arrived at by some dynamic cognitive algebra (Anderson, 1974), forms the cognitive response. Himmelfarb (1974), supporting the

linear discrepancy model (referring to it as information integration), raised this same issue with regard to apparent resistance effects in persuasion: "Resistance effects cannot simply be inferred from differences in the overall attitudinal response" (p. 413). The relationship between belief trajectories and cognitive responses needs to be determined.

The elaboration likelihood model (ELM; Petty & Cacioppo, 1986) suggests that "a given variable may play different roles in the persuasion process" (O'Keefe, 2002, p. 161). The roles that source credibility and discrepancy play in discrepancy models are not fully resolved. In the studies that have been reviewed, discrepancy appears to have induced central processing in some research and peripheral processing in other research. On one hand, it seems that discrepancy causes beliefs almost automatically, as if a response to a cognitive algebra mechanism: Note that Kaplowitz and Fink's (1991) finding that focus of attention (source vs. reasons) and alleged size of the behavioral sample on which the expectations of the source's position were based had little effect on the relation between discrepancy and P_I. On the other hand, the psychological-discrepancy-discounting model has a role for psychological discrepancy, which may seem to suggest elaboration and resistance could also be associated with levels of attention or other factors (Fink et al., 1983). In addition, a relationship between discrepancy and counterargument production has been found (e.g., Brock, 1967; Kaplowitz & Fink, 1995), but this relationship does not seem integral to the relationship between discrepancy and belief position. Research to clarify the role of cognitive elaboration in discrepancy processes would be valuable for formulating a more complete model of discrepancy and belief change.

Cognitive Dissonance

If, as Aronson et al. (1963) and Bochner and Insko (1966) proposed, dissonance is caused by receipt of discrepant messages, the stress or tension associated with dissonance should be present after receipt of such messages, and greater discrepancy should cause greater dissonance. Furthermore, misattribution of stress should eliminate associated belief change (Drachman & Worchel, 1976; Fazio, Zanna, & Cooper, 1977; Pittman, 1975; Zanna & Cooper, 1974) as well as the oscillations that could indicate dissonance and regret (Walster, 1964). Research to clarify the role that dissonance plays in discrepancy is long overdue.

The analysis of social processes needs to be more carefully investigated. Long-term effects due to messages that differ in discrepancy need to incorporate the two "laboratory unavailable" responses to dissonance mentioned by Bochner and Insko (1966).

Involvement

Laroche's (1977) model included involvement as a key factor. Chung et al. (2008) used two topics that differed in level of involvement, and some important differences in model parameters between these topics were found; however, the topics differed in many unspecified ways, so that conclusions concerning the differences due to involvement must be tentative. Given the extensive research on and theory regarding involvement and belief change (e.g., Freedman, 1964; Johnson & Eagly, 1989) and given the intriguing findings in Chung et al. (2008) experimentally manipulating involvement seems to be a necessary next step to clarify its role in the discrepancy-belief change process.

Methodological Wish List

Measurement

The next steps in theory construction regarding discrepancy will benefit from significant improvements in methodology. The discrepancy models in the sciences, some of which were briefly mentioned earlier, rely on conventional, agreed-on measurement rules, which are lacking in belief-change research. Furthermore, the scales that form the basis for the International System of Units (ISU; meter, kilogram, second, ampere, kelvin, candela, and mole) all have a lower bound of zero and have, in principle, no upper bound (although in practice there may be an upper bound); other scientific quantities are defined in terms of these fundamental units. The need addressed here is not just to create more reliable measures but measures that have greater precision and that can be used to derive other measures within a specified theoretical framework (see Torgerson, 1958).

Following this logic of scientific measurement, Woelfel and Fink (1980) examined cultural and cognitive processes using distance (in their case, psychological and cultural distance), time, and related concepts to formulate theory. The study of discrepancy of beliefs, with discrepancy considered as a distance, can readily be studied using equations that are tied to fundamental measurements, such as those of distance and time. The recommendation here is to create and utilize a *system* of measures, rather than separate scales (typically measurement by fiat; Torgerson, 1958), that is tied to theory.

Dynamic Models and Longitudinal Designs

Dynamic models are best for explicating processes, which are typically written as mathematical equations. Longitudinal research designs (e.g., panel studies, time-series designs, pooled cross-sectional time-series designs) used to estimate dynamic models are generally not applied to the study of belief change, but they can be and should be; Chung and colleagues' (2008) work is an exception. To understand process, we must see it unfold over time. Static models can only get us so far.

Multidimensional Models

Finally, we note that a message can induce change in concepts that are unmentioned in the message as well as change along dimensions other than the belief-position dimension. A multidimensional framework can examine both of these kinds of changes (see Dinauer & Fink, 2005; Woelfel & Fink, 1980). By focusing almost exclusively on belief position, we have not seen the whole picture, which a multidimensional analysis can provide.

Conclusion

Studying the effect of discrepant messages on belief change would have seemed, at the onset, to be an easy and straightforward task. After years of considering this issue, and after different researchers, theories, and models have been brought to bear on it, there have been advances with regard to the shape of the relationship, the factors that do and do not play a role, as well as the temporal parameters of the process. There are significant questions that remain, and, alas (or hooray!), more research is needed.

References

Anderson, N. H. (1974). Cognitive algebra: Integration theory applied to social attribution. In L. Berkowitz (Ed.), *Advances in experimental social psychology* (Vol. 7, pp. 1–101). New York, NY: Academic Press.

Anderson, N. H., & Hovland, C. (1957). The representation of order effects in communication research. In C. Hovland, W. Mandell, E. H. Campbell, T. Brock, A. S. Luchins, A. R. Cohen, et al. (Eds.), *The order of presentation in persuasion* (pp. 158–169). New Haven, CT: Yale University Press.

Aronson, E., Turner, J. A., & Carlsmith, J. M. (1963). Communicator credibility and communication discrepancy as determinants of opinion change. *Journal of Abnormal and Social Psychology, 67,* 31–36.

Bar-Meir, G. (2011). *Basics of fluid mechanics.* Chicago, IL: Bar-Meir. Retrieved from www.potto.org/FM/fluidMechanics.pdf

Berlo, D. K. (1960). *The process of communication.* New York, NY: Holt, Rinehart, & Winston.

Bochner, S., & Insko, C. A. (1966). Communicator discrepancy, source credibility, and opinion change. *Journal of Personality and Social Psychology, 4,* 614–621.

Brock, T. C. (1967). Communication discrepancy and intent to persuade as determinants of counterargument production. *Journal of Experimental Social Psychology, 3,* 296–309.

Chung, S., & Fink, E. L. (2008). The cognitive dynamics of beliefs: The effect of information on message processing. *Human Communication Research, 34,* 477–504.

Chung, S., Fink, E. L., & Kaplowitz, S. A. (2008). The comparative statics and dynamics of beliefs: The effect of message discrepancy and source credibility. *Communication Monographs, 75,* 158–189.

Cook, T. D. (1969). Competence, counterarguing, and attitude change. *Journal of Personality, 37,* 342–358.

Corman, S. R. (1996). Cellular automata as models of unintended consequences of organizational communication. In J. H. Watt & C. A. VanLear (Eds.), *Dynamic patterns in communication processes* (pp. 191–212). Thousand Oaks, CA: Sage.

Danes, J. E., Hunter, J. E., & Woelfel, J. (1978). Mass communication and belief change: A test of three mathematical models. *Human Communication Research, 4,* 243–252.

Dinauer, L. D., & Fink, E. L. (2005). Inter-attitude structure and attitude dynamics: A comparison of the hierarchical and Galileo spatial-linkage models. *Human Communication Research, 31,* 1–32.

Drachman, D., & Worchel, S. (1976). Misattribution of dissonance arousal as a means of dissonance reduction. *Sociometry, 39,* 53–59.

Eagly, A. H., & Chaiken, S. (1993). *The psychology of attitudes.* Fort Worth, TX: Harcourt, Brace, Jovanovich.

Eagly, A. H., & Telaak, K. (1972). Width of the latitude of acceptance as a determinant of attitude change. *Journal of Personality and Social Psychology, 23,* 388–397.

Edwards, K., & Smith, E. E. (1996). A disconfirmation bias in the evaluation of arguments. *Journal of Personality and Social Psychology, 71,* 5–24.

Eiser, J. R. (1994). Toward a dynamic conception of attitude consistency and change. In R. R. Vallacher & A. Nowak (Eds.), *Dynamical systems in social psychology* (pp. 197–218). New York, NY: Academic Press.

Fazio, R. H., Zanna, M. P., & Cooper, J. (1977). Dissonance and self-perception: An integrative view of each theory's proper domain of application. *Journal of Experimental Social Psychology, 13,* 464–479.

Festinger, L. (1957). *A theory of cognitive dissonance.* Evanston, IL: Row, Peterson.

Fink, E. L., & Kaplowitz, S. A. (1993). Oscillation in beliefs and cognitive networks. In G. A. Barnett & W. Richards (Eds.), *Progress in communication sciences* (Vol. 12, pp. 247–272). Norwood, NJ: Ablex.

Fink, E. L., Kaplowitz, S. A., & Bauer, C. L. (1983). Positional discrepancy, psychological discrepancy, and attitude change: Experimental tests of some mathematical models. *Communication Monographs, 50,* 413–430.

Fink, E. L., Kaplowitz, S. A., & Hubbard, S. E. (2002). Oscillation in beliefs and decisions. In J. P. Dillard & M. Pfau (Eds.), *The persuasion handbook: Theory and practice* (pp. 17–37). Thousand Oaks, CA: Sage.

Flay, B. R. (1978). Catastrophe theory in social psychology: Some applications to attitudes and social behavior. *Behavioral Science, 23,* 335–350.

Freedman, J. L. (1964). Involvement, discrepancy, and opinion change. *Journal of Abnormal and Social Psychology, 69,* 290–295.

Gilbert, D. T., Krull, D. S., & Malone, P. S. (1990). Unbelieving the unbelievable: Some problems with the rejection of false information. *Journal of Personality and Social Psychology, 59,* 601–613.

Himmelfarb, S. (1974). "Resistance" to persuasion induced by information integration. In S. Himmelfarb & A. H. Eagly (Eds.), *Readings in attitude change* (pp. 413–419). New York, NY: Wiley.

Hovland, C. I., & Weiss, W. (1951). The influence of source credibility on communication effectiveness. *Public Opinion Quarterly, 15,* 635–650.

Hunter, J. E., Levine, R. L., & Sayers, S. E. (1976). Attitude change in hierarchical belief systems and its relationship to persuasibility, dogmatism, and rigidity. *Human Communication Research, 3,* 299–324.

Jaccard, J. (1981). Towards theories of persuasion and belief change. *Journal of Personality and Social Psychology, 40,* 260–269.

Johnson, B. T., & Eagly, A. H. (1989). The effects of involvement on persuasion: A meta-analysis. *Psychological Bulletin, 106,* 290–314.

Kaplowitz, S. A., & Fink, E. L. (with Mulcrone, J., Atkin, D., & Dabil, S.). (1991). Disentangling the effects of discrepant and disconfirming information. *Social Psychology Quarterly, 54,* 191–207.

Kaplowitz, S. A., & Fink, E. L. (1995). [Message discrepancy, source credibility and the trajectories of attitude change]. Unpublished raw data.

Kaplowitz, S. A., & Fink, E. L. (1996). Cybernetics of attitudes and decisions. In J. Watt & C. A. Van Lear (Eds.), *Dynamic patterns in communication processes* (pp. 277–300). Thousand Oaks, CA: Sage.

Kaplowitz, S. A., & Fink, E. L. (1997). Message discrepancy and persuasion. In G. A. Barnett & F. J. Boster (Eds.), *Progress in communication sciences* (Vol. 13, pp. 75–106). Greenwich, CT: Ablex.

Kaplowitz, S. A., Fink, E. L., Armstrong, G. B., & Bauer, C. L. (1986). Message discrepancy and the persistence of attitude change: Implications of an information integration model. *Journal of Experimental Social Psychology, 22,* 507–530.

Kaplowitz, S. A., Fink, E. L., & Bauer, C. L. (1983). A dynamic model of the effect of discrepant information on unidimensional attitude change. *Behavioral Science, 28,* 233–250.

Knight, R. D. (2007). *Physics for scientists and engineers: A strategic approach* (2nd ed., Vol. 2). Boston, MA: Addison Wesley.

Laroche, M. (1977). A model of attitude change in groups following a persuasive communication: An attempt at formalizing research findings. *Behavioral Science, 22,* 246–257.

Latané, B., & Nowak, A. (1994). Attitudes as catastrophes: From dimensions to categories with increasing involvement. In R. R. Vallacher & A. Nowak (Eds.), *Dynamical systems in social psychology* (pp. 219–249). San Diego, CA: Academic Press.

Lave, C. A., & March, J. G. (1993). *An introduction to models in the social sciences.* Lanham, MD: University Press of America.

McGreevy, S. E. (1996). *Cognitive oscillations, need for closure, and the social influence process: The roles of cognition and motivation during decision making.* Unpublished doctoral dissertation, University of Maryland, College Park.

McGuire, W. J. (1985). Attitudes and attitude change. In G. Lindzey & E. Aronson (Eds.), *The handbook of social psychology* (3rd ed., Vol. 2, pp. 233–346). New York, NY: Random House.

Miller, N. (1965). Involvement and dogmatism as inhibitors of attitude change. *Journal of Experimental Social Psychology, 1,* 121–132.

O'Keefe, D. J. (2002). *Persuasion theory and research* (2nd ed.). Thousand Oaks, CA: Sage.

Pacanowsky, M. (1976). Salt passage research: The state of the art. *Journal of Communication, 26*(4), 31–36.

Petty, R. E., & Cacioppo, J. T. (1981). *Attitudes and persuasion: Classic and contemporary approaches.* Dubuque, IA: Wm. C. Brown.

Petty, R. E., & Cacioppo, J. T. (1986). *Communication and persuasion: Central and peripheral routes to attitude change.* New York, NY: Springer-Verlag.

Pittman, T. S. (1975). Attribution of arousal as a mediator in dissonance reduction. *Journal of Experimental Social Psychology, 11,* 53–63.

Saltiel, J., & Woelfel, J. (1975). Inertia in cognitive processes: The role of accumulated information in attitude change. *Human Communication Research, 1,* 333–344.

Shannon, C. E., & Weaver, W. (1949). *The mathematical theory of communication.* Urbana, NY: University of Illinois Press.

Sherif, C. W., & Sherif, M. (Eds.). (1967). *Attitude, ego-involvement, and change.* New York, NY: Wiley.

Sherif, C. W., Sherif, M., & Nebergall, G. (1965). *Attitude and attitude change: The social judgment-involvement approach.* Philadelphia, PA: Saunders.

Sherif, M., & Hovland, C. I. (1961). *Social judgment: Assimilation and contrast effects in communication and attitude change.* New Haven, CT: Yale University Press.

Smith, R. A., & Fink, E. L. (2010). Compliance dynamics within a simulated friendship network I: The effects of agency, tactic, and node centrality. *Human Communication Research, 36,* 232–260.

Torgerson, W. S. (1958). *Theory and methods of scaling.* New York, NY: Wiley.

Toy, D. (1982). Monitoring communication effects: A cognitive structure/cognitive response approach. *Journal of Consumer Research, 9,* 66–76.

Van der Maas, H. L. J., Kolstein, R., & van der Plight, J. (2003). Sudden transition in attitude. *Sociological Methods and Research, 32,* 125–152.

Walster, E. (1964). The temporal sequence of post-decision processes. In L. Festinger (Ed.), *Conflict, decision, and dissonance* (pp. 112–128). Stanford, CA: Stanford University Press.

Wang, M.-L. T. (1993). *The cognitive effects of stereotype modification.* Unpublished doctoral dissertation, University of Maryland, College Park.

Woelfel, J., & Fink, E. L. (1980). *The measurement of communication processes: Galileo theory and method.* New York, NY: Academic Press.

Zanna, M. P., & Cooper, J. (1974). Dissonance and the pill: An attributional approach to studying the arousal properties of dissonance. *Journal of Personality and Social Psychology, 29,* 703–709.

Zimbardo, P. G. (1960). Involvement and communication discrepancy as determinants of opinion conformity. *Journal of Abnormal and Social Psychology, 60,* 86–94.

CHAPTER 7

Functional Attitude Theory

Christopher Carpenter, Franklin J. Boster, and Kyle R. Andrews

Oratory is the art of enchanting the soul, and therefore he who would be an orator has to learn the differences of human souls—they are so many and of such a nature, and from them come the differences between man and man.

Plato, "Phaedrus"
(360 BCE/1993 CE, p. 84)

Plato proposed that a speaker who wishes to persuade others effectively must not assume that the same persuasive appeal works for everyone. He asserted that each person had a particular type of soul and that to change attitudes, persuasive efforts must be tailored to each. This concept of tailoring persuasive appeals to the needs of individual audience members finds modern expression in a group of persuasion theories identified as functional theories of attitudes.

In the 1950s, two groups of scholars developed attitude theories proposing that attitudes serve different functions (Katz, 1960; Smith, Bruner, & White, 1956). They posited that people develop attitudes in order to serve their goals, and that although any particular attitude might serve multiple functions, it would generally serve

one more than the others. They theorized that although two people might have an attitude with the exact same valence, that attitude might serve very different functions for each person. For example, Varda might have a positive attitude toward BMWs because they are sturdily built vehicles that help her save money on car repairs, whereas Clover might have a positive attitude toward BMWs because he thinks they will help him impress women.

Smith et al. (1956) focused on trying to understand the relationships between attitudes and personality. Taking a clinical perspective, they conducted in-depth interviews to try to understand the personality of 10 men based on their attitudes toward the Soviet Union. From the interviews they then derived inductively their typology of attitude functions.

Working independently, and from the then-dominant perspectives in psychology (psychoanalysis and behaviorism), Katz (1960) and colleagues (Katz, Sarnoff, & McClintock, 1956; Sarnoff & Katz, 1954) derived attitude functions deductively. Katz's goal was to define attitude functions as a means of increasing the effectiveness of persuasive appeals. He reasoned that if a persuasive appeal targeted the function that an attitude served for a particular person, then that persuasive appeal would be much more likely to change, shape, or reinforce the attitude in the direction that the speaker desired. For example, if a car salesperson, Craig, was trying to sell a new BMW to Varda, he would be more likely to make the sale if he emphasized the reliability of the car rather than how attractive people thought it was. On the other hand, if Clover was looking at cars, Craig would do well to point out how attractive the car was rather than bore him with statistics about gas mileage.

An implication of these positions is that understanding attitude functions allows influencing agents to tailor messages to audience members rather than merely target messages to an audience. Miller and Steinberg (1975) argued that communication varies along a dimension of the quantity of individuating information persons have and use about those with whom they are communicating. Rather than targeting cultural-level information about the audience (e.g., country of origin) or sociological level information (e.g., profession or SES), influencing agents who understand the function(s) that an attitude serves for a particular target can tailor their persuasive approach. Such an approach was conjectured to have a higher probability of success than alternative approaches.

After the first wave of functional research by Katz (1960) and Smith and colleagues (1956) to explicate functional attitude theories, these theories were "in a state of hibernation for some two decades" (Snyder & Debono, 1985, p. 597). Beginning in the 1980s, these theories underwent a revival and have subsequently inspired a great deal of empirical work on matching persuasive messages to functions in a second wave of functional attitude research. This chapter examines different approaches to using functional theories to understand persuasion by first examining the initial typology of functions constructed by Katz (1960) and Smith et al. (1956) in the first wave of functional attitude theory research. Then the contemporary approaches that attempt to determine attitude functions for

the purposes of targeting persuasive messages that represent a second wave will be explored. Finally, a third wave of functional attitude research that conceives of the attitude functions as processes to be modeled in order to help determine which functions should be considered separate functions will be discussed before turning to suggestions for future research.

The Initial Set of Attitude Functions

Despite the fact that the two groups of scholars worked independently, both Katz (1960) and Smith et al. (1956) derived similar lists of functions. They generally used different terms, but there was considerable conceptual overlap in their ideas. Most theorists identify five unique functions. In these formulations, the concept of an attitude function is that of a qualitative variable (i.e., attitude function) with each function being conceived as a value of that variable (e.g., ego-defensive, utilitarian, etc.) in much the same way as one would think of a qualitative variable such as religious preference having various different values (Judaism, Islam, Christianity, Hinduism, Buddhism, etc.). Although Katz and Smith et al. discussed the possibility of an attitude serving multiple functions, nevertheless, these values of the variable (functions) still are conceived as mutually exclusive. To extend the analogy with religious preference, an attitude that serves multiple functions for a person might be akin to someone who lists more than one religious preference. Such a person might be unusual; nevertheless, such a response is not impossible. The five functions are described next.

Utilitarian Attitudes

Attitudes that serve a utilitarian function (termed object appraisal by Smith et al., 1956) are formed and held in order to provide persons with an efficient way to distinguish objects that bring pleasure and objects that produce pain (Katz, 1960). Hence, utilitarian functions serve to help people maximize utility. These attitudes are rooted in a desire to satisfy personal needs and desires. For example, Varda's attitude toward BMWs has a utilitarian function because she is focused on the practical aspects of the car, such as its reliability and the money she might save on repairs. If influencing agents wanted to tailor messages to an audience whose target attitude serves a utilitarian function, they would emphasize the ways in which that which is advocated improves the audience's life. For example, politicians who emphasize the number of jobs they secure through defense contracts are targeting a utilitarian function.

Social-Adjustive

Although Katz discussed the application of social influences to a variety of functions, he did not include it as a separate function. On the other hand, Smith et al. (1956) described the social-adjustive function as a means of regulating relationships. Attitudes serving a social-adjustive function facilitate the ability to interact with desirable social group members or to impress attractive others. In the BMW example, Clover's attitude toward BMWs serves a social adjustive function because he is concerned with whether or not his car will make him attractive to women. A politician who wanted to target an audience's social-adjustive function might emphasize a descriptive norm that is both shared by the audience's peer group and that supports her position on a pivotal issue.

Value-Expressive

Attitudes with a value-expressive function facilitate the expression of people's abstract values (Katz, 1960). A value-expressive attitude facilitates a person's ability to voice and remain consistent with their values. Unlike utilitarian attitudes, they do not provide direct, concrete rewards or punishments. And, unlike social-adjustive attitudes, a value-expressive attitude does not promote the needs of fitting in with a group or impression management. Value-expressive functions differ from utilitarian or social goals because one does not derive any benefit, construed narrowly, from having such attitudes, save a sense of satisfaction that one has been consistent with one's principles. If a car salesperson wanted to sell a BMW to an environmentalist whose attitude(s) toward BMWs served a value-expressive function, the salesperson might focus on the BMW Corporation's efforts to support green technology. Of course, in addition to knowing that an attitude serves a value-expressive function, one must also know which value is being served by the attitude in order to target a persuasive message (Maio & Olson, 2000). Even if an attitude toward BMWs serves a value-expressive function, mentioning the corporation's efforts to use green technology might not be persuasive if the audience's BMW attitude is anchored to values concerned with equality and fair labor practices rather than environmentalism.

Ego-Defensive

According to Katz (1960), attitudes that serve an ego-defensive function (externalization for Smith et al., 1956) allow people to avoid acknowledging unpleasant aspects of self or of the external world. Ego-defensive attitudes can promote protecting self-esteem. Threats to self-esteem can include personal failings or poor behavior. Katz argued that such attitudes often involved rationalizing and other defense mechanisms. One scenario in which an attitude toward BMWs serves an ego-defensive function would be one in which someone had a positive attitude toward BMWs because of frustration resulting from an inability to earn occupational advancement. The car could instill a feeling of importance despite being passed over for promotion. Katz's research in this area focused on those who held negative attitudes toward minority groups as a means of increasing their own self-esteem. He and his colleagues argued that these attitudes might be changed by helping the audience gain self-insight into the defense mechanisms supported by these attitudes (Stotland, Katz, & Patchen, 1959).

Knowledge

Attitudes that serve a knowledge function help people gain greater understanding of the structure and operation of their world (Katz, 1960). Katz noted that the world that people inhabit is extremely complex, and that attitudes might facilitate making sense of that world without serving needs other than understanding. Herek (1987) argued that Smith and colleagues' (1956) object appraisal function represents a combination of both Katz's utilitarian and the knowledge functions because Smith et al. argued that people organize the world for the purpose of reaching utilitarian goals. Other scholars propose that the knowledge function drives attitudes that serve for no purpose other than learning about the world as an end in itself, predicated on a basic need to know (Locander & Spivey, 1978). Someone might have an attitude about candidates in a presidential election in Bolivia not because it affects their interests or expresses their values but because they try to make sense of South American politics. Similarly, an attitude toward BMWs may emerge because of an interest in the auto industry. Katz argued that these attitudes can be changed by explaining how an audience's understanding of the world is inadequate and how a different attitude provides a more accurate world view.

Summary

It is important to emphasize that although this list contains the most commonly described attitude functions, it may not be comprehensive.

Both Katz (1960) and Smith et al. (1956) hint at the existence of functions that they did not identify. In this spirit, Clary, Snyder, Ridge, Copeland, Stukas, Haugen, and Miene (1998) suggest that the ego-defensive function may be divided into attitudes that defend self-esteem from attacks and attitudes that promote self-esteem. Furthermore, Locander and Spivey (1978) attempted to measure Katz's functions and found that there were people whose attitude toward some objects did not serve any of the functions mentioned previously. Although both Katz (1960) and Smith et al. (1956) suggested the possibility of an attitude serving multiple functions, this possibility was not investigated systematically until techniques of measuring and inducing the various functions were developed in order to successfully target functions with persuasive messages. The second wave of theory and research that developed methods of identifying functions for the purpose of matching messages to functions to increase message persuasiveness is discussed next.

Functions as Variables

Some scholars argue that the study of attitude functions was neglected for two decades because the seminal initial work (Katz, 1960; Smith et al., 1956) failed to supply useful methods of studying the phenomenon (Snyder & Debono, 1985). Specifically, Smith et al. (1956) conducted lengthy interviews, and such a methodological approach does not lend itself to empirical investigations with samples sufficient to provide precise estimates of effects. Moreover, it is viewed commonly as being more subjective than required for a rigorous study of the phenomenon. Katz and colleagues attempted to explore the ego-defensive function using authoritarianism as an indicator of the ego-defensive function (Katz et al., 1956; Sarnoff & Katz, 1954). These studies yielded inconsistent results, and perhaps for that reason others did not pursue this line of inquiry. One influential attempt at remedying this state of affairs was Herek's (1986) neofunctional approach, and it involved reconceptualizing attitude functions in a way that would encourage empirical investigation.

Herek's Neofunctional Approach

Herek (1986) proposed that the concept of attitude functions should be expanded beyond the personality centered-approach of Smith et al. (1956) and the categorical approach discussed by Katz (1960). In his reconceptualization of attitude functions each function is construed as a quantitative dimension such that any attitude serves all functions to varying degrees. Thus, for Herek, attitudes serve multiple functions and the extent to which each attitude serves multiple functions can be measured. Consequently, the relationships among attitude functions can be investigated empirically and quantitatively.

Herek (1986) also proposed a new typology of attitude functions. Specifically, he posited that conceptual clarity may be gained by distinguishing two categories of attitude functions. The first category includes the evaluative functions, which are associated with gaining rewards and avoiding punishments. These attitude functions provide people with a means of organizing objects and events by self-interest. Herek distinguished three types: experiential and specific, experiential and schematic, and anticipatory-evaluative. Experiential and specific attitudes are formed by and directed at a single object of a category of attitude objects based on one or more encounters with that specific object. Varda might encounter a poorly maintained BMW driven by her friend Erin, and from that experience Varda might develop an experiential and specific negative attitude toward Erin's BMW as a means of assisting her in avoiding accepting rides in dangerous and unreliable automobiles. On the other hand, Varda's attitude toward Erin's BMW would not necessarily generalize to all BMWs. If Varda formed a positive view of BMWs based on having driven and ridden in many others that she found to be safe and dependable, she would have developed an experiential-schematic attitude.

Such attitudes represent the inductive development of an attitude toward a category of attitude objects based on personally encountering and evaluating many specific cases of the attitude object. In contrast, the anticipatory-evaluative function serves to inform people concerning the rewards or punishments that might accompany attitude objects, but they do not arise from any actual experience with these objects. Instead, one estimates the rewards and punishments, and the extent of them, that would result from an encounter with an attitude object. If Varda had never encountered a BMW, but had she heard positive reviews of its safety and reliability from trusted sources, she might develop a positive attitude that functions in an anticipatory-evaluative manner. Notably, these three functions that are grouped under the evaluative category are all similar to Katz's (1960) utilitarian function.

The other category of attitude functions identified by Herek (1986) is termed "expressive." They include the social-adjustive, the value-expressive, and defensive functions identified by other theorists. Specifically, the social-adjustive and the value-expressive functions are similar to those to which Katz (1960) attaches the same labels, and the defensive function is similar to Katz's ego-defensive function. The expression to others of these attitudes, rather than the utilitarian character of attitudes that serve evaluative functions, provides benefit for those who hold them. Herek's use of this categorization scheme to understand more clearly the attitudes persons have toward those with AIDS is a particularly useful application of this set of distinctions (see Herek, 2000 for a review).

In addition to conceiving of the functions as quantitative variables and providing an original classification scheme, Herek (1986) rejected the idea that functions are stable within individuals but across contexts. He argued that functions may be related to personality variables, and thus, that certain personality characteristics would be associated with a higher likelihood of an attitude serving a particular function. For example, Snyder and Debono (1985) proposed that people who are likely to engage in extensive self-monitoring are also likely to have attitudes that serve a social-adjustive purpose. Moreover, Herek extended the personality approach by proposing that characteristics of the attitude topic might influence the likelihood that a particular topic would be associated with a particular function. For example, Shavitt (1990) found that attitudes toward air-conditioners were most likely to serve utilitarian functions. Finally, Herek (1986) argued that situations could also make particular attitude functions salient. For example, he argued that social-adjustive functions were likely to predominate with attitudes toward one's friends. In one application of this approach, Shavitt, Swan, Lowrey, and Wanke (1994) found that particular functions can be primed. These various approaches that conceive of attitude functions as variables have been used to craft tailored messages. The tailoring research using these methods will be examined next.

The Functional Matching Hypothesis

Katz (1960) argued that an important application of research on attitude functions is tailoring messages to functions. He believed that knowing what function an attitude served would enable the persuader to focus suasory effort on arguments relevant to the needs of the audience. His proposal has come to be known as the functional matching hypothesis. Since the 1980s, a great deal of research has been conducted examining the effectiveness of matching messages to functions using strategies based on three methods of targeting attitude functions identified by Herek (1986).

Personality

The most common method of targeting attitude functions began with Smith and colleagues' (1956) assumption that attitude functions are associated with personality. The earliest research

in this area was done by Katz and his colleagues (Katz, McClintock, & Sarnoff, 1957; Stotland et al., 1959), and their work attempted to measure authoritarianism using a variety of measures (California F-Scale, MMPI conformity items, thematic apperception tests, and sentence completion measures). They believed that those who were more authoritarian would be more likely to have ego-defensive attitudes toward racial minority groups. The variety of tests did not offer convergent validity of their construct; some were consistent with the effectiveness of targeting ego-defensive attitudes and some were not.

More consistent results have been found using self-monitoring as an indicator of social-adjustive attitudes (see Debono, 2000, for a review). Initially, it is worth noting that the self-monitoring scale (Snyder, 1974; Snyder & Gangestead, 1986), the primary means of assessing the trait, lacks construct and content validity (Dillard & Hunter, 1989). Despite these measurement problems, a number of studies have used the scale to predict attitude functions. Snyder and Debono (1985) conducted the initial experiment, arguing that because self-monitoring is a personality construct that is associated with adapting oneself to gain the social approval of others, those high in this trait would be more likely to have highly social-adjustive attitudes. They hypothesized that those low in self-monitoring would hold more value-expressive attitudes because low self-monitors tend to look inward for their attitudes rather than to the expectations of others. They used scores on the self-monitoring scale to create two groups, one high in self-monitoring and one low in self-monitoring. They found that for low self-monitors, advertising messages that focused on product quality were substantially more persuasive than those that focused on social status; but that for high self-monitors, advertising that focused on social status was more persuasive than advertising that focused on product quality.

Following their seminal work, a number of studies have used self-monitoring to explore the types of messages that match social-adjustive and value-expressive attitudes (e.g., Debono, 1987; Debono & Rubin, 1995; Debono & Snyder, 1989). Debono and Rubin (1995) found that high self-monitors preferred cheese from France to cheese from Kansas regardless of taste, but that low self-monitors preferred the cheese with superior flavor, being relatively uninfluenced by the country of origin. They argued that high self-monitors responded to the country of origin because imported cheese was perceived to be of higher status than domestic cheese, whereas low self-monitors were influenced by their reaction to the cheese's taste. Debono and Snyder (1989) found that high self-monitors preferred an attractive automobile, whereas low self-monitors preferred an ugly automobile. They reasoned that the high self-monitors had social-adjustive attitudes and therefore chose their automobiles based on what would impress others. They claimed that the low self-monitors chose the less attractive car because they associated less attractive cars with more reliable cars.

Although it makes intuitive sense that high self-monitors would be more likely to have social-adjustive attitudes, it is less clear what to expect from low self-monitors. Most scholars investigating self-monitoring and attitude functions argue that low self-monitors will be more likely to have value-expressive functions (Debono, 1987; Debono & Harnish, 1988; Debono & Telesca, 1990; Petty & Wegener, 1998; Snyder & Debono, 1985). Yet, these studies target value-expressive attitudes with utilitarian appeals that focus on the quality of products rather than on an abstract value. Given the results that most investigators have reported using utilitarian appeals with low self-monitors, some (Dutta-Bergman, 2003, Shavitt, Lowrey, & Han, 1992) have argued that low self-monitors' attitudes are more likely to be utilitarian than value-expressive. On the other hand, Lavine and Snyder (1996) were able to show that for low self-monitors a value-based appeal was more successful than an image-based appeal. It appears that although high self-monitors are consistently able to be persuaded using messages targeting the

social-adjustive function, the functions of attitudes served by low self-monitors are both conceptually and empirically less clear. Furthermore, Hullet and Boster (2001) found that measures of value-expressive functions and social-adjustive functions were uncorrelated. This finding suggests that there are people who are able to possess attitudes that are both social-adjustive and value-expressive, one but not the other, or neither. Additionally, as noted previously, Herek's (1986) neo-functional approach emphasized the possibility of multifunctional attitudes.

Attitude Objects

Although the personality approach to studying attitude functions remains the most popular, some have examined Herek's (1986) suggestion that attitudes toward some topics or objects are inherently likely to serve single functions. For example, Shavitt and colleagues have pursued this path (Shavitt, 1990; Shavitt, Lowrey, & Han, 1992). Shavitt noted that in Snyder and Debono's (1985) self-monitoring studies, there were several consumer products that did not produce the results predicted by the functional matching hypothesis. She proposed that some objects (e.g., aspirin) are likely to serve, and only serve, a utilitarian function; whereas, other objects (e.g., automobiles) might serve a variety of functions, at which point one's personality might be more likely to predict attitude functions. She reasoned that for unifunctional objects, persuasive messages that matched those functions would be more persuasive than those that did not. After using a thought-listing task coupled with questionnaire data to identify the predominant function served by various objects, she gave subjects the task of reading advertisements for some of those objects. The advertisements either matched or mismatched the objects' function. Results indicated that the typical functional matching effect occurred; the advertisements were more persuasive when they matched the functions associated with their products. In subsequent experiments, Shavitt et al. (1992) found that self-monitoring exerted a strong effect on the type of functions associated with particular consumer products only when the product was multifunctional. It appears that personality differences are only useful for predicting attitudes for products that are likely to serve multiple functions. No matter how high one might score on the self-monitoring scale, one wants aspirin to alleviate a headache, not to impress friends.

Situation

Some investigators have attempted to determine if situations can be structured to increase the salience of attitude functions. Shavitt, Swan, Lowry, and Wänke (1994) administered a survey that either highlighted sensory experiences or social concerns in order to induce either utilitarian functions or social-adjustive functions. Utilitarian functions were primed by asking the subjects to rate how good or bad a variety of experiences made them feel on scales ranging from "makes me feel very bad" to "makes me feel very good" (p. 143). Social-adjustive functions were primed by asking the subjects to rate a number of events based on how good of an impression the event would make on hypothetical observers of the event. They found evidence consistent with a functional matching effect for the functions they primed.

Katz (1960) noted, "The most general statement that can be made concerning attitude arousal is that it is dependent upon the excitation of some need in the individual, or some relevant cue in the environment" (p. 176). Following Katz, Julka, and Marsh (2005) argue that the best way to induce any specific attitude function is to heed Katz's (1960) suggestion that attitudes change when the need that the operative attitude function serves is frustrated. Rather than attempting to measure pre-existing functions, they suggest frustrating the operative attitude function, and then providing a persuasive message (organ donation in this case) that would allow the audience to satisfy the need that had been frustrated. To induce a need to express attitudes consistent

with their values, some subjects were given a rigged values survey that indicated that they were not living up to their values. The investigators believed that this tactic would increase their motivation to couple their attitudes and their values. To induce the knowledge function, some subjects were given confusing instructions for a card game. They found evidence consistent with the functional matching effect such that targeting messages at the value function was more persuasive for those who had value-expressive motivation induced than those who had knowledge motivation induced. Alternatively, the knowledge targeted message was more persuasive for those who had the knowledge motivation induced than those who had the value-expressive motivation induced. Furthermore, they found this functional matching effect was stronger for the conditions in which these functions were frustrated than other conditions in which these functions were merely made salient by using a simple values survey with no feedback (value-expressive functions were salient but not aroused) or giving them easy to understand instructions for a card game (knowledge function were salient but not aroused).

Measuring Functions

Several scholars (Clary & Snyder, 1992; Clary, Snyder, Ridge, Copeland, Stukas, Haugen, & Miene, 1998; Clary, Snyder, Ridge, Miene, & Haugen, 1994) have tested the functional matching hypothesis using Herek's (1987) method of measuring attitude functions by self-report. Clary and Snyder's (1992) work provides an example. Their volunteer functions inventory (VFI) was designed to assess five different motivations for engaging in volunteerism based on the five previously described functions. They tested the functional matching effect with five different videotaped messages promoting volunteerism that were each designed to target one of the five functions. They used the subjects' scores on the VFI to assign a message to them that either matched the function with which their attitude was most associated or the function with which their attitude was least associated. If the message matched the function identified by one's highest score on the VFI, then it was more persuasive than if it matched their lowest score. Subsequently, they replicated this effect for brochures. Clary et al. (1994) conducted a similar study using the VFI to measure the primary function served by the subjects' attitudes. They found that functional matching was also associated with higher ratings of trustworthiness toward the source of the message and a stronger belief that the message addressed their individual goals. These studies are unique in that they created messages to target all five of the previously elucidated functions rather than targeting a subset of the traditional five functions (e.g., using the self-monitoring scale to target either the social-adjustive functions or utilitarian function, Snyder & Debono, 1985). Although the VFI is a promising tool for targeting messages supporting volunteering, in order to use the functional measurement approach to tailor messages in other contexts, a more general instrument is needed, one that is not specific to a particular attitude object.

Several attempts have been made to produce such a measure. Herek's (1987) items are topic specific, Herek making the argument that although his measure can be adapted to other domains, the wording may need to be changed from topic to topic to reflect the specifics of that domain. Alternatively, Locander and Spivey (1978) produced evidence consistent with the validity of a general measure of Katz's (1960) four functions, but their measure was developed assuming that the only source of an attitude function is personality, this instrument being an attempt to measure features of personality thought to be linked with particular functions. Thus, the instrument neglects the influence of the attitude object and the situational features that also impact attitude function. Franc and Brkljačić (2005) also present a general measure, but it is limited in that it assesses only the utilitarian, social-expressive, and value-expressive functions. Consequently, it provides a foundation on which to build indicators of the knowledge function and the ego-defensive function. If attitude functions can be measured effectively, the influence of personality, object, and situation can be estimated and theory developed to explain their varying effects.

Explanations for the Functional Matching Hypothesis

The majority of studies examining the functional matching hypothesis have found evidence consistent with its predictions regardless of the source of the attitude function. Although the effect appears robust, explanations for it remain uncertain. Lavine and Snyder (1996) argued that the effect arises because of biased processing. Specifically, when the audience receives a functionally matched message, they are predicted to perceive the message as of higher quality and to produce more favorable message-relevant thoughts than when they are exposed to a mismatched message. Furthermore, Lavine and Snyder predicted that perceptions of message quality would mediate the relationship between functional matching and attitudes, and they found evidence consistent with these hypotheses in two studies examining attitudes toward voting.

The elaboration likelihood model (ELM; Petty & Cacioppo, 1986) has also been used to explain the functional matching hypothesis results. There is inconsistency, however, in deriving predictions from the ELM. Snyder and Debono (1985) propose that functional matching operates as a peripheral cue such that those who are not processing centrally employ the heuristic cue that matched arguments are better regardless of quality. If a message produces attitude change via means other than message content, it follows from the ELM that peripheral processes are operative. Debono (1987, study 2) found that evidence consistent with this reasoning. Specifically, functional matching increased the persuasiveness of a message even when the speaker produced no actual arguments.

Alternatively, Debono and Harnish (1988) argued that functional matching increases depth of processing so that mismatched messages are processed peripherally and matched messages are processed centrally. They found, consistent with ELM predictions, that when a message provided a functional match, argument strength had a stronger impact on the persuasiveness of the message than when the message did not provide a functional match. Furthermore, consistent with the ELM-based hypothesis of increased processing, they found that the ratio of positive to negative thoughts generated by their subjects was associated strongly with post-message attitudes when the message matched functions but not when the message failed to match functions. This latter effect was not replicated, however, by Debono (1987).

In their second study, Petty and Wegener (1998) found evidence consistent with the ELM explanation as the effects of argument strength and functional matching were limited to those low in need for cognition. They argued that if the audience is motivated strongly to process arguments carefully and thoroughly (in this case, those who chronically process centrally due to their high need for cognition), functional matching will not affect the depth of processing the message. Functional matching is anticipated to increase the effect of argument strength for only those low in need for cognition (i.e., for those for whom the default is limited processing). On the other hand, in their first study in this article, Petty and Wegener (1998) found that functional matching did increase the persuasiveness of strong arguments and decrease the persuasiveness of weak arguments. Yet, there was also a strong main effect for functional matching such that matched arguments were *less* persuasive than mismatched arguments. Thus, this experiment failed to replicate functional matching hypothesis predictions that matching is expected to increase the persuasiveness of the arguments. Given the inconsistency of these results, the ELM may not be adequate as an explanation of this phenomenon (cf., Stiff & Boster, 1987).

Others have offered a provocative alternative derived from the unimodel (Thompson, Kruglanski, & Spiegel, 2000). The unimodel posits that the functional matching effect results from functionally matched messages providing information that is relevant to the audience. According to Thompson et al., attitude functions serve to determine what kind of information is relevant to the audience's goals. Information that is irrelevant is ignored just as easily as information from bad arguments. No studies have been published reporting a critical test of this unimodel prediction as compared to the various ELM predictions, but Hullett (2002, 2004) has found consistently that the functional matching effect is mediated by the perception that the message is relevant to one's values.

Structure of Attitude Functions

Katz (1960) and Smith et al. (1956) produced similar lists of functions. Herek (1986) divided them up somewhat differently but other than expanding the types of utilitarian functions and dropping the knowledge function, he produced a similar list. More recent scholarship has begun to question the adequacy of that list (Hullett & Boster, 2001; Maio & Olson, 2000; Watt, Maio, Haddock, & Johnson, 2008).

Maio and Olson (2000) argued that utilitarian attitudes are not conceptually distinct from value-expressive attitudes because attitudes that are based on maximizing utility require some value to determine what is good and bad for the individual. They found that their subjects' attitudes toward attending a proposed music festival immediately before finals were substantially correlated with utilitarian values related to enjoyment and negatively related to utilitarian values related to achievement. They found that just as responses to appeals based on other values more commonly associated with value-expressive attitudes were substantially related to the specific values that were targeted, targeting utilitarian values operated the same way. It is also worth noting that these investigators were following up on an important point they had made previously (Maio & Olson, 1994); namely, that knowing that an attitude is value-expressive does not allow functional matching in and of itself. Rather, one must know the specific targeted value. One could determine that the target of a message has a value-expressive function for that attitude, but if the message was not targeted at the correct value, it would fail to persuade.

Although Maio and Olson (2000) argued that utilitarian attitudes may simply be value-expressive attitudes with a particular utilitarian value, Hullett and Boster (2001) make a similar argument such that social-adjustive attitudes are a particular type of value-expressive attitudes. They argued that people with social-adjustive attitudes are simply pursuing an other-directed value (the extent to which the individual's values conform to the wishes of others). They found that when the message was based on supporting conformity, the degree to which the target had other-directed values was related directly to agreement with the message.

The bulk of the research that has demonstrated a successful functional matching effect in the second wave of functional attitude research has been conducted on utilitarian, social-adjustive, or value-expressive attitudes (see Clary & Snyder, 1992 and Julka & Marsh, 2006 for exceptions). If utilitarian, social-adjustive, and value-expressive attitudes are all simply value-expressive attitudes, all this line of research has demonstrated is that it is more effective to target the value that the individual associates with the attitude than to target a value the audience either does not support or does not associate with the attitude being targeted. In order to determine if any given proposed function is actually a separate function, it would be helpful to return to Katz's (1960) original purpose of delineating functions; namely, to determine if the processes by which attitudes change differ based on the function. In an early statement of functional attitude theory, Katz and Stotland (1959) discussed the possibility of attitude functions varying based on the intervening variables between the function and the attitude. The third wave of functional attitude research examines the different types of cognitive processes that occur when different attitude functions predominate or are salient (Hullett, 2002; 2004; 2006, Hullett & Boster 2001; La France & Boster, 2001; Lapinski & Boster, 2001). These studies can be used to demonstrate which functions produce the same cognitive processes, and thus could be profitably combined, and which produce different cognitive processes and should therefore be distinguished.

Although the ego-defensive function produced the most research in the initial phase of functional attitude research (e.g. Katz, McClintock, & Sarnoff, 1957; Katz, Sarnoff, & McClintock, 1956), it is the most understudied function in the second wave of functional attitude theory research, a wave ushered in by the extensive use of the self-monitoring scale (Snyder & Debono, 1985). Lapinski and Boster (2001) sought to address this lacuna by employing causal modeling to understand the cognitive processes that occur when an ego-defensive attitude is challenged. Rather than exploring how to target ego-defensive attitudes, they modeled the process by which ego-defensive attitudes become more resistant to change, focusing on how people defend their ego from a message that attacks a pivotal aspect of their self-image. In addition to the inherent benefit of studying resistance to persuasion, their work suggests future work focusing on reducing the processes that cause resistance. They found evidence consistent with a causal chain in which the degree to which a message is ego-threatening produces predominantly negative thoughts in the audience. The production of negative thoughts leads to message discounting and then source derogation. Finally, increasing source derogation resulted in an increasingly negative attitude. This model describes a serial process that people experience in order to protect their ego from a message that suggests a discrepancy between their behavior and their self-image. This process is different from the processes identified by Hullett (Hullett, 2002, 2004; Hullett & Boster, 2001) concerning value-expressive, social-adjustive, and utilitarian functions.

Hullett and Boster (2001) examined messages that targeted the social-adjustive and value-expressive functions. When the message advocated conformity, the relationship between the extent to which the audience valued conformity and their agreement with the message was mediated by perceptions of message quality (although the extent to which they valued other-directedness did have a direct effect on message acceptance). When they used a message that advocated self-direction (values associated with independence and following one's own desires), the relationship between that value and message acceptance was again mediated by perceptions of message quality. Lavine and Snyder (1996) found a similar effect for social-adjustive and value-expressive functions such that perceptions of message quality mediated the relationship between the functional match of the message and message acceptance.

Hullett (2002) expanded this process-oriented approach by measuring the extent to which targets of a value-expressive message actually held that value and the extent to which the message was relevant to the basis of their attitude. Hullett found that the extent to which the audience held a value influenced the extent to which they viewed the message targeting that value as relevant to their attitudes, which then increased their perceptions of message quality. His analysis suggests a process in which the audience initially determines if a message is relevant to the values associated with their attitudes, and then the extent to which the message is relevant determines the audience's subjective determination of the quality of the message. As before, message quality perceptions directly influence message acceptance. Hullett (2004) went on to demonstrate that this process occurs for other-directed values (similar to the basis of the social-adjustive function) and self-centered values (similar to the

basis of the utilitarian function), suggesting that regardless of the value that is targeted, the same process occurs. Hullett also found that regardless of which value the persuasive message targeted, if the message was perceived to be relevant to one's reasons for holding the attitude, it was associated with guilt arousal, which increased message acceptance independent of the impact of message relevance on perceptions of message quality.

These studies on the cognitive processes underlying different functions are consistent with the perspective that value-expressive, utilitarian, and social-adjustive attitudes all seem to be changed via the same processes (Hullett, 2002, 2004; Hullett & Boster, 2001) and thus may not represent different functions. On the other hand, the research by Lapinski and Boster (2001) on the unique processes associated with ego-defensive attitudes, suggests that this function may be a theoretically distinct attitude function. The remaining function of the original five, the knowledge function (Katz, 1960), has only been the focus of a small number of studies (Clary et al., 1998; Clary et al., 1994; Clary & Snyder, 1992; Julka & Marsh, 2006). The studies by Clary and colleagues have all been basic functional matching studies that did not investigate whether or not the knowledge function was associated with a different process. Julka and Marsh's (2006) study did not investigate the process by which attitudes with a knowledge function change, but they did find that the knowledge function could be induced similarly to how the value-expressive function could be induced (e.g., by causing the audience to feel that they had failed to reach the goal associated with each function). It remains to be seen whether the processes associated with the knowledge function simply represent another value and could be subsumed as another type of value-expressive attitudes or if there are unique cognitive processes associated with the knowledge function that would require a unique message strategy as the ego-defensive function seems to require.

Challenges

Theoretical Challenges

Hullett (2002, 2004) found evidence consistent with the perspective that value-relevant, social-adjustive, and utilitarian functions all engage similar, serial cognitive processes. Critical tests are needed to compare some of the ELM predictions with the more complex causal processes Hullett examined. In general, not enough attention has been paid to the cognitive processes that generate the functional matching effect. Unless and until functional attitude scholars advance from focusing on mere functional matching effects to trying to understand the causal processes associated with the different functions as initiated by the third wave of functional attitude research, progress will not be made toward a comprehensive functional theory of attitudes.

As with much persuasion research, the studies that emerge from viewing attitude functions as a process are cross-sectional, and have the corresponding limitations in the strength of the causal inferences that can be drawn from this method of data collection. And, although future research would profit from longitudinal data collection, it would profit even more if longitudinal data sets emerged from designs derived from dynamic theories. Meeting this condition would require that the structural equations implicit in Hullett and Boster's (2001) and Lapinski and Boster's (2001) papers be replaced by change equations or differential equations detailing the processes by which each variable in these cross-sectional models change. Theory of this level of sophistication would then dictate many features of design and data collection, as well as provide straightforward tests of the model (cf., Boster, Mayer, Hunter, & Hale, 1980; Boster, Hunter, Mongeau, & Fryrear, 1982).

Several investigators have also found that messages can be used to make attitudes more relevant to particular functions. La France and Boster (2001) found that the attitude functions in their study changed to become more experiential schematic and less experiential specific after exposure to a message that targeted the attitudes associated with the functions they measured. Hullett (2004) found that messages explicitly linking a particular attitude to a value can increase the value-relevance of a particular attitude. Theories integrating both the effects of functions on message processing and the effects of messages on the function(s) served by attitudes would formalize functional attitude theory and provide a degree of specificity and theoretical precision that would move it beyond being a mere approach to understanding attitudes.

Practical Challenges

Functional attitude theories suggest that in order to persuade someone, influencing agents must plot the cognitive structure of an attitude, determine the function(s) that the attitude serves, and tailor a message accordingly. The theory and technology necessary to perform these tasks effectively remain elusive. Cognitive structure is difficult to access; mapping it will prove more challenging. Advances in the technology of tailoring messages to the individual (Maibach, Maxfield, Ladin, & Slater, 1996) require that targets respond to lengthy questionnaires. Despite these difficulties, targeted research projects have the potential to enhance understanding of these features of the persuasion process.

Targeting functions provides a more precise means of tailoring messages to targets than previous approaches. Miller and Steinberg (1975) argue that to adapt a message to an audience one can use information about them that exists along a continuum ranging from broad cultural-level knowledge to individuating information about the target. A recent review of the tailoring research (Hawkins, Kreuter, Resnicow, Fishbein, & Dijkstra, 2008) suggests that the ideal way to tailor to the audience is to use individuating information and calls for more research on the *processes* involved that can make tailoring more effective. Research using attitude functions to tailor messages allows message targeting at more individuated level information.

The majority of the experiments that identify attitude functions as a means of tailoring persuasive messages examine attitude formation (e.g. Snyder & Debono, 1985). A small number have examined attitude change (e.g., Lavine & Snyder, 1996). None, however, have pursued attitude functions as a means of making attitudes more resistant to suasory appeals. Maio and Olson (1995) report that value-expressive attitudes have stronger value-attitude links than do attitudes that serve other functions (cf., Blankenship & Wegener, 2008). It may be that particular functions confer stronger resistance than others, for example, Katz (1960) suggested that ego-defensive attitudes may be particularly resistant to change because these functions are tied to one's sense of self-esteem, which people are strongly motivated to protect. Research exploring the functions most likely to produce resistance, or the conditions under which any given function is most likely to result in decreased yielding, coupled with the means of changing those functions has the potential to provide a unique means of increasing resistance to persuasion.

Conclusion

A logically coherent, comprehensive, and empirically predictive functional attitude theory remains one of the unfulfilled goals of early persuasion research. Although the theoretical and technical hurdles can be daunting, substantial conceptual and empirical progress has been made in the last two decades. Sustaining and building on these recent successes is pivotal if the promise of Smith and colleagues' (1956) seminal work and Katz's (1960) work is to be realized, and the study of the functional theory of attitudes is to become a linchpin of persuasion

theory. Future advances of this sort would fulfill Plato's recommendation that orators adapt their messages to the soul of their listener.

References

Blankenship, K. L., & Wegener, D. T. (2008). Opening the mind to close it: Considering a message in light of important values increases message processing and later resistance to change. *Journal of Personality and Social Psychology, 94,* 196–213.

Boster, F. J., Fryrear, J. E., Mongeau, P. A., & Hunter, J. E. (1982). An unequal speaking linear discrepancy model: Implications for polarity shift. In M. Burgoon (Ed.), *Communication yearbook 6* (pp. 395–418). Beverly Hills, CA: Sage.

Boster, F. J., Mayer, M. E., Hunter, J. E., & Hale, J. L. (1980). Expanding the persuasive arguments explanation of the polarity shift: A linear discrepancy model. In D. Nimmo (Ed.), *Communication yearbook 4* (pp. 165–176). New Brunswick, NJ: Transaction Books.

Clary, E. G., & Snyder, M. (1992). Persuasive communications strategies for recruiting volunteers. In D. R. Young, R. M. Hollister, & V. A. Hodgkinson (Eds.), *Governing, leading, and managing nonprofit organizations: New insights from research and practice* (pp. 121–137). San Francisco, CA: Jossey-Bass.

Clary, E. G., Snyder, M., Ridge, R., Copeland, J. Stukas, A. A., Haugen, J., et al. (1998). Understanding and assessing the motivations of volunteers: A functional approach. *Journal of Personality and Social Psychology, 74,* 1516–1530.

Clary, E. G., Snyder, M., Ridge, R., Miene, P. K., & Haugen, J. A. (1994). Matching messages to motives in persuasion: A functional approach to promoting volunteerism. *Journal of Applied Social Psychology, 24,* 1129–1149.

Debono, K. G. (1987). Investigating the social-adjustive and value-expressive functions of attitudes: Implications for persuasion processes. *Journal of Personality and Social Psychology, 52,* 279–287.

Debono, K. G. (2000). Attitude functions and consumer psychology: Understanding perceptions of product quality. In G. R. Maio & J. M. Olson (Eds.), *Why we evaluate: Functions of attitudes* (pp. 195–221). Mahwah, NJ: Erlbaum.

Debono, K. G., & Harnish, R. J. (1988). Source expertise, source attractiveness, and the processing of persuasive information: A functional approach. *Journal of Personality and Social Psychology, 55,* 541–546.

Debono, K. G. & Rubin, K. (1995). Country of origin and perceptions of product quality: An individual difference perspective. *Basic and Applied Social Psychology, 17,* 239–247.

Debono, K. G., & Snyder, M. (1989). Understanding consumer decision-making processes: The role of form and function in product evaluation. *Journal of Applied Social Psychology, 19,* 416–424.

Debono, K. G., & Telesca, C. (1990). The influence of source physical attractiveness on advertising effectiveness: A functional perspective. *Journal of Applied Social Psychology, 20,* 1383–1395.

Dillard, J. P., & Hunter, J. E. (1989). On the use and interpretation of the emotional empathy scale, the self-consciousness scale, and the self-monitoring scale. *Communication Research, 16,* 104–129.

Dutta-Bergman, M. J. (2003). The linear interaction model of personality effects in health communication. *Health Communication, 15,* 101–116.

Franc, R., & Brkljačić, T. (2005). Self-report measure of attitude functions: Instrumental attitudes towards condom use and value-expressive attitudes towards voting? *Review of Psychology, 12,* 147–154.

Hawkins, R. P., Kreuter, M., Resnicow, K., Fishbein, M., & Dijkstra, A. (2008). Understanding tailoring in communicating about health. *Health Education Research, 23,* 454–466.

Herek, G. M. (1986). The instrumentality of attitudes: Toward a neofunctional theory. *Journal of Social Issues, 42,* 99–114.

Herek, G. M. (1987). Can functions be measured? A new perspective on the functional approach to attitudes. *Social Psychology Quarterly, 50,* 285–303.

Herek, G. M. (2000). The social construction of attitudes: Functional consensus and divergence in the U.S. public's reactions to AIDS. In G. R. Maio & J. M. Olson (Eds.), *Why we evaluate: Functions of attitudes* (pp. 325–364). Mahwah, NJ: Erlbaum.

Hullett, C. R. (2002). Charting the process underlying the change of value-expressive attitudes: The importance of value-relevance in predicting the matching effect. *Communication Monographs, 69,* 158–178.

Hullett, C. R. (2004). Using functional theory to promote sexually transmitted disease (STD) testing: The impact of value-expressive messages and guilt. *Communication Research, 31,* 363–396.

Hullett, C. R. (2006). Using functional theory to promote HIV testing: The impact of value-expressive messages, uncertainty, and fear. *Health Communication, 20,* 57–67.

Hullett, C. R., & Boster, F. J. (2001). Matching messages to the values underlying value-expressive and social-adjustive attitudes: Reconciling and old theory with a contemporary measurement approach. *Communication Monographs, 68,* 133–153.

Julka, D. L., & Marsh, K. L. (2005). An attitude functions approach to increasing organ-donation participation. *Journal of Applied Social Psychology, 35,* 821–849.

Katz, D. (1960). The functional approach to the study of attitudes. *Public Opinion Quarterly, 24,* 163–204.

Katz, D., McClintock, C., & Sarnoff, I. (1957). The measurement of ego defense as related to attitude change. *Journal of Personality, 25,* 465–474.

Katz, D., Sarnoff, I., & McClintock, C. (1956). Ego-defense and attitude change. *Human Relations, 9,* 27–45.

Katz, D., & Stotland, E. (1959). A preliminary statement to a theory of attitude structure and change. In S. Koch (Ed.), *Psychology: A study of a science* (pp. 423–475). New York, NY: McGraw-Hill.

La France, B. H., & Boster, F. J. (2001). To match or mismatch? That is only one important question. *Communication Monographs, 68,* 211–234.

Lapinski, M. K., & Boster, F. J. (2001). Modeling the ego-defensive functions of attitudes. *Communication Monographs, 68,* 314–324.

Lavine, H., & Snyder, M. (1996). Cognitive processing and the functional matching effect in persuasion: The mediating role of subjective perceptions of message quality. *Journal of Experimental Social Psychology, 32,* 580–604.

Lennox, R. D., & Wolfe, R. N. (1984). Revision of the self-monitoring scale. *Journal of Personality and Social Psychology, 46,* 1349–1364.

Locander, W. B., & Spivey, W. A. (1978). A functional approach to attitude measurement. *Journal of Marketing Research, 15,* 576–587.

Maibach, E., Maxfield, A., Ladin, K., & Slater, M. (1996). Translating health psychology into effective health communication: The American healthstyles audience segmentation project. *Journal of Health Psychology, 1,* 261–277.

Maio, G. R., & Olson, J. M. (1994). Value-attitude-behaviour relations: The moderating role of attitude functions. *British Journal of Social Psychology, 33,* 301–312.

Maio, G. R., & Olson, J. M. (1995). Relations between values, attitudes, and behavior intentions: The moderating role of attitude function. *Journal of Experimental Social Psychology, 31,* 266–285.

Maio, G. R., & Olson, J. M. (2000). What is a "value-expressie" attitude? In G. R. Maio & J. M. Olson (Eds.), *Why we evaluate: Functions of attitudes* (pp. 249–269). Mahwah, NJ: Erlbaum.

Miller, G. R., & Steinberg, M. (1975). *Between people: A new analysis of interpersonal communication.* Chicago, IL: Social Science Research.

Petty, R. E., & Cacioppo, J. T. (1986). *Communication and persuasion: Central and peripheral routes to attitude change.* New York, NY: Springer-Verlag.

Petty, R. E., & Wegener, D. T. (1998). Matching versus mismatching attitude functions: Implications for scrutiny of persuasive messages. *Personality and Social Psychology Bulletin, 24,* 227–240.

Plato. (1993). *Symposium and Phaedrus* (B. Jowett, Trans.). New York, NY: Dover. (Original work 360 BCE)

Sarnoff, I., & Katz, D. (1954). The motivational bases of attitude change. *Journal of Abnormal and Social Psychology, 49,* 115–124.

Shavitt, S. (1990). The role of attitude objects in attitude functions. *Journal of Experimental Social Psychology, 26,* 124–148.

Shavitt, S., Lowrey, T. M., & Han, S. P. (1992). Attitude functions in advertising: The interactive role of products and self-monitoring. *Journal of Consumer Psychology, 1,* 337–364.

Shavitt, S., Swan, S., Lowrey, T. M., Wanke, M. (1994). The interaction of endorser attractiveness and involvement in persuasion depends on the goal that guides message processing. *Journal of Consumer Psychology, 3,* 137–162.

Smith, M. B., Bruner, J. S., & White, R. W. (1956). *Opinions and personality.* New York, NY: Wiley.

Snyder, M. (1974). Self-monitoring of expressive behavior. *Journal of Personality and Social Psychology, 30,* 526–537.

Snyder, M., & DeBono, K. G. (1985). Appeals to image and claims about quality: Understanding the psychology of advertising. *Journal of Personality and Social Psychology, 49,* 586–597.

Snyder, M., & Gangestead, S. (1986). On the nature of self-monitoring: Matters of assessment, matters of validity. *Journal of Personality and Social Psychology, 51,* 125–139.

Stiff, J. B. & Boster, F. J. (1987). Cognitive processing: Additional thoughts and a reply to Petty, Kasmer, Haugtvedt, and Cacioppo. *Communication Monographs, 54,* 250–256.

Stotland, E., Katz, D., & Patchen, M. (1959). The reduction of prejudice though the arousal of self-insight. *Journal of Personality, 27,* 507–531.

Thompson, E. P., Kruglanski, A. W., & Spiegel, S. (2000). Attitudes as knowledge structures and persuasion as specific case of subjective knowledge acquisition. In G. R. Maio & J. M. Olson (Eds.), *Why we evaluate: Functions of attitudes* (pp. 59–96). Mahwah, NJ: Erlbaum.

Watt, S. E., Maio, G. R., Haddock, G., & Johnson, B. T. (2008). Attitude functions in persuasion: Matching, involvement, self-affirmation, and hierarchy. In W. D. Crano & R. Prislin (Eds.), *Attitudes and attitude change* (pp. 189–211). New York, NY: Psychology Press.

CHAPTER 8

Reasoned Action Theory

Persuasion as Belief-Based Behavior Change

Marco Yzer

Introduction

Almost 50 years after its inception, reasoned action theory continues to serve as a foundation for persuasion research. The popularity of the theory lies in its direct applicability to the question of how exposure to persuasive information leads to behavior change. Despite its wide use and long history, reasoned action is a dynamic theory with a number of unresolved issues. As this chapter will show, some of these issues reflect misconceptions of theoretical propositions or misuse of research recommendations, whereas others indicate opportunities for theoretical advancement.

Reasoned action theory explains behavior by identifying the primary determinants of behavior and the sources of these determinant variables, and by organizing the relations between these variables. The theory is marked by a sequence of reformulations that build on one another in a developmental fashion. These are the theory of reasoned action (Fishbein & Ajzen, 1975), the theory of planned behavior (Ajzen, 1985), and the integrative model of behavioral

prediction (Fishbein, 2000). The theory's current formulation, graphically displayed in Figure 8.1., is described as the reasoned action approach to explaining and changing behavior (Fishbein & Ajzen, 2010). In this chapter I use the term reasoned action theory to refer to the current formulation of the theory and to propositions that apply to all formulations of the theory.

The objectives of this chapter are to make clear how reasoned action theory contributes to a better understanding of persuasion processes and outcomes, and to identify accomplishments of and opportunities for research in the reasoned action tradition. Because of its relevance for persuasion scholarship, I will first highlight the reasoned action hypothesis that behavior change originates from beliefs about the behavior. Next I will discuss key propositions within the historical context in which they were developed, issues related to conceptualization and operationalization of the theory's components, and opportunities for future research. The range of issues included in this review addresses the decades-long time frame during which persuasion scholars have explicitly used core reasoned action

Figure 8.1 Components of Reasoned Action Theory and Their Relations

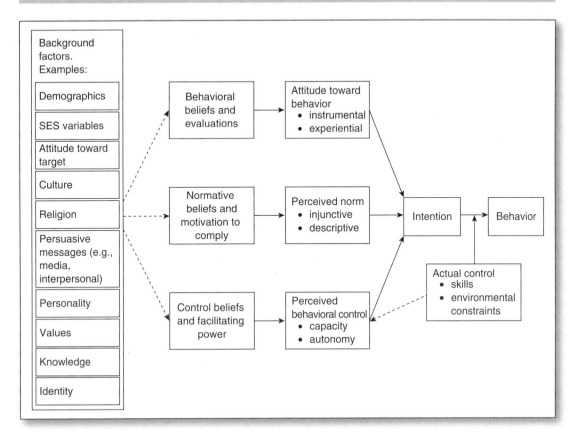

concepts. The research I review here is illustrative rather than exhaustive, by necessity, as few other behavioral theories have generated more research.

The Reasoned Action Perspective on Persuasion

Beliefs that people hold about a behavior play a central role in reasoned action explanations of behavior. In Fishbein and Ajzen's (2010) words, "human social behavior follows reasonably and often spontaneously from the information or beliefs people possess about the behavior under consideration. These beliefs originate in a variety of sources, such as personal experience, formal education, radio, newspapers, TV, the Internet and other media, and interactions with family and friends. . . . No matter how beliefs associated with a given behavior are acquired, they serve to guide the decision to perform or not perform the behavior in question" (p. 20).

When people act on beliefs that they have formed about a behavior, they engage in a reasoned, but not necessarily rational process. For example, someone suffering from paranoid personality disorder may lock the door of his office because he believes that his colleagues are conspiring against him. This person acts in a reasoned manner on a belief, even though others would deem his belief irrational. Regardless whether beliefs are irrational, incorrect (because based on false information), or motivationally biased, once beliefs are formed they are the cognitive basis from which behavior reasonably follows (Blank & Hennessy, 2012; Fishbein & Ajzen, 2010).

Beliefs affect behavior through a sequence of effects. Specific beliefs about a behavior inform attitude, perceived norm, and perceived behavioral control regarding the behavior, which in turn determine intention to perform the behavior. If one has the necessary abilities to perform the behavior and if there are no situational obstacles that impede behavioral performance, then intention should lead to behavior. The conceptualization of behavior formation as a process makes clear that a persuasive message cannot directly change behavior. Although the ultimate objective of persuasive messages is to reinforce or change a particular behavior, persuasive messages at best create or change beliefs. When beliefs are appropriately selected, changes in those beliefs should affect attitude, perceived norm, or perceived behavioral control, which in turn should affect intention and behavior. Those beliefs that most strongly discriminate between people who do and do not (intend to) perform a particular behavior, are the choice candidates to address in persuasive messages (Fishbein & Ajzen, 2010; Fishbein & Yzer, 2003).

In terms of reasoned action theory, persuasion thus concerns the effects of exposure to a persuasive message on beliefs about performing a behavior, and through effects on those beliefs on behavior. Clearly, then, the precision with which one can predict behavior is directly relevant for persuasion scholarship. The remainder of this chapter will therefore be used to review the ability of reasoned action theory to predict behavior. For this purpose it is useful to first discuss the historical context in which reasoned action theory was developed.

Historical Context

In the early 20th century there was widespread consensus that attitude should matter as a basis for human behavior. For example, most contemporary definitions emphasized attitude as a tendency to act (for an overview see Allport, 1935). By the 1960s, however, accumulated empirical support for the hypothesis that people act on their attitude was inconsistent at best, with many studies reporting no effect of attitude on behavior at all. As a result, many scholars questioned the usefulness of attitude for behavioral prediction. Most widely cited in this regard is Wicker (1969), who, on a review of studies that correlated self-reported attitude with lagged observations of behavior, concluded that it is unlikely that people act on their attitude. In counterpoint, others argued that measurement issues were at least in part responsible for weak correlations between attitude and behavioral data. Particularly pertinent is Triandis's (1964) finding that the prediction of behavior from attitude improved when measures of attitude and behavior represented the same dimensions.

The debate on the question whether attitude predicts behavior helps understand the origins of reasoned action propositions. In effect, what was under discussion was whether contemporary attitude theory offered valid hypotheses about how thoughts, feelings, and behavior regarding an object are associated. Fishbein observed that the confusion surrounding the attitude-behavior relation had to do with the wide range of different variables that were included under the umbrella label of "attitude." Similar to Thurstone (1928), Fishbein (1967) viewed attitude as "a relatively simple unidimensional concept, referring to the amount of affect for or against a psychosocial object" (p. 478). Building on Dulany's (1968) theory of propositional control over verbal responses, he argued that attitude should be separated from its antecedents and consequences. Moreover, in order to improve prediction of behavior, he urged scholars to focus on the relations between these variables, that is, beliefs, attitude, behavioral intention, and behavior (Fishbein, 1963, 1967).

A number of principles have been developed to aid such inquiry (e.g., Ajzen & Fishbein, 1973). A first holds that prediction of behavior (e.g., running) is more precise than prediction of behavioral categories (e.g., exercise) or goals (e.g., losing weight). Exercise includes many different behaviors, and each of these behaviors may be associated with quite different beliefs. From the author's perspective, for example, running is fun but swimming is not. Whether or not I will report to like and engage in exercise therefore depends on whether I think about running, swimming, or both when asked about my exercise. Similarly, losing weight is a goal that can be achieved by many different behaviors, and one may hold positive beliefs about losing weight yet in fact not achieve that goal because necessary dieting and exercise behaviors are not performed due to negative beliefs about those behaviors.

Second, prediction of specific behaviors is more precise than prediction of general behaviors. Levels of specificity vary by the extent to which a behavioral definition includes each of four components, that is, action (e.g., running), target (e.g., at a 9-minute per mile pace), context (e.g., on a treadmill at the YMCA), and time (e.g., twice a week). Clearly, "running" can be interpreted more broadly than "running twice a week at a 9-minute pace on a treadmill at the YMCA." When two people think about "running," they may therefore think about quite different behaviors, each associated with different, behavior-specific beliefs. It is for this reason that persuasive messages are more effective when they promote a specific behavior and its underlying beliefs than a general, more broadly interpretable behavior (Fishbein, 2000).

Third, and known as the compatibility principle, prediction of behavior improves when behavior is measured at the same level of specificity as beliefs, attitude, and intention (cf. Triandis, 1964). For example, intention to recycle hazardous materials may not correlate with frequency of recycling batteries, because people may intend to perform the more general behavior of recycling hazardous materials but not intend to perform the specific behavior of recycling batteries.

Adherence to these principles should improve the precision of behavioral prediction, and consequently, the effectiveness of persuasive efforts. Remarkably, however, although these principles are as relevant for the prediction of behavior

today as when they were first introduced, they continue to be violated in research that applies reasoned action theory (Hale, Householder, & Greene, 2002; Trafimow, 2004). This has important implications. For example, it has been shown that measurement in accordance with the compatibility principle strengthens relations among reasoned action variables, which suggests that studies that do not adhere to this principle underestimate the ability of reasoned action variables to explain intention and behavior (Cooke & Sheeran, 2004; van den Putte, 1993).

Key Components and Their Relations

Reasoned action theory has three structural parts that together explain behavior formation: (a) the prediction of behavior from behavioral intention; (b) the explanation of intention as a function of attitude, perceived norm, perceived behavioral control, and their underlying beliefs; and (c) the exposition of beliefs as originating from a multitude of potential sources. I will use this partition to structure a discussion of issues related to each reasoned action component and the proposed relations between components.

Behavior

The precision with which behavior can be predicted improves when specific behaviors rather than behavioral categories or goals are measured, and when the behavior that one wants to predict is measured at the same level of specificity as the variables that are used to predict it. Another noteworthy measurement issue has to do with the question whether behavior should be observed or assessed with self-report measures.

Whereas for pragmatic reasons most reasoned action research uses self-reports of behavior, observed behavior has an intuitive appeal because it does not, or at least to a lesser extent, suffer from validity issues known to affect self-reports of behavior (Albarracín et al., 2001). Key among those is that self-reports of behavior can be exaggerated (e.g., male's reports of sexual activity; Brown & Sinclair, 1999) or understated (e.g., reports of at-risk health behavior; Newell, Girgis, Sanson-Fisher, & Savolainen, 1999). Regardless of whether these biases are deliberate or reflect fallible cognitive estimation processes (Brown & Sinclair, 1999), they render behavioral self-reports less than perfectly accurate. This does not mean that prediction of observed behavior is always more precise than prediction of self-reported behavior.

Consider, for example, Armitage's (2005) study of physical activity among members of a gym. Armitage measured attitude, perceived norm, perceived control, and intention at baseline with items framed in terms of "participating in regular physical activity." At a three-month follow-up he assessed behavior by both asking gym members enrolled in his study "How often have you participated in regular physical activity in the last 3 months?" and by electronically logging gym entrance. Clearly, baseline measures were more compatible with the self-report behavior measure than with the observed behavior measure. As just one example, when people think about regular physical exercise, they may think about activities outside the gym that are not reflected in records of gym attendance, but that likely are reflected in self-reports of physical exercise. In support of this contention Armitage found a stronger correlation of intention to participate in regular physical exercise with self-reported regular physical exercise, $r = .51$, than with records of gym attendance, $r = .42$. This finding has been corroborated in meta-analytic research (Armitage & Conner, 2001; but see Webb & Sheeran, 2006).

A moment's reflection shows that the attitude, perceived norm, perceived control, and intention measures that Armitage used would have been more compatible with, and thus more predictive of, the self-report behavior measure used three months after baseline if the former would have

asked about "participating in regular physical activity *in the next three months.*" This is an issue that affects many prospective studies. Interestingly, however, discussions about improving behavioral prediction predominantly focus on variables that possibly moderate effects of reasoned action variables on self-reported behavior, and remain largely silent on measurement of behavior itself (for a notable exception, see Falk, Berkman, Whalen, & Lieberman, 2011). To be sure, moderator analysis has important potential for determining when the theory's propositions are particularly likely to apply, which not only directs investigators to appropriate application but also suggests areas for further theory development (Weinstein & Rothman, 2005). Even so, the scarcity of work that tests the validity of self-report behavior measures, for example, by assessing compatibility between behavioral determinant and behavior measures, is striking (Albarracín et al., 2001).

Behavioral Intention

Behavioral intention is the most immediate determinant of behavior. It is defined as people's readiness to perform a behavior: "Intentions are assumed to capture the motivational factors that influence a behavior; they are indications of how hard people are willing to try, of how much of an effort they are planning to exert, in order to perform the behavior" (Ajzen, 1985, p. 181). Intention is indicated by the subjective probability of behavioral performance, that is, by people's estimate of how likely it is that they will or will not perform a particular behavior. Examples of widely used intention items are *How likely is it that you . . .* (followed by the definition of the behavior under investigation; scale anchors *I definitely will not—I definitely will*) and *I intend to . . .* (scale anchors *I completely disagree—I completely agree*).

The intention concept and its operationalization have not been universally accepted, however. Concerned about the sufficiency of intention as the only variable that directly determines behavior, investigators have proposed several alternative intention concepts and measures. This section reviews three such measures.

Warshaw and Davis (1985) proposed that behavioral expectations, or people's self-predictions regarding their behavior, are superior to behavioral intention in predicting behavior, because behavioral expectations take possible barriers to behavioral performance into account more so than intention. Items such as *I expect to* . . . and *I will* . . . (scale anchors *highly unlikely to highly likely*) are commonly used to measure behavioral expectation. Empirical findings suggest that behavioral expectation measures do not outperform intention measures (Armitage & Conner, 2001; Fishbein & Stasson, 1990; Sheeran & Orbell, 1998; but see Sheppard, Hartwick, & Warshaw, 1988), and it is not uncommon to combine the two types of measures into a single intention scale (e.g., Fielding, McDonald, & Louis, 2008).

Gibbons, Gerrard, Blanton, and Russell (1998) proposed behavioral willingness as another alternative for intention. Gibbons and colleagues argued that an intention to act implies rational deliberation, whereas behavior often is irrational and triggered by situational factors. Developed in the context of health-risky behavior, the behavioral willingness hypothesis holds that people may intend to engage in safe behavior, but be willing to engage in risky behavior if the situation would offer opportunities for doing so. For example, someone may intend to have no more than three drinks at a party, but drink more when at the party an attractive person offers a fourth drink. Similar to this example, behavioral willingness measures ask whether people would be willing to engage in a particular behavior given a particular scenario, that is, under specified circumstances. It is therefore unclear whether behavioral willingness is truly different from intention or simply a more specific intention (Fishbein & Ajzen, 2010).

Gollwitzer's (1999) concept of implementation intentions offers a greater contribution to behavioral prediction. Implementation intentions are highly specific plans people make about when, where, and how to act on a motivation to act, that is, on their intention to act. There is evidence that implementation intentions improve the prediction of behavior (e.g., Ziegelmann, Luszczynska, Lippke, & Schwarzer, 2007), but not always (e.g., Budden & Sagarin, 2007; for a review, see Gollwitzer & Sheeran, 2006). Instead of a viable alternative to the intention variable, implementation intentions are perhaps better interpreted as a useful moderator, such that people who formed positive intentions are more likely to act on their intentions if they have also thought about how to implement their plans.

Predicting Behavior From Intention

Reasoned action theory has been able to account for behavior with a good measure of success. For example, meta-analyses of studies that prospectively examined behavior found intention-behavior correlations to average around $r = .45$ (e.g., Albarracín et al., 2001; Armitage & Conner, 2001; Cooke & Sheeran, 2004; Hagger, Chatzisarantis, & Biddle, 2002; Sheeran & Orbell, 1998; Sheppard et al., 1998). Whereas these average correlations usefully indicate the theory's general ability to account for behavior, it is important to understand which factors increase or decrease the strength of association between intention and behavior. Before discussing two such factors, I first address an important methodological implication of the hypothesis that intention predicts behavior.

Testing Prediction

To test the hypothesis that intention *predicts* behavior, behavior should be measured some time after the variables that theoretically predict it were measured. Because behavior assessed at a certain time point indicates what people did at that same time (for observed behavior) or have done prior to that time (for self-reported behavior), correlating cross-sectional intention and behavior data produces a causal inference problem (Huebner, Neilands, Rebchook, & Kegeles, 2011; Webb & Sheeran, 2006; Weinstein, 2007). A cross-sectional intention-behavior correlation indicates the extent to which intention is consistent with people's past behavior, and should not be interpreted as prediction of future behavior. Unfortunately, intention-behavior correlations obtained from cross-sectional designs are still being published as tests of behavioral prediction (e.g., de Bruijn, Kremers, Schaalma, Van Mechelen, & Brug, 2005; Keats, Culos-Reed, Courneya, & McBride, 2007; Kiviniemi, Voss-Humke, & Seifert, 2007).

Lagged measurement is challenging, both for methodological and budgetary reasons. It is therefore not surprising that cross-sectional studies greatly outnumber prospective studies. For example, Albarracín and colleagues (2001) collected 96 samples for their meta-analysis, but of these, only 23 could be used to test the theory's ability to predict behavior. Similarly, Armitage and Conner (2001) obtained correlations from 185 samples, yet only 44 of these provided lagged intention-behavior correlations, and of the 33 samples that Cooke and French (2008) analyzed, 19 could be used to test intention effects on behavior (but see Hagger et al., 2002, for a higher ratio). This means that although reasoned action theory was designed to predict behavior, it is primarily used to explain intention. This gives pause for reflection: Despite the thousands of reasoned action studies now in existence, only a fraction provides a convincing test of this key aspect of the theory.

Moderators of Intention Effects on Behavior

At least two factors determine the strength of intention-behavior relations. To begin, intention should affect behavior to the extent that intention is temporally stable. If between assessments of intention and behavior nothing happens that might change someone's intention, then intention data should predict behavioral data. However, if intention changes between assessments

because, for example, someone is exposed to a persuasive message, then the behavior data reflect an intention formed after intention data were obtained. The longer the gap between assessments of intention and behavior, the more likely it is that intention changes, thereby attenuating the intention-behavior correlation. Sheeran and colleagues (Sheeran & Orbell, 1998; Sheeran, Orbell, & Trafimow, 1999) found empirical support for this idea. For example, in a meta-analysis of 28 prospective condom use studies, Sheeran and Orbell (1998) found that intention-behavior relations were stronger when the time between measurement of intention and behavior was short rather than long. Note, however, that there is no gold standard for the optimal time lag between intention and behavior assessments, in part because it is near impossible to predict when people will be exposed to factors that influence their intention.

The relation between intention and behavior is also conditional on actual control over behavioral performance (Ajzen, 1985; Fishbein & Ajzen, 2010). People are thought to have actual control over behavioral performance when they have the necessary skills and when the situation does not impose constraints on behavioral performance. Thus, when despite positive intentions people do not perform a behavior, behavioral nonperformance is not a motivational problem but a problem of competence (i.e., deficient skills or abilities) and means (i.e., presence of environmental constraints). It is here where the aforementioned implementation intentions prove useful; actual behavior is more likely when people plan how and when to act on their intention (Norman & Conner, 2005; van Osch et al., 2009), possibly because planning requires people to consider the skills it takes and the obstacles they are up against when they would perform a particular behavior.

Attitude and Behavioral Beliefs

Attitude is an evaluation of performing a future behavior in terms of "favor or disfavor, good or bad, like or dislike" (Fishbein & Ajzen, 2010, p. 78). Although attitude is typically analyzed with a single composite scale, attitude is thought to have two aspects, namely an instrumental (or cognitive) aspect, indicated by perceptions of, for example, how foolish or wise, useful or useless performing a behavior is, and an experiential (or affective) aspect, indicated by how unpleasant or pleasant, unenjoyable or enjoyable performing the behavior is perceived to be. The relative importance of instrumental and experiential aspects of attitude as determinants of intention have clear implications for persuasive messages; if instrumental attitude matters most, a message should emphasize the usefulness of the recommended behavior, but if experiential attitude is more important, a message should emphasize how enjoyable the behavior is. Unfortunately, however, because published reports often do not make clear whether attitude was measured with instrumental, experiential, or both types of items, inferences about when instrumental and experiential attitude contribute to behavioral prediction cannot be made with full confidence. The question whether differential impact is predictable thus deserves more systematic inquiry than it has received thus far.

According to reasoned action theory, attitude formation is the process by which a potentially large set of specific beliefs, which has associated with a behavior over time, informs an overall sense of favorableness toward the behavior. Consistent with expectancy-value perspectives, attitude is a multiplicative combination of behavioral beliefs, which are perceptions of the likelihood that performing a particular behavior will have certain consequences, and an evaluation of those consequences in terms of good or bad. For example, two persons may both believe that if they use a tanning bed, they will get a tan. In addition, person A thinks that being tanned is good, but person B does not. In this single belief example, both person A and person B think that using a tanning bed will give them a tan, but because their opposite evaluations of being tanned person A's attitude toward using a tanning bed is positive

and person B's attitude is negative. This makes clear that both beliefs about behavioral consequences and evaluations of those consequences need to be considered to determine favorableness toward a behavior. It also makes clear that to change attitude, persuasive messages can address beliefs about the likelihood of particular consequences of a behavior but also address evaluations of those consequences. For example, suppose that people already believe that unprotected sex may lead to gonorrhea but do not evaluate gonorrhea as a very serious disease. In this case, a message does not need to argue that unprotected sex can lead to gonorrhea, but can improve attitude toward using condoms if a message convinces that gonorrhea is quite serious.

Although belief-evaluation product terms have been found to correlate strongly with attitude (Albarracín et al., 2001), they typically do not explain much more variance in attitude than the separate behavioral beliefs (e.g., Armitage, Conner, Loach, & Willetts, 1999). For this reason, most investigators only assess behavioral beliefs, or the perceived likelihood of behavioral consequences. Note, however, that for statistical reasons product terms are unlikely to be associated with large effects in regression analysis, which is the method commonly used to test reasoned action (Ajzen & Fishbein, 2008; Yzer, 2007). We should be careful not to abandon conceptual ideas on the basis of empirical results if those results reflect statistical artifacts.

Perceived Norm and Normative Beliefs

To capture the influence of people's social environment on their intention to perform a particular behavior, Fishbein and Ajzen (1975; Ajzen & Fishbein, 1973; Fishbein, 1967) proposed the concept of subjective norm as a second determinant of behavioral intention. In the theory of reasoned action (Fishbein & Ajzen, 1975) subjective norm is the extent to which I believe that other people think that I should or should not engage in a particular behavior. Other scholars refer to subjective norm as injunctive norm (Cialdini, Reno, & Kallgren, 1990), and in recent years, reasoned action theorists have used "injunctive norm" rather than "subjective norm" to indicate expected approval or disapproval from others (Fishbein, 2000; Fishbein & Ajzen, 2010).

The question whether subjective norm is able to capture all relevant perceived social influence has been controversial. This question in large part stemmed from empirical findings in which subjective norm contributed little to the explanation of intention (Albarracín et al., 2001; Cooke & French, 2008; Hagger et al., 2002). Note, however, that there is evidence that subjective norm matters in collectivistic populations (Giles, Liddell, & Bydawell, 2005; Lee & Green, 1991), in younger samples (Albarracín, Kumkale, & Johnson, 2004; van den Putte, 1993), and for behaviors that have salient social aspects (Cooke & French, 2008; Finlay, Trafimow, & Moroi, 1999), which implies that normative messages can have strong persuasive potential for some identified segments and behaviors. Even so, because much work found relatively small subjective norm effects, many investigators have tested alternative normative measures, including, among others, personal norm, verbal approval, social support, and descriptive norm (e.g., Larimer, Turner, Mallett, & Geisner, 2004; van den Putte, Yzer, & Brunsting, 2005).

In recognition of a need to expand the scope of the normative component, reasoned action theory currently posits a perceived norm component that is the composite of injunctive and descriptive norms (see also Fishbein, 2000). The descriptive norm indicates the extent to which I believe that other people perform a particular behavior themselves (Cialdini, Reno, & Kallgren, 1990). A meta-analysis of 14 correlations showed that descriptive norms explained variance in behavioral intention that subjective norms did not, supporting the discriminant validity of the descriptive norm variable (Rivis & Sheeran, 2003). In addition, injunctive and descriptive

norms can have differential effects (Larimer et al., 2004), not only in magnitude but also in direction (Jacobson, Mortensen, & Cialdini, 2011). Thus, although in the context of reasoned action theory, injunctive and descriptive norms can be analyzed with a composite perceived norm scale, it may prove useful to also examine the effects of these variables separately.

Injunctive and descriptive norm measures tap normative perceptions regarding "most people who are important to me." Perceived norm thus reflects perceived social pressure to perform or not to perform a behavior that is generalized across specific referents. It is a function of beliefs about particular individuals; whether particular individuals think I should perform a behavior (injunctive normative beliefs) or whether those individuals perform the behavior themselves (descriptive normative beliefs). However, believing that a particular individual prescribes a certain behavior will not matter if one does not care what that individual thinks, that is, if one is not motivated to comply with that individual. For example, someone affected by diabetes may expect that her doctor will approve her injecting insulin, but also believe that her friends will disapprove, or believe that her insulin-dependent friends do not self-inject. If it is more important for her to do what her peers want her to do than what her doctor wants her to do, then she will experience an overall sense of pressure against injecting insulin.

In more general terms, perceived norm is a function of normative beliefs about particular individuals weighed by the extent to which someone wants to comply with those individuals. However, as discussed in the context of multiplicative composites of behavioral beliefs and their evaluations, effects of product terms are hard to demonstrate in regression analysis. Reasoned action research often relies on regression analysis, which explains why there is not much evidence to support multiplicative composites of normative beliefs and motivation to comply (Fishbein & Ajzen, 2010). The usefulness of normative beliefs and motivation to comply should not be rejected if a lack of empirical support for these measures is caused by a statistical artifact. For example, Giles and colleagues (2005) examined both normative beliefs and motivation to comply regarding condom use in a sample of Zulu adults. Their analysis allowed them to identify important sources of influence, which in turn could inform decisions about who to target in behavior change interventions.

Perceived Behavioral Control and Control Beliefs

Concerned that the theory of reasoned action's focus on volitional behavior unnecessarily restricted the scope of the theory, Ajzen (1985) argued that the theory could also predict non-volitional behavior if it would address perceptions of control over behavioral performance. His inclusion of a perceived behavioral control variable as an additional determinant of intention and behavior established the theory of planned behavior (Ajzen, 1985, 1991). Perceived behavioral control was initially defined as ". . . people's perception of the ease or difficulty of performing the behaviour of interest" (Ajzen, 1991, p. 183), and "compatible with . . . perceived self-efficacy" (p. 184). Consistent with this definition, items widely used to measure perceived behavioral control ask how much control people believe they have over performing a behavior, how easy or difficult they believe performing the behavior will be, or how confident they are that they can perform the behavior.

The proposed equivalence of perceived control, perceived difficulty, and self-efficacy has been the subject of considerable debate. Arguments in that debate for the most part are based on empirical tests of the dimensionality of perceived behavior control. A common finding from such tests is that confidence-framed items and control-framed items load onto separate factors (e.g., Armitage & Conner, 1999; Kraft, Rise, Sutton, & Røysamb, 2005). Importantly, these two factors are often interpreted as indicating "perceived behavioral

control" and "self-efficacy," suggesting a theoretical distinction between the two (Norman & Hoyle, 2004; Terry & O'Leary, 1995). Building on this idea, investigators have used the two item clusters to explore whether perceived behavioral control or self-efficacy offers a better explanation of intention or behavior (e.g., Pertl et al., 2010; Rodgers, Conner, & Murray, 2008).

The contention that perceived behavioral control and self-efficacy are theoretically distinct is unconvincing, however, if based solely on empirical criteria (such as proportions of variance explained) and without careful consideration of what these concepts are supposed to mean. For example, Terry and O'Leary (1995) purported to contrast perceived control and self-efficacy, but only used easy-difficult items to measure self-efficacy. It is not clear, however, why easy-difficult items are best seen as self-efficacy. Indeed, there is evidence that at least in some behavioral domains, easy-difficult is more closely related with attitude (Kraft et al., 2005; Yzer, Hennessy, & Fishbein, 2004) or intention (Rhodes & Courneya, 2003) than with control. Thus, whereas control items often load on two separate factors, this by itself does not irrefutably confirm the conceptual separation of perceived control and self-efficacy. Rhodes and Courneya (2003) warn in this regard against backward theorizing: ". . . items should be created to indicate theoretical concepts; theoretical concepts should not be created to indicate items!" (p. 80).

Fishbein and Ajzen (2010) similarly observe that ". . . although there is good empirical evidence that items meant to assess perceived behavioral control can be separated into two factors, identifying them as self-efficacy expectations and perceived control is misleading and unjustified" (p. 165). They argue that self-efficacy (Bandura, 1997) and perceived behavioral control are conceptually similar; both center on people's perception of whether they can carry out a particular behavior. Consistent with this, reasoned action theory posits that perceived behavioral control/self-efficacy is a latent variable that has two aspects, namely capacity and autonomy. Capacity is indicated by items asking people how certain they are that they can perform a behavior. Autonomy is indicated by items asking people how much they feel that performing a behavior is up to them. Capacity and autonomy can be congruent, but there are situations in which they are not. For example, someone may believe that the decision to climb a tall building is up to him, but feel certain that he cannot do so because he is afraid of heights. Depending on the purpose of the investigation, capacity and autonomy thus can be combined or analyzed separately. Similarly, to enhance perceived behavioral control over a behavior, persuasive messages can focus on skill building, emphasize autonomous decision-making, or do both. The appeal of a multiaspect interpretation of perceived behavioral control is that it clarifies its conceptual definition, and refocuses our attention to the possibility of additive contributions of capacity and autonomy to behavioral prediction rather than superiority of one over the other. It also is a new idea, and thus should be a priority in future research.

The belief basis of perceived behavioral control consists of control beliefs (i.e., the perceived likelihood of having particular resources and opportunities for behavioral performance) and perceived power (i.e., the extent to which those resources and opportunities facilitate or obstruct behavioral performance). Perceived behavioral control is proposed to be the sum of the control beliefs-perceived power product terms. The belief basis of perceived behavior control has received curiously little research attention (see, e.g., Armitage & Conner, 2001). Therefore, and also considering the recent reconceptualization of perceived behavior control, systematic tests of control beliefs offer good opportunities for theoretical advancement.

Explaining Intention

Reviews of studies on determinants of intention have found multiple correlations in the $R = .55-.70$ range (e.g., Albarracín et al., 2001; Armitage & Conner, 2001; Hagger et al., 2002; Rivis &

Sheeran, 2003; van den Putte, 1993). These results are impressive, particularly considering that they are based on studies that differ considerably in inclusion and measurement of predictor variables. At the same time, it should be noted that these multiple correlations reflect the effects of direct measures of attitude, perceived norm, and/or perceived behavioral control on intention. Relatively few studies have examined the role of beliefs in intention formation. Van den Putte (1993), for example, reports that of the 150 independent samples he analyzed, only 18 measured both behavioral beliefs and attitude, and only 13 measured both normative beliefs and subjective norm. The curious neglect of beliefs is disconcerting, because beliefs are the basis of persuasive messages that seek to change behavior.

A possible explanation for this phenomenon is that because of the availability of attitude, perceived norm, perceived behavioral control, and intention measure templates (e.g., Fishbein & Ajzen, 2010), designing measures of these four variables is a fairly straightforward affair. However, determining which beliefs are salient in a particular population is not as straightforward: ". . . although an investigator can sit in her or his office and develop measures of attitudes, perceived norms and [perceived behavioral control], she or he cannot tell you what a given population (or a given person) believes about performing a given behavior. Thus one must go to members of that population to identify salient outcome, normative and [control] beliefs" (Fishbein, 2000, p. 276). Recommendations for belief elicitation procedures are also available, however, (Ajzen & Fishbein, 1980; Fishbein & Ajzen, 2010), and there thus is no good reason for disregarding beliefs if one seeks to explain intention.

Background Factors and the Question of Sufficiency

Beliefs originate from a large number of sources. Interaction with other people, engagement with media messages, growing up in a particular culture, membership of a religious community, and even gender and personality, for example, can all play a role in forming and shaping beliefs about a particular behavior. In the language of reasoned action theory, these variables are background factors, which are possibly but not necessarily related with beliefs. Similarly, background factors do not affect intention and behavior directly, but indirectly through beliefs. Thus, for example, if gender is empirically associated with intention or behavior, gender also should be correlated with beliefs, that is, men and women should hold different beliefs (Fishbein, 1967; Fishbein & Ajzen, 2010). Such findings can usefully inform decisions about which beliefs to target in different gender segments.

The conceptualization of background factors is directly relevant for a persistent debate on the question whether reasoned action variables are sufficient for explaining intention and behavior (for review, see Fishbein & Ajzen, 2010, chapter 9). Relevant for the present discussion of background factors is a substantial body of research that proposed an extension of the theory to better account for intention. Specifically, a number of different variables have been suggested as a fourth determinant variable in addition to attitude, perceived norm, and perceived behavioral control, including, among many others, gender, self-identity, and culture. Such research efforts are commendable to the extent that they promote theoretical development. However, many recommendations for extending reasoned action theory do not start from compelling conceptual arguments, but instead rely on empirical markers such as change in proportion of explained variance. The logic that if a particular variable explains variance in intention, it must be an important predictor has important statistical problems (Trafimow, 2004). A correlation between a particular variable and intention therefore does not conclusively prove that the variable is a predictor of intention and not a background factor.

New Directions and Opportunities for Future Research

The thousands of reasoned action studies now in existence address only a limited number of questions and use only a limited number of methodologies. For example, studies that explain intention far outnumber studies that prospectively examine behavior and studies that examine beliefs; and studies that use survey methodology far outnumber experimental studies. Although survey-based tests of intention usefully show whether in a particular population intention to perform a particular behavior is guided by attitude, perceived norm or perceived behavioral control, belief-based and behavioral analyses are at least as interesting to persuasion scholars. In addition, there are other questions that should appear more prominently on research agendas than they have thus far. Two of these have to do with developing hypotheses about when reasoned action variables will predict which behaviors, and how reasoned action can inform message design.

Predicting Prediction

Reasoned action theory proposes that to predict intention and behavior only a small number of variables need to be considered. Because each behavior is substantively unique, which of these variables most critically guide a particular behavior in a particular population is an empirical question. Clear research recommendations have been developed for identifying those critical variables (e.g., Fishbein & Ajzen, 2010; Fishbein & Yzer, 2003), and there is evidence that interventions that follow these recommendations can effectively change behavior (e.g., Albarracín et al., 2005).

Although the basic assumption of the uniqueness of each behavior is true in principle, the implication that identification of a behavior's critical predictor is an empirical question is not altogether satisfactory. Both for scholarly and intervention purposes, it would be more advantageous if prediction could be predicted, that is, if it would be possible to hypothesize which reasoned action variable will predict a particular behavior in a particular population. There is some evidence that this is a realistic objective. For example, experimental work has corroborated behavior and population features that determine the predictive power of perceived norm (Jacobson, Mortensen, & Cialdini, 2011; Trafimow & Fishbein, 1994).

One can turn to other theory to derive principles that can help understand when specific reasoned action variables will explain behavior (Fishbein & Ajzen, 2010; Weinstein & Rothman, 2005). For example, Lutchyn and Yzer (2011) used construal level theory (Trope & Liberman, 2003) to test the implications of changing the time component of behavioral definitions for the relative importance of behavioral and control beliefs. Construal level theory proposes that people use abstract terms to construe behaviors that are to be performed some time in the future. Construals of such distant behaviors emphasize the "why" aspects of behavior, and describe behavior in terms of the value or desirability of a behavioral outcome, or in reasoned action terms, behavioral beliefs. In contrast, construals of near future behaviors are more concrete and represent the "how" aspect of the behavior. They reflect feasibility of the behavior, or in reasoned action terms, control beliefs. Lutchyn and Yzer (2011) found that the salience of beliefs is a function of time frame, such that when the time component in a behavioral definition moves from the near to the distant future, the salience of behavioral beliefs increases and the salience of control beliefs decreases. These findings have implications for message design. To motivate distant behavior, messages need to address behavioral consequences. For example, a message sent in September to motivate people to get a flu shot right before the flu season's expected onset

in December can emphasize the benefits of getting a flu shot. To affect near future behavior, for example, getting a flu shot this week, messages should include references to control beliefs, for example, information about where one can get free flu shots.

Moving Beyond Message Content

Interventionists can use reasoned action theory to identify the behavioral, normative, and/or control beliefs that guide people's behavior. It is these beliefs that messages should address. The theory thus is a tool for informing message *content*. It was not designed to inform the next necessary question in the message design process; which audiovisual, narrative, duration, and other stylistic message features will change the beliefs addressed in the message? Fishbein and Ajzen (2010) commented thus on the boundaries of reasoned action theory: "Selection of appropriate primary beliefs is perhaps our theory's most important contribution to behavior change interventions. The theory offers little guidance as to the specific strategies that will most effectively bring about the desired changes in behavioral, normative, or control beliefs. Such guidance must come from outside our theory" (p. 367).

Some guidance is available. The literature on communication campaigns, for example, offers excellent overviews of components and design steps of successful campaigns (Rice & Atkin, 2009). Similarly, scholars have addressed the complementary nature of behavior change and message effects theories for the purpose of improving cancer prevention (Cappella, 2006). Such work highlights that message development involves decisions about both content and creative design, and that different theories are to be used to inform each of these decisions. Which theories in particular complement reasoned action theory is a relatively unexplored question, but one that if answered can greatly advance understanding of persuasive messages.

Conclusion

Seen through a reasoned action lens, persuasion is belief-based behavior change. Therefore, the better one understands which beliefs cause behavior by what process, the better able one is to design successful messages. The review presented in this chapter discussed that if used correctly, reasoned action theory can identify the beliefs that explain why people do or do not perform a particular behavior. It also identified a number of issues that if addressed can deepen our understanding of behavioral prediction. Akin to how reasoned action theory was first conceived, to address these issues, an outward-looking strategy that draws on complementary theory will generate greatest progress. The challenge for future research is twofold; more precise predictions about how and when reasoned action variables predict intention and behavior are needed, and in addition, message design strategies that can change these variables need to be identified. These are challenges that promise exciting research, significant theoretical advancement, and effective practical application.

References

Ajzen, I. (1985). From intentions to actions: A theory of planned behavior. In J. Kuhl & J. Beckman (Eds.), *Action-control: From cognition to behavior* (pp. 11–39). Heidelberg, Germany: Springer.

Ajzen, I. (1991). The theory of planned behavior. *Organizational Behavior and Human Decision Processes, 50,* 179–211.

Ajzen, I., & Fishbein, M. (1973). Attitudinal and normative variables as predictors of specific behavior. *Journal of Personality and Social Psychology, 27,* 41–57.

Ajzen, I., & Fishbein, M. (1980). *Understanding attitudes and predicting social behavior.* Englewood Cliffs, NJ: Prentice-Hall.

Ajzen, I., & Fishbein, M. (2008). Scaling and testing multiplicative combinations in the expectancy-value model of attitudes. *Journal of Applied Social Psychology, 38,* 2222–2247.

Albarracín, D., Gillette, J. C., Earl, A. N., Glasman, L. R., Durantini, M. R., & Ho, M. H. (2005). A test of major assumptions about behavior change: A comprehensive look at HIV prevention interventions since the beginning of the epidemic. *Psychological Bulletin, 131,* 856–897.

Albarracín, D., Johnson, B. T., Fishbein, M., & Muellerleile, P. (2001). Theories of reasoned action and planned behavior as models of condom use: A meta-analysis. *Psychological Bulletin, 127,* 142–161.

Albarracín, D., Kumkale, G. T., & Johnson, B. T. (2004). Influences of social power and resources on condom use decisions: A research synthesis. *AIDS Care, 16,* 700–723.

Allport, G. W. (1935). Attitudes. In C. Murchison (Ed.), *Handbook of social psychology* (pp. 798–844). Worcester, MA: Clark University Press.

Armitage, C. J. (2005). Can the theory of planned behavior predict the maintenance of physical activity? *Health Psychology, 24,* 235–245.

Armitage, C. J., & Conner, M. (1999). Distinguishing perceptions of control from self-efficacy: Predicting consumption of a low fat diet using the theory of planned behavior. *Journal of Applied Social Psychology, 29,* 72–90.

Armitage, C. J., & Conner, M. (2001). Efficacy of the theory of planned behavior: A meta-analytic review. *British Journal of Social Psychology, 40,* 471–499.

Armitage, C. J., Conner, M., Loach, J., & Willetts, D. (1999). Different perceptions of control: Applying an extended theory of planned behavior to legal and illegal drug use. *Basic and Applied Social Psychology, 21,* 301–316.

Bandura, A. (1997). *Self-efficacy: The exercise of control.* New York, NY: Freeman.

Blank, M., & Hennessy, M. (2012). A reasoned action approach to HIV prevention for persons with serious mental illness. *The Annals of the American Academy of Political and Social Science, 640,* 173–188.

Brown, N. R., & Sinclair, R. C. (1999). Estimating number of lifetime sexual partners: Men and women do it differently. *Journal of Sex Research, 36,* 292–297.

Budden, J. S., & Sagarin, B. J. (2007). Implementation intentions, occupational stress, and the exercise intention-behavior relationship. *Journal of Occupational Health Psychology, 12,* 391–401.

Cappella, J. N. (2006). Integrating message effects and behavior change theories: Organizing comments and unanswered questions. *Journal of Communication, 56,* S265–S279.

Cialdini, R. B., Reno, R. R., & Kallgren, C. A. (1990). A focus theory of normative conduct: Recycling the concept of norms to reduce littering in public places. *Journal of Personality and Social Psychology, 58,* 1015–1026.

Cooke, R., & French, D. P. (2008). How well do the theory of reasoned action and theory of planned behaviour predict intentions and attendance at screening programmes? A meta-analysis. *Psychology & Health, 23,* 745–765.

Cooke, R., & Sheeran, P. (2004). Moderation of cognition-intention and cognition-behaviour relations: A meta-analysis of properties of variables from the theory of planned behavior. *British Journal of Social Psychology, 43,* 159–186.

Courneya, K. S., & McAuley, E. (1993). Predicting physical activity from intention: Conceptual and methodological issues. *Journal of Sport and Exercise Psychology, 15,* 50–62.

De Bruijn, G. J., Kremers, S. P. J., Schaalma, H., van Mechelen, W., & Brug, J. (2005). Determinants of adolescent bicycle use for transportation and snacking behaviour. *Preventive Medicine, 40,* 658–667.

Dulany, D. E. (1968). Awareness, rules, and prepositional control: A confrontation with S-R behavior theory. In D. Horton & T. Dixon (Eds.), *Verbal behavior and general behavior theory* (pp. 340–387). Englewood Cliffs, NJ: Prentice-Hall.

Falk, E. B., Berkman, E. T., Whalen, D., & Lieberman, M. D. (2011). Neural activity during health messaging predicts reductions in smoking above and beyond self-report. *Health Psychology, 30,* 177–185.

Fielding, K. S., McDonald, R., & Louis, W. R. (2008). Theory of planned behaviour, identity and intentions to engage in environmental activism. *Journal of Environmental Psychology, 28,* 318–326.

Finlay, K. A., Trafimow, D., & Moroi, E. (1999). The importance of subjective norms on intentions to perform health behaviors. *Journal of Applied Social Psychology, 29,* 2381–2393.

Fishbein, M. (1963). An investigation of the relationships between beliefs about an object and the attitude toward that object. *Human Relations, 16,* 233–240.

Fishbein, M. (1967). Attitude and the prediction of behavior. In M. Fishbein (Ed.), *Readings in attitude theory and measurement* (pp. 477–492). New York, NY: Wiley.

Fishbein, M. (2000). The role of theory in HIV prevention. *AIDS Care, 12,* 273–278.

Fishbein, M., & Ajzen, I. (1975). *Belief, attitude, intention, and behavior: An introduction to theory and research.* Reading, MA: Addison-Wesley.

Fishbein, M., & Ajzen, I. (2010). *Predicting and changing behavior: The reasoned action approach.* New York, NY: Psychology Press.

Fishbein, M., & Stasson, M. (1990). The role of desires, self-predictions, and perceived control in the prediction of training session attendance. *Journal of Applied Social Psychology, 20,* 173–198.

Fishbein, M., & Yzer, M. C. (2003). Using theory to design effective health behavior interventions. *Communication Theory, 13,* 164–183.

Gibbons, F. X., Gerrard, M., Blanton, H., & Russell, D. W. (1998). Reasoned action and social reaction: Willingness and intention as independent predictors of health risk. *Journal of Personality and Social Psychology, 74,* 1164–1180.

Giles, M., Liddell, C., & Bydawell, M. (2005). Condom use in African adolescents: The role of individual and group factors. *AIDS Care, 17,* 729–739.

Gollwitzer, P. M. (1999). Implementation intentions: Strong effects of simple plans. *American Psychologist, 54,* 493–503.

Gollwitzer, P. M., & Sheeran, P. (2006). Implementation intentions and goal achievement: A meta-analysis of effects and processes. *Advances in Experimental Social Psychology, 38,* 69–119.

Hagger, M. S., Chatzisarantis, N. L. D., & Biddle, S. J. H. (2002). A meta-analytic review of the theories of reasoned action and planned behavior in physical activity: Predictive validity and the contribution of additional variables. *Journal of Sport and Exercise Psychology, 24,* 3–32.

Hale, J. L., Householder, B. J., & Greene, K. L. (2002). The theory of reasoned action. In J. P. Dillard & M. Pfau (Eds.), *The persuasion handbook: Developments in theory and practice* (pp. 259–286). Thousand Oaks, CA: Sage.

Huebner, D. M., Neilands, T. B., Rebchook, G. M., & Kegeles, S. M. (2011). Sorting through chickens and eggs: A longitudinal examination of the associations between attitudes, norms, and sexual risk behavior. *Health Psychology, 30,* 110–118.

Jacobson, R. P., Mortensen, C. R., & Cialdini, R. B. (2011). Bodies obliged and unbound: Differentiated response tendencies for injunctive and descriptive social norms. *Journal of Personality and Social Psychology, 100,* 433–448.

Keats, M. R., Culos-Reed, S. N., Courneya, K. S., & McBride, M. (2007). Understanding physical activity in adolescent cancer survivors: An application of the theory of planned behavior. *Psycho-oncology, 16,* 448–457.

Kiviniemi, M. T., Voss-Humke, A. M., & Seifert, A. L. (2007). How do I feel about the behavior? The interplay of affective associations with behaviors and cognitive beliefs as influences on physical activity behavior. *Health Psychology, 26,* 152–158.

Kraft, P., Rise, J., Sutton, S., & Røysamb, E. (2005). Perceived difficulty in the theory of planned behaviour: Perceived behavioural control or affective attitude? *British Journal of Social Psychology, 44,* 479–496.

Larimer, M. E., Turner, A. P., Mallett, K. A., & Geisner, I. M. (2004). Predicting drinking behavior and alcohol-related problems among fraternity and sorority members: Examining the role of descriptive and injunctive norms. *Psychology of Addictive Behaviors, 18,* 203–212.

Lee, C., & Green, R. T. (1990). A cross-cultural examination of the Fishbein behavioral intention model. *Journal of International Business Studies, 22,* 289–305.

Lutchyn, Y., & Yzer, M. (2011). Applying Temporal Construal Theory to the Theory of Planned Behavior to examine time frame effects on belief generation. *Journal of Health Communication, 16,* 595–606.

Newell, S., Girgis, A., Sanson-Fisher, R. W., & Savolainen, N. J. (1999). The accuracy of self-reported health behaviors and risk factors relating to cancer and cardiovascular disease in the general population: A critical review. *American Journal of Preventive Medicine, 17,* 211–229.

Norman, P., & Conner, M. (2005). The Theory of Planned Behavior and exercise: Evidence for the mediating and moderating roles of planning on intention-behavior relationships. *Journal of Sport and Exercise Psychology, 27,* 488–504.

Norman, P., & Hoyle, S. (2004). The theory of planned behavior and breast self-examination: Distinguishing between perceived control and self-efficacy. *Journal of Applied Social Psychology, 34,* 694–708.

Pertl, M., Hevey, D., Thomas, K., Craig, A., Ni Chuinneagain, S., & Maher, L. (2010). Differential effects of self-efficacy and perceived behavioral control on intention to perform skin cancer related health behaviors. *Health Education Research, 25,* 769–779.

Rhodes, R. E., & Courneya, K. S. (2003). Investigating multiple components of attitude, subjective norm, and perceived control: An examination of the theory of planned behaviour in the exercise domain. *British Journal of Social Psychology, 42,* 129–146.

Rice, R. E., & Atkin, C. K. (2009). Public communication campaigns: Theoretical principles and practical applications. In J. Bryant & M. B. Oliver (Eds.), *Media effects: Advances in theory and research* (3rd ed., pp. 436–468). New York, NY: Routledge.

Rivis, A., & Sheeran, P. (2003). Descriptive norms as an additional predictor in the theory of planned behaviour: A meta-analysis. *Current Psychology, 22,* 218–233.

Rodgers, W. M., Conner, M., & Murray, T. C. (2008). Distinguishing among perceived control, perceived difficulty, and self-efficacy as determinants of intentions and behaviours. *British Journal of Social Psychology, 47,* 607–630.

Sheeran, P., & Orbell, S. (1998). Do intentions predict condom use? Meta-analysis and examination of six moderator variables. *British Journal of Social Psychology, 37,* 231–250.

Sheeran, P., Orbell, S., & Trafimow, D. (1999). Does the temporal stability of behavioral intentions moderate intention-behavior and past behavior-future behavior relations? *Personality and Social Psychology Bulletin, 25,* 721–730.

Sheeran, P., & Taylor, S. (1999). Predicting intentions to use condoms: A meta-analysis and comparison of the theories of reasoned action and planned behavior. *Journal of Applied Social Psychology, 29,* 1624–1675.

Sheppard, B. H., Hartwick, J., & Warshaw, P. R. (1988). The theory of reasoned action: A meta-analysis of past research with recommendations for modifications and future research. *Journal of Consumer Research, 15,* 325–342.

Terry, D. J., & O'Leary, J. E. (1995). The theory of planned behavior: The effects of perceived behavioural control and self-efficacy. *British Journal of Social Psychology, 34,* 199–220.

Thurstone, L. L. (1928). Attitudes can be measured. *The American Journal of Sociology, 33*, 529–554.

Trafimow, D. (2004). Problems with change in R^2 as applied to theory of reasoned action research. *British Journal of Social Psychology, 43*, 515–530.

Trafimow, D., & Fishbein, M. (1994). The moderating effect of behavior type on the subjective norm-behavior relationship. *Journal of Social Psychology, 134*, 755–763.

Triandis, H. C. (1964). Exploratory factor analyses of the behavioral component of social attitudes. *Journal of Abnormal and Social Psychology, 68*, 420–430.

Trope, Y., & Liberman, N. (2003). Temporal construal. *Psychological Review, 110*, 403–421.

Van den Putte, B. (1993). *On the theory of reasoned action.* Unpublished doctoral dissertation, University of Amsterdam, the Netherlands.

Van den Putte, B., Yzer, M. C., & Brunsting, S. (2005). Social influences on smoking cessation: A comparison of the effect of six social influence variables. *Preventive Medicine, 41*, 186–193.

Van Osch, L., Beenackers, M., Reubsaet, A., Lechner, L., Candel, M., & de Vries, H. (2009). Action planning as predictor of health protective and health risk behavior: An investigation of fruit and snack consumption. *International Journal of Behavioral Nutrition and Physical Activity, 6*, 69.

Warshaw, P. R., & Davis, F. D. (1985). Disentangling behavioral intention and behavioral expectation. *Journal of Experimental Social Psychology, 21*, 213–228.

Webb, T. L., & Sheeran, P. (2006). Does changing behavioral intentions engender behavior change? A meta-analysis of the experimental evidence. *Psychological Bulletin, 132*, 249–268.

Weinstein, N. D. (2007). Misleading tests of health behavior theories. *Annals of Behavioral Medicine, 33*, 1–10.

Weinstein, N. D., & Rothman, A. J. (2005). Revitalizing research on health behavior theories. *Health Education Research, 20*, 294–297.

Wicker, A. W. (1969). Attitudes versus actions: The relationship of verbal and overt behavioral responses to attitude objects. *Journal of Social Issues, 25*, 41–78.

Yzer, M. C. (2007). Does perceived control moderate attitudinal and normative effects on intention? A review of conceptual and methodological issues. In I. Ajzen, D. Albarracin, & R. Hornik (Eds.), *Prediction and change of health behavior: Applying the reasoned action approach* (pp. 107–123). Mahwah, NJ: Erlbaum.

Yzer, M. C., Hennessy, M., & Fishbein, M. (2004). The usefulness of perceived difficulty for health research. *Psychology, Health and Medicine, 9*, 149–162.

Ziegelmann, J. P., Luszczynska, A., Lippke, S., & Schwarzer, R. (2007). Are goal intentions or implementation intentions better predictors of health behavior? A longitudinal study in orthopedic rehabilitation. *Rehabilitation Psychology, 52*, 97–102.

CHAPTER 9

The Elaboration Likelihood Model

Daniel J. O'Keefe

The elaboration likelihood model (ELM) of persuasion is a "dual process" approach to social information-processing phenomena that is focused specifically on persuasion (Petty & Cacioppo, 1986; Petty & Wegener, 1999). The central idea of the ELM is that two different basic kinds of persuasion processes can be engaged, depending on the degree to which the message recipient engages in "elaboration" of (systematic thinking about) information relevant to the persuasive topic. The development of the ELM has broken new ground in the study of persuasion processes, and offers important advances over previous work. In what follows, the nature of elaboration is described, the two persuasion processes are detailed, the ELM's analysis of multiple roles for persuasion variables is described, and directions for future research are sketched.

Elaboration

The ELM suggests that, under different conditions, receivers will vary in the degree to which they are likely to engage in issue-relevant thinking ("elaboration"). Sometimes receivers will engage in a great deal of elaboration—attending carefully to the message's arguments and evidence, reflecting on other arguments they remember, and so forth. But on other occasions, receivers will not do so much thinking about the persuasive message.

The most straightforward means of assessing the amount of elaboration is the "thought-listing" technique: Immediately following the receipt of a persuasive message, receivers are simply asked to list the thoughts that occurred to them during the communication (for a broad review of such techniques, see Cacioppo, von Hippel, & Ernst, 1997). The number of issue-relevant thoughts reported provides at least a rough index of the amount of issue-relevant thinking. And those issue-relevant thoughts can also be classified in various ways, most notably in terms of their favorability to the advocated position.

The degree of elaboration thus forms a continuum, from extremely high elaboration to little or no elaboration. A variety of factors influence the amount of elaboration that message recipients undertake, with these usefully divided into influences on elaboration *motivation* (the desire to engage in issue-relevant thinking) and elaboration *ability* (the capability for issue-relevant thinking).

Elaboration motivation can be influenced by a great many factors, but two can serve here as illustrations. One is the receiver's level of involvement with the persuasive issue, where involvement is understood as the degree of direct personal relevance of the topic to the message recipient. As involvement increases, elaboration motivation increases. That is, as a given issue becomes increasingly personally relevant to a receiver, the receiver's motivation for engaging in thoughtful consideration of that issue increases (e.g., Petty, Cacioppo, & Schumann, 1983).

Second, elaboration motivation is influenced by the receiver's level of need for cognition. "Need for cognition" is an individual-difference variable concerning the degree to which persons engage in and enjoy thinking. As need for cognition increases, elaboration motivation increases (for a review, see Cacioppo, Petty, Feinstein, & Jarvis, 1996, pp. 229–231). That is, people who generally enjoy thinking hard are on the whole more likely to be motivated to process persuasive messages closely.

Elaboration ability is also influenced by a number of different factors. One such influence is the receiver's amount of prior knowledge about the topic. As receivers know more about the topic, they can engage in greater elaboration (e.g., Laczniak, Muehling, & Carlson, 1991). A lack of relevant background knowledge can plainly interfere with one's ability to think carefully about an issue.

A second influence on elaboration ability is the presence of a distraction in the persuasion setting—some distracting stimulus or task. In experimental research, distractions have included such things as having an audio message be accompanied by static or beep sounds, or having receivers monitor a bank of flashing lights. Under conditions that would otherwise produce relatively high elaboration, distraction interferes with such issue-relevant thinking (for a review, see Petty & Cacioppo, 1986, pp. 61–68).

The amount of elaboration in which a receiver engages is influenced jointly by elaboration motivation and elaboration ability. A receiver might have the desire to attend closely to a message (elaboration motivation) but be prevented from doing so (e.g., by the presence of a distraction). When elaboration motivation and ability align, the contrast is striking. Imagine, on the one hand, a low need-for-cognition receiver, encountering a message that's not very involving, on a topic about which the receiver knows relatively little, while keeping one eye on the television set—plainly the recipe for very low elaboration. By contrast, a knowledgeable and high need-for-cognition individual encountering a message on a highly involving topic, with nothing to distract from attending closely to the message, is likely to undertake considerable elaboration.

Now one might be tempted to think that where little or no elaboration is occurring, little or no persuasion can occur, given that the receiver is not very engaged with the message. But the ELM proposes that persuasion can take place at any point along the elaboration continuum, even under conditions of very low elaboration—but it suggests that the nature of persuasion varies depending on the degree of elaboration. This idea is expressed by the ELM's two "routes to persuasion."

Elaboration and the Two Routes to Persuasion

According to the ELM, different kinds of persuasion processes are activated, depending on how much elaboration occurs. To bring out the basic idea, the ELM describes two fundamentally different routes to persuasion: the central route and the peripheral route. As a brief overview: The central route is activated when elaboration is relatively high; when persuasion is achieved through the central route, it comes about through elaboration, that is, through issue-relevant thinking. The peripheral route is activated when elaboration is relatively low; when persuasion is achieved through the peripheral route, it commonly comes about through the receiver's use of mental short-cuts ("heuristics") rather than thoughtful examination of issue-relevant considerations.

The Central Route

In central-route persuasion (i.e., when elaboration is relatively high), the outcomes of persuasive efforts will depend most centrally on the predominant valence of the receiver's issue-relevant thoughts. If the message evokes predominantly negative thoughts about the advocated view, then little or no attitude change is likely to occur. But if the message leads the receiver to have predominantly positive thoughts about the advocated position, then the message is likely to be relatively successful in changing the receiver's attitudes in the desired direction.

Two notable factors influence elaboration valence (the relative positivity of the evoked thoughts). One is whether the message advocates a pro-attitudinal position—one toward which the receiver is already favorably inclined—or a counterattitudinal position. With pro-attitudinal messages, recipients will presumably ordinarily be inclined to have favorable thoughts about the position advocated; when the message advocates a counterattitudinal position, receivers will generally be inclined to have unfavorable thoughts about the advocated view. Thus, everything else being equal, one expects pro-attitudinal messages to evoke predominantly favorable thoughts, and counterattitudinal messages to evoke predominantly unfavorable thoughts.

A second influence on elaboration valence is argument strength, that is, the quality (strength) of the arguments advanced in the message. Under conditions of high elaboration, message recipients are closely scrutinizing the message contents, and the valence of receivers' elaboration will naturally reflect the results of such scrutiny. If close examination of the message reveals weak arguments, dubious reasoning, poor evidence, and the like, predominantly

negative elaboration is likely; if the message is found to contain powerful arguments, sound reasoning, good evidence, and the like, then predominantly positive elaboration is more likely. That is, under conditions of high elaboration, argument quality influences the evaluative direction of elaboration and hence influences persuasive success (e.g., Petty & Cacioppo, 1984; Petty, Cacioppo, & Goldman, 1981; Petty, Cacioppo, & Schumann, 1983).

The Peripheral Route

In peripheral-route persuasion (i.e., when elaboration is relatively low), the outcomes of persuasive efforts do not depend on the receiver's issue-relevant thinking—after all, with low elaboration, there isn't much such thinking. Instead, persuasive effects arise through some other mechanism. A variety of such peripheral-route mechanisms have been suggested, but the one with the greatest research attention is the receiver's use of heuristics, that is, simple rules—which don't require much thinking—for deciding whether to agree with the advocated view. These heuristics are activated by "peripheral cues," extrinsic aspects of the communication situation.

These heuristics are not ordinarily consciously articulated, but the workings of heuristics can be inferred from the observable influence of peripheral cues on persuasive outcomes. The ELM underwrites a specific prediction about the effect of peripheral cues, namely, that the influence of peripheral cues will be greater under conditions of relatively low elaboration likelihood (e.g., lower involvement) or under conditions in which the cue is relatively more salient. The primary evidence for the operation of heuristic principles consists of research results conforming to just such patterns of effect (for some discussion, see Bless & Schwarz, 1999).

One such heuristic is based on the communicator's apparent credibility, and if expressed explicitly, would amount to a principle such as "statements by credible sources can be trusted."

When this heuristic is activated, higher-credibility communicators are more persuasive than lower-credibility communicators. Consistent with ELM expectations, the peripheral cue of credibility has been found to have greater impact on persuasive outcomes when elaboration likelihood is relatively low (e.g., Petty, Cacioppo, & Goldman, 1981; Rhine & Severance, 1970) or when credibility cues are less salient (e.g., Andreoli & Worchel, 1978).

A second heuristic is activated by the recipient's liking for the communicator, and might be expressed as "people I like usually have correct opinions." When this heuristic is activated, liked communicators are more persuasive than disliked communicators. Consistent with ELM expectations, the persuasive advantage of liked communicators over disliked communicators diminishes as involvement increases (e.g., Chaiken, 1980, Experiment 1; Petty, Cacioppo, & Schumann, 1983) or as the salience of liking cues varies (e.g., Chaiken & Eagly, 1983).

A third heuristic is activated by other people's reactions to the message, and can be expressed as a belief such as "if other people believe it, then it's probably true." When this heuristic is employed, the approving reactions of others enhance message effectiveness (and disapproving reactions should impair effectiveness). A number of studies have confirmed the operation of such a consensus heuristic in persuasion (for a review, see Axsom, Yates, & Chaiken, 1987).

As can be seen from these three examples, heuristics are mental shortcuts for message recipients. Rather than engaging in extensive thinking about the message topic and the merits of the arguments, instead receivers can decide what to think by relying on such simple considerations as the communicator's expertise or likeability or the reactions of other people.

The Two Routes Illustrated

A classic illustration of the differences between the central and peripheral routes to persuasion is provided by Petty, Cacioppo, and Goldman's (1981) experiment, in which three factors were varied: the receiver's level of involvement, the expertise of the communicator, and argument quality. The participants were college undergraduates, and the persuasive messages advocated the adoption of senior comprehensive examinations as a college graduation requirement. Involvement was varied by having the message advocate adoption of that requirement either at the receiver's own university (high involvement) or at a distant university (low involvement).

High-involvement receivers were significantly affected by the quality of the arguments (being more persuaded by strong arguments than by weak arguments), but were not significantly influenced by the communicator's degree of expertise. By contrast, low-involvement receivers were more affected by expertise variations (being more persuaded by the high expertise source than by the low) than by variations in argument quality. That is, where receivers were inclined to engage in extensive elaboration (by virtue of involvement), argument quality was more influential than was the peripheral cue of expertise. But where receivers were not inclined to invest the cognitive effort in close scrutiny of the message, the peripheral cue had more influence.

As this study illustrates, persuasion can be obtained either through a central route (involving relatively high elaboration) or through a peripheral route (where little elaboration occurs). But the factors influencing persuasive success are different in the two routes.

It should be emphasized that the two routes to persuasion are not conceived of as two rigidly different categories of persuasion, but rather as prototypical extremes at the ends of an elaboration continuum. For example, at intermediate levels of elaboration, one expects some complex mixture of central-route and peripheral-route processes. Thus the ELM does not claim that (for example) peripheral cues have no influence on persuasive outcomes under conditions of high elaboration, but rather simply that as elaboration increases, the influence of peripheral cues decreases and the influence of elaboration valence increases.

Consequences of the Route to Persuasion

Although persuasion can be achieved either through central or peripheral routes, the ELM emphasizes that these two ways of achieving persuasion are not identical in their consequences. Broadly speaking, the attitude change obtained through central-route persuasion is likely to be more enduring over time, more resistant to counterpersuasion, and more directive of subsequent behavior (for reviews and discussion, see Petty & Cacioppo, 1986, pp. 173–195; Petty, Haugtvedt, & Smith, 1995; Petty & Wegener, 1999, pp. 61–63).

One way of characterizing these effects is to say that central-route persuasion produces stronger attitudes than does peripheral-route persuasion. The attitudes resulting from these two routes might not necessarily be evaluatively any more extreme (for example, central-route and peripheral-route persuasion might yield equally positive attitudes), but those attitudes could differ with respect to attitude strength. (For discussion of strength-related attitude properties and effects, see Bassili, 2008; Farc & Sagarin, 2009; Petty & Krosnick, 1995; Visser, Bizer, & Krosnick, 2006.)

The plain implication for persuaders is that central-route persuasion, though perhaps more difficult to achieve (because it requires ensuring greater elaboration by message recipients), brings long-term benefits, in the form of attitudes that are more stable over time and are more likely to exert an influence on behavior.

Multiple Roles for Persuasion Variables

One important contribution of the ELM to the general understanding of persuasion is its

emphasizing that a given variable might play different roles in persuasion under different conditions. From the perspective of the ELM, a variable might influence persuasion in three general ways. First, it might affect the degree of elaboration (and thus influence the degree to which central-route or peripheral-route processes are engaged). Second, it might serve as a peripheral cue (and so influence persuasive outcomes when peripheral-route persuasion is occurring). Third, it might influence the valence of elaboration (and so influence persuasive outcomes when central-route persuasion is occurring). (Some presentations of the ELM provide a more elaborated list of possible roles [e.g., Petty & Wegener, 1999, p. 51], but the three identified here will serve for present purposes [see O'Keefe, 2002, pp. 164–165].)

The question naturally arises, however, as to exactly *when* a given variable is likely to serve in one or another of these roles. The ELM offers a general rule of thumb for anticipating the likely function for a given variable, based on the overall likelihood of elaboration (Petty, Wegener, Fabrigar, Priester, & Cacioppo, 1993, p. 354). When elaboration likelihood is low, then if a variable affects attitude change, it most likely does so by serving as a peripheral cue. When elaboration likelihood is high, then any effects of a variable on attitude change are likely to come about through influencing elaboration valence. And when elaboration likelihood is moderate, then any effects of a variable on attitude change are likely to arise from affecting the degree of elaboration (as when some aspect of the persuasive situation suggests that closer scrutiny of the message will be worthwhile).

One might wonder about the degree to which this ELM rule of thumb is genuinely informative, because it amounts to little more than a restatement of the distinction between the two routes to persuasion. For instance, the proffered principle says in effect that "when elaboration is low, attitude change happens through peripheral processes and so anything that affects attitude change under such conditions does so by serving as a peripheral cue." This might appear to verge on a tautology, in which by definition something that influences attitude change under conditions of low elaboration must be operating as a peripheral cue. The value of this rule of thumb thus turns on the degree to which one can independently assess whether peripheral or central processes are engaged, and such independent assessments are elusive (as acknowledged by Petty & Briñol, 2006, p. 217).

However, the ELM's analysis does point to distinctive predictions about the different roles of a given variable, predictions derived from the operation of moderating variables. For example, if the physical attractiveness of a communicator in an advertisement is processed as a peripheral cue (and so activates a general liking heuristic), then the nature of the advertised product is unlikely to influence the cue's effects. By contrast, if attractiveness influences elaboration valence because of being processed as an argument, then attractiveness's effects should obtain for some products (namely, those for which attractiveness is a plausible argument, such as beauty products) but not for others (Petty & Briñol, 2006, p. 218). The implication is that by examining the observed effects of a moderator variable, one can distinguish whether a given property is activating a heuristic or influencing elaboration valence.

The larger point to be noticed is that the ELM draws attention to the mistake of thinking that a given variable can influence persuasive outcomes through only one pathway. For example, the credibility of the communicator might serve as a peripheral cue (and so activate a credibility-based heuristic)—but it could also influence the amount of elaboration, as when the communicator's apparent expertise leads receivers to think that it will be worthwhile to pay closer attention to the message's arguments. Recognizing this complexity of persuasion processes represents an especially important contribution of the ELM.

Future Research

As fruitful as the ELM has been as a framework for stimulating research, at least three areas of research deserve future attention: the nature of argument quality, the nature of involvement, and the relationship of central and peripheral processes.

The Nature of Argument Quality

In ELM research, the nature of argument quality (or argument strength) has not been a focus of explicit attention, because argument quality variations have been defined in terms of persuasive effects. That is, a high-quality argument is one that, in pretesting, is relatively more persuasive (compared to a low-quality argument) under conditions of high elaboration.

This way of defining argument quality reflects the role that argument quality has played in ELM research designs. In ELM research, argument quality variations have been used "primarily as a methodological tool to examine whether some other variable increases or decreases message scrutiny, not to examine the determinants of argument cogency per se" (Petty & Wegener, 1998, p. 352). The idea is that if message receivers are sensitive to argument quality variations (as displayed by their being more persuaded by high-quality arguments than by low-quality arguments), then those receivers must have been engaged in close message processing (relatively high elaboration). For example, in Petty, Cacioppo, and Goldman's (1981) classic study discussed earlier, argument quality variations affected persuasive outcomes under conditions of high involvement but not under conditions of low involvement; the inference to be drawn is that under conditions of higher involvement, audiences were more closely processing the message and so were more attentive to argument quality variations.

But a thorough understanding of persuasion processes requires some analysis of the nature of these argument quality variations. As a way of seeing the importance of this matter, consider: What advice would the ELM offer to a persuader presenting a counterattitudinal message to an audience likely to engage in a great deal of elaboration? Presumably the advice would be "use high-quality arguments." But because argument quality has been defined in terms of effects (a high-quality argument is one that persuades under conditions of high elaboration), this advice amounts to saying "to be persuasive under conditions of high elaboration, use arguments that will be persuasive"—which is obviously unhelpful (for some elaboration of this line of reasoning, see O'Keefe, 2002, 2003). And, unfortunately, the experimental messages used in ELM experiments appear to have confounded a great many different appeal variations, making it challenging to identify just which features might have been responsible for the observed effects.

However, research has identified the active ingredient in ELM messages as a variation in the perceived desirability of the outcomes associated with the advocated view (Areni & Lutz, 1988; Hustinx, van Enschot, & Hoeken, 2007; van Enschot-van Dijk, Hustinx, & Hoeken, 2003; see also Johnson, Smith-McLallen, Killeya, & Levin, 2004). So (for example) when receiver involvement is low, the persuasiveness of a message is relatively unaffected by variation in the desirability of the outcomes, whereas when involvement is high, persuasive success is significantly influenced by whether the outcomes are thought to be highly desirable or only slightly desirable. That is, under conditions of high elaboration, receivers are led to have more positive thoughts about the advocated view when the message's arguments indicate that the advocated view will have outcomes that the receivers think are relatively desirable than they do when the arguments point to outcomes that are not so desirable—but this difference is muted under conditions of low elaboration.

That outcome desirability should turn out to be a key determinant of the persuasiveness of

arguments under conditions of high involvement—that is, direct personal relevance—is perhaps not entirely surprising. When the outcomes affect the message recipient directly, the desirability of the outcomes becomes especially important.

The open question is whether *other* message variations might function in a way similar to outcome desirability. That is, are there other quality-related features of persuasive appeals that function as outcome desirability does—features whose variation makes relatively little difference to persuasive outcomes under conditions of low elaboration, but whose variation makes a more substantial difference under conditions of high elaboration?

One candidate that naturally comes to mind is outcome *likelihood*. A general expectancy-value conception of attitudes would suggest that attitudes are a joint function of evaluative judgments (how desirable the attitude object's characteristics are seen to be) and likelihood judgments (the likelihood with which those characteristics are associated with the object). Correspondingly, one might expect that messages varying in the depicted likelihood of outcomes might have effects parallel to those of messages varying in the depicted desirability of outcomes: variation in outcome likelihood might make a greater difference to persuasiveness under conditions of high elaboration than under conditions of low elaboration.

There is not much direct evidence concerning whether the effects of outcome-likelihood variations are moderated in this way by involvement. However, the general research evidence concerning the persuasive effects of outcome-likelihood variation is not very encouraging. Some research finds that outcome-likelihood variations have persuasive effects akin to those of outcome-desirability variations (e.g., Witte & Allen, 2000), but other studies have found very different patterns of effects (e.g., Johnson et al., 2004; Smith-McLallen, 2005). Perhaps only under yet-to-be-discovered conditions do variations in outcome likelihood function in ways akin to outcome desirability.

In any case, the general question remains open: There may be additional quality-related message characteristics—beyond outcome desirability—that enhance message persuasiveness under conditions of high elaboration. Identification of such message properties would represent an important advance in the understanding of persuasion generally and argument quality specifically.

The Nature of Involvement

In persuasion research, the concept of "involvement" has been used by a variety of theoretical frameworks to describe variations in the relationship that receivers have to the message topic. The most notable historical example is social judgment theory's use of the concept of "ego-involvement" (Sherif, Sherif, & Nebergall, 1965). The ELM has extended this tradition in its emphasis on the role of involvement as an influence on elaboration likelihood. But various commentators have suggested distinguishing different kinds of "involvement," on the grounds that different varieties of involvement have different effects on persuasion processes.

For example, Johnson and Eagly (1989) distinguished value-relevant involvement (in which abstract values are engaged) and outcome-relevant involvement (in which concrete short-term outcomes or goals are involved). Their meta-analytic evidence suggested that value-relevant involvement leads receivers to defend their opinions when exposed to counterattitudinal messages, regardless of whether the message contains strong or weak arguments. By contrast, outcome-relevant involvement produces the pattern of effects expected by the ELM, in which variations in argument strength produce corresponding variations in persuasive effects. Johnson and Eagly's argument thus is that the ELM describes the role that one kind of involvement plays in persuasion, namely, outcome-relevant involvement, but does not capture the effects of variations in value-relevant involvement. Petty and

Cacioppo (1990), however, have argued that the same process might underlie these apparently divergent patterns of effect (for some further discussion, see Johnson & Eagly, 1990; Levin, Nichols, & Johnson, 2000; Petty & Cacioppo, 1990; Petty, Cacioppo, & Haugtvedt, 1992; see also Park, Levine, Westermann, Orfgen, & Foregger, 2007).

As another example, Slater (2002) has approached the task of clarifying involvement's role in persuasion not by starting with different kinds of "involvement" but by starting with different kinds of message processing—and then working backward to consider how different kinds of involvement (and other factors) might influence the different sorts of processing. Slater's analysis includes such processing varieties as "outcome-based processing" (motivated by the goal of self-interest assessment), "value-affirmative processing" (motivated by the goal of value reinforcement), and "hedonic processing" (motivated by the goal of entertainment)—with these influenced by, respectively, outcome relevance (akin to "outcome-relevant involvement"), value centrality (akin to "value-relevant involvement"), and narrative interest. Slater (2002, p. 179) thus argues that "simply distinguishing value-relevant involvement from the issue- or outcome-relevant involvement manipulated in ELM research does not go far enough."

The larger point is that involvement (simpliciter) is a concept that is insufficiently well-articulated to do the work asked of it. Although a broad distinction between value-relevant and outcome-relevant involvement has merit, further conceptual and empirical work is surely to be welcomed.

The Relationship of Central and Peripheral Processes

One prominent alternative to the ELM has been Kruglanski and Thompson's (1999b) "uni-model" of persuasion, which suggests that the ELM's two routes to persuasion are in fact not fundamentally different: In each route, receivers try to reach conclusions about what to believe, using whatever evidence is available. In the two persuasion routes, different kinds of evidence are employed (peripheral cues in the peripheral route, message arguments in the central route), but from the point of view of the unimodel, these are not actually two fundamentally different processes. In each route there is a process of reasoning to conclusions based on evidence, and thus a unitary picture—a "unimodel"—will suffice.

This underlying similarity, it is argued, has been obscured in ELM research by virtue of a confounding of the contrast between cue and arguments and the contrast between simple and complex inputs. From the unimodel point of view, both peripheral cues and message arguments can vary in their complexity (ease of processing, brevity, etc.). The argument is that in ELM research, peripheral cues have typically been quite simple and arguments have typically been quite complex. This produces differences in how these two inputs are processed, but (the suggestion is) if cues and arguments are made equally complex, then they will be seen to be processed identically and produce identical effects. This unity of underlying processing thus is taken to undermine the ELM's distinction between the two persuasion processes.

As an illustration of research supporting the unimodel's view, Kruglanski and Thompson (1999b, Study 1) found that when communicator expertise information was relatively lengthy, expertise influenced the attitudes of receivers for whom the topic was personally relevant but not the attitudes of receivers for whom the topic was not relevant. That is, topic relevance and expertise interacted in exactly the same way as topic relevance and argument quality did in earlier ELM studies. The apparent implication is that peripheral cues (such as expertise) and message arguments function identically in persuasion, once the level of complexity of each is equalized. (For some presentations of the unimodel and related research, see Erb & Kruglanski, 2005; Erb, Pierro, Mannetti, Spiegel, & Kruglanski, 2007; Kruglanski, Chen, Pierro, Mannetti, Erb, & Spiegel, 2006;

Kruglanski, Erb, Pierro, Mannetti, & Chun, 2006; Kruglanski & Thompson, 1999a, 1999b.)

The unimodel raises both empirical and conceptual issues concerning the ELM, and these issues are sufficiently complicated that it will take some time to sort them out. (For some discussion of these and related issues, see, e.g., Chaiken, Duckworth, & Darke, 1999; Petty & Briñol, 2006; Petty, Wheeler, & Bizer, 1999; Wegener & Claypool, 1999.) Empirically, it is not yet clear exactly when (or, indeed, whether) the ELM and the unimodel make genuinely different predictions. That is, there is at present some uncertainty about just what sort of empirical findings will represent confirmation of one view and disconfirmation of the other. Consider, for instance, the just-mentioned finding indicating that complex information about source expertise had more influence on persuasive outcomes when the topic was personally relevant to receivers than when it was not (Kruglanski & Thompson, 1999b, Study 1). From a unimodel perspective, this is taken to be inconsistent with the ELM, because the ELM is assumed to expect that source cues will have a smaller influence on persuasion as topic relevance increases. But—bearing in mind that a given variable might affect persuasion through various pathways—the ELM might explain this result in several ways, including the possibility that expertise information was processed as an argument or provoked elaboration of self-generated (as opposed to message) arguments (Petty, Wheeler, & Bizer, 1999, pp. 159–160). The general point is that it is not yet clear whether (or exactly how) the ELM and the unimodel can be made to offer contrasting empirical predictions.

Conceptually, the unimodel points to some aspects of the ELM that are not clear. Consider, for example, the question of whether it is true by definition that peripheral cues are easy to process. If part of the very concept of a peripheral cue is that it is easy to process, then it does not make sense to speak of there being any "confounding" of cues and simplicity—and so the unimodel's suggestion that there might be complex cues is conceptually malformed. On the other hand, if peripheral cues are *not* by definition easy to process, then it becomes more plausible to explore, as the unimodel suggests, the effects of hard-to-process peripheral cues.

In sum, the unimodel has raised valuable issues concerning the ELM. Continuing attention to these issues offers the promise of better-articulated conceptual frameworks and more finely tuned empirical predictions.

The ELM: A Model of Attitude Change, Not Persuasion

The ELM can be placed in a broader context by noticing that it is better described as a theory of attitude change than as a theory of persuasion. To be sure, influencing attitudes is often an important aspect of persuasion. Attitudes influence what products people buy, what policies they prefer, what candidates they favor—and so persuaders often have the goal of ensuring that people have the desired attitudes.

However, attitude change is only part of persuasion. To see the difference, consider that one common challenge persuaders face is the task of getting people to act consistently with their current attitudes. For example, people often have positive attitudes about regular exercise, recycling, energy conservation, and so forth—but nevertheless fail to act consistently with those attitudes. In such cases, persuaders don't need to convince people of the desirability of the action ("Recycling is really a good thing to do"); that is, persuaders don't need to focus on changing attitudes. Instead, the advocate's task is to somehow get people to act on existing attitudes.

A variety of research findings bear on identifying and addressing such persuasive challenges. For example, sometimes the problem may be that normative considerations override personal attitudes ("Nobody else in my neighborhood recycles"), or that people don't know how to perform the behavior ("I'm confused by the different categories of trash"). [Some readers will detect here echoes of the theory of planned behavior and its variants (Fishbein & Ajzen, 2010).] Or perhaps people can be induced to feel hypocritical about their failure to act consistently with their attitudes, with these feelings then motivating subsequent attitude-consistent behavior (e.g., Stone & Fernandez, 2008). Or the problem might be that people haven't thought about exactly how they will perform the behavior, and so encouraging explicit behavioral planning could address the problem (e.g., Gollwitzer & Sheeran, 2006). That is, the larger literature on persuasion offers many resources for addressing the circumstance in which the desired attitudes are in place but the corresponding behavior is not occurring.

To be sure, the ELM is not entirely silent on how persuaders might proceed in such situations. For example, as discussed earlier, some evidence suggests that attitudes shaped through central-route processes are more likely to be expressed in subsequent behavior than are those arising from peripheral-route processes. Correspondingly, one might encourage persuaders to pursue central-route persuasion so as to maximize the chances of subsequent attitude-consistent behavior.

But inducing attitude-consistent behavior is not necessarily always a matter only of strengthening attitudes. Sometimes, even when people have (what appear to be) perfectly strong attitudes, they nevertheless fail to act on them—for example, when they believe themselves incapable of performing the desired action. In such situations, persuaders need guidance not readily supplied by the ELM.

Conclusion

The ELM has proven a remarkably fertile theoretical framework. Its central contribution is the recognition of the variable character of issue-relevant thinking—and from that has flowed a stream of research findings and conceptual insights that has permanently enriched the understanding of persuasion. The model does not offer a comprehensive account of all persuasion-related phenomena, and open questions certainly remain. But the ELM unquestionably represents a significant advance in the study of persuasion.

References

Andreoli, V., & Worchel, S. (1978). Effects of media, communicator, and message position on attitude change. *Public Opinion Quarterly, 42,* 59–70. Retrieved May 1, 2012, from http://www.jstor.org/stable/2748091

Areni, C. S., & Lutz, R. J. (1988). The role of argument quality in the elaboration likelihood model. *Advances in Consumer Research, 15,* 197–203.

Axsom, D., Yates, S., & Chaiken, S. (1987). Audience response as a heuristic cue in persuasion. *Journal of Personality and Social Psychology, 53,* 30–40.

Bassili, J. N. (2008). Attitude strength. In W. D. Crano & R. Prislin (Eds.), *Attitudes and attitude change* (pp. 237–260). New York, NY: Psychology Press.

Bless, H., & Schwarz, N. (1999). Sufficient and necessary conditions in dual-process models: The case of mood and information processing. In S. Chaiken & Y. Trope (Eds.), *Dual-process models in social psychology* (pp. 423–440). New York, NY: Guilford.

Cacioppo, J. T., Petty, R. E., Feinstein, J. A., & Jarvis, W. B. G. (1996). Dispositional differences in cognitive motivation: The life and times of individuals varying in need for cognition. *Psychological Bulletin, 119,* 197–253.

Cacioppo, J. T., von Hippel, W., & Ernst, J. M. (1997). Mapping cognitive structures and processes through verbal content: The thought-listing technique. *Journal of Consulting and Clinical Psychology, 65,* 928–940.

Chaiken, S. (1980). Heuristic versus systematic information processing and the use of source versus message cues in persuasion. *Journal of Personality and Social Psychology, 39,* 752–766.

Chaiken, S., Duckworth, K. L., & Darke, P. (1999). When parsimony fails . . . *Psychological Inquiry, 10,* 118–123.

Chaiken, S., & Eagly, A. H. (1983). Communication modality as a determinant of persuasion: The role of communicator salience. *Journal of Personality and Social Psychology, 45,* 241–256.

Erb, H.-P., & Kruglanski, A. W. (2005). Persuasion: Ein oder zwei processe? [Persuasion: One or two processes?]. *Zeitschrift fur Sozialpsychologie, 36,* 117–133.

Erb, H.-P., Pierro, A., Mannetti, L., Spiegel, S., & Kruglanski, A. W. (2007). Biassed processing of persuasive information: On the functional equivalence of cues and message arguments. *European Journal of Social Psychology, 37,* 1057–1075.

Farc, M. M., & Sagarin, B. J. (2009). Using attitude strength to predict registration and voting behavior in the 2004 US presidential elections. *Basic and Applied Social Psychology, 31,* 160–173.

Fishbein, M., & Ajzen, I. (2010). *Predicting and changing behavior: The reasoned action approach.* New York, NY: Psychology Press.

Gollwitzer, P. M., & Sheeran, P. (2006). Implementation intentions and goal achievement: A meta-analysis of effects and processes. In M. P. Zanna (Ed.), *Advances in experimental social psychology* (vol. 38, pp. 69–120). San Diego, CA: Elsevier Academic Press.

Hustinx, L., van Enschot, R., & Hoeken, H. (2007). Argument quality in the elaboration likelihood model: An empirical study of strong and weak arguments in a persuasive message. In F. H. van Eemeren, J. A. Blair, C. A. Willard, & B. Garssen (Eds.), *Proceedings of the sixth conference of the International Society for the Study of Argumentation* (pp. 651–657). Amsterdam: Sic Sat.

Johnson, B. T., & Eagly, A. H. (1989). Effects of involvement on persuasion: A meta-analysis. *Psychological Bulletin, 106,* 290–314.

Johnson, B. T., & Eagly, A. H. (1990). Involvement and persuasion: Types, traditions, and the evidence. *Psychological Bulletin, 107,* 375–384.

Johnson, B. T., Smith-McLallen, A., Killeya, L. A., & Levin, K. D. (2004). Truth or consequences: Overcoming resistance to persuasion with positive thinking. In E. S. Knowles & J. A. Linn (Eds.), *Resistance and persuasion* (pp. 215–233). Mahwah, NJ: Erlbaum.

Kruglanski, A. W., Chen, X., Pierro, A., Mannetti, L., Erb, H.-P., & Spiegel, S. (2006). Persuasion according to the unimodel: Implications for cancer communication. *Journal of Communication, 56,* S105–S122. doi: 10.1111/j.1460-2466.2006.00285.x

Kruglanski, A. W., Erb, H.-P., Pierro, A., Mannetti, L., & Chun, W. Y. (2006). On parametric continuities in the world of binary either ors. *Psychological Inquiry, 17,* 153–165.

Kruglanski, A. W., & Thompson, E. P. (1999a). The illusory second mode or, the cue is the message. *Psychological Inquiry, 10,* 182–193.

Kruglanski, A. W., & Thompson, E. P. (1999b). Persuasion by a single route: A view from the unimodel. *Psychological Inquiry, 10,* 83–109.

Laczniak, R. N., Muehling, D. D., & Carlson, L. (1991). Effects of motivation and ability on ad-induced cognitive processing. In R. Holman (Ed.), *Proceedings of the 1991 conference of the American Academy of Advertising* (pp. 81–87). New York, NY: D'Arcy Masius Benton and Bowles.

Levin, K. D., Nichols, D. R., & Johnson, B. T. (2000). Involvement and persuasion: Attitude functions for the motivated processor. In G. R. Maio & J. M. Olson (Eds.), *Why we evaluate: Functions of attitudes* (pp. 163–194). Mahwah, NJ: Erlbaum.

O'Keefe, D. J. (2002). *Persuasion: Theory and research* (2nd ed.). Thousand Oaks, CA: Sage.

O'Keefe, D. J. (2003). Message properties, mediating states, and manipulation checks: Claims, evidence, and data analysis in experimental persuasive message effects research. *Communication Theory, 13,* 251–274.

Park, H. S., Levine, T. R., Westermann, C. Y. K., Orfgen, T., & Foregger, S. (2007). The effects of argument quality and involvement type on attitude formation and attitude change: A test of dual-process and social judgment predictions. *Human Communication Research, 33,* 81–102.

Petty, R. E., & Briñol, P. (2006). Understanding social judgment: Multiple systems and processes. *Psychological Inquiry, 17,* 217–223.

Petty, R. E., & Cacioppo, J. T. (1984). The effects of involvement on responses to argument quantity and quality: Central and peripheral routes to persuasion. *Journal of Personality and Social Psychology, 46,* 69–81.

Petty, R. E., & Cacioppo, J. T. (1986). *Communication and persuasion: Central and peripheral routes to attitude change.* New York, NY: Springer-Verlag.

Petty, R. E., & Cacioppo, J. T. (1990). Involvement and persuasion: Tradition versus integration. *Psychological Bulletin, 107,* 367–374.

Petty, R. E., Cacioppo, J. T., & Goldman, R. (1981). Personal involvement as a determinant of argument-based persuasion. *Journal of Personality and Social Psychology, 41,* 847–855.

Petty, R. E., Cacioppo, J. T., & Haugtvedt, C. P. (1992). Ego-involvement and persuasion: An appreciative look at the Sherifs' contribution to the study of self-relevance and attitude change. In D. Granberg & G. Sarup (Eds.), *Social judgment and intergroup relations: Essays in honor of Muzafer Sherif* (pp. 147–174). New York, NY: Springer-Verlag.

Petty, R. E., Cacioppo, J. T., & Schumann, D. (1983). Central and peripheral routes to advertising effectiveness: The moderating role of involvement. *Journal of Consumer Research, 10,* 135–146. Retrieved May 1, 2012, from http://www.jstor.org/stable/2488919

Petty, R. E., Haugtvedt, C. P., & Smith, S. M. (1995). Elaboration as a determinant of attitude strength: Creating attitudes that are persistent, resistant, and predictive of behavior. In R. E. Petty & J. A. Krosnick (Eds.), *Attitude strength: Antecedents and consequences* (pp. 93–130). Mahwah, NJ: Erlbaum.

Petty, R. E., & Krosnick, J. A. (Eds.). (1995). *Attitude strength: Antecedents and consequences.* Mahwah, NJ: Erlbaum.

Petty, R. E., & Wegener, D. T. (1998). Attitude change: Multiple roles for persuasion variables. In D. T. Gilbert, S. T. Fiske, & G. Lindzey (Eds.), *Handbook of social psychology* (4th ed., Vol. 1, pp. 323–390). Boston, MA: McGraw-Hill.

Petty, R. E., & Wegener, D. T. (1999). The elaboration likelihood model: Current status and controversies. In S. Chaiken & Y. Trope (Eds.), *Dual-process models in social psychology* (pp. 41–72). New York, NY: Guilford.

Petty, R. E., Wegener, D. T., Fabrigar, L. R., Priester, J. R., & Cacioppo, J. T. (1993). Conceptual and methodological issues in the elaboration likelihood model of persuasion: A reply to the Michigan State critics. *Communication Theory, 3,* 336–362.

Petty, R. E., Wheeler, S. C., & Bizer, G. Y. (1999). Is there one persuasion process or more? Lumping versus splitting in attitude change theories. *Psychological Inquiry, 10,* 156–163.

Rhine, R. J., & Severance, L. J. (1970). Ego-involvement, discrepancy, source credibility, and attitude change. *Journal of Personality and Social Psychology, 16,* 175–190.

Sherif, C. W., Sherif, M., & Nebergall, R. E. (1965). *Attitude and attitude change: The social judgment-involvement approach.* Philadelphia: W. B. Saunders.

Slater, M. D. (2002). Involvement as goal-directed strategic processing: Extending the elaboration likelihood model. In J. P. Dillard & M. Pfau (Eds.), *The persuasion handbook: Developments in theory and practice* (pp. 175–194). Thousand Oaks, CA: Sage.

Smith-McLallen, A. (2005). *Is it true? (When) does it matter? The roles of likelihood and desirability in argument judgments and attitudes.* (Doctoral dissertation). Retrieved from UMI. (UMI No. AAT-3187759)

Stone, J., & Fernandez, N. C. (2008). To practice what we preach: The use of hypocrisy and cognitive dissonance to motivate behavior change. *Social and Personality Psychology Compass, 2,* 1024–1051.

van Enschot-van Dijk, R., Hustinx, L., & Hoeken, H. (2003). The concept of argument quality in the elaboration likelihood model: A normative and empirical approach to Petty and Cacioppo's "strong" and "weak" arguments. In F. H. van Eemeren, J. A. Blair, C. A. Willard, & A. F. Snoeck Henkemans (Eds.), *Anyone who has a view: Theoretical contributions to the study of argumentation* (pp. 319–335). Amsterdam: Kluwer.

Visser, P. S., Bizer, G. Y., & Krosnick, J. A. (2006). Exploring the latent structure of strength-related attitude attributes. In M. P. Zanna (Ed.), *Advances in experimental social psychology* (Vol. 38, pp. 1–68). San Diego, CA: Elsevier Academic Press.

Wegener, D. T., & Claypool, H. M. (1999). The elaboration continuum by any other name does not smell as sweet. *Psychological Inquiry, 10,* 176–181.

Witte, K., & Allen, M. (2000). A meta-analysis of fear appeals: Implications for effective public health campaigns. *Health Education and Behavior, 27,* 591–615.

CHAPTER 10

Affect and Persuasion

James Price Dillard and Kiwon Seo

ognitive approaches to understanding human thought and action have embraced a model of mind-as-computer (Miller, 2003). Indeed, in areas such as artificial intelligence, one of the primary tools of the trade is computer simulation. The mind-as-computer metaphor pointed the way to understanding persuasive processes in terms of input processes, comprehension, associative memory, decision making, depth of processing, and recall: All of which led to improved understanding of how messages create change in individuals. But, as data accrued and theoretical boundaries were tested, it became apparent that something crucial was missing: Computers didn't feel. In sharp contrast, humans are often, perhaps always, experiencing some kind of affect. Some research has shown that pre-existing moods caused research participants to respond to persuasive messages in very different ways. Other lines of inquiry established that the feelings produced by persuasive messages undergird purchasing behaviors, voting, and health decisions.

What is meant by affect? The first section of this chapter reviews how that term has been used. The theoretical perspectives that correspond with different usage are also considered. The second segment explores questions of message design and message effects as they pertain to affect. It aims to illustrate the issues that are most central to research on emotion and persuasion. The third and final portion considers what future research might look like by focusing attention on practices and ideas that have retarded research as well as those that are likely to yield the greatest benefit as we move forward.

Conceptions of Affect

Affect is an umbrella term that is meant to encompass feelings of all sorts. Beneath that umbrella lie some important distinctions that implicitly and explicitly guide the questions that researchers ask about affect as well as their corresponding answers. Gaining an appreciation of the research requires a closer examination of the various ways in which affect has been conceptualized.

Bipolar Valence

One approach to thinking about affect is in terms of valence, where valence means a contrast between good and bad or pleasant and unpleasant. The strongest version of the valence perspective is bipolar model. On this view, affect is invariably located at some point on a continuum that ranges from positive at one end of the scale and negative at the other. Here, the underlying theoretical concept of affect is hydraulic: For every unit of good feeling that accrues to an individual, one unit of bad feeling is displaced.

Categorical Valence

A less stringent assumption can be seen in studies in which good and bad feelings are considered separately, as when research participants are asked how good they feel and, in a separate question, how bad they feel (e.g., Watson & Clark, 1994). In these cases, the conceptual relationship between valenced categories is one of conceptual independence. Studying the effects of emotion on persuasion typically means using positive and negative feelings as predictors.

Valence Plus Arousal

Another tradition of affect research expands on the valence-only models by adding an arousal dimension. These pleasure-arousal (PA) models view valence as the hedonic tone of the experience and arousal as the subjective experience of energy versus lassitude. Together, pleasure and arousal are thought to define "core" or elemental aspects of all affective experience (Russell & Feldman Barrett, 1999). Some theorists see value in asserting the existence of an affective circumplex. Pragmatically, this means that pleasure and arousal are orthogonal to one another. Any and all affects are arrayed in a circle defined by terms that are roughly equidistant from the point at which the two dimensions cross. Thus, all affects can be understood in terms of their location. In this view, depression is defined in terms of unpleasantness and low arousal. Joy is both pleasant and energetic. One inarguable problem for the PA models lie in the placement of anger

and fear, both of which occupy the same space in the unpleasant–high arousal quadrant of the circumplex. They have also been justly criticized as atheoretical in that they are inductive findings derived entirely from the application of dimension reduction algorithms to judgments of the frequency or similarity of affect words. Despite these shortcomings, the PA models have maintained a place in the research literature for 40 or more years.

Discrete Emotions and Appraisal Theories

In simple terms, the discrete emotions approach casts affect as a set of qualitatively distinct states that vary in intensity. Individuals may experience more or less happiness, sadness, or jealousy, but each emotion is categorically different from every other emotion. One way in which they are distinct is their causes.

Cognitive appraisal theories are frameworks for understanding discrete emotions. There are several such theories, but they all agree that emotions arise from a particular form of cognition known as appraisals (Scherer, Schorr, & Johnstone, 2001). At the broadest level, appraisals are judgments of the extent to which relevant aspects of the environment are configured so as to promote or inhibit an individual's goals, where goals range in abstraction from survival to arriving at work on time. When the person-environment relationship is seen as relevant and goal congruent, positive emotions follow. Conversely, perceptions of relevance and goal incongruence yield negative emotions. But, there is a host of other appraisals too that, in combination, create unique constellations of appraisals that define different emotions. For instance, joy/happiness derives from the belief that (1) some event has transpired that is (2) compatible with a previously existing goal (e.g., Roseman, 2001). Guilt is the product of knowledge that one has failed to meet some personally relevant standard for behavior. Other possible appraisals might be expressed as the answers to questions such as: How certain is the event (e.g., past vs. future)? What is the cause (e.g., self vs. other)? Can I control it (e.g., high vs. low)? Was it fair/legitimate (e.g., high vs. low)? Emotion theorists disagree about how the content and number of appraisals that are required for a theory of emotion. However, they agree on the larger point that each of the emotions results from an exclusive pattern of antecedent judgments.

Emotions themselves can be thought of as distinctive, patterned responses that are observable in six domains.

- One of them is *subjective experience.* Fear feels different from anger, which feels different from elation.
- Emotions are also represented in the *physiological domain,* which includes changes in: blood flow to different areas of the body, blood pressure, heart rate, nervous system activation, and muscle tension.
- *Neurological activity* in distinct brain regions is associated with different emotions (Phan, Wager, Taylor, & Liberzon, 2002).
- Emotions correspond with alterations in *expression.* The most obvious of these alterations are facial expressions, but other aspects of behavior, such as gait and body lean, are expressive as well. This point underscores an often unappreciated feature of emotion: They are not merely internal phenomena. Rather, emotional states produce behaviors that are seen and interpreted by others.
- Emotions bring about changes in *cognition.* Fear, for example, narrows the perceptual field and focuses attention on the threatening stimulus. Happiness enables associations across conceptual categories.
- Emotions prompt change in the realm of *motivation.* Although all emotions energize behavioral tendency in terms of approach or avoidance (except, perhaps, contentment),

the motivations associated with particular emotions are best conceptualized at a more specific level. Disgust causes people to recoil, hope prompts engagement, and team pride encourages embrace. In other words, each emotion is functionally different and behaviorally specific form of approach or avoidance.

One important question that has been raised about appraisal models is the order in which the cognitive judgments occur. Lazarus (1991) draws a line between two groups of judgments: Primary appraisals—relevance and goal congruity—have to do with the nature and significance of the event. Secondary appraisals, which include notions of accountability and coping potential, have more to do with defining the options for behavioral response. Another writer, Scherer (1984), suggests that appraisals are sequenced such that they move from rudimentary evaluations, such as novelty and the intrinsic pleasantness of the event, through more cognitively complex judgments, including cause, power, and legitimacy. His multistep model does not require that every appraisal take place. Steps can be skipped. But, the overall process is thought to occur in a strict order. Whether one supposes two-steps or several in the appraisal process, the assumption that appraisals are ordered implies questions concerning the speed at which the process unfolds.

An answer can be had by turning attention to the function of emotions. From an evolutionary perspective, emotions are decision-making programs that accept input in terms of appraisal information, then output directions for behavior. They are designed, evolutionarily speaking, to provide adaptive solutions to problems that occurred with regularity in the physical and social environment that produced *homo sapiens* (Tooby & Cosmides, 2008). A key part of the argument here is that those problems were recurrent. Though they might take many different forms, threats to individuals' well-being occurred with reliable frequency. And, obstacles to goal achievement presented themselves on a regular basis. Due to the persistence of these problems, humans developed emotions as a standardized means for recognizing and addressing them. One of the primary advantages of emotions over cognition is their speed. Relatively speaking, emotions are very fast. This can be a distinct benefit when circumstances require an immediate response. It may prove disadvantageous when an immediate impulse calls for behavior in one direction, but a more considered examination of the situation suggests the reverse. Because persuasive messages so often prompt several emotional and cognitive responses, studying persuasive effects requires that researchers recognize and test for multiple, possibly conflicting, reactions to messages.

Understanding Persuasion and Emotion

An Appraisal Model of Persuasion

As previously described, the focus of appraisal theories is the link between a specific type of cognition (i.e., appraisals) and a particular type of affective response (i.e., emotions). The theoretical machinery designed to explain that linkage is now well-developed and widely accepted. But, theories of appraisal are not theories of persuasion. To render them applicable to the issues that are the focus of this volume, persuasion researchers have attempted to extend the framework at both ends of the appraisal-emotion sequence (see Figure 10.1). For example, messages may be viewed as representations of past, current, or future environments such that they instigate appraisals. Indeed, manipulations of message content to achieve variations in valence and probability of an outcome are remarkably similar to appraisals of goal congruence and relevance (i.e., Lazarus's primary appraisals). However, where appraisal research emphasizes the overall content of the circumstances, persuasion inquiry has recognized the importance of noncontent features such as style and structure (e.g., Shen & Bigsby, this volume). The model in Figure 10.1. also extends the appraisal process by considering standard persuasion outcomes—beliefs, attitudes, intentions, and behavior—as potential consequences of emotion (see chapter 4 in this volume for a discussion of the relationships among various persuasion outcomes). These additions have allowed researchers to pose theoretically engaging questions such as: What message features provoke emotional response? How exactly do emotions influence persuasion? The next two sections examine those questions in more detail.

Figure 10.1   An Appraisal Model of Persuasion

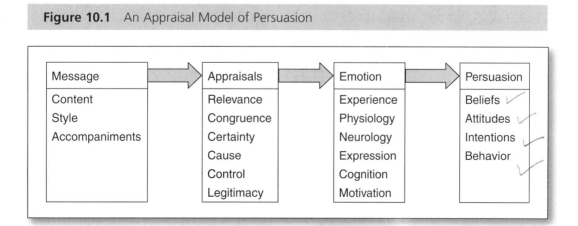

Message Features That May Evoke Emotions

Content

As Shen and Bigsby (chapter 2 of this volume) note, content can be thought of as the topic of a message, the theme of an appeal, or, in some cases, the story that is being told. Appraisal theory is especially useful for identifying message content that might arouse emotion. Table 10.1. presents a summary of appraisals and their corresponding emotions at two levels of abstraction. *Molar* appraisals are global summaries of the cognitions that precede emotion. They are often helpful shorthand, but only insofar as they are used with awareness that they summarize a more precise and complex set of judgments. The column labeled *molecular* illustrates this point by offering a more detailed description of their underlying components. Both are useful for understanding the antecedents of emotional arousal and, hence, for message design. However, there are at least two respects in which Table 10.1. is limited.

For one, controversy regarding what should be counted as an emotion and what should not is

unlikely to be resolved in the near future. Even so, probably there is agreement that the table is missing some elements that might be important to the study of persuasion and affect. For example, a more exhaustive account would include the self-conscious emotions of guilt, shame, pride, and embarrassment. Because these feelings may figure prominently in consequential contexts such as democratic action (Iyer, Schmader, & Lickel, 2007) and the radicalization of terrorists (McCauley & Moskalenko, 2008), they warrant the attention of persuasion researchers. Another set of missing entries in Table 10.1. is those emotions that are not experienced, but only anticipated. Lindsey, Yun, and Hill (2007) offer a case in point when they demonstrate that anticipated guilt may provide the motivation for helping unknown others (see also Wang, 2011). Thus, Table 10.1. is intended as an illustration, one that is helpful primarily for its heuristic value.

The distance between events and appraisals also merits mention. Whereas it is tempting to assume that audience members generally grasp the intended meaning of messages, such a presumption can be wildly off the mark. One classic example can be seen in the literature on fear appeals, which for many years simply assumed

Table 10.1 Emotions and Their Cognitive Antecedents

Emotions	Appraisals	
	Molar	**Molecular**
Fear	Danger	High probability of severe harm
Anger	Social offense	Unwarranted obstruction of goal
Sadness	Loss	Irrevocable failure to meet goal
Happiness	Progress	Acute movement toward goal
Hope	Potential progress	Change in the likelihood of goal achievement
Contentment	Satisfaction	Goal has been met

Source: Adapted from "The persuasive influence of emotion in cancer prevention and detection messages," by J. P. Dillard and R. Nabi, 2006, *Journal of Communication, 56,* p. 123-139. Copyright 2006 by Wiley. Adapted with permission.

that message content that was considered scary by the message designer would be fear-inducing in the message recipient. When attention was given to the gap between message content and emotional response, it became clear that threat appeals, rather than fear appeals, would be a more appropriate title for that research literature because that terminology avoids conflating message features with their expected effects (see chapter 12 in this volume). As appraisal theory makes plain, any given message may evoke distinct emotional effects in different recipients. The presentation of specific message content does not guarantee evocation of particular emotions.

Style

Whereas message content refers to *what* the message is about, style is *how* that content is expressed. Classically, this has meant a focus on language. The advent of mediated messages, however, has broadened the meaning of style to include ideas such as editing, point of view, and pacing.

With regard to language, one of the most prolific areas of inquiry has been that of framing. This is the idea that stylistic variations shape understanding by selecting, then making salient, certain aspects of a perceived reality to the exclusion of other elements (Entman, 1993). The concept is broad enough that it now refers to several distinct lines of research. One of these draws primarily from the tradition of journalism and mass communication. To wit, news coverage is *thematically framed* when it emphasizes context broadly by presenting evidence that is collective, abstract, and general. *Episodically framed* news stories focus on concrete events and specific cases (note the parallels here with research on narrative; see chapter 13 in this volume).

Although most existing research on news framing hews to a cognitive perspective, more recent work highlights emotional reactions. For instance, Aarøe's (2011) analysis of news coverage of a controversial Danish law revealed that episodic framing produced stronger expressions

of compassion, pity, anger, and disgust (relative to thematic framing). The same pattern, for the same emotions, has been reported for persuasive messages that make an explicit case against mandatory minimum sentencing (Gross, 2008). Major's (2011) data show heightened anger and diminished happiness for thematically framed messages about lung cancer and obesity. More complex findings appear in Gross and D'Ambrosio (2004), who describe framing effects on responses to the 1992 Los Angeles riots that are contingent on person factors such as political orientation (liberal vs. conservative). After reading a message that emphasized individual responsibility, conservatives experienced more anger than liberals. The reverse pattern held the two groups consumed a message that highlighted the situational causes of the riots. These statistical interactions underscore the appraisal theory notion that emotional responses are the result of the interplay between stimulus and person. Hence, while message features *may* produce main effects, theory and research indicate that it would be ill-advised to expect simplicity as a regular occurrence.

The term *framing* has also been used to distinguish messages that contrast the potential for favorable outcomes with those that highlight undesirable consequences. More specifically, *gain-framed* messages emphasize the benefits of compliance with the advocacy, which may include avoiding harm. Appeals that are *loss-framed* highlight the unattractive consequences of failure to comply or the potential loss of attaining wanted outcomes. Although the genesis of this distinction lies in Kahneman and Tversky's (1979) prospect theory, its' application to persuasion is appreciably different from their work on decision-making (O'Keefe & Jensen, 2006).

Only a few studies have investigated the ability of gain- and loss-framed appeals to evoke affect. Millar and Millar (2000) report that gain frames produced more favorable reactions than did loss frames. However, their bipolar measure of affect rendered it impossible to tease out the effects of frame on emotions of positive and negative feelings independent of one another. Similarly, Schneider et al. (2001) assessed only negative affects, fear and anxiety, which precluded the possibility of testing for an effect of gain-framing on positive emotions. Studies that utilized a discrete emotions approach present a clearer picture. Shen and Dillard (2007) describe positive effects of gain (vs. loss) framing on happiness and negative effects on disgust, anger, fear, and sadness. Cho and Boster (2008) found functionally identical results for the same set of emotions. At first blush, this overall pattern of results might appear to be most parsimoniously interpreted by the valence-only model of affect. However, to do so would be to overlook important variation with the categories of positive and negative, as well as the unique effects of discrete emotions on persuasion.

Accompaniments

All persuasive messages contain or imply content. Even seemingly vacuous advertisements that present no more than a brand name on a blank page are understood to be promoting a particular product or service. There are other message features, such as imagery, that may accompany message content even though they do not stand on their own. The choice of the term *accompaniments* is not intended to imply triviality. In fact, it may be that they are capable of powerful effects on the elicitation of emotion. Nonetheless, they are mainly used to support or amplify the verbal portions of messages.

Probably the most extensive theoretical analysis of imagery is offered by Zillmann's (1999) exemplification theory, which posits that individuals form and maintain beliefs about phenomena based on samplings of direct or indirect experience. Exemplars are defined as informational units that are representative of some phenomena. For instance, a news story about a particular smoker may exemplify the category of persons who smoke. A series of studies demonstrates that the addition of a picture to a news story is sufficient to elevate perceptions of risk of melanoma, farm failure, roller coasters, and tick-borne diseases (the findings are summarized in Zillmann, 2006). Although many persuasive efforts target outcomes other than beliefs about risk, Zillmann's data imply the potential for a broader array of effects, including emotional arousal. Indeed, Banerjee, Greene, and Yanovitzky's (2011) research shows a dosage effect of images on surprise such that before-and-after images of cocaine users provoked more surprise as a function of the number of images.

There are features of accompaniments that may themselves be considered stylistic. For example, the size of an image may influence emotional arousal. Research using clips of people engaged in potentially arousing activities, such as piloting a fighter plane and driving in the Indianapolis 500, reported that viewers were more excited and perceived more danger when watching the clips on larger versus small screens (Lombard, Reich, Grabe, Bracken, & Ditton, 2000).

Research Designs and the Elicitation of Affect

Generally speaking, there are two kinds of research paradigms used to study persuasion and affect. In the first, messages are designed with the intention of provoking particular emotions. For example, fear/threat appeals may contain content that describes the likelihood and severity of some hazard if the message recipient fails to comply with the advocacy. Research designs that vary message features for the purpose of eliciting emotion may be referred to as *message-induced affect* approaches. These designs and their corresponding theory focus on pathos as a rhetorical proof or, equivalently, the study of emotional appeals.

Of course, even very brief messages vary on a multitude of dimensions including content, structure, pacing, language, imagery, and so on. Such complexity greatly complicates the problem of causal inference. Which message features are responsible for evoking the intended emotions?

And, when other feelings are created, which message features brought them about? Some traction on the inference problem can be gained by including multiple messages of any given sort in the research. If they comprise a representative set, one should expect some consistency of effects across the set for the message feature under study. To the extent that the other message features are really unimportant, they should show little or no consistency of effect.

A different research paradigm separates the message from the affect induction altogether (e.g., Anghelcev & Sar, 2011). One common instantiation of this approach is the Life Event Inventory Task (Schwarz & Clore, 1983), an experimental procedure in which participants are asked to recall and write briefly about a past event that caused them to experience a particular emotion. Subsequently, participants are presented with a persuasive message. The phrase *message-irrelevant affect* has been used to describe these research designs in order to emphasize that the induced emotions have no logical connection to the message. Indeed, one key feature of many investigations is an effort to obfuscate in the minds of the participants any perceived linkage between the affect induction and the persuasive message. This is usually achieved by informing participants that they are taking part in two unrelated studies, one that deals with emotional memories and one that focuses on something else, such as message evaluation.

From the standpoint of causal inference, procedures like the Life Event Inventory Task are attractive in that specific emotions clearly occur prior to message processing. One can then presumably draw uncluttered inferences concerning how emotions influence message processing. This is an interesting question, but it is different from that of how message-induced emotions might bring about persuasion. And, of course, many communication researchers are less interested in supposedly pure manipulations of emotion and more concerned with how the affect that is induced by one message might shape

processing of a subsequent persuasion effect. For example, Chang (2011) examined how affect induced by a magazine editorial influenced reactions to an advertisement that was presented after the editorial. Because of its correspondence with real-world media contexts, the use of messages to evoke feelings in message-irrelevant affect designs enhances external validity. However, they also present challenges to internal validity as a result of the complexity of the affect-inducing stimulus.

The Effects of Affect

Evidence of Effects

For at least two millennia, students of suasory discourse have embraced the idea that emotions can persuade (Aristotle, 2007). Evidence of this point can be seen in the analysis of emotional appeals by early rhetoricians, including Aristotle, and can be traced through history to the present time. But, the more nuanced question—how should the emotion-persuasion link be analyzed and understood?—is still under debate. There are several options to consider. From the perspective of the dimensional valence model, the affects vary along a single dimension (positive vs. negative) and should be tested accordingly. That is, researchers should measure affective responses on a series of semantic differential scales, then correlate the sum of those scales with the persuasion outcome of interest. The categorical valence model directs researchers to similar options, except that positive and negative affects are measured independently of one another and treated as two separate predictors. The pleasure-arousal model, also a dimensional model, ordains the use of two sets of bipolar scales and, thus, two continuous predictors: Pleasant (vs. unpleasant) and arousal (vs. subdued). The discrete emotions position insists that each emotion is defined by a different function and different response patterns. Thus, emotions must be measured individually, and their effects on persuasion must be evaluated using methods that allow for unique effects to manifest themselves.

To date, there are many existing studies that test the relationship between affect and persuasion. Only a subset has produced evidence that can be used to differentiate the various models of affect. Studies that assess emotions on only bipolar scales must be excluded because the measurement procedures assume, rather than test, the structure of affect. If affects are measured on a positive versus negative scale, researchers cannot then unscramble the differences between sadness and anger or hope and happiness because those distinctions are lost at the moment of data collection. The same problem extends to pleasure-arousal models, except that there are two dimensions rather than one. In fact, the only data that can be used to empirically evaluate the worth of the different models come from investigations that utilize discrete emotion procedures. It is possible to aggregate specific emotions into larger categories, such as pleasant and unpleasant, but impossible work in the other direction, that is, to disassemble global affective judgments into discrete elements.

There are four types of evidence in the persuasion literature that distinguish the discrete emotions model from the alternatives. Each is illustrated next using investigations from different contexts:

1. *There is variation in the effects of negative emotions.* Although public opinion remains divided about the wisdom of a Western-led war with Iraq, there is no question that a sizeable portion of the U.S. population is critical of their government's action. In a survey of undergraduate U.S. citizens, Iyer, Schmader, and Lickel (2007) examined the associations of anger, guilt, and shame with intentions for political action. They found that both anger and shame predicted intentions to advocate withdrawal from Iraq, while the association with guilt was nonsignificant. The results are instructive in that they illustrate how two negative emotions can exert independent effects on a single intention,

and, in the same analysis, a third negative emotion may show no significant effect at all. In further illustration of this same general point, Nan (2009, p. 437) presents results showing that anger toward public service announcements is counter-persuasive, while guilt seems to generate agreement with the message. These findings too are at odds with any model of affect that anticipates uniform effects within valence-defined categories, that is, the bipolar valence model, the categorical valence model, and the pleasure dimension of the PA model.

2. *There is variation in the effects of positive emotions.* Participants in the Kim, Park, and Schwarz (2010) were asked to list three life events that were either peaceful or exciting. Then, under the guise of a separate study, data were gathered on their evaluations of a message that promoted a vacation to Japan. There were two versions of the advertisement. One of them emphasized the possibilities for adventure and excitement via exposure to anime/manga, electronics, and Japanese drumming, while the other promised a serene and tranquil experience focused on hot springs, tea ceremonies, and religious traditions. Responses to the question "I would like to take a vacation in this country" were most favorable when message content matched the pre-existing emotional state. In other words, the effects of these two positive emotions were reversed as a function of message content. Nan (2009, Table 2) also provides evidence of the independent, and generally opposing, effects of two other positive emotions. In her data, happiness is associated with greater persuasion, and contentment with less.

3. *Discrete emotion models exhibit better predictive power than the alternatives.* In one of the few direct comparisons of affect models, Dillard and Peck (2001) examined emotional reactions to public service announcements on a variety of prosocial topics, such as exercise, charitable giving, and avoiding contraction of HIV. They conducted two series of regression analyses, each of which used perceived effectiveness of the messages as the

criterion variable. In the discrete emotions analyses, anger, fear, sadness, guilt, happiness, and contentment were used as separate predictors. For the valence analyses, anger, fear, sadness, and guilt were combined to form a single, negative-affect predictor; happiness and contentment were combined to form a single, positive affect variable. A ratio of the R^2 change for each set of equations permitted a judgment of the relative predictor power of each affect model. The discrete emotions analysis was superior to the valence analysis by a factor of two.

4. *Different emotions produce different persuasion outcomes.* Appraisal theory presupposes that emotions are means of solving functionally distinct types of problems. From that premise, it seems reasonable to infer that different emotions would produce different persuasive outcomes. An illustration of these variations is offered by Brader (2005), in an experiment conducted in the context of a Democratic primary race for governor. Two messages were designed, both of which manipulated various nonverbal cues to create either enthusiasm or fear. More concretely, one message paired uplifting music and images of children with message content that described conditions that were "good and getting better" (p. 392). The other appeal, which argued that things were "bad and getting worse," (p. 392) was accompanied by tense music and pictures of violence. In a crossed design, both messages were attributed to both candidates. The data revealed that the enthusiasm message solidified pre-existing voter preferences and dramatically increased intention to vote (a 29% increase). In contrast, the fear message was more effective at changing voter preferences, but had no significant influence on intention to vote.

The research cited in preceding paragraphs is illustrative: Much more evidence exists. The research that appears in the literature prior to 2001 is summarized by Dillard and Meijnders (2002). And, accrual of data since that time has only supported the conclusion that a discrete emotions perspective is not merely preferable, but

rather, necessary for understanding the effects of emotion on persuasion (e.g., Huddy, Feldman, Taber, & Lahav, 2005; Lerner, Gonzalez, Small, & Fischhoff, 2003; Lerner & Keltner, 2000).

Mechanisms of Effect

The appraisal model of persuasion (Figure 10.1.) depicts movement from emotion to persuasion outcome with a simple, single arrow. However, because emotions are complex states that implicate a host of perceptual, cognitive, physiological, and motivational systems, they might influence the persuasion process through multiple means (Dillard & Nabi, 2006).

Perhaps the simplest claim regarding the mechanism is that emotions can have a direct effect on persuasion outcomes (Dillard & Nabi, 2006). This idea traces back to the assumption that stimulation of an action tendency is a defining feature of any emotional response. Each emotion has some implications for action that can be understood as approach/engagement or avoidance/withdrawal. These motivational tendencies are guides to behavior with direct implications for attitudes and intentions. However, because emotions are evolutionarily designed to solve *specific* problems, the action tendency associated with each emotion is a more specific variation on one, the other, or both of those two broad themes. Table 10.2. provides a summary of emotions and their predominant action tendencies. The qualifier *predominant* is important in this application because action tendencies vary as a function of context. For example, the predominant action tendency for fear is acquiescence. But, under some circumstances, fear motivates aggression. The table also attempts to elaborate on the point that action tendencies can be analyzed at both the general and specific levels. At the general level, anger and happiness are both approach emotions in that they prompt engagement with the emotion-inducing stimulus. However, at the specific level, they are quite different from one another. The logic of the direct effects mechanism predicts that action

Table 10.2 Emotions and Their Action Tendencies

Emotions	General[a]	Specific
Fear	Avoid	Acquiesce
Anger	Approach	Attack
Sadness	Avoid	Review plan/convalesce
Happiness	Approach	Bask/bond
Hope	Approach	Renew effort
Contentment	Avoid	Immobility

a. These should be understood as approach/engage and avoidance/withdrawal.

tendency effects will be moderated by various aspects of the advocacy or the context in which the message is presented.

Another class of mechanisms reflects heightened sensitivity to appraisal-relevant message features. The most commonly observed type of effect is matching, in which emotion-consistent beliefs are amplified by the evocation of the corresponding emotion. Just as perceived risk induces fear, fear increases estimates of risk. Conversely, prior instigation of anger attenuates perceived risk (Lerner et al., 2003). Kim et al. (2010) describe matching effects for pre-message emotions and subsequent issue judgments that are mediated by expectancies, a specific form of belief. Turner (2007) reports findings in which matching effects for anger carry over to politically oriented action tendencies, including signing a petition, talking to friends, and organizing an event.

There is also evidence of emotional inductions that can activate the behavioral approach and avoidance systems, which, in turn, render audience members sensitive to noncontent message features. Using the Life Event Inventory procedure, Yan, Dillard, and Shen (2010) demonstrate a variation on the sensitization phenomenon such that when sadness or fear are used to stimulate the behavioral inhibition system, loss framed messages become more persuasive.

In parallel, inducing anger or happiness—both of which are approach emotions—activates the behavioral approach system and causes gain-framed messages to be evaluated more favorably (Yan, Dillard, Shen, in press).

Emotions can also influence the way in which messages are processed. Specifically, emotions of different sorts might propel individuals toward or away from a message topic, a phenomenon that Nabi's (1999) cognitive-functional model (CFM) characterizes as *motivated attention*. In the same vein, message consumers may try to regulate the emotion via *motivated processing* (Nabi, 1999). Based on the type of emotion experienced, motivated attention sets a baseline attention level that will either impede (for avoidance emotions, like fear) or facilitate (for approach emotions, like anger) subsequent information processing. Expectation of reassurance from the message might then further shape style of processing. For example, given anger's nature, the CFM predicts that it is likely to promote closer information processing. Fear is likely to promote more message scrutiny only when reassurance cues are unavailable. Huddy and Gunnthorsdottir (2000) suggest that message-induced emotion effects may be limited to message recipients who are knowledgeable about and involved with the issue.

Although the data on matching effects are appealing, Agrawal and Duhacheck (2010) suggest that they may be overridden, at least in some cases, by motivated processing. In their research, shame or guilt was evoked by describing others either observing or suffering from the negative consequences of binge drinking. The others-as-observers perspective produced shame because message recipients were presented as behaving in way that yielded unfavorable judgments of their friends and family. In contrast, when friends and family were described as bearing the costs of the research participants irresponsible behavior, the participants reported feeling guilt. Antidrinking messages that were matched on induced emotion, yielded *mismatched* persuasive effects presumably because participants were motivated to counterargue against appeals that further threatened their sense of self.

Other Themes in the Research Literature

Affect and Attitudes

The concept of attitude is inextricably bound up with that of evaluation. And, of course, so is affect. The fact that the two concepts both draw on valence as an underlying concept has meant that, at certain points in history of social science, researchers made little or no distinction between them. For example, the original version of the theory of reasoned action viewed affect and attitude as essentially synonymous (Fishbein & Ajzen, 1975). However, in subsequent years, theorists developed meaningful grounds on which to differentiate the two. One of the most compelling expositions is offered by Zanna and Rempel (1988) who show that the utility of treating (1) attitude as a summary cognitive judgment regarding the goodness-badness of a mental object and (2) affect as one or more feeling states that may influence attitude. Their position aligns perfectly with the appraisal model of persuasion given in Figure 10.1., and it has clear implications for the measurement of both attitude and affect. To wit, attitude is appropriately assessed

via judgments of good or bad, favorable or unfavorable, and like or dislike, all of which capture the cognitive aspect of evaluations. In contrast, measures that index responses such as anxious, pleasant, tense, happy, and sad may be appropriate for the assessment of emotion, but they are invalid indicators of attitude. Some investigations continue to intermingle measures of affect and attitude, thereby diminishing the interpretability of their results.

The Affect Heuristic

Heuristics are short-cut decision-making rules that come into play when a more detailed analysis of persuasive circumstance is unwarranted or impossible. For instance, when faced with a nonfunctional computer, many people defer to the recommendation of their IT specialist rather than spend time themselves learning the technology of personal computers, disassembling their machine, then locating and fixing the problem themselves. Pertinent to this chapter is the claim that individuals often rely on an affect heuristic: A feeling that captures the positive or negative aspect of a stimulus (Slovic & Peters, 2006). This definition seems to carry on the tradition of conflating affect and attitude. However, the terminology and theorizing are more contemporary. Experiments conducted on the affect heuristic manipulate variables, such as time pressure, that are held to govern the activation of other cognitive heuristics (Slovic, Finucane, Peters, & MacGregor, 2002). Indeed, the results show parallel effects. However, the affect heuristic is defined in terms of feelings rather than cognition. This bears some similarity to the notion of signal value, that is, the idea that subjective experience is the means by which conscious awareness is informed of the change in the physiological, expressive, cognitive, and, motivational domains (described in more detail below). But, work on the affect heuristic seems to reject the conception of specific emotions. Despite its application to risk assessment, which is normally associated with fear, research on the affect heuristic makes only a distinction between positive and negative affect. In the final analysis, the notion of an affect heuristic has been successful at stimulating research. However, it seems to bring together concepts from appraisal theory, cognitive theory, and the valence approach in ways that are fundamentally incompatible with one another. Thus, it is difficult to know how to locate the research in a more general framework.

Issues for Future Research

The Regrettable Persistence of Valence Models

Taken together, the reasons to prefer a discrete emotions perspective over the alternative conceptions are quite strong (Nabi, 2010). It seems clear that continued dependence on valence models is a mistake. Nonetheless, the valence model still appears in the literature with remarkable regularity—a circumstance that seems to call for explanation.

One way of accounting for this curiosity is to recognize that valence judgments are salient throughout life. They are learned early, then practiced regularly. Rudimentary processes such as the startle response are quickly followed by an assessment of the intrinsic pleasantness of stimuli (Scherer, 1984). And, as theories such as reasoned action tell us, even many initially complex decisions ultimately reduce to good versus bad judgments (chapter 8 in this volume). Jointly, these facts of life may bring valence judgments to the forefront of human consciousness, where they are as likely to bias the views of social scientists as they are lay persons.

Another reason for the endurance of the valence perspective may lie with the methods that are commonly employed in studies of affect. Atheoretical applications of exploratory factor analysis to emotion data typically produce one positive emotion factor and one negative emotion factor. To generate an example, undergraduate students at Penn State were asked to react to a one-page print advertisement regarding participation in an education program that would render them eligible for a free tablet personal computer (Seo & Dillard, 2012). The message recipients provided information regarding their emotional reactions as well as estimates of their intention to take part in the program. Next, the emotion data were submitted to a principle axis factor analysis followed by oblique rotation. Table 10.3. gives the loadings for the pattern matrix, which are reasonably clear and perfectly typical: There are two factors, one composed of

Table 10.3 Pattern Matrix of a Principal Axis Analysis of Emotion Data

Emotion	Factor 1	Factor 2
Happiness	**.63**	−.12
Contentment	**.73**	.12
Anger	−.18	**.73**
Sadness	.01	**.77**
Fear	.08	**.46**

Note: N = 455. Emotion judgments were made on 0 = *None of this feeling* to 4 = *A great deal of this feeling* using multiple items for each affect: Happiness (happy, excited, eager, and cheerful; α = .90), contentment (content, calm, satisfied, and tranquil; α = .71), anger (angry, irritated, annoyed, and aggravated; α = .88), sadness (sad, dreary, and dismal; α = .50), and fear (fearful, afraid, and scared; α = .85).

positive emotions and the other consisting of negative emotions. This simple, intuitive solution looks as if it conforms perfectly with the valence model of affect. In line with the factor analytic findings, we created two variables to represent positive and negative affect (i.e., happiness + contentment and anger + sadness + fear). These two variables were then used as predictors of intention to participate in the education program for personal computer (sample item: *If I can, I will take part in the Free Tablet PC Program*). The regression analysis yielded standardized coefficients of .40, $p < .05$, for positive affect and $-.23$, $p < .05$ for negative affect. Anyone looking at these results might conclude that positive affect promotes persuasion, while negative affect has an inhibitory effect.

But, there is a fly in the ointment. The purpose of factor analysis is to group things together that are similar. If the factor analytic findings constitute a useful description of reality, then the elements of each factor must show similar effects. To test for this pattern, a second regression analysis was conducted in which each of the emotions was used as separate predictors of intention. The results showed that the emotions that made up the positive emotion factor did not show consistent relationships with behavioral intention. Happiness was directly associated with intention ($\beta = .62$, $p < .05$), but contentment showed the opposite relationship ($\beta = -.20$, $p < .05$). Thus, the positive emotions did not exhibit similar effects. Attention to the negative emotions yielded a complementary conclusion: Anger was significantly and inversely related to intention ($\beta = -.14$, $p < .05$), but the weights for sadness and fear were functionally zero ($\beta = -.03$ and $\beta = -.04$, both nonsignificant). Hence, the negative emotions did not exhibit similar effects. Overall then, the exploratory factor analysis encourages grouping the data in a way that produces inaccurate conclusions and obscures the true nature of the data. In contrast, allowing theory to direct the analysis provides a justifiably variegated approach to the analysis.

Given their ubiquity and endurance, it seems that valence models must be capturing something

of use. But, what that might be is not evident. It would be far more useful to reject this simplification of emotional influence and get on with the business of refining theory and conducting research that is equal in nuance to human experience.

The Value of Research on Style and Accompaniments

Most of the time, content is king: Genuine differences in message content evoke different cognitive and emotional responses, as well as varying degrees of persuasion (although, of course, these differences must be perceived). It is not the least surprising that many applied persuasion campaigns undertake formative research with the goal of identifying substantive arguments to support the goal of changing beliefs, attitudes, and behavior (chapter 17 in this volume). There is little reason to question the desirability of this aim. However, there is at least one significant barrier to achieving it.

Argument novelty has been posited to a necessary condition for persuasion (Morley & Walker, 1987). Minimally, new arguments carry more weight than those that have been heard before (Prochaska, Johnson, & Lee, 1998, p. 68). In some persuasive domains, argument novelty may be an infinite resource. Political campaigns come quickly to mind: They are endlessly creative because they are so frequently unbeholden to facts. In other areas, practical or ethical considerations constrain the available pool of novel arguments. Health-related persuasion surely ought to be limited to the facts as they are understood by the community of science. This means that the claim that smoking causes cancer has been repeated so many times that it may be virtually impossible to find an audience for whom the claim is novel. Hence, persuasion practitioners who aim to reduce risky health behaviors, diminish crime, or encourage physical activity may have few alternatives other than style and accompaniments in the production of effective campaigns.

This is not to suggest that efforts to devise compelling arguments should be abandoned. Rather, it implies that, if campaigns are to maximize their impact, they must consider message features in addition to argumentative content. To the extent that those features mold parts of the persuasive process, it is likely that their influence derives from emotional arousal. The graphic imagery that appears on cigarette packages in some non-U.S. countries, is an opportunity to understand the interplay of emotion and persuasion, as well as a possible means of improving public health. In this same vein, the well-established tendency for human facial expression to create emotional contagion has not generated a body of persuasion research that is commensurate with the power of the concept. Anthropomorphic inclinations that produce imposition of human faces on nonhuman objects offers intriguing possibilities (Landwehr, McGill, & Hermann, 2011). Not to be overlooked are the more subtle aspects of the visual experience, such as color and script style (Wakefield, Germain, & Durkin, 2008) or camera angle (Giessner, Ryan, Schubert, & van Quaquebeke, 2011).

In short, efforts to enhance our understanding of stylistic issues are needed. Such research can be intellectually provocative and theoretically stimulating. In some applied settings, it may be the only available means of enhancing persuasive effectiveness.

Conclusion

The artist Vincent van Gogh said "Let's not forget that the little emotions are the great captains of our lives and we obey them without realizing it." He was certainly correct in identifying emotion as a powerful determinant of human action. Indeed, much of this chapter has reviewed research that accords perfectly with van Gogh's assertion. Yet, on his last point—that "we obey them without realizing it"—van Gogh may have overstepped. Message consumers do have the ability to defuse emotion-induced judgments and action tendencies by

monitoring their feelings and recognizing the causes of those affects. Communication researchers have the opportunity to create theory that links messages features with emotional response and emotional response with important persuasion outcomes. The development of a scientific account of emotion and persuasion is a worthy aim in its own right. To the extent that it enables audience members to better understand and manage the relationship between persuasive appeals and emotion impact, it furthers the goals of creating more effective citizens, more critical consumers, and more successful decision makers.

References

Aarøe, L. (2011). Investigating frame strength: The case of episodic and thematic frames. *Political Communication, 28,* 207–226.

Agrawal, N., & Duhachek, A. (2010). Emotional compatibility and the effectiveness of anti-drinking messages: A defensive processing perspective on shame and guilt. *Journal of Marketing Research, 47,* 263–273.

Anghelcev, G., & Sar, S. (2011). The influence of pre-existing audience mood on message relevance and the effectiveness of health PSAs: Differential effects by message type. *Journalism & Mass Communication Quarterly, 88,* 481–501.

Aristotle. (2007). *On rhetoric: A theory of civic discourse* (George A. Kennedy, Trans., 2nd ed.). New York, NY: Oxford University.

Banerjee, S. C., Greene, K., & Yanovitzky, I. (2011). Sensation seeking and dosage effect: An exploration of the role of surprise in anti-cocaine messages. *Journal of Substance Abuse, 16,* 1–13.

Brader, T. (2005). Striking a responsive chord: How political ads motivate and persuade voters by appealing to emotions. *American Journal of Political Science, 49,* 388–405.

Chang, C. (2011). The influence of editorial liking and editorial-induced affect on evaluations of subsequent ads. *Journal of Advertising, 40,* 45–58.

Cho, H., & Boster, F. J. (2008). Effects of gain versus loss frame antidrug ads on adolescents. *Journal of Communication, 58,* 428–446.

Dillard, J. P., & Meijnders, A. (2002). Persuasion and the structure of affect. In J. P. Dillard &

M. W. Pfau (Eds.), *The persuasion handbook: Developments in theory and practice* (pp. 309–328). Thousand Oaks, CA: Sage.

Dillard, J. P., & Nabi, R. (2006). The persuasive influence of emotion in cancer prevention and detection messages. *Journal of Communication, 56,* s123–s139.

Dillard, J. P., & Peck, E. (2001). Persuasion and the structure of affect: Dual systems and discrete emotions as complementary models. *Human Communication Research, 27,* 38–68.

Entman, R. M. (1993). Framing: Toward clarification of a fractured paradigm. *Journal of Communication, 43,* 51–58.

Fishbein, M., & Ajzen, I. (1975). *Belief, attitude, intention, and behavior.* Reading, MA: Addison-Wesley.

Giessner, S. R., Ryan, M. K., Schubert, T. W., & van Quaquebeke, N. (2011). The power of pictures: Vertical angles in power pictures. *Media Psychology, 14,* 442–464.

Gross, K. (2008). Framing persuasive appeals: Episodic and thematic framing, emotional response, and policy opinion. *Political Psychology, 29,* 169–192.

Gross, K., & D'Ambrosio, L. (2004). Framing emotional response. *Political Psychology, 25,* 1–29.

Huddy, L., Feldman, S., Taber, C., & Lahav, G. (2005). Threat, anxiety, and support of anti-terrorism policies. *American Journal of Political Science, 49,* 610–625.

Huddy, L., & Gunnthorsdottir, A. H. (2000). The persuasive effects of emotive visual imagery: Superficial manipulation or the product of passionate reason? *Political Psychology, 21,* 745–778.

Iyer, A., Schmader, T., & Lickel, B. (2007). Why individuals protest the perceived transgressions of their country: The role of anger, shame, and guilt. *Personality and Social Psychology Bulletin, 33,* 572–587.

Kahneman, D., & Tversky, A. (1979). Prospect theory: An analysis of decision under risk. *Econometrica, 47,* 263–291.

Kim, H., Park, K., & Schwarz, N. (2010). Will this trip really be exciting? The role of incidental emotions in product evaluation. *Journal of Consumer Research, 36,* 983–991.

Landwehr, J. R., McGill, A. L., & Hermann, A. (2011). It's got the look: The effect of friendly and aggressive "facial" expressions on product liking and sales. *Journal of Marketing, 75,* 132–146.

Lazarus, R. S. (1991). *Emotion and adaptation.* New York, NY: Oxford University Press.

Lerner, J. S., Gonzalez, R. M., Small, D. A., & Fischhoff, B. (2003). Effects of fear and anger on perceived risks of terrorism: A national field experiment. *Psychological Science, 14,* 144–150.

Lerner, J. S., & Keltner, D. (2000). Beyond valence: Toward a model of emotion-specific influences on judgment and choice. *Cognition and Emotion, 14,* 473–493.

Lerner, J. S., & Tiedens, L. Z. (2006). Portrait of the angry decision maker: How appraisal tendencies shape anger's influence on cognition. *Journal of Behavioral Decision Making, 19,* 115–137.

Lindsey, L. L. M., Yun, K, A., & Hill, J. B. (2007). Anticipated guilt as motivation to help unknown others: An examination of empathy as a moderator. *Communication Research, 34,* 468–480.

Lombard, M., Reich, R. D., Grabe, M. E., Bracken, C. C., & Ditton, T. B. (2000). Presence and television: The role of screen size. Human Communication Research, 26, 75–98.

Major, L. H. (2011). The mediating role of emotions in the relationship between frames and attribution of responsibility for health problems. *Journalism and Mass Communication Quarterly, 88,* 502–522.

McCauley, C., & Moskalenko, S. (2008). Mechanisms of political radicalization: Pathways toward terrorism. *Terrorism and Political Violence, 20,* 415–433.

Millar, M., & Millar, K. (2000). Promoting safe driving behavior: The influence of message framing and issue involvement. *Journal of Applied Social Psychology, 30,* 853–866.

Miller, G. A. (2003). The cognitive revolution: A historical perspective. *Trends in Cognitive Sciences, 7,* 141–144

Morley, D. D., & Walker, K. (1987). The role of importance, novelty, and plausibility in producing belief change. *Communication Monographs, 54,* 436–442.

Nabi, R. L. (1999). A cognitive-functional model for the effects of discrete negative emotions on information processing, attitude change, and recall. *Communication Theory, 9,* 292–320.

Nabi, R. L. (2010). The case for emphasizing discrete emotions in communication research. *Communication Monographs, 77,* 153–159.

Nan, X. (2009). Emotional responses to televised PSAs and their influence on persuasion: An investigation of the moderating role of faith in intuition. *Communication Studies, 5,* 426–442.

O'Keefe, D. J., & Jensen, J. D. (2006). The advantages of compliance or the disadvantages of noncompliance? A meta-analytic review of the relative persuasive effectiveness of gain-framed and loss-framed messages. *Communication Yearbook, 30,* 1–43.

Phan, K. L., Wager, T., Taylor, S. F., & Liberzon, I. (2002). Functional neuroanatomy of emotion: A meta-analysis of emotion activation studies in PET and fMRI. *NeuroImage, 16,* 331–348.

Prochaska, J. O., Johnson, S., & Lee, P. (1998). The transtheoretical model of behavior change. In S. A. Schumaker, E. B. Schron, J. K. Ockene, & W. L. McBee (Eds.), *The handbook of health behavior change* (pp. 59–84), 2nd ed. New York, NY: Springer.

Roseman, I. J. (2001). A model of appraisal in the emotion system: Integrating theory, research, and applications. In K. R. Scherer, A. Schorr, & T. Johnstone (Eds.), *Appraisal processes in emotion: Theory, methods, research* (pp. 68–91). New York, NY: Oxford University Press.

Russell, J. A., & Feldman Barrett, L. (1999). Core affect, prototypical emotional episodes, and other things called *emotion*: Dissecting the elephant. *Journal of Personality and Social Psychology, 76,* 805–819.

Scherer, K. R. (1984). On the nature and function of emotion: A component process approach. In K. R. Scherer, & P. Ekman (Eds.), *Approaches to emotion* (pp. 293–317). Hillsdale, NJ: Erlbaum.

Scherer, K. R., Schorr, A., & Johnstone, T. (Eds.). (2001). *Appraisal processes in emotion: Theory, methods, research.* New York, NY: Oxford University Press.

Schneider, T. R., Salovey, P., Apanovitch, A. M., Pizarro, J., McCarthy, D., Zullo, J., et al. (2001). The effects of message framing and ethnic targeting on mammography use among low-income women. *Health Psychology, 20,* 256–266.

Schwarz, N., & Clore, G. L. (1983). Mood, misattribution, and judgments of well-being: Informative and directive functions of affective states. *Journal of Personality and Social Psychology, 45,* 513–523.

Seo, K., & Dillard, J. P. (2012). (Unpublished data). University Park: Pennsylvania State University.

Shen, L., & Dillard, J. P. (2007). The influence of behavior inhibition/approach systems and message framing on the processing of persuasive health messages. *Communication Research, 34,* 433–467.

Slovic, P., Finucane, M. L., Peters, E., & MacGregor, D. G. (2002). The affect heuristic. In T. Gilovich, D. Griffin, & D. Kahneman (Eds.), *Heuristics and biases: The psychology of intuitive judgment* (pp. 397–420). New York, NY: Cambridge University Press.

Slovic, P., & Peters, E. (2006). Risk perception and affect. *Current Directions in Psychogical Science, 15,* 322–325.

Tooby, J., & Cosmides, L. (2008). The evolutionary psychology of the emotions and their relationship to internal regulatory variables. In M. Lewis, J. M. Haviland-Jones, & L. F. Barrett (Eds.), *Handbook of emotions* (3rd ed., pp. 114–137.) New York, NY: Guilford.

Turner, M. M. (2007). Using emotion in risk communication: The Anger Activism Model. *Public Relations Review, 33,* 114–119.

Wakefield, M. A., Germain, D., & Durkin, S. J. (2008). How does increasingly plainer cigarette packaging influence adult smokers' perceptions about brand preference? An experimental study. *Tobacco Control, 17,* 416–421.

Wang, X. (2011). The role of anticpated guilt in intentions to register as organ donors and to discuss organ donation with family. *Health Communication, 26,* 683–690.

Watson, D., & Clark, L. A. (1994). *The PANAS-X: Manual for the positive and negative affect schedule-Expanded Form.* Iowa City: University of Iowa.

Yan, C., Dillard, J. P., & Shen, F. (2010). The effects of mood, message framing, and behavioral advocacy on persuasion. *Journal of Communication, 60,* 344–363.

Yan, C., Dillard, J. P., & Shen, F. (in press). Emotion, motivation, and the persuasive effects of message framing. *Journal of Communication.*

Zanna, M. P., & Rempel, J. K. (1988). Attitudes: A new look at an old concept. In D. Bar-Tal & A. W. Kruglanski (Eds.), *The social psychology of knowledge* (pp. 315–334). Cambridge, UK: Cambridge University Press.

Zillmann, D. (1999). Exemplification theory: Judging the whole by some of its parts. *Media Psychology, 1,* 69–94.

Zillmann, D. (2006). Exemplification effects in the promotion of safety and health. *Journal of Communication, 56,* S221–S237.

CHAPTER 11

Reactance Theory and Persuasion

Brian L. Quick, Lijiang Shen, and James Price Dillard

S ir Isaac Newton famously claimed that for every action there is an equal and opposite reaction. It is doubtful that he had persuasion in mind when formulating his third law of motion, but, the principle alerts us to the parallel possibility that suasory efforts may too instigate reactions that run counter to the intended action of the message. Quite apart from the laws of motion, the literature suggests that opposing reactions may vary greatly in degree. Some appeals are so effective that the counter-reaction is scarcely measurable. Others may produce no discernable persuasive change, perhaps because the action and reaction are closely balanced. In still other cases, the predominant response is counterpersuasion, a condition that has come to be known as a boomerang effect.

All of these outcomes are of interest to persuasion researchers, but boomerangs and failure to persuade are both common and pragmatically frustrating. The perspective that is most frequently called on to give account of them is psychological reactance theory (PRT; Brehm, 1966). Consequently, this chapter reviews and synthesizes work on this landmark theory. It proceeds by first considering the theory's original formulation alongside the empirical research done to test it. The second section focuses on refinement of the theory, before turning, in the third movement, to contemporary research. Following from that, directions are offered for future inquiry.

Overview of Reactance Theory and Classic Research

There are four components to reactance theory: Freedom, threat to freedom, reactance, and restoration of freedom. *Freedoms* are beliefs about the ways in which one can behave. Brehm and Brehm (1981) argue that freedoms are "not 'abstract considerations,' but concrete behavioral realities" (p. 12). Nonetheless, freedom is defined broadly to include actions as well as emotions and attitudes (Brehm, 1966). In other words, freedom to do, freedom to feel, or freedom to hold a particular evaluation, or not to. Individuals possess freedoms only to the extent that they have knowledge of them and perceive that they are capable of enacting the behavior.

Given that an individual perceives a specific freedom, anything that makes it more difficult for him or her to exercise that freedom constitutes a *threat* (Brehm, 1966; Brehm & Brehm, 1981). Even an impersonal event, such as the weather can be viewed as a threat, if it renders the exercise of a freedom more difficult. However, social influence as a threat is most pertinent to questions of persuasive communication. Important to understanding the theory is recognition that the term threat is used narrowly to mean threat-to-freedom, and not threats as used in everyday language, nor threats to well-being used in research on fear/threat appeals, or threats as a forewarning of social influence in research on inoculation.

Psychological *reactance* is "the motivational state that is hypothesized to occur when a freedom is eliminated or threatened with elimination" (Brehm & Brehm, 1981, p. 37). This is the key mediator and central explanatory mechanism of the theory. Its proposed existence follows from the assumption that humans place a high value on choice, autonomy, and control. As reflected in many worn phrases, people seek to be the captains of their own destinies, the masters of their own fates.

The fourth component of the theory is *restoration*. PRT contends that when a perceived freedom is eliminated or threatened with elimination, the individual will be motivated to reestablish that freedom. Direct restoration of the freedom involves doing the forbidden act. In addition, freedoms may be restored indirectly by increasing liking for the threatened choice (Brehm, Stires, Sensenig, & Shaban, 1966; Hammock & Brehm, 1966), derogating the source of threat (Kohn & Barnes, 1977; Schwarz, Frey, & Kumpf, 1980; Smith, 1977; Worchel, 1974), denying the existence of the threat (Worchel & Andreoli, 1974; Worchel, Andreoli, & Archer, 1976), or by exercising a different freedom to gain feeling of control and choice (Wicklund, 1974). (See Quick & Stephenson, 2007b for a measure of various means for restoring reactance.)

Corollaries of Reactance Theory

PRT is built around four principles (Brehm, 1966). The first specifies that reactance can only be aroused if individuals believe they have freedom over a particular outcome. An early study illustrating PRT's first principle was conducted by Wicklund and Brehm (1968), in which participants were asked to evaluate a job applicant. Their results revealed differences among high competent individuals following exposure to the freedom-threatening condition. That is, competent individuals exposed to the freedom-threatening communication resulted in greater reactance than exposure to the non-freedom-threatening condition. No significant difference emerged for non-competent individuals (Wicklund & Brehm, 1968). In other words, for individuals aware of their abilities, exposure to freedom-threatening messages resulted in heightened reactance.

Principle two pertains to the relationship between the importance of a freedom and the magnitude of reactance. Specifically, PRT asserts that as the threatened behavior increases in attractiveness, so does the amount of reactance aroused. Brehm and Weinraub (1977) recruited toddlers to participate in an experiment in which 2-year-olds were presented with two toys. However, one of these toys was placed behind a transparent barrier, whereas the other was next to the barrier. As expected, when the toys were different in shape, as opposed to similar in shape, consistent with the second principle, preference for the obstructed toy was heightened among boys. However, this hypothesized finding was not true for the girls. As will be shown in the subsequent pages, more recent work has shown a relationship between the importance of the threatened freedom and reactance arousal.

The third principle states that reactance increases as the number of freedom threats increases. Although conceptually cogent, extant PRT research is inconsistent in supporting this principle (for a review, see Brehm & Brehm, 1981). One such study finding support for threat intensity on reactance was conducted by Heller, Pallak, and Picek (1973). In their project, in line with PRT, as persuasive intent and freedom threats increased, participants' attitude change in the opposite direction spiked. These researchers reasoned that perceiving a message as a freedom threat results in maladaptive responses such as unfavorable attitudes toward the advocacy.

The fourth principle maintains that as implied threats are present, the magnitude of reactance will increase (Brehm, 1966; Brehm & Brehm, 1981). Implied threats are often communicated in the form of a persuasive message. An earlier study conducted by Reich and Robertson (1979) examined littering behaviors following exposure to variations in freedom-threatening language. Specifically, in their three-study experiment, they found individuals presented with messages featuring explicit commands such as "Don't you dare litter" resulted in greater littering than exposure to messages featuring appeals to social norms. As shown earlier, their study provides support for the fourth principle of PRT in that as implied threats increase, reactance arousal increases. However, it should be noted that the previously mentioned research in support of these four principles was conducted without measuring reactance. That is, these researchers merely hypothesized the presence of reactance given the outcomes believed to be linked to this aversive state. As will be shown later in this chapter, following a validated operationalization of psychological reactance (Dillard & Shen, 2005), more recent work has begun and continues to test the four theoretical principles advanced by Brehm (1966).

Progress in Refining Reactance Theory

The Nature of Reactance

Conceptually speaking, reactance was defined primarily in terms of its antecedents and outcomes. For example, reactance is the result of the collision between a freedom and a threat to freedom. Nearer the end of the process, reactance is the state that is responsible for efforts to restore freedom. In either case, it has been defined in terms of either what causes or what effect it has, but not what it is. Apart from a brief mention of the possibility that individuals "may be aware of hostile and aggressive feelings" (Brehm, 1966, p. 9), if the level of reactance arousal is high, the nature of reactance itself is rarely addressed. Brehm's apparent reluctance to explicate the principle mechanism of the theory may have followed his estimate of its potential for measurement. According to Brehm and Brehm (1981), "reactance has the status of an intervening, hypothetical variable. . . . We *cannot* [emphasis added] measure reactance directly, but hypothesizing its existence allows us to predict a variety of behavioral effects" (p. 37).

The position that reactance cannot be measured is logically consequential. In effect, it assigns reactance to a black box. Message features go in the box and outcomes emerge, but the operations within the box itself remain mysterious and unknowable. When results match with theoretical predictions, then it is assumed that the process-in-a-box must have occurred. But, when results do not work out as expected, then the failure must be with the messages, the circumstances, the sample, or something other than the box. Indeed, it has been common to invoke reactance as the explanation for a failed persuasion attempt. In this regard, it became the default assumption for any persuasive effort that produced a boomerang or a no-effect finding. It is better to have a black-box theory than no theory at all. But, it is vastly preferable to understand and measure the workings inside the box. Only then can the entire theoretical process be open to empirical test. Hence, it was important to understand the nature of reactance in order that it might be assessed directly.

Since the time of Brehm's writings, scholars have applied ideas drawn from reactance theory to a number of different domains. In the course of analyzing and extending the theory, reactance has, implicitly and explicitly, been defined in several different ways. Dillard and Shen (2005) describe four views. In the first, reactance is purely cognitive. Research in the cognitive response tradition adopted this perspective (e.g., Petty & Cacioppo, 1986), as did work on the clinical manifestations of reactance (Kelly & Nauta, 1997). One advantage to conceiving of reactance in this way is that it immediately becomes measurable through a variety of self-report techniques. The means that is most obviously relevant to questions of persuasion is the widely used thought-listing technique (Petty & Cacioppo, 1986). This purely cognitive view suggests that reactance can be conceived of and operationalized as counter-arguing.

Second, citing similarities between antecedents of reactance and cognitive appraisals that lead to anger, some writers suggest that reactance might be considered, in whole or in part, as an emotion (Dillard & Meijnders, 2002; Nabi, 2002). This claim aligned well with Brehm's description of reactance as the experience of hostile and aggressive feelings (Seltzer, 1983; White & Zimbardo, 1980; Wicklund, 1974). In this view then, reactance is more or less synonymous with the family of concepts that index varying degrees of anger (e.g., irritation, annoyance, and rage). From this perspective, reactance might be operationalized in various ways, including asking individuals to make a judgment on a close-ended scale regarding the degree to which they are experiencing anger.

A third logical option holds that reactance might be considered as both affect *and* cognition. Though unrelated to reactance per se, one example of this type of thinking can be seen in Leventhal's (1970) parallel processing model. He posits that individuals have both cognitive and emotional reactions to persuasive health messages and that those reactions have unique effects on message acceptance. Evidence consistent with both points can be found in studies of cognitive and emotional responses to public

service announcements (Dillard & Peck, 2000, 2001; Dillard, Plotnick, Godbold, Freimuth, & Edgar, 1996; Stephenson, 2003; Witte, 1994).

A final possibility also suggests that reactance has both cognitive and affective components. However, unlike the previous position, which specified distinct effects, in this fourth perspective, cognition and affect are intertwined. In fact, they are intertwined to such a degree that their effects on persuasion cannot be disentangled. This view conceives of reactance as an alloy of its components, rather than a simple sum of distinct elements (as is implied by the previous position).

Dillard and Shen (2005) report on a research project designed to test each of the four alternatives. The study itself utilized two messages: One that promoted the use of dental floss and the other that encouraged university students to curb their alcohol intake. For both messages, the data clearly favored the intertwined model over the alternatives. Hence, the authors concluded that reactance was in fact measureable and that it could be modeled as a combination of anger and negative cognitions.

Several studies provided additional support for this conclusion. For example, Rains and Turner (2007) conducted an investigation that pitted the intertwined model against the dual-process model, as well as a fifth alternative in which anger preceded negative cognition. Across their two health-related studies, the intertwined model showed the best fit to the data. In a research project that examined exercise behaviors, Quick and Considine (2008) tested and found support for the intertwined model in a sample comprised of members of a health and fitness center. Additional, complementary findings can be seen in Quick and Stephenson (2007a) and Shen (2010a). Given the many variations across studies in terms of messages and samples, and the apparent consistency of findings, the intertwined model seems to provide a workable representation of reactance itself and, thus, an operational means of moving away from black-box theorizing.

Measuring Reactance

The method (discussed earlier) for measuring the components of reactance involves two procedures (Dillard & Shen, 2005). One uses Likert scales to assess anger. For example, respondents were asked: *To what extent did the message that you just read make you feel . . . angry/irritated/ annoyed/aggravated: 0 = none of this feeling, 4 = a great deal of this feeling.* The complementary procedure asks respondents to list any thoughts that they had while reading the message. The results were coded by research assistants in a four-step process that unitized the data, then screened out self-reports of emotion as well as cognitions that were unrelated to the message or topic.

Although not the primary focus of her study, Lindsey (2005) developed a measure of reactance to bone marrow donation messages using a four-item scale informed by Hong's (Hong & Faedda, 1996) Psychological Reactance Scale. The items were: *I am uncomfortable that I am being told how to feel about bone marrow donation; I do not like that I am being told how to feel about bone marrow donation; It irritates me that the message told me how to feel about bone marrow donation; I dislike that I am being told how to feel about bone marrow donation.* In terms of the economics of research, the potential advantages of the four-item measure are apparent: It provides a brief index that could be easily incorporated into surveys without the expensive and laborious tasks of gathering and coding free-response data.

Quick (2012) undertook a comparative analysis of the two methods in terms of reliability and validity (by evaluating each in a nomothetic network with a freedom threat, attitude, motivation, and source appraisal). Both approaches exhibited satisfactory reliability. Both were also sensitive to variations in forceful language and both predicted attitude, motivation, and source appraisal in theoretically meaningful ways. Quick recommends continued use of the Dillard and Shen (2005) measure on the basis of its relatively greater reliability and validity as well as the fact

that the association between the two approaches is low: The four-item measures correlate only .23 and .22 with anger and negative cognitions respectively . Most importantly, he recommends the Dillard and Shen (2005) measure as it distinguishes reactance and freedom threat as distinct entities, whereas Lindsay's (2005) measure combined these concepts. In order to be consistent with PRT (Brehm, 1966), a freedom threat must precede reactance. For this reason, combining a freedom threat with reactance does not permit researchers the opportunity to examine the relationship between them, which is discussed in greater detail later in this chapter. His recommendation, while reasoned, leaves open the question of how to more efficiently assess reactance.

One option explored by Rains and Turner (2007) and by Quick and Stephenson (2008), involves participant coding of their own cognitive responses. This generally precludes fine-grained analyses that unitize, then screen out emotions and irrelevant cognitions, because of the training time required to carry out the layers of classification. But, due to the fact that thought listing often contains ambiguous language, research participants may be in a uniquely valid position to judge the valence of their own reports. To wit, when confronted with a cognitive response such as "Is that claim supported by science?" researchers are forced to guess as to whether the query is critical or supportive. In principle, research participants have more direct access to their own evaluations, and can, conceivably, provide more valid judgments. Of course, focused research is needed to evaluate the veracity of this speculation.

Reactance as an Individual Difference

Psychological reactance was first conceived as situation specific (Brehm, 1966; Wicklund, 1974). Accordingly, most of the classic reactance research was done on situational reactance, such as alternative restriction and forced choice and in social influence settings (see Burgoon, Alvaro, Grandpre, & Voulodakis, 2002, for a review). However, Brehm and Brehm (1981) recognized that reactance could be conceptualized as a trait too, a position consistent with the theory's assumption that people vary in the strength of their needs for autonomy and self-determination (Wicklund, 1974).

Several attempts have been made to develop scales to measure reactance proneness (Dowd, Milne, & Wise, 1991; Hong, 1992; Hong & Faedda, 1996; Hong & Page, 1989; Merz, 1983). Merz (1983) developed the first self-report measure, which showed promising results, but later work yielded inconsistent factor structures (see Donnell, Thomas, & Buboltz, 2001; Hong & Ostini, 1989; Tucker & Byers, 1987). Subsequently, Dowd et al. (1991) developed the Therapeutic Reactance Scale for clinical purposes. However, the two-factor solution lacked a simple structure, and several of the items exhibited poor correspondence with the theoretical construct of reactance (cf. Buboltz, Thomas, & Donnell, 2002).

Dissatisfied with existing measures, Hong and Page (1989) translated (German to English) and revised Merz's (1983) questionnaire, thereby creating the 14-item Hong Psychological Reactance Scale (HPRS). The first investigation of the scale structure yielded a four-factor solution whose factors were labeled Freedom of Choice, Conformity Reactance, Behavioral Freedom, and Reactance to Advice and Recommendations. Subsequent efforts also produced structurally similar results after discarding three items (Hong, 1992; Hong & Faedda, 1996). Although it is not clear that the individual factors are sufficiently reliable to justify scientific application, there is evidence that the overall sum of the items is a useful, single indicator of proclivity to experience reactance (Brown, Finney, & France, 2011; Shen & Dillard, 2005). The set of items formed well-fitting, second-order factor model that exhibited parallelism across both theoretically relevant and tangential reference indicators (e.g., attitude vs. biological sex; Shen & Dillard), or in a bifactor framework, they formed a single general factor that captured the variances beyond the common residual variances explained by specific factors (Brown et al.; Table 11.1. provides the items).

Table 11.1 Items for the Hong Psychological Reactance Scale (Hong & Faedda, 1996)

1. I become frustrated when I am unable to make free and independent decisions.
2. It irritates me when someone points out things which are obvious to me.
3. I become angry when my freedom of choice is restricted.
4. Regulations trigger a sense of resistance in me.
5. I find contradicting others stimulating.
6. When something is prohibited, I usually think, "That's exactly what I am going to do".
7. I resist the attempts of others to influence me.
8. It makes me angry when another person is held up as a role model for me to follow.
9. When someone forces me to do something, I feel like doing the opposite.
10. I consider advice from others to be an intrusion.
11. Advice and recommendations usually induce me to do just the opposite.

Source: Abridged and modified from "Refinement of the Hong Psychological Reactance Scale," by S. M. Hong and S. Faedda, 1996, *Educational & Psychological Measurement*, *56*, p. 177, Copyright 1996 by Sage Publications.

Research indicates that trait reactant individuals are autonomous, independent, nonconformist, self-determined, and somewhat rebellious (Dowd, Wallbrown, Sanders, & Yesenosky, 1994; Hong & Faedda, 1996; Miller, Burgoon, Grandpre, & Alvaro, 2006; Miller & Quick, 2010). In line with these characteristics, research supports a positive association between reactance proneness and anger, autonomy, denial, dominance, independence, interpersonal mistrust, intolerance, negative cognitions, nonconformity, and self-sufficiency (e.g., Dowd et al., 1994; Seibel & Dowd, 2001).

For the sake of clarity, it is worth emphasizing one final point regarding reactance as an individual difference. Specifically, the HPRS does not capture a steady state form of reactance. Rather, the HPRS assesses sensitivity and responsiveness to circumstances and messages that may be seen as curtailing autonomy. Individual differences in reactance are differences in propensity to experience the process specified by reactance theory. Accordingly, measurements via the HPRS might be expected to contribute to predicting responses to persuasive messages either (1) above and beyond messages effects alone or (2) in conjunction with them. Research pertaining to trait reactance as both a main effect and as a moderator is considered in more detail later in this chapter.

Modeling the Reactance Process

Although research has modeled the freedom threat induction check as both an endogenous and exogenous variable, Quick and his colleagues encouraged PRT researchers to treat freedom threat and reactance measures both as mediators (Quick & Considine, 2008; Quick & Stephenson, 2008). That is, they advocate modeling reactance as a two-step process featuring a freedom threat as induction check followed by reactance. Although many alternatives are possible, Quick and colleagues have used four items (drawn from Dillard & Shen, 2005) and provided consistent evidence of their reliability and validity. The four items are given in Table 11.2.

Table 11.2   Items to Measure Perceived Threat to Freedom

1. The message threatened my freedom to choose.
2. The message tried to make a decision for me.
3. The message tried to manipulate me.
4. The message tried to pressure me.

The reasoning behind including the freedom threat induction check is that individuals could reasonably express anger and negative cognitions for any number of reasons having nothing to do with a threatened or eliminated freedom (e.g., fallacious reasoning or noncredible sources). To fully test the process proposed by PRT, researchers should ensure that the antecedents under investigation are directly related to a freedom threat, which in turn predicts reactance. Inclusion of the threat induction check creates a more demanding and theoretically precise test of the theoretical process under scrutiny. Modeling this portion of the process is akin to opening another viewing window on the contents of the black box. It has considerable practical application too in that it permits persuasion practitioners to trace the effects of their appeals or campaigns through the process from beginning to end. Recent demonstrations of the utility of this two-step logic can be found in Quick and Kim (2009); Quick, Scott, and Ledbetter (2011), and Quick (2012).

Summary

Whereas classic reactance research generally adopted a black box approach to process, contemporary inquiry has made significant strides toward understanding the process more directly. Recent advances directly measuring threat to freedom and reactance allow researchers to trace the effects of individual differences and message variations through the multiple steps proposed by PRT.

Contemporary Research on Reactance Effects

A good deal of recent research examines message and audience features associated with psychological reactance. This section reviews that literature for the purpose of highlighting factors that are likely to increase or decrease reactance.

Inducing Reactance

Domineering Language

One of the most obvious predictions of PRT is that high pressure communicators will induce reactance. But, how exactly, is pressure exerted? One common means of answering this question has been to experimentally manipulate the language of the persuasive appeal. For example, in high pressure conditions, individuals are told to "Stop the denial!" or "Any reasonable person would agree that not exercising is a problem!" (Dillard & Shen, 2005; Grandpre, Alvaro, Burgoon, Miller, & Hall, 2003; Quick & Kim, 2009; Rains & Turner, 2007). The ineffectiveness of using this type of language has been reported within the context of alcohol consumption (Bensley & Wu, 1991; Rains & Turner, 2007), drug use (Burgoon, Alvaro, Broneck, Miller, Grandpre, Hall, et al., 2002), exercise (Miller, Lane, Deatrick, Young, & Potts, 2007; Quick & Considine, 2008; Quick & Stephenson, 2008), meningitis (Rains & Turner, 2007), sunscreen (Buller, Borland, & Burgoon, 1998; Quick & Stephenson, 2008), strep throat (Rains & Turner, 2007), and tobacco use (Grandpre et al., 2003).

The research assessing the ineffectiveness of controlling language has benefited from several studies sampling from various demographics. For example, Rains and Turner (2007) found exposure to freedom-threatening language resulted in greater reactance in her two-study experiment utilizing college students. Similarly, Quick and colleagues discovered that domineering language was perceived as a freedom threat among adolescent (Quick & Kim, 2009), college

student (Quick & Stephenson, 2008), and adult samples (Quick & Considine, 2008) across multiple topics. Additionally, Henriksen, Dauphinee, Wang, and Fortmann (2006) discovered that adolescents exposed to ads containing strong language, such as "Buy our product. It will kill you," "Think. Don't smoke!" and "Tobacco is whacko if you're a teen," received poor evaluations, thus resulting in increased curiosity toward cigarettes. Overall, while the labels identifying this language feature are inconsistent (e.g., controlling, dogmatic, forceful, threat-to-choice language), each demonstrates the ineffectiveness of intense language in persuasion.

Intent to Persuade

Several classic studies demonstrate that manipulations of perceived intent to persuade produces results that are consistent with the theoretical predictions of reactance theory (e.g., Heller et al., 1973; Kohn & Barnes, 1977). More contemporary evidence of the negative impact of intent can be found in Benoit's (1998) meta-analysis, which reported a homogeneous effect across 12 investigations. Wood and Quinn (2003) describe a subsequent meta-analysis that shows diminished postmessage attitude change in forewarned conditions. Their results suggest that counter-persuasion effects may be limited to high-involvement topics, a side condition that seems to have been anticipated by PRT's claim that importance of the freedom enhances reactance. Evidence can also be drawn from the impact of threat (of influence attempt) on inducing resistance in inoculation research (chapter 14 in this volume).

There are, however, two important qualifications to the research on intent. One is that the data base is relatively small. Thus, it precludes strong tests of distinctions among types of forewarning. That is, warning of a pending message, warning of the topic of a pending message, and warning of the topic of the message as well as its position (i.e., counter- vs. pro-attitudinal). Second, none of the available studies utilized a methodology that directly assessed reactance or located it in a process model. While this is true of much reactance research, as discussed earlier in this chapter, it limits the confidence with which one can claim that reactance is implicated in persuasion or boomerang effects.

Narrative

Many of the messages that have been used to study reactance consist of arguments and evidence. But, research on narrative tells us that stories may also be an effective means of inducing change in beliefs and attitudes (chapter 13 in this volume). Moyer-Gusé (2008) theorized that one of the reasons for narrative effectiveness is the relative inhibition of reactance. This is thought to occur to the extent that the narrative form obfuscates persuasive intent. Indeed, Moyer-Gusé and Nabi (2010) found that perceived persuasive intent was positively associated with reactance for individuals exposed to a dramatic narrative. Hence, individual differences in perceived persuasive intent were in evidence even though a single narrative message was presented. Those differences corresponded directly with reactance.

One complicating factor is that their index of reactance was composed of items such as *The show tried to pressure me to think a certain way* and *The show tried to force its opinions on me.* The item content suggests a closer correspondence with threat to freedom (see Table 11.2.) than to reactance as it has been discussed in this chapter. But, either way, the measure taps an important piece of the reactance process. And, the findings suggest that when individuals perceived that an entertainment program was attempting to influence their health attitudes, then threat-to-freedom or reactance was likely to follow. In sum, even if, on average, narratives are less likely to induce reactance than argument, individuals exposed to narrative may still experience something like reactance as a result of trait-type differences.

Magnitude of the Request

Recent PRT research suggests the magnitude of the request, as well as emphasizing the gains or losses of performing an act (see Quick & Bates, 2010; Reinhart, Marshall, Feeley, & Tutzauer, 2007), influences the degree of reactance arousal. For instance, Rains and Turner's (2007) results suggest that as the magnitude of the request increased [ranged from small requests (e.g., reporting unclean conditions on campus) to large requests (e.g., donating $250 each semester to fund a sanitization company)], psychological reactance also increased.

Reactance Proneness as an Audience Segmentation Variable

As noted by Atkin and Salmon (chapter 17 this volume), the purpose behind segmenting an audience is to create groups of similar individuals. One reason to seek similarity is that group membership may correspond with the target of change. Another is that group similarity may indicate a propensity for members of the group to make similar responses to any given message.

On the first point, recent work suggests reactance proneness should be considered when segmenting at-risk audiences in public health campaigns (Miller et al., 2006; Miller & Quick, 2010; Quick, Bates, & Quinlan, 2009). Specifically, Miller et al. (2006) made a strong case for segmenting audiences by reactance proneness as they found it to be a "prominent predictor" of smoking in adolescents (p. 246). More recently, Miller and Quick (2010) report that reactant-prone individuals were more likely to use tobacco products and engage in risky sex than low-reactant prone individuals. Importantly, these researchers found reactance proneness to be a better predictor of certain risky behaviors than sensation seeking, an individual, characterized as individuals seeking out novel, arousing, emotionally complex, or intense situations (Stephenson et al., 1999). For years, sensation seeking has been a primary segmentation variable for illicit drug use as well as other hedonic behaviors, including risky sex and tobacco use. Thus, despite a positive correlation between the traits ($r = .34–.38$ in Miller & Quick, 2010, and in Quick & Stephenson, 2008), it is intriguing that reactance seems to predict certain risky behaviors with greater power than sensation seeking.

The second reason to utilize reactance proneness as an audience segmentation variable emphasizes the potential for high or low reactance prone individuals to respond similarly within group but differently between groups. In other words, trait reactance may interact with message features. A few studies report just such an effect, but sometimes in a form more complex than anticipated. For instance, Dillard and Shen (2005) found that trait reactance moderated the effect of domineering language on reactance, such that high reactant individuals were significantly more sensitive to linguistic variations than were low reactant individuals. However, the interaction was observed for a message on the use of dental floss, but not one on reducing binge drinking.

Quick and Stephenson (2008) applied the multigroup method to test for differences in the association between message features, freedom threat, reactance, and a motivation to perform the advocated behavior. In doing so, they discovered that the association between a freedom threat and reactance was stronger for high trait reactant individuals than low trait reactant individuals within the context of sunscreen promotion. However, this finding was not replicated within the context of exercise. From this research, it appears that reactance proneness influences how individuals process persuasive messages, although these differences are not consistent across contexts/topics.

With partial empirical support for reactance proneness as a moderator of PRT, questions remain about why this individual difference variable impacts the message processing of freedom-threatening messages within some contexts but not others. One explanation for this inconsistency could be the importance of an issue. Recently, Quick et al. (2011) discovered that trait reactance was positively associated with a freedom threat within the context of organ donation. Moreover, among high trait reactant individuals

with low issue involvement toward the issue, exposure to the message increased perceptions of a freedom threat compared to individuals with high issue involvement. A criticism of this study is their broad conceptualization of involvement. Specific types, such as impression-, outcome-, and value-relevant involvement (Johnson & Eagly, 1989, 1990), might render different effects on reactance arousal.

Diminishing Reactance

Choice-Enhancing Postscripts

Just as domineering and controlling language induces reactance, the presence of choices tends to diminish it. Brehm and Brehm (1981) reviewed the impact of choice on reactance. Choice can impact reactance from the dispositional as well as situational perspectives. The dispositional approach considers individual differences in external versus internal locus of control. The basic argument is there is an interaction between locus of control and language used in counseling: Controlling and directive language is more effective for externals; and nondirective and unstructured language works better for internals (Abramowitz, Abramowitz, Roback, & Jackson, 1974; Kilman, Albert, & Sotile, 1975). The situational approach examines the outcomes of the presence of choice. Gordon (1976) found that choice led to significantly more perceived value of a clinical treatment, as well as more relaxation. Kanfer and Grimm (1978) found that free choice participants (choices offered and preference honored) improved significantly more than lost choice participants (choice offered, but preference not honored); however, no choice participants (choices not offered) did not differ significantly from either group.

However, without a measure of reactance, these studies cannot rule out the possibility that these results could have been produced due to cognitive dissonance, which unfortunately did not have a measure either. Miller et al. (2007) examined the impact of postscripts that restore one's freedom. Basically, a restoration postscript tells the recipient, "the choice is yours. You are free to decide for yourself"; while a filler postscript does not contain such an argument. Their results showed that the restoration postscript significantly reduced perceived threat to freedom. However, the authors did not report the impact of the postscript on negative cognition or anger, or on the persuasion outcomes. Although the evidence could have been stronger, this research has important implications for research and practice at the same time. Theoretically speaking, such research is consistent with the theorization of Brehm and Brehm (1981). Practically speaking, this offers a cost-effective means of message design to reduce psychological reactance.

Empathy

Given that reactance can be considered as an alloy of anger and negative cognition (Dillard & Shen, 2005), messages that inhibit unintended anger and reduce counter-argument should diminish reactance as well. It has been proposed that empathy-arousing messages fall into that strategy (Shen, 2010b, 2011). Empathy during message processing is defined as a perception-action process that occurs when the perception of the characters' state automatically activates the recipients' vicarious experience of the characters' state, situation, and objectives. Such empathic responses are conceptualized to have three components: perspective taking, emotional contagion, and identification (Shen, 2010a). Perspective taking means that the message recipients adopt the viewpoint of the message and its source, which means counter-argument is less likely. Emotional contagion means that the recipient's emotional experiences would be similar to those portrayed in the message, thus less unintended emotions (including anger).

The function of empathy lies in social bonding and relationship development, which indicates that it contradicts or inhibits the core relational theme for anger (a demeaning offense against me

and mine, Lazarus, 1991). Identification with the persuasive message means that the recipients tend to consider the persuasive attempt as less external, which reduces perceived threat to freedom, hence mitigating psychological reactance. There has been empirical evidence that in addition to a direct impact on persuasion, state empathy indeed mitigates psychological reactance (Shen, 2010b, 2011). Shen also identified three message features that are believed to induce empathy: the degree to which a message portrays characters' pain and suffering, the degree to which the message is realistic, and the degree to which the message is affect-laden. These studies provided initial evidence that empathy can be an effective means to reduce reactance.

Sensation Value

Message sensation value refers to "the degree to which formal and content audio-visual features of a message elicit sensory, affective, and arousal responses" (Palmgreen, Donohew, Lorch, Rogus, Helme, & Grant, 1991, p. 219), with sensation value being a critical determinant in message effectiveness. Messages high in sensation value elevate arousal or stimulation due to being dramatic, exciting, and novel (Morgan, Palmgreen, Stephenson, Lorch, & Hoyle, 2003). Similarly, perceived message sensation value refers to a message recipient's judgments of message sensation value along three dimensions (Palmgreen, Stephenson, Everett, Baseheart, & Francies, 2002): dramatic impact, emotional arousal, and novelty. Kang, Cappella, & Fishbein (2006) advance the intriguing argument that high sensation value messages can distract audiences from refuting the argument, that is, reduce counter-arguing, thereby enhancing ad persuasiveness. The results are complex. They show an interaction between argument quality, message sensation value, risk for marijuana use such that high risk adolescents judged the high quality–high sensation value messages as particularly ineffective. As the authors note, one challenge to interpretation lies with the fact that the high quality argument messages contained five times more commands than the low quality argument messages. A reactance perspective might suggest that this aspect of the message reduced persuasive impact especially among the pro-attitudinal (i.e., high risk group).

Working in the same area, Quick (in press) explicitly examined the relationship between the three dimensions of perceived message sensation value and reactance. His study of anti-marijuana messages showed no observable effect for either dramatic impact and emotional arousal. However, perceived novelty did significantly reduce reactance levels. Hence, the available data, though few in number, indicate that message novelty may be an effective means of preventing reactance effects. This knowledge provides direction for research and application, but cannot alone solve the context-bound problem of developing genuinely new reasons for behavior change.

Reactance as a Persuasive Strategy

Quick and colleagues (2009) argued that arousing reactance could serve as a motivator for individuals to support clean indoor air policies. They discovered that as individuals' anger increased following exposure to secondhand smoke, they were more likely to support clean indoor air policies. Therefore, as a rhetorical strategy, Quick et al. advocated the use of messages emphasizing the violation of one's right to breathable air could be an effective strategy, which in turn would motivate individuals to actively support clean indoor air initiatives. Mining a similar conceptual vein, Turner (2007) presents a framework for understanding political action that is motivated by choice-reduced anger.

A similar application of reactance-based persuasion can be seen in the "truth" campaign, a successful long-term effort to discourage smoking among Florida youth (Bauer, Johnson, Hopkins, & Brooks, 2000; Siegel & Biener, 2000). Interestingly, the website notes explicitly the potential for reactance effects: "Tell someone not to do something and they will. . . . We're not

here to tell people not to smoke, because, well, it doesn't work" (truth®, 2012). However, the anti-smoking ads themselves leverage reactance effects by portraying the tobacco industry as controlling and deceptive (Farrelly, Davis, Haviland, Messeri, & Healton, 2005). One message underscores industry efforts to manipulate adolescents in this way:

> In response to the fact that 5 million people around the world die annually due to tobacco, individuals outside of a major tobacco company sing and dance to a catchy song suggesting the ingredients in cigarettes, the health costs associated with smoking, and the number of deaths annually must be a typo. At the end of the ad, one of the performers say, "Wait, there is no way there is that many typos."

The campaign itself was a notable applied success. More intensive study of the messages using contemporary methods for assessing reactance could provide insight into the basis for that achievement.

New Directions for PRT Research

In keeping with the themes developed throughout this chapter, we see several promising possibilities for future research. Foremost among them is working toward a better understanding of the message features that enhance and diminish reactance. As currently formulated, many of the message concepts discussed in this chapter have their roots in lay perceptions of language rather than crafted scientific theories. A turn toward sociolinguist frameworks, such as politeness theory, or basic interpersonal communication theory might provide a perspective on message design that would move PRT in a forward direction.

Future research might also assess reactance proneness as a moderator variable in large-scale campaigns in much the same way sensation seeking has been examined in the past. In theory, reactance proneness appears to be an especially important segmentation strategy for adolescents and young adults, in particular because this is an age when reactance arousal is heightened (see Brehm & Brehm, 1981; Burgoon, Alvaro, Grandpre, et al., 2002; Woller, Buboltz, & Loveland, 2007). Answers to at least two questions are needed before it can be concluded that trait reactance is a useful general strategy: (1) To what extent, if any, is it empirically distinct from sensation seeking? (2) Can trait reactance predict patterns of message choice and consumption (as has been done so effectively for sensation seeking)?

Future research should seek to understand reactance as a strategy of empowerment. By broadening depictions of reactance as a potentially useful state, not just an aversive state, social influence researchers might be able to capitalize on opportunities to infuse change, particularly among adolescents who value their freedom and strongly oppose persuasive attempts aimed at reducing these freedoms. Understanding reactance as the basis for change is surely equal in importance to its role as a force for counterpersuasion.

Finally, we reemphasize the value of studying reactance as a process. Mass communication research might also benefit from application of PRT. Extant work has hypothesized that PRT can play a pivotal role in media selection, particularly among adolescents (Bushman & Cantor, 2003; Scharrer & Leone, 2008; Sneegas & Plank, 1998). Essentially, these researchers assert that media ratings restricting individuals from viewing particular programs or playing certain videogames enhance the attractiveness of the content (referred to as forbidden-fruit effect). Like other classic studies of PRT, media selection is limited by its reliance on outcomes associated with reactance rather than measuring the state directly. Media effect research would benefit from this approach, just as classic PRT inquiry has advanced by focusing on mediating processes.

Conclusion

As of this writing, reactance theory is almost half a century old. The fact that it still inspires questions and motivates research is testimony to the power of its ideas. Looking back, there is ample evidence that PRT has made signal contributions to our understanding of persuasion. As efforts are made to further refine the theory and to meld it with ongoing research, we anticipate that its value to future generations of persuasion researchers will equal or exceed its past achievements.

References

Abramowitz, C. V., Abramowitz, S. I., Roback, H. B., & Jackson, C. (1974). Differential effectiveness of directive and non-directive group therapies as a function of client internal-external control. *Journal of Consulting and Clinical Psychology, 42,* 849–853.

Bauer, U. E., Johnson, T. M., Hopkins, R. S., & Brooks, R. G. (2000). Changes in youth cigarette use and intentions following implementation of a tobacco control program: Findings from the Florida Youth Tobacco Survey, 1998–2000. *The Journal of the American Medical Association, 284,* 723–728.

Benoit, W. L. (1998). Forewarning and persuasion. In M. Allen & R. W. Preiss (Eds.), *Persuasion: Advances through meta-analysis* (pp. 139–154). Cresskill, NJ: Hampton Press.

Bensley, L. S., & Wu, R. (1991). The role of psychological reactance in drinking following alcohol prevention messages. *Journal of Applied Social Psychology, 21,* 1111–1124.

Brehm, J. W. (1966). *A theory of psychological reactance.* New York, NY: Academic Press.

Brehm, J. W., & Brehm, S. S. (1981). *Psychological reactance: A theory of freedom and control.* San Diego, CA: Academic Press.

Brehm, J. W., Stires, L. K., Sensenig, J., & Shaban, J. (1996). The attractiveness of an eliminated choice alternative. *Journal of Experimental Social Psychology, 2,* 301–313.

Brehm, S. S., & Weinraub, M. (1977). Physical barriers and psychological reactance: 2-year-olds' responses to threats to freedom. *Journal of Personality and Social Psychology, 35,* 830–836.

Brown, A. R., Finney, S. J., & France, M. K. (2011). Using the bifactor model to assess the dimensionality of the Hong Psychological Reactance Scale. *Educational and Psychological Measurement 71*(1), 170–185.

Brugoon, M., Alvaro, E., Broneck, K., Miller, C., Grandpre, J. R., Hall, J. R., & Frank, C. A. (2002). Using interactive media tools to test substance abuse prevention messages. In W. D. Crano & M. Burgoon (Eds.), *Mass media and drug prevention: Classic and contemporary theories and research* (pp. 67–87). Mahwah, NJ: Erlbaum.

Buboltz, W. C., Thomas, A., & Donnell, A. J. (2002). Evaluating the factor structure and internal consistency reliability of the therapeutic reactance scale. *Journal of Counseling & Development, 80,* 120–125.

Buller, D. B., Borland, R., & Burgoon, M. (1998). Impact of behavioral intention on effectiveness of message features: Evidence from the family sun safety project. *Human Communication Research, 24,* 433–453.

Burgoon, M., Alvaro, E., Grandpre, J., & Voulodakis, M. (2002). Revisiting the theory of psychological reactance: Communicating threats to attitudinal freedom. In J. P. Dillard & M. Pfau (Eds.), *The persuasion handbook: Developments in theory and practice* (pp. 213–232). Thousand Oaks, CA: Sage.

Bushman, B. J., & Cantor, J. (2003). Media ratings for violence and sex: Implications for policymakers and parents. *American Psychologist, 58,* 130–141.

Dillard, J. P., & Meijnders, A. (2002). Persuasion and the structure of affect. In J. P. Dillard and M. Pfau (Eds.), *The persuasion handbook: Developments in theory and research* (pp. 309–327). Thousand Oaks, CA: Sage.

Dillard, J. P., & Peck. E. (2000). Affect and persuasion: Emotional responses to public service announcements. *Communication Research, 27,* 461–495.

Dillard, J. P., & Peck. E. (2001). Persuasion and the structure of affect: Dual systems and discrete emotions as complementary models. *Human Communication Research, 27,* 38–68.

Dillard, J. P., Plotnick, C. A., Godbold, L. C., Freimuth, V. S., & Edgar, T. (1996). The multiple affective consequences of AIDS PSAs: Fear appeals do more than scare people. *Communication Research, 23,* 44–72.

Dillard, J. P., & Shen, L. (2005). On the nature of reactance and its role in persuasive health communication. *Communication Monographs, 72,* 144–168.

Donnell, A. J., Thomas, A., & Buboltz, W. (2001). Psychological reactance: Factor structure and internal consistency of the questionnaire for the measurement of psychological reactance. *The Journal of Social Psychology, 14,* 679–687.

Dowd, E. T., Milne, C. R., & Wise, S. L. (1991). The therapeutic reactance scale: A measure of psychological reactance. *Journal of Counseling & Development, 69,* 541–545.

Dowd, E. T., Wallbrown, F., Sanders, D., & Yesenosky, J. M. (1994). Psychological reactance and its relationship to normal personality variables. *Cognitive Therapy and Research, 18,* 601–612.

Farrelly, M. C., Davis, K. C., Haviland, M. L., Messeri, P., & Healton, C. G. (2005). Evidence of a dose-response relationship between "truth" antismoking ads and youth smoking prevalence. *American Journal of Public Health, 95,* 425–431.

Gordon, R. M. (1976). Effects of volunteering and responsibility on perceived value and effectiveness of a clinical treatment. *Journal of Consulting and Clinical Psychology, 44,* 799–801.

Grandpre, J. R., Alvaro, E. M., Burgoon, M., Miller, C. H., & Hall, J. R. (2003). Adolescent reactance and anti-smoking campaigns: A theoretical approach. *Health Communication, 15,* 349–366.

Hammock, T., & Brehm, J. W. (1966). The attractiveness of choice alternatives when freedom to choose is eliminated by a social agent. *Journal of Personality, 34,* 546–554.

Heller, J. F., Pallak, M. S., & Picek, J. M. (1973). The interactive effects of intent and threat on boomerang attitude change. *Journal of Personality and Social Psychology, 26,* 273–279.

Henriksen, L., Dauphinee, A., Wang, Y., & Fortmann, S. (2006). Tobacco companies' antismoking ads and adolescent reactance: Test of a boomerang effect. *Tobacco Control, 15,* 13–18.

Hong, S. M. (1992). Hong's Psychological Reactance Scale: A further factor analytic validation. *Psychological Reports, 70,* 512–514.

Hong, S. M., & Faedda, S. (1996). Refinement of the Hong psychological reactance scale. *Educational and Psychological Measurement, 56,* 173–182.

Hong, S. M., & Ostini, R. (1989). Further evaluation of Merz's psychological reactance scale. *Psychological Reports, 64,* 707–710.

Hong, S. M., & Page, S. (1989). A psychological reactance scale: Development, factor structure and reliability. *Psychological Reports, 64,* 1323–1326.

Johnson, B. T., & Eagly, A. H. (1989). Effects of involvement on persuasion: A meta-analysis. *Psychological Bulletin, 106,* 290–314.

Johnson, B. T., & Eagly, A. H. (1990). Involvement and persuasion: Types, traditions, and the evidence. *Psychological Bulletin, 107,* 375–384.

Kanfer, F. H., & Grimm, L. G. (1978). Freedom of choice and behavioral change. *Journal of Consulting and Clinical Psychology, 46,* 873–878.

Kang, Y., Cappella, J. N., & Fishbein, M. (2006). The attentional mechanism of message sensation value: Interaction between message sensation value and argument quality on message effectiveness. *Communication Monographs, 73,* 351–378.

Kelly, A. E., & Nauta, M. M. (1997). Reactance and thought suppression. *Personality and Social Psychology Bulletin, 23,* 1123–1132.

Kilman, P. R., Albert, B. M., & Sotile, W. M. (1975). Relationship between locus of control, structure of therapy, and outcome. *Journal of Consulting and Clinical Psychology, 43,* 588.

Kohn, P. M., & Barnes, G. E. (1977). Subject variables and reactance to persuasive communications about drugs. *European Journal of Social Psychology, 7,* 97–109.

Lazarus, R. S. (1991). *Emotion and adaptation.* New York, NY: Oxford University Press.

Leventhal, H. (1970). Findings and theory in the study of fear communications. In L. Berkowitz (Ed.), *Advances in experimental social psychology* (Vol. 5, pp. 119–186). New York, NY: Academic Press.

Lindsey, L. L. M. (2005). Anticipated guilt as behavioral motivation: An examination of appeals to help unknown others through bone marrow donation. *Human Communication Research, 31,* 453–481.

Merz, J. (1983). A questionnaire for the measurement of psychological reactance [in German]. *Diagnostica, 29,* 75–82.

Miller, C. H, Burgoon, M., Grandpre, J. R., & Alvaro, E. M. (2006). Identifying principal risk factors for the initiation of adolescent smoking behaviors: The significance of psychological reactance. *Health Communication, 19,* 241–252.

Miller, C. H., Lane, L. T., Deatrick, L. M., Young, A. M., & Potts, K. A. (2007). Psychological reactance and promotional health messages: The effects of controlling language, lexical concreteness, and the restoration of freedom. *Human Communication Research, 33,* 219–240.

Miller, C. H., & Quick, B. L., (2010). Sensation seeking and psychological reactance as health risk predictors for an emerging adult population. *Health Communication, 25,* 266–275.

Morgan, S. E., Palmgreen, P., Stephenson, M. T., Lorch, E. P., & Hoyle, R. H. (2003). The relationship between message sensation value and perceived message sensation value: The effect of formal message features on subjective evaluations of anti-drug public service announcements. *Journal of Communication, 53,* 512–526.

Moyer-Gusé, E. (2008). Toward a theory of entertainment in persuasion: Explaining the persuasive effects of EE messages. *Communication Theory, 18,* 407–425.

Moyer-Gusé, E., & Nabi, R. L. (2010). Explaining the effects of narrative in an entertainment television program: Overcoming resistance to persuasion. *Human Communication Research, 36,* 26–52.

Nabi, R. L. (2002). Discrete emotions and persuasion. In J. P. Dillard & M. Pfau (Eds.), *The persuasion handbook: Developments in theory and research* (pp. 289–308). Thousand Oaks, CA: Sage.

Palmgreen, P., Donohew, L., Lorch, E, P., Rogus, M., Helme, D., & Grant, N. (1991). Sensation seeking, message sensation value, and drug use as mediators of ad effectiveness. *Health Communication, 3,* 217–227.

Palmgreen, P., Stephenson, M. T., Everett, M. W., Baseheart, J. R., & Francies, R. (2002). Perceived message sensation value (PMSV) and the dimensions and validation of a PMSV scale. *Health Communication, 14,* 403–428.

Petty, R. E., & Cacioppo, J. T. (1986). *Communication and persuasion: Central and peripheral routes to attitude change.* New York, NY: Springer-Verlag.

Quick, B. L. (2012). What is the best measure of psychological reactance? An empirical test of two measures. *Health Communication, 27,* 1–9.

Quick, B. L. (in press). Perceived message sensation value and psychological reactance: A test of the dominant thought disruption hypothesis. *Journal of Health Communication.*

Quick, B. L., & Bates, B. R. (2010). The use of gain- or loss-frame messages and efficacy appeals to dissuade excessive alcohol consumption among college students: A test of psychological reactance theory. *Journal of Health Communication, 15,* 603–628.

Quick, B. L., Bates, B. R., & Quinlan, M. R. (2009). The utility of anger in promoting clean indoor air policies. *Health Communication, 24,* 548–561.

Quick, B. L., & Considine, J. R. (2008). Examining the use of forceful language when designing exercise advertisements for adults: A test of conceptualizing reactance arousal as a two-step process. *Health Communication, 23,* 483–491.

Quick, B. L., & Kim, D. K. (2009). Examining reactance and reactance restoration with Korean adolescents: A test of psychological reactance within a collectivist culture. *Communication Research, 36,* 765–782.

Quick, B. L., Scott, A. M., & Ledbetter, A. (2011). A close examination of trait reactance and issue involvement as moderators of psychological reactance theory. *Journal of Health Communication, 16,* 660–679.

Quick, B. L., & Stephenson, M. T. (2007a). Further evidence that psychological reactance can be modeled as a combination of anger and negative cognitions. *Communication Research, 34,* 255–276.

Quick, B. L., & Stephenson, M. T. (2007b). The reactance restoration scale (RSS): A measure of direct and indirect restoration. *Communication Research Reports, 24,* 131–138.

Quick, B. L., & Stephenson, M. T. (2008). Examining the role of trait reactance and sensation seeking on reactance-inducing messages, reactance, and reactance restoration. *Human Communication Research, 34,* 448–476.

Rains, S. A., & Turner, M. (2007). Psychological reactance and persuasive health communication: A test and extension of the intertwined model. *Human Communication Research, 33,* 241–269.

Reich, J. W., & Robertson, J. L. (1979). Reactance and norm appeal in anti-littering messages. *Journal of Applied Social Psychology, 9,* 91–101.

Reinhart, A. M., Marshall, H. M., Feeley, T. H., & Tutzauer, F. (2007). The persuasive effects of message framing in organ donation: The mediating role of psychological reactance. *Communication Monographs, 74,* 229–255.

Scharrer, E., & Leone, R. (2008). First-person shooters and the third-person effect. *Human Communication Research, 34,* 210–233.

Schwarz, N., Frey, D., & Kumpf, M. (1980). Interactive effects of writing and reading a persuasive essay on attitude change and selective exposure. *Journal of Experimental Social Psychology, 16,* 1–17.

Seibel, C. A., & Dowd, E. T. (2001). Personality characteristics associated with psychological reactance. *Journal of Clinical Psychology, 57,* 963–969.

Seltzer, L. F. (1983). Influencing the "shape" of resistance: An experimental exploration of paradoxical directives and psychological reactance. *Basic and Applied Social Psychology, 4,* 47–71.

Shen, L. (2010a). Mitigating psychological reactance: The role of message-induced empathy in persuasion. *Human Communication Research, 36,* 397–422.

Shen, L. (2010b). On a scale of state empathy during message processing. *Western Journal of Communication, 74,* 504–524.

Shen, L. (2011). The effectiveness of fear- vs. empathy-arousing anti-smoking PSAs. *Health Communication, 26,* 404–415.

Shen, L., & Dillard, J. P. (2005). Psychometric properties of the Hong Psychological Reactance Scale. *Journal of Personality Assessment, 85,* 74–81.

Siegel, M., & Biener, L. (2000). The impact of an anti-smoking media campaign on progression to established smoking: Results of a longitudinal youth study. *American Journal of Public Health, 90,* 380–386.

Smith, M. J. (1977). The effects of threats to attitudinal freedom as a function of message quality and initial receiver attitude. *Communication Monographs, 44,* 196–206.

Sneegas, J. E., & Plank, T. A. (1998). Gender differences in pre-adolescent reactance to age-categorized television advisory labels. *Journal of Broadcasting & Electronic Media, 42,* 423–434.

Stephenson, M. T. (2003). Examining adolescents' responses to antimarijuana PSAs. *Human Communication Research, 29,* 343–369.

Stephenson, M. T., Palmgreen, P., Hoyle, R. H., Donohew, L., Lorch, E., & Colon, S. E. (1999). Short-term effects of an anti-marijuana media campaign targeting high sensation seeking adolescents. *Journal of Applied Communication Research, 27,* 175–195.

truth®. (2012). *About Us.* Retrieved March 9, 2012, from http://www.thetruth.com/about/

Tucker, R. K., & Byers, P. Y. (1987). Factorial validity of Merz's psychological reactance scale. *Psychological Reports, 61,* 811–815.

Turner, M. M. (2007). Using emotion to prevent risky behavior: The anger activism model. *Public Relations Review, 33,* 114–119.

White, G. L., & Zimbardo, P. G. (1980). The effects of threat of surveillance and actual surveillance on expressed opinion toward marijuana. *Journal of Social Psychology, 111,* 49–61.

Wicklund, R. A. (1974). *Freedom and reactance.* Potomac, MD: Lawrence Erlbaum.

Wicklund, R. A., & Brehm, J. W. (1968). Attitude change as a function of felt competence and threat to attitudinal freedom. *Journal of Experimental Social Psychology, 4,* 64–75.

Witte, K. (1994). Fear control and danger control: A test of the Extended Parallel Process Model (EPPM). *Communication Monographs, 61,* 113–134.

Woller, K. M. P., Buboltz, Jr., W. C., & Loveland, J. M. (2007). Psychological reactance: Examination across age, ethnicity, and gender. *American Journal of Psychology, 120,* 15–24.

Wood, W., & Quinn, J. M. (2003). Forewarned and forearmed? Two meta-analytic syntheses of forewarnings of influence appeals. *Psychological Bulletin, 129,* 119–138.

Worchel, S. (1974). The effect of three types of arbitrary thwarting on the instigation to aggression. *Journal of Personality, 42,* 300–318.

Worchel, S., & Andreoli, V. (1974). Attribution of causality as a means of restoring behavioral freedom. *Journal of Personality and Social Psychology, 29,* 237–245.

Worchel, S., Andreoli, V. A., & Archer, R. (1976). When is a favor a threat to freedom: The effects of attribution and importance of freedom on reciprocity. *Journal of Personality, 44,* 294–310.

CHAPTER 12

Fear Appeals

Paul A. Mongeau

The half-life of social science theory and research is notoriously short. Scholars have a seemingly insatiable need to focus on new, different, and unique ideas, even if they represent old wine in new academic skins. The study of persuasion, however, seems immune to this short attention span. This may be because the nature of attitudes; how they are shaped, reinforced, and changed; and how they are (un) related to behaviors are, relatively speaking, less strongly influenced by social and cultural changes. As a consequence, the social scientific study of many persuasion theories and concepts has relatively long histories. What is more, the study of fear appeals is among the oldest in all such persuasion research.

The chapter's primary goal is to review social science fear appeals theory and research. Despite considerable uncertainty in the early years, general conclusions of the effectiveness of fear appeals have become more optimistic in the past few decades. Fear appeals work, at least for most audiences and most contexts. Disagreements abound, however, concerning why fear appeals work (and why they don't). I will conclude that one reason that this is the case is that the explanations have not been given a fair test. Therefore, this chapter will spend more time considering explanations than the actual

research. Before doing so, two fundamental issues—the nature of emotions and the nature of fear appeals—are considered.

Emotions and Persuasion

There is a general consensus that emotions are an amalgam of cognitive, physiological, and behavioral elements (Bradley & Lang, 2000; Nabi, 2002; Shiota & Kalat, 2011). The relative importance of these elements in the production of emotion, however, has been the source of considerable disagreement (e.g., Zajonc, 1980, versus Lazarus, 1982). Cognitively based views of emotions tend to ignore physiological processes (e.g., Witte, 1992). Psychophysiological views of emotion, on the other hand, largely ignore cognition and typically consider emotion to be identifiable solely from physiological measures (e.g., Williams et al., 2001). Although it is important to integrate, and truly balance, physiological, behavioral, and cognitive elements in the production and effects of emotion (Bradley & Lang, 2000), actually finding scholarship that actually does so is rare.

The persuasion literature generally considers emotions from a cognitive perspective (Nabi, 2002). Given this focus, emotions have four particularly useful characteristics (Guerrero,

Andersen, & Trost, 1998). First, emotions involve a rapid cognitive evaluation of environmental changes. The emotion of fear, for example, necessitates identifying a threat to health and well-being (e.g., Leventhal, 1970). Second, emotions reflect an affective evaluation of the environmental change. Changes that reflect positively on health and well-being generally generate positive emotions (e.g., joy or love), while environmental changes that reflect poorly on us likely generate negative emotions (e.g., jealousy or fear). Third, even from a cognitive perspective, there is an understanding that emotions involve physiological responses. Finally, and most relevant to persuasion, emotions have a behavioral component; that is, "The primary function of emotion is to guide behavior" (Dillard & Meijnders, 2002, p. 318).

Defining Fear, Threat, and Fear Appeals

Given this view of emotions, it is important to define fear and associated terms. Witte defined fear as "a negatively-valenced emotion accompanied by a high level of arousal and is elicited by a threat that is perceived to be significant and personally relevant" (Witte, 1992, p. 331; see also Easterling & Leventhal, 1989). This definition highlights three important points. First and most simply, fear is an emotion. Second, the experience of fear involves, by definition, physiological arousal (e.g., increases in heart rate, respiration rate, blood pressure as well as pupil dilation and releases of adrenaline; Guerrero et al., 1998). Thus, an approach to fear appeals that ignores physiology is missing an important element of the emotional process. Finally, Witte's (1992) definition suggests an important link between fear and threat. I consider this distinction and its implications for the construction of fear appeals next.

Despite important differences between fear and threat, these terms have been used synonymously throughout the history of fear appeals

(Witte, 1992; see, for example, Hovland, Janis, & Kelly, 1953). Fear is an internal characteristic, that is, a negative emotion that is thought to intervene between fear appeals and responses (Hovland et al., 1953; Witte, 1992). Threat, on the other hand, is an environmental characteristic that represents something that portends negative consequences for the individual. Thus, messages depict a threat, that when processed by the receiver, creates fear.

The distinction between fear and threat has clear implications for the construction of fear appeals. According to Rogers (1975, 1983 and most scholars that followed), fear appeals contain two parts: a threat component and a coping component. Each of these components is further subdivided into two parts. First, fear appeals depict an environmental *threat* to recipients' health and well-being. In most fear appeal manipulations, the depicted threat to well-being is physical (e.g., second-hand smoke causes cancer). More specifically, through intense verbal text often (but not necessarily) accompanied by vivid graphics (e.g., gruesome photographs), researchers typically manipulate the threat's *severity* (e.g., lack of adequate dental hygiene cases great pain from toothaches, mouth infections, decayed teeth and painful trips to the dentist; Janis & Feshbach, 1953). The second threat component is *susceptibility* (or vulnerability) that indicates that the environmental threat is likely to strike unless preventative action is taken (e.g., painful outcomes will occur unless message recommendations are followed; Janis & Feshbach).

Fear appeals initially depict a threat to the receivers' health and/or well-being. This message component, according to some (but not all) fear appeal explanations, generates the emotion of fear in the audience members (e.g., Hovland et al., 1953; Witte, 1992). For a fear appeal to be persuasive (i.e., generate responses in the direction of message recommendations), however, it must also indicate how audience members can *avoid* the threat. Therefore, the second fear appeal component is the *coping component* (Rogers, 1975, 1983; Witte, 1992) that includes both response efficacy and self-efficacy information. First, response efficacy represents "the availability and effectiveness of a coping response that might reduce or eliminate the noxious stimulus" (Rogers, 1975, p. 97). Second, self-efficacy represents the extent to which the recipient has the ability to perform the recommended behavior (Rogers, 1983). Self-efficacy is important, for example, in the case of smoking cessation. A tobacco smoker might understand that smoking dramatically increases the probability of contracting several nasty diseases (high perceived noxiousness and vulnerability) and that smoking cessation reduces those probabilities (high perceived response efficacy). If the recipient, however, considers smoking an addiction, a lack of self-efficacy would likely interfere with enacting the recommended coping behavior. In short, current thinking suggests that in order to be effective, fear appeals must not only depict a serious and imminent threat, but must also provide the individual with a way of *avoiding* that threat.

Do Fear Appeals Work?

The social scientific study of fear appeals begins, for all intents and purposes, with Janis and Feshbach's (1953) seminal investigation (also described in Hovland et al., 1953). In their study, they presented the entire freshman class of large Connecticut high school (in intact classrooms) with minimal, moderate, or strong fear appeals concerning dental hygiene (i.e., proper tooth brushing technique and equipment) or a control message. Their results indicated that as the strength of the fear appeal increased, behavior change in the week following message reception decreased. In short, they reported a negative linear relationship between fear appeals and behavior change.

As in other cases where an initial study generates counterintuitive results (e.g., LaPiere, 1934), considerable fear appeal research ensued over the next two decades. Most studies during this time generated positive linear relationships between

fear appeals and attitude and behavior change. On the other hand, some studies from that era (i.e., Goldstein, 1959; Janis & Terwilliger, 1962; Leventhal & Watts, 1966) were consistent with Janis & Feshbach's (1953) results (i.e., a negative linear relationships between fear appeal strength and attitude change).

When I began reading the fear appeal literature in the early 1980s, reviews typically included wailing and gnashing of teeth as authors described incongruous and confusing results (e.g., Smith, 1982). This confusion stemmed, in large part, from the contradictory results among those early fear appeal studies. Over the past three decades, reviewers of the fear appeal literature have become more positive. Early meta-analyses (Boster & Mongeau, 1984; Sutton, 1982) suggested that the literature was not as confusing or as scattered as the previous reviews suggested. In addition, an important methodological milestone in clarifying the effects of fear appeals is Rogers's (1975, 1983) explication of the fear appeal manipulation (described earlier). A large majority of performed studies after Rogers' clarification of the structure of fear appeals report *positive* linear relationship between the strength of a fear appeal and message acceptance (see Witte & Allen, 2000).

Recent meta-analyses (e.g., Witte & Allen, 2000) indicate that the accumulated research clearly suggests that fear-arousing messages work, at least for most audiences and on most occasions. (This caveat is an important one that will be discussed later in the chapter.) In summarizing their meta-analytic results, Witte and Allen conclude:

> In sum, the stronger the fear appeal, the greater the attitude, intention and behavior changes. Similarly, the stronger the severity and susceptibility in the message, the more attitude, intention, and behavior changes. Finally, the stronger the response efficacy and self-efficacy in a message, the stronger the attitudes, intentions, and behaviors toward the recommended response. (p. 598)

Fear Appeal Explanations

Over the past several decades, several explanations attempted to elucidate fear appeals successes and failures. Therefore, this section describes and evaluates five historically important approaches to fear appeals: the drive model (Hovland et al., 1953), the parallel response model (Leventhal, 1970), the protection motivation explanation (Rogers, 1975, 1983), the extended parallel processing model (Witte, 1992), and the stage model (Stroebe, 2000). These explanations reflect predominant contemporary social science paradigms. In the 1950s and 1960s, the predominant explanation (the drive model; e.g., Hovland et al., 1953; Janis, 1967; McGuire, 1969) reflected classical condition and learning paradigms. Through the 1970s and beyond, as the cognitive revolution challenged, and eventually superseded, the reinforcement paradigm (G. A. Miller, 2003), fear appeal explanations quickly followed suit. During this time, fear appeal explanations swung from entirely emotion and reinforcement-based, to presenting a balance between emotion and cognitive foci, to finally becoming entirely cognitive (and, thus, representing threat appeal explanations as previously defined), where consideration of emotion processes waned. It is only relatively recently that the emotion of fear has returned to the study of fear appeals, but only from a cognitive perspective.

Another interesting aspect of these explanations is that rather than representing entirely new formulations, each attempt builds on, and includes elements from, earlier explanations. This is an interesting choice as the explication of each new explanation generally involves a scholarly thrashing of the predecessors.

The Drive Model

As with several other topics, the social scientific study of fear appeals largely begins with Hovland et al.'s (1953) *Communication and Persuasion.*

Their fear appeal chapter offered considerable speculation (in part because there were very few data beyond Janis & Feshbach, 1953) concerning the persuasive effects of fear appeals. The chapter introduced many concepts that remain at the forefront of fear appeal scholarship today. Moreover, their drive model dominated the fear appeals conversation for over 20 years. Although its predictions are inconsistent with the accumulated data, it remains important bedrock on which the foundations of other explanations are built.

Working from the classical conditioning paradigm, Hovland et al.'s (1953) *drive model*, depicts fear as a drive; that is, a negatively valenced state that an individual is motivated to avoid or (once experienced) eliminate. The explanation claims that the threat presented in a persuasive message initiates fear as a drive state. The emotional arousal generates a search for, and effort to work through, several strategies to reduce the drive. Whatever strategy is successful in reducing the drive state is considered a reward, thereby increasing the probability that it will be repeated in the future (Hovland et al., 1953). If rehearsing and advocating message recommendations reduces fear, they will be integrated into the receiver's cognitive structure (i.e., attitude and behavior change occur) and this strategy will represent the preferred option for processing future messages. If, on the other hand, rehearsing message recommendations fails to reduce the drive, audience members will attempt alternative strategies. For example, Hovland et al. suggest that the receiver might attempt to disregard the message (i.e., inattentiveness), derogate the message source, or minimize or ignore the threat. Of course, if receivers take this route, attitude and behavior change seems unlikely. Again, if any of these alternative strategies are successful in reducing drive, it is rewarding and represents the response of choice in similar future situations.

From the drive model, Hovland et al. (1953) predicted a curvilinear (i.e., inverted-U shaped) relationship between the strength of a fear appeal and attitude and behavior change. Specifically, "from zero to some moderate level, acceptance tends to increase, but as emotional tension mounts to higher levels, acceptance tends to decrease" (Hovland et al., 1953, pp. 83–84). In short, the drive model predicts that greatest levels of attitude and behavior change will occur when fear appeals are moderate (when compared to when they are either low or high).

Two noteworthy extensions of the drive model are Janis's (1967) "family of curves" and McGuire's (1968, 1969) two-factor explanation. Janis argues that fear arousal creates competing forces of vigilance to the threat, on the one hand, and hypervigilance (i.e., interference) on the other. Increasing fear arousal facilitates audience members' motivation and ability to process the persuasive message, however, as fear arousal increases further, facilitating factors are countered by interference (e.g., defensive avoidance through counterarguing in a search for loopholes; Janis, 1967, p. 176). The point on the arousal continuum at which inhibiting factors outweigh facilitating factors varies across messages and audiences, resulting in a *family of curves* where the function's peak falls at different points on an emotional arousal continuum.

McGuire (1968, 1969), on the other hand, argued that when a persuasive message creates fear, the emotion can act as a cue or as a drive. As a cue, receivers depend on learned responses that interfere with message reception and acceptance. On the other hand, as a drive, fear motivates receivers to avoid the threat and is thought to facilitate message acceptance. Both drive and cue functions increase monotonically as fear arousal increases, but at differing rates. This combination of competing forces leads to the predicted inverted U-shaped relationship.

Evaluating the Drive Model

One important criticism of the drive model focuses on the representation of fear as a drive. Equating these terms essentially places emotion in the same category as hunger or thirst. Thus, although it refers to emotional arousal, does little more than wave its hand toward emotion as it is considered in more recent theory and research.

What is more, the curvilinear prediction between fear appeal strength and responses derived from the drive model was doomed from the beginning. Although social science theorizing at the day was replete with inverted-U-shaped functions (Leventhal, 1970), pairing the drive model with a curvilinear relationship was a curious choice. The most complete data that Hovland et al. (1953) reported was the negative linear relationship on behavior change from Janis and Feshbach (1953). It is difficult to shoehorn these data into the drive model's inverted U-shaped function. Hovland et al. claim that the negative linear relationship represents the downward slope in the inverted-U (see also Janis, 1967). For this to be the case, however, Janis and Feshbach's *minimal* appeal would have to be at least moderate on some objective fear arousal continuum. This supposition is handicapped because Hovland et al. also went into great detail describing the truly mundane nature of the *minimal* appeal. In summary, evidence consistent with the curvilinear relationship in subsequent research is virtually nonexistent (Boster & Mongeau, 1984; Witte & Allen, 2000), although I will argue later that the methods typically used in fear appeal studies do not fully test the model.

Given the drive model's inability to explain the accumulated data, subsequent explanations attempted to explain both positive linear and negative linear relationships between the strength of fear appeals and responses. Specifically, similar to McGuire's (1968) two-factor approach, these explanations present multiple ways of processing fear-arousing messages (e.g., Das, de Wit, & Stroebe, 2003; Leventhal, 1970; Witte, 1993). Typically, one way of dealing with fear appeals facilitates message acceptance while the other inhibits it. Moreover, over time, the next generation of explanations focused increasingly on the cognitive, rather than affective, processes.

Parallel Response Model

Although other explanations appeared in the interim (e.g., G. R. Miller, 1963), the second historically important fear appeal explanation is the parallel response model (Leventhal, 1970, 1971). This explanation acts as a bridge between the largely affectively focused drive model and the more recent, cognitively oriented, explanations. Specifically, the parallel response model suggests that audience members will deal with the depicted threat in one of two ways: fear control or danger control.

Fear Control

In fear control, internal affective responses (e.g., physiological arousal) are interpreted as a sign of fear. When further cognitive work suggests that there is nothing to be done to avoid the threat, audience members will look internally to reduce emotional arousal. Leventhal (1970) argues that a wide variety of responses might occur during fear control (e.g., defensive reactions, eating or drinking to interfere with emotional responses, or reinterpreting the arousal). Audience members' internal focus likely inhibits focusing on, elaborating about, and accepting message recommendations. When audience members engage in fear control, then, the strength of fear appeals should be inversely related to attitude and behavior change.

Danger Control

Danger control represents a problem-solving process whereby recipients consider how to deal with the message threat. Information guiding problem-solving typically comes from the message itself, though other sources of information (e.g., memory, coping abilities, and emotional responses) are also important, particularly as the problem-solving process develops (Leventhal, 1970). In other words, danger control increases the probability that receivers will attend to, elaborate on, and accept message recommendations. Therefore, when audience members engage in danger control, the strength of fear appeals should be positively correlated with attitude and behavior change.

As the model's label suggests, danger control's problem solving process works parallel to, and independently from, fear control emotional processes. Thus, emotional arousal (i.e., fear) should be positively correlated with attitude and behavior change, however, this relationship is spurious as both responses are caused by the message (Leventhal, 1970). Thus, fear appeals generate *both* fear and adaptive responses; however, they are not causally related.

Evaluating the Parallel Processing Model

The primary value of the parallel processing model is historical, as it was the first explanation to clearly and explicitly separate cognitive from affective responses to a fear appeal. Therefore, the parallel processing explanation provided a logical explanation for the inconsistencies in fear appeal studies of the time. Specifically, studies generating negative relationships between fear appeals and attitude change (e.g., Janis & Feshbach, 1953) produced fear control while studies producing positive correlations (e.g., G. R. Miller & Hewgill, 1966) produced danger control.

Although this explanation facilitated thinking about fear appeals' persuasive successes and failures, it had one serious flaw. Specifically, it lacked the specificity necessary to generate clear predictions and tests (Beck & Frankel, 1981; Boster & Mongeau, 1984; Rogers, 1975). Specifically, Leventhal (1970, 1971) neither developed operationalizations fear control and danger control, nor specified the conditions under which each would operate. (Ironically, Leventhal criticized both Janis' family of curves explanation and the drive model on the same grounds.) Leventhal predicted that the strength of fear appeals would generally be positively related to attitude and behavior change. Sternthal and Craig (1974), however, used the same explanation to predict an inverted-U-shaped relationship between fear appeal strength and attitude and behavior change. Specifically, danger control would predominate from low to some moderate level of emotional arousal after which fear control would take over. Given the lack of specificity in construct specification and predictions, it is impossible to differentiate, or test, these predictions.

Therefore, although historically important for extending thinking about fear appeal processing, the parallel response model is not testable. Following the trend sweeping the social sciences, the next family of explanations (e.g., Beck & Frankel, 1981; Rogers, 1975) posited that attitude and behavior change was an exclusive function of the cognitive processing of fear appeals and virtually ignored emotional arousal (Witte, 1992). Although fear and perceptions of threat are "intricately and reciprocally related" (Witte & Allen, 2000, p. 592), the emotion of fear went AWOL from fear appeals for nearly two decades.

Protection Motivation Explanation

Rogers (1975) attributed the inconsistent fear appeal results to the haphazard manner in which fear appeals had been conceptualized and operationalized. Thus, the primary contribution of Rogers' (1975, 1983) protection motivation explanation (both original and revised) is the specification of fear appeal components. Although these components had been previously described several times (e.g., Hovland et al., 1953; Janis, 1967; Leventhal, 1970), Rogers's systematic descriptions generated greater consistency in the development of fear appeals and, perhaps, study results.

As previously noted, Rogers (1975, 1983) described fear appeal as containing four components (severity, susceptibility, self-efficacy, and response efficacy). Working from an expectancy value perspective (cf., chapter 8 in this volume), the protection motivation explanation posits that receivers evaluate messages along each message component (i.e., perceived severity, perceived susceptibility, perceived response efficacy, and perceived self-efficacy). In the initial formulation, these perceptual variables combined multiplicatively to create protection

motivation, an intervening variable that "arouses, sustains, and directs activity" (Rogers, 1975, p. 94). Protection motivation, in turn, directly influences behavior change. Thus, protection motivation (akin to behavioral intention) replaces fear as the mediating variable between fear appeals and responses. "Our emphasis on 'protection motivation' rather than 'fear' is designed to emphasize the importance of cognitive processes rather than visceral ones" (Rogers, 1983, p. 169).

In short, the protection motivation explanation initially predicted a threat by efficacy interaction on attitude and behavior change. When either threat or efficacy levels are zero (e.g., either the threat is weak or if the coping response is ineffective), no attitude or behavior change is predicted to occur. Messages that present a severe threat that is likely to strike the audience member will be persuasive *only* if they are combined with recommended coping responses that are effective in avoiding the threat and that are in the receiver's behavioral repertoire.

Evaluating the Protection Motivation Explanation

The primary strength of the protection motivation explanation is the specification of fear appeal components; particularly the bifurcation of threat and coping components. Although they were discussed earlier (e.g., Hovland et al., 1953), Rogers's (1975, 1983) conceptualizations and operationalizations represent important grounding for subsequent theoretical frames (e.g., Stroebe, 2000; Witte, 1993).

The revised protection motivation explanation is relatively difficult to evaluate as it relates to fear appeals because it extends beyond persuasive messages to include other information sources (e.g., intrapersonal and social) relevant to coping. Thus, the revised explanation includes, but extends far beyond fear appeals. As a consequence, recent meta-analytic studies (Floyd, Prentice-Dunn, & Rogers, 2000; Milne, Sheeran, & Orbell, 2000) do not speak directly to the issue of fear appeals. One issue is clear, however. The multiplicative combination of cognitive meditational variables (i.e., perceived severity, perceived susceptibility, and perceived response efficacy, and perceived self efficacy) from the original protection motivation explanation has been rejected (Rogers, 1983). Factors influence responses separately rather than in combination (Floyd et al., 2000; Milne et al., 2000; Rogers, 1983).

Witte (1993) claims that an important limitation of the protection motivation explanation is that it foregrounds cognitive (especially subjective expected utility) processes while giving emotions only a tertiary role. For example, in the revised protection motivation model, fear influences protection motivation only as a function of perceptions of threat and efficacy (Rogers, 1983). In short, with the protection motivation explanations, the pendulum had swung entirely from an emotional position (where fear alone mediated the effectiveness of fear appeals) to nearly an entirely cognitive one (where the only cognitive concepts were of consequence).

Extended Parallel Processing Model

Witte (1992) lamented the erosion of fear and, more broadly, affective processes from fear appeal explanations. To reverse this trend, Witte created the extended parallel processing model (or EPPM), which attempted to balance cognitive and affective processes. This balance was attempted by combining elements from the drive, parallel processing, and protection motivation explanations. Specifically,

Leventhal's model forms the basis of the theory. PMT explains the danger control side of the model (i.e., when and why fear appeals work), and portions of Janis and McGuire's explanations can be accounted for under the fear control side of the model (i.e., when and why fear appeals fail). (Witte & Allen, 2000, p. 594)

In short, the parallel processing model (Leventhal, 1970) differentiated fear control from danger control, however, it failed to specify when each would operate. The EPPM (Witte, 1992) uses protection motivation components to fill this gap. Specifically, the EPPM predicts that when threat is weak, no attitude or behavior change will occur because receivers are unmotivated to engage in active message processing. If the message threat is either weak or remote (or both), there is no need to attend to, and/or heed, message recommendations (i.e., no threat, no sweat).

When the threat depicted in the message is both severe *and* likely to strike, receivers will experience fear (Witte, 1992). Fear creates further increases in perceived threat and motivates receivers to look for ways of avoiding it. Whether audience members engage in fear control or danger control, then, depends on the message's coping component. Specifically, if threat is high and efficacy is low (the recommended coping response is ineffective and/or the receiver is unable to perform it), fear increases greatly and participants are predicted to engage in fear control. Fear control processes include any of several forms of defensive avoidance, such as message avoidance and not thinking about the issue in the future (Witte, 1992). Under these conditions, attitude and behavior change in the direction of message recommendations is unlikely as participants focus on emotional reactions.

When both threat and efficacy are strong, on the other hand, receivers are predicted to engage in danger control. In doing so, receivers engage in unbiased cognitive processing of message content in choosing responses (Witte, 1992). Under these conditions, attitude, intention, and behavior change in the direction of message recommendations are predicted to occur.

In summary, in the EPPM, "threat-by-efficacy interactions are the fundamental determinants of study outcomes" (Witte, 1992, p. 330). Specifically, the model predicts a multiplicative interaction between threat and efficacy where both threat and efficacy have to be present for attitude, behavior, or intention change to occur. In any other combination of threat and efficacy, little or no change in attitude, behavior, or intention is expected. If threat is low, receivers are unmotivated to process the message. If threat is high and efficacy low, fear control processes predominate.

Evaluating the Extended Parallel Processing Model

Witte and Allen's (2000) meta-analysis seems to be of two minds. The meta-analytic results comparing the four EPPM conditions (i.e., high threat-high efficacy, high threat-low efficacy, low threat-high efficacy, and low threat-low efficacy) indicate main effects for both threat and efficacy, but no interaction effect. Specifically, consistent with the EPPM, the high threat-high efficacy condition produced the greatest attitude change. Inconsistent with model predictions, the low threat-high efficacy and high threat-low efficacy conditions both generated greater attitude change than did the low threat-low efficacy condition. (The EPPM predicts that all three of these conditions should generate equal amounts of attitude change, though for different reasons.) In short, although the EPPM predicts a multiplicative interaction between threat and efficacy, these results suggested an additive process where threat and efficacy separately influence responses.

In an effort to save the EPPM's multiplicative prediction, Witte and Allen (2000) performed effects-coded analyses pitting the predicted multiplicative model with the additive model suggested by the data. Using unreported contrasts to represent the two effects, Witte and Allen report that *both* the additive and multiplicative patterns significantly predicted outcomes, suggesting that the predicted multiplicative model might fit the data after all. The flaw in that logic, however, is that the two models' predictions are strongly interrelated. Specifically, the multiplicative interaction contains the two main effects from the additive model. Therefore, any set of effects codes representing the additive model will correlate strongly with those

representing the multiplicative model.[1] In such a case, it would be nearly impossible to generate effect-code models that could differentiate these two sets of predictions.

In summary, the accumulated data appear similar to tests of the original formulation of the protection motivation explanation. When considering the separate impact of predictor variables, the data match predictions reasonably well. Both threat and efficacy positively influence attitude and behavior change. When considering the *specific combinations* of threat and efficacy, however, the accumulated data do not fit predictions as clearly. Specifically, the "off" cells (i.e., high threat-low efficacy and low threat-high efficacy) produce greater attitude change than the model predicts. Why this might be and how it could be explained from the EPPM perspective remains unclear.

The Stage Model of Fear Appeals

The most recent explanation for fear appeals is the stage model (e.g., de Hoog, Stroebe, & de Wit, 2007; Das et al., 2003; Stroebe, 2000); not to be confused with the transtheoretical (or stages of change) model (see Prochaska & DiClemente, 2005). As is typical for this literature, the stage model combines concepts from earlier explanations (e.g., parallel response, protection motivation, and the EPPM) but also combines them with the dual-process model of message processing (Chaiken, 1980), stress-coping explanations (e.g., Lazarus & Folkman, 1984), and models of message evaluation, evidence, and inference (e.g., Kunda, 1987). The model is quite recent, more complex than its predecessors, and relatively untested. Therefore, this review will be brief.

Like the other explanations, the stage model assumes that fear appeal components include threat (i.e., severity and susceptibility) and coping (i.e., response and self-efficacy). These components are presented, and processed, in stages (thus the explanation's label) with threat assessments potentially influencing subsequent efficacy assessments (Das et al., 2003; Stroebe, 2000). The stage model considers threat components (i.e., severity and susceptibility) as differentially influencing depth of message processing (heuristic or systematic), receiver's processing goals (i.e., accuracy or defensive), and persuasive outcomes (i.e., attitude or behavior change). For example, while both severity and susceptibility are predicted to influence attitudes, only susceptibility is predicted to influence behaviors and intentions. What is more, both the processing of the threat and efficacy message components are predicted to be biased (the threat component negatively and the efficacy component positively). When threat is strong, audience members will attempt to counterargue and find logical flaws (loopholes) in message arguments (Das et al., 2003; Stroebe, 2000). Failing to find such loopholes, receivers will likely accept *any* coping response unless it is totally implausible and/or impossible to enact. Such a positive bias allows the receiver to feel good in the face of a severe threat.

Evaluating the Stage Model

The stage model is intriguing; however, evaluating it is difficult, first, because few published studies directly test it and, second, its predictions are slippery. For example, de Hoog et al. (2007) assert several times that main effects either *could* or *should* be moderated. Thus, it is not clear whether main effects or interaction effects should influence responses. The body of studies in the de Hoog et al. meta-analysis included only those studies that manipulated *either* severity or susceptibility or manipulated both, but separately (i.e., studies that confounded severity and susceptibility, e.g., Janis & Feshbach, 1953 and all of Witte's work, were not analyzed). Meta-analytic results (de Hoog et al.) indicate that several predictions were inconsistent with meta-analytic results. For example, susceptibility predicted behaviors, but not attitudes (as expected), however, severity significantly predicted attitudes (where only efficacy judgments were supposed to

have the influence). Finally, although response efficacy predicted attitudes, but not behaviors, self efficacy predicted both attitudes and behaviors (while only the former was predicted).

The Current State of Fear Appeal Theory and Research

On the whole, the current state of fear appeal theory and research is simultaneously clear and confused. The results of several meta-analytic investigations are relatively clear. Fear appeals work, for most audiences and messages. As Witte and Allen (2000) noted, both the strength of fear appeals (including both severity and susceptibility) and the efficacy of the coping response (both self-efficacy and response efficacy) influence experienced fear, attitudes, intentions, and behaviors.

That fear appeals work *for most audiences and messages*, however, represents an important caveat to this conclusion. Witte and Allen (2000) report that, in most all cases, effect sizes vary more across studies than is expected by chance alone. Such heterogeneity in study effect sizes suggests that fear appeals are more effective for some topics and for some audiences than they are for others, due presumably to some unknown moderator variable (or variables). Consideration of such variables will be taken up shortly.

Why Don't Fear Appeal Explanations Work?

Given the state of the literature, a summary evaluation of fear appeal explanations has not changed substantially since 1984 when Boster and Mongeau claimed "none of the fear appeal explanations are consistent with the available evidence" (p. 366). Fear appeals work (most of the time at least), but it is safe to say that fear appeal explanations do not. Specifically, the drive model never came close to explaining the data; the parallel processing model was untestable; and predictions from the most recent explanations (i.e., protection motivation, extended parallel processing, and stage models) were inconsistent with how various fear appeal components (i.e., severity, susceptibility, self-efficacy, and response-efficacy) influence attitude, intention, and behavior change (de Hoog et al., 2007; Rogers, 1983; Witte & Allen, 2000).

There are several potential reasons why fear appeal explanations don't match the accumulated data. Some of these reasons center on the nature of the explanations themselves, while other reasons are a function of the research methods used to test them. I will consider each of these factors in turn.

Issues Relevant to the Explanations Themselves

There are at least three factors associated with fear appeal explanations (both what they have and what they lack) that likely lead to their demise. First, ever since Hovland and colleagues' (1953) seminal work, each new fear appeal explanation has taken something from previous work, changed it and/or combined it with other perspectives and/or concepts, in order to develop something *new*. Parallel processing was built with bricks from the drive model. The EPPM combined parts of the drive, parallel response, and protection motivation explanations. Most recently, the stage model combined elements from all these explanations with several other persuasion concepts (e.g., Chaiken, 1980). In short, instead of becoming more consistent, terse, and compelling over time, fear appeal explanations are becoming more bloated, convoluted, and no closer to explaining the accumulated data. Such a state of affairs is due, in part, to the perpetration of several central constructs that are poorly conceptualized and operationalized (e.g., fear control, danger control, and defensive avoidance). What is more, one has to question whether the accumulated data necessitate this level of conceptual complexity.

A second shortcoming of fear appeal explanations is that they consistently highlight cognition and shortchange physiological aspects of emotion. This cognitive focus likely reflects social science paradigm shift over the past half-century. This shift has generated considerable useful inquiry and theory (e.g., G. A. Miller, 2003) in many scholarly areas, including persuasion (see, e.g., Eagly & Chaiken, 1993, and many chapters in this volume). On the other hand, the concept of fear (and emotion more generally), particularly the concept of physiological arousal, has faded into the background. This leaves explanations of how fear appeals work (or don't work) simplistic and incomplete.

With the exception of the EPPM, recent fear appeal explanations are more accurately characterized as threat appeal explanations (Witte, 1992) as they focus nearly exclusively on the cognitive processing of messages. Largely gone is any consideration of arousal (e.g., physiological or emotional) or emotional labeling. Even within the EPPM, physiological processes given a tertiary role, guiding message rejection more than message acceptance (Witte, 1992).

Given the imbalance between cognitive and emotional (particularly physiological) factors in fear appeal explanations, we know more about danger control (i.e., message acceptance) than we do about fear control (and message rejection). Moreover, much of the thinking on the fear control centers on defensive avoidance, both of which are particularly poorly defined constructs. Rather than constructs used to make predictions, fear control and defensive avoidance are typically utilized to explain (after the fact) the failure of a fear appeal. What is more, discussions of defensive avoidance frequently include a variety of responses that likely stem from different (cognitive or emotional or both) processes that occur during message processing, long afterward, or both. Different defensive avoidance processes likely produce different outcomes, but this claim has not been adequately considered or tested. As it stands, defensive avoidance seems to be more of a post-hoc shorthand description of study outcomes rather than a compelling theoretical variable. Although the accumulated data appear consistent with danger control processes, greater theory and research needs to focus on fear control processes as well.

A third area where fear appeal explanations are lacking is the consideration of moderator variables (i.e., any variable that influences the direction and/or strength of relationship between two other variables; Stiff & Mongeau, 2003). When I teach persuasion, each major topic typically involves discussing at least one moderator variable (e.g., vested interest as a moderator of the attitude-behavior relationship; Sivacek & Crano, 1982). The recent study of fear appeals is an exception. Consideration of moderator variables is important given the heterogeneity of fear appeal effects (Witte & Allen, 2000). Although early fear appeal research considered several moderator variables (e.g., source credibility, trait anxiety, participant age, etc.; Boster & Mongeau, 1984), the study of such variables has largely died. (One exception is trait anxiety, see Hale, Lemieux, & Mongeau, 1995; Witte & Morrison, 2000.)

Despite the dearth of moderator variables in modern fear appeal research, future research might fruitfully investigate several important candidates. One potentially important moderator variable is the novelty of the threat. Fear appeal explanations suggest that describing the severity and susceptibility of the threat are important components of fear appeals. Recent research, however, suggests that this might not be the case (Nabi, Roskos-Ewoldsen, & Carpentier, 2008). When the threat is new to the audience, the threat component is indeed likely critically important to a fear appeal's success. What we don't know is whether it is necessary to remind audience members of a threat they are already aware of. During the Cuban Missile Crisis, did U.S. residents really need to be reminded of the dangers of a nuclear attack to convince them to build a basement bomb shelter? In the present, do tobacco smokers really need to be reminded of the health threats of their habit in order to motivate them to change? Nabi et al. suggest that when the threat is well-known to participants,

that presenting only the efficacy information can be more persuasive, and produce less reactance, than presenting the full fear appeal. Although their results are somewhat equivocal (they work better for men when the issue is testicular self-examination than for women for breast self-examination), they do suggest that this is an important issue for future fear appeal research.

A second set of moderator variables relevant to the effectiveness of fear appeals represent the nature of the recommended behavioral change. The fear appeal literature (and persuasion in general) seems to assume that message factors work in a *one-size-fits-all* fashion. This is a questionable assumption because, first, effect sizes differ across studies and, second, behavioral changes differ dramatically across message topics. Some changes are drastic, occur over time, and require consistent maintenance (e.g., dietary change to reduce blood cholesterol levels; Prochaska & DiClemente, 2005). In such cases, not only must an individual decide to make drastic changes in one's diet, but must consistently maintain those changes when making daily dietary decisions. Other behavioral changes only need to be made once and following that decision, no further elaboration is likely necessary (e.g., signing an organ donation card). The nature of the successful persuasive message (or campaign) is likely quite different if the behavior in question is ongoing rather than discrete. Also, eliminating a behavior (e.g., quitting smoking) might involve fundamentally different persuasion processes than initiating behaviors (e.g., starting an exercise regime; Floyd et al., 2000).

Another aspect of behavioral change that fear appeal explanations fail to consider is the receiver's *readiness* to make a change. Smoking cessation, for example, is likely a long and complicated process requiring several stages (e.g., Prochaska & DiClemente's, 2005, pre-contemplation, contemplation, and preparation stages). Convincing a smoker that they *should* quit likely has to precede convincing people *how* to quit. Put another way, where an individual might be in the *process* of change or their readiness for making a major multibehavioral, longitudinal change are likely important moderators of the effectiveness of fear appeals. These are issues discussed in detail by the transtheoretical (stages of change) explanation (Prochaska & DiClemente, not to be confused with the stages of change model discussed earlier, Stroebe, 2000).

Reasons Centering on Research Methods

Fear appeal explanations have changed dramatically since Janis and Feshbach's (1953) drive model. The research methods used to test these explanations, however, have changed less drastically. Thus, a second set of reasons why fear appeal explanations don't work lies not with the explanations themselves, but with the predominant methods used to test them. Specifically, the operationalization of fear arousal (i.e., perceived fear) seems particularly problematic.

Put simply, the drive model and the EPPM suggest, essentially, that the fear appeal's threat component creates the emotion of fear while the coping component is supposed to reduce it. The operational definition of perceived fear (in most studies) is a self-report measure of how much fear (or concern or worry) participants experienced during message reception (Witte & Allen, 2000; for exceptions, however, see Dillard & Anderson, 2004; Mewborn & Rogers, 1979). Many times self-report measure of perceived fear represents little more than a manipulation check rather than an important theoretical variable in and of itself.

There are two problems with the self-report measure of fear in such an experimental design. First, the *perceived fear* judgment participants make is inherently ambiguous. Given a typical fear appeal, recipients are likely calm at the beginning of the message, emotionally aroused in the middle (after processing the threat component), and relatively calm at the end (after processing an effective coping component). If this is indeed the case, how does he or she respond to an item asking, after the fact, how much fear (or concern or worry) they experienced during the message? If the actual level of fear varied (perhaps dramatically) during the message, what does such an overall measure really tell us?

Moreover, given the typical post-test only design used in most fear appeal studies, not only are self-report data ambiguous, they are unable to capture a great deal of important information. As a fear appeal explanation, the EPPM centers on the creation and reduction of emotional arousal as a central determinant of attitude and behavior change. The typical (post-test only) fear appeal study provides no data that speak to this critically important point. Put another way, researchers need to utilize physiological, rather than exclusively self-report indicators of fear arousal and reduction.

If physiological measures of fear arousal are so important to testing fear appeal explanations, why are self-report measures the norm? Certainly they are less expensive, don't require sophisticated equipment, and are easier to interpret. Moreover, Witte claims that self-report measures are the preferred operational definition of fear because they are likely more sensitive than physiological measures "because self-rated fear is more global in nature and more adequately reflects an overall emotional state, while physiological arousal fluctuates substantially during the presentation of a fear appeal" (Witte, 1992, p. 331).

There are three curious aspects to Witte's (1992) claim about the superiority of self-report measures of fear. First, she was describing Rogers's (1983) view from the protection motivation explanation, which is disinterested in fear as an explanatory construct. Second, Witte admits that the correlation between self-report and physiological indicators of fear in Mewborn & Rogers (1979) is "quite modest" (p. 346). Clearly, one indicator cannot simply stand in for another. Finally, and most important, the EPPM predicts that the creation of emotional arousal and its reduction are central to determining fear control or danger control processes. Therefore, the substantial fluctuations of arousal during processing of a fear appeal are critically important data rather than unnecessary noise.

Summary Comments

In summary, the accumulated fear appeal literature indicate that this message type works for most audiences and topics, however, the predictions made by fear appeal explanations do not clearly match the accumulated data. Fear appeal explanations, however, have not been given a fair test in large part because of the inadequate operational definitions and research designs. Specifically, due largely to the highly cognitive nature of the entire literature, the important physiological processes presumed to mediate the relationship between fear appeals and responses have gone dramatically understudied.

Future fear appeal research, then, should gather physiological data concerning the arousal and reduction of fear during message processing. Some fear appeal explanations rely heavily on physiological responses such that a full accounting of these formulations is impossible without the messier, more complex data. Once collected, I suspect that physiological data will likely require additional theory building. As researchers generate evidence as to how physiology is involved (or not involved) in the processing of fear appeals, existing explanations will almost certainly be found wanting. Explanations that truly balance cognitive and physiological components of emotion are clearly needed to advance fear appeal scholarship to the next level. As Bradley and Lang (2000) note, "As a bare minimum, an experiment should include a sample measure from each major system: overt acts, language, and physiology" (p. 245).

Notes

1. For example, assume that the additive contrasts were −1, 0, 0, and +1 for the low-low, low-high,

high-low, high-high conditions respectively. For the multiplicative model, assume contrasts of -1, -1, -1, and +3 for the same conditions. Given that the multiplicative model contains the same main effects as the additive models, these two sets of contrasts are very strongly correlated ($r = .82$).

References

Beck, K. H., & Frankel, A. (1981). A conceptualization of threat communications and protective health behavior. *Social Psychology Quarterly, 44,* 204–217. Retrieved May 4, 2012, from http://www.jstor.org/stable/3033834

Boster, F.J., & Mongeau, P. (1984). Fear-arousing persuasive messages. In R. N. Bostrom (Ed.), *Communication yearbook 8* (pp. 330–375). Newbury Park, CA: Sage.

Bradley, M. M. & Lang, P. J. (2000). Measuring emotion: Behavior, feeling, and physiology. In R. D. Lang, L. Nadel, & G. Ahern (Eds.), *Cognitive neuroscience of emotion* (pp. 242–276). New York, NY: Oxford University Press.

Chaiken, S. (1980). Heuristic versus systematic information processing and the use of source versus message cues in persuasion. *Journal of Personality & Social Psychology, 39,* 752–766. doi: 10.1037/0022-3514.39.5.752

Das, E. H. H. J., de Wit, J. B. F., & Stroebe, W. (2003). Fear appeals motivate acceptance of action recommendations: Evidence for a positive bias in the processing of persuasive messages. *Personality and Social Psychology Bulletin, 29,* 650–664. doi: 10.1177/0146167203029005009

de Hoog, N., Stroebe, W., & de Wit, Jon B. F. (2007). Impact of vulnerability to severity of a health risk on processing and acceptance of fear-arousing communications: A meta-analysis. *Review of General Psychology 11,* 258–285. doi: 10.1037/1089-2680.11.3.258

Dillard, J. P., & Anderson, J. W. (2004). The role of fear in persuasion. *Psychology and Marketing, 21,* 909–926. doi: 10.1002/mar.20041

Dillard, J. P., & Meijnders, A. (2002). Persuasion and the structure of affect. In J. P. Dillard & M. Pfau (Eds.), *The persuasion handbook: Developments in theory and practice* (pp. 309–327). Thousand Oaks, CA: Sage.

Eagly, A. H., & Chaiken, S. (1993). *Psychology of attitudes*. Belmont, CA: Wadsworth.

Easterling, D. V., & Leventhal, H. (1989). Contribution of concrete cognition to emotion: Neutral symptoms as elicitors of worry about cancer. *Journal of Applied Psychology, 74,* 787–796. doi: 10.1037/0021 9010.74.5.787

Floyd, D. L., Prentice-Dunn, S., & Rogers, R. W. (2000). A meta-analysis of research on Protection Motivation Theory. *Journal of Applied Social Psychology, 30,* 407–429. doi: 10.1111/j.1559-1816.2000. tb02323.x

Goldstein, M. J. (1959). The relationship between coping and avoiding behavior and response to fear arousing propaganda. *Journal of Abnormal and Social Psychology, 58,* 247–252. doi: 10.1037/ h0044492

Guerrero, L. K., Andersen, P. A., & Trost, M. R. (1998). Communication and emotion: Basic concepts and approaches. In P. A. Andersen & L. K. Guerrero (Eds.), *Handbook of communication and emotion: Research, theory, applications, and contexts* (pp. 5–27). San Diego, CA: Academic Press.

Hale, J. L., Lemieux, R., & Mongeau, P. A. (1995). Cognitive processing of fear-arousing message content. *Communication Research, 22,* 459–474. doi: 10.1177/009365095022004004

Hovland, C., Janis, I., & Kelly, H. (1953). *Communication and persuasion.* New Haven, CT: Yale University Press.

Janis, I. L. (1967). Effects of fear arousal on attitude change: Recent developments in theory and research. In L. Berkowitz (Ed.), *Advances in experimental social psychology* (Vol. 3; pp. 167–222). New York, NY: Academic Press.

Janis, I. L., & Feshbach, S. (1953). Effects of fear-arousing communications. *The Journal of Abnormal and Social Psychology, 48,* 78–92. doi: 10.1037/h0060732

Janis, I. L., & Terwilliger, R. F. (1962). An experimental study of psychological resistance to fear arousing communications. *The Journal of Abnormal and Social Psychology, 65,* 403–410. doi: 10.1037/ h0047601

Kunda, A. (1987). Motivated inference: Self-serving generation and evaluation of causal theories. *Journal of Personality and Social Psychology, 53,* 636–647. doi: 10.1037/0022-3514.53.4.636

LaPiere, R. T. (1934). Attitudes vs. actions. *Social Forces, 13,* 230–237. Retrieved May 5, 2012, from http://www.jstor.org/stable/2570339

Lazarus, R. S. (1982). Thoughts on the relations between emotion and cognition. *American Psychologist, 37,* 1019–1024. doi: 10.1037/0003 066X.37.9.1019

Lazarus, R. S., & Folkman, S. (1984). *Stress, appraisal, and coping.* New York, NY: Springer.

Leventhal, H. (1970). Findings and theory in the study of fear communications. In L. Berkowitz (Ed.), *Advances in experimental social psychology* (Vol. 5, pp. 119–186). New York, NY: Academic Press.

Leventhal, H. (1971). Fear appeals and persuasion: The differentiation of a motivational construct. *American Journal of Public Health, 61,* 1208–1224. doi: 10.2105/AJPH.61.6.1208

Leventhal, H., & Watts, J. C. (1966). Sources of resistance to fear-arousing communications on smoking and lung cancer. *Journal of Personality, 34,* 155–175. doi: 10.1111/j.1467-6494.1966.tb01706.x

McGuire, W. J. (1968). Personality and susceptibility to social influence. In E. Borgatta, W. L. Lambert (Eds.), *Handbook of personality theory and research* (pp. 1130–1187). Boston: Rand McNally.

McGuire, W. J. (1969). The nature of attitudes and attitude change. In G. L. Lindzey & E. Aronson (Eds.), *The handbook of social psychology* (2nd ed., pp. 136–314). Reading, MA: Addison-Wesley.

Mewborn, C. R., & Rogers, R. W. (1979). Effects of threatening and reassuring components of fear appeals on physiological and verbal measures of emotions and attitudes. *Journal of Experimental Social Psychology, 15,* 242–253. doi.org/10.1016/ 0022-1031(79)90035-0

Miller, G. A. (2003). The cognitive revolution: A historical perspective. *TRENDS in Cognitive Science, 7,* 141–144. doi:10.1016/S1364-6613(03)00029-9

Miller, G. R. (1963). Studies on the use of fear appeals: A summary and analysis. *Central States Speech Journal, 14,* 117–125. doi: 10.1080/1051097630 9362689

Miller, G. R., & Hewgill, M. A. (1966). Some recent research on fear-arousing message appeals. *Speech Monographs, 33,* 377–391. doi: 10.1080/0363775 6609375505

Milne, S., Sheeran, P., & Orbell, S. (2000). Prediction and intervention in health-related behavior: A meta-analytic review of protection motivation theory. *Journal of Applied Social Psychology, 30,* 106–143. doi: 10.1111/j.1559-1816.2000.tb02308.x

Nabi, R. L. (2002). Discrete emotions and persuasion. In J. P. Dillard & M. Pfau (Eds.), *The persuasion* handbook: *Developments in theory and practice* (pp. 289–308). Thousand Oaks, CA: Sage.

Nabi, R. L., Roskos-Ewoldsen, D., & Carpentier, F. D. (2008). Subjective knowledge and fear appeal effectiveness: Implications for message design. *Health Communication, 23*, 191–201. doi: 10.1080/10410230701808327

Prochaska, J. O., & DiClemente, C. C. (2005). The transtheoretical approach. In J. C. Norcross and M. R. Goldfried (Eds.), *Handbook of psychotherapy integration* (2nd ed., pp. 141–171). New York, NY: Oxford University Press.

Rogers, R. W. (1975). A protection motivation theory of fear appeals and attitude change. *Journal of Psychology: Interdisciplinary and Applied, 91*, 93–114. doi: 10.1080/00223980.1975.9915803

Rogers, R. W. (1983). Cognitive and physiological processes in fear appeals and attitude change: A revised theory of protection motivation. In J. Cacioppo & R. Petty (Eds.), *Social psychophysiology* (pp. 153–176). New York, NY: Guilford.

Shiota, M. N., & Kalat, J. W. (2011). *Emotion* (2nd ed.). Belmont, CA: Cengage.

Sivacek, J., & Crano, W. D. (1982). Vested interest as a moderator of attitude–behavior consistency. *Journal of Personality and Social Psychology, 43*, 210–221. doi: 10.1037/0022-3514.43.2.210

Smith, M. J. (1982). *Persuasion and human action: A review and critique of social influence theories.* Belmont, CA: Wadsworth.

Sternthal, F., & Craig, C. (1974). Fear apples: Revisited and revised: A comparative analysis. *Journal of Consumer Research, 1*(3), 22–34. Retrieved May 4, 2012, from http://www.jstor.org/stable/2488776

Stiff, J. B., & Mongeau, P. A. (2003). *Persuasive communication* (2nd ed.). New York, NY: Guilford.

Stroebe, W. (2000). *Social psychology and health* (2nd ed.). Buckingham, UK: Open University Press.

Sutton, S. R. (1982). Fear-arousing communications: A critical examination of theory and research. In J. R. Eisner (Ed.), *Social psychology and behavioral medicine* (pp. 303–337). New York, NY: John Wiley.

Williams, L. M., Phillips, M. L. Brammer, M. J., Skerrett, D., Lagopoulos, J., Rennie, C., et al. (2001). Arousal dissociates amygdala and hippocampal fear responses: Evidence from simultaneous fMRI and skin conductance recording. *NeuroImage, 14*, 1070–1079. doi.org/10.1006/nimg.2001.0904

Witte, K. (1992). Putting the fear back into fear appeals: The extended parallel process model. *Communication Monographs, 59*, 329–349. doi: 10.1080/03637759209376276

Witte, K. (1993). Message and conceptual confounds in fear appeals: The role of threat, fear, and efficacy. *Southern Journal of Communication, 58*, 147–155. doi: 10.1080/10417949309372896

Witte, K., & Allen, M. (2000). A meta-analysis of fear appeals: Implications for effective public health campaigns. *Health Education & Behavior, 27*, 591–615. doi: 10.1177/109019810002700506

Witte, K., & Morrison, K. (2000). Examining the influence of trait anxiety/repression-sensitization on individuals' reactions to fear appeals. *Western Journal of Communication, 64*, 1–27. doi: 10.1080/10570310009374661

Zajonc, R. B. (1980). Feeling and thinking: Preferences need no inferences. *American Psychologist, 35*, 151–175. doi: 10.1037/0003-066X.35.2.151

CHAPTER 13

Narrative Persuasion

Helena Bilandzic and Rick Busselle

In the context of persuasion, narrative is most commonly considered in opposition to argumentation. This separation likely began with Aristotle's distinction between logos and pathos, which has come to represent the domain of logic and reason on one hand, and emotion, poetry, and stories on the other (Herrick, 1997). Throughout much of the 20th century, persuasion connoted argument—the putting forth of claims and supporting evidence linked by rational or logical coherence (Salvador, 1994; Zarefsky, 1990). Conversely, narrative was thought of as a description of events and characters (Abbott, 2002; Bruner, 1986) presented possibly to enlighten, certainly to entertain. This distinction between persuasion and narrative also is reflected in the view of audiences as processing information in either a paradigmatic or narrative mode (Bruner, 1986). In the paradigmatic mode, audience members are thought to gather information, weigh facts, and evaluate arguments; while in the narrative mode, they are assumed to focus on understanding causally and chronologically related events played out by sentient characters (Padgett & Allen, 1997).

This dichotomy between argument and narrative may be heuristically useful. However, there are risks inherent in a two-mode view of messages or processing (Keren & Schul, 2009): Exclusionary definitions fail to recognize the presence of narrative elements in arguments and rhetorical elements in narratives. Consider that an argument may contain information, such as an example (e.g., Gibson & Zillmann, 1994), which audience members may process the same way they do narrative information. Similarly, a narrative may contain persuasive information that takes the form of an argument (e.g., Hoeken & Hustinx, 2009) or claims and evidence (e.g., Dahlstrom, 2010).

Narrative persuasion may not be a mutually exclusive alternative to other persuasive, rhetorical forms, or an alternative to traditional advertising or health messages. Instead, one can approach narrative persuasion from the perspective that much of human communication and interaction, including many forms of persuasive messages, contain narrative elements or may activate in audiences processes associated with narrative comprehension (Schank & Abelson, 1995; Schank & Berman, 2002). Over the past decade, research in advertising, health communication, and entertainment education has incorporated theoretical and methodological elements of narrative persuasion (e.g., Durkin & Wakefield, 2008; Escalas, 2007; Moyer-Gusé, 2008). Given this, our approach in this chapter is to explore how narrative elements manifest in different types of persuasive content, the degree to which people are aware of persuasive intent when diffused in narratives, and the mechanisms leading to narrative persuasion.

Defining Narrative in Light of Persuasion

Narrative can be thought of, again broadly, as symbolic representation of events (Abbott, 2002; Ryan, 2007, see also Escalas, 1998). Abbott (2002) illustrates how a narrative can be as brief as a single sentence, such as "I fell down." Explicitly, this communicates the occurrence of an event and suggests states that precede and follow: The narrator was standing and then, as a result of some mishap, found him- or herself on the ground. Similarly, a sketch of a ship wrecked on a rocky shore suggests that the vessel once sailed and that something happened, possibly a storm, which led to its current state. This definition of narrative can easily be applied to a broad range of potentially persuasive content, from a novel like *Uncle Tom's Cabin*, often cited as changing attitudes about slavery prior to the United States' Civil War (Strange, 2002) to a photograph of a wrecked automobile accompanied by a textual reference to alcohol. This broad definition of narrative emphasizes two elements that are not necessarily associated with other persuasive forms: the suggestion of a character or characters and the representation of an event or events. In the shipwreck example, the sketch may not include any humans. Yet, the ship's passengers—at least a crew—are implied, as is the driver of a wrecked automobile.

Audiences do not receive stories passively. Instead, readers, viewers, or listeners construct the story's meaning in their own mind; the result is referred to as the "realization" of the story (Oatley, 2002). Story realization is the audience member's cognitive and emotional understanding of events based on the text and their own pre-existing, relevant knowledge of the topic (Busselle & Bilandzic, 2008; Graesser, Olde, & Klettke, 2002). While the elements of

the story exist in a text, the realization of the story exists in the mind of audience members as they experience the narrative. Bordwell (1985) describes a story as "the imaginary construct we create progressively and retroactively . . . the developing result of picking up narrative cues, applying schemata, and framing and testing hypotheses" (p. 49, also see Zwaan, Langston, & Graesser, 1995).

A minimalist definition of narrative as a representation of events will include a range of media formats, such as images, phrases, and advertisements, even though they commonly would not be thought of as narratives. Certainly, the depiction of a parent putting a bandage on a child's scrape suggests characters and events, as well as several emotions. Such "drama ads" communicate a product's features "through a story-like format" (Wentzel, Tomczak, & Herrmann, 2010, p. 511). Advertisements or marketing messages containing testimonials and examples also may take a narrative form when a typical person describes an experience with a product or situation (e.g., Martin, Wentzel, & Tomczak, 2008).

An alternative to this plot-focused definition is to consider narrative as a portrayal of the inner world of a character—his or her views, perspectives, emotions, motivations, or goals (Fludernik, 1996). Narrative that is based on this "experientiality" is independent of plot. For example, brief testimonials from cancer patients (e.g., Kreuter et al., 2010) about their current state represent a narrative. This definition emphasizes the notion of empathy (Zillmann, 1994, 2006) or identification with a character (Cohen, 2001; Murphy, Frank, Moran, & Patnoe-Woodley, 2011), which also are processes central to narrative experiences. Here, even a fear appeal message may be considered a narrative if, for example, it includes some type of victim statement (e.g., Slater, 1999). Considering that consumers of stories are often deeply moved by characters, it makes sense to extend the definition of narrative in this way.

Ultimately, narrative persuasion can be defined as any influence on beliefs, attitudes, or actions brought about by a narrative message through processes associated with narrative comprehension or engagement. With this broad definition in mind, we turn to the differences between rhetoric and narrative persuasion.

Narrative Versus Non-narrative Persuasion

A primary question among persuasion scholars has focused on the relative effectiveness of messages presented in a narrative form compared to those taking a non-narrative form. This is a complex question because non-narrative messages intended to persuade can use different strategies, such as presenting statistical evidence, reasoned arguments, or non-narrative, celebrity endorsements. Similarly, potentially persuasive narratives can vary in many ways, as previously described, as well as with respect to the mere quality of the story (Green & Brock, 2002).

A number of studies have compared narrative to non-narrative persuasive messages. Kreuter et al. (2010) found that a narrative about the importance of mammography in breast cancer detection and survival told by survivors was more effective than a comparable informational video with respect to recall and behavioral intention, but not actual behavior. However, Kreuter et al. (2010) note that the non-narrative message was relatively ineffective in its persuasive influence, generally, as well as in comparison to the narrative version. Similarly, while de Wit, Das, and Vet (2008) found a narrative message superior to statistical evidence in increasing perceived risk and severity of contracting hepatitis B virus, they note that the statistical evidence message was no different from a control message that contained no evidence. Ricketts, Shanteau, McSpadden, & Fernandez-Medina, (2010) found that participants who read swing-set assembly instructions containing brief stories of playground injuries exhibited more safety behaviors than participants who read instructions without stories. Braverman (2008) found that narrative testimonials about drinking water in order to

lose weight (Studies 1 and 3) and about alcohol abuse (Study 2) were more persuasive than statistical evidence about these topics. However, the difference was present only among participants who were less involved in the issue, implicating a heuristic process. Niederdeppe, Shapiro, and Porticella (2011) found a narrative about the causes of obesity to be more effective in prompting external attributions than a non-narrative summary explanation containing similar information. However, the effect was found only among politically liberal participants.

A number of studies also have found narrative messages to be equal or inferior to messages taking a narrative form. Kopfman, Smith, Ah Yun, and Hodges, (1998) found that statistical evidence messages about organ donation were evaluated more positively (e.g., credibility, appropriateness) and lead to more positive attitudes about signing an organ donor card than a similar narrative message. However, the organ donation narrative produced greater anxiety among participants than the non-narrative regarding the need for an organ transplant. Dunlop, Wakefield, and Kashima (2010) recently found no advantage of a narrative over an advocacy format in storyboards for advertisements about smoking cessation or the importance of protecting oneself from sunburn. Similarly, Baesler and Burgoon (1994) found statistical evidence to be no more effective than narratives in influencing beliefs about juvenile delinquency. Greene and Brinn (2003) found statistical evidence to be more effective than narrative message in reducing tanning bed usage, and that difference was greater one month later.

A meta-analysis (Allen & Preiss, 1997) suggested that statistical evidence is more persuasive than narrative evidence, while a more recent meta-analysis did not reveal any significant differences between statistical and narrative messages when all outcome measures were pooled, and a stronger effect of narratives compared to statistical evidence when attitudes as outcome measures were singled out (Reinhart & Feeley, 2007).

At present, results about the effectiveness of narratives versus non-narrative formats are somewhat contradictory. However, as with most communication issues, the most effective message form likely depends on a number of situational factors, such as ideology (Niederdeppe, Shapiro, & Porticella, 2011), involvement in the message or the topic (Braverman, 2008), the nature of the non-narrative evidence to which the narrative is being compared (Greene & Brinn, 2003), whether the message is congruent or incongruent with the individual's existing attitude (Slater & Rouner, 1996), as well as the temporal distance between exposure and outcome measurement (e.g., Appel & Richter, 2007; Cody & Lee, 1990; Kreuter et al., 2010). Studies that compare narrative to non-narrative messages suggest that progress lies in asking when and under what conditions narrative messages are appropriate and what makes them more and less effective. We now turn to these issues.

The Integration of Narrative and Persuasive Content

We suggested earlier that strictly distinguishing between arguments and narratives does not account for the variety of ways the two formats can be intertwined. A closer look is required to identify typical combinations, which may have different implications for effects.

Probably the purest form is the story that is created with the intention of persuading. For example, in traditionally designed entertainment-education (E-E) narratives, the story is proscriptively designed to include a transitional character who initially exhibits negative behavior and then is rewarded for positive behavior change (Bandura, 2004; Sabido, 2004). It is the entire story that is thought to have persuasive power, rather than any individual fact or facts. Advertisements and public service announcements also may take a narrative form. Such ads have been formally recognized by the advertising industry as "drama" or "narrative" ads (Escalas, 1998; Wentzel, Tomczak, & Herrmann, 2010).

Second, stories may have been created for entertainment purposes, but are recognized as having persuasive potential, even though its intended purpose was to attract and entertain an audience (e.g., Slater, Rouner, & Long, 2006). For example, Moyer-Gusé, Chung, and Jain (2011) recently demonstrated the ability of an episode of *Sex and the City* to increase discussions about sexually transmitted infections.

Third, instead of the story itself being the persuasive message, information intended to influence the audience may be embedded in a story (Dahlstrom, 2010; Greenberg, Salmon, Patel, Beck, & Cole, 2004; Hoeken & Hustinx, 2009). This sometimes takes the form of a highly integrated, complex storyline focusing on a topic, such as breast cancer (Hether, Huang, Beck, Murphy, & Valente, 2008) or organ donation (e.g., Morgan, King, Smith, & Ivic, 2010; Morgan, Movius, & Cody, 2009) imbedded in an entertainment program. However, the persuasive message also may be less central or even tangential to the overall plot (Valente et al., 2007), or take the form of nothing more than the insertion of a brand name or product image into a story (e.g., de Gregorio & Sung, 2010) or a piece of information related to a social issue or topic, such as the failure rate of condoms (Collins, Elliott, Berry, Kanouse, & Hunter, 2003).

Finally, a narrative example or testimonial may be inserted into a message that is not necessarily narrative in its overall form. Zillmann and colleagues (Gibson & Zillmann, 1994; Zillmann & Brosius, 2000) have demonstrated that the insertion of a narrative example into a news report can increase the report's influence on perceptions of the report's topic. Similarly, testimonials in which an individual shares an anecdote or experience often take a narrative form (Braverman, 2008; Brosius & Bathelt, 1994; Slater, 2002).

For two reasons, it is important to consider how narrative and persuasive content are combined. First, research has recognized that the extent to which the persuasive information is integrated into the story is important, with greater integration positively related to the magnitude of influence (e.g., Cowley & Barron, 2008; Dahlstrom, 2010; Fisch, 2000; Russell, 2002). However, the extent of integration is to some extent dependent on the type of persuasion outcome under consideration. For example, from a failed condom storyline in the sitcom *Friends* (Collins et al., 2003), audience members may have learned the simple fact that condoms have a nontrivial failure rate. But they also may have gained insight into the complications of unintended pregnancy on the lives of sexual partners. That is, the fact of the condom failure rate may be integrated superficially (e.g., mentioned in a conversion between two minor characters) or deeply (e.g., motivating the central plot line of several episodes). Regardless, of that particular fact, insight about the complications of unintended pregnancy may be integrated deeply into the plot and available to the audience, independent of specific facts that are or are not stated.

Second, in argumentation, it matters whether audience members are forced to draw their own conclusions or conclusions are drawn for them (Hovland & Mandell, 1952). Similarly, it matters whether the persuasive message associated with a narrative is expressed implicitly or explicitly. *Explicit statements* represent everything that belongs to the story proper, such as, events, characters, settings; all of these can be elaborated or counterargued. The same is true for explicit facts in the story, such as the existence of a rare disease or the causes of lung cancer. They may even be explicitly verbalized positions, such as when a mother warns her son against using alcohol. *Implicit statements*, on the other hand, are expressed by the whole story, its facts, events, and character developments. Here, the story provides grounds for inferences about the story's overall message (e.g., by simply showing the consequences of an accident in which four friends of the drunk driver have been killed), but does not state the position explicitly. Explicit messages can be argued against—implicit messages need to be inferred before counterarguing can occur. Thus, messages that are implicitly contained in the story may be somewhat insulated from counterarguing,

a topic to which we will return in detail in the following. Explicit messages also have greater potential for being perceived as controlling or manipulative by audience members. Awareness of persuasive intent, in turn, is an important determinant of resistance.

Awareness of Persuasive Intent and Resistance

Some persuasive narratives come from sources openly committed to changing the audience's view to match their own. Explicit persuasive intent is present in communicative forms, such as narrative advertisements or public service announcements. Implicit persuasive intent is present in formats such as entertainment-education programs. Narratives with no explicit or implicit persuasive intent, such as *House, MD,* or *CSI,* also may influence audience's views, as suggested by cultivation research (Morgan & Shanahan, 2010).

When audience members detect persuasive intent, issues of resistance (Knowles & Linn, 2004), reactance (Brehm & Brehm, 1981; Dillard & Shen, 2005), and counterarguing (Petty & Cacioppo, 1979; Petty, Tormala, & Rucker, 2004) become relevant. Resistance is a reaction against change, and more specifically, both the motivation to withstand pressures to change, as well as the actual outcome of not having been changed by a pressure (Knowles & Linn, 2004). Resistance is articulated in several ways (Knowles & Linn, 2004): (1) as heightened scrutiny, where people become more alert when confronted with a persuasive message and carefully consider it in a more critical way than usual; as (2) distrust, where people meet a message with caution when it comes from a source perceived to be persuasive and, apart from negative affect, also generate disbelief in the message; and (3) as reactance, which is negative affect against the perception of persuasive influence and the motivation to counteract that pressure. A slightly different articulation comes from Dillard and Shen (2005;

see also Shen & Dillard, 2005) who describe reactance as an "intermingling" of negative cognition (counterarguing) and emotion (anger).

Among the most convincing arguments for using stories to achieve persuasive goals is their ability to communicate a persuasive message while minimizing reactance, resistance, or counterarguing in audience members. For example, stories may be perceived as lacking a persuasive intent altogether (Moyer-Gusé, 2008), or provide a compelling diversion from the persuasive message (Slater & Rouner, 2002). If an explicit persuasive message is absent, or is not perceived, and the frame that is available is an entertaining one, unfavorable reactions like reactance, distrust, or scrutiny are less likely (Dal Cin, Zanna, & Fong, 2004). Readers or viewers do not expect to be influenced by these stories, and are thought to lower their guard. Dal Cin, Zanna, and Fong (2004) suggest that narrative messages fly "under the radar."

Which type of resistance occurs and how much it jeopardizes the potential for influence appears to depend on the extent to which persuasive intent is evident within the story (Slater & Rouner, 2002). Moyer-Gusé (2008) and Moyer-Gusé and Nabi (2010) have developed a model that explains how entertainment-education messages overcome resistance. Reactance is lowered (1) by disguising the persuasive intent within the narrative structure, (2) through parasocial interaction with sympathetic characters who make the persuasive message seem less authoritative, less controlling, and more acceptable for the target group, and, for the same reasons, (3) through the audience's liking or identifying with a central character. In this model, selective avoidance is overridden by transportation into the narrative and identifying with characters. Also, perceived similarity and identification reduce the perception of invulnerability, which is another form of resistance. Similar to Slater and Rouner (2002) and Green and Brock (2000), Moyer-Gusé (2008) sees transportation and identification as phenomena that reduce counterarguing (for a detailed discussion of counterarguing, see the next section).

Mechanisms of Narrative Persuasion

The key to investigating the influence of narratives is to understand the mechanisms that lead to the adoption of narrative assertions. The potential of stories to educate has been supported by the fact that stories are more easily remembered than abstract principles (Schank & Abelson, 2005). Story events and characters are linked with each other through personal, causal, temporal, and spatial associations, which facilitate retrieval of more complex sequences; one need only remember a single story rather than a litany of unrelated facts (Green & Brock, 2005). In a similar vein, narrative can be considered as a basic mode of communication (Bruner, 1986) that best suits the way humans think and remember.

Apart from this general advantage of stories, most models of narrative persuasion assume that some sort of activity on the part of the reader or viewer mediates the persuasive effect of stories: Readers or viewers of narrative counterargue less, elaborate more, make use of imagery, and vicariously experience the characters' fates. While these four mechanisms of narrative persuasion are plausible, they are generally not discussed in conjunction or within a unified theoretical framework; also, they have received different amounts of scholarly attention, which is reflected in our synthesis that follows.

Counterarguing

The most prevalent explanation for a narrative's persuasive potential is the premise that narrative forms of persuasion inhibit counterarguing. This premise warrants consideration because the relationship between a narrative and a counterargument depends on awareness of persuasive intent, the availability of a target for counterarguing, the nature of involvement in a narrative context, and how counterarguing is measured.

Counterarguing typically is defined as the generation of direct rebuttals toward an overtly persuasive message or in response to a counterattitudinal statement (e.g., Jacks & Cameron, 2003; Wellins & McGinnies, 1977). Cacioppo (1979, Experiment 2) defined counterarguments as "statements directed against the *advocated position* that mentioned specific unfavorable consequences . . . alternative methods, challenges to the validity of arguments in the message, and statements of affect opposing the advocated position . . . " (p. 494, fn. 7). Bohner, Ruder, and Erb (2002) defined counterarguing as thoughts relevant to a persuasive message and unfavorable with respect to an issue.

Counterarguing in the context of narratives has been operationalized in two ways. First, one method uses a thought-listing task to directly document audience members' thoughts—including counterarguments—about a narrative. Kopfman et al. (1998) found that, while narrative messages were no more effective than statistical arguments in garnering behavioral intention about organ donation, participants who read a persuasive narrative listed fewer thoughts of all types (negative, neutral, and positive) about the topic than those who read a statistical argument. However, the prevalence of negative thoughts, indicating counterarguing was not statistically different between participants who read the two different message forms.

Slater, Rouner, and Long (2006) had participants list thoughts about the main themes of television drama programs (gay marriage and capital punishment) after viewing. They found little evidence that participants counterargued with these themes, suggesting either an absence of counterarguments or that counterarguments were focused elsewhere. Green and Brock (2000) asked participants to list thoughts about a narrative in which a young girl is murdered at a shopping mall. They concluded that, "[a]lthough participants were clearly thinking about and reacting to the story, it was impossible to code these thoughts as favorable or unfavorable toward the focal belief items" (2000, p. 707). Niederdeppe, Shapiro, and Porticella (2011) distinguished between cognitive and emotional counterarguments and found that political liberals were both less likely to produce cognitive counterarguments to a narrative about the societal causes of obesity and were more supportive than conservatives of the argument that societal factors influence obesity.

Second, several studies used summary measures of counterarguing, asking audience members to estimate, for example, how much they "wanted to 'argue back' with what was going on onscreen" (Moyer-Gusé, Chung, & Jain, 2011, p. 395), or "found myself thinking of ways I disagreed with what was being presented" (Moyer-Gusé & Nabi, 2010, p. 36). Using this method, Moyer-Gusé, Chung, and Jain (2011) found counterarguing with the program about sexually transmitted infections negatively related to the intention to discuss and discussions about the topic. Further, counterarguing moderated the relation between identification with characters and intentions to discuss the topic.

There are advantages and disadvantages to both measures, which will become evident as we proceed. For now it is sufficient to point out that summary measures provide an indication of counterarguing, but obfuscate the target of counterarguments. Conversely, thought lists provide a more direct indication of the target of participants' thoughts allowing researchers to distinguish between thoughts about the persuasive target and other aspects of the narrative. However, selecting thought categories and establishing intercoder reliability can be problematic.

Three factors complicate our understanding of counterarguing in a narrative context. First, engaging with a narrative involves processes and motivations different from those involved in processing overtly persuasive messages. Second, the persuasive elements in a narrative may vary with respect to their availability to an audience member's awareness and therefore their availability as the target of a counterargument. Third, the nature of involvement in a narrative is not the same as involvement in an overtly persuasive argument. We address each of these issues in turn.

In narrative comprehension, the primary cognitive activity is constructing mental models to represent characters, situations, and ultimately the meaning of the text (Graesser, Olde, & Klettke, 2002; van Dijk & Kintsch, 1983; Zwaan, Langston, & Graesser, 1995). Conversely, engaging with a persuasive argument requires consideration of claims and evaluation of evidence (Bruner, 1986; Zarefsky, 1990). To the extent that these are separate cognitive activities, they put separate demands on cognitive capacity and are more likely to interfere with than complement each other.

Related to this is the idea that humans are Spinozan processors when evaluating the truth status of information (Gilbert, 1991). Evidence suggests that humans initially accept information, and then evaluate the veracity of that information only when and if motivated to do so (Bradley & Shapiro, 2005; Gilbert, 1991; Gilbert, Krull, & Malone, 1990). This suggests that rather than *suspending* disbelief when engaging with a narrative, audiences must *construct* disbelief (Prentice, Gerrig, & Bailis, 1997). The implication for narrative persuasion is that for someone engaged in a fictional story, the initial truth status of an event, character, or situation is neither real nor unreal. Instead, events and characters simply are accepted. Their status as fictional products only becomes relevant to the audience member if something prompts evaluation about the truth or realism of story assertions (Busselle & Bilandzic, 2008). Such a prompt may take the form of awareness of persuasive intent (Nabi, 2002), an observed inconsistency within the text (Oatley, 2002), or an inconsistency between the text and an audience member's background knowledge or experience (Busselle & Bilandzic, 2008).

For example, consider a program in which a police officer says that she and her partner must recover a stolen snake-bite antidote because "millions are bitten by poisonous snakes annually." An audience member may counterargue the premise that snake bites are so prevalent ("millions") or become aware that the program is sponsored by, for example, an outdoor safety organization. However, such consideration of veracity or persuasive motive requires cognitive energy beyond that necessary for comprehending the narrative and also requires a shift of cognitive focus toward evaluative processes rather than narrative comprehension. This refocusing should interfere with the story's progression. Subsequently, the audience's engagement in the narrative experience should be compromised (Busselle & Bilandzic, 2008; Green & Brock, 2002), along with enjoyment of the narrative experience itself (Busselle & Bilandzic, 2009; Green, Brock, & Kaufman, 2004); all of which point toward acceptance rather than critical scrutiny as the default processing mode.

A second issue relates to the various possible targets of counterarguing and their availability to the audience. Typically in advertisements and PSAs, the persuasive intent is obvious to the audience and the advocated position is explicitly articulated. This is true even when the message takes a narrative form. This avails to the audience the motivation and opportunity to counterargue, as well as a target for that argument. Conversely, many narratives do not offer explicit advocated positions, but simply show what happens to characters facing certain problems. Essentially, such stories show lived experiences that are difficult to argue against (Oatley, 2002). Here, the story itself makes no assertion about how representative or typical a case may be—it shows specific people in specific situations, at a specific time and location. It is possible to argue that such a portrayal is unlike reality or unlikely to happen in reality. This may occur, for example, when events seem incoherent (Oatley, 2002) or behaviors and characters seem unrealistic (Busselle & Bilandzic, 2008). But, again, this requires the additional cognitive work of abstraction and generalization. Further, such counterarguing may be focused more on the representation's authenticity than on a specific advocated persuasive position. In some cases, audiences may infer a story's point or morale, and use the inference for counterargument. It is unlikely, however, that an audience member is more than minimally aware of such thematic points as they process the narrative (Graesser, Olde, & Klettke, 2002). Indeed, a story's thematic point (e.g., one must take risks to gain rewards) may be unavailable to the audience until the story is near or at its conclusion.

The third point we will take up related to counterarguing is the issue of involvement in a narrative versus involvement in an overtly persuasive message. In attitude change models, such as the Elaboration-Likelihood-Model (Petty & Cacioppo, 1986), high involvement creates a mind set in audience members that fosters attention to the message and scrutiny of argument quality. People who are involved make connections between themselves and the content, compare and judge media content against their prior knowledge and experiences, and are motivated toward thorough evaluation. This, in turn, means higher involvement is positively related to the likelihood that an individual will scrutinize the content for persuasive intent, accuracy, and agreement with their own views.

Conversely, in narrative processing, the dominant processing experience is transportation or narrative engagement—a state of intense cognitive and emotional focus on the story (Green & Brock, 2000; Busselle & Bilandzic, 2009). This form of engagement is different from involvement in that it does not necessarily activate the recipient's self-concept, experiences, and lifeworld. The character and plot of "Harry Potter" does not in any way refer to or reflect an average adult's situation; nonetheless, readers may be highly transported into the plot and feel with the young protagonist. On the other hand, involvement and narrative engagement are similar in that they represent intense, active processing. A transported reader vividly relives the story in her mind, extracts meaning from the story without consciously investing effort, elaborates the story text, and understands hints and clues provided by the story by drawing inferences. In this sense, engagement in a narrative parallels involvement in a persuasive message but without the assumption that the audience's

ego is implicated. This suggests that the relationship between engagement in a narrative and involvement in an overtly persuasive message is surprisingly oppositional. While involvement *enables* counterarguing with overtly persuasive messages, involvement in the form of narrative engagement or transportation is a mechanism that *prevents* counterarguing: When audiences focus their mental capacity on processing the narrative, they should have neither the ability nor the motivation to counterargue (Green & Brock, 2000; Slater & Rouner, 2002).

To sum up, the suppression of counterarguing, facilitated by a text's narrative properties and a reader's narrative engagement, has been discussed as the most important mechanism for narrative persuasion. As we have demonstrated, it is not easy to determine the target of counterarguing in a narrative. It seems to be necessary to separate the story itself from the persuasive message. However, such a separation suggests a more complex conceptualization of counterarguing, one in which counterarguing, when it does occur, may be targeted toward elements of the imbedded or implied persuasive message, or toward elements of the narrative itself, such as plot or character development that may be unrelated to an intended persuasive point.

Elaboration and Inference

Elaboration of a persuasive message is considered an important factor in persuasion (Petty & Cacioppo, 1986). It describes the extent to which someone is engaging in issue-relevant thinking and thorough weighing of argument quality. If the arguments stands up to this critical scrutiny, the persuasive message should change beliefs and attitudes. Issue involvement may increase the likelihood of elaboration by increasing the motivation to attend to and process information (Petty & Wegener, 1999).

However, as we have previously argued, involvement is not sufficient to describe narrative processing. Slater and Rouner (2002) suggested replacing involvement with the more suitable notion of engagement or transportation in their Extended ELM (E-ELM). In this model, elaboration is an outcome of engagement (not involvement) and that changes attitudes and behavior. Similarly, the Transportation-Imagery-Model (Green & Brock, 2000) assumes that "all mental systems and capacities become focused on events occurring in the narrative" (p. 701). However, Green and Brock (2000) derive different consequences from this intensive focus on the story. It is not elaboration of story content that enhances persuasive effects (as is the case in the E-ELM), because there is no rational evaluation of arguments. Rather, strong immersion into a story reduces counterarguments against story assertions, creates a lifelike experience, and provides strong connections with characters, all of which facilitate narrative persuasion. However, elaboration may still be compatible with the assumptions put forward by the Transportation-Imagery-Model.

Approaches that are concerned with elaboration seem to build on a capacity model of human information processing (e.g., Lang, 2009). Deploying more resources to a task (manifested as involvement, or transportation) improves task performance (elaboration). There is a limited pool of resources, which is divided between the story itself and the persuasive message. The capacity model by Fisch (2000, 2009) is useful here. It explains how children learn educational content embedded in stories. It assumes that both the story itself (events, characters, locations, time, etc.) and the educational content draw on a limited pool of capacity available in working memory. If story and educational content are not related to each other, the two tasks will compete for resources. In general, comprehension of the story will be prioritized in resource allocation. In contrast, when educational content is not tangential, but integral to the story (in other words, important for the development of the plot or the actions of the characters), there will be synergies between processing story and processing the educational content.

The smaller the distance between story and educational content, the better the educational content will be comprehended. Although this model is concerned with children, the same principle should apply to adults. It should be recognized that there is a bit of a paradox here regarding a narrative and the integration of educational and persuasive content into that narrative: A story is likely little affected by information that is not integrated, but that information likely has little persuasive or educational influence. Conversely, when information is highly integrated, the information is likely to have greater influence, but it also has greater impact on the narrative, which may in turn render the narrative less interesting or engaging. For example, an action film with an un-integrated comment about casual sex likely will have little impact on audience attitudes about sexual behavior. But an action film with a strong safe-sex theme likely is not a typical action film, and may border on romance, drama, or tragedy, and may be less engaging to an audience that anticipated an action film.

When there is no explicit persuasive message to attend to and process, processing should first and foremost be directed at the story elements—changes in characters, time, location, events, causality (Zwaan, Langston, & Graesser, 1995). In order to make the story coherent, readers or viewers make inferences where the story does not provide enough information (e.g., Graesser, Wiemer-Hastings, & Wiemer-Hastings, 2001). The more capacity is used to process the story, the richer the mental model of the story should be. It makes sense to assume that people who are more immersed in a story also make more inferences about the implications of the story events. More immersion also means that readers are more affected by negative outcomes and story endings. In this case, people may engage in "anomalous replotting" (Gerrig, 1993) or counterfactual thinking (Tal-Or, Boninger, Poran, & Gleicher, 2004)—a cognitive activity of imagining a different course of events that may have prevented the negative outcome. However, it is difficult to imagine repotting before a story has concluded. Thus, elaboration, inferences and re-plotting should be increased when people are engaged, and any of these cognitive activities may lead to more persuasion.

Elaboration is stimulated by personal involvement—when people think that an issue is relevant, or when it relates to their own lives and experiences. Evoking personal memories and experiences is also well-known as resonance in other fields, such psychology of reading (Seilman & Larsen, 1989) or cultivation (Morgan, Shanahan, & Signorielli, 2009). Personal relevance may induce central processing and increase persuasive effects (Petty & Cacioppo, 1986), and add autobiographical emotions to the emotions evoked by the narrative (Oatley, 2002).

While transportation and involvement have similar properties regarding the intensity of information processing and also clear differences regarding references to the self, they most often are not considered simultaneously. However, there are some exceptions. For example, Prentice, Gerrig, and Bailis (1997) explored the role of familiarity of story setting for processing fictional texts and found that unfamiliar settings support narrative effects. When readers are familiar with the setting and read unsupported assertions in a story (corresponding to weak arguments), they are more prone to critically assess the content and reject the assertions. Wheeler, Green, and Brock (1999) failed to find the same effect of familiarity in an exact replication, but did find support for closer scrutiny of texts in familiar settings. Green (2004) found that previous experience (i.e., having a homosexual friend or family member and reading story with a homosexual protagonist) increased transportation, but did not alter its effects on beliefs. Strange and Leung (1999) found that being reminded by a narrative ("remindings") of people one knows in real life facilitates the story's effect on responsibility attribution.

Bilandzic (2006) argued that the consistency of prior experience with the story is important. The model put forward by Bilandzic predicts that persuasive effects of narratives should be weakened by prior experiences that diverge from the narrative and facilitated by prior experiences that are consistent with the narrative. Specifically, divergent prior experiences produce a critical mode of viewing, which is characterized by the increased occurrence of negative thoughts about the narrative and noticing flaws in the narrative. Critical mode lowers narrative engagement, as well as narrative effects. In contrast, consistent prior experiences reinforce narrative engagement and produce an "enhanced engagement" mode of viewing, in which autobiographical memories and emotions mesh together with emotions elicited by the story and produce even stronger narrative engagement than in a situation where there is no match between the story and one's experiences. The enhanced engagement mode should reduce counterarguing and strengthen narrative effects.

The concept of self-referencing also deals with personal experiences, but places emphasis on how processing of information changes when the information is considered in conjunction with self-relevant information (Escalas, 2007). One explanation for how self-referencing affects processing is that it induces elaboration and turns the reader's attention toward argument quality. Effects only occur when strong arguments are present (e.g., Burnkrant & Unnava, 1989). Other research however suggests that self-referencing binds cognitive resources and levels the influence of argument quality (e.g., Sujan, Bettman, & Baumgartner, 1993). To resolve this disparity in research, Escalas (2007) differentiates between analytical and narrative self-referencing. In analytical referencing, information is related to self-structure in memory and leads to more attention to argument quality. Narrative referencing, in contrast, evokes autobiographical memories that are replayed in the mind. These thoughts are similar to stories and can transport the reader into past events, which leaves less capacity for scrutinizing argument quality and should facilitate persuasion. This version of the relation with the self is even more potent than simply being involved, because readers or viewers actively generate or retrieve a complete and self-specific story in their mind, and are transported into their own specific construction.

Altogether, elaboration and inference represent cognitive activities of the audience associated with deeper reflection of the story and higher persuasive outcomes. While these cognitive activities can be stimulated by any kind of story, they are certainly encouraged by ambiguous plots or characters, and open or negative endings. A crucial question concerns the nature of elaboration. In a narrow sense, elaboration can be understood as thinking about the arguments of a persuasive message. However, as we have pointed out already, narratives do not always contain arguments, for example, if, in Fisch's (2009) terms, the distance between educational content and story is small. In this case, it is likely that people will elaborate the persuasive message by thinking about the story itself, or the fate of the characters (for example, the alcohol-related death of the protagonist's husband). In this sense, it is useful to define elaboration in a broader way, as thinking about an issue rather than scrutinizing argument quality.

Imagery

In their Transportation-Imagery-Model, Green and Brock (2002) place imagery at the center of narrative persuasion. Narrative texts are considered to be influential if they evoke "measureable images" (Green & Brock, 2002, p. 321). Readers are led by the narrative to generate visual, mental representations of a narrative scene that has qualities similar to a representation elicited by external stimuli. These images are generated during or after exposure and can be "recalled, recognized, and responded to" (p. 321), which explains their potential for effects. Images have to be connected and evoked in a strong transportive experience and be firmly connected to the story plot in order to have effects—otherwise they would be random images that do not contribute to the progress and the experience of the narrative. The belief-changing mechanism, then, is that images

take on a specific meaning in the experience of a narrative. Images have specific implications for beliefs, and by leading readers to infer these, images may oppose and change existing beliefs. For example, the image of a violent psychiatric patient stabbing a little girl to death supports the belief that stronger security measures are necessary for those patients to protect society (Green & Brock, 2000).

Consequently, imagery production is an integral part of the transportation scale. However, the imagery subscale has proven less predictive of effects than the overall transportation scale (Green & Brock, 2000). This may mean that imagery is only effective if it occurs in the context of transportive experiences (this is the interpretation of the authors: Green & Brock, 2005, p. 129). Alternatively, the same results may be explained by considering imagery production as one possible mechanism of narrative impact; other aspects (that react to imagery as a content feature) override the actual amount of imagery production (for example, strong emotional narrative experience). In a different study reported by Green and Brock (2005) the rated quality of imagery did have a mediating effect on beliefs (Livingston, 2003).

Another explanation for why imagery may be influential is that it is difficult to counterargue against images (Mazzocco & Brock, 2006). This is similar to the way a narrative may be to some extent immune from counterarguing in a narrow sense. In contrast to rhetorical argumentation, the criterion of an image is not whether it is logically correct or not. A strong emotional image persists in the reader's mind regardless of reality status—it is the *idea* that a little girl may be stabbed to death that changes attitudes rather than the *fact* that it did or did not happen.

Mazzocco and Brock (2006) argue that imagery may be effective due to three processes: First, images can be encoded dually (analogically and symbolically) and thus be better remembered; second, they may award reality status to fictional or unbelievable events; third, they provide experiences that are close to sensations. The authors also offer explanations that show how images may impact or alter the processing mode following the ELM. Images may be used as peripheral cues for attitude formation. We do not need an argument when we have an image. Mazzocco and Brock (2006) also suggest that images are highly accessible and may act as peripheral cues that create enduring effects even in peripheral processing. But central processing may also be strengthened with images when they are heavily related to the theme of the message, they may entail a more thorough processing of the message and increase central persuasive effects. Both paths are equally plausible and probably depend on the specific characteristics of the image and the message.

Rather than relying on peripheral processing, one may also argue that imagery is an argument in and of itself, which may be used to form a judgment and save the reader or viewer from having to consider the full range of rhetoric arguments (Mazzocco & Brock, 2006). This is plausible in the example of *Murder in the Mall* (Green & Brock, 2000), where the image of the mental patient stabbing the girl is closely connected to or even stands for the more restrictive attitudes about criminal mental patients.

Further, audiovisual material should support imagery construction in a way that is different from textual content. Mazzocco and Brock (2006) distinguish between image representations that automatically result in mental images, which is the case in pictorial stimuli (television, photos, etc.). The other case entails a more effortful construction of mental images from nonpictorial stimuli that require "imaginal elaboration." Image elaboration competes for resources with the process of elaborating of a text's arguments. Only if sufficient cognitive resources are available are images processed properly and influence on persuasive outcomes possible. This would support Green and Brock's (2002) assertion that imagery can only have influence when related to the plot and combined with a transportive experience: If the plot is closely related to the images used, we can expect synergies in processing the

plot and in processing the images. This is in parallel to Fisch's (2009) contention that the distance between story and educational content matters. Then, we may regard transportation as greater investment in processing the story, which should result in increased resource availability.

Summing up, imagery is an important characteristic of all audiovisual stories and, to varying degrees, of written or audio stories. There are good theoretical arguments suggesting images influence persuasion outcomes. It stands to reason that not all imagery has this potential. For example, descriptions of a landscape or a room will create images, but are likely to be irrelevant to persuasion. On the other hand, strong transportive experiences are possible without any imagery, for example, a detailed portrayal of a character's feeling and thoughts; their inner world. It seems that imagery is neither a necessary nor a sufficient direct condition for narrative engagement; in many cases, however, it may provide the basis for readers and viewers to react emotionally, to engage with the narrative and care for the characters, and subsequently for narrative effects.

Vicarious Experience

Media narratives provide rich depictions of social experience, containing behaviors, motivations, emotions, situational, and socials contexts to which audiences usually do not have access. By understanding narratives, following the fates, successes, and failures of characters, by emoting for and identifying with the characters—essentially, by reliving the story in their minds—audiences may experience social life vicariously. Social Cognitive Theory (Bandura, 1986) provides a good theoretical background for this. By observing models in the media, audience members learn how successful a particular behavior is for achieving one's goals, and whether it is easy or hard to perform (Bandura, 2004, 2009). Processes of identification support vicarious learning: First, similarity to the model is important for viewers to accept a behavior as manageable within one's own capabilities. If the model's capabilities are perceived to be different from one's own, vicarious experience is less influential (Pajares, Prestin, Chen, & Nabi, 2009). Second, if people process narratives in a transportive mode, they typically are able to take on the perspective of a character and see the narrative through this character's eyes (identification as perspective taking, Cohen, 2001).

A consequence of this perspective taking is that people are able to deeply understand the emotions and the motivations of a character, and understand the joys of succeeding or the sadness of failing as if it was happening to themselves (Busselle & Bilandzic, 2008). Thus, perspective taking should increase a message's effectiveness as people care for the characters and internalize outcome expectancies. Also, perspective taking should help with acquiring self-efficacy: The story is perceived with reduced distance as the narrative experience resembles direct personal experience and the audience perceives the events as if they were part of the action themselves (Green & Brock, 2000). In Entertainment-Education approaches, positive and negative models are strategically constructed for this purpose; transitional characters offer an opportunity for the audience to experience the change from an undesirable behavior to a desirable one, as well as the motivations and intricacies of that change (Singhal & Rogers, 1999). Indeed, narrative engagement has been integrated in Entertainment-Education approaches to capture the specific potential for persuasion (e.g., Moyer-Gusé, 2008).

Mar and Oatley (2008) decrease the distance between the model and the audience by stating that stories (they focus literary on stories) are "simulations of selves in the social world" (p. 173). While reading a story, people experience thoughts and emotions implied by the story, and in doing so, simulate the story in their minds. The stories themselves, Mar and Oatley argue, offer complex models of the human social world and allow readers to understand other people's

motivations, thoughts, and feelings. In contrast to Social Cognitive Theory, the focus is not on behaviors, but on sympathetic and empathetic growth (i.e., learning to understand and anticipate other people's states of mind and feel compassion with their fates) and on the acquisition of social knowledge (i.e., norms and values in a given society).

This final mechanism of narrative persuasion may be the one that moves away most from rhetoric persuasion and comes closest to narrative persuasion as an independent field. Only narratives can provide grounds to simulate a self in a possible world; and only narratives carry a dense array of social information. At the same time, these subtle experiences and effects are somewhat difficult to capture in empirical research. Especially since social knowledge is omnipresent, it may be difficult to trace the effects of single exposures or, in the long term, to single out the specific influence of media.

Conclusions and Suggestions for the Future

People have probably always used narratives when attempting to persuade, and narratives have always had the potential to be persuasive. Thus, it is somewhat surprising that over the past century, with the exception of propaganda, narrative persuasion has received relatively little research attention. On the other hand, the separation of narratives from overt argumentation is understandable, because, as we have articulated in this chapter, narratives are fundamentally different from their non-narrative counterparts. When comprehending a narrative, audience members must focus on characters and events, rather than arguments and evidence, in order to construct a coherent story. This process is different from that involved in comprehending arguments and evidence, requiring its own cognitive resources and involving separate psychological mechanisms. Fortunately, over the past decade this trend has reversed and scholarship focused on narrative persuasion has progressed quickly. In that time the focus has shifted from comparing the effectiveness of narrative and non-narrative formats to exploring mechanisms that allow narratives to persuade, processes that mediate effects, and individual differences that may render audience members more or less susceptible.

We can conclude that the form a persuasive narrative may take varies in three important ways. First is the level of integration between the story and the persuasive message. High integration is evident when the story itself *is* the persuasive message, for example, when a story conveys a lesson or morale or when PSAs or advertisements take a narrative form. Low integration is evident when a piece of information or a product appears in a narrative but is only tangentially linked to the narrative's main plot or theme. Second is the extent to which awareness of persuasive intent is available to the audience. At one end of this continuum may be cases in which neither the content nor the setting suggest persuasive intent, such as when one sits down to watch a medical drama program for entertainment purposes (as opposed to in a research setting). On the other hand, the persuasive purpose of a 30-second commercial or PSA likely is obvious to most audiences, excepting children. A third way that a potentially persuasive narrative may vary is in the extent to which the persuasive point is made explicitly in the story or is left to the audience to infer. Of course these three variations in form are interrelated and related to both engagement in the narrative and involvement with the narrative's persuasive message. Research is needed to better understand how integration, explicitness and awareness of persuasive intent interact with each other and with other phenomena such as involvement, reactance, and counterarguing.

As we have argued, engagement in a narrative should serve a function that is oppositional to involvement in a persuasive argument. Individuals who are highly involved in a persuasive argument likely focus on critical evaluation of claims and evidence. Conversely, individuals highly engaged in a narrative should be unmotivated and, to some extent, incapable of critical scrutiny, especially scrutiny targeted toward a persuasive argument that is implied and peripheral to the narrative's main storyline. Research is needed to further investigate how all of these factors interact with each other and intervene in a narrative's persuasive influence. For example, extant theorizing suggests that reactance and counterarguing are incompatible with persuasive messages presented in a narrative form. While some empirical evidence of this exists, it is not clear exactly how to conceive of the relationship between narrative form and counterarguing. We might think of narratives as inhibiting resistance in the sense that counterarguing may be initiated but narrative comprehension interferes with development and elaboration of counterarguments. Alternatively, narratives may prevent counterarguing in the sense that the presence of a narrative interferes with the initiation of critical evaluation.

Finally, one may not even suspect persuasive intent because of narrative form, but may find aspects of the narrative that are unrelated to the persuasive point objectionable in some way and counterargue with those targets (for example, an unrealistic plot or an inconsistent character). At this point it is not safe to assume that all forms of counterarguing necessarily decrease persuasive effects. It is possible that, for example, counterarguments focused away from a narrative's persuasive purpose may inhibit resistance to the intended persuasive message or increase the likelihood that the persuasive message will be processed heuristically, in turn facilitating persuasive effects. This is consistent with the basic assumption of the Transportation-Imagery-Model (Green & Brock, 2000) that intense engagement in a narrative reduces capacity and ability for critical scrutiny, which essentially means that the persuasive message is processed heuristically when audiences are primarily engaged with the narrative. Indeed, to the extent that becoming highly engaged in a narrative is similar to a real-life experience, it is possible that that real-life experience includes heuristically processed information about people, behaviors, and products, again facilitating persuasive influence. Further research into both the processes and the conditions under which the processes occur is warranted.

Narrative engagement appears to be an important mediator in persuasive effects. More research is needed to better understand the precise nature of transportation, such as whether it originates from identification or imagery, and whether it is the same phenomenon when engaging with a 30-second advertisement or PSA, situation comedy, or a longer dramatic television program or motion picture. Similarly, research is needed to better understand the role of imagery in stories with strong visual descriptions versus those focused on the inner world of characters, as well as in different media, such as written short stories versus 3-D movies.

Thus far, the effects of narrative persuasive are discussed in terms of attitudes, beliefs, and behaviors. However, the insight gained through identification with characters and experienced events may be a fundamentally different kind of effect, one specific to narratives. Research investigating insight as an outcome of narrative experience is warranted.

Ultimately, research in the merged domains of persuasion and narrative have important implications for theoretical understanding and practical application in health communication, entertainment-education, and marketing, as well as areas in which narrative effects traditionally have not been conceived as a form of persuasion.

References

Abbott, H. P. (2002). *The Cambridge introduction to narrative.* Cambridge, UK: Cambridge University Press.

Allen, M., & Preiss, R. W. (1997). Comparing the persuasiveness of narrative and statistical evidence using meta-analysis. *Communication Research Reports, 14,* 125–131.

Appel, M., & Richter, T. (2007). Persuasive effects of fictional narratives increase over time. *Media Psychology, 10,* 113–134.

Baesler, E., & Burgoon, J. (1994). The temporal effects of story and statistical evidence on belief change. *Communication Research, 21,* 582–602.

Bandura, A. (1986). *Social foundation of thought and action: A social cognitive theory.* Englewood Cliffs, NJ: Prentice-Hall.

Bandura, A. (2004). Social cognitive theory for personal and social change by enabling media. In A. Singhal, M. J. Cody, E. M. Rogers, & M. Sabido (Eds.), *Entertainment-education and social change: History, research, and practice* (pp. 75–96). Mahwah, NJ: Erlbaum.

Bandura, A. (2009). Social cognitive theory of mass communication. In J. Bryant & M. B. Oliver (Eds.), *Media effects: Advances in theory and research* (pp. 94–124). Los Angeles, CA: Erlbaum.

Bilandzic, H. (2006). The perception of distance in the cultivation process: A theoretical consideration of the relationship between television content, processing experience, and perceived distance. *Communication Theory, 16,* 333–355.

Bohner, G., Ruder, M., & Erb, H. (2002). When expertise backfires: Contrast and assimilation effects in persuasion. *British Journal of Social Psychology, 41,* 495–519.

Bordwell, D. (1985). *Narration in the fiction film.* Madison: University of Wisconsin Press.

Bradley, S., & Shapiro, M. A. (2005). Parsing reality: The interactive effects of complex syntax and time pressure on cognitive processing of television scenarios. *Media Psychology, 6,* 307–333.

Braverman, J. (2008). Testimonials versus informational persuasive messages: The moderating effect of delivery mode and personal involvement. *Communication Research, 35,* 666–694.

Brehm, S., & Brehm, J. (1981). *Psychological reactance: A theory of freedom and control.* New York, NY: Academic Press.

Brosius, H. B., & Bathelt, A. (1994). The utility of exemplars in persuasive communications. *Communication Research, 21,* 48–78.

Bruner, J. (1986). *Actual minds, possible worlds.* Cambridge, MA: Harvard University Press.

Burnkrant, R. E., & Unnava, H. R. (1989). Self-referencing. A strategy for increasing processing of message content. *Personality and Social Psychology Bulletin, 15,* 628–638.

Busselle, R. W., & Bilandzic, H. (2008). Fictionality and perceived realism in experiencing stories: A model of narrative comprehension and engagement. *Communication Theory, 18*, 255–280.

Busselle, R. W., & Bilandzic, H. (2009). Measuring narrative engagement. *Media Psychology, 12*, 321–347.

Cacioppo, J. T. (1979). The effects of exogenous changes in heart rate on facilitation of thought and resistance to persuasion. *Journal of Personality and Social Psychology, 37*, 489–498.

Cody, R., & Lee, C. (1990). Behaviors, beliefs, and intentions in skin cancer prevention. *Journal of Behavioral Medicine, 13*, 373–389.

Cohen, J. (2001). Defining identification: A theoretical look at the identification of audiences with media characters. *Mass Communication and Society, 4*, 245–264.

Collins, R. L., Elliott, M. N., Berry, S. H., Kanouse, D. E., & Hunter, S. B. (2003). Entertainment television as a healthy sex educator: The impact of condom-efficacy information in an episode of *Friends. Pediatrics, 112*, 1115–1121.

Cowley, E., & Barron, C. (2008). When product placement goes wrong: The effects of program liking and placement prominence. *Journal of Advertising, 37*, 89–98.

Dahlstrom, M. (2010). The role of causality in information acceptance in narratives: An example from science communication. *Communication Research, 37*, 857–875.

Dal Cin, S., Zanna, M. P., & Fong, G. T. (2004). Narrative persuasion and overcoming resistance. In E. S. Knowles & J. A. Linn (Eds.), *Resistance and persuasion* (pp. 175–191). Mawah, NJ: Erlbaum.

De Gregorio, F., & Sung, Y. J. (2010). Understanding attitudes toward and behaviors in response to product placement: A consumer socialization framework. *Journal of Advertising, 39*, 83–96.

De Wit, J. B. F., Das, E., & Vet, R. (2008). What works best: Objective statistics or a personal testimonial? An assessment of the persuasive effects of different types of message evidence on risk perception. *Health Psychology, 27*, 110–115.

Dillard, J. P., & Shen, L. J. (2005). On the nature of reactance and its role in persuasive health communication. *Communication Monographs, 72*, 144–168.

Dunlop, S. M., Wakefield, M., & Kashima, Y. (2010). Pathways to persuasion: Cognitive and experiential responses to health-promoting mass media messages. *Communication Research, 37*, 133–164.

Durkin, S., & Wakefield, M. (2008). Interrupting a narrative transportation experience: Program placement effects on responses to antismoking advertising. *Journal of Health Communication, 13*, 667–680.

Escalas, J. E. (1998). Advertising narratives: What are they and how do they work? In B. Stern (Ed.), *Representing consumers: Voices, views, and visions* (pp. 1–23). New York, NY: Routledge & Kegan Paul.

Escalas, J. E. (2007). Self-referencing and persuasion: Narrative transportation versus analytical elaboration. *Journal of Consumer Research, 33*, 421–429.

Fisch, S. M. (2000). A capacity model of children's comprehension of educational content on television. *Media Psychology, 2*, 63–91.

Fisch, S. M. (2009). Educational television and interactive media for children. In J. Bryant & M. B. Oliver (Eds.), *Media effects: Advances in theory and research* (pp. 402–435). New York, NY: Routledge.

Fludernik, M. (1996). *Towards a natural narratology.* London, UK: Routledge.

Gerrig, R. J. (1993). *Experiencing narrative worlds.* New Haven, CT: Yale University Press.

Gibson, R., & Zillmann, D. (1994). Exaggerated versus representative exemplification in news reports: Perceptions of issues and personal consequences. *Communication Research, 21*, 603–624.

Gilbert, D. T. (1991). How mental systems believe. *American Psychologist, 46*, 107–119.

Gilbert, D. T., Krull, D. S., & Malone, P. S. (1990). Unbelieving the unbelievable: Some problems in the rejection of false information. *Journal of Personality and Social Psychology, 59*, 601–613.

Graesser, A. C., Olde, B., & Klettke, B. (2002). How does the mind construct and represent stories? In M. C. Green, J. J. Strange, & T. C. Brock (Eds.), *Narrative impact: Social and cognitive foundations* (pp. 229–262). Mahwah, NJ: Erlbaum.

Graesser, A. C., Wiemer-Hastings, P., & Wiemer-Hastings, K. (2001). Constructing inferences and relations during text comprehension. In J. S. T. Sanders & W. Spooren (Ed.), *Text representation: Linguistic and psycholinguistic aspects* (pp. 249–271). Amsterdam, The Netherlands: John Benjamins.

Greene, K., & Brinn, L. S. (2003). Messages influencing college women's tanning bed use: Statistical versus narrative evidence format and a self-assessment to increase perceived susceptibility. *Journal of Health Communication, 8*, 443–461.

Green, M. C. (2004). Transportation into narrative worlds: The role of prior knowledge and perceived realism. *Discourse Processes, 38,* 247–266.

Green, M. C., & Brock, T. C. (2000). The role of transportation in the persuasiveness of public narratives. *Journal of Personality and Social Psychology, 79,* 701–721.

Green, M. C., & Brock, T. C. (2002). In the mind's eye: Transportation-imagery model of narrative persuasion. In M. C. Green, J. J. Strange, & T. C. Brock (Eds.), *Narrative impact: Social and cognitive foundations* (pp. 315–341). Mahwah, NJ: Erlbaum.

Green, M. C., & Brock, T. C. (2005). Persuasiveness of narratives. In T. C. Brock & M. C. Green (Eds.), *Persuasion: Psychological insights and perspectives* (2nd ed., pp. 117–142). Thousand Oaks, CA: Sage.

Green, M. C., Brock, T. C., & Kaufman, G. F. (2004). Understanding media enjoyment: The role of transportation into narrative worlds. *Communication Theory, 14,* 311–327.

Greenberg, B. S., Salmon, C. T., Patel, D., Beck, V., & Cole, G. (2004). Evolution of and E-E research agenda. In A. Singhal, M. Cody, E. Rogers, & M. Sabido (Eds.), *Entertainment-education and social change: History research and practice.* (pp. 191–206). Mahwah, NJ: Erlbaum.

Herrick, J. A. (1997). *The history and theory of rhetoric: An introduction.* Scottsdale, AZ: Gorsuch Scarisbrick.

Hether, H. J., Huang, G. C., Beck, V., Murphy, S. T., & Valente, T. W. (2008). Entertainment-education in a media-saturated environment: Examining the impact of single and multiple exposures to breast cancer storylines on two popular medical dramas. *Journal of Health Communication, 13,* 808–823.

Hoeken, H., & Hustinx, L. (2009). When is statistical evidence superior to anecdotal evidence in supporting probability claims? The role of argument type. *Human Communication Research, 35,* 491–510.

Hovland, C. I., & Mandell, W. (1952). An experimental comparison of conclusion-drawing by the communicator and by the audience. *Journal of Abnormal and Social Psychology, 47,* 581–588.

Jacks, Z. J., & Cameron, K. A. (2003). Strategies for resisting persuasion. *Basic and Applied Social Psychology, 25,* 145–161.

Keren, G., & Schul, Y. (2009). Two is not always better than one. *Perspectives on Psychological Science, 4,* 533–550.

Knowles, E. S., & Linn, J. A. (2004). The importance of resistance to persuasion. In E. S. Knowles & J. A. Linn (Eds.), *Resistance and persuasion* (pp. 3–9). Mahwah, NJ: Erlbaum.

Kopfman, J. E., Smith, S. W., Ah Yun, J. K., & Hodges, A. (1998). Affective and cognitive reactions to narrative versus statistical evidence organ donation messages. *Journal of Applied Communication Research, 26,* 279–300.

Kreuter, M. W., Holmes, K., Alcaraz, K., Kalesan, B., Rath, S., Richert, M., et al. (2010). Comparing narrative and informational videos to increase mammography in low-income African American women. *Patient Education and Counseling, 81,* S6–S14.

Lang, A. (2009). The limited capacity model of motivated mediated message processing. In R. L. Nabi & M. B. Oliver (Eds.), *Media processes and effects* (pp. 193–204). Los Angeles, CA: Sage.

Livingston, S. D. (1993). *Mechanisms of attitude change in narrative versus rhetorical persuasion.* Unpublished master's thesis, Columbus, Ohio State University.

Mar, R. A., & Oatley, K. (2008). The function of fiction is the abstraction and simulation of social experience. *Perspectives on Psychological Science, 3,* 173–192.

Martin, B. A. S., Wentzel, D., & Tomczak, T. (2008). Effects of susceptibility to normative influence and type of testimonial on attitudes toward print advertising. *Journal of Advertising, 37,* 29–43.

Mazzocco, P. J., & Brock, T. C. (2006). Understanding the role of mental imagery in persuasion: A cognitive resources model. In L. R. Kahle & C. H. Kim (Eds.), *Image and psychology of marketing communication* (pp. 65–78). Mahway, NJ: Erlbaum.

Morgan, M., & Shanahan, J. (2010). The state of cultivation. *Journal of Broadcasting and Electronic Media, 54,* 337–355.

Morgan, M., Shanahan, J., & Signorielli, N. (2009). Growing up with television: Cultivation processes. In J. Bryant & M. B. Oliver (Eds.), *Media effects: Advances in theory and research* (pp. 34–49). Los Angeles, CA: Erlbaum.

Morgan, S. E., King, A. J., Smith, J. R., & Ivic, R. (2010). A kernel of truth? The impact of television storylines exploiting myths about organ donation on the public's willingness to donate. *Journal of Communication, 60,* 778–796.

Morgan, S. E., Movius, L., & Cody, M. J. (2009). The power of narratives: The effect of entertainment television organ donation storylines on the attitudes, knowledge, and behaviors of donors and nondonors. *Journal of Communication, 59,* 135–151.

Moyer-Gusé, E. (2008). Toward a theory of entertainment persuasion: Explaining the persuasive effects of entertainment-education messages. *Communication Theory, 18,* 407–425.

Moyer-Gusé, E., Chung, A. H., & Jain, P. (2011). Identification with characters and discussion of taboo topics after exposure to an entertainment narrative about sexual health. *Journal of Communication, 61,* 387–406.

Moyer-Gusé, E., & Nabi, R. (2010). Explaining the effects of narrative in and entertainment television program: Overcoming resistance to persuasion. *Human Communication Research, 36,* 26–52.

Murphy, S. T., Frank, L. B., Moran, M. B., & Patnoe-Woodley, P. (2011). Involved, transported, or emotional? Exploring the determinants of change in knowledge, attitudes, and behavior in entertainment-education. *Journal of Communication, 61,* 407–430.

Nabi, R. L. (2002). Discrete emotions and persuasion. In J. P. Dillard & M. Pfau (Eds.), *The persuasion handbook. Developments in theory and practice* (pp. 289–308). Thousand Oaks, CA: Sage.

Niederdeppe, J., Shapiro, M. A., & Porticella, N. (2011). Attributions of responsibility for obesity: Narrative communication reduces reactive counterarguing among liberals. *Human Communication Research, 37,* 295–323.

Nuland, S. (1994). *How we die: Murder and serenity* (pp. 118–139). New York, NY: Knopf.

Oatley, K. (2002). Emotions and the story worlds of fiction. In M. C. Green, J. J. Strange, & T. C. Brock (Eds.), *Narrative impact: Social and cognitive foundations* (pp. 39–69). Mahwah, NJ: Erlbaum.

Padgett, D., & Allen, D. (1997). Communicating experiences: A narrative approach to creating service brand image. *Journal of Advertising, 26,* 49–62.

Pajares, F., Prestin, A., Chen, J., & Nabi, R. L. (2009). Social Cognitive Theory and media effects. In R. L. Nabi & M. B. Oliver (Eds.), *Media processes and effects* (pp. 283–298). Los Angeles, CA: Sage.

Petty, R. E., & Cacioppo, J. T. (1979). Issue involvement can increase or decrease persuasion by enhancing message-relevant cognitive responses. *Journal of Personality and Social Psychology, 37*(10), 1915–1926.

Petty, R. E., & Cacioppo, J. T. (1986). *Communication and persuasion: Central and peripheral routes to attitude change.* New York, NY: Springer-Verlag.

Petty, R. E., Tormala, Z. L., & Rucker, D. D. (2004). Resisting persuasion by counterarguing: An attitude strength perspective. In J. Jost, M. Banaji, R. Mahzarin, & D. Prentice (Eds.), *Perspectivism in social psychology: The yin and yang of scientific progress. APA Science Series. APA Decade of Behavior Series* (Vol. 15, pp. 37–51). Washington DC: American Psychological Association.

Petty, R. E., & Wegener, D. T. (1999). The Elaboration Likelihood Model: Current status and controversies. In S. Chaiken & Y. Trope (Eds.), *Dual-process-theories in social psychology* (pp. 41–72). New York, NY: Guilford Press.

Prentice, D. A., Gerrig, R. J., & Bailis, D. S. (1997). What readers bring to the processing of fictional texts. *Psychonomic Bulletin and Review, 4,* 416–420.

Reinhart, A., & Feeley, T. (2007, November 15). *Comparing the persuasive effects of narrative versus statistical messages: A meta-analytic review.* Paper presented at the annual meeting of the NCA 93rd Annual Convention, Chicago, IL.

Ricketts, M., Shanteau, J., McSpadden, B., & Fernandez-Medina, K. M. (2010). Using stories to battle unintentional injuries: Narratives in safety and health communication. *Social Science and Medicine, 70,* 1441–1449.

Russell, C. (2002). Investigating the effectiveness of product placements in television shows: The role of modality and plot connection congruence on brand memory and attitude. *Journal of Consumer Research, 29,* 306–318.

Ryan, M. (2007). Toward a definition of narrative. In D. Herman (Ed.), *Cambridge companion to narrative* (pp. 22–35). Cambridge, UK: Cambridge University Press.

Sabido, M. (2004). The origins of entertainment education. In A. Singhal, M. J. Cody, M. Sabido, A. Singhal, & E. M. Rogers (Eds.), *Entertainment education and social change: History, research, and practice* (pp. 61–74). Mahwah, NJ: Erlbaum.

Salvador, M. (1994). The rhetorical genesis of Ralph Nader: A functional exploration of narrative and argument in public discourse. *Southern Communication Journal, 59,* 227–239.

Schank, R. C., & Abelson, R. P. (1995). Knowledge and memory: The real story. In R. S. Wyer, Jr. (Ed.),

Knowledge and memory: The real story (pp. 1–85). Hillsdale, NJ: Erlbaum.

Schank, R. C., & Berman, T. R. (2002). The pervasive role of stories in knowledge and action. In M. C. Green, J. J. Strange, & T. C. Brock (Eds.), *Narrative impact: Social and cognitive foundations* (pp. 315–341). Mahwah, NJ: Erlbaum.

Seilman, U., & Larsen, S. F. (1989). Personal resonance to literature: A study of remindings while reading. *Poetics, 18,* 165–177.

Shen, L., & Dillard, J. (2005). Psychometric properties of the Hong psychological reactance scale. *Journal of Personality Assessment, 85,* 74–81.

Singhal, A., & Rogers, E. M. (1999). *Entertainment-Education: A communication strategy for social change.* Mahwah, NJ: Erlbaum.

Slater, M. D. (1999). Drinking and driving PSAs: A content analysis of behavioral influence strategies. *Journal of Alcohol and Drug Education, 44,* 68–81.

Slater, M. D. (2002). Entertainment education and the persuasive impact of narratives. In M. C. Green, J. J. Strange, & T. C. Brock (Eds.), *Narrative impact: Social and cognitive foundations* (pp. 157–181). Mahwah, NJ: Erlbaum.

Slater, M. D., & Rouner, D. (1996). Value-affirmative and value-protective processing of alcohol education messages that include statistical evidence or anecdotes. *Communication Research, 23,* 210–235.

Slater, M. D., & Rouner, D. (2002). Entertainment-education and elaboration likelihood: Understanding the processing of narrative persuasion. *Communication Theory, 12,* 173–191.

Slater, M. D., Rouner, D., & Long, M. (2006). Television dramas and support for controversial public policies: Effects and mechanisms. *Journal of Communication, 56,* 235–252.

Strange, J. (2002). How fictional tales wag real-world beliefs: Models and mechanisms of narrative influence. In M. C. Green, J. J. Strange, & T. C. Brock (Eds.), *Narrative impact: Social and cognitive foundations* (pp. 263–286). Mahwah, NJ: Erlbaum.

Strange, J. J., & Leung, C. C. (1999). How anecdotal accounts in news and in fiction can influence judgments of a social problem's urgency, causes, and cures. *Personality and Social Psychology Bulletin, 25,* 436–449.

Sujan, M., Bettman, J. R., & Baumgartner, H. (1993). Influencing consumer judgments via autobiographical memories: A self-referencing perspective. *Journal of Marketing Research, 30,* 422–436.

Tal-Or, N., Boninger, D. S., Poran, A., & Gleicher, F. (2004). Counterfactual thinking as a mechanism in narrative persuasion. *Human Communication Research, 30,* 301–328.

Valente, T. W., Murphy, S., Huang, G., Gusek, J., Greene, J., & Beck, V. (2007). Evaluating a minor storyline on ER about teen obesity, hypertension, and 5 a day. *Journal of Health Communication, 12,* 551–566.

Van Dijk, T. A., & Kintsch, W. (1983). *Strategies of discourse comprehension.* New York, NY: Academic Press.

Wellins, R., & McGinnies, E. (1977). Counterarguing and selective exposure to persuasion. *Journal of Social Psychology, 103,* 115–127.

Wentzel, D., Tomczak, T., & Herrmann, A. (2010). The moderating effect of manipulative intent and cognitive resources on the evaluation of narrative ads. *Psychology of Marketing, 27,* 510–530.

Wheeler, S. C., Green, M. C., & Brock, T. C. (1999). Fictional narratives change beliefs: Replications of Prentice, Gerrig, and Bailis (1997) with mixed corroboration. *Psychonomic Bulletin and Review, 6,* 136–141.

Zarefsky, D. (1990). Future directions on argumentation theory and practice. In R. Trapp and J. Scheutz (Eds.), *Perspectives on argumentation: Essays in honor of Wayne Brockriede* (pp. 287–297). Prospect Heights, IL: Waveland Press.

Zillmann, D. (1994). Mechanisms of emotional involvement with drama. *Poetics, 23,* 33–51.

Zillmann, D. (2006). Empathy: Affective reactivity to others' emotional experiences. In J. Bryant & P. Vorderer (Eds.), *Psychology of entertainment* (pp. 151–181). Mahwah, NJ: Erlbaum.

Zillmann, D., & Brosius, H.-B. (2000). *Exemplification in communication: The influence of case reports on the perception of issues.* Mahwah, NJ: Erlbaum.

Zwaan, R. A., Langston, M. C., & Graesser, A. C. (1995). The construction of situation models in narrative comprehension: An event-indexing model. *Psychological Science, 6,* 292–297.

CHAPTER 14

Inoculation Theory

Josh Compton

After Michael Pfau and I offered what was, prior to this chapter, the most comprehensive narrative review of inoculation scholarship (Compton & Pfau, 2005), we concluded that inoculation, while a mature theory, was "far from retiring" (p. 136). We predicted prodigious theory development and application, and as this review will show, this happened and is happening. Researchers continue to propel inoculation scholarship forward in quantity and theoretical depth. Some scholarship confirms findings from the first years of the theory; other discoveries challenge fundamental assumptions about resistance in general and inoculation theory in particular. And all the while, the original analogy is pulled and stretched.

Inoculation theory maintains a complicated relationship with its analogical namesake. More than rhetorical flourish, the analogy was intended to serve, in the words of its creator, as inoculation's "theoretical point of departure" (McGuire, 1964, p. 222). There is a logic in analogy—an *analogic* (Holyoak & Thagard, 1995, p. 2) unique to theorizing with analogy—that, in inoculation theory, weaves biological resistance processes with persuasion resistance processes. While some resistance dynamics line up neatly, others have looser connections, and still others seem, at least at first glance, to be independent of the analogy. Although one-to-one connections between characteristics of sources and targets are not requirements for analogical transfer, when they are present, they are useful (Holyoak & Thagard, 1995). After identifying purported gaps between the two resistances, some have called for reconsideration of the analogy (e.g., Wood, 2007).

Because of the historical and contemporary importance of the analogy in inoculation theory's story, the analogy will never be far from our considerations in this chapter. Initially, the chapter focuses on how the early model of inoculation held tightly to the analogy to explain how inoculation confers resistance. After considering *how*, the chapter turns to *where* by tracing inoculation theory's applications in health, politics, and commerce. Next, the basic model and its analogical premises are confronted in a survey of some of the most important contemporary issues facing the theory as the chapter outlines analogical connections with mediators, moderators, and outcomes. The chapter concludes with a suggested agenda for the next generations of inoculation scholarship—an agenda that recognizes *and* challenges inherent assumptions of the analogy.

The Basic Model

McGuire (1964) named and explained his resistance model with a medical analogy, noting how persuasion inoculation parallels medical inoculation. Consider, for example, an annual flu shot. A flu shot injects weakened versions of influenza virus—weakened to avert infection but strong enough to activate resistance. In a medical inoculation, resistance results from protective responses, such as the production of antibodies, triggered by threat. Similarly, during persuasion inoculation, pretreatment messages offer weakened versions of counterarguments—again, weakened to prevent persuasion but strong enough to activate protective responses. In a persuasion inoculation, resistance results from protective responses, such as the production of refutations to counterarguments, triggered by threat (McGuire, 1964). In both cases, resistance mechanisms, motivated by threat, confer protection against future attacks.

In this basic model, we find tight connections between medical and persuasion inoculations. Future threatening viruses are linked to future threatening persuasive challenges; weakened viruses reflect weakened counterarguments; and antibodies that come to the rescue in medical inoculations mirror refutations during persuasion inoculations. Under the assumptions of the basic model of inoculation theory, the medical analogy is explicatory. It neatly serves as an explanation for inoculation-conferred resistance that is as simple—or, as we would later discover, as complex—as we wish.

The prototypical inoculation pretreatment is a two-sided message, often called a *refutational* pretreatment, to contrast with a one-sided message, or *supportive* pretreatment (McGuire, 1964). To return to the medical analogy: An example of a supportive pretreatment against the threat of disease would be a vitamin regimen—a way to boost health before facing a potentially harmful virus (McGuire, 1964). In contrast, refutational pretreatments raise persuasive challenges: counterarguments, or arguments that challenge existing positions, beliefs, or attitudes. These counterarguments are weakened by refutations—becoming like weakened viruses in some medical inoculations (McGuire, 1964).

McGuire and his colleagues designed a series of experiments in the early 1960s to compare resistance conferred by refutational pretreatments to other pretreatments (e.g., supportive) or to no pretreatments (no message-control). Refutational pretreatments were superior in conferring resistance to subsequent challenges (McGuire, 1964).

Demonstrating resistance requires some inverted logic. Tests must confirm persuasion in order to assess resistance. So, as with tests of persuasion, inoculation studies need to show that the attack message used in the study was actually persuasive. But with resistance research, the key question is whether a pretreatment rendered the attack *less* persuasive. McGuire's standard research design—and most subsequent research designs in contemporary inoculation scholarship—enables this type of scrutiny: All participants are exposed to an attack message or messages, but only some receive pretreatment messages prior to the attack. This design allows researchers to assess whether the attack was actually persuasive *and* to assess whether the pretreatment (e.g., the refutational inoculation message) mitigated the persuasiveness of the attack.

This design allowed for comparisons of inoculation and control conditions, and also, different types of resistance pretreatments. For example, McGuire and his colleagues compared *refutational-same* and *refutational-different* inoculation pretreatments. *Refutational-same* raise and refute the same arguments that later are used in the attack message; *refutational-different* raise and refute novel arguments, not included in the attack. Both approaches confer resistance, which means that inoculation is not limited to refuting the same arguments later used in the attack (McGuire, 1964).

McGuire's inoculation theory offered a more nuanced understanding of the resistance effect of two-sided messages. Researchers had confirmed that two-sided messages could offer "an advanced basis for ignoring or discounting [opposing messages]" and that this preparation somehow "inoculated" recipients (Lumsdaine & Janis, 1953, p. 318). McGuire's theory moved past *that* refutational pretreatments work into *how* refutational pretreatments work. And an explanation of *how*, consistent with the basic model derived from the analogy, turns attention to threat and counterarguing—a catalyst (threat) and an activity (counterarguing) of inoculation-conferred resistance.

Threat and Counterarguing

Threat

Threat in inoculation is not a message property, but instead, a response to a message. It is recognized vulnerability, a perception that an existing position, once thought safe from change, may be at risk. In medical inoculation, the presence of an antigen motivates antibody production. In persuasion inoculation, we find something similar: The mere presence of unexpected challenges to an existing position, or counterarguments, threatens perceived security of that existing position. McGuire called this threat *implicit* threat (McGuire, 1964).

We also find an additional threat motivator in many inoculation messages: a forewarning of impending persuasive attacks. In McGuire's terms, this is *explicit* threat (McGuire, 1964). In most inoculation studies, a forewarning comes at the beginning of the inoculation message, although recent studies have used forewarnings at the end of a message, too (e.g., Ivanov et al., 2011). Regardless of where the forewarning occurs, the basic message is: Although you currently hold the right position on this issue, you will face future persuasive attacks, and such challenges may change your position. With both types of threat—implicit and explicit—potential vulnerability is exposed, motivating a process (or, as we later discovered, *processes*) of resistance.

Counterarguing

The collective generation of counterarguments and refutations, post-inoculation pretreatment, is a process called *counterarguing*. It is important to distinguish this conceptualization of counterarguing with material in an inoculation pretreatment. A pretreatment message does, indeed, present counterarguments and, usually, refutations, as a two-sided approach. But counterarguing *as a process* extends the argumentation modeled in pretreatment messages to activity *after* the pretreatment. Something dynamic happens: Those inoculated begin to counterargue on their own, raising and refuting additional arguments about the issue (see Compton & Pfau, 2005, McGuire, 1964). This process of counterarguing—modeled in the pretreatment and then continued—is tightly connected to our medical analogy. Refutations function much like antibodies, attacking and weakening offending antigens.

This is the basic model of inoculation-conferred resistance to influence: raising and refuting challenges confers resistance to future stronger challenges by (1) revealing vulnerability of the position (threat) through an explicit forewarning and/or the presence of counterarguments, which motivates (2) counterarguing (i.e., raising and refuting additional arguments about the issue *in addition to* arguments in the pretreatment).

Study after study in the 1960s confirmed that inoculation confers resistance to persuasion (McGuire, 1964). Yet, two unresolved limitations likely impeded inoculation's development in the immediate years following its introduction: (1) a lack of empirical confirmation of *how* inoculation conferred resistance (e.g., threat and counterarguing); and (2) the restricted use of inoculation with cultural truisms.

The analogy bore the burden of explaining inoculation. A weakened offending antigen threatens, which motivates a protection response—in biology and, McGuire reasoned, in persuasion. And yet, threat was only assumed in the early years of the theory (Compton & Pfau, 2005). Counterarguing was treated similarly to threat—also assumed, for the most part. One study (Papageorgis & McGuire, 1961) attempted to measure counterarguing by having participants make a list of arguments that supported their position, but this way of assessing post-inoculation cognitions did not support inoculation's effect on counterarguing.

Threat and counterarguing fit the logic (or *analogic*, Holyoak & Thagard, 1995) of the analogy, but in early research, lacked empirical support as explanatories. However, beginning with Pfau and Burgoon (1988) and continuing through recent inoculation scholarship, scholars have measured elicited threat and post-inoculation counterarguing. The most commonly used threat measure is a Likert-type scale with items such as *nonthreatening/threatening* and *not harmful/harmful* (e.g., Ivanov et al., in press). Counterarguing is often assessed using some variation of thought listing (i.e., asking participants to put into words thoughts that went through their heads; e.g., Parker, Ivanov, & Compton, 2012). Confirmation of threat and counterarguing helped propel inoculation scholarship forward, encouraging inoculation's resurgence as an active research program in the late 1970s (led by M. Burgoon and colleagues) and then again in the 1990s (led by Pfau and colleagues).

Scholars clarified threat and counterarguing, but what of inoculation's perceived restriction to cultural truisms? McGuire's early work with inoculation did not advance beyond cultural truisms, or "beliefs that are so widely shared within the person's social milieu that [the person] would not have heard them attacked, and indeed, would doubt that an attack were possible" (McGuire, 1964, p. 201). McGuire chose cultural truisms as the issue domain of inoculation to keep, as close as possible, the analogy connection. Cultural truisms represented "a 'germ-free' ideological environment" (McGuire, 1964, p. 200), and this, he reasoned, enabled tests of resistance with issues people had never heard attacked and avoided complications suggested by selective exposure predictions. Early inoculation studies explored issues such as teeth brushing and benefits of penicillin.

McGuire's decision to use cultural truisms limited inoculation's application to noncontroversial issue domains—by design. But later, Pryor and Steinfatt (1978) challenged McGuire's reasoning that restricted inoculation to cultural truisms, pointing out that an application to controversial issues remains consistent with the analogic, so long as *new* counterarguments are raised in the inoculation message. Their interpretation allowed extensions of inoculation beyond the boundaries of uncontended issues (cultural truisms), while remaining consistent with the analogic. A survey of subsequent inoculation scholarship shows inoculation's success with a wide-range of controversial issues, including legalizing marijuana (e.g., Pfau et al., 2009), banning testing on animals (Nabi, 2003), and support for U.S. involvement in the Iraq War (Pfau et al., 2008). Building from the basic model and confirming its efficacy against more provocative issues paved the way for dynamic applications of inoculation—particularly in health, politics, and commerce.

Applications of the Theory

Health

Inoculation theory's application to health issues is apt, if in name only. Indeed, even when inoculation theory was restricted to cultural truisms, its earliest studied issues were often health-related (e.g., dental hygiene, X-rays). But inoculation's potential as an applied health strategy was more fully realized when it was extended beyond the laboratory and into the field (see Ivanov, 2011). No health issue demonstrates this better than inoculation-informed antismoking campaigns. Not only did inoculation help children with low-self esteem resist pressures to smoke (Pfau, Van Bockern, & Kang, 1992), but also some attitudinal effects lasted 20 months after inoculation pretreatments (Pfau & Van Bockern, 1994). This ground-breaking study set precedence for using inoculation to inform health campaigns, and it offered a more focused approach than Richard Evans' *social inoculation* (see Wallack & Corbett, 1987), which uses multiple activities—often employing refutational messages—but fails to measure the key variable of threat.

Building from inoculation's established efficacy as a preventative strategy with smoking, Godbold and Pfau (2000) found inoculation also helped children combat alcohol influences. Specially designed normative inoculation messages gave children a more accurate perspective of how many of their peers were drinking, although inoculation did not enhance attitudinal resistance to alcohol advertising, perhaps because researchers weren't able to elicit more threat with the inoculation condition (Godbold & Pfau, 2000). Parker, Ivanov, and Compton (2012) found inoculation conferred resistance to challenges to college students' condom use attitudes. They also found a cross-protection effect: Inoculating against challenges to condom use attitudes also conferred protection of binge drinking attitudes.

Politics

Applied research confirms inoculation offers an effective, innovative political campaign strategy—a preemptive approach to protect image and secure votes (see Pfau & Kenski, 1990). Inoculation preempts effects of attacks on candidate image and their positions (Pfau & Burgoon, 1988; Pfau, Kenski, Nitz, & Sorenson, 1990), including attacks raised in debates (An & Pfau, 2004), and its effects extend beyond attitudes and into intended actions—with some voters, boosting likelihood of voting and information seeking (Pfau, Park, Holbert, & Cho, 2001). Other research explores inoculation's effects on specific political issues. Pfau and his colleagues assessed inoculation's efficacy in securing support for U.S. involvement in Iraq against the influence of photographs (Pfau, Haigh, Fifrick, et al., 2006) and news visuals (Pfau, Haigh, Shannon, et al., 2008). Inoculation reduced influences of photographs,

but only with females (Pfau et al., 2006); against news visuals, inoculation boosted threat and counterarguing but did not impact attitudes (Pfau et al., 2008). Turning their attention specifically to inoculation's effects on political dialogue, Lin and Pfau (2007) confirmed its efficacy against spiral of silence effects, or the stifling effect of perceiving that one's opinion is in the minority (see Noelle-Neumann, 1993). Inoculation boosted confidence, encouraged speaking out, and bolstered positions against challenges (Lin & Pfau, 2007).

Commerce

Inoculation can inform corporate communication, public relations, and marketing. Inoculation messages in employee literature bolster organizational identity, commitment, conscientiousness, and sportsmanship (Haigh & Pfau, 2006); corporate issue-advocacy campaigns have inoculative effects (Burgoon, Pfau, & Birk, 1995); and pre-crisis inoculation protects image after a crisis (Wan & Pfau, 2004; Wigley & Pfau, 2010b).

Inoculation can either help or thwart marketing. Companies can inoculate against their competitor's comparison ads with higher-involving products (Pfau, 1992) and can inoculate against attacks based on country-of-origin (COO), even when multiple attacks are launched (Ivanov, Pfau, & Parker, 2009a). But inoculation can also help consumers resist marketing efforts. Inoculating against front-group stealth campaigns (groups of companies with misleading, innocuous names) protects against their influence (Lim & Ki, 2007; Pfau et al., 2007), and inoculating against credit card marketing protects college students from some potentially negative effects (Compton & Pfau, 2004).

Clearly, inoculation's efficacy is not restricted to cultural truisms. In health, politics, commerce, and a host of other domains (some of which remain unexplored or underexplored), inoculation confers resistance to influence. And often, applied findings are consistent with McGuire's original theorizing: Inoculation messages elicit threat, boost counterarguing, and confer resistance.

And yet, we also see ways the basic model is stretched or even challenged in applied scholarship. Sometimes inoculation pretreatments enhance threat and counterarguing but fail to confer resistance (e.g., Pfau et al., 2008). Some political inoculation studies found inoculation protects attitudes against attacks, but also derogates the sources of the attack messages (e.g., Pfau et al., 1990), an effect not clearly connected to the analogy. To further explore how such findings fit within a larger conversation of inoculation in laboratory and field studies, we review key issues in contemporary inoculation theory next.

Issues in Contemporary Inoculation Theory

Inoculation is a classic persuasion theory—"the grandparent theory of resistance to attitude change" (Eagly & Chaiken, 1993, p. 561)—and it continues to have contemporary relevance. Some contemporary inoculation issues reflect components of the original model, while others stretch the model into new domains and mechanisms.

Consider, for example, how contemporary work with the issue of timing has supported *and* challenged assumptions of the analogy. Timing involves two separate yet related issues: What is the optimum amount of time between pretreatment and attack, and how long do inoculation effects last? These are issues of *timing* and *decay*, respectively (Compton & Pfau, 2005). As McGuire (1964) first reasoned, those inoculated need some time between pretreatment and attack for resistance to strengthen, (e.g., through continued counterarguing). The connection to the medical inoculation is tight: A body needs time to produce antibodies, for example, after it is alerted to an offending agent. But, with time, those inoculated likely forget *and* lose motivation to counterargue (Insko, 1967).

Much of the early inoculation research used short delays: a matter of seconds (e.g., McGuire, 1961a) or days (e.g., McGuire, 1961b). But more recent research has extended the delay between pretreatment and attack to weeks (e.g., Ivanov et al., in press) or even up to 21 months (Pfau & Van Bockern, 1994). Now, a common delay between pretreatment and attack is about two weeks (e.g., Ivanov et al., in press). Banas and Rains's (2010) meta-analysis suggested that the ideal length of the delay between pretreatment and attack does not line up with how McGuire (1964) and others (e.g., Compton & Pfau, 2005) have theorized. Instead of finding that resistance gradually increases after the pretreatment before eventually dropping off, Banas and Rains found no difference between immediate and moderate delays, with resistance diminishing after about two weeks.

If inoculation effects eventually wear off, wouldn't booster sessions be a way to prolong resistance? It was an idea first proposed by McGuire (1964), and it is continued in more recent scholarship; but to date, effects of boosters on resistance are mild, at best, from early work (e.g., McGuire, 1961) through more recent study (e.g., Pfau et al., 1997). Have we lost an analogical link? Then again, perhaps boosters *can* enhance inoculation, but we haven't yet discovered optimal timing of when to boost (Compton & Pfau, 2005).

While some scholars have focused on dynamics of inoculation in contemporary studies, such as timing, others turn to mechanisms of resistance. Banas and Rains's (2010) meta-analysis of inoculation theory scholarship, which analyzed decades of laboratory studies, supported the basic model in some ways, but failed to find support for other key predictions. Among their findings, results supported inoculation's comparative advantage over supportive pretreatments and no pretreatment (control), as well as inoculation's ability to confer resistance to refutational-same and refutational-different attacks. However, in regard to the basic model, results failed to find impacts of elicited threat on resistance. (The researchers point out that power was low for their test of threat.)

Results of Banas and Rains's (2010) meta-analysis and other studies that confront the basic model warrant another look at the analogy. Has the analogy outlived its usefulness? Or do we need to fine-tune the way we are referencing the analogy in our theorizing and scholarship? A review of issues in contemporary inoculation theory, including an overview of what we know of inoculation theory's moderators, mediators, and outcomes, helps to offer some answers to these and other questions.

Moderators: Pre-attitude, Involvement, Self-Efficacy

Pre-attitude

Pre-attitude is an especially important moderator in the process of inoculation. Because inoculation is a preventative strategy, the target attitude must be in place *before* inoculation (Compton & Pfau, 2005; McGuire, 1964). When the intended attitude is not in place, inoculation messages can have a persuasive effect, but such an application of inoculation messages is not consistent with the domain of the theory (Wood, 2007). Pre-attitude, then, is a moderator of unique importance, serving as both a moderator during inoculation and as a necessary condition for inoculation.

Most contemporary inoculation scholarship assesses pre-attitude and then accounts for pre-attitude in analysis (e.g., treating it as a covariate, e.g., Pfau et al., 2009). Taking an even more precise look at pre-attitude, Ivanov, Pfau, and Parker (2009b) examined attitude bases (affective or cognitive) and subsequent effects on pretreatment message strategies (affective or cognitive), finding that matching the base of an attitude to message strategy is most effective (e.g., an affective-based inoculation pretreatment message is more effective with an affective-based attitude).

Perceived Involvement

When inoculation scholars study involvement, they are usually studying people's perceived involvement with an issue. Pfau and his colleagues (1997) once reasoned: "[I]nvolvement holds the key to inoculation's terrain" (p. 210), theorizing that when involvement levels are too high, people will not experience more threat. On the other hand, if involvement levels are too low, people will not care enough about the issue to experience threat. Consequently, because threat is a requisite for inoculation, low and high involvement levels should counter inoculation. Moderate involvement levels, they concluded, are most susceptible to inoculation pretreatments—those moderately involved care enough, but not too much, to experience threat. In a departure from the basic model, results of their study suggested involvement, and not threat, directly led to counterarguing, and with low- and high-involvement issues, they found a direct path from involvement to resistance (Pfau et al., 1997). Banas and Raines's (2010) meta-analysis failed to find support for involvement levels enhancing resistance, although power was low (.12).

Later, Pfau and colleagues found that pre-inoculation involvement levels lead to resistance by working through anger and not traditional mechanisms of threat or counterarguing (Pfau et al., 2001). Even when looking at specific types of initial involvement, most involvement types "bypassed the mechanisms of threat and counterarguing, and instead, exert[ed] a direct impact on elicited anger, attitude strength, and resistance to persuasive attacks" (Pfau et al., 2010, p. 12).

Self-Efficacy

One's perception of self-efficacy can affect inoculation. Higher levels of pre-inoculation self-efficacy boost resistance when inoculation messages use anger appeals, but when inoculation messages use rational appeals, a moderate level of self-efficacy is optimal; when self-efficacy is low, inoculation messages that use happiness appeals are most effective (Pfau et al., 2001). Extant theory does not offer much clarity as to *why* these differences emerged.

Of these moderators, pre-attitude fits the medical analogy most clearly. Just as people cannot be inoculated against a disease they already have, people cannot be inoculated against a position they already hold. Identifying the presence and valence of an attitude is a crucial first step in successful inoculation. The connection is less clear with involvement and self-efficacy as moderators of inoculation. However, treating the two variables as mediators of inoculation may offer a better fit. This is a possibility we explore next, in addition to the mediators suggested by the basic model.

Mediators in the Basic Model: Threat and Counterarguing

Threat

We have argued before that threat is required for inoculation (Compton & Pfau, 2005), something first proposed by McGuire in his original explanations for how inoculation works (McGuire, 1964). Without threat, resistance is not inoculation-conferred resistance—whether implicit (from exposure to counterattitudinal content in the pretreatment message) and/or explicit (a product of a forewarning). To date, research has failed to differentiate how much independent threat is caused by each (Wood, 2007).

Recently, scholars have turned attention to constructing more focused manipulations of threat (see Banas & Rains, 2010) to generate more threat. In most inoculation research, threat levels fail to exceed moderate ranges (Compton & Pfau, 2005). To elicit more threat, researchers have varied language intensity in pretreatment messages (Pfau et al., 2010), constructed affective-negative pretreatments (Pfau et al., 2009), and exploited the force of psychological reactance (Ivanov et al., 2011). From such research, we have learned that stronger language does not necessarily enhance threat (Pfau et al., 2010), affective-negative messages can generate more threat than affective-positive messages (Pfau et al., 2009), and boosting reactance during inoculation boosts resistance

(Ivanov et al., 2011). Studies like these are illuminating not only the role of threat, but also, the larger processes of inoculation itself.

Counterarguing

Scholars began regularly measuring counterarguing output in the 1990s, and more recently, have taken an even closer look at this process of inoculation-conferred resistance. Results indicate most post-inoculation refutational preemption is cognitive (Pfau, et al., 2009; Wigley & Pfau, 2010a), but when affective counterarguments are generated, they are strong (Wigley & Pfau, 2010a).

Since the earliest research, scholars assumed that counterargument output grows in the days following inoculation pretreatments, and then begins to decay (McGuire, 1964). As Insko (1967) pointed out, those inoculated need time to generate "belief-bolstering material" (p. 316), but their motivation to bolster the belief also diminishes with time. Yet these assumptions about counterarguing have not received consistent empirical support. Instead, inoculation messages appear to immediately boost counterarguing (Pfau et al., 2006; Pfau et al., 2009). One study found counterarguing lasts for at least 44 days, and then plays an active role during resistance to the attack message (Pfau et al., 2004, 2006), while another study found that counterarguing output dissipates after about two weeks (Pfau et al., 2009). Some research shows that inoculation elicits more counterarguing, but counterarguing doesn't directly lead to resistance (e.g., Pfau et al., 2008).

Moderators Beyond the Basic Model: Involvement, Self-Efficacy, Affect, and Talk

Perceived Involvement

Earlier research assessed initial involvement levels on resistance—that is, how involved people were with the issue *prior* to the inoculation pretreatment. Beginning in 2004, researchers began assessing perceived involvement as a product of inoculation pretreatments—a dynamic variable elicited by the inoculation message (e.g., Compton & Pfau, 2004). Researchers wondered if the active process of issue consideration (e.g., counterarguing) motivated by inoculation treatment messages leads to changes that go beyond attitude strength. And that is what they found. A single inoculation pretreatment message can enhance perceived involvement with a target issue (e.g., Compton & Pfau, 2004, 2008; Pfau et al., 2004, 2005, 2009). Pfau and colleagues (2004) found elicited involvement to boost resistance through traditional mechanisms: pretreatments enhanced threat, which then enhanced involvement, which then lead to resistance through counterarguing and attitude accessibility.

Self-Efficacy

As with issue involvement, the first inoculation studies to explore self-efficacy treated it as an independent variable only—perceptions of self-efficacy held *prior* to inoculation (Pfau et al., 2001). Later, researchers assessed self-efficacy as a dependent variable, finding that pretreatments enhance perceptions of self-efficacy (Pfau et al., 2009). We can assume that perceived self-efficacy enhances resistance, but to date, its function as a moderator can only be inferred. It is a product of inoculation pretreatments, but not yet clearly linked to the process of inoculation.

Affect

For much of inoculation's development, and despite threat's importance as a motivator, inoculation-conferred resistance was viewed primarily through a cognitive lens—raising and refuting counterarguments to strengthen positions (McGuire, 1964). But beginning in the 2000s, researchers began taking closer looks at affect.

The earliest affect inoculation research (Pfau et al., 2001) found anger boosts, while happiness weakens, resistance. We know from more recent research that inoculation is optimized "when the

refutational preemption component of inoculation messages feature arguments supported by hard evidence in addition to the use of affect triggers which signal that goals may be thwarted" (Pfau et al., 2009, p. 93). Additionally, inoculation makes people less fearful immediately after the pretreatment, and as the process continues, those inoculated get angrier and less happy (Pfau et al., 2009).

Precise effects of affect—and of different types of affect—during inoculation are difficult to pin down. We are in early stages of understanding affect in inoculation. And yet, some consistencies are beginning to emerge. Consider, for example, findings that point to unique and important roles of anger during (e.g., Ivanov et al., 2011; Pfau et al., 2001)—and even after—(Pfau et al., 2009) the inoculation process. Ivanov and Miller and colleagues (2011) approached anger with an innovative twist, turning to another classic theory of persuasion: reactance (see Brehm, 1966). Reactance describes how persuasion efforts can fail when message recipients interpret persuasive attempts as threats to their freedoms. Reactance, then, can be an obstacle to persuasion. But building on recent findings by Dillard and Shen (2005) that conceptualized reactance as anger and negative cognitions, Ivanov and Miller and colleagues *exploited* reactance instead of trying to avoid it. They designed inoculation messages specifically to elicit anger by framing the future persuasive attack as a threat to freedom, and this, in conjunction with the negative cognitions consistent with how inoculation confers resistance (counterarguing), resulted in enhanced resistance. Evidence is accumulating that anger plays an important role in inoculation-conferred resistance, consistent with a growing body of research that suggests, in a more general sense, inoculation pretreatments are triggering emotions and feelings, and these affect dimensions are affecting resistance.

Post-inoculation Talk

Usually, scholars assume that counterarguing in inoculation is "an internal process" (Pfau et al.,

2006, p. 144), or a "silent dialogue" (Wigley & Pfau, 2010a, p. 218). Yet recent evidence suggests inoculation also triggers *external* dialogue. Post-inoculation, people talk about the issue with their friends and family (Compton & Pfau, 2004; Ivanov et al., in press), even about beliefs that they perceive to be minority positions (Lin & Pfau, 2007). Building off of these findings, scholars built a case for *why* inoculation increases talk, surmising when people are shaken by the threat process of inoculation and buoyed by the preemptive refutation, this causes them to turn to their friends for support (to alleviate threat) or advocacy (to pass along the newly acquired refutational content; Compton & Pfau, 2009). Compton and Pfau (2009) also suggested that post-inoculation talk plays a role in how inoculation confers resistance—a conclusion that has since been empirically supported (Ivanov et al., in press). Talking about the issue seems to strengthen attitudes about the issue.

Does the analogy allow for new moderators such as affect and talk? Yes, it does, although connections may not be as immediately clear as those between refutations and antibodies, viruses, and counterarguments. For example, with affect, the best analog may be psychoneuroimmunology (PNI), a field of immunity research that explores dynamic relationships between emotions and immunity responses, including the influence of emotions on vaccination efficacy (see Kiecolt-Glaser, McGuire, Robles, & Glaser, 2002). Affect, in both cases, determines immunity. Considering new inoculation moderators can be consistent with the analogy when we maintain a focus on the two main components—threat and counter-arguing—and adopt a more nuanced view of biological inoculation.

Outcomes: Attitudes, Self-Efficacy, Behavioral Intentions

Attitudes

For many inoculation scholars, the most important benchmark for inoculation's efficacy is whether a target attitude, postattack, demonstrates resistance to persuasion. The simple question is: Was the attack message more persuasive to those who did not receive an inoculation pretreatment compared to those who did? Beginning in the 2000s, researchers also began to assess inoculation's impacts on attitude dimensions beyond valence, exploring attitude strength (e.g., Pfau et al., 2003), certainty (e.g., Pfau et al., 2004), and confidence (e.g., Compton & Pfau, 2004). These attitudinal dimensions have been used—in conjunction with attitudes toward an issue—as measures of conferred resistance.

Behavioral Intentions

Inoculation scholars have also assessed inoculation's impacts on behavioral intentions, particularly in applied scholarship. As examples: inoculating against credit card marketing message affects credit behaviors like efforts to increase credit card debt (Compton & Pfau, 2004), and inoculation in a political context can affect voting intentions (e.g., Pfau, Park, Holbert, & Cho, 2001).

Alternative and Supplementary Explanations for Resistance

Source Derogation

Tannenbaum's congruity research in the 1960s examined how source derogation impacts resistance (e.g., Tannenbaum & Norris, 1965), and source derogation is sometimes considered a competing explanation for resistance to influence. But instead of treating it as an alternative resistance process, some inoculation scholars have considered source derogation as an outcome of inoculation (e.g., Ivanov et al., 2011), although successful inoculation does not always derogate sources of attack messages (e.g., Pfau et al., 2007). One early inoculation study even attempted to link source derogation to the medical analogy: "Extending the biological 'inoculation' analogy with some cautions, we are then asking the question: 'Does the prestige and status of the physician who administers a drug alter the effectiveness of the drug in combating disease?" (Anderson, 1967, p. 351). We may find that inoculation-elicited counterarguing does just that by not only raising refutations of issue-specific counterarguments, but also, refutations of the source's credibility.

Attitude Accessibility

Attitude accessibility (see Fazio, 1986), or how quickly one engages an attitude upon encountering an issue, has been proposed as an alternative explanation for how inoculation works. Scholars speculated that inoculation increases the speed of retrieval for the target attitude, functioning as a resistance mechanism. And indeed, scholars have found inoculation increases attitude accessibility, which then strengthens resistance (Pfau et al., 2004; Pfau et al., 2003). But instead of considering attitude accessibility an alternative explanation, researchers concluded traditional components of inoculation (threat and counterarguing) and attitude accessibility were "somewhat independent . . . but to an even greater extent overlapping" (Pfau et al., 2004, p. 347) because both paths begin with threat and involvement.

Associative Networks

Inoculation scholars have turned to associative attitude networks (see Anderson, 1983) to explore how cognitive and affective nodes are created and linked to issues during inoculation. Much of the logic explored in associative networks mirrors that of counterarguing. With associative network research, scholars have used concept maps to illustrate changes to attitudinal nodes. Through this research, scholars have determined inoculation adds more nodes and linkages, and these alterations to the network enhance resistance (Pfau et al., 2005). But another study failed to confirm similar effects. They did find, however, affective-negative pretreatments add more cognitive nodes—more than affective-positive or even

cognitive pretreatments (Pfau et al., 2009). Scholars are at early stages of understanding these issues, but it appears dramatic inoculation effects may be attributed to subtle shifts in attitude structures.

SEM: Clarity and Mystery

One promising development in better understanding the inoculation process is the use of structural equation modeling (SEM) to identify and link variables of resistance (e.g., Pfau et al., 2004). But while SEM has added conceptual clarity, it has also revealed one of inoculation's continuing confounding mysteries: a direct path from inoculation pretreatments to resistance—a path independent of conventional mechanisms (threat and counterarguing) and, to date, proposed alternative explanations (e.g., attitude accessibility; see Compton & Pfau, 2005). In one SEM study, this path represented 14% of variance in attitude toward the issue (Pfau et al., 2004). This mystery path suggests we have not identified significant processes of inoculation (Insko, 1967), or our current efforts to measure inoculation are not optimal (Compton & Pfau, 2005). Or, both.

To better account for this and other as-yet-undefined processes at work in inoculation, more research is needed. This chapter concludes with proposed directions for future inoculation scholarship, including some new areas that emerge from a closer scrutiny of the basic analogic of inoculation theory.

New Directions in Inoculation Research

Pretreatments: Message Variations

Threat

McGuire once noted: "An obvious way of threatening . . . is by pre-exposure to weakened forms of attacking arguments" (1964, p. 201).

In many ways, threat triggers have not ventured too far from this "obvious" way. Weakened counterarguments, in conjunction with an explicit forewarning, are what, purportedly, elicit threat. Fortunately, scholars have begun to consider less obvious ways of inducing threat—and results are promising. Some of this research looks at manipulations of the traditional forewarning (e.g., Ivanov et al., 2011), and we should also continue to think beyond forewarnings as we develop new ways of generating threat (e.g., triggering reactance, Ivanov et al.). Further exploration of narratives and visuals (e.g., video, animation) seems particularly promising (Compton & Pfau, 2005), including vivid dramatizations of pressure to change issue positions, which may enhance perceived vulnerability beyond that of the conventional written message (e.g., Pfau, Van Bockern, & Kang, 1992).

Refutational Preemption

To date, differentiation in pretreatment message content is mostly on the basis of cognitive and affective appeals, including emotion-specific inductions, such as anger and happiness (e.g., Pfau et al., 2009), or affect intensity of counterarguments and refutations (Nabi, 2003). Other research has explored variations in argument strength (e.g., strong counterarguments with weak refutations; Compton & Pfau, 2004). But other manipulations have received less attention. For example, McGuire and his colleagues explored differences between passive and active refutations of counterarguments as part of an inoculation pretreatment (e.g., McGuire, 1961b), but this has received little attention in contemporary inoculation scholarship. In some ways, this is surprising, as the active/passive dichotomy may be useful analogs for medical inoculation variations (i.e., actively vs. passively acquired immunity). Future research should also consider effects of more implicit inoculation message refutations. For example, editorial cartoons and other types of political humor are often dependent on receivers making connections and drawing conclusions.

Could subtle argumentation function in an inoculation message, or is inoculation more effective when conclusions are clearly drawn during refutational preemption?

Process: Macro- and Microconsiderations

Affect

The trajectory of affect research in the story of inoculation scholarship is encouraging. First efforts confirmed that affect matters during inoculation (e.g., Pfau et al., 2001), and then, that specific emotions play roles during inoculation (Pfau et al., 2009). Most recently, by turning to other classic theories of persuasion for insight, we are learning with precision not just that affect matters, but how specific emotions mingle with traditional processes of resistance (e.g., threat and counterarguing) to elicit resistance (Ivanov et al., 2011). What we need next is a broader picture of which specific emotions are playing a role in inoculation-conferred resistance and when.

Post-inoculation Talk

New theorizing and research with word-of-mouth communication in general, and post-inoculation talk (PIT) in particular, offer an exciting shift from intrapersonal dynamics to interpersonal ones. Just as some biological inoculations can pass from person to person (see Compton & Pfau, 2009), persuasion inoculations may also be contagious. Compton and Pfau (2009) articulated the theorizing behind inoculation's effects on talk. More recently, Ivanov and colleagues (in press) confirmed that those inoculated are likely to talk about the issues *and* that this post-inoculation talk has a strengthening effect on the resistance of those inoculated. Next, innovative research designs are needed to trace and track post-inoculation talk as messages move along interpersonal networks. This type of research could reveal whether PIT serves more of an advocacy function (passing along issue content) or even, as Compton and Pfau (2009) suggested, an inoculative function (eliciting threat by passing along both counterarguments and refutations, and ultimately, spreading inoculation). Inoculation gives people something to talk about—and the motivation to do it.

Umbrella of Protection

Since McGuire's original model, scholars have touted inoculation's ability to confer a wide sphere of protection against persuasive attacks (Compton & Pfau, 2005; McGuire, 1964), confirming that inoculation pretreatments protect against same *and* novel arguments (see Banas & Rains, 2010). But more recently, scholars have found that inoculation's protection extends beyond specific arguments and into novel issue domains. Parker, Ivanov, and Compton (2012) confirmed inoculating against challenges to college students' condom use attitudes also protects binge drinking attitudes—even when only one of the issues is mentioned in the pretreatment message. They suggest further exploration of attitude structures and linkages to better understand this cross-protection.

For example, in their empirical test of attitudinal hierarchies and spatial-linkage models (e.g., Galileo model), Dinauer and Fink (2005) found more support for a spatial-linkage model, suggesting that attitudes can affect one another regardless of their position in an attitude hierarchy. Change in one attitude leads to change in related attitudes. Approaching attitudes and their structures may help to explain wider-ranging effects of inoculation than previously realized. And, notably, this line of research is consistent with some medical inoculations that have cross-protection effects, whereas inoculating against one threat provides protection against related threats.

Outcomes: Iatrogenic Effects?

Successful medical inoculation is contingent on a body's defense mechanisms recognizing and then confronting a threatening agent, or antigen. Presumably, successful persuasion inoculation—if consistent with the conventional model—also requires recognition of threat. But what if a side effect of inoculation is that it makes people *too* responsive to defending a position? This is one of many potential side effects of inoculation that warrant consideration in future scholarship. In medical terms, we might call these *iatrogenic effects*, or side-effects caused by a pretreatment protocol. Other possibilities include: Does inoculation lead to increased cynicism by inadvertently (or advertently) fostering source derogation? Does inoculation lead to a heuristic that dismisses rather than thoughtfully refutes challenges? If research demonstrates iatrogenic effects, the next step will be to identify ways of alleviating negative side effects—perhaps even inoculating against them.

Of course, with any future inoculation scholarship, manipulations to inoculation should not be atheoretical. Boundary conditions—as initially proposed by McGuire and clarified in the subsequent decades of research—should be considered. Additionally, following in the same vein as scholarship that has explored inoculation and attitude accessibility (e.g., Pfau et al., 2004) and psychological reactance (Ivanov et al., 2011), scholars should turn to additional theoretical processes when doing inoculation research.

Conclusion

As we have surveyed more than 50 years of inoculation scholarship and looked ahead to future developments of the theory, we have returned to the original medical analogy for comparison and contrast. While several arguments can be made against the analogy, two fundamental challenges include: (1) Some key variables of inoculation—including forewarnings and refutations (e.g., Wood, 2007)—do not have clear analogs with medical inoculation; and (2) the analogy may overemphasize cognitive dimensions, namely, counterarguing, to secure its parallel with antibodies in medical inoculations.

But even with these objections, the analogy is more instructive than restrictive. As to the first objection, the two main processes of inoculation—threat and protective responses to threat—have clear analogs, even if some *manifestations* of these processes may not. For example: Forewarning in persuasion inoculation may not have a clear analog with the medical analogy, but threat does, and threat, not forewarning, is the requisite component. In hindsight, it appears we may have clouded operationalizations of threat in previous research by not delineating threat from forewarning. Clearer definitions of threat (a process of inoculation) and forewarning (one possible threat trigger) will be helpful as we continue inoculation's development.

As to the second major concern, inoculation scholarship did focus mostly on cognitive processes at work in resistance during the early years of theory development. But now, with increased attention to affect, this isn't so much a problem with the analogy as it is an effect of how much we want to nuance the analogy. The analogy does not limit inoculation explanations to counterarguing. As previously mentioned, antibodies triggered during medical inoculations can be likened to the counterarguing process of persuasion inoculation. But the key descriptor is *likened*, not *limited*. Counterarguing is *a* resistance response triggered by the presence of counterattitudinal content, but it is not the only resistance response (see, for example, reactance, Ivanov et al., 2011). Indeed, some of the most current work with medical inoculations examines ways of conferring resistance with vaccines that not only motivate increased production of antibodies, but also other protection components, such as memory cells and protective proteins. Broadening persuasion inoculation's scope to include new aspects of resistance is not only consistent with medical inoculations, but even encouraged by new developments in immunology.

My current take on the analogy debate is this: The inoculation analogy is both limiting and flexible enough. It is limiting in the sense that it constrains inoculation as a preemptive strategy of resistance. It is also limiting by defining a process of resistance that stems from threat. But the analogy is also flexible enough to account for a wide range of defense-building processes against a wide range of attacks. What is needed next is to continue expanding our conceptualization of inoculation-conferred resistance while respecting its inherent boundary conditions, and the original analogy helps us do that in some ways McGuire first proposed and in new ways he might have never imagined. An observation he and a colleague made at the conclusion of one of the earliest inoculation studies continues to resonate: "Pursuit of the medical analogy suggests many further questions" (McGuire & Papageorgis, 1962, p. 33). I couldn't agree more.

References

An, C., & Pfau, M. (2004). The efficacy of inoculation in televised political debates. *Journal of Communication, 54*(3), 421–436.

Anderson, J. R. (1983). *The architecture of cognition.* Cambridge, MA: Harvard University Press.

Anderson, L. R. (1967). Belief defense produced by derogation of message source. *Journal of Experimental Social Psychology, 3*, 349–360.

Banas, J. A., & Rains, S. A. (2010). A meta-analysis of research on inoculation theory. *Communication Monographs, 77*(3), 281–311.

Burgoon, M., Pfau, M., & Birk, T. (1995). An inoculation theory explanation for the effects of corporate issue/advocacy advertising campaigns. *Communication Research, 22*(4), 485–505.

Compton, J., & Pfau, M. (2004). Use of inoculation to foster resistance to credit card marketing targeting college students. *Journal of Applied Communication Research, 32*(4), 343–364.

Compton, J., & Pfau, M. (2005). Inoculation theory of resistance to influence at maturity: Recent progress in theory development and application and suggestions for future research. In P. J. Kalbfleisch (Ed.), *Communication yearbook* (Vol. 29, pp. 97–145). Mahwah, NJ: Erlbaum.

Compton, J., & Pfau, M. (2009). Spreading inoculation: Inoculation, resistance to influence, and word-of-mouth communication. *Communication Theory, 19*(1), 9–28.

Dinauer, L. D., & Fink, E. L. (2005). Interattitude structure and attitude dynamics: A comparison of the hierarchical and Galileo spatial-linkage models. *Human Communication Research, 31,* 1–32.

Eagly, A. H., & Chaiken, S. (1993). *The psychology of attitudes.* New York, NY: Harcourt Brace Jovanovich.

Fazio, R. H. (1986). How do attitudes guide behavior? In R. H. Sorrentino & E. T. Higgins (Eds.), *The handbook of motivation and cognition: Foundations of social behavior* (pp. 204–243). New York, NY: Guiliford Press.

Godbold, L. C., & Pfau, M. (2000). Conferring resistance to peer pressure among adolescents: Using inoculation theory to discourage alcohol use. *Communication Research, 27*(4), 411–437.

Haigh, M. M., & Pfau, M. (2006). Bolstering organizational identity, commitment, and citizenship behaviors through the process of inoculation. *International Journal of Organizational Analysis, 14,* 295–316.

Holyoak, K. J., & Thagard, P. (1995). *Mental leaps: Analogy in creative thought.* Cambridge, MA: MIT Press.

Insko, C. A. (1967). *Theories of attitude change.* New York, NY: Appleton-Century-Crofts.

Ivanov, B. (2011). Designing inoculation messages for health communication campaigns. In H. Cho (Ed.), *Health communication message design: Theory and practice* (pp. 73–93). Los Angeles, CA: Sage.

Ivanov, B., & Miller, C. H. (with Sims, J. D., Harrison, K. J., Compton, J., Parker, K. A., et al. (2011, November). *Boosting the potency of resistance: Combining the motivational forces of inoculation and psychological reactance.* Paper presented at the annual convention of the National Communication Association, New Orleans, LA.

Ivanov, B., Miller, C. H., Compton, J., Averbeck, J. M., Harrison, K. J., Sims, J. D. et al. (in press). *Effects of post-inoculation talk on resistance to influence. Journal of Communication.*

Ivanov, B., Pfau, M., & Parker, K. A. (2009a). Can inoculation withstand multiple attacks? An examination of the effectiveness of the inoculation strategy compared to the supportive and restoration strategies. *Communication Research, 36*(5), 655–676.

Ivanov, B., Pfau, M., & Parker, K. A. (2009b). The attitude base as a moderator of the effectiveness of inoculation strategy. *Communication Monographs, 76*(1), 47–72.

Kiecolt-Glaser, J. K., McGuire, L., Robles, T. F., & Glaser, R. (2002). Psychoneuroimmunology: Psychological influences on immune function and health. *Journal of Consulting and Clinical Psychology, 70*(3), 537–547.

Lim, J. S., & Ki, E.-J. (2007). Resistance to ethically suspicious parody video on YouTube: A test of inoculation theory. *Journalism and Mass Communication Quarterly, 84*(4), 713–728.

Lin, W.-K., & Pfau, M. (2007). Can inoculation work against the spiral of silence? A study of public opinion on the future of Taiwan. *International Journal of Public Opinion Research, 19*(2), 155–172.

Lumsdaine, A. A., & Janis, I. L. (1953). Resistance to 'counterpropaganda' produced by one-sided and two-sided 'propaganda' presentations. *Public Opinion Quarterly, 17*(3), 311–318.

McGuire, W. J. (1961a). The effectiveness of supportive and refutational defenses in immunizing and restoring beliefs against persuasion. *Sociometry, 24*(2), 184–197.

McGuire, W. J. (1961b). Resistance to persuasion conferred by active and passive prior refutation of same and alternative counterarguments. *Journal of Abnormal and Social Psychology, 63*(2), 326–332.

McGuire, W. J. (1964). Inducing resistance to persuasion: Some contemporary approaches. In L. Berkowitz (Ed.), *Advances in experimental social psychology* (Vol. 1, pp. 191–229). New York, NY: Academic Press.

McGuire, W. J., & Papageorgis, D. (1961). The relative efficacy of various types of prior belief-defense in producing immunity against persuasion. *Journal of Abnormal and Social Psychology, 62*(2), 327–337.

McGuire, W. J., & Papageorgis, D. (1962). Effectiveness of forewarning in developing resistance to persuasion. *Public Opinion Quarterly, 26*(1), 24–34.

Nabi, R. L. (2003). "Feeling" resistance: Exploring the role of emotionally evocative visuals in inducing inoculation. *Media Psychology, 5*(2), 199–223.

Noelle-Neumann, E. (1993). *The spiral of silence: Public opinion, our social skin.* Chicago, IL: University of Chicago Press.

Papageorgis, D., & McGuire, W. J. (1961). The generality of immunity to persuasion produced by pre-exposure to weakened counterarguments. *Journal of Abnormal and Social Psychology, 62,* 475–481.

Parker, K. A., Ivanov, B., & Compton, J. (2012). Inoculation's efficacy with young adults' risky behaviors: Can inoculation confer cross-protection over related but untreated issues? *Health Communication, 27*(3): 223–233.

Pfau, M. (1992). The potential of inoculation in promoting resistance to the effectiveness of comparative advertising messages. *Communication Quarterly, 40*(1), 26–44.

Pfau, M. (1997). Inoculation model of resistance to influence. In G. A. Barnett & F. J. Boster (Eds.), *Progress in communication sciences: Advances in persuasion* (Vol. 13, pp. 133–171). Greenwich, CT: Ablex.

Pfau, M., Banas, J., Semmler, S. M., Deatrick, L., Lane, L., Mason, A., et al. (2010). Role and impact of involvement and enhanced threat in resistance. *Communication Quarterly, 58*(1), 1–18.

Pfau, M., & Burgoon, M. (1988). Inoculation in political campaign communication. *Human Communication Research, 15*(1), 91–111.

Pfau, M., Compton, J., Parker, K. A., An, C., Wittenberg, E. M., Ferguson, M., et al. (2006). The conundrum of the timing of counterarguing effects in resistance: Strategies to boost the persistence of counterarguing output. *Communication Quarterly, 54*(2), 143–156.

Pfau, M., Compton, J., Parker, K. A., Wittenberg, E. M., An, C., Ferguson, M., et al. (2004). The traditional explanation for resistance versus attitude accessibility: Do they trigger distinct or overlapping processes of resistance? *Human Communication Research, 30*(3), 329–360.

Pfau, M., Haigh, M., Fifrick, A., Holl, D., Tedesco, A., Cope, J., et al. (2006). The effects of print news photographs of the casualties of war. *Journalism and Mass Communication Quarterly, 83*(1), 150–168.

Pfau, M., Haigh, M. M., Shannon, T., Tones, T., Mercurio, D., Williams, R., et al. (2008). The influence of television news depictions on the images of war on viewers. *Journal of Broadcasting and Electronic Media, 52*(2), 303–322.

Pfau, M., Haigh, M. M., Sims, J., & Wigley, S. (2007). The influence of corporate front-group stealth campaigns. *Communication Research, 34*(1), 73–99.

Pfau, M., Holbert, R. L., Szabo, E. A., & Kaminski, K. (2002). Issue-advocacy versus candidate advertising: Effects on candidate preferences and democratic process. *Journal of Communication, 52*(2), 301–315.

Pfau, M., Ivanov, B., Houston, B., Haigh, M., Sims, J., Gilchrist, E., et al. (2005). Inoculation and mental processing: The instrumental role of associative networks in the process of resistance to counter-attitudinal influence. *Communication Monographs, 72*(4), 414–441.

Pfau, M., & Kenski, H. C. (1990). *Attack politics: Strategy and defense.* New York, NY: Praeger.

Pfau, M., Kenski, H. C., Nitz, M., & Sorenson, J. (1990). Efficacy of inoculation messages in promoting resistance to political attack messages: Application to direct mail. *Communication Monographs, 57*(1), 1–12.

Pfau, M., Park, D., Holbert, R. L., & Cho, J. (2001). The effects of party- and PAC-sponsored issue advertising and the potential of inoculation to combat its impact on the democratic process. *American Behavioral Scientist, 44*(12), 2379–2397.

Pfau, M., Roskos-Ewoldsen, D., Wood, M., Yin, S., Cho, J., Kerr-Hsin, L., et al. (2003). Attitude accessibility as an alternative explanation for how inoculation confers resistance. *Communication Monographs, 70*(1), 39–51.

Pfau, M., Semmler, S. M., Deatrick, L., Mason, A., Nisbett, G., Lane, L., et al. (2009). Nuances about the role and impact of affect in inoculation. *Communication Monographs, 76*(1), 73–98.

Pfau, M., Szabo, E. A., Anderson, J., Morrill, J., Zubric, J., & Wan, H. H. (2001). The role and impact of affect in the process of resistance to persuasion. *Human Communication Research, 27*(2), 216–252.

Pfau, M., Tusing, K. J., Koerner, A. F., Lee, W., Godbold, L. C., Penaloza, L. J., et al. (1997). Enriching the inoculation construct: The role of critical components in the process of resistance. *Human Communication Research, 24*(2), 187–215.

Pfau, M., Van Bockern, S., & Kang, J. G. (1992). Use of inoculation to promote resistance to smoking initiation among adolescents. *Communication Monographs, 59*(3), 213–230.

Pfau, M., & Van Bockern, S. (1994). The persistence of inoculation in conferring resistance to smoking initiation among adolescents: The second year. *Human Communication Research, 20*(3), 413–430.

Poole, M. S., & Hunter, J. E. (1979). Change in hierarchically organized attitudes. In D. Nimmo (Ed.), *Communication yearbook 3* (pp. 157–176). New Brunswick, NJ: Transaction Books.

Pryor, B., & Steinfatt, T. M. (1978). The effects of initial belief level on inoculation theory and its proposed mechanisms. *Human Communication Research, 4,* 217–230.

Tannenbaum, P. H., & Norris, E. L. (1965). Effects of combining congruity principle strategies for the reduction of persuasion. *Sociometry, 28*(2), 145–157.

Wallack, L., & Corbett, K. (1987). Alcohol, tobacco and marijuana use among youth: An overview of epidemiological program and policy trends. *Health Education Quarterly, 14,* 223–249.

Wan, H.-H., & Pfau, M. (2004). The relative effectiveness of inoculation, bolstering, and combined approaches in crisis communication. *Journal of Public Relations Research, 16*(3), 301–328.

Wigley, S., & Pfau, M. (2010a). Arguing with emotion: A closer look at affect and the inoculation process. *Communication Research Reports, 27*(3), 217–229.

Wigley, S., & Pfau, M. (2010b). Communicating before a crisis: An exploration of bolstering, CSR, and inoculation practices. In W. T. Coombs & S. J. Holladay (Eds.), *The handbook of crisis communication* (pp. 568–590). Malden, MA: Wiley.

Wood, M. L. M. (2007). Rethinking the inoculation analogy: Effects on subjects with differing preexisting attitudes. *Human Communication Research, 33*(3), 357–378.

CHAPTER 15

Supportive and Persuasive Communication

Theoretical Intersections

Graham D. Bodie

This chapter highlights various associations among *persuasion* and *supportive communication* research. Social support and persuasion play critical roles in a host of contexts and settings, serving essential functions in families, places of work, schools, and communities. Persuasion and support also serve as contexts in which to explore issues related to health, gender, and cultural differences, and mediated message production and processing. Thus, the sheer number of potential parallels between these literatures precludes my ability to entertain exhaustion. Instead, I forward several similarities I view as having the greatest potential to spark creative cross-fertilization and to improve our understanding of what makes human communication possible. Specifically, this chapter focuses on how research in persuasion and social support have advanced our understanding of the (1) nature of messages and their effects, (2) character of message production and processing and the interactions within which these occur, and (3) relationships within which supportive and persuasive interactions are nested. A final section outlines directions

for future research that can add richness to the individual persuasion and support literatures as well as help advance more general theory development. In order to frame these larger sections, I begin this chapter by offering a definition of supportive communication and draw from it parallels to work in persuasion.

What Is Supportive Communication?

The study of social support continues to be dominated by three primary perspectives (MacGeorge, Feng, & Burleson, 2011). Scholars who study social support as a sociological phenomenon primarily focus on social integration, while the psychological perspective primarily focuses on *perceived* support, or the degree to which one perceives his or her social network as available if needed. A major feature that differentiates communication-focused scholarship on social support from the extensive sociological and psychological literatures is its explicit focus on peculiarities of *enacted* support

(Goldsmith, 2004). More specifically, research on supportive communication is concerned with "the *messages* through which people both seek and express support . . . the *interactions* in which supportive messages are produced and interpreted . . . [and] the *relationships* that are created by and contextualize . . . supportive interactions" (Burleson, Albrecht, Goldsmith, & Sarason, 1994, p. xviii; emphases in original). Given these foci are basic issues of interpersonal communication scholarship more generally (Knapp, Daly, Albada, & Miller, 2002), it is not surprising that those who study compliance gaining, persuasion, and interpersonal influence show similar interests (Dillard, Anderson, & Knobloch, 2001; Wilson, 2010).

The Nature of Messages and Their Effects

When people attempt to persuade or comfort others, they do so by using particular message features, some of which "more consistently lead to goal attainment than do others" (Burleson, 2010, p. 152). This section is comprised of two subsections; the first outlines features of advice and comforting messages found to reliably predict relevant outcomes, while the second reviews those relevant outcomes.

Message Content

Numerous studies have sought to identify helpful forms of supportive behavior, and synthetic reviews of these empirical findings provide considerable insight about the behavioral features that distinguish more versus less helpful supportive efforts (e.g., MacGeorge et al., 2011). There are similar bodies of research focused on documenting various techniques for enhancing compliance (e.g., Wilson, 2002) and message features that enhance attitude and behavioral change more generally (e.g., D. J. O'Keefe, 2002). Indeed, this chapter's focus on connecting the support and persuasion literatures is not unique,

as there is a long tradition of psychotherapy research equating affect change with changing underlying attitudes (for review, see Perrin, Heesacker, Pendley, & Smith, 2010). Although therapeutic change and attitude change are not identical, I find this particular connection interesting and useful for communication scholarship insofar as it provides the insight that promoting change (in the most general sense) is often catalyzed by a range of specific message features that may not be unique to a particular context (i.e., persuasion or support). In other words, perhaps there exist a set of fundamental features of messages that cut across contexts, the discovery of which might aid in more general theory development. In what follows I explore research on advice as a type of instrumental support and research on person centeredness in the context of emotional support, both of which have borrowed from and can help extend what we know about the effects of messages in the context of persuasion and can shed light onto more fundamental features of messages that assist change.

Features of Advice Messages

Advice is considered both a form social support insofar as it is relevant to helping others solve problems and as a form of persuasion insofar as advisors are recommending a particular action (Feng & MacGeorge, 2006). Thus, it is not surprising that scholars interested in advice as a type of supportive communication have borrowed heavily from work in persuasion. For instance, early work on advice focused on the inherently face threatening nature of these interactions and how messages might be crafted to attend to threats to face (Goldsmith, 1994; Goldsmith & MacGeorge, 2000); similar concerns are found in work on persuasion (e.g., Applegate & Woods, 1991) and compliance gaining (Baxter, 1984; see also Wilson, Aleman, & Leatham, 1998, who consider advice as a form of compliance gaining). Although research generally supports the facework paradigm, critics suggest that "precise linguistic strategies that consistently reduce perceived face-threat have been inconclusive" (MacGeorge, Feng, Butler, & Budarz, 2004, p. 44). Indeed, invoking the term facework focuses attention primarily on message style rather than message substance, causing researchers to focus on message strategies over features (see D. J. O'Keefe, 1994).

Current work that attempts to uncover specific ways in which advice messages can reduce threats to face and increase the effectiveness of advice also borrows heavily from persuasion. For instance, research by MacGeorge and her colleagues provides four ways in which advice content can vary—usefulness (comprehensibility, relevance), feasibility (ability to be accomplished), absence of limitations, and efficacy (likelihood the advice will be effective at addressing the problem); these specific features of advice messages are consistently stronger predictors of advice outcomes than more generic strategies of facework (MacGeorge, Feng, & Thompson, 2008). In an extension of this work, Feng and Burleson (2008), borrowing from persuasion the concept of explicitness (see D. J. O'Keefe, 1999), found that advice was perceived as more effective when the efficacy, feasibility, and absence of limitations of the advice message was stated explicitly. Thus, it appears that comprehensible and relevant messages that present a solution perceived as feasible, efficacious, and absent of limitations are likely to instill change (i.e., doing or believing something differently than if left alone) more readily than messages without these characteristics; and it helps even more if these components are clearly and unambiguously stated.

Person Centeredness

Person centeredness (PC) is a general quality of messages and refers to the degree to which "messages take into account and adapt to the subjective, emotional, and relational aspects of communicative contexts" (Burleson, 2007, p. 113). Over 30 years of research in the context of emotional support shows that messages higher in PC are perceived as better and produce better outcomes than messages lower in PC; a smaller set of studies supports heightened effectiveness for person-centered persuasive messages (see Burleson, 2007). Higher person-centered messages are those that illustrate recognition of an interlocutor's goals while also reflecting the goals of the sender and aspects unique to that situation (see Table 15.1). Thus, PC captures more than adaptation to the *person*. Indeed, PC was originally labeled "listener-adapted persuasive strategies" (B. J. O'Keefe & Delia, 1979, p. 231), an oversimplification quickly revised to acknowledge that messages (like people) are more or less complex, with complexity a product of the number of relevant interpersonal goals addressed in the message (B. J. O'Keefe & Delia, 1982). That is, messages can vary in "the degree to which and manner in which multiple goals are addressed in the message" (B. J. O'Keefe, 1988, p. 81). By addressing multiple goals, influencers and helpers alike stand to be more successful in changing beliefs and behaviors. Indeed, research shows clear and consistent advantages of attending to multiple interaction goals (e.g., giving explicit advice while also mitigating face concerns, listening attentively to another's distress while also attending to concerns about one's own emotional well-being), and the next section reviews these effects and their relations to message quality.

Message Effects

The nature and structure of message effects has a long history, and the subject is so vast that it has garnered much more attention than can be afforded here. For the sake of this chapter, I will discuss two broad classes of message effects (Bodie, Burleson, & Jones, 2012; Dillard, Shen, & Vail, 2007; Dillard, Weber, & Vail, 2007; Goldsmith, 2004; MacGeorge et al., 2004; D. J. O'Keefe, 1994). The first class of effects can be labeled *message evaluations* (ME), judgments or reactions to the message and/or its sender. Assessments of ME in studies of persuasion typically focus on the extent to which a

Table 15.1 Examples of Low and High Person-Centered Messages

Persuasion (Request for Extension)

Low PC

Professor Griffin, you *have* to give me an extension on the term paper assignment. I've been so busy with so many things lately and I haven't had a chance to work on it. I'm on the social events committee at my frat house and had to help plan a party last week. The week before that, there was a big paint ball tournament. And before that, I had a huge exam in a *really* important class in my major. So, I haven't had a chance to start working on the term paper. I really need an extension on this assignment; I have to get a good grade on it. I'll turn it in next week, OK?

High PC

Professor Griffin, can I talk with you about the term paper assignment? I really love the topic you suggested for my paper; it's so interesting and I'm learning so much! I've found a tremendous amount of material on this topic. I want to master all the material and write a really excellent paper, but to do that, I'm going to need a little more time than you originally allowed. You told us that we should make this paper something that we are proud of, and I really want to do that. So do you suppose I can turn the paper in next week? I know the extra time will allow me to produce an excellent paper, and one I think you'll enjoy reading.

Comforting (Relationship Breakup)

Low PC

Ben broke up with you? He's an idiot! But, this isn't the end of the world, you know. I mean, it's not the worst thing that could happen to you, and to be honest, I think you'll be better off without Ben. Anyway, there are tons of cute guys on this campus, you know, lots of fish in the sea. You just gotta get out there and catch another one! Keep in mind that no guy is worth getting all worked up about. I mean, it's just not that big a deal, not at this point in life. You can do a lot better than Ben. Just remember that Ben isn't worth any heartache and you'll stop being so depressed about the whole thing.

High PC

Barb broke up with you? Oh man! I'm really sorry; I know you must be hurting right now. Do you want to talk about it? You were together a long time and were really involved with her, so you must have some real heartache. This just sucks; I'm really sorry, man. The same thing happened to me last year, and I remember how rotten it makes you feel. It's especially tough when it's sudden like that. It's probably gonna take some time to work through it – after all, breaking up is a really hard thing. I know it may not mean very much right now, but keep in mind that you've got some good friends here – people who really care about you. I'm here whenever you want to talk about things.

Notes: I obtained these messages from my advisor, Brant Burleson, early in my doctoral program at Purdue. I will forever be grateful for his influence on my thinking as a scholar of human communication.

message is favorably evaluated in reference to its persuasive potential using scales tapping evaluations of either the message attributes (e.g., *logical–illogical*) or the likely outcomes of those messages (e.g., *persuasive–not persuasive*; Dillard & Sun, 2008). In contrast, evaluations of comforting messages generally focus on the constructs of helpfulness (e.g., *helpful–unhelpful*), sensitivity (e.g., *sensitive–insensitive*), and supportiveness (e.g., *supportive–unsupportive*; see Goldsmith, McDermott, & Alexander, 2000). Not surprisingly, various aspects of message quality (like those previously reviewed) have been found to influence evaluations of both persuasive (Dillard, 2003) and supportive (MacGeorge et al., 2011) messages.

The second class of effects can be characterized as *message outcomes* (MO), which includes a range of effects happening *after* the message. Persuasive messages are generally created to change or stabilize attitudes (or determinants of attitudes such as beliefs and evaluations, see Fishbein & Ajzen, 1975), behavioral intentions, and actions, whereas supportive messages generally aim to generate cognitive (e.g., appraisals), affective (e.g., emotions), and/or behavioral (e.g., coping) change (see Burleson, 2009). Backing research that finds ME is a function of message characteristics, advice is more likely to be implemented and, thus, lead to desired change (e.g., assist in coping) if it is efficacious, feasible, and absent of limitations (MacGeorge et al., 2008). Likewise, high person-centered messages are more persuasive (e.g., Waldron & Applegate, 1998) and are shown to enhance emotional improvement (Jones & Guerrero, 2001) compared to low person-centered messages; in the context of emotional support, low person-centered messages can further exacerbate stress reactivity (Bodie, in press-b).

A primary strategy in both persuasion and supportive communication research has been to focus on ME, a strategy that makes two primary assumptions: (1) whatever affects ME will similarly affect MO, and (2) ME is a causal antecedent

of outcomes. Synthesizing relevant persuasion research to date, Dillard, Weber, and Vail (2007) found that the association between ME and MO was substantial ($r = .41$). Dillard, Shen, and Vail (2007) subsequently reported five studies that consistently supported ME as a causal antecedent of MO. A recent two-study report found similar results for the relationship between supportive message evaluations and outcomes (Bodie, Burleson, et al., 2012). Overall, then, it appears that a strong connection between evaluations and outcomes exists in at least two communication contexts, and it seems reasonable to assume that this association extends to other communication contexts as well.

This finding has important methodological and conceptual implications. Although assessing ME is generally much easier, safer, and cheaper than is assessing MO, outcomes are generally of greatest practical interest. Practitioners of persuasion and support want to know what to say in order to change the attitudes and feeling states of others, not just whether message features are *perceived* to be better. Of course message evaluations are interesting and important in their own right, and there exist a host of potential evaluations that can be made of supportive and persuasive messages. Likewise, if we were to focus on outcomes to the exclusion of effects such as perceived comprehension known to influence these outcomes, we would miss out on important opportunities to advance theory and practice (see Berger, 1989).

Beyond Effects: How Messages "Work" Within Interaction

However useful theories of supportive messages have been in explicating the features that are evaluated more positively and typically help or hinder outcomes, only recently have these theories been incorporated into more comprehensive theories of how messages "work" (i.e., have their effects). One of the earliest attempts was Burleson and Goldsmith's (1998) theory of conversationally induced reappraisals, which proposes that successful comforting messages work by changing the implications of the person-environment relationship for the recipient's coping ability and general well-being (Jones & Wirtz, 2006). In a similar manner, influence scholars have shown the utility of appraisal-based theories for the study of how influence messages operate to create certain emotional responses (Dillard, Kinney, & Cruz, 1996). In contrast to strategy-based frameworks that attempt to match messages to "a predefined and static environmental circumstance," appraisal theories suggest that messages work by "discursively constructing useful appraisals of particular person-environment configurations" (Burleson & Goldsmith, 1998, p. 259). Thus, an important contribution of appraisal theories is to shift our focus from static message effects to the interactions in which messages are more or less efficacious.

Supportive and Persuasive Interactions

Supportive and persuasive interactions are most commonly described using phase models. For instance, the interactive coping model forwarded by Barbee and her colleagues (Barbee, 1990; Barbee & Cunningham, 1995; Barbee et al., 1993; Derlega, Barbee, & Winstead, 1994) outlines four phases of supportive interaction—*support activation, support provision, target reactions,* and *helper responses*—and persuasive interaction is discussed with somewhat similar phases (e.g., compliance solicitation, resistance; Sanders & Fitch, 2001). To date, however, only a handful of studies have actually investigated supportive or persuasive interactions in the ways implied by these models. Research suggests, for instance, that advice has more positive outcomes when directly solicited (e.g., Goldsmith, 2000) and when prefaced by highly person-centered emotional support and adequate problem analysis (Feng, 2009). Likewise, a number of studies

have investigated "sequential request strategies" (D. J. O'Keefe, 2002) and general principles explaining how and why people change and adapt (or fail to do so) when initial persuasive attempts are unsuccessful (e.g., Hample & Dallinger, 1998). Nevertheless, much persuasive and supportive communication research utilizes methodological tools such as paper and pencil surveys that are far from "interactive" at their core (Jones & Guerrero, 2001; Wilson, 2002). The primary strategy used to explore support and persuasion as interactive phenomena is to explore how people produce and process messages in the service of interaction goals.

Message Production

Dillard and Solomon (2000) describe four message production processes, namely situation comprehension, goal formation, planning, and behavioral enactment. To these processes, Burleson and Planalp (2000) suggest two others, monitoring and reencoding. Thus, variability in the content and quality of influence or supportive messages can be explained as a function of abilities to define the situation, form relevant intentions to achieve some purpose, generate cognitive representations of action plans, carry out the action plan(s), observe and evaluate the outcomes of the generated action, and, if necessary, alter goals, plans, and actions. Given that most research to date has focused on the first two of these processes, the sections that follow are necessarily limited, and others are encouraged to explore the contributions of support and persuasion to planning, enactment, monitoring, and encoding processes.

Situation Comprehension

In general, people who view their social milieu in more complex ways are better able to produce messages that take into account a greater number of contextual features and contingencies. *Interpersonal cognitive complexity* (ICC) is a stable individual difference that represents this ability to comprehend and process social information, including messages (Burleson & Caplan, 1998). Perceivers with higher ICC have more differentiated, abstract, and organized constructs (or schemas) for processing social information and, thus, have more advanced social perception skills than do less complex perceivers. Considerable research indicates that ICC is positively associated with the ability to generate sophisticated supportive and persuasive messages (for review, see Burleson & Caplan, 1998). Thus, ICC is a domain specific general ability to "size up" people and situations (Burleson & Bodie, 2008). Although domain is usually not cast at the level of communicative context, it is possible that interpersonal influence and supportive contexts constitute domains of knowledge. Indeed, it is easy to imagine a person who has a high level of ICC (i.e., can "size up people") but little knowledge of how attitude or affect change occurs.

Other variables that seem to describe ways in which individuals are likely to "size up" persuasive and supportive interactions can be classed into what scholars call *implicit theories* or how individuals structure their beliefs about a particular phenomenon. Burleson and Planalp (2000), for instance, discuss implicit theories of emotion—how the individual thinks emotion works—which seem highly relevant to the supportive context. Indeed, the support attempts of individuals who believe emotions cannot be changed or that they dissipate over time irrespective of communicative efforts should vary drastically from those of individuals who see emotions as pliable and able to be manipulated through talk. Similarly, B. J. O'Keefe (1988) discusses implicit theories of communication, or how the individual structures the workings of communication; similar ideas have been forwarded about persuasion (Roskos-Ewoldsen, 1997) and other elements of communication (e.g., listening; Bodie, St. Cyr, Pence, Rold, & Honeycutt, 2012). In general, implicit theories offer an explanatory link between goals and message outcomes; in other words, two individuals may have a similar

goal in mind (e.g., to gain compliance from a friend) but produce drastically different messages in order to obtain that goal because each views the purpose of communicating differently in that situation (see also Planalp & Knie, 2002).

Goal Generation

The specific nature of goals—"future states of affairs that an individual is committed to maintaining or bringing about" (Dillard et al., 2001, p. 433)—has been a standard focus of both persuasion and supportive communication research. Interpersonal influence scholars typically talk about primary and secondary goals (Dillard, 1990) with primary goals (e.g., gaining assistance) referring to goals that motivate interpersonal influence, and secondary goals (e.g., identity goals) those that constrain behavior. In general, to the extent that putative support providers have "a desire to modify the target's behavior," they hold a primary goal similar to that of compliance seekers. Interestingly, although "give advice" is often listed as a primary influence goal (for review, see Wilson, 2002, Table 5.1), to "be supportive" is usually listed as a secondary goal (Meyer, 2004).

For the support context, two primary goals have been identified. Individuals are said to primarily be emotion- or problem-focused, though a variety of subgoals under each category have been documented (e.g., MacGeorge, 2001) as have various ways in which these goals might be accomplished (e.g., avoid embarrassing talk about emotions versus given her the right advice about how to solve the problem; Burleson & Gilstrap, 2002). In addition, scholars recognize several secondary goals of support, including resource goals (e.g., the relationship may suffer if support seeking and provision are imbalanced in a relationship), arousal goals (e.g., the need to protect one's own emotional well-being), and interaction goals (e.g., the need to protect the other's face; Goldsmith, 1992). Indeed, the need to accomplish multiple, often competing, goals is a fundamental characteristic of supportive (Goldsmith, 1992), compliance gaining (Wilson, 2002), and interpersonal influence (Dillard, 1990) interactions.

Regardless of interaction context, a focus on goals provides scholars with a "highly proximal generative mechanisms for [explaining] the messages people produce" (Burleson & Gilstrap, 2002, p. 44). Indeed, the "sine qua non of goal categories . . . is their ability to conjoin otherwise isolated actions into coherent, connected, rule-guided (and in some cases sequential) patterns" (Hoffman, Mischel, & Mazze, 1981, p. 212). Moreover, invoking the notion of goals allows scholars to explain how variables such as ICC impact message production ability—individuals who are more cognitively complex see communicative situations in more complex ways and are thus better able to generate more complex goals for social interaction and think about how to integrate seemingly inconsistent goals (e.g., advise and save face; see Dillard, 1997, for an extended discussion of the benefits of the goal construct).

What still remains somewhat elusive, however, is exactly how goals arise and change over the course of interaction. Wilson's (1990) cognitive rules (CR) model is a general theory of goal formation that has been applied in the context of interpersonal influence with similar implications for supportive interactions. The CR model proposes that goal-relevant knowledge is stored in long-term memory within nodes that represent concepts (e.g., people, traits, settings). Cognitive rules link various interaction goals (e.g., give advice) with these various concept nodes. So, when faced with a situation that calls forth a primary goal and other situational features that make salient various secondary goals, the CR model proposes that certain cognitive rules are activated and, thus, are more likely to be employed than other, less salient cognitive rules. This might help explain why, for instance, men tend to employ less helpful forms of support, especially with other men—although a primary goal of helping his friend work through his emotions "pushes," a secondary identity or relational resource goal might "pull" back certain (more effective) strategies (cf. Burleson, Holmstrom, & Gilstrap, 2005).

Finally, although this review has focused solely on message production *abilities*, research clearly shows that *motivation* is an equally important contributor to effective message production (Berger, 1996). Burleson, Holmstrom, and Gilstrap (2005) identified three types or components of motivation for supportive message production: "*goal motivation*, or the desire to achieve a particular social outcome (such as relieving the emotional distress of another); *effectance motivation*, or the level of confidence a person has in his or her ability to achieve an outcome (such as improving another's affective state); and *normative motivation*, or the desire to behave in role-appropriate ways (such as saying the correct things when comforting others, according to salient social norms)" (pp. 470–471). Interestingly, a focus on ability and motivation is also evident in the literature on message processing, and it is to that literature we now turn.

Message Processing

Researchers studying supportive communication have borrowed extensively from the persuasion literature to explain variability in message effects. Scholars interested in variability in advice receptiveness have found that advice is better received when offered by more expert and relationally close individuals who have a stronger influence history with the recipient (Feng & MacGeorge, 2006); these variables map conceptually to credibility, similarity, and authority found to improve the likelihood of persuasive success (see D. J. O'Keefe, 2002). Likewise, although substantial research indicates that highly person-centered comforting messages are evaluated more positively and have more positive outcomes than less person-centered messages, growing evidence indicates that the effect of PC is moderated by several demographic factors (e.g., recipient's ethnicity), personality traits and cognitive factors (e.g., ICC), and features of the interactional context (e.g., recipient's need for support; for review, see Bodie & Burleson, 2008). Recently, my research has focused on exploring the degree to which these moderating variables can be more succinctly organized under a "dual-process" framework. The primary contribution of this work is to suggest message effects are a joint function of message content and how these messages are attended to and processed.

The General Dual-Process Framework

Dual-process theories, regardless of whether they are directed at explaining person perception, stereotyping, decision making, or communicative functions, assert that information processing lies on a continuum, with "[the] anchors of this continuum [reflecting] the 'duality' invoked by these" theories (Moskowitz, Skurnik, & Galinsky, 1999, p. 13). These anchors have been labeled mindless/mindful, top-down/bottom-up, automatic/intentional, effortless/effortful, holistic/analytic, and systematic/heuristic, just to name a few. But these dichotomies often obscure the notion that processing lies on a continuum, and, thus, varies in extent as opposed to being simply high or low. In my work, I have chosen to refer to this variation as elaboration in line with a popular dual-process theory of persuasion (Wegener & Claypool, 2000).

In general, as elaboration increases, recipients begin to more carefully reflect on the content of issue-relevant information, thoughtfully consider this information in relation to prior ideas, and give closer attention to multiple aspects of the communicative context. When elaboration is high, change is said to occur through "high thought" mechanisms. As elaboration decreases, cues not directly related to the issue at hand begin to have a larger influence on communication outcomes through mechanisms of change that require relatively little thought. With regard to explaining variation in message outcomes in particular, dual-process theories postulate that (1) multiple factors influence the amount of elaboration accorded by recipients, and (2) the effects of communicative structures (i.e., source, message, context, recipient) on outcomes vary as

a function of elaboration (see Holmstrom et al., 2011). In particular, dual-process theories hold that message content has the strongest effect on outcomes when recipients are both *motivated* to attend to the message and possess the *ability* to consider its content thoughtfully.

Contextually-Based Dual-Process Theories

The most well-known variant of dual-process theories outlines the role of processing in explaining persuasive message outcomes (ELM) (see chapter 9 in this volume). To explain why variables (e.g., credibility) seemed to sometimes effect persuasion outcomes and sometimes not, Petty and Cacioppo (1986), borrowing from more general cognitive response theories, set forth the idea that persuasion works through a variety of mechanisms, some of which involve cognitive elaboration and some of which do not involve much thinking at all to accomplish. Grounded in this approach, my doctoral committee chair and I (Bodie & Burleson, 2008) organized the variables found to moderate the effects of message content on outcomes, suggesting these variables have their effects by either (1) influencing the recipient's ability and/or motivation to systematically process these messages or (2) serving as cues that quickly trigger responses to the message.

To date, the general logic of dual-process thinking has been applied to the processing and outcomes of varied forms of support, including informational support (Feng & MacGeorge, 2010), everyday emotional support (Bodie, in press-a; Bodie, Burleson, Gill-Rosier, et al., 2011; Bodie, Burleson, Holmstrom, et al., 2011, Study 2; Holmstrom et al., 2011), grief management (Bodie, Burleson, Holmstrom, et al., 2011, Study 1; Rack, Burleson, Bodie, Holmstrom, & Servaty, 2008), and the management of stress during a public speaking task (Bodie, in press-b). The theory aims to explain why various elements of supportive interactions have the effects they do with particular others on specific occasions. The core thesis of this theory is that the elements of supportive interactions produce certain effects as a joint function of the intrinsic properties of these elements (e.g., the sophistication of supportive messages) and how these elements are processed cognitively by their recipients (e.g., systematically vs. superficially).

Dual-process theories of persuasion like the ELM have been accurately critiqued for several reasons. First, these theories often treat the nature of message quality as a methodological as opposed to theoretical concern (see chapter 9 in this volume). The dual-process theory of supportive message outcomes borrows from the extensive research in the context of supportive communication on message quality and shows that effects predicted by the general dual-process framework are supported. By using a strong theory of supportive message content, our theory does "more than [providing] a means of indirectly assessing the amount of elaboration that has occurred" (D. J. O'Keefe, 2002, p. 156); thus, dual-process theories of persuasive message effects might borrow from our research to help fill a lack of "understanding quality-related message features [and] their roles in persuasion" (p. 166).

Second, dual-process theories have been critiqued for assuming that high elaboration processes operate when motivation and ability are high as opposed to actually testing the underlying change processes. Our theory also borrows extensively from theories of emotion and coping to pinpoint when and why certain operative mechanisms will underlie affect change and other important outcomes. In particular, current research suggests specific mechanisms and attempts to set forth a priori hypotheses to test whether those mechanisms are primarily responsible for mediating the relationship between various aspects of the supportive environment and various effects and outcomes. For instance, I (Bodie, in press-a) recently explored the degree to which the cognitively demanding affect change mechanism reappraisal is more likely to operate when processing motivation is high than when low. To manipulate motivation, I exposed participants to either a moderately severe academic failure situation (students imagined failing a class required for entry into the major) or a mildly severe academic failure situation (students imagined receiving a "C" on an in-class reading quiz constituting 1% of the course grade). The key test was whether motivation moderated the degree to which reappraisal mediated the impact of PC on anticipated affect improvement (AAI). Results showed that, similar to the Jones and Wirtz (2006) study that originally tested Burleson and Goldsmith's theory, the combination of positive emotion words and situation reappraisal partially mediated the PC-AAI effect; however, this was only true for participants exposed to a moderately severe academic stressor. The mediated model did not fit for low motivation participants.

Summary

When communication scholars discuss social support or persuasion, it is almost always within the context of interaction (Barbee & Cunningham, 1995; Burleson, Albrecht, et al., 1994; Dillard et al., 2001; Sanders & Fitch, 2001; Wilson, 2002, 2010). In general, the focus on interaction draws attention to how people seek, produce, receive, process, and respond to comfort and influence. The sequential structure of these interactions also highlights the need to investigate how they unfold over time, the multiple variables likely to moderate the impact of message quality on outcomes, and the mediating variables that link messages and effects. As this work has been conducted, we have learned valuable information, including the role of these interactions in initiating, maintaining, and transforming the relationships within which they are nested.

The Role of Support and Influence in Relationships

Just as individuals produce and process messages in the pursuit of relevant interaction goals, so too do individuals pursue relationships for particular reasons. This perspective, typically called the functional approach to interpersonal relationships, "stresses what certain relationships typically *do* for people and, consequently, what people come to look to those relationships *for*" (Burleson, Metts, & Kirch, 2000, p. 245). Although people come to and remain in relationships for a variety of reasons, interpersonal needs theory (Schutz, 1958) suggests that close relationships primarily serve needs for affection (the need to love and feel loved), inclusion (the need to belong), and control (the need to feel in control of one's life). Since communication is "the means through which people both pursue and service relevant relationship functions" (Burleson & Samter, 1994, p. 62), it seems likely that both supportive and persuasive communication allow relational partners to meet individual and relational needs. Indeed, people value the ability of relational partners to influence and support appropriately and both are used frequently by relational partners having real implications for relationship quality.

Meeting Relational Needs Through Persuasion and Support

Individuals meet relational needs and fulfill relational functions through a variety of behaviors, each of which can be classified as either affective or instrumental in orientation (Burleson & Samter, 1990). Affectively oriented skills like comforting and ego-support primarily reference abilities to effectively manage feelings and emotions, whereas instrumentally oriented skills like informing and persuading are primarily focused on the management of activities and behaviors. In general, people report both affective and instrumental communication skills as important for close relationships, though people typically rate affectively oriented skills like comforting as more important than instrumental skills like persuading. These main effects are, however, qualified by characteristics of the relationship under question. In general, the importance of communication skills increases

linearly as a function of relational closeness from casual friendships or acquaintanceships to best friends (Westmyer & Myers, 1996).

Likewise, Burleson et al. (1996) reported that affectively oriented skills were seen as substantially more important in romantic partners than in friends, whereas instrumental skills of romantic partners were seen as only somewhat more important than those of friends. Finally, Holmstrom (2009) found that although affectively oriented skills were more important for female friends than for male friends, instrumental skills did not differ as a function of sex of friend. These latter results suggest that the communication skills relevant to meeting relational needs depend on relationship type (perhaps because different relationships serve different functions), but that affectively oriented communication skills are especially relevant in and are an expected part of highly intimate relationships (see also Cunningham & Barbee, 2000; Sprecher & Regan, 2002).

Of course, this does not mean that influence is an unimportant part of highly intimate relationships. In addition to being supportive, individuals expect their friends, romantic partners, and other close relational partners to provide a positive source of influence (Dillard et al., 2001). So, during initial interactions, we are likely primed to look for both supportive and persuasive behaviors and to assess the degree to which these behaviors signal a "good" friend or partner. Likewise, over the course of our friendship or romantic involvement, our close others influence us with respect to a range of important and consequential behaviors and attitudes. The famous MBRS study (Miller, Boster, Roloff, & Seibold, 1977), which set the agenda for compliance gaining throughout the 1980s, was born out of the developmental perspective on interpersonal communication and provided the first evidence that individuals tailor their influence tactics based on perceived relational intimacy (see Baxter & Bylund, 2004; Wilson, 2010).

Interestingly, and contrary to politeness theory, research suggests that greater politeness is used in relationships that are marked by more closeness (Baxter, 1984). In a similar manner, the way in which individuals go about influencing others signals how they feel about their relationship. For instance, relational partners who feel more subjectively close are more likely to use influence tactics that invoke the importance of the relationship to the behavior or attitude under question (Orina, Wood, & Simpson, 2002). So, it appears that both supportive and persuasive communication are used within relationships of various types and help fulfill different functions in those relationships. Likewise, supportive and persuasive messages display a fundamental feature of human communication more generally— they "[function] to establish relationships when . . . produced or processed in ways that suggest the formation or escalation of a personal bond between interaction partners . . . [and] maintain relationships when . . . production or processing reinforces and sustains preexisting levels of involvement" (Solomon & Vangelisti, 2010, p. 327).

Directions for Future Research

The purpose of this final section is to identify specific areas for future research. I have organized these areas of future research within the same framework as earlier, first exploring needed work on the nature of messages and their effects, followed by needed work on interaction, and ending with needed work on relationships. A final, short section proposes a more general set of questions aiming to point future work toward discovering broader connections.

The Nature of Messages and Their Effects

Both supportive communication and persuasion scholars have generated useful theories of messages that outline potential ways in which messages can vary and, thus, have their effects. As the sections in this chapter suggest, change— whether it be therapeutic or attitudinal—is fostered by messages that are tailored to meet multiple goals and perceived as useful, feasible, absent of limitations, and efficacious. Of course, aspects of messages such as argument explicitness or person centeredness are context dependent, and our field would undeniably profit from investigating how specific messages invoke these broad concepts across a range of contexts. Indeed, the call to move compliance gaining research from a *strategy-based* to a *feature-based* approach was not made recently (D. J. O'Keefe, 1994), though persuasion research still seems to lag behind support research in investigating specific features of messages likely to impact recipients. Thus, persuasion scholars are likely to gain from recognizing and utilizing the rich research of support scholars who, for the past 30 years, have "emphasized theoretically driven descriptions of . . . messages, descriptions focused on underlying differentiating features" (D. J. O'Keefe, 1994, p. 63).

Beyond identifying features of individual messages more likely to promote change, scholars should focus their attention to the sequential placement of these various message features and how placement within an interaction can influence outcomes. Compliance gaining research has a rich history of studying strategies, such as door-in-the-face and foot-in-the-door, while work in social support has largely ignored how features like person centeredness might be more or less helpful depending on when they come in an interaction (see Feng, 2009). While doing this important research, scholars should attend to theoretical mechanisms that can explain why certain sequential patterns are more effective than others and attempt to integrate this work within more holistic frameworks that focus on more than a single strategy or set of similar strategies (e.g., Cialdini, 2001).

Finally, scholars of persuasive and supportive communication have much to learn from each other with respect to the nature of effects and outcomes. Unfortunately, little research in either context attends to distinctions among various *evaluations* made of messages or to the potential for each unique type of evaluation to be distinctly related to some outcomes but not others. Likewise, there are several important *outcomes* of both persuasive and supportive messages, though certain outcomes are studied more readily than others. For instance, supportive communication research tends to focus on emotional improvement with less attention afforded to the impact of messages on long-term coping potential, while work in persuasion tends to focus on attitude change with less attention afforded to behaviors. Thus, although each literature has independently generated myriad variables describing message *evaluations* and message *outcomes*, the classification of these variables into a more cogent theoretical model and its subsequent testing still await. Indeed, much more attention should be paid to the conceptualization and operationalization of a vast range of evaluations and outcomes and the particular causal sequence of these factors in social interaction (Bodie, Burleson, et al., 2012; Dillard, Weber, et al., 2007). In addition, attention should be afforded to the similarities and differences among outcomes assessed in persuasive and supportive contexts. Doing so should help generate more integrated theoretical accounts of perceived and actual effects of messages of various types.

Messages Within Interaction

Just as there is little reason to doubt the importance of mapping various features of messages and how these features impact a range of evaluations and outcomes, there is little reason to doubt the inherently interactive nature of persuasion and support. This interactive nature has most readily been studied from the vantage point of the individual and how she produces and processes messages. Research bearing on the nature of message production has vast implications for supportive and persuasive communication. In general, models of message production and the research exploring them highlight the importance of individual abilities to interpret

situations, formulate plans to achieve multiple goals derived from these interpretations, and continually monitor the situation so as to decrease the likelihood plans are thwarted. To date, research has primarily focused on the individual formulation of goals. Thus, focusing more on the planning, monitoring, and reencoding processes should bolster theory development for supportive and persuasive communication as well as, more generally, how people (and their goals) within interaction change over time. Likewise, research should attend to the various types of motivation that provoke a felt need to support or persuade others and the degree to which they are equally salient across contexts.

The nature of message processing has primarily been examined from the dual-process framework. As reviewed earlier in the chapter, a recently developed dual-process theory of supportive message processing not only addresses concerns raised by critics of this framework in the context of persuasion, but it also extends the scope of the influential dual-process approach outside the realm of persuasion. Indeed, the dual-process framework appears to have general utility in suggesting modifications to theories of supportive interaction, though the specific ways in which thinking influences the supportive encounter may be theory dependent. Likewise, our theory has more general utility and value for addressing a range of important theoretical questions about communication (see also Bodie, Burleson, et al., 2012): Why do particular messages have certain effects with certain people in particular contexts, but different effects with different people in other contexts? How do messages influence cognitive, affective, and behavioral outcomes? How and why do these messages work—or fail to work? And, why do some supportive and persuasive episodes and interactions have extended, lasting effects, while others do not?

These important questions aside, and even with the vast amount of knowledge generated from a focus on supportive and persuasive message production and processing, we know precious little about how these parts work together within interaction. There are certainly a host of useful theories that can effectively frame studies for each context (e.g., attribution theory; MacGeorge, 2001; Wilson, Cruz, Marshall, & Roa, 1993), but more synergistic and ambitious work of theorizing interaction at more global levels should be preferred when possible.

Interactions Within Relationships

Scholars of persuasive and supportive communication alike recognize the ubiquity and importance of these episodes to relationships, and research reporting on the importance individuals place on communication skills seems to support this recognition; that is, relational partners value both affectively and instrumentally oriented skills in a variety of close relationships. The importance placed on skills is not without its consequences, either. Research has shown, for instance, that those who highly value affectively oriented skills are less lonely, better accepted, and more liked than those who place less importance on these skills (Burleson & Samter, 1990; Samter, 1992). Results of other studies have indicated that similarity in relational partners' communication values predicts satisfaction in both friendship and romantic relationships (Burleson, Kunkel, & Birch, 1994). Of course, most of the research and theories directed at understanding relationship formation and maintenance "prominently feature intrapersonal or cognitive processes, whereas the dynamics of interpersonal interaction are often less well developed. Consequently, the corpus of work tends to portray relationships as two individuals coming together, rather than an evolving dyadic social unit" (Solomon & Vangelisti, 2010, p. 338). It seems, therefore, that the degree to which our understanding of supportive and persuasive communication can illuminate the formation and maintenance of relationships is still an issue open for empirical and theoretical scrutiny.

Consequently, much more work should be conducted that attempts to understand persuasion and support as it occurs in everyday life and within important relationships of various types. Although simple survey studies might still usefully answer some remaining questions, the more arduous (and potentially rewarding) work of assessing patterns of interaction and how these patterns develop and change over the course of a relationship is needed. This work will necessarily entail going beyond investigating individual perceptions and looking at how individuals within relationships act, react, and interact to co-create meaning.

Broader Future Research Potential

This chapter set out to highlight important associations among persuasion and social support research. In service of these goals I defined supportive communication and its focus on messages, interactions, and relationships, then reviewed the extant literature that illustrates connections to work in persuasion in these areas of emphasis. A key to understanding how and why I chose the connections I did lies in the fact that this chapter is framed within a message-centered approach to interpersonal communication, which assumes "there is one underlying nature of communication" (Burleson, 2010, p. 158). Both persuasive and supportive communication are aimed at instilling change in one or more interlocutors, though social support and influence interactions each represent a unique context within which to discover the nature of change and the nature of communication that can promote change.

But, if persuasion and social support constitute unique contexts, what makes them different? And, perhaps more important, what makes them similar? Answering these questions should go a long way toward uncovering essential aspects of how the supportive and persuasive messages we produce and process have the effects they do within particular interactions and relationships. Certainly, several scholars have noted that, for instance, advice is one of "the many reasons people seek compliance from others" (Wilson, 2010, p. 219); thus, at least one form of supportive communication (advice) is perceived as conceptually similar to one form of persuasive communication (compliance gaining). But what fundamental dimensions underlie any differences and similarities? One possible answer comes from the work of Dillard and Solomon (2000) who assert that influence episodes can be described as "those in which self-benefit is high while other-benefit is low" (p. 170). To the extent that supportive episodes constitute a "natural antipode" of this conceptual space (i.e., these episodes are high on other-benefit and low on self-benefit), we might glean greater insight into one potential dimension that can explain variation in message quality, message production, message processing, and how communication contributes to change. Certainly future work should begin to answer these broader questions toward a fuller understanding of what makes human communication possible, and I hope this chapter contributes in some small way toward that goal.

References

Applegate, J. L., & Woods, E. (1991). Construct system development and attention to face wants in persuasive situations. *Southern Communication Journal, 56,* 194–204. doi: 10.1080/10417949109372830

Barbee, A. P. (1990). Interactive coping: The cheering-up process in close relationships. In S. Duck (Ed.), *Personal relationships and social support* (pp. 46–65). London, UK: Sage.

Barbee, A. P., & Cunningham, M. R. (1995). An experimental approach to social support communications: Interaction coping in close relationships. *Communication Yearbook, 18,* 381–413.

Barbee, A. P., Cunningham, M. R., Winstead, B. A., Derlega, V. J., Gulley, M. R., Yankeelov, P. A., & Druen, P. B. (1993). Effects of gender role expectations on the social support process. *Journal of Social Issues, 49*(3), 175–190. doi: 10.1111/j.1540 4560.1993.tb01175.x

Baxter, L. A. (1984). An investigation of compliance-gaining as politeness. *Human Communication Research, 10,* 427–456. doi: 10.1111/j.1468-2958 .1984.tb00026.x

Baxter, L. A., & Bylund, C. (2004). Social influence in close relationships. In J. S. Seiter & H. Gass (Eds.), *Perspectives on persuasion, social influence, and compliance-gaining* (pp. 317–336). Boston, MA: Allyn & Bacon.

Berger, C. R. (1989). Goals, plans, and discourse comprehension. In J. J. Bradac (Ed.), *Message effects in communication science* (pp. 75–101). Newbury Park, CA: Sage.

Berger, C. R. (1996). The hierarchy principle in strategic communication. *Communication Theory, 6,* 111–142. doi: 10.1111/j.1468-2885.1996.tb00123.x

Bodie, G. D. (in press-a). The role of thinking in the comforting process: An empirical test of a dual-process framework. *Communication Research.*

Bodie, G. D. (in press-b). Task stressfulness moderates the effects of verbal person centeredness on cardiovascular reactivity: A dual-process account of the reactivity hypothesis. *Health Communication.*

Bodie, G. D., & Burleson, B. R. (2008). Explaining variations in the effects of supportive messages: A dual-process framework. *Communication Yearbook, 32,* 355–398.

Bodie, G. D., Burleson, B. R., Gill-Rosier, J. N., McCullough, J. D., Holmstrom, A. J., Rack, J. J., et al. (2011). Explaining the impact of attachment style on evaluations of supportive messages: A dual-process framework. *Communication Research, 38,* 228–247. doi: 10.1177/0093650210362678

Bodie, G. D., Burleson, B. R., Holmstrom, A. J., Rack, J. J., McCullough, J. D., Hanasono, L., et al. (2011). Effects of cognitive complexity and emotional upset on processing supportive messages: Two tests of a dual-process theory of supportive communication outcomes. *Human Communication Research, 37,* 350–376. doi: 10.1111/j.1468-2958.2011.01405.x

Bodie, G. D., Burleson, B. R., & Jones, S. M. (2012). Explaining the relationships among message quality, message evaluations, and message outcomes: A dual-process approach. *Communication Monographs, 79,* 1–22. doi: 10.1080/03637751.2011.646491

Bodie, G. D., St. Cyr, K., Pence, M., Rold, M., & Honeycutt, J. M. (2012). Listening competence in initial interactions I: Distinguishing between what listening is and what listeners do. *International Journal of Listening, 26,* 1–28. doi: 10.1080/10904018.2012 .639645

Burleson, B. R. (2007). Constructivism: A general theory of communication skill. In B. B. Whaley & W. Samter (Eds.), *Explaining communication: Contemporary theories and exemplars* (pp. 105–128). Mahwah, NJ: Erlbaum.

Burleson, B. R. (2009). Understanding the outcomes of supportive communication: A dual-process approach. *Journal of Social and Personal Relationships, 26,* 21–38. doi: 10.1177/0265407509105519

Burleson, B. R. (2010). The nature of interpersonal communication: A message-centered approach. In C. R. Berger, M. E. Roloff, & D. R. Roskos-Ewoldsen (Eds.), *The Handbook of Communication Science* (pp. 145–163). Los Angeles, CA: Sage.

Burleson, B. R., Albrecht, T. L., Goldsmith, D., & Sarason, I. G. (1994). Introduction: The communication of social support. In B. R. Burleson, T. L. Albrecht, & I. G. Sarason (Eds.), *Communication of social support: Messages, interactions, relationships, and community* (pp. xi–xxx). Thousand Oaks, CA: Sage.

Burleson, B. R., & Bodie, G. D. (2008). Constructivism and interpersonal processes. In W. Donsbach (Ed.), *The international encyclopedia of communication* (Vol. 3, pp. 950–954). Oxford, UK: Blackwell.

Burleson, B. R., & Caplan, S. E. (1998). Cognitive complexity. In J. C. McCroskey, J. A. Daly, M. M. Martin, & M. J. Beatty (Eds.), *Communication and personality: Trait perspectives* (pp. 230–286). Cresskill, NJ: Hampton Press.

Burleson, B. R., & Gilstrap, C. M. (2002). Explaining sex differences in interaction goals in support situations: Some mediating effects of expressivity and instrumentality. *Communication Reports, 15,* 43–55. doi: 10.1080/08934210209367751

Burleson, B. R., & Goldsmith, D. J. (1998). How the comforting process works: Alleviating emotional distress through conversationally induced reappraisals. In P. A. Andersen & L. K. Guerrero (Eds.), *Handbook of communication and emotion: Research, theory, applications, and contexts* (pp. 245–280). San Diego, CA: Academic Press.

Burleson, B. R., Holmstrom, A. J., & Gilstrap, C. M. (2005). "Guys can't say that to guys": Four experiments assessing the normative motivation account for deficiencies in the emotional support provided by men. *Communication Monographs, 72,* 468–501. doi: 10.1080/03637750500322636

Burleson, B. R., Kunkel, A. W., & Birch, J. D. (1994). Thoughts about talk in romantic relationships: Similarity makes for attraction (and happiness, too). *Communication Quarterly, 42,* 259–273. doi: 10.1080/01463379409369933

Burleson, B. R., Kunkel, A. W., Samter, W., & Werking, K. J. (1996). Men's and women's evaluations of communication skills in personal relationships: When sex differences make a difference— and when they don't. *Journal of Social and Personal Relationships, 13,* 201–224. doi: 10.1177/0265407596132003

Burleson, B. R., Metts, S., & Kirch, M. W. (2000). Communication in close relationships. In C. Hendrick & S. S. Hendrick (Eds.), *Close relationships: A sourcebook* (pp. 244–258). Thousand Oaks, CA: Sage.

Burleson, B. R., & Planalp, S. (2000). Producing emotion(al) messages. *Communication Theory, 10,* 221–250. doi: 10.1111/j.1468-2885.2000.tb00191.x

Burleson, B. R., & Samter, W. (1990). Effects of cognitive complexity on the perceived importance of communication skills in friends. *Communication Research, 17,* 165–182. doi: 10.1177/009365090017002

Burleson, B. R., & Samter, W. (1994). A social skills approach to relationship maintenance: How individual differences in communication skills affect the achievement of relationship functions. In D. J. Canary & L. Stafford (Eds.), *Communication and relational maintenance* (pp. 61–90). San Diego, CA: Academic Press.

Cialdini, R. B. (2001). *Influence: Science and practice* (4th ed.). Boston, MA: Allyn & Bacon.

Cunningham, M. R., & Barbee, A. P. (2000). Social support. In C. Hendrick & S. S. Hendrick (Eds.), *Close relationships: A sourcebook* (pp. 272–285). Thousand Oaks, CA: Sage.

Derlega, V. J., Barbee, A. P., & Winstead, B. A. (1994). Friendship, gender, and social support: Laboratory studies of supportive interactions. In B. R. Burleson, T. L. Albrecht, & I. G. Sarason (Eds.), *Communication of social support: Messages, interactions, relationships, and community* (pp. 136–151). Thousand Oaks, CA: Sage.

Dillard, J. P. (1990). Primary and secondary goals in interpersonal influence. In M. J. Cody & M. L. McLaughlin (Eds.), *Psychology of tactical communication* (pp. 70–90). Clevendon, UK: Multilingual Matters.

Dillard, J. P. (1997). Explicating the goal construct: Tools for theorists. In J. O. Greene (Ed.), *Message production: Advances in communication theory* (pp. 47–69). Mahwah, NJ: Erlbaum.

Dillard, J. P. (2003). Persuasion as a social skill. In J. O. Greene & B. R. Burleson (Eds.), *Handbook of communication and social interaction skills* (pp. 479–514). Mahwah, NJ: Erlbaum.

Dillard, J. P., Anderson, J. W., & Knobloch, L. (2001). Interpersonal influence. In M. L. Knapp & J. A. Daly (Eds.), *Handbook of interpersonal communication* (pp. 425–474). Thousand Oaks, CA: Sage.

Dillard, J. P., Kinney, T. A., & Cruz, M. G. (1996). Influence, appraisals, and emotions in close relationships. *Communication Monographs, 63,* 105–130. doi: 10.1080/03637759609376382

Dillard, J. P., Shen, L., & Vail, R. G. (2007). Does perceived message effectiveness cause persuasion or vice versa? 17 consistent answers. *Human Communication Research, 33,* 467–488. doi: 10.1111/j.1468-2958 .2007.00308.x

Dillard, J. P., & Solomon, D. H. (2000). Conceptualizing context in message-production research. *Communication Theory, 10,* 167–175. doi: 10.1111/j.1468-2885.2000.tb00186.x

Dillard, J. P., & Sun, Y. (2008). The perceived effectiveness of persuasive message: Questions of structure, referent, and bias. *Journal of Health Communication, 13,* 149–168. doi: 10.1080/10810730701854060

Dillard, J. P., Weber, K. M., & Vail, R. G. (2007). The relationship between the perceived and actual effectiveness of persuasive messages: A meta-analysis with implications for formative campaign research. *Journal of Communication, 57,* 613–631. doi: 10.1111/j.1460-2466.2007.00360.x

Feng, B. (2009). Testing an integrated model of advice-giving in supportive interactions. *Human Communication Research, 35,* 115–129. doi: 10.1111/j.1468-2958.2008.01340.x

Feng, B., & Burleson, B. R. (2008). The effects of argument explicitness on responses to advice in supportive interactions. *Communication Research, 35,* 849–874. doi: 10.1177/0093650208324274

Feng, B., & MacGeorge, E. L. (2006). Predicting receptiveness to advice: Characteristics of the problem, the advice-giver, and the recipient. *Southern Communication Journal, 71,* 67–85. doi: 10.1080/10417940500503548

Feng, B., & MacGeorge, E. L. (2010). The influences of message and source factors on advice outcomes. *Communication Research, 37,* 576–598. doi: 10.1177/0093650210368258

Fishbein, M., & Ajzen, I. (1975). *Belief, attitude, intention, and behavior: An introduction to theory and research.* Reading, MA: Addison-Wesley.

Goldsmith, D. J. (1992). Managing conflicting goals in supportive interaction: An integrative theoretical framework. *Communication Research, 19,* 264–286. doi: 10.1177/009365092019002007

Goldsmith, D. J. (1994). The role of facework in supportive communication. In B. R. Burleson, T. L. Albrecht, & I. G. Sarason (Eds.), *Communication of social support: Messages, interactions, relationships, and community* (pp. 29–49). Thousand Oaks, CA: Sage.

Goldsmith, D. J. (2000). Soliciting advice: The role of sequential placement in mitigating face threat. *Communication Monographs, 67,* 1–19. doi: 10.1080/03637750009376492

Goldsmith, D. J. (2004). *Communicating social support.* New York, NY: Cambridge University Press.

Goldsmith, D. J., & MacGeorge, E. L. (2000). The impact of politeness and relationship on perceived quality of advice about a problem. *Human Communication Research, 26,* 234–263. doi: 10.1111/j.1468-2958.2000.tb00757.x

Goldsmith, D. J., McDermott, V. M., & Alexander, S. C. (2000). Helpful, supportive, and sensitive: Measuring the evaluation of enacted support in personal relationships. *Journal of Social and Personal Relationships, 17,* 369–391. doi: 10.1177/026540 7500173004

Hample, D., & Dallinger, J. M. (1998). On the etiology of the rebuff phenomenon: Why are persuasive messages less polite after rebuffs? *Communication Studies, 49,* 305–321. doi: 10.1080/10510979 809368541

Hoffman, C., Mischel, W., & Mazze, K. (1981). The role of purpose in the organization of information about behavior: Trait-based versus goal-based categories in person cognition. *Journal of Personality and Social Psychology, 40,* 211–225. doi: 10.1037/0022-3514.40.2.211

Holmstrom, A. J. (2009). Sex and gender similarities and differences in communication values in same-sex and cross-sex friendships. *Communication Quarterly, 57,* 224–238. doi: 10.1080/01463370902889455

Holmstrom, A. J., Bodie, G. D., Burleson, B. R., Rack, J. J., McCullough, J. D., Hanasono, L. K., et al. (2011). *Testing a dual-process theory of supportive communication outcomes: How source, message, contextual, and recipient factors influence outcomes in support situations.* Manuscript submitted for publication.

Jones, S. M., & Guerrero, L. K. (2001). Nonverbal immediacy and verbal person-centeredness in the emotional support process. *Human Communication Research, 4,* 567–596. doi:10.1111/j.1468-2958.2001.tb00793.x

Jones, S. M., & Wirtz, J. (2006). How does the comforting process work? An empirical test of an appraisal-based model of comforting. *Human Communication Research, 32,* 217–243. doi:10.1111/j.1468-2958.2006.00274.x

Knapp, M. L., Daly, J. A., Albada, K. F., & Miller, G. R. (2002). Background and current trends in the study of interpersonal communication. In M. L. Knapp & J. A. Daly (Eds.), *Handbook of interpersonal communication* (3rd ed., pp. 3–20). Thousand Oaks, CA: Sage.

MacGeorge, E. L. (2001). Support providers' interaction goals: The influence of attributions and emotions. *Communication Monographs, 68,* 72–97. doi:10.1080/03637750128050

MacGeorge, E. L., Feng, B., & Burleson, B. R. (2011). Supportive communication. In M. L. Knapp & J. A. Daly (Eds.), *Handbook of Interpersonal Communication* (4th ed., pp. 317–354). Thousand Oaks, CA: Sage.

MacGeorge, E. L., Feng, B., Butler, G. L., & Budarz, S. K. (2004). Understanding advice in supportive interactions: Beyond the facework and message evaluation paradigm. *Human Communication Research, 30,* 42–70. doi:10.1111/j.1468-2958.2004.tb00724.x

MacGeorge, E. L., Feng, B., & Thompson, E. R. (2008). "Good" and "Bad" advice: How to advise more effectively. In M. T. Motley (Ed.), *Studies in applied interpersonal communication* (145–164). Thousand Oaks, CA: Sage.

Meyer, J. R. (2004). Effect of verbal aggressiveness on the perceived importance of secondary goals in messages. *Communication Studies, 55,* 168–184. doi:10.1080/10510970409388611

Miller, G. R., Boster, F. J., Roloff, M. E., & Seibold, D. (1977). Compliance-gaining message strategies: A typology and some findings concerning effects of situation differences. *Communication Monographs, 44,* 37–51. doi:10.1080/03637757709390113

Moskowitz, G. B., Skurnik, I., & Galinsky, A. D. (1999). The history of dual-process notions, and the future of preconscious control. In S. Chaiken & Y. Trope (Eds.), *Dual-process theories in social psychology* (pp. 12–36). New York, NY: Guilford.

O'Keefe, B. J. (1988). The logic of message design: Individual differences in reasoning about communication. *Communication Monographs, 55,* 80–103. doi:10.1080/03637758809376159

O'Keefe, B. J., & Delia, J. G. (1979). Construct comprehensiveness and cognitive complexity as predictors of the number and strategic adaptation of arguments and appeals in a persuasive message. *Communication Monographs, 46,* 231–240. doi:10.1080/03637757909376009

O'Keefe, B. J., & Delia, J. G. (1982). Impression formation and message production. In M. E. Roloff & C. R. Berger (Eds.), *Social cognition and communication* (pp. 33–72). Beverly Hills, CA: Sage.

O'Keefe, D. J. (1994). From strategy-based to feature-based analyses of compliance-gaining message classification and production. *Communication Theory, 4,* 61–68. doi:10.1111/j.1468-2885.1994.tb00082.x

O'Keefe, D. J. (1999). Argumentation explicitness and persuasive effect: A meta-analytic review of the effects of citing information sources in persuasive messages. In F. H. Ivan Eemeren, R. Grootendorst, J. A. Blair, & C. A. Willard (Eds.), *Proceedings of the fourth international conference of the International Society for the Study of Argumentation* (pp. 611–617). Amsterdam, The Netherlands: Sic Sat.

O'Keefe, D. J. (2002). *Persuasion: Theory and research* (2nd ed.). Thousand Oaks, CA: Sage.

Orina, M. M., Wood, W., & Simpson, J. (2002). Strategies of influence in close relationships. *Journal of Experimental Social Psychology, 38,* 459–472. doi:10.1016/S0022-1031(02)00015-X

Perrin, P. B., Heesacker, M., Pendley, C., & Smith, M. B. (2010). Social influence processes and persuasion in psychotherapy and counseling. In J. E. Maddux & J. P. Tangney (Eds.), *Social Psychological Foundations of Clinical Psychology* (pp. 441–460). New York, NY: Guilford.

Petty, R. E., & Cacioppo, J. T. (1986). *Communication and persuasion: Central and peripheral routes to attitude change.* New York, NY: Springer-Verlag.

Planalp, S., & Knie, K. (2002). Integrating verbal and nonverbal emotion(al) messages. In S. R. Fussell (Ed.), *The verbal communication of emotions: Interdisciplinary perspectives* (pp. 50–71). Mahwah, NJ: Erlbaum.

Rack, J. J., Burleson, B. R., Bodie, G. D., Holmstrom, A. J., & Servaty, H. L. (2008). Bereaved adults' evaluations of grief management messages: Effects of message person centeredness, recipient individual differences, and contextual factors. *Death Studies, 32,* 399–427. doi: 10.1080/07481180 802006711

Roskos-Ewoldsen, D. R. (1997). Implicit theories of persuasion. *Human Communication Research, 24,* 31–63. doi: 10.1111/j.1468-2958.1997.tb00586.x

Samter, W. (1992). Communicative characteristics of the lonely person's friendship circle. *Communication Research, 19,* 212–239. doi: 10.1177/0093650 92019002005

Sanders, R. E., & Fitch, K. L. (2001). The actual practice of compliance-seeking. *Communication Theory, 11,* 263–289. doi: 10.1111/j.1468-2885.2001.tb00243.x

Schutz, W. C. (1958). *The interpersonal underworld.* Palo Alto, CA: Science and Behavior Books.

Solomon, D. H., & Vangelisti, A. L. (2010). Establishing and maintaining relationships. In C. R. Berger, M. E. Roloff, & D. R. Roskos-Ewoldsen (Eds.), *The handbook of communication science* (pp. 327–344). Los Angeles, CA: Sage.

Sprecher, S., & Regan, P. C. (2002). Liking some things (in some people) more than others: Partner preferences in romantic relationships and friendships.

Journal of Social and Personal Relationships, 19, 463–481. doi: 10.1177/0265407502019004048

Waldron, V. R., & Applegate, J. L. (1998). Person-centered tactics during verbal disagreements: Effects on student perceptions of persuasiveness and social attraction. *Communication Education, 47,* 53–66. doi: 10.1080/03634529809379110

Wegener, D. T., & Claypool, H. M. (2000). The elaboration continuum by any other name does not smell as sweet. *Psychological Inquiry, 10,* 176–181. doi: http://www.jstor.org/stable/1449238

Westmyer, S. A., & Myers, S. A. (1996). Communication skills and social support messages across friendship levels. *Communication Research Reports, 13,* 191–197. doi: 10.1080/08824099609362086

Wilson, S. R. (1990). Development and test of a cognitive rules model of interaction goals. *Communication Monographs,* 57, 81–103. doi: 10.1080/03637759 009376188

Wilson, S. R. (2002). *Seeking and resisting compliance: Why people say what they do when trying to influence others.* Thousand Oaks, CA: Sage.

Wilson, S. R. (2010). Seeking and resisting compliance. In C. R. Berger, M. E. Roloff, & D. R. Roskos-Ewoldsen (Eds.), *The Handbook of Communication Science* (2nd ed., pp. 219–235). Los Angeles, CA: Sage.

Wilson, S. R., Aleman, C. G., & Leatham, G. B. (1998). Identity implications of influence goals: A revised analysis of face-threatening acts and application to seeking compliance with same-sex friends. *Human Communication Research, 25,* 64–96.

Wilson, S. R., Cruz, M. G., Marshall, L. J., & Roa, N. (1993). An attributional analysis of compliance-gaining interactions. *Communication Monographs, 60,* 352–372. doi: 10.1080/03637759309376317

PART III

Contexts, Settings, and Applications

CHAPTER 16

Political Persuasion

Richard M. Perloff

Politics has always been about persuasion, for better and sometimes for worse. The storied Founding Fathers, who publicly lamented the formation of campaigns and political parties, engaged in vitriolic persuasive attacks against members of opposing groups, with Jefferson and Hamilton leading the persuasive charge. Persuasion played an increasing role in 19th century presidential election campaigns from Jackson to McKinley. It was harnessed by Lincoln, in eloquent egalitarian speeches that still arouse emotions today, but also by prejudiced political figures who argued in favor of slavery or against immigrants' rights. But it was not until the 20th century that American politics and persuasion became synonymous in the public mind, with the advent of broadcast media, political consulting, and the nattering gaggle of speechwriters, pollsters, fund-raisers, political journalists, and other exemplars of the institutionalization of politics.

Contemporary political persuasion is played out on a media terrain. In the 21st century, as Iyengar (2004) observes, "American politics is almost exclusively a mediated experience. The role of the citizen has evolved from occasional foot soldier and activist to spectator" (p. 254). Citizens are necessarily objects of mediated persuasive appeals. Leaders recognize that they must harness the news and persuasive media to sway public opinion, resulting in a continuous and complex interplay of influence among elites, voters, and an increasingly polymorphous media.

Political persuasion at once repels and intrigues the public. Commentators on Fox News rail against the "powerful liberal media," fanning passions among conservative viewers. Liberals, who frequently gravitate to the more politically congenial National Public Radio (Iyengar & Hahn, 2009), invoke the value-laded term "propaganda" with impunity as they recall the Bush administration's campaign to convince the American public that Iraq possessed weapons of mass destruction. Yet the onset of the quadrennial presidential election campaign, with the ritualistic appearance of candidates in snowy Iowa and New Hampshire, titillates even jaded political aficionados, many of whom will predictably lament the onslaught of negative advertisements, viewed as "the electronic equivalent of the plague" (West, 2010, p. 70). Living in a media democracy, citizens have developed a multitude of lay theories about the impact of political persuasion, as well as normative evaluations of its role in American political life. Some of these theories are thoughtful, others are intuitively reasonable if simplistic, while still others are downright kooky. Citizens have every right to articulate their notions of political persuasion effects, and our democracy is richer for their sharing these perspectives in conversations. It is the job of social scientists to articulate comprehensive models of political persuasion, test them empirically, and engage in the difficult but important task of integrating the facts of persuasion with the ideals of democracy in an effort to reach a reasoned assessment of the state of political persuasive communication today. This chapter is designed to systematically examine these issues.

The scholarly study of political persuasion in America dates back to the 1920s when Lippmann (1922) theorized about media effects on "pictures in our heads" and Lasswell (1927) described the nature of World War I propaganda during a time when writers worried that democratic society was "run by an unseen engineer" (p. 222). Scholars categorized propaganda effects, most famously in the "ABCs of propaganda analysis," a listing of seven propagandistic devices, including name-calling, transfer, and testimonial (Jowett & O'Donnell, 2006). The techniques, while overly general from a social scientific perspective, remain relevant today, with name-calling studied under the rubric of negative advertising, transfer under accessibility of associations, and testimonial within the source credibility heading. The nascent study of propaganda took an abrupt turn with the 1944 publication of Lazarsfeld, Berelson, and Gaudet's study of communication effects in Erie County, Ohio, which uncovered little evidence of strong media effects, but considerably more support for interpersonal influence, a somewhat surprising turn of events that contrasted sharply with the gloom and doom of the early propaganda studies.

The term "propaganda" fell out of favor at the end of the World War II, its benighted orientation out of step with the cheerful zeitgeist of the 1950s. Suddenly, persuasion was a favored term. The study of persuasion gained academic respectability with Hovland, Janis, and Kelley's (1953) experimental studies of communication and attitudes. Yet as the 1950s came to a close, the academic community seemed to foreclose the possibility of strong political persuasive influences with the publication of Klapper's (1960) proclamation of limited effects, ironically published just before the celebrated Kennedy-Nixon debates affected the outcome of the 1960 election. It became increasingly impossible to deny media effects in the wake of the endless stream of vivid television images of racial brutality, Vietnam casualties, and political assassinations, as well as political advertisements, famously exemplified by "Daisy" in 1964 and 1968, as McGinnis (1969) described in his classic account of the selling of the recently remodeled Richard Nixon.

Emboldened by their intuition that television had strong influences and motivated to develop a new disciplinary approach to political communication, mass communication researchers sought to empirically overturn the limited effects legacy of Klapper, which Bartels called "one of the most noticeable embarrassments of modern social science" (quoted in Callaghan & Schnell, 2005, p. 2). With increasing evidence of media impact on political cognitions (Becker, McCombs, & McLeod, 1975) and growing recognition that political communication operated on macrolevels that had been hitherto ignored (Chaffee, 1975), the interdisciplinary field of political communication was born. Political persuasion is a subset of this field and a vital area of study.

The academic study of political persuasion is a multifaceted arena that operates on different levels of analysis, involves complex questions of causation, and presents distinctive methodological challenges. In addition, political persuasion calls on storied historical narratives, blurs the lines between persuasion and communication, and raises knotty normative concerns. Each of these deserves brief consideration.

First, political persuasion occurs on different levels. It operates on the microlevel, as when a television commercial alters a voter's attitude, the dyadic level, showcased by communication network effects on political deliberation (Huckfeldt, Johnson, & Sprague, 2004), and the macrolevel, exemplified by presidential speech effects on public opinion or multiple influences of primaries on the institutionalization of political consulting. Political persuasion can also occur on micro- and macrolevels simultaneously, as when Internet-relayed protests about the 2009 corrupt Iranian election helped mobilize citizens and transformed the Iranian electoral context.

Second, in political persuasion the arrows of causal influence flow in different directions. Normatively, political persuasion should start with both the electorate, where citizens persuade political leaders to implement policies that reflect the public will, and elites, as when politicians convince the public to support critical foreign policy initiatives. The media are an important and complex link between public and elites. Empirically, media political content can produce changes in public attitudes, public opinion can drive media coverage, both may be a product of elite governmental influence, or each may operate under specific contingent conditions. One of the great challenges of political persuasion research is to sort out cause and effect. Needless to say, it is not easy.

Third, the study of political persuasion presents unique methodological problems. In surveys of media effects, researchers measure exposure by self-report. However, respondents may misremember the source, reporting that they learned a fact from a debate when they actually acquired it from news coverage of the debate. In addition, recall may not be a valid measure of exposure to a particular message. Voters can fail to recall seeing a political ad, but actually have had exposure to it, or assume they saw the ad when they in fact did not (Valentino, Hutchings, & Williams, 2004). What's more, media exposure is increasingly confounded with pre-existing attitudes, with those exposed to a particular media outlet more likely to harbor attitudes congenial with the outlet than those not exposed (Bennett & Iyengar, 2008). Thus, regular views of Fox News differ from nonviewers in both exposure and strength of conservative Republican attitudes.

Fourth, political persuasion calls on rich historical narratives, more so than other persuasion arenas. The Founding Fathers, Lincoln, the World War II generation, Ronald Reagan, and time-honored family values are invoked to convince Americans to cast votes or partake in political causes. At the same time, historical perspectives are contested, contentious, and fraught with multiple meanings.

A fifth complexity involves the degree to which political message content falls under a traditional persuasion rubric, which emphasizes a communicator's intent to persuade (O'Keefe, 2002). If we examine the sender's motives, we find that political journalism is sometimes less concerned with persuasion than with informing or entertaining mass audiences. Yet if we focus on audience effects, we discover abundant evidence that news sets agendas, primes attitudes, and influences political evaluations. News, therefore, falls along the border of communication and persuasion. Even this distinction is muddied by increasing tendencies of news programs to promote particular points of view. Fox and MSNBC are prominent examples of news organizations whose talk shows promulgate political perspectives. Some of their programming, as well as those of ideological blogs, can be regarded as persuasion, although it is useful to differentiate political persuasion from propaganda and manipulation, which have different definitional features (Perloff, 2010).

Finally, political persuasion raises difficult value-laden questions. Political leaders have exploited persuasion to attain horrific ends, as is painfully evident from reviewing its uses by despots from Adolf Hitler to Saddam Hussein to Mahmoud Ahmadinejad. Yet charismatic persuaders have long harnessed the symbols of political communication for laudable purposes. Through the poetry of his words and moral clarity of his message, Martin Luther King Jr. mobilized masses of people to challenge a racially prejudiced status quo. On a less grandiose level, politicians rely on persuasion to make their case to voters, frequently bending rhetoric to suit audience predispositions. Thus, political communication raises a host of complex value-tinged questions, and these underlie social scientific questions of effects. Do campaigns enhance the art of argumentation or rely on shibboleth and poll-tested synecdoche to influence voters? Do campaigns encourage or discourage open-minded consideration of alternative points of view? Does political persuasion manipulate voters or deliver what they want? These questions are hardly new. Appeals to sophistry and logos date back to ancient Greece. Discussions of the morality of persuasion recall Plato's metaphor of the cave. Scurrilous political attacks were commonplace in 18th-century America. Normative assumptions about values, such as deliberation and freedom of speech, play a distinctive role in the study of processes and effects of this persuasion genre.

Theoretical Perspectives on Political Persuasion Effects

Source Approaches

> We have to be very clear on this point: that the response is to the image, not to the man ... It's not what's **there** that counts, it's what's projected—and carrying it one step further, it's not what **he** projects but rather what the voter receives. It's not the man we we have to change, but rather the **received impression.**

> Raymond K. Price, speechwriter
> for Richard Nixon's 1968
> presidential campaign, quoted in
> McGinnis (1969, p. 37)

Credibility—or for consultants like Price, the manufacturing of credibility—plays a critical role in contemporary political persuasion. Persuasion research has identified three components of credibility: **expertise, trustworthiness,** and **good will** (McCroskey & Teven, 1999). Each is salient in different political contexts, as is illustrated by these three anecdotal examples.

Richard Nixon employed expertise in the 1972 election, with his consultants reasoning that the gruff, chronically distrustful Nixon was not a likable figure. As his adviser Roger Ailes famously quipped, voters regarded Nixon as "a bore, a pain in the ass ... who was forty-two years old the day he was born. They figure other kids got footballs for Christmas. Nixon got a briefcase and he loved it" (McGinnis, 1969, p. 103). Consequently the campaign ads emphasized not that "you like Nixon," but "you need Nixon" (Diamond & Bates, 1992, p. 180). Messages focused on his experience, competence, and accomplishments, such as traveling to China. He trounced the morally admirable, but politically hapless, George McGovern. Four years later, the nation reeling from Watergate, Jimmy Carter promised that he would never lie to the American people. Trustworthiness became his mantra. Appearing with his evangelical smile, the born again Christian and political incarnate of *The Waltons* character John-Boy (Nimmo & Combs, 1980), strode to the White House with an earnest, faith-based manner that contrasted with Gerald Ford, whose pardoning of Nixon cast doubts on his trustworthiness in the eyes of many voters. Carter edged Ford in a close election, only to lose in 1980 to Ronald Reagan, whose communication skills helped convey likability and charm to the majority of the electorate.

Good will, the third of the credibility triumvirate, came to the fore in the 1992 election, when the electorate, reeling from recession, sought a candidate who could empathize with its economic woes. Enter Governor Bill Clinton of Arkansas, who conveyed good will in a presidential town hall debate, turning, Oprah-style, to a questioner who asked how the national debt had personally affected each of the candidate's lives. After gently asking her to explain how the debt had affected her, he displayed empathy toward the plight of the questioner and others hurt by the national recession, thereby enhancing his connection with the audience.

Although there are no hard data demonstrating that these dimensions of credibility influenced vote decisions in 1960, 1976, and 1992, the plethora of credibility research and studies of presidential debates (Denton & Holloway, 1996) suggests they certainly played a role in voters' presidential evaluations. Source factors could be similarly summoned to explain the roles candidate image played in more recent elections, such as Bush's "aw shucks" likability in 2000 and Obama's dynamism in 2008. Complicating matters, the elaboration likelihood model (Petty & Wegener, 1999) stipulates that source factors can serve as a cue, argument, or catalyst for processing, depending on the extent of elaboration likelihood.

Message Perspectives

Announcer: (quiet symphonic music, accompanied by a video of boats pulling out of the harbor in the early morning, against a clean city skyline) It's morning again in America. Today, more men and women (video clip of a smiling businessman stepping out of a taxi on a New York street in the morning . . .) will go to work than ever before in our country's history . . . (video clip of newspaper boy throwing papers from his bike in a suburb . . .) With interest rates at about half the record highs of 1980, nearly 2,000 families today will buy new homes (video of a man and his young son, with a spring in their steps, carrying a rug into their new home) . . . . It's morning again in America (photo of a lit White House at dusk).

> 1984 advertisement for
> President Ronald Reagan,
> Westen (2007, pp. 73–74)

Reagan's advertisement is emblematic of successful campaign spots. It contains some of the major attributes of the persuasive political message: **compelling narrative, evidence,** and a **strategic frame.** A persuasive narrative contains a

structure that can be easily comprehended and has clearly defined protagonists and antagonists, a coherent storyline, a moral lesson, and rich metaphors (Westen, 2007). Political narratives typically promulgate myths, "dramatic, socially constructed realities. . . . that people accept as permanent" (Nimmo & Combs, 1980, p. 16). Myths are the stuff of politics, whether cultivated by Barack Obama in 2008 (a multicultural outsider who can restore the voice of the people to Washington) or Tea Party conservatives in 2010 (antigovernment crusaders harking back to the spirit of 1775 who will restore the voice of the people to Washington). Narratives with mythic attributes can transport individuals to historically exalted places and, through the act of transportation, influence attitudes (Green & Brock, 2005). Stories with vivid anecdotes and compelling themes can also change attitudes (Kopfman, Smith, Ah Yun, & Hodges, 1998). Narratives are influential when they promote associations between candidates and time-honored values, as well as contain optimistic themes.

More prosaic message attributes also influence political evaluations. Evidence—factual assertions and quantitative data—can serve as an effective device in political persuasion. Presidential debates from Kennedy-Nixon to McCain-Obama have featured candidates' use of evidence to bolster arguments or serve as peripheral cues. Plausible evidence can exert potent effects on attitudes (Reynolds & Reynolds, 2002), although there is never a guarantee the evidence cited is factually correct; indeed, it frequently can be inaccurate, but sadly compelling.

Framing, an additional ingredient of political messages that has stimulated considerable research, has especially important implications for political persuasion. Given that most political issues are complex and multilayered, they can be defined in different ways, an ambiguity that political communicators frequently exploit. A frame is the central organizing theme that communicators harness to suggest what underlies a multifaceted, controversial issue (Gamson, 1989). Contemporary politics is a contest among competing frames in which the three main actors in political communication—leaders, media, and the public—symbolically joust to determine which frame will dominate discourse and ultimately influence policy.

Framing is a time-honored political pursuit, long part of the warp and woof of American political campaigns. One of the earliest framing battles in American history occurred at the Constitutional Convention in Philadelphia in 1787. The Federalist frame emphasized that "an independent representative model of government was necessary to guard against excessive democracy," while the anti-Federalists centered on the "threat to liberty" and dangers posed by government consolidation (Callaghan & Schnell, 2005, p. 3). In our own day, we encounter framing debates on a multitude of issues, ranging from Obama's health care reform (cost control for the middle-class or European-style socialism?) to the New York City mosque (insensitivity to victims of 9/11 or First Amendment-enshrined freedom of religion?). Some scholars find frames to be a useful heuristic to describe the ways that government can manipulate public opinion in a manner that furthers its ideological goals. Of course, manipulation is a value-laden term, and frames are also used by citizens groups to challenge government's perspective on an issue (Druckman, 2001).

Framing is a broad, but fuzzy, concept that operates on multiple levels. It is less a theory than an elastic concept with rich, cross-cutting applications. This has been a foundational strength, but a source of frustration to researchers who understandably want to classify a concept for use in empirical study. In political persuasion, where frames operate on a narrower level than in the whole of political communication, we have more certainty. There is abundant evidence that frames influence political attributions, perceived issue importance, tolerance, and a variety of political cognitions (e.g., Callaghan & Schnell, 2005; Iyengar, 1991; Nelson, Clawson, & Oxley, 1997). Why do frames work? What happens inside the head of voters when they process divergent frames? Scholars have gathered data to advance

three mediating mechanisms (Slothuus, 2008). The first is accessibility, the view that frames make certain attributes more accessible, while pushing others to the background. A second view emphasizes belief importance, whereby frames make some considerations seem more relevant than others, leading them to be accorded more weight in a citizen's decision-making calculus. A third account is belief change; rather than altering perceived importance, frames provide new arguments on behalf of a particular viewpoint.

Although pinpointing processes has some practical utility to message strategists, its primary import has been to differentiate competing theories of political psychology. Researchers who argue in favor of accessibility view framing as analogous to priming, contending that political opinions are superficial, tilting with the political wind, capable of being manipulated by consultants who can cleverly call attention to "top-of-the-head" considerations. Those who advance the belief importance interpretation view framing as more mindful, requiring the deployment of more thoughtful or at least targeted messages that address importance considerations (Nelson et al., 1997). These scholars are also at pains to differentiate framing from persuasion, which they argue involves changes in belief content or evaluations of the attitude object. Frames, they argue, are not the same as arguments, an underpinning of the third approach, which emphasizes that framing is a subset of persuasion because it works by delivering new information or *changing* the cognitive content of an individual's political beliefs. Framing, belief importance advocates note, works by altering information that is already part of memory.

The latter debate—is framing persuasion?—is redolent of the academic battles of the 1970s, in which researchers argued that agenda-setting and other cognitive effects were theoretically new media influences that did not fall under the traditional persuasion rubric (Becker, McCombs, & McLeod, 1975). Scholars were at pains to differentiate these cognitive effects from attitudinal influences, both because the former seemed to showcase stronger media influences (ones not emphasized by bête noire Klapper) and because they allowed the nascent field of political communication to claim a turf that differentiated it from the time-honored terrain of social psychology. There are subtle differences between framing and persuasion. Frames differ from arguments in certain respects and when frames appear in news stories that are not intended to change viewers' attitudes on the topic, they blur the line between communication and persuasion. In addition, unlike persuasion, which focuses on attitude change, framing affects interpretations (Tewksbury & Scheufele, 2009). However, it strains credulity to argue that framing is not an element of—or at least overlaps with—persuasion. Political candidates seek to frame issues in ways that will get them elected. The political environment is awash in battles among elites, media, and activist groups, each trying to convince the public to frame an issue in a particular way. Interpretations, the object of message frames, can potently influence attitudes.

A more substantive issue is the nature of framing effects. Scholars have speculated that the public may be highly susceptible to framing effects; political leaders, the argument goes, may be able to alter frames in subtle ways that allow them to manipulate public opinion to their advantage. The resilience of attitudes (and closed-mindedness of partisans) suggests that elites have a more difficult job exploiting frames to their advantage than is commonly assumed. Moreover, a casual review of the difficulty that recent presidents have had framing issues in ways that are palatable to the public—one recalls Clinton's and Obama's health care reform campaigns and Bush's post-2003 effort to rally the public around the Iraq War—illustrate the problems with this hypodermic needle model-style argument. Yet to say frames have few effects is to discount an abundant empirical literature. Elite frames can mold public opinion, particularly, theory suggests, when the frame is relevant or applicable to an existing political schema, when it resonates with existing values, or when it connects two ideas that were

previously not linked in the public mind (Nesbit, 2010; Price & Tewksbury, 1997). When we take this to the macrolevel, we find that causal arrows can operate in multiple directions. Elite frames definitely influence the public, but public—and perceived public—frames cajole leaders into taking particular positions. Frames advocated by activist groups also influence elites and citizens, and the media's ways of framing the frames add another layer of influence.

Channel Factors

> The hidden ground of American politics is now a simultaneous information environment that extends to the entire planet.... This charismatic image has replaced the goals and the parties and the policies.
>
> McLuhan (1976/2010)

McLuhan's comment encapsulates the notion that the modality in which political communication occurs—the mass media and now the Internet—is the essential feature of contemporary politics. It also underscores the widespread perception that images and appearances have supplanted political substance. For persuasion researchers, the question turns on whether a particular channel or modality—the term has never been adequately defined—has distinctive persuasive effects. Channel effects have intrigued scholars ever since it was widely reported that radio listeners believed that the verbally combative Nixon won the first presidential debate, while those who viewed the encounter on television perceived that the telegenic JFK emerged victorious. It is arguably the most famous of all communication research results and has been discussed endlessly over the years. Although scholars place credence in the finding (Kraus, 1996), it is not entirely clear what it means. Does television favor the low intensity "cool" candidate, as McLuhan (1964) argued? Or, stated in more contemporary terms, does television, a visual medium, confer persuasive advantage on a candidate whose pleasant visual appearance seems to match the formal features of the medium? Did the 1960 results instead reflect a rejection of Nixon's idiosyncratic mannerisms, or was it an interaction effect reflecting approval of a candidate whose nonverbal communication matched his verbal arguments? More complexly, does this effect generalize to other candidates and other elections?

Television has undoubtedly changed the persuasive discourse of election campaigns, but how it has done so and facts supporting this hypothesis have been hard to come by. Jamieson (2003) has argued that by taking political rhetoric from the town center and moving it to the living room, television has personalized political speech, increasing its intimacy and conversational style. Others contend, based on the vividness effect (Taylor & Thompson, 1982), that by placing a premium on vivid, cognitively accessible information, televised political messages should be more impactful than the same messages delivered via other media. There have been few studies addressing these issues, although Chaiken and Eagly's (1976) finding that an easy message is most compelling when videotaped and a difficult message most persuasive when written is a notable exception. It helps explain the rhetorical success of Ronald Reagan, whose compellingly simple rhetoric seemed to match the conventions of television, while also shedding light on the shortcomings of Jimmy Carter, whose complex messages seemed peculiarly unsuited to the television medium (Hart, 1984).

It is possible that there are persuasive benefits associated with contemporary channel features, such as high-definition television, with its credibility-inducing effects (Bracken, 2006), as well as texting and social networking sites, used heavily by Obama in 2008 (Kenski, Hardy, & Jamieson, 2010). In any event, whatever persuasive effects particular channels exert are strongly influenced by the nature of the message, as well as contextual features, such as number of individuals physically (or in the case of Facebook, virtually)

present. It remains an empirical question as to whether use of Internet channels invigorates or retards civic debate, although there is some meta-analytic evidence suggesting that Internet use has a small positive effect on engagement (Boulianne, 2009).

Receivers

> Voting is a matter of the heart, what you **feel** about someone, rather than a matter of the mind. (The mind) takes what the heart feels, and interprets it.
>
>   Political consultant Robert
>   Goodman, quoted in Diamond &
>   Bates (1992, p. 311)

Dual-process theories of persuasion, such as the elaboration likelihood model (Petty & Wegener, 1999), offer a useful framework for viewing the complex psychology of the political receiver. The ELM stipulates that there are two routes by which people process information—central and peripheral. Motivation and ability determine the degree to which individuals trek down the central and peripheral paths. Persuasive message strategies can be derived from the processes by which individuals elaborate on communications.

When voters lack motivation or ability to centrally process political messages, they rely on peripheral cues or heuristics, superficial strategies that make them vulnerable to disingenuous appeals. A telling anecdotal example of this occurred in a low-involving Illinois primary election some years back, in which voters preferred candidates with smooth-sounding names (Fairchild and Hart) to those with less euphonious names (Sangmeister and Pucinksi), only to be learn to their apparent dismay that Fairchild and Hart were followers of extremist politician Lyndon LaRouche (O'Sullivan, Chen, Mohapatra, Sigelman, & Lewis, 1988). Presumably, their reliance on a simple cue—euphony of candidate names—led voters down the primrose peripheral path of persuasion, an outcome at odds with normative democratic theory.

There is some empirical evidence consistent with ELM predictions. Candidate physical appearance—similarity and attractiveness—seem to exert particularly strong effects under low-involving conditions (Bailenson, Iyengar, Yee, & Collins, 2008; Rosenberg & McCafferty, 1987). Mere exposure also promotes electoral success in elections that may reasonably be regarded as low involvement. Candidates who spent more money in these races were more likely to get elected than opponents with less financial largesse (Grush, McKeough, & Ahlering, 1978). Repeated political exposure, working through a series of low-level cognitive processes, seems to have produced liking, thereby influencing voting behavior. In a similar fashion, weak political frames are more likely to influence opinions when individuals lack knowledge or ability, although even those low in elaboration likelihood prefer strong to weak frames, a finding that offers some solace to proponents of contemporary democracy (Chong & Druckman, 2007).

Citizens low in political ability or knowledge also may be susceptible to indirect persuasion effects via the impact of presumed influence (Gunther & Storey, 2003). According to this view, exposure to mass media leads individuals to assume that others are strongly influenced by persuasive media messages. By a process analogous to social proof (Cialdini, 2001), individuals presume that such influence is commonplace and normative; this in turn pushes receivers to accept the message. During presidential primaries, low involvement/low ability receivers may presume that media stories that favor the front-runner potently influence public opinion, leading them to leap on the bandwagon and support the leading candidate. Notice that "bandwagon," a classic propaganda effect articulated by 1930s scholars, is still invoked some 80 years later, but is explained in more sophisticated and careful ways.

In concert with ELM predictions, there is also evidence that voters who are high in elaboration likelihood are more likely to systematically process political information than those on the low end of the elaboration likelihood continuum. Voters high in political sophistication based their post 9/11 evaluations of former President George W. Bush on their defense policy preferences. Their less politically sophisticated counterparts seemed less motivated or able to base evaluations of Bush on policy predispositions. They increased positive evaluations of Bush, but not apparently because of systematic consideration of policy issues. Instead, they experienced a "rally around the flag" effect, transferring enhanced patriotic feelings to presidential evaluations (Ladd, 2007).

It would seem as if low-involved, low-ability voters are easily swayed by simple—sometimes misleading—persuasive appeals, displaying the type of susceptibility to persuasion that worries democratic theorists. Research would seem to offer some support for Churchill's quip that "the best argument against democracy is a five-minute conversation with the average voter." Yet this overstates matters. Voters who are low in elaboration likelihood lack the motivation to attend to political messages, and one cannot be influenced by a message to which one has not been exposed (presumed influence notwithstanding). Theoretically, these voters are more susceptible to McGuire's (1968) yielding than reception mediator—more likely to yield to a persuasive message than to carefully attend to it. Political awareness intersects with elaboration likelihood to determine persuasion effects. Complicating matters, factors such as the intensity of political information and deviance of messages from the status quo also intervene, moderating the impact of elaboration likelihood and awareness on attitude change (Zaller, 1992).

Do political media then manipulate low elaboration voters? The answer is complicated. Under some conditions, low-involved, low-ability voters suspend beliefs, allowing themselves to be taken in by misleading information. Under other conditions, they consciously opt to rely on heuristics, such as political party or a judgment that if negatively valued lobbyists support a proposal, it should be opposed for this reason (Kinder, 1998). It is difficult to determine when judgments represent irrational voting and when they constitute a rational decision-making strategy. Suffice it to say that sometimes low-involved voters get taken for a ride, suckered in by their reliance on unctuous political cues.

On the other end of the continuum, it appears as if highly involved, high-ability voters adopt a more rational approach, taking into account policy predispositions or systematically processing persuasive messages. For example, in 2008, Independent voters whose conservative views on social issues would ordinarily propel them to a Republican candidate took a serious look at Obama. John Butler, owner of a floral shop near Youngstown, Ohio, typified these voters. Living in a region of the country hit hard by the economic downturn, Butler said he had no choice but to lay off 25 of his 26 employees and cancel his health insurance policy. "I looked at my situation and realized I couldn't afford to vote for McCain. I was as shocked as anyone," he said (Belkin, 2008, p. A5). A similar dynamic operated in 2010, this time to the detriment of the Democrats. Significant numbers of Independent voters, concerned about the economy and reasoning that the party in power was responsible for job losses, voted Republican in the midterm elections (Calmes & Thee-Brenan, 2010).

Yet high-involved, high-ability voters also tend to have strong preexisting attitudes, which can render them susceptible to emotional appeals (Brader, 2006). These attitudes can be based on sophisticated ideological schema or they may be well-learned prejudices, which can overcome the pull of material self-interest. Sears and his colleagues have consistently found that symbolically evoked predispositions, such as party identification, anti-communist attitudes, and racial prejudice, powerfully influence electoral behavior (Sears, 1993). This leads to what ELM theorists felicitously call "biased processing." Complementing classic studies of confirmatory biases (Lord, Ross, & Lepper, 1979), political psychologists report that individuals

routinely engage in biased searches of electoral information, increasing their support for prior preferences even after exposure to contradictory information (Redlawsk, 2002). Biased processing is more likely when individuals harbor strong political attitudes.

Yet in contemporary politics, where the electorate is divided between "red states" and "blue states," *selectivity* is frequently the order of the day. Displaying what psychologists call "de facto selectivity," voters are more likely to communicate with those who share their political predispositions than those with who disagree (Mutz, 2006). We live in political worlds that kindly reinforce what we know to be true. What is more, selective exposure can produce more polarized political attitudes (Stroud, 2010). Conservative Republicans who tune into more conservative media programs hold more polarized attitudes than other Republican conservatives. Liberal Democrats who are exposed to more liberal media outlets hold more polarized attitudes, compared to other liberal Democrats (Stroud, 2010). Yet although partisans do seek out opinion-reinforcing information, they do not necessarily avoid sources that provide politically dissonant information (Garrett, 2009). And Independent voters, who may be looking for signs of nonpartisanship in political candidates, can be open to persuasive messages containing persuasive arguments and cues.

Thus, the persuasive effects of political communications are best conceptualized as interactive, involving "a set of joint contingencies among message, receiver, and source factors" (Iyengar, 2004, p. 252). Source credibility, message, and channel factors discussed previously rarely exert main effects in the contemporary political world, but, instead, intersect with receiver characteristics such as those identified by persuasion theories, like the ELM and social judgment perspectives. Such intersections can be politically consequential, as when individuals tune into a politically congruent blog and become more convinced of the moral superiority of their political position. Glenn Beck and

Sarah Palin appeal to scores of conservative Americans, offering nostrums that resonate with individuals who feel adrift in a system that they feel is dominated by hostile forces (Leibovich, 2010). Although political consultants may not express this in social scientific terms, they seem to be exquisitely aware of these contingencies. Republicans have mobilized evangelical Christians, relying on strong goodness of fit between their pro-life messages and voters' attitudes. Democrats have activated Latino and African American voters, employing credible same-race communicators. Strategists have sought to access symbolic affect in voters, hoping they will translate attitudes into voting behavior.

Conclusions

Viewed a half-century later, Klapper's work serves as a time-honored bookend for the field of political persuasion. His conclusions captured a kernel of truth in his own era, which presaged the emergence of television news and exploitation of media technologies for political campaigning. As he suggested, mass media do operate within "a nexus of mediating factors" (p. 8). They can create attitudes when people lack opinions—or possess nonattitudes (Converse, 1970). Media can also form attitudes via processes of political socialization (McLeod & Shah, 2009). Yet although Klapper appreciated the nuanced complexity of political persuasion, he operated from a rather vapid conceptual orientation. The multitude of theoretical perspectives and research findings that have emerged over the past half century have enriched our understanding of political persuasion effects. And, as has been frequently observed, Klapper's pessimistic account of media effects understated the power of contemporary political communication. Reinforcement effects can be politically consequential, when they pull behavior in line with attitudes, enticing voters (evangelical Christians in 2004 and droves of African Americans in 2008) to cast votes in favor of ideologically congruent candidates. Attitude-strengthening

influences may matter a great deal in presidential primaries, which attract the politically motivated, whose attitudes are primed for reinforcement effects. Campaign messages that exert a large effect on a small number of voters may be of considerable importance in close presidential elections like 1976 and 2000, as well as in a host of local races, where targeted campaign ads can propel more financially well-heeled candidates to victory. Outside the election season, agenda-setting, priming, and framing effects can influence the vicissitudes of public opinion on topics ranging from the Iraq War to the public option in health care.

When involvement is moderate and attitudes are not strong, voters will weigh political arguments, their processing a function of the political environment in which they reside. Yet in America, the political milieu is frequently fractious, contested, and freighted with rhetorical flourish. Given that the environment is intensely partisan, voters themselves have strong symbolic predispositions, and many vote against rather than for a candidate, it may be more useful to approach the persuasion quandary in terms of how candidates *overcome* voters' resistance to persuasion rather than how they push them toward message acceptance (Knowles & Linn, 2004). Politicians do this in a variety of ways, such as by reframing a message to minimize resistance, confronting resistance by offering politically palatable slogans, or disrupting resistance through distraction. They also strive to define the terrain of the election. "Campaigns," Kinder (2003) observes, "are not so much debates over a common set of issues as they are struggles to define what the election is about" (p. 365). Once candidates have successfully framed a campaign as revolving around a particular issue—change in 2008, Democrats' responsibility for the economic downturn in 2010—they have set the persuasive stage for subsequent messages. Candidates then craft specific messages that meld source, message, and channel factors with situationally appropriate receiver characteristics (partisanship, prejudices, fears, and anxieties).

In a political world that is "out of sight" and "out of mind" (Lippmann, 1922) but that is experienced in deeply symbolic ways, the most enduring campaign appeals are frequently those rich in symbolic meanings. "The cognitive match between symbolic meaning and predisposition" is an important factor determining when symbolic meaning influences political predispositions (Sears, 1993, p. 131). And once again the focus is on meaning. Whether we call it framing, cue-activating, or political transportation, the conclusion that emerges repeatedly is that persuaders win elections by controlling the symbolic meaning of the issue du jour.

Normative Conundrums

A discussion of political persuasion would not be complete without discussing normative issues that lie at the heart of so many questions about communication effects. Of the many value-laced questions that are discussed, the ones that strike at the core of democratic engagement involve campaign negativity. Do campaigns polarize voters, exacerbating partisan sentiments? Do uncivil candidate attacks inhibit citizen involvement? Do campaigns close rather than open political minds?

Many scholars take a dim view of contemporary campaigns. They argue that the proliferation of extreme political voices on cable television and the Internet exacerbate partisanship, strengthening polarized attitudes (Sunstein, 2001). Selective exposure magnifies this tendency. What's more, as Bennett and Iyengar (2008) observe:

But while as recently as 25 years ago, these partisans would have been hard pressed to find overtly partisan sources of information, today the task is relatively simple. In the case of Republicans, all they need to do is tune in to Fox News or the *O'Reilly Factor*. The new, more diversified information environment makes it not only more feasible for consumers to seek out news they might find agreeable but also provides a

strong economic incentive for news organizations to cater to their viewers' political preferences. (p. 720)

Enhanced tendencies toward selective exposure also reduce the odds that partisans will encounter information that challenges their political viewpoints. Tuned into websites that can communicate false information, they lack the opportunity, as Mill (1859/1956) famously stated, to gain "the clearer perception and livelier impression of truth produced by its collision with error." Thus, passionate liberals, tuned into websites that claimed Republican Vice President candidate Sarah Palin had faked her pregnancy may have subscribed to this notion for a time. Staunch conservatives may have chosen not to attend to information that countered the viral falsehood that Obama was a Muslim.

What's more, in an effort to rouse partisan animus, campaigns deploy negative ads and uncivil attacks. American politics is a combat sport characterized by spectacularly nasty attacks on candidates for public office. Negative ads reinforce partisan attitudes and demobilize voters (Ansolabehere & Iyengar, 1995). Uncivil political discussion can decrease tolerance for an opposing political view (Mutz & Reeves, 2005). Convinced that this is the way to win elections, candidates deliberately raise divisive wedge issues to influence persuadable voters (Hillygus & Shields, 2008). In a series of intriguing studies, Simon (2002) compared the electoral success of partisan campaigns, in which the candidate focused on his or her most effective political themes with those that sought to create dialogue, such as by discussing issues on which the opponent's stand approximated that of the median voter or through inoculation, which mentioned, but counterargued, a potential political liability. Campaigns that focused on dialogue cost a candidate an average of 21 percentage points, or approximately one fifth of the voting public. Simon argues that, whatever the merits for the political system, it is rational for a candidate to deemphasize thoughtful dialogue in favor of a more narrow partisan approach.

Ruminating on problems such as these, Miller (2005) lamented, in an article aptly entitled "Is persuasion dead?" that "marshalling a case to persuade those who start from a different position is a lost art. Hearing what's right in the other side's argument seems a superfluous thing that can only cause trouble, like an appendix. Politicos huddle with like-minded souls in opinion cocoons that seem impervious to facts."

In contrast, optimists put forth an alternative viewpoint. One set of counterarguments is empirically based: The public is less psychologically selective and polarized than critics suggest. Research finds that selective avoidance is not the norm. People do not shy away from politically incongruent information (Garrett, 2009; Holbert, Garrett, & Gleason, 2010). Most Americans commonly encounter political disagreements (Huckfeldt et al., 2004). In recent years, Americans have become more similar to one another in their social attitudes, not more different (Fiorina & Levendusky, 2006). Even the argument that negative advertisements adversely influence election outcomes has been questioned. After reviewing 111 studies, Lau, Sigelman, and Rovner (2007) reported that there is no significant evidence that negative campaigning propels attacking candidates to victory. Negative campaigns do reduce political efficacy and trust in government, but do not depress voter turnout.

Others have pointed out that negative ads have more issue content than positive spots (Geer, 2006). They also turn the normative argument around, contending that both negative messages and partisan attitudes can have salutary effects. Negative ads engage the thought processes of voters in a way that blander positive spots cannot (Brader, 2006). Uncivil negative messages can exert positive effects on political interest (Brooks & Geer, 2007), while intense campaigns promote open-minded thinking (Kam, 2006). Partisanship, which feeds off strident negative messages, can be good for the political system. Partisans, not the politically ambivalent, partake in political causes (Mutz, 2006).They knock on doors in election campaigns, organize new political parties (for example, the Green Party and Tea Party), and run for political office.

It is a controversial debate. Political persuasion is fraught with complexities and conundrums. Interpersonal discussions about politics contain internal contradictions. Dialogue with politically divergent others can increase tolerance, but produce ambivalence that inhibits participation in politics (Mutz, 2006). Lobbying can advance the needs of the little guy, but more often than not elevates the interests of economic elites (Hacker & Pierson, 2010). Political communication can be good for some types of democratic outcomes and bad for others. There are tensions and contradictions in the practice of political persuasion, all the more so in advanced media democracies such as the United States.

Unresolved Issues and Future Research

In the first book chapter on political persuasion that appeared in a communication handbook, Sears and Whitney (1973) focused on such persuasion concepts as communicator credibility, selective exposure, perceptual biases, and partisan attitudes. Plus la change, plus la meme chose. Yet their chapter differs from a contemporary account in two ways. First, Sears and Whitney argued that Americans exhibited a positivity bias, a predisposition to favorably evaluate politicians. Quite the opposite tendency exists today. Second, reflecting the knowledge base circa 1973, their chapter did not discuss communication concepts (e.g., framing), explicate theoretical linkages between cognitive processes and media effects, or document the many complex influences political media exert on attitudes. The field has come a long way in the past four decades.

Even so, there remain unanswered questions, the resolution of which can advance political communication scholarship. In the remainder of the chapter, I propose a variety of directions, guided by the venerable source-message-channel-receiver rubric.

Source Approaches

Research on verbal dimensions of credibility would be usefully complemented by studies of nonverbal, visual features, exemplified by the three categories of expressive displays of political leaders: anger/threat, fear/evasion, and happiness/reassurance (e.g., Sullivan & Masters, 1988; see also Grabe & Bucy, 2009). An interdisciplinary program of research (Lanzetta et al., 1985) has documented the facial characteristics associated with each of these categories of political emotions (e.g., open eyelids for anger, lowered, furrowed eyebrows for fear, and raised eyebrows for happiness). At the same time, these studies have shown that expressive displays can influence political attitudes. Conspicuously absent has been research, directed by persuasion theories, that examines their impact on political communicator credibility, as well as the ways these expressive displays influence affective information processing (Dillard & Peck, 2000; Neuman, Marcus, Crigler, & MacKuen, 2007), particularly as it occurs in different electoral contexts and diverse cultures, characterized as they are by different rules of emotional engagement.

Message Perspectives

With the exception of inoculation (Banas & Rains, 2010), which has been systematically examined, there have been strikingly few tests of major persuasion theories in the political domain. Predictions from the elaboration likelihood model, neoassociation approaches, and even the theory of reasoned action have been inadequately explored in the political sphere. Thus, it is difficult to conduct meta-analyses of the political persuasion literature. Although we know a great

deal about political cognition and affect, we know much less about how these processes translate to message strategies. It would be useful to derive communication effects hypotheses from differential conceptualizations of affect, encompassing affective priming, symbolic politics, and online processing models. Guided by the ELM, researchers should conduct a series of studies, using different methodologies, to determine whether peripheral cues exert a stronger impact under low than high political involvement, and the types of cues that are particularly impactful under low elaboration conditions.

Although the ELM is notoriously vague in spelling out the types of arguments that are effective under high involvement/ability conditions, it does predict that self-interested appeals should be maximally effective under high personal relevance, as the earlier example of the Obama voter in 2008 suggests but does not empirically document. More broadly, it would be useful to explore the impact of symbolic narratives, examining the way they can transport partisans and energize political imaginations in ways that the Tea Party seems to have done as of late. Framing research could benefit from microstudies that explicitly test message strategies derived from differential underlying processes (i.e., accessibility, belief importance, and belief change), as well as macro-research that identifies the conditions under which elite, activist, and public frames exert the strongest impact on political outcomes.

Channel Factors

Research on the communication channel should flourish in coming years in view of volcanic changes in political technology. Social media sites like Facebook seemed to have played a key role in the Tunisian and Egyptian revolts, galvanizing activists and producing seismic shifts in public attitudes (Preston, 2011). In a similar fashion, Obama's use of social networking sites is widely believed to have mobilized and influenced waves of young political participants. Yet we lack knowledge of the processes by which this occurred. While researchers can't easily study campaigns or revolutions in vivo, they can test hypotheses in experimental settings. Experiments could test predictions about web 2.0 political influence, with hypotheses exploring whether influence occurs through central processing, virtual opinion leaders and multiple step flows, presumed influence, social proof (Cialdini, 2001), or combinations thereof.

At the same time, research should probe channel effects associated with traditional political media formats. Guided by conceptualizations of digital rhetoric that emphasize anonymity, interactivity, as well as spatial characteristics (Gurak & Antonijevic, 2009), studies could probe whether negative advertising has different effects on the Internet than on television and how perceivers process leader expressive displays when conveyed on YouTube rather than television screens.

Receivers

There is no consensus on which individuals are most susceptible to political persuasion. Some scholars argue that voters least knowledgeable about politics are most influenced, while others maintain that the highly sophisticated are most susceptible because they can better comprehend political communications; still others contend it is those in the middle of the distribution who are most likely to change their attitudes in response to political messages (Hillygus, 2010). Like the search for the holy grail or the most persuadable types of people, this is a fool's errand, given the complexity, situational influences, and difficulties in measuring political personality traits. The ELM reminds us that individuals on both ends of the elaboration likelihood continuum are susceptible to influence. Perhaps the most useful research strategy is to study political influence in situs, testing theoretical predictions in particular contexts, in this way

accumulating a conceptually driven answer to these array of questions.

At the same time, the emphasis on the current yin and yang of political persuasion—deliberation and polarization—suggests possible direction for research. We need to better understand the processes by which deliberation produces more open-minded thinking, as well as the psychological processes underlying polarization. Studies should provide an in-depth examination of how and why individuals become psychologically entrenched in political positions, as well as ways to nudge them toward greater tolerance. While critics appropriately worry that polarization can produce cynicism, a more nuanced approach emphasizes that political polarization, with its focus on clear-cut issue positions, can promote deeper processing of political issues. Moderators of polarization effects, such as gender (with female voters sometimes engaged by civil, but not strident, attacks; see Brooks & Geer, 2009), are ripe for the exploring. Research in this tradition can clarify the functions and dysfunctions of political polarization. Empirical extensions to non-American contexts—an arena in which political communication scholarship is frequently devoid of guiding conceptualizations—would be a welcome addition to the literature.

Finally, on a more phenomenological note, it would be interesting to simply talk to American citizens and ask them how they feel about politics. One might learn unexpected things from talking to people, such as the issues they find politically meaningful—no doubt different from those covered in the mainstream media—as well as their conceptual explanations and emotional triggers. There is much that we know about how people construct the political world, as well as media effects on citizen constructions (Armoudian & Crigler, 2010). This literature should be instructive in revitalizing research programs exploring how individuals from different demographic and cultural groups interpret political events.

Normative and Empirical Issues

There remains no scholarly consensus on just what role political persuasion *ought* to play in contemporary democracy. Some theorists argue that communication should promote deliberative thought (Gastil, 2008). Others assert persuasion is less about deliberation than about offering candidates systematic opportunities to make their case. Some utilitarian philosophers would applaud the system, pointing to the benefits conferred by availability of communication technologies that reach hundreds of millions of citizens. Still others would lament the diminished sense of political community on which a thriving democracy depends (Sandel, 2009). Even if all agree that the system is designed to improve the political good, there exists no consensus on the meaning of "good." Does good mean promoting civic harmony? Does it refer to negative messages, which allow for systemic criticism of incumbents' records? Does it involve the discovery of truth and its wide diffusion to the electorate? And if it involves all these things, where does one strike the optimum balance?

The existence of different philosophical prescriptions is inevitable. It would be naive to expect consensus. But it would be useful to gain greater clarity on the normative assumptions that underlie explorations of "is" and "ought" questions. One frequently detects a tendency to accept, even reify, particular approaches. Deliberation and deliberative democracy are lionized. Habermas' work (1987) is treated as gospel. It sometimes seems to be taken for granted that democratic outcomes will be advanced through thoughtful deliberation. Yet, as Hibbing and Theiss-Morse (2002) pungently note, most Americans do not want to be involved in deliberative conversations. Americans favor representative democracy, hoping their representatives will place the voice of the people ahead of self-interest. What's more, deliberation's critics argue, discursive attempts at conflict resolution can polarize people when attitudes are strong. Political persuasion scholarship would benefit from recognition that there is a pluralism of normative approaches and research can usefully clarify assumptions derived from these perspectives (Jacobs, Cook, & Delli Carpini, 2009).

Research can usefully lay out the empirical facts on the ground at a particular political moment and in this way shed light on normative prescriptions. If we find that during times of polarization, political discourse contains more personalized than issue-based attacks and its effects are more scabrous than salutary, this suggests that the system would be served by encouraging more civility. If, on the other hand, we find that polarization produces more participation than cynicism, this suggests a different normative course. And if the truth lies primarily in a host of contingent conditions, this too has important implications. Just as we have social and cultivation-based media indicators, we also need political communication indicators that document the communicative consequences of institutional and systemic changes. These empirical facts provide a systematic way of tracking the impact of exogenous forces on diverse political outcomes.

Research on topics like these can advance the science of political persuasion, while also shedding light on normative questions that lie at the heart of the democratic enterprise. As presently practiced, political campaigns are dirty and imperfect, yet also capable of achieving goals that advance the polity. "Democratic politics," Huckfeldt and his colleagues (2004) conclude, "is a frequently messy business, filled with contentious issues, perplexing dilemmas, and seemingly irresolvable disputes." And, they add, "this is the way that it must be," (p. 202).

Must it?

References

Ansolabehere, S., & Iyengar, S. (1995). *Going negative: How political advertisements shrink and polarize the electorate.* New York, NY: Free Press.

Armoudian, M., & Crigler, A. N. (2010). Constructing the vote: Media effects in a constructionist model.

In J. E. Leighley (Ed.), *The Oxford handbook of American elections and political behavior* (pp. 300–325). New York, NY: Oxford University Press.

Bailenson, J. N., Iyengar, S., Yee, N., & Collins, N. A. (2008). Facial similarity between voters and candidates causes influence. *Public Opinion Quarterly, 72,* 935–961.

Banas, J. A., & Rains, S. A. (2010). A meta-analysis of research on inoculation theory. *Communication Monographs, 2010, 77,* 281–311.

Becker, L. B., McCombs, M. E, & McLeod, J. M. (1975). The development of political cognitions. In S. H. Chaffee (Ed.), *Political communication: Strategies for research* (pp. 21–63). Newbury Park, CA: Sage.

Belkin, D. (2008, November 1). In Ohio, downturn upends old loyalties. *The Wall Street Journal,* A5.

Bennett, W. L., & Iyengar, S. (2008). A new era of minimal effects? The changing foundations of political communication. *Journal of Communication, 58,* 707–731.

Boulianne, S. (2009). Does Internet use affect engagement: A meta-analysis of research. *Political Communication, 26,* 193–211.

Bracken, C. C. (2006). Perceived source credibility of local television news: The impact of television form and presence. *Journal of Broadcasting and Electronic Media, 50,* 723–741.

Brader, T. (2006). *Campaigning for hearts and minds: How emotional appeals in political ads work.* Chicago, IL: University of Chicago Press.

Brooks, D. J., & Geer, J. G. (2007). Beyond negativity: The effects of incivility on the electorate. *American Journal of Political Science, 51,* 1–16.

Brooks, D. J., & Geer, J. G. (2009). Comments on chapter one. In P. S. Nivola & D. W. Brady (Eds.), *Red **and** blue nation? Consequences and correction of America's polarized politics* (pp. 34–40). Baltimore, MD: Brookings Institution Press.

Callaghan, K., & Schnell, F. (2005). Introduction: Framing political issues in American politics. In K. Callaghan & F. Schnell (Eds.), *Framing American politics* (pp. 1–17). Pittsburgh, PA: University of Pittsburgh Press.

Calmes, J., & Thee-Brenan, M. (2010, November 3). Democrats lose support among women and Independents, polls show. *The New York Times,* P7.

Chaffee, S. H. (Ed.). (1975). *Political communication: Issues and strategies for research.* Beverly Hills, CA: Sage.

Chaiken, S., & Eagly, A. (1976). Communication modality as a determinant of message persuasiveness and message comprehensibility. *Journal of Personality and Social Psychology, 34,* 605–614.

Chong, D., & Druckman, J. N. (2007). Framing public opinion in competitive democracies. *American Political Science Review, 101,* 637–655.

Cialdini, R. B. (2001). *Influence: Science and practice* (4th ed.) Boston, MA: Allyn & Bacon.

Converse, P. (1970). Attitudes and non-attitudes: Continuation of a dialogue. In E. R. Tufte (Ed.), *The quantitative analysis of social problems* (pp. 168–189). Reading, MA: Addison-Wesley.

Denton, R. E., Jr. & Holloway, R. L. (1996). Clinton and the town hall meetings: Mediated conversation and the risk of being "in touch." In R. E. Denton & R. L. Holloway (Eds.), *The Clinton presidency: Images, issues, and communication strategies* (pp. 17–41). Westport, CT: Praeger.

Diamond, E., & Bates, S. (1992). *The spot: The rise of political advertising on television* (3rd ed.). Cambridge, MA: MIT Press.

Dillard, J. P., & Peck, E. (2000). Affect and persuasion: Emotional responses to public service announcements. *Communication Research, 27,* 461–495.

Druckman, J. N. (2001). On the limits of framing effects: Who can frame? *Journal of Politics, 63,* 1041–1066.

Fiorina, M. P., & Levendusky, M. S. (2006). Disconnected: The political class versus the people. In P. S. Nivola & D. W. Brady (Eds.), *Red and blue nation? Characteristics and causes of America's polarized politics* (pp. 49–71). Baltimore, MA: Brookings Institution Press.

Gamson, W. A. (1989). News as framing: Comments on Graber. *American Behavioral Scientist, 33,* 157–161.

Garrett, R. K. (2009). Politically motivated reinforcement seeking: Reframing the selective exposure debate. *Journal of Communication, 59,* 676–699.

Gastil, J. (2008). *Political communication and deliberation.* Thousand Oaks, CA: Sage.

Geer, J. G. (2006). *In defense of negativity: Attack ads in presidential campaigns.* Chicago, IL: University of Chicago Press.

Grabe, M. E., & Bucy, E. P. (2009). *Image bite politics: News and the visual framing of elections.* New York, NY: Oxford University Press.

Green, M. C., & Brock, T. C. (2005). Persuasiveness of narratives. In T. C. Brock & M. C. Green (Eds.),

Persuasion: Psychological insights and perspectives (pp. 117–142). Thousand Oaks, CA: Sage.

Grush, J. E., McKeough, K. L., & Ahlering, R. F. (1978). Extrapolating laboratory exposure research to actual political elections. *Journal of Personality and Social Psychology, 36,* 257–270.

Gunther, A. C., & Storey, J. D. (2003). The influence of presumed influence. *Journal of Communication, 53,* 199–215.

Gurak, L. J., & Antonijevic, S. (2009). Digital rhetoric and public discourse. In A. A. Lunsford, K. H. Wilson, & R. A. Eberly (Eds.), *The Sage handbook of rhetorical studies* (pp. 497–507). Thousand Oaks, CA: Sage.

Habermas, J. (1987). *A theory of communicative action* (Vol. 2). Boston, MA: Beacon Press.

Hacker, J. S., & Pierson, P. (2010). *Winner-take-all politics: How Washington made the rich richer—and turned its back on the middle class.* New York, NY: Simon & Schuster.

Hart, R. P. (1984). *Verbal style and the presidency: A computer-based analysis.* Orlando, FL: Academic Press.

Hibbing, J. R., & Theiss-Morse, E. (2002). *Stealth democracy: Americans' beliefs about how government should work.* Cambridge, UK: Cambridge University Press.

Hillygus, D. S. (2010). Campaign effects on vote choice. In J. E. Leighley (Ed.), *The Oxford handbook of American elections and political behavior* (pp. 326–345). New York, NY: Oxford University Press.

Hillygus, D. S., & Shields, T. G. (2008). *The persuadable voter: Wedge issues in presidential campaigns.* Princeton, NJ: Princeton University Press.

Holbert, R. L., Garrett, R. K., & Gleason, L. S. (2010). A new era of minimal effects? A response to Bennett and Iyengar. *Journal of Communication, 60,* 15–34.

Hovland, C. I., Janis, I. L., & Kelley, H. H. (1953). *Communication and persuasion: Psychological studies of opinion change.* New Haven, CT: Yale University Press.

Huckfeldt, R., Johnson, P. E., & Sprague, J. (2004). *Political disagreement: The survival of diverse opinions within communication networks.* Cambridge, UK: Cambridge University Press.

Iyengar, S. (1991). *Is anyone responsible? How television frames political issues.* Chicago, IL: University of Chicago Press.

Iyengar, S. (2004). Engineering consent: The renaissance of mass communications research in politics. In J. T. Jost, M. R. Banaji, & D. A. Prentice (Eds.), *Perspectivism in social psychology: The yin and yang of scientific progress* (pp. 247–257). Washington DC: American Psychological Association.

Iyengar, S., & Hahn, K. S. (2009). Red media, blue media: Evidence of ideological selectivity in media use. *Journal of Communication, 59,* 19–39.

Jacobs, L. R., Cook, F. L., & Delli Carpini, M. X. (2009). *Talking together: Public deliberation and political participation in America.* Chicago, IL: University of Chicago Press.

Jamieson, K. H. (2003). *The press effect: Politicians, journalists, and the stories that shape the political world.* New York, NY: Oxford University Press.

Jowett, G. S., & O'Donnell, V. (2006). *Propaganda and persuasion* (4th ed.). Thousand Oaks, CA: Sage.

Kam, C. D. (2006). Political campaigns and open-minded thinking. *Journal of Politics, 68,* 931–945.

Kenski, K., Hardy, B. W., & Jamieson, K. H. (2010). *The Obama victory: How media, money, and message shaped the 2008 election.* New York, NY: Oxford University Press.

Kinder, D. R. (1998). Communication and opinion. In N. W. Polsby (Ed.), *Annual Review of Political Science, 1,* 167–197. Palo Alto, CA: Annual Reviews.

Kinder, D. R. (2003). Communication and politics in the age of information. In D. O. Sears, L. Huddy, & R. Jervis (Eds.), *Oxford handbook of political psychology* (pp. 357–393). New York, NY: Oxford University Press.

Klapper, J. T. (1960). *The effects of mass communication.* New York, NY: Free Press.

Knowles, E. S., & Linn, J. A. (2004). Approach-avoidance model of persuasion: Alpha and omega strategies for change. In E. S. Knowles & J. A. Linn (Eds.), *Resistance and persuasion* (pp. 117–148). Mahwah, NJ: Erlbaum.

Kopfman, J. E., Smith, S. W., Ah Yun, J. K., & Hodges, A. (1998). Affective and cognitive reactions to narrative versus statistical evidence organ donation messages. *Journal of Applied Communication Research, 26,* 279–300.

Kraus, S. (1996). Winners of the first 1960 televised presidential debate between Kennedy and Nixon. *Journal of Communication, 46,* 78–96.

Ladd, J. M. (2007). Predispositions and public support for the president during the war on terrorism. *Public Opinion Quarterly, 71,* 511–538.

Lanzetta, J. T., Sullivan, D. G., Masters, R. D., & McHugo, G. J. (1985). Emotional and cognitive responses to televised images of political leaders.

In S. Kraus & R. M. Perloff (Eds.), *Mass media and political thought: An information-processing approach* (pp. 85–116). Beverly Hills, CA: Sage.

Lasswell, H. D. (1927). *Propaganda technique in the world war.* New York, NY: Knopf.

Lazarsfeld, P. F., Berelson, B., & Gaudet, H. (1944). *The people's choice: How the voter makes up his mind in a presidential campaign.* New York, NY: Columbia University Press.

Lau, R. R., Sigelman, L., & Rovner, I. B. (2007). The effects of negative political campaigns: A meta-analytic reassessment. *Journal of Politics, 69,* 1176–1209.

Leibovich, M. (2010, October 3). Being Glenn Beck. *The New York Times Magazine,* 35–41, 53–54, 57.

Lippmann, W. (1922). *Public opinion.* New York, NY: Free Press.

Lord, C. G., Ross, L., & Lepper, M. R. (1979). Biased assimilation and attitude polarization: The effects of prior theories on subsequently considered evidence. *Journal of Personality and Social Psychology, 37,* 2098–2109.

McCroskey, J. C., & Teven, J. J. (1999). Goodwill: A reexamination of the construct and its measurement. *Communication Monographs, 66,* 90–103.

McGinniss, J. (1969). *The selling of the president 1968.* New York, NY: Trident Press.

McGuire, W. J. (1968). Personality and susceptibility to social influence. In E. F. Borgatta & W. W. Lambert (Eds.), *Handbook of personality theory and research* (pp. 1130–1187). Chicago, IL: Rand McNally.

McLeod, J. M., & Shah, D. V. (2009). Communication and political socialization: Challenges and opportunities for research. *Political Communication, 26,* 1–10.

McLuhan, M. (1964). *Understanding media: The extensions of man.* New York, NY: McGraw-Hill.

McLuhan, M. (2010, September 26). Op-ed at 40: Four decades of argument and illustration. *The New York Times,* p. 3. (Reprinted from *The New York Times,* September 23, 1976).

Mill, J. S. (1956/1859). *On liberty.* Indianapolis: Bobbs-Merrill. (Original work published 1859)

Miller, M. (2005, June 4). Is persuasion dead? *The New York Times.* Retrieved May 7, 2012, from http://www.nytimes.com/2005/06/04/opinion/04miller_oped.html

Mutz, D. C. (2006). *Hearing the other side: Deliberative versus participatory democracy.* Cambridge, UK: Cambridge University Press.

Mutz, D. C., & Reeves, B. (2005). The new videomalaise: Effects of televised incivility on political trust. *American Political Science Review, 99,* 1–15.

Nelson, T. E., Clawson, R. A., & Oxley, Z. M. (1997). Media framing of a civil liberties conflict and its effect on tolerance. *American Political Science Review, 91,* 567–583.

Nesbit, M. C. (2010). Knowledge into action: Framing the debates over climate change and poverty. In P. D'Angelo & J. A. Kuypers (Eds.), *Doing news framing analysis: Empirical and theoretical perspectives* (pp. 43–83). New York, NY: Routledge.

Neuman, W. R., Marcus, G. E., Crigler, A. N., & MacKuen, M. (Eds.). (2007). *The affect effect: Dynamics of emotion in political thinking and behavior.* Chicago, IL: University of Chicago.

Nimmo, D., & Combs, J. E. (1980). *Subliminal politics: Myths and mythmakers in America.* Englewood Cliffs, NJ: Prentice-Hall.

O'Keefe, D. J. (2002). *Persuasion: Theory and research* (2nd ed.). Thousand Oaks, CA: Sage.

O'Sullivan, C. S., Chen, A., Mohapatra, S., Sigelman, L., & Lewis, E. (1988). Voting in ignorance: The politics of smooth-sounding names. *Journal of Applied Social Psychology, 18,* 1094–1106.

Perloff, R. M. (2010). *The dynamics of persuasion: Communication and attitudes in the 21st century* (4th ed.) New York, NY: Routledge.

Petty, R. E., & Wegener, D. T. (1999). The elaboration likelihood model: Current status and controversies. In S. Chaiken & Y. Trope (Eds.), *Dual-process theories in social psychology* (pp. 41–72). New York, NY: Guilford.

Preston, J. (2011, February 15). While Facebook plays a start role in the revolts, its executives stay offstage. *The New York Times,* A10.

Price, V., & Tewksbury, D. (1997). News values and public opinion: A theoretical account of media priming and framing. In G. A. Barnett & F. J. Boster (Eds.), *Progress in the communication sciences* (Vol. 13, pp. 173–212). New York, NY: Ablex.

Redlawsk, D. P. (2002). Hot cognition or cool consideration? Testing the effects of motivated reasoning on political decision making. *Journal of Politics, 64,* 1021–1044.

Reynolds, R. A., & Reynolds, J. L. (2002). Evidence. In J. P. Dillard & M. Pfau (Eds.), *The persuasion handbook: Developments in theory and practice* (pp. 427–444). Thousand Oaks, CA: Sage.

Rosenberg, S. W., with McAfferty, P. (1987). The image and the vote: Manipulating voters' preferences. *Public Opinion Quarterly, 57,* 31–47.

Sandel, M. J. (2009). *Justice: What's the right thing to do?* New York, NY: Farrar, Strauss, and Giroux.

Sears, D. O. (1993). Symbolic politics: A socio-psychological theory. In S. Iyengar & W. J. McGuire (Eds.), *Explorations in political psychology* (pp. 113–149). Durham, NC: Duke University Press.

Sears, D. O., & Whitney, R. E. (1973). Political persuasion. In I. de Sola Pool, F. W. Frey, W. Schramm, N. Maccoby, & E. B. Parker (Eds.), *Handbook of communication* (pp. 253–289). Chicago, IL: Rand NcNally.

Simon, A. F. (2002). *The winning message: Candidate behavior, campaign discourse, and democracy.* Cambridge, UK: Cambridge University Press.

Slothuus, R. (2008). More than weighting cognitive importance: A dual-process model of issue framing effects. *Political Psychology, 29,* 1–28.

Stroud, N. J. (2010). Polarization and partisan selective exposure. *Journal of Communication, 60,* 556–576.

Sullivan, D. G., & Masters, R. D. (1988). "Happy warriors": Leaders' facial displays, viewers' emotions, and political support. *American Journal of Political Science, 32,* 345–368.

Sunstein, C. (2001). *Republic.com.* Princeton, NJ: Princeton University Press.

Taylor, S. E., & Thompson, S. C. (1982). Stalking the elusive "vividness" effect. *Psychological Review, 89,* 155–181.

Tewksbury, D., & Scheufele, D. A. (2009). News framing theory and research. In J. Bryant & M. B. Oliver (Eds.), *Media effects: Advances in theory and research* (3rd ed., pp. 17–33). New York, NY: Routledge.

Valentino, N. A., Hutchings, V. L., & Williams, D. (2004). The impact of political advertising on knowledge, Internet information seeking, and candidate preference. *Journal of Communication, 54,* 337–354.

West, D. M. (2010). *Air wars: Television advertising in election campaigns, 1952–2008* (5th ed.). Washington DC: CQ Press.

Westen, D. (2007). *The political brain: The role of emotion in deciding the fate of the nation.* New York, NY: Public Affairs.

Zaller, J. R. (1992). *The nature and origins of mass opinion.* Cambridge, UK: Cambridge University Press.

CHAPTER 17

Persuasive Strategies in Health Campaigns

Charles K. Atkin and Charles T. Salmon

The dawn of health campaigns in the United States can be traced back almost three hundred years, when Reverend Cotton Mather successfully promoted public inoculations during Boston's smallpox epidemic of 1721. The temperance movement in the 1800s tenaciously battled alcohol problems by swaying public opinion to support legal restrictions (ultimately resulting in nationwide prohibition), rather than persuading individuals to drink responsibly (Paisley & Atkin, 2012).

In the past half-century, health topics have dominated the public communication campaign agenda, with concerted efforts to prevent smoking, drug use, drunk driving, AIDS, cancer, and obesity. Certain campaigns have attained significant effects on health behavior, while many other campaign efforts have met with only limited success. This chapter will examine factors that determine the degree of persuasive impact of health campaigns.

Health campaigns seek to influence attitudes and behaviors in sizable audiences via strategic development and dissemination of an array of multichannel mediated messages, for purposes of benefitting individuals and/or society. Campaigns utilize systematic frameworks and fundamental strategic principles that have evolved over the past half century. Campaign designers analyze the situation, set objectives, devise strategies, and create a set of messages that are disseminated via mass media, new technologies, and supplemental interpersonal networks.

Theoretical Foundations of Campaigns

In order to better understand and explain the influence of health campaigns, researchers and strategists have focused on the unique nature of campaigns relative to other persuasive contexts. Those who study and design health campaigns have drawn on perhaps an increasing variety of theoretical perspectives to guide their conceptualizations of campaign influence processes.

Distinctive Features of Campaigns

The health campaign constitutes a relatively distinctive form of persuasive communication, due to the nature of health topic and the nature of campaigning. First, the domain of health is composed of a *disparate array of problems*, and the unique medical, political, and social aspects of each type of disease or unhealthy practice tend to shape the communication objectives and strategies. Various health-related behaviors and outcomes lend themselves to a differential focus on promotion, prevention, cessation, detection, and/or treatment; for example, campaigners may address certain problems by positively promoting healthy actions while other problems are better suited to use of threats for preventing risky behaviors.

Second, the nature of health campaigning poses a different challenge than conventional forms of persuasion because campaigners are ethically bound to reach the most unhealthy segments of the population. Unlike commercial and political campaigns that focus on the most promising prospects whom are already favorably predisposed, health campaigns must give priority to influencing resistant audiences who do not practice the healthy behavior and are not interested in doing so. Because people in greatest need of change are most difficult to change, the campaigners must allocate resources to low-yield segments and supplement direct messages with messages aimed at those who can exert interpersonal influence or institute environmental change.

Third, campaigns tend to be media based, which means that *message exposure* becomes a very important stage of response; Hornik (2002) regards lack of exposure as a key factor limiting campaign effects. The uses and gratifications perspective originally developed by Blumler and Katz (1973) provides useful insights into the motivations that lead to selection of messages and utilization of media content (Rubin, 2009). Prominent placement and pervasive quantity of messages may be needed to ensure that the audience encounters the messages, while message qualities such as personal relevance and entertainment value help to attract attention. For example, stylistic factors are important in reaching the key audience of sensation seekers, who prefer visual messages that are novel, fast-paced, explicit, and intense (Palmgreen, Donohew, &

Harrington, 2001). Compelling cues and promos may be necessary to motivate people to seek out messages in channels that are not regularly perused. Defensive avoidance of exposure is a major barrier when message content is inconsistent with predispositions.

Fourth, campaigns tend to feature a *substantial quantity of diverse messages* to be created and coordinated, which affords the campaign team an opportunity to employ a variety of persuasive strategies. With so many message executions, the designer isn't confined to a single approach, but can choose to utilize a mixture of both implicit and explicit conclusions, gain and loss frames, or one-sided and two-sided arguments as tactics in various campaign contexts. Moreover, campaigns tend to disseminate messages over a lengthy period of time, ranging from several weeks to several decades. This timespan enables utilization of prolonged repetition of message executions, combinations of concentrated and dispersed message placement patterns, and sequential compliance techniques.

The persisting and pervasive dissemination of campaign messages featuring certain predominant themes has potential to shape conceptions of reality through cultivation processes (Morgan, 2009). Frequent exposure may cultivate beliefs about the prevalence of various health problems, social norms for practicing promoted as well as proscribed health behaviors addressed in the messages, and expectations of experiencing positive and negative consequences that are regularly portrayed. Similarly, a sustained quantity of prominently placed news items about a health problem or policy solution can raise the salience of these issues through agenda-setting processes (McCombs, 2004). Campaigns are typically able to make only a limited contribution to the media visibility of a health topic, but focused campaign efforts can raise policy issues higher on the media agenda.

Finally, the large quantity of messages enables a campaign to reach multiple intended audiences, as discussed, the audience analysis section of this chapter. Audiences typically are defined and profiled through segmentation analysis that seeks to identify clusters of individuals who are likely to react in a relatively uniform manner to a given campaign message. It should be noted that high-quantity, broad-scale message dissemination often reaches unintended audiences; the problem of unintended effects is discussed near the end of the chapter.

Key Theoretical Perspectives

Health campaign strategies are based on a broad range of theories from the fields of social psychology, public health, communication, and marketing. The applicable conceptualizations can be arrayed in three basic clusters: social marketing and diffusion, health behavior, and the communication-persuasion matrix.

Campaign strategies derived from *social marketing* typically apply the following approaches: an audience-centered consumer orientation, a sophisticated segmentation of the overall population in to target audiences, a calculated attempt to attractively package pro-health products (while minimizing personal adoption costs), a pragmatic focus on attainable objectives, and a combination of direct persuasion, policy change, and interpersonal communication to influence behavior (Andreasen, 1995, 2006; Kotler & Lee, 2008; McKenzie-Mohr, 2011). *Social norms marketing* narrowly applies a pro-health form of promotion with messages demonstrating the underestimated popularity of desirable practices, such as responsible drinking (Perkins, 2002). The social marketing approach blends well with the diffusion of innovations theory, which highlights the ideas of relative advantage and trialability of recommended behaviors, moving adopters through stages, opinion leadership for advancing the adoption process via multistep flows through interpersonal channels and social networks (Rogers, 2003).

The segmenting and staging components of social marketing and diffusion approaches are reflected in the popular transtheoretical model (Prochaska & Velicer, 1997), which features different stages (precontemplation, contemplation, preparation, action, or maintenance) that shape subaudience readiness to attempt, adopt, or sustain health behaviors. Campaigns typically need to have multiple strategies to influence subaudiences who have progressed to each stage.

McGuire's (2001) classic communication-persuasion matrix specifies an individual-level array of communication concepts that can be utilized by health campaign strategists. This basic input-output model arranges the conventional *input variables* (source, message, channel, and receiver) on one axis crossed by a lengthy series of *output variables* ranging from exposure and processing, to learning and yielding, and finally to enactment of recommended behaviors on the other axis. Among inputs, McGuire emphasizes that campaign impact is importantly determined by source credibility, persuasive appeals to a broad array of motives, message repetition, and multiple paths to persuasion. His matrix serves as a comprehensive organizing structure for a broad range of persuasion theories explaining both input and output processes pertinent to campaigns.

A cluster of *health behavior* perspectives, which have typically been adapted from social psychology theories and models, have been applied to health campaign strategies. The theory of planned behavior (Ajzen, 1991) is an extension of the theory of reasoned action (Azjen & Fishbein, 1980). The TRA, which has been frequently applied to the health context, formulates a combination of personal attitudes, perceived norms of influential others, and motivation to comply as predictors of intended behavior. A key underlying mechanism is based on the expectancy-value equation, which postulates attitudes are predicted by likelihood beliefs about certain consequences of a behavior, multiplied by one's evaluation of those consequences. The TRA shares similarities with the health belief model (Janz & Becker, 1984); the HBM components of perceived susceptibility multiplied by severity of consequences are particularly pertinent to designing health threat appeals (Stephenson & Witte, 2001).

The TPB is centrally applicable to health because it bridges the significant gap between intentions and behavior by adding the concept of perceived behavioral control, which originates from Bandura's (1997) self-efficacy theory. Self-efficacy is a key component of Social Cognitive Theory (Bandura, 1986), which illuminates media influence processes via source role models, explicitly demonstrated behaviors, and depiction of vicarious reinforcement.

In the communication discipline, Fishbein and Cappella (2006) and Cappella and associates (2001) have developed an integrative theory of behavior change that integrates HBM, SCT, and TRA to specify how external variables, individual differences, and underlying beliefs contribute to differential influence pathways for outcome behaviors, *intentions*, attitudes, norms, and self-efficacy.

Audience Analysis and Campaign Design

Identifying Audience Segments

Health campaign design begins with a conceptual assessment of the situation to determine opportunities and barriers and to identify which behaviors would to be performed by which people (Atkin & Salmon, 2010; Silk, Atkin, & Salmon, 2011). Rather than attempting to reach the broad public, campaign designers typically identify specific segments of the overall population. There are two major strategic advantages of subdividing the public in terms of demographic characteristics, predispositions, personality traits, and social contexts. First, campaign efficiency is improved if subsets of the audience can be prioritized according to their (a) degree of centrality to attaining the campaign's objectives, and (b) degree of receptivity to being influenced to adopt the recommendations. Second, effectiveness is increased if message content, form and style, and channels are adapted to the attributes and abilities of subgroups.

The design specifies *focal segments* of the population whose health practices are at issue, and the primary *focal health behaviors* that the campaign ultimately seeks to influence. The next step is to trace backward from the focal behaviors to identify the proximate and distal determinants, and then create *models* of the pathways of influence via attitudes, beliefs, knowledge, social influences, and environmental forces. The next phase is to examine the model from a *communication* perspective, specifying *intended audiences* that can be directly reached) and *target behaviors* (ranging from preliminary acts to focal practices) that can be influenced by campaign messages. This requires a comprehensive plan for combining the myriad strategic components subject to manipulation by the campaigner, drawing on the three clusters of theories.

Formative Evaluation

The application of general campaign design principles depends on an understanding of the specific health context (especially types of audiences and types of products), so effective design usually requires extensive formative evaluation inputs (Atkin & Freimuth, 2012). In the early stages of campaign development, designers collect background information about the focal segments and interpersonal influencers, using statistical databases and custom surveys to measure audience predispositions and their evaluations of prospective sources and appeals.

Formative evaluation provides strategists with information about the nature of the existing problematic behaviors to be addressed by the campaign and the "product line" of responses to be promoted. Audience predispositions toward prospective recommended actions can be assessed in order to select the most promising options. In order to achieve bottom-line behavioral objectives, campaign messages must first have an impact on preliminary or intermediate variables along the response chain. Formative research illuminates the following variables for key segments of intended audiences: (1) entry-level awareness, knowledge, and literacy related to the health topic; (2) beliefs and perceptions pertaining to barriers and opportunities affecting performance of a behavior, to likelihood expectations of experiencing beneficial and harmful outcomes, and to social support; (3) existing attitudes and values, notably evaluations of outcomes and opinions about policy options; (4) salience factors, such as level of involvement in the health topic, agenda ranking of a policy issue, and relative weighting of various outcomes; (5) self-efficacy and confidence in implementation skills; and (6) media channel usage and topical interpersonal communication. Researchers also obtain rating scores for prospective source messengers and message appeals.

As message concepts are being refined and rough versions are created, qualitative reactions are obtained in focus group discussion sessions, and supplemental quantitative ratings of perceived effectiveness are measured in message testing laboratories. A meta-analysis performed by Dillard, Weber, and Vail (2007) found that pretest ratings correlated +.41 with actual message effects, indicating that perceived effectiveness is a moderately strong predictor.

Direct Effects on Focal Audience Segments

Receptivity to a health campaign may be considered as a continuum. Campaigns tend to achieve the strongest impact when disseminating trigger or reinforcement messages designed to promote healthy practices among those who are already favorably predisposed (e.g., adoption of five-a-day fruit and vegetable consumption by already health conscious-persons). A somewhat less receptive (but more important) target is composed of "at risk" people who might try an unhealthy behavior in the near future (e.g., drug use among teens whose peers are experimenting with drugs). On the other hand, those committed to unhealthy practices tend not to be readily

influenced by directly targeted campaigns, so a heavy investment of resources to induce immediate discontinuation is likely to yield a marginal payoff.

Campaigners also need to consider demographic, social, and psychological-based subgroups (e.g., high vs. low in income, social support, or sensation seeking). Influencing these varied population segments may require a complex combination of narrowly customized messages, along with widely applicable multitargeted messages presenting broad appeals and optimally ambiguous recommended actions.

The nature of the health problem dictates the broad parameters of the focal audience to be influenced (e.g., adolescents in an antidrug campaign, middle-aged women in a breast cancer campaign). Because audience receptivity tends to be a more central determinant of campaign effectiveness than the potency of the campaign stimuli, there will be differential success depending on which segment is targeted. To achieve the maximum degree of communication effects, campaign designers often focus on receptive target audiences ready to be influenced to perform the practice.

Indirect Pathways of Influence

It is often valuable for health campaigns to supplement the predominant direct approach (educating and persuading the focal segment) by influencing additional target audiences who can indirectly exert interpersonal influence or help reform environmental conditions that shape the behaviors of the focal segment (Atkin & Salmon, 2010). Thus, campaigners can profitably invest effort and resources in campaign initiatives aimed at (1) direct impact on *interpersonal influencers* and (2) *policy-makers* (direct impact on those who make policy combined with indirect impact via interested publics who attempt to influence them). Mass media campaigns have considerable potential for producing effects on institutions and groups at the national and community level as well as motivating personal influencers in close contact with individuals in the focal segment. These influencers can provide positive and negative reinforcement, shape opportunities, facilitate behavior with reminders at opportune moments, serve as role models, and exercise control (by making rules, monitoring behavior, and enforcing consequences). Furthermore, influencers can customize their messages to the unique needs and values of the individual.

Interpersonal Influencers

An important goal of campaigns is to stimulate interpersonal influence attempts by inspiring, prompting, and empowering influencers. Influencers are similar to opinion leaders, but are in a position to exercise means control as well as utilizing persuasion. For example, a variety of peer and authority figures are in a position to personally educate, persuade, or control the prime focal segment of high-risk adolescents: parents, siblings, friends, coworkers, bosses, teachers, club leaders, coaches, medical personnel, and police officers. More generally, interpersonal networks can play a key role in preventing unhealthy practices, assisting with cessation efforts, and encouraging screening visits. Some influencers are responsive to negative appeals that arouse concern about harmful consequences to those they are trying to help behave appropriately. Consequently, a portion of campaign messages can be designed to motivate various interveners, facilitators and enforcers to take positive action . . . or at least to dissuade them from emboldening unhealthy choices. The effectiveness of social network-oriented media campaigns, typically targeted to friends and family members of the focal individuals to be influenced, is reviewed in the health domain by Abroms and Maibach (2008).

Societal Policy Makers

Individuals' decisions about health practices are clearly shaped by the constraints and opportunities in their daily environment, such as monetary expenses, rules, laws, social pressures, community services, entertainment role models, and commercial messages. Through the interventions of government, business, educational, medical, media, religious, and community organizations, many of these potent forces can be engineered to increase the likelihood of healthy choices or discourage unhealthy practices. Key initiatives include direct service delivery, restrictions on advertising and marketing practices, and the imposition of taxes. Consider the example of smoking: substantial reductions in tobacco use have been attained by instituting policies that increase monetary cost, decrease locations where smoking is permitted, broaden availability of cessation assistance programs, reduce smoking depictions in movies, and tightly restrict ads that promote cigarettes. More fundamental long-range approaches might attempt to reduce health disparities by reducing poverty, improving schools, broadening access to the health care system, or enhancing employment opportunities.

Thus, an important campaign approach is to aim messages at constituencies that can influence government and corporate policy makers, who are in a position to formulate policies that shape the environment for health behaviors. Strategically, this approach relies primarily on a two-step pathway from the campaign to the constituency to the policy makers. First, the campaign seeks to influence public opinion within population segments that are inclined to be involved in addressing the health issue. To facilitate the second step, the campaign provides guidance on techniques to use in contacting and persuading those who determine policy, such as letter writing, petition signing, testifying, boycotting, protesting, or voting. Campaign organizers may also cite public opinion poll findings (or commission custom polls) to demonstrate support for the advocated position. As a supplement, the campaigners may create elaborate persuasive messages (e.g., position paper, testimony, mailing, op-ed piece) that are designed to be submitted directly to the policy makers.

Reformers have developed tactics that combine community organizing and mass media publicity to advance healthy public policies through the *media advocacy* techniques. News coverage of health can shape both the public agenda and the policy agenda pertaining to new initiatives, rules, and laws related to health in society. An important strategy involves changing the public's beliefs about the effectiveness of policies and interventions that are advanced, which leads to supportive public opinion (and direct pressure) that can help convince institutional leaders to formulate and implement societal constraints and opportunities.

The four primary activities involved in media advocacy include (1) developing an overall strategy that involves formulation of policy options, identification of stakeholders that have power to create relevant change and apply pressure, and development of messages for these stakeholders; (2) setting the agenda by gaining access to the news media through feature stories, staged news events, and editorial commentary; (3) shaping the debate by framing public health problems as policy issues, by emphasizing social accountability, and by providing evidence for the broader claims; and (4) advancing the policy by maintaining interest, pressure, and coverage over time (Wallack & Dorfman, 2001).

Over the past 25 years, activists seeking to influence public and private sector policy makers to enact reforms that address health problems have concentrated their efforts on smoking, drinking, and breast cancer. Substantial success has been attained in influencing federal and local governments to impose alcohol and tobacco control measures, and to obtain funding for breast cancer prevention research. Policy-oriented campaigns aimed at businesses have also been effective, as shown in a recent analysis health-related advocacy campaigns aimed at changing corporate practices in the alcohol, tobacco, food, pharmaceutical, automobile, and firearms domains; the study concludes that campaigns achieved policy or mobilization outcomes contributing to health and safety improvements in these types of companies (Freudenberg, Bradley, & Serrano, 2009).

Prevention Versus Promotion

Campaigns are generally designed with measurable objectives specifying behavioral responses by audience members. In the health arena, the focal behavior is usually a specific practice or discrete action. However, there are numerous intermediate responses that might be targeted, such as awareness, knowledge, salience priorities, beliefs, expectancies, values, and attitudes; campaigns may seek to change key variables along the pathways leading to the focal behavior. The two fundamental approaches are promotion of healthy behavior or prevention or cessation of unhealthy behavior. Traditionally, prevention campaigns more often present fear appeals highlighting negative consequences of an unhealthy behavior, rather than promoting the desirability of a positive alternative. The negatively oriented prevention approach is more potent for topics where harmful outcomes are genuinely ominous.

The social marketing perspective is more applicable to promoting positive behavior rather than directly combating unhealthy behavior; this approach promises rewarding gains from attractive "products." Product promotion is better suited for attractive concepts, such as the "designated driver" or "staircase exercising," rather than for less compelling concepts, such as "alcohol abstinence" or "drug-free lifestyle." In developing behavioral recommendations in promotional campaigns, designers can draw on an array of options from the "product line." These target responses vary in palatability based on degree of effort, sacrifice, and monetary expense; in determining the degree of difficulty of the product to be promoted, a central strategic consideration is receptiveness of the focal segment. The prolonged nature of campaigns enables the use of gradually escalating sequential request strategies over a period of months or even years. Campaigns have potential to overcome defensive responses to difficult products by initially featuring simpler or softer products that fall within the audience's latitude of acceptability.

Persuasive Strategies

Although designers typically include some *awareness* messages and a few *instructional* messages in the campaign mix, *persuasive* messages constitute the central type of content in health campaigns. Campaigns feature persuasive appeals derived from McGuire's matrix or health behavior models, such as the theory of planned behavior. These theories provide numerous lines of argumentation to convince the audience to adopt the advocated action or avoid the proscribed behavior. For target audiences that are already favorably inclined toward the recommended behavior, the campaign has the relatively simple persuasive task of reinforcing existing predispositions (e.g., strengthening a positive attitude, promoting postbehavior consolidation, and motivating behavioral maintenance over time). However, for the least healthy segments of society who are most in need of attitude and behavior change, the campaign strategists face a distinct challenge in achieving impact. Because a lengthy campaign generally disseminates a broad array of persuasive messages, strategists have ample opportunity to develop and refine a variety of appeals built around motivational incentives designed to influence attitudes and behaviors.

Incentive Appeals

In creating and presenting persuasive appeals on health topics, the initial strategic decision involves message framing (O'Keefe & Jensen, 2007; Quick & Bates, 2010). For most direct attempts to influence health behaviors, strategists face a basic choice between motivating the audience with prospects of experiencing consequences that are generally regarded as desirable or undesirable. In gain-framed approaches, the messages present incentives that promise the audience that performing a healthy practice (or not performing an unhealthy practice) will either attain a valued outcome or avoid an undesirable outcome; by contrast, loss-framed message appeals argue that performing an unhealthy practice (or not performing a healthy practice) will lead to either attainment of an undesirable outcome or nonattainment of a desirable outcome. The most prevalent strategies in health campaigns are threats of losses from performing a proscribed practice and promises of gains from performing a recommended practice.

In health campaigns, the most widely used design frameworks employ a basic expectancy-value mechanism, wherein attitudinal and behavioral responses are contingent on each individual's valuation of outcomes promoted in campaign messages. Messages typically focus on the two expectancy-value components of outcomes: the subjective probability of a consequence occurring and the degree of positive or negative valence of that outcome. For the conventional loss-framed messages threatening undesirable consequences, the operational formula derived from the health belief model is the summation of *susceptibility x severity* across various outcomes. The prime communication objectives are (1) to change expectancy beliefs to a higher level of probability, (2) to intensify the negativity or positivity of the valence, and (3) heighten the salience of detrimental or beneficial outcomes associated with engaging in recommended practices.

The basic dimensions of incentives include physical health, economic, legal, social, psychological/aspirational, and effort; each has potential positive and negative valuations based on audience predispositions. The most frequently used dimension in health campaigns is physical health, with negatively valued threats (particularly death, illness, and injury) featured more often than positive promises, such as wellness.

Campaigns have increasingly diversified negative incentive strategies to include appeals to include the other undesirable dimensions (e.g., psychological regret, social rejection, monetary cost). Moreover, diversification has increasingly broadened the emphasis on positive incentives (e.g., valued states such as self-esteem, altruism, and efficiency).

Negative Appeals

Health campaigns rely heavily on loss-framed messages focusing on undesirable consequences associated with initiating or continuing an unhealthy practice (Stephenson & Witte, 2001). Instead of primarily emphasizing intense fear appeals, health messages might also pose threats of a less severe nature and present negative incentives beyond the physical health domain. For health topics where there are no compelling consequences (e.g., low probability of a genuinely strong valence), the next best approach is to select a mildly valenced incentive that is highly probable. In the case of drug campaigns, minor negative physical incentives might be loss of stamina, weight gain, and physiological addiction. Other messages might feature negative social incentives (e.g., looking uncool, alienating friends, incurring peer disapproval, losing the trust of parents, or deviating from social norms), negative psychological incentives (e.g., reduced ability to concentrate, low grades, feeling lazy and unmotivated, losing control, and making bad decisions, as well as anxiety about getting caught or experiencing harm, guilt, and loss of self-respect), economic incentives (e.g., diminished job prospects, fines, the cumulative cost of purchasing drugs, and inability to spend money on other needs and desires) and legal incentives (penalties for violating laws and policies, such as incarceration, loss of driver's license, or suspension from school).

Positive Appeals

Campaigns can also diversify beyond the traditional reliance on fear appeals by presenting a higher proportion of gain-frame incentives. For many of the negative consequences of performing the proscribed practice, there is a mirror-image positive outcome that can be promised for performing the healthy alternative. In the physical health dimension, drug abstinence messages might offer prospects ranging from a longer lifespan to enhanced athletic performance. Similarly, psychological incentives might promise outcomes like gaining control over one's life, achieving a positive self-image, attaining one's goals, or feeling secure. Social incentives might include being cool, gaining approval and respect, forming deeper friendships, building trust with parents, and being a good role model. The social norms marketing approach (DeJong & Smith, 2012; Perkins, 2002) is a widely used strategy in promoting responsible drinking on college campuses; messages typically feature statistical evidence to demonstrate that a majority students perform or approve of healthy practices (e.g., use of the designated driver arrangement, or approval of a four-drink limit on celebratory occasions).

Multiple Appeals

There might be dozens of persuasive appeals that are potentially effective on a given health topic, so it is advantageous for campaigners to use a large variety of appeals rather than relying on a handful of incentives. A major campaign's capacity for conveying multiple appeals allows dissemination of diverse messages; this provides several distinct reasons for the individual to comply or to influence multiple segments of the target audience via media channels where precise targeting is difficult. In identifying incentives to be presented, the key criteria are the salience of the promised or threatened consequences, the malleability of beliefs about the likelihood of experiencing these outcomes, and the potential persuasiveness of the arguments that can be advanced (Cappella et al., 2001). For messages about familiar health subjects, it is important to include novel appeals to complement the standard arguments. Preproduction research can test basic concepts to determine the effectiveness of each one and to examine optimum combinations, and pretesting research can compare the relative influence of executions of various appeals.

Evidence

People tend to be defensive when processing threatening messages about the subject of their personal health, which may be manifested by reactance, counterarguing, or denial of applicability (Stephenson & Witte, 2001). Thus, there is a priority for providing credible evidence to buttress claims about susceptibility, especially concerning risk level of harmful physical consequences. Formative evaluation is helpful in determining which types of individuals are influenced by health messages that use hard information (e.g., citing statistics, offering documentation, and quoting experts), and which segments are more responsive to visual imagery (e.g., exemplars, dramatized specimen cases, and testimonials). Health message designers take care to demonstrate how the evidence is relevant to the situation experienced by the target audience, and are cautious about using extreme claims (e.g., singular cases, implausible statistics, or excessive gore) or contested information. Not only might these elements strain credulity and arouse suspicion, but such content may be challenged by critics on contentious health issues.

One-Sided Versus Two-Sided Campaign Messages

Compliance with behavioral recommendations is impeded by a variety of disadvantages perceived by the audience, notably effort in adopting healthy practices and forsaking the pleasures of unhealthy practices. The strategist is faced with the questions of whether and how to handle these drawbacks. Across major phases of a campaign, the one-sided strategy would consistently ignore the disadvantages and present only the case favoring the healthy behavior or opposing the unhealthy competition; campaigns typically disseminate mostly one-sided messages. The high quantity of campaign messages enables apportionment of some messages to the two-sided strategy.

In a two-sided message, the elements of the opposing case are strategically raised and discounted in order to counteract current misgivings and future challenges, using techniques such as refuting inaccurate information or diminishing the salience of a drawback. The conditions of the typical health campaign context favor a judicious inclusion of two-sided appeals for several reasons: (1) key disadvantages of certain healthy practices are already widely recognized, (2) priority target audience segments are experiencing the benefits of unhealthy practices, (3) media and interpersonal channels frequently convey messages promoting the advantages of unhealthy practices. Formative evaluation is helpful in precisely determining the extent to which the "other side" is familiar to various audiences.

Message Qualities

Designing mediated health campaign messages involves the strategic selection of substantive material and the creative production of stylistic features. In developing the combination of message components, the campaign designer may seek to emphasize up to five influential message qualities. First, *credibility* is primarily conveyed by the trustworthiness and competence of the source and the provision of convincing evidence. Second, the style and ideas should be presented in an *engaging* manner via selection of interesting or arousing substantive content combined with attractive and entertaining stylistic execution; this is a key factor because many people regard health topics as inherently dull. The third dimension emphasizes selection of material and stylistic devices that are personally *involving* and *relevant* (e.g., portrayals of familiar settings, engrossing narratives, or personally tailored information), so receivers regard the behavioral recommendation as applicable to their own health situation and needs. The fourth element is *understandability,* with simple, explicit, and detailed presentation of health content that is comprehensive and comprehensible to receivers. For persuasive messages, the fifth factor is *motivational incentives,* as previously described.

Message Sources

Most health messages prominently depict source messengers, and most identify the campaign's sponsor as well. The *messenger* is the model or character in the message that delivers information, demonstrates behavior, or provides a testimonial. Salmon and Atkin (2003) provide a lengthy discussion of the strengths and weaknesses of various types of messengers in health campaigns. Messengers can substantially enhance the quality of message content by performing in an engaging manner, imparting trust- or competence-based credibility, and possessing characteristics that are relevant to key audience segments. In the health campaign context, three key contributions of source messengers are (1) increasing breadth of exposure by attracting attention in the cluttered media environment (2) facilitating comprehension through personalization or modeling of unfamiliar or complex health behavior recommendations, and (3) augmenting visibility and memorability of the campaign over sustained periods of time. Zillmann's (2006) exemplification theory presents a detailed examination of the mechanisms that healthy and unhealthy exemplars appearing in mediated messages use to convey risk perceptions, elicit reactivity, and motivate protective action.

Eight types of messengers are typically featured in campaign messages: celebrities, health experts (e.g., doctors/researchers), professional performers (e.g., models/actors), ordinary people (e.g., blue-collar males), public officials (e.g., political leaders), organizational executives (e.g., hospital administrator), specially experienced individuals (e.g., victims/survivors), or distinctive characters (e.g., animated/costumed figures). Selection of each messenger depends on the predispositions of the target audience, persuasion mechanism underlying the strategy, and type of message. Awareness messages tend to present celebrities, characters, and public officials to draw attention and make a superficial impression; instruction messages are more likely to depict performers and health organization executives to describe or demonstrate how to carry out complex behaviors; and persuasion messages may more often feature ordinary people for purposes of relevance and identification, experts for delivering evidence, and experienced individuals for reinforced or cautionary role modeling.

Each source has its advantages and drawbacks. For example, a researcher or medical authority would strengthen the expertise dimension, but would probably be less engaging due to the delivery of technical information. In contrast, a message that features a popular celebrity can draw great interest to a campaign message, especially if the celebrity conveys experiential competence or relevance as a victim or survivor of the health problem. Indeed, certain celebrities are highly respected and perceived to be trustworthy on various health topics, while other celebrities may engender skepticism, distract from message content, have an unhealthy image, or lose their luster before the campaign concludes. Ordinary people serving as source presenters may be perceived by the audience to be similar and thus relevant and perhaps trustworthy as a role model, but may lack perceived competence or attractiveness. Despite certain drawbacks, the personalized, credible, and engaging qualities of a source figure offer clear advantages over presenting message material without a manifest messenger or only with attribution to an impersonal organization.

The large number of message executions over a lengthy campaign enables the strategist can deploy a substantial collection of source messengers. Multiple messengers have potential for increasing the odds of success, by leveraging the complementary strengths of each type to serve certain functions for diverse audience segments. However, this tactic may increase the risk information overload and undermine continuity across message executions. It should be noted that continuity can still be attained by highlighting the sponsoring organization via prominent name identification, logo, and other symbols. Aside from this provision of branding linkages across disparate campaign stimuli, some widely recognized sponsors can also draw attention to the messages and enhance the credibility or relevance the content.

Mediated Communication Channels

To disseminate messages, health campaigns employ an ever-richer variety of channels encompassing the three basic categories of traditional mass media, conventional minimedia, and interactive technologies. Among mass media, campaigners have customarily relied on television, radio, newspapers, and magazines, specifically broadcast spots, news items, feature stories, and entertainment program inserts. The minimedia play a supplemental role via secondary message vehicles, including billboards, pamphlets, posters, slide shows, direct mailings, and automated phone calls. The importance of new technology channels for health campaigning has rapidly increased, with widespread utilization of websites, email listserves, serious games, and social media (notably Facebook), as well as emerging use of mobile phones, tablets, Twitter, and blogs.

In assessing the dozens of options for channeling campaign messages, designers take into consideration advantages and drawbacks along a number of communicative dimensions. Salmon and Atkin (2003) discuss channel differences in terms of *reach* (proportion of population exposed to the message), *specializability* (narrowcasting to specific subgroups or tailoring to individuals), *interactivity* (receiver participation and stimulus adaptation during processing), *personalization* (human relational nature of source-receiver interaction), *decodability* (mental effort required

for processing stimulus), *depth* (channel capacity for conveying detailed and complex content), *credibility* (believability of material conveyed), *agenda-setting* (potency of channel for raising salience priority of issues), *accessibility* (ease of placing messages in channel), and *economy* (low cost for producing and disseminating stimuli).

Channel selection is most often governed by the usage patterns of target audiences and the nature of the message and topic, within the constraints of available resources. Health campaigners find it more practical to stage a pseudo-event that generates irregular news coverage than to raise funds to purchase time or space in the ideal media vehicle, and they will place a PSA on a low-rated mature adult radio station than on a hot teen station due to ready accessibility. Certain topics pertaining to health and safety attain free publicity because they are inherently attractive to reporters and editors working in traditional media, such as newspapers, women's magazines, radio talk shows, and TV newsrooms.

Indeed, accessibility and economy are major reasons why typically underfunded health campaigners embrace new technologies. Although message production expenses can be substantial for elaborate website features and for sophisticated games, little cost is incurred for many forms of dissemination via digital media. There are several additional compelling reasons for the rise of digital media channels, notably depth capacity, interactivity, and tailoring (Edgar, Noar, & Freimuth, 2007; Parker & Thorson, 2009; Rice & Atkin, 2009). Unlike traditional media vehicles that are limited to a certain number of pages per issue or minutes per day, digital media have remarkable *depth capacity* for storing information that can be retrieved by website users or experienced by game players. Websites are an especially important channel for people that are highly involved in health topics, such as health opinion leaders seeking to stay well-informed or individuals diagnosed with an illness pursuing treatment information.

Interactivity enables the user and source to use monologue, responsive dialog, mutual discourse and feedback, involving a wide array of specific design features, such as surveys, games, services, email, hyperlinks, and chat rooms (Rice & Atkin, 2009). For example, online health-related support groups provide social support and help boost self-efficacy.

Thousands of health games on computers, consoles, websites, and mobile apps have been developed to teach skills, boost self-efficacy, and simulate role-playing. Lieberman's (2012) overview of studies and meta-analyses indicates that health games have positive effects on behavior change related to physical activity, nutrition, mental health, safer sex negotiation, disease self-management, and adherence to one's treatment plan. Health games are especially attractive to the younger population segments that are harder to reach and influence through traditional channels. The interactive, observational, experiential, and absorbing nature of game playing has enormous potential for advanced applications to health, such as utilizing sophisticated avatars and 3-D body model characters.

Digital media facilitate *tailoring* of individually customized messages that reflect each person's predispositions and abilities (Noar, Harrington, & Aldrich, 2009; Rimer & Kreuter, 2006). Online screening questionnaires assess factors such as readiness stage, stylistic tastes, knowledge levels, and current beliefs, and then direct them to *narrow-cast* messages. Not only does this approach increase the likelihood of learning and persuasion, but it decreases the possibility of boomerang effects. Mobile phone calling and texting are well-suited to offer tailored, wide-reaching, interactive, and continuing campaign interventions (Cole-Lewis & Kershaw, 2010).

There are a number of other ways to utilize new media for health campaigns. Online public service messages include brief banner ads, solicitations to click through to a website, streamed PSA spots, or long-form video messages on YouTube. Paid health promotion ads on social media sites have greater potential for impact because of more prominent placement and more precise targeting. Blogs link together users with similar information needs and concerns to share their views and experiences, while wikis support collaboration among campaign members. Podcasts can provide relevant audio information to motivated audiences, and Twitter provides updates and protocol reminders to campaign-specific followers.

Messages placed in the mainstream media can attract the attention of many informal influencers, who can then exert an indirect influence on the focal individuals. Health issues gaining visibility in the news media can benefit from the agenda-setting effect (e.g., the obesity epidemic), whereby problems and solutions are perceived as more urgent and significant. This is particularly important in media advocacy strategies targeted at opinion leaders and policy makers.

Entertainment-education, the practice of embedding health-related material in popular entertainment programming or creating entertainment content as a vehicle for health education, attracts large audiences and conveys information in a relevant and credible manner. This approach has proved quite successful in promoting health in less developed countries (Singhal, Cody, Rogers, & Sabido, 2004), and it also has been used in the United States to promote safety belts, use of designated drivers, safe sex, and drug abstinence as well as dealing with youth-oriented topics such as alcohol and obesity prevention.

There are tens of thousands of websites offering a wide variety of health materials; in addition to prepackaged pages and video clips, the interactive capacity enables campaign message tailoring. Tailored messages are constructed via diagnostic questionnaires that gather each individual's background information (e.g., capabilities, stage of readiness, stylistic taste, knowledge level, and current beliefs) and translate the data into individually customized messages (Noar et al., 2009; Rimer & Kreuter, 2006). Not only does this approach increase the likelihood of learning and persuasion, but it decreases the possibility of boomerang effects.

Quantitative Dissemination Factors

Five major aspects of strategic message dissemination are the total volume of messages, the amount of repetition, the prominence of placement, the scheduling of message presentation, and temporal length of the campaign. A substantial *volume* of stimuli helps attain adequate reach and frequency of exposure, as well as comprehension, recognition, and image formation. Message saturation also conveys the significance of the problem addressed in the campaign, which heightens agenda setting and salience. A certain level of *repetition* of specific executions facilitates message comprehension and positive affect toward the product, but high repetition eventually produces wear-out and diminishing returns.

Placement *prominence* of messages in conspicuous positions within media vehicles (e.g., newspaper front page, heavily traveled billboard locations, or high-rank search engine websites) serves to enhance both exposure levels and perceived significance. Another quantitative consideration involves the *scheduling* of a fixed number of presentations; depending on the situation, campaign messages may be most effectively concentrated over a short duration, dispersed thinly over a lengthy period, or distributed in intermittent bursts of "flighting" or "pulsing." In terms of the calendar, there are critical "timing points" when the audience is more likely to be attentive or active in information-seeking.

Regarding the overall *length* of the campaign, the challenging task of gaining audience attention and compliance often requires exceptional persistence of effort over long periods of time to attain a critical mass of exposures to produce impact. In many cases, perpetual campaigning is necessary because focal segments of the population are in constant need of influence as newcomers enter the priority audience, backsliders revert to prior misbehavior, evolvers gradually adopt practices at a slow pace, and vacillators need regular reinforcement.

To maximize quantity, campaigners seek to gain media access via monetary support from government and industry (to fund paid placements and leveraged media slots), aggressive lobbying for free public service time or space, skillful use of public relations techniques for generating entertainment and journalistic coverage, and reliance on low-cost channels of communication, such as websites and social media. The Ad Council creates more PSA messages that address health issues than for any other topic. Finally, the reach of a campaign is often boosted by sensitizing audiences to appropriate content already available in the media and by stimulating information-seeking from specialty sources.

Campaign Effectiveness

Researchers have assessed the impact of media-based health campaigns using survey and field experimental designs over the past several decades. The findings from many empirical studies have been summarized in literature reviews and meta-analyses, the most recent of which include Lundgren and McMakin (2009), Rice and Atkin (2009), Atkin and Salmon (2010), Green and Tones (2010), Webb, Joseph, Yardley, and Michie (2010), Rice and Atkin (2011), Silk et al. (2011), Phillips, Ulleberg, and Vaa (2011), Snyder and LaCroix (2012), and Paisley and Atkin (2012). The preponderance of evidence shows that conventional campaigns typically have limited direct effects on most health behaviors; specifically, campaigns are capable of exerting moderate to powerful influence on cognitive outcomes, but less influence on attitudinal behavioral outcomes. Further, the degree of impact on behavior tends to occur in proportion to such factors as dose of information, duration of campaign activities, integration of mass and interpersonal communication systems, and supplementation of social-change strategies, such as enforcement and engineering. Societal level outcomes in the form of policy changes have also been attained, but isolating the campaign input is difficult.

A campaign may not attain a strong impact for many reasons. Audience resistance barriers arise at each stage of response, from exposure to behavioral implementation. A major problem is simply reaching the audience and attaining attention to the messages (Hornik, 2002). Exposed audience members are lost at each subsequent response stage, due to defensive responses, such as misperception of susceptibility to threatened consequences, denial of applicability of message incentives to self, defensive counterarguing against persuasive appeals, rejection of unappealing behavioral recommendations, and sheer inertial lethargy. Public communication campaign outcomes tends to diminish when receivers regard messages as offensive, boring, preachy, confusing, irritating, misleading, irrelevant, uninformative, unbelievable, or unmotivating.

Salmon and Murray-Johnson (2001) make distinctions among various types of campaign effectiveness, including *definitional effectiveness* (e.g., getting a social phenomenon defined as a social problem or elevating it on the public agenda), *contextual effectiveness* (e.g., impact within particular contexts, such as education vs. enforcement vs. engineering), *cost-effectiveness* comparison (e.g., prevention vs. treatment, addressing certain problems over others), and *programmatic effectiveness* (e.g., testing campaign outcomes relative to stated goals and objectives).

Rather than being defined in absolute terms, campaign effectiveness is often defined relative to pre-campaign expectations. Although campaign planners may be tempted to set readily attained goals, lowering the bar does not necessarily improve campaign performance. Nevertheless, Fishbein (1996) advances the pragmatic argument that realistically small effect sizes should be set for media campaign so that obtaining effects is achievable.

Future Research Agenda

Fortunately for the next wave of campaign scholars, numerous theoretical and practical challenges remain to be addressed if health campaigns are to be more successful. Investigations are needed answer the following questions pertaining to campaign design and implementation.

What is the optimum *mix of message content themes*? Health campaigns typically use multiple persuasive strategies, but what is the most effective ratio of gain-frame versus loss-frame messages, one-sided versus two-sided appeals, and physical health versus nonhealth incentives? Second, what is the most effective balance of *direct* versus *indirect strategies* in health contexts? Campaigns increasingly rely on messages targeted to *interpersonal influencers* and on *media advocacy* approaches aimed at the general public and policy makers, but what is the appropriate way for these approaches to be intermingled? Third, how can campaigns *communicate effectively with young people*, who exhibit fundamentally different appraisals of risk and future consequences, who are using radically different interactive and personal media, and who are deeply embedded in peer networks?

Fourth, what is the impact of various *quantities of campaign messages?* What is the critical mass of stimuli needed to achieve meaningful effects on key outcomes, and what is the optimum frequency of repetition for a particular message execution? Fifth, what is the relative impact of various *channels for disseminating messages*? Specifically, what are the appropriate roles to be played by traditional media versus new technologies, and which of dozens of digital media devices can make meaningful contributions to health? Sixth, how can strategists reduce counterproductive effects at the individual and society levels? Promotion of cancer screening may lead to a rise in detrimental tests and treatments, recommending sunscreen use may produce a false sense of protection, fear appeals may create anxiety rather than coping responses, and depicting drugs as forbidden fruit may arouse curiosity. Finally, how can campaigns effectively overcome the *unhealthy influences of entertainment, news, and advertising messages* on high-profile health issues, such as drinking, smoking, safe sex, and violence?

Conclusion

Most experts conclude that contemporary public communication campaigns attain a modest rather than strong impact. This appears to be the case for health campaigns, which are characterized by limited effects on the health behaviors in most cases. The inability to attain strong impact can be traced to meager dissemination budgets, unsophisticated application of theory and models, and poorly conceived strategic approaches. It is also due to the difficulty of the task facing the health campaigner in surmounting the challenge of influencing resistant people to adopt difficult practices or sacrifice pleasurable activities.

In these situations, the pragmatic strategy may be to emphasize relatively attainable impacts: aiming at the more receptive focal segments, promoting more palatable positive products perceived to have a favorable benefit-cost ratio, creatively generating free publicity, and shifting campaign resources to indirect pathways that facilitate and control behavior of the focal segment via interpersonal, network, organizational, and societal influences. These emphases are not playing the expectations game, but can lead to substantive improvements in effectiveness. More generally, the degree of campaign success can be enhanced via greater diversification of influence pathways, of recommended behaviors, and of persuasive appeals beyond the approaches conventionally used in health campaigns. In addition, campaign strategists should realize that the optimum campaign mix incorporates elements to supplement persuasive appeals for influencing attitudes and behaviors; there are important roles for messages that simply impart new knowledge, enhance salience, deliver educational lessons, provide reminders to act, and stimulate information seeking.

Despite the array of barriers that diminish campaign effectiveness, the research literature shows important success stories over the past several decades. Health campaigns have made significant contributions to the progress in addressing pressing problems, such as smoking, seat belt use, drunk driving, AIDS, drug use, and heart disease. These effective campaigns tend to be characterized by theoretical guidance and rigorous evaluation, substantial quantity of message dissemination over sustained periods, widespread receptivity to the advocated action and accompanying persuasive incentives, and supplementation of mediated messages by campaign-stimulated factors, such as informal interpersonal influences and social engineering policy initiatives.

With the increasing implementation of increasingly sophisticated strategies and the rising societal priority of healthier behavior, there is a sound basis for optimism that campaigns can produce stronger impacts in the future. The ideas outlined in this chapter offer some promising approaches for scholars and practitioners to consider in developing the next generation of health campaigns.

References

Abroms, L. C., & Maibach, E. W. (2008). The effectiveness of mass communication to change public behavior. *Annual Review of Public Health, 29*, 219–234.

Ajzen, I. (1991). The theory of planned behavior. *Organizational Behavior and Human Decision Processes, 50*(2), 179–211.

Ajzen, I., & Fishbein, M. (1980). *Understanding attitudes and predicting social behavior.* Englewood Cliffs, NJ: Prentice-Hall.

Andreasen, A. (1995). *Marketing social change: Changing behavior to promote health, social development, and the environment.* San Francisco, CA: Jossey-Bass.

Andreasen, A. (2006). *Social marketing in the 21st century.* Thousand Oaks, CA: Sage.

Atkin, C. (1994). Designing persuasive health messages. In L. Sechrest, T. Backer, E. Rogers, T. Campbell, & M. Grady (Eds.), *Effective dissemination of clinical health information.* Rockville, MD: Department of Health and Human Services.

Atkin, C., & Freimuth, V. (2012). Guidelines for formative evaluation research in campaign design. In R. E. Rice & C. Atkin (Eds.), *Public communication campaigns* (4th ed., pp. 53–68). Thousand Oaks, CA: Sage.

Atkin, C. K., & Salmon, C. (2010). Communication campaigns. In C. Berger, M. Roloff, & D. Roskos-Ewoldsen (Eds.), *Handbook of communication science* (2nd ed., pp. 419–435). Thousand Oaks, CA: Sage.

Bandura, A. (1986). *Social foundations of thought and action: A social cognitive theory.* Englewood Cliffs, NJ: Prentice Hall.

Bandura, A. (1997). *Self-efficacy: The exercise of control.* New York, NY: W. H. Freeman.

Blumler, J. G., & Katz, E. (1973). *The uses of mass communications: Current perspectives on gratifications research.* Beverly Hills, CA: Sage.

Cappella, J., Fishbein, M., Hornik, R., Ahern, R. K., & Sayeed, S. (2001). Using theory to select messages in anti-drug media campaigns: Reasoned action and media priming. In R. E. Rice & C. K. Atkin (Eds.), *Public communication campaigns* (3rd ed., pp. 214–230). Thousand Oaks, CA: Sage.

Cole-Lewis, H., & Kershaw, T. (2010, January). Text messaging as a tool for behavior change in disease prevention and management. *Epidemiologic Reviews,* http://epirev.oxfordjournals.org/cgi/content/abstract/mxq004v1

DeJong, W., & Smith, S. (2012). Truth in advertising: Social norms marketing campaigns to reduce college student drinking. In R. E. Rice & C. Atkin (Eds.) *Public communication campaigns* (4th ed., pp. 177–188). Thousand Oaks, CA: Sage.

Dillard, J. P., Weber, K. M., & Vail, R. (2007). The relationship between the perceived and actual effectiveness of persuasive messages: A meta-analysis with implications for formative campaign research. *Journal of Communication, 57*(4), 613–631.

Edgar, T., Noar, S., & Freimuth, V. (2007). *Communication perspectives on HIV/AIDS for the 21st century.* Mahwah, NJ: Erlbaum.

Fishbein, M. (1996). Great expectations, or do we ask too much from community-level interventions? *American Journal of Public Health, 86*(8), 1075–1076.

Fishbein, M., & Cappella, J. N. (2006). The role of theory in developing effective health communications. *Journal of Communication, 56*(Supplement), S1–S17.

Freudenberg, N., Bradley, S. P., Serrano, M. (2009). Public health campaigns to change industry practices that damage health: An analysis of 12 case studies. *Health Education & Behavior, 36*, 230–249.

Green, G., & Tones, K. (2010). *Health promotion: Planning and strategies* (2nd ed.). London, UK: Sage.

Hornik, R. (2002). *Public health communication.* Mahwah, NJ: Erlbaum.

Janz, N. K., & Becker, H. M. (1984). The health belief model: A decade later. *Health Education Quarterly, 11*, 1–47.

Kotler, P., & Lee, N. (2008). *Social marketing: Influencing behaviors for good.* Thousand Oaks, CA: Sage.

Lieberman, D. A. (2012). Designing digital games, social media, and mobile technologies to motivate and support health behavior change. In R. E. Rice & C. K. Atkin (Eds.), *Public communication campaigns* (4th ed., pp. 275–290). Thousand Oaks, CA: Sage.

Lundgren, R. E., & McMakin, A. H. (2009). *Risk communication: a handbook for communicating environmental, safety, and health risks.* Hoboken, NJ: Wiley.

McCombs, M. (2004). *Setting the agenda: The mass media and public opinion.* Malden, MA: Blackwell.

McGuire, W. (2001). Input and output variables currently promising for constructing persuasive communications. In R. E. Rice & C. K. Atkin (Eds.), *Public communication campaigns* (3rd ed., pp. 22–48). Thousand Oaks, CA: Sage.

McKenzie-Mohr, D. (2011). *Fostering sustainable behavior: An introduction to community-based social marketing.* Gabriola Island, BC, Canada: New Society.

Morgan, M. (2009). "Cultivation analysis and media effects." In R. L. Nabi & M. B. Oliver (Eds.), *The Sage handbook of media processes and effects* (pp. 69–82). Thousand Oaks, CA: Sage.

Noar, S. M., Harrington, N. G., & Aldrich, R. (2009). The role of message tailoring in the development of persuasive health communication messages. In C. S. Beck (Ed.), *Communication yearbook 33* (pp. 73–133). New York, NY: Erlbaum.

O'Keefe, D. J., & Jensen, J. D. (2007). The relative persuasiveness of gain-framed and loss-framed messages for encouraging disease prevention behaviors: A meta-analytic review. *Journal of Health Communication, 12*, 623–644.

Paisley, W., & Atkin, C. K. (2012). Public communication campaigns: The American experience. In R. E. Rice & C. K. Atkin (Eds.), *Public Communication Campaigns* (4th ed., pp. 21–34). Thousand Oaks, CA: Sage.

Palmgreen, P., Donohew, L., & Harrington, N. G. (2001). Sensation seeking in antidrug campaign and message design. In R. E. Rice & C. K. Atkin (Eds.), *Public communication campaigns* (3rd ed., pp. 300–308). Thousand Oaks, CA: Sage.

Parker, J. C., & Thorson, E. (2009). *Health communication in the new media landscape.* New York, NY: Springer.

Perkins, H. W. (2002). Social norms and the prevention of alcohol misuse in collegiate contexts. *Journal of Studies on Alcohol, 63*(14), 163–172.

Phillips, R. O., Ulleberg, P., & Vaa, T. (2011). Meta-analysis of the effect of road safety campaigns on accidents. *Accident Analysis and Prevention, 43,* 1204–1218.

Prochaska, J., & Velicer, W. (1997). The Transtheoretical Model of health behavior change. *American Journal of Health Promotion, 12,* 38–48.

Quick, B., & Bates, B. (2010). The use of gain- or loss-frame messages and efficacy appeals to dissuade excessive alcohol consumption among college students: A test of psychological reactance theory. *Journal of Health Communication, 15,* 603–628.

Rice, R. E., & Atkin, C. K. (2009). Public communication campaigns: Theoretical principals and practical applications. In J. Bryant & M. Oliver (Eds.), *Media effects: Advances in theory and research* (3rd ed., pp. 436–468). Hillsdale, NJ: Erlbaum.

Rice, R. E., & Atkin, C. K. (2011). Communication campaigns. *Oxford Bibliographies Online (Communication).* doi: 10.1093/OBO/9780199756841-0055

Rimer, B., & Kreuter, M. W. (2006). Advancing tailored health communication: A persuasion and message effects perspective. *Journal of Communication, 56,* S184–S201.

Rogers, E. M. (2003). *Diffusion of innovations* (5th ed.). New York, NY: Free Press.

Rubin, A. M. (2009). Uses and gratifications: An evolving perspective of media effects." In R. Nabi & M. B. Oliver (Eds.) *The Sage handbook of media processes and effects* (pp. 147–160). Thousand Oaks, CA: Sage.

Salmon, C., & Atkin, C. K. (2003). Media campaigns for health promotion. In T. L. Thompson, A. M. Dorsey, K. I. Miller, & R. Parrott, R. (Eds.), *Handbook of health communication* (pp. 472–494). Mahwah, NJ: Erlbaum.

Salmon, C., & Murray-Johnson, L. (2001). Communication campaign effectiveness: Some critical distinctions. In R. E. Rice & C. K. Atkin (Eds.), *Public communication campaigns* (3rd ed., pp. 168–180). Thousand Oaks, CA: Sage.

Silk, K., Atkin, C. K., & Salmon, C. (2011). Developing effective media campaigns for health promotion. In T. L. Thompson, R. Parrott, & J. Nussbaum (Eds.), *Handbook of health communication* (2nd ed., pp. 203–219). Hillsdale, NJ: Erlbaum.

Singhal, A., Cody, M., Rogers, E., & Sabido, M. (2004). *Entertainment-education and social change: History, research, and practice.* Mahwah, NJ: Erlbaum.

Snyder, L. B., & LaCroix, J. M. (2012). How effective are mediated health campaigns? A synthesis of meta-analyses. In R. E. Rice & C. K. Atkin (Eds.), *Public Communication Campaigns* (4th ed., pp. 113–130). Thousand Oaks, CA: Sage.

Stephenson, M., & Witte, K. (2001). Creating fear in a risky world: Generating effective health risk messages. In R. E. Rice & C. K. Atkin (Eds.), *Public communication campaigns* (3rd ed., pp. 88–102). Thousand Oaks, CA: Sage.

Wallack, L., & Dorfman, L. (2001). Putting policy into health communication: The role of media advocacy. In R. E. Rice & C. K. Atkin (Eds.), *Public communication campaigns* (3rd ed., pp. 389–401). Thousand Oaks, CA: Sage.

Webb, T. L., Joseph, J., Yardley, L. & Michie, S. (2010). Using the Internet to promote health behavior change: A systematic review and meta-analysis of the impact of theoretical basis, use of behavior change techniques, and mode of delivery on efficacy. *Journal of Medical Internet Research, 12*(1), e4. Retrieved May 9, 2012, from http://www.jmir.org/2010/1/e4

Zillmann, D. (2006). Exemplification effects in the promotion of safety and health. *Journal of Communication, 56,* S221–237.

The Siren's Call

Mass Media and Drug Prevention

William D. Crano, Jason T. Siegel, and Eusebio M. Alvaro

The appeal of the mass media in drug prevention rests on the prospect that a single crusade, executed properly, will cheaply and effectively resolve the exasperating and seemingly intractable problems of illicit substance use. This magic bullet mentality is understandable and possibly even correct, though the evidence of the past century's efforts offers faint encouragement that we will arrive at this enchanted outcome any time soon. Our purpose in writing this chapter is to review some of applications of the mass media in drug prevention, to identify possible reasons for their inconsistent effects, and to suggest means of arriving at more positive preventive outcomes. This plan involves reconsideration of a general theory of message effects whose consistent implementation may foster development of campaigns that deliver on their promise to attenuate the problem of drug misuse.

Analyzing and integrating the fit of past campaigns with recommendations of contemporary theory is complicated by research operations that often involved only a weak association with established theories and untested assumptions about the mindset and usage status of the intended audience. The sometimes tenuous theoretical underpinnings of the many early mass-mediated prevention campaigns, and the less than optimal evaluation techniques adopted, surely impeded progress (Crano, 2010; Fishbein et al., 2002; McGuire, 1991). Identifying these shortcomings may facilitate development of informed guidelines leading to more sure and rapid progress, for although the promise of the mass media in drug prevention has largely gone unrealized, the jury is still out regarding the *possible* efficacy of the general approach in the critical arena of drug prevention.

Common Problems Whose Solution May Lead to Progress

Mis- or Nonapplication of Theory and Level of Analysis

For those steeped in the hypothetico-deductive approach of modern social science, it may come as a surprise that many past mass-mediated anti-drug interventions were based on little more than horse sense and uninformed assumptions of campaign targets' general susceptibility to common messages. Even campaigns that adopted empirically established models of attitude formation or change often neglected to make use of a consistent theory of message effects in their message-development strategy. In the present context, a theory of message effects is a model of the factors involved in attitude change, and the features of the communication that must be present in addressing these factors. It stands to reason that if some degree of resistance to a counterattitudinal message is expected, it may prove useful to understand something about the resistance processes that are brought on line when a persuasive message is encoded. Messages should be designed in full cognizance of this expected resistance or counterargumentation. Following the theory of reasoned action (TRA; Fishbein & Ajzen, 2010), for example, one might have a clear idea that changing attitudes or subjective norms may affect intentions and subsequent behaviors.

However, the theory does not reveal how one designs persuasive messages to accomplish these changes in attitude or perceived subjective norms. It was not designed to do so. These message factors thus remain speculative, dependent more on preference than established theory and research. This is not a shortcoming of the TRA; rather, it is the result of a lack of an empirically established theory of message construction, and it may be the heart of past failures. The issue is one of level of analysis (Doise, 1986). The typical theory of attitude formation and change is explicit about the factors that must be affected if a communication is to bring about change, but with few exceptions, these theories adopt a strict receiver orientation. That is, the explanatory mechanism for change is almost always located in the intended receiver, rather than among the variables the campaign organizer can actually control (but see Palmgreen, Stephenson, Everett, Baseheart, & Francies, 2002; Stephenson & Palmgreen, 2001).

The common theories of change operate at a metalevel, but the mircolevel advice often is lacking. This is not a fault of the common theories; rather, this lack of message specificity suggests the need to develop more precise models of the persuasion process, and the message features required to interface with these processes to effect change. Not many such models exist, but there are some, and they should be used and refined in light of current knowledge.

There are, of course, positive examples of theory-guided, empirical, mass media research that amply illustrate the potential of strategies that meld a theory of attitude formation and change with a theory of message construction (see Atkin, 2002; Atkin & Wallack, 1990; Donohew, 2006; Palmgreen & Donohew, 2010; Salmon & Atkin, 2003), but in general, campaigns that satisfy both of these requirements are the exception rather than the rule. If a mass media antidrug persuasion campaign is to succeed, it should be built on a reasonable and empirically established theory of attitude formation or change, which is paired with a reasonable and empirically established theory of message construction. Of course, recognizing receiver characteristics that might affect message reception, especially usage status in the case of illicit substance prevention, also must be a central feature of the antidrug media campaign (Crano, Siegel, Alvaro, Lac, & Hemovich, 2008b; Crano, Siegel, Alvaro, & Patel, 2007). Ignoring either can spell disaster for any mass mediated persuasion attempt.

Consider, for example, the recent National Youth Anti-drug Mass Media Campaign (henceforth, the Campaign). The budget of the Campaign exceeded a billion dollars (http://www .whitehouse.gov/ondcp/anti-drug-media-campaign), but its results were not nearly as positive as hoped. The Campaign was theory based and focused on a specific audience of adolescents at risk of initiating drug use (marijuana was most frequently targeted, though inhalants and amphetamines also were featured). It attained an exceptionally high frequency of message exposure. Almost all known media were used in its unprecedented ad blitz, which carried over four years, nationwide. The goal of the Campaign was to reduce adolescent drug initiation and misuse, an ambition that had remained unfulfilled over the years. Most of the elements were in place, but structural features of the Campaign imperiled its outcome.

Those familiar with the ads produced in this program would find it difficult to discern a through-line in the messages used in this heroic, four-year, ultimately unsuccessful effort (Hornick, Jacobsohn, Orwin, Piesse, & Kalton, 2008). Although the guiding theoretical rationale was in place from the start, the Campaign's ads did not appear to be based on a clear theory of messaging, and this resulted in a damaging lack of commonality of persuasive approach and a series of persuasive ads that did not seem particularly persuasive. Both outcomes were perhaps inevitable, given the nature of the process by which the ads were created and deployed. Although developed by well-regarded marketing firms, the communications did not speak with a common voice, nor were they based on a clear idea of the factors that might be involved adolescents' accepting or rejecting an anti-drug message.

This resulted in a series of one-off communications whose only commonality was their frequency of exposure. Absence of a consistent theme did not permit program developers to connect the many ads that were created, which might have reduced resistance and added to their impact. This shortcoming was not a signal feature of the Campaign. *Any* mass media persuasion campaign that is not framed by a strong theoretical view of how and why particular ads will operate is inevitably prone to failure, because even if some effective communications are developed, their effects will not cumulate owing to their haphazard appearance and ultimate dilution in a sea of failed messages. Intuition is not a substitute for empirical research when persuasion via well-developed messages is a sought-for outcome. Because a message attracts attention, is salient, funny, artistic, colorful, memorable, or charming does not necessarily imply that it will be persuasive. None of these features can substitute for strong theory and empirical research when deciding on the likely outcome of a message—or a full-blown media campaign.

Iatrogenesis

An unfortunate, if not inevitable sequel of a failed persuasion campaign is an outcome that is diametrically opposite to that intended (Cho & Salmon, 2007). Iatrogenic effects in response to mass mediated prevention ads are not new. Researchers in communication and psychology have been aware of boomerang or contrast effects in response to persuasive messages for many years. Sherif and Hovland (1961), for example, developed an interesting model based on earlier psychophysical research to explain unwanted and often unanticipated changes in response to persuasive messages, and they were not the first. Commenting on mass persuasion and education efforts more than 80 years ago, Payne (1931, pp. 219–220) found that "The proposed introduction of narcotic education into the public schools, like sex education, raises some questions. One of the most serious of these is the reputed danger of stimulating the curiosity and adventure interest of the child through emphasizing either negatively or positively the unusual effects of drugs upon both mind and body."

Forty years later, a Canadian report noted the "Speed Kills" campaign that aired in North America in the late 1960s may have had more "attractive than deterrent power" (Commission of Inquiry, 1970). In 1973, the National Commission on Marijuana and Drug Abuse made many recommendations to President Richard Nixon based on a two-year study of the problem, noting that drug prevention efforts might *"merely stimulate youthful interest in drugs"* (Feingold & Knapp, 1977). In the mid-1980s, a pre-launch article in the *British Medical Journal* noted that a forthcoming U.K. campaign might be "more than a waste of money;" rather, it was feared that it would stimulate curiosity in drugs and thereby increase their use (Hanson, 1985; Home Office, 1984).

Reactance

Over the years and across diverse literatures, various explanations have been offered for the iatrogenic effects of antidrug campaigns. Brehm's (1966) psychological reactance theory provides a plausible explanation for these outcomes (Brehm & Brehm, 1981; Burgoon, Alvaro, Grandpre, & Voloudakis, 2003), especially on respondent samples concerned with independence threats. Persuasive communication may be viewed in PRT terms as representing an inherent threat to freedom. When a perceived freedom is threatened by a message proscribing an attitude or behavior, people may experience motivating pressures to reestablish that freedom (Heilman & Toffler, 1976). PRT-based research has found that reactance arousing messages have a negative effect on persuasion (Burgoon et al., 2003; Dillard & Shen, 2005; Grandpre et al., 2003; Miller, Burgoon, Grandpre, & Alvaro, 2006; Quick & Stephenson, 2007). While not explicitly based on PRT, Comello and Slater (2011) presented encouraging findings on the potential of messages that enhance feelings of autonomy to facilitate drug resistance. In their study, students exposed to autonomy-supportive print ads from the Campaign evidenced greater accessibility of the belief that marijuana use was inconsistent with autonomy, and were less willing to use the substance.

Awareness of Persuasive Intent

We have known for some time that participants aware of an influencing agent's intent to persuade will prove more resistant to persuasion (Allyn & Festinger, 1961; Wood & Quinn, 2003). Walster and Festinger (1962), for example, showed that an "overheard" persuasive communication concerned with an issue on which the individual was highly vested was significantly more persuasive than directly focused or irrelevant messages, a result later replicated and expanded by Brock and Becker (1965). These studies indicate that the more explicit the intent to persuade, the less persuasive is the appeal, *if* the target is concerned about the issue, and the message is not perceived as unduly propagandistic. All bets are off if these conditions are not met. It stands to reason, then, that the less explicit the intent to persuade, the more receptive is the target.

Crano and associates (2007) built on this possibility in creating a minimal "overhead communication" manipulation to influence subjects' responses to anti-inhalant messages in a mass mediated experiment. Embedded in an antibullying video, a maneuver designed to minimize suspicion and experimental demand effects, middle school participants saw a video message that began with either, "Are you in the sixth, seventh, or eighth grade?" or "Parents, do you have a young teen at home?" The message target was reiterated four times throughout the video with statements such as either "Your child . . ." or "Parents" or "Students." For resolutely abstinent non-users, the indirectly targeted message (analogous to an overheard communication) was not expected to impart any greater influence than the direct message, as either would be of minor relevance to them. However, an inhalant-relevant communication was expected to be highly relevant for inhalant users, and for non-users at high risk for initiation. Both hypotheses were supported: the direct or indirect feature of the message had no effect on resolute non-users; however, it significantly affected the attitudes of those for whom the message was relevant. The "indirect" manipulation, less than a dozen words, caused increased positivity of ad evaluations of adolescent inhalant users and those at high initiation risk; positive message evaluation, in turn, predicted significantly lower intentions to use inhalants.

Curiosity

Curiosity is perhaps the oldest, yet least-researched explanation for the iatrogenic effects of antidrug campaigns. As Sheppard, Goodstadt, and Willet (1987, p. 197) put it: "education raises levels of awareness, leading to curiosity which in turn leads to experimentation." Although there is little research directly examining the extent to which iatrogenic antidrug campaign effects are predicated on increased curiosity about drugs, a study by Lancaster (2004) studied the impact of general messages about drugs on curiosity. Drawing on the model of product curiosity, Lancaster found that exposure to mediated messages about drugs increased awareness of drugs, interest in drugs, and uncertainty about drug use. She argued this process may lead to a higher intent to use drugs, especially among those at risk for use.

Resistance Enhancement

A relatively unexplored, but nonetheless serious outcome of successful resistance, if not an iatrogenic reaction to antidrug media, is suggested in recent research by Tormala in his resistance appraisals model (RAM: Tormala, 2008; Tormala & Petty, 2002, 2004). The RAM holds that people's attitude certainty increases as a result of their successfully resisting strong persuasive messages. The stronger the resisted message, the greater the augmentation of certainty and subsequent resistance. Thus, attitudes strengthened as a result of successfully resisting messages perceived as strong are likely to persist, to prove resistant to change, and to show a stronger link with behavior (Petty & Krosnick, 1995).

Arguably, ads would be perceived as strong if presented as part of a nationwide mass media saturation campaign and attributed to a well-known agency of drug prevention. However, if the ads were not compelling, and hence were resisted, enhanced (pro-drug) attitude certainty would be expected among at-risk nonusers and users. According to the RAM, then, in addition to the iatrogenic effects reported in the evaluation of this campaign by Hornik and colleagues (2008; see also Orwin et al., 2006), the Campaign's failed persuasion attempts created greater resistance to future drug prevention appeals than

was evident before their ads aired. It is possible in drug prevention that nothing sometimes is better than something.

Normative Considerations

Social norming is a yet another common explanation for iatrogenic effects. A test of the social norming hypothesis was afforded by examining the Campaign's evaluation data. Jacobsohn (2005) assessed the extent to which estimates of perceived marijuana use were associated with campaign exposure and found the exposure/marijuana use relationship was mediated by increased-use perceptions. In line with social norms theory (Berkowitz, 1997; Perkins & Berkowitz, 1986), she proposed that the meta-message that marijuana use is prevalent had a greater impact on use than the explicit anti-marijuana message. The social norming explanation has drawn considerable interest from prevention scientists. If targets of large-scale persuasive prevention interventions assume that the problem under attack is widespread, or normative, and if complying with normative demands is considered desirable, then reversing the perception that a targeted behavior is widespread may prove a useful avenue of prevention.

There is little doubt that adolescents appear to overestimate their peers' involvement in substance misuse (Wolfson, 2000). The Campaign may have fallen prey to this problem, but research has demonstrated massive normative misperception, even with illicit inhalants, which received little attention in the Campaign. For example, Crano, Gilbert, Alvaro, and Siegel (2008a) found that less than 5% of their sixth-grade respondents reported ever having used inhalants, but estimated nearly 40% of their friends had done so. A slightly higher proportion (< 10%) of the study's seventh-grade respondents reported lifetime inhalant misuse, but estimated that more than 50% of their friends had used these substances to get high. This apparent normative misperception may have been motivated, as users estimated significantly higher "friends' usage" rates than nonusers. It is reasonable to assume that users' friends indeed might have been more likely to use inhalants than nonusers' friends, but the extent of the discrepancy strains credulity.

Blanton's deviance regulation model (DRM) provides the clearest empirically supported method of taking advantage of normative misperceptions in prevention (Blanton & Burkley, 2008; Blanton & Christie, 2003; Blanton, Stuart, & VandenEijnden, 2001). The DRM assumes that people develop images of prototypical persons as a result of the behaviors in which they engage. The image formed of a person described as a marathon runner, for example, is different from that of a chess whiz, or a regular marijuana user. Theoretically, if we engage in behaviors similar to those of the prototype (chess whiz, etc.), others will associate us with the prototype. People attempt to maintain a positive identity by acting in accord with, or contrary to, these implicit positive or negative images.

Because actions that deviate from the norm are viewed as particularly informative, the DRM suggests that people will deviate from (antisocial) norms if by doing so they stand out and are associated with positive prototypes; however, they will avoid deviating from (prosocial) norms if by doing so they become associated with negative images (persons or positions). The model suggests that messages should be framed on the basis of each group's (or, better, each individual's) perception of the normative nature of substance misuse or abstinence. For example, if an undesirable behavior (e.g., marijuana use) is viewed as normative by the individual ("Everyone does it"), the model suggests communications will be most effective if they adopt a positive persuasive frame that promotes the desirable attributes and behaviors of those who *deviate* from the norm ("Teens who refuse to use marijuana are acting responsibly, maturely . . . "). However, if usage is viewed as nonnormative, then a negative frame is indicated ("Marijuana is rarely used in this school. Why be an outsider?") This frame emphasizes the negative consequences of deviating from the norm.

Blanton and colleagues' research suggests the utility of the DRM, and hopefully will be widely adopted in the future.

What Is to Be Done?

The picture of antidrug mass media campaigns that has been drawn to this point is not particularly appealing, but it does supply direction for future campaign developers. In general, most prior campaigns did not live up to their potential. To change this longstanding state of affairs requires a reconsideration of approach. Repeating the same procedures and expecting different results would seem to fit Einstein's definition of insanity. Taking advantage of all that went before in mass media and drug prevention requires reconsideration of strategies and tactics, starting with reflection on the fundamental functions persuasive messages are meant to serve. Almost by definition, poorly constructed messages will not persuade. In some circumstances, such communications, as has been shown, have produced results opposite to those intended. But how are persuasive messages created? To answer this question requires a return to theories and research in which the fundamental form of the persuasive communication was deliberated. We choose to focus on the work of Carl Hovland and his Yale Communication and Attitude Change Program, which he founded at the end of World War II, and whose impact is felt even today in communication and social psychology (McGuire, 1996). While we do not subscribe to all features of Hovland's model of the nature of the persuasive communication, especially its almost singular commitment to a strong behaviorist orientation, the fundamental conception of the factors that must be included in a communication, if it is to persuade, strike us as persuasive (McGuire, 2003). These message features are honored more in the breech than in today's practice, but as has been suggested, common practice does not have much to show for the past 50 years' efforts in mass-mediated drug prevention. If a lack of clear focus on the construction of persuasive communications is at least in part responsible for past failures, then it makes sense to consider the factors that make a message persuasive.

Hovland insisted that a message must fulfill three functions if it to succeed in persuading. It must raise a question in the mind of the receiver about the validity of an established belief; it must provide an answer to that question at odds with the belief (after all, we are considering persuasion, a change of belief, not reinforcement of held-beliefs); and it must provide some compensation or reinforcement for accepting the proffered alternative (vs. continued resistance and maintenance of the original belief).

Following Hovland's lead (see especially Hovland, 1954; Hovland, Janis, & Kelley, 1953; Hovland, Lumsdaine, & Sheffield, 1949; Sherif & Hovland, 1961), these three components must be included in any and every message that is intended to persuade. They do not exhaust the list of desired features in a communication; rather, they are the minimum necessary requirements of a persuasive message. The focus is directed to persuasion, or attitude change, not attitude formation, for which recent research on evaluative conditioning seems more ideally suited. In persuasion, the receiver holds a position more or less strongly, which is more or less contrary to that advocated in the communication. In *attitude formation*, the critical belief, if it exists, is ill-formed and not strongly held.

Assuming attention to the message, a big assumption whose consideration is beyond the scope of this chapter (see Crano, 2012; Johnson & Eagly, 1990; McGuire, 2000), the first requirement that the message raise a question in the target's mind regarding the validity of his or her belief flows naturally from this assumption. Without raising a question, there is little conflict, and subsequently little force for change. If the message fails to raise a question, the persuasion process never begins. This first requirement does not imply that the questioning produces change—it is merely the first step in the process. The message need not raise the question subtly,

but it must do so credibly and unmistakably. Not many would judge the Truth anti-smoking campaign as subtle, but there is reasonable evidence that it is effective (Farrelly, Davis, Haviland, Messeri, & Healton, 2005).

The second requirement of the persuasive communication, that it answers the question it has raised, also flows naturally from the notion that the persuasion process is directive. It is not sufficient merely to stimulate a question. It is necessary that receivers accept the recommended answer. Without providing the answer, the communication is unlikely to achieve much in mass communication contexts. The answer to the question raised in the initial phase of the persuasive message process must be difficult to resist if it is to prevail (that is, if the attitude is to be changed). This requirement, too, is premised on Hovland's view of persuasion dynamics, which maintains that the influence target will raise counterarguments in response to communications that call beliefs into question. The intensity of counterargumentation is theorized to be dependent in part on the centrality or personal relevance of the attitude under persuasive attack. If the attitude is not attached to a highly vested outcome, resistance may be minimal; with highly relevant attitude objects, however, strong resistance can be expected (Crano, 1997; Lehman & Crano, 2002; Visser, Bizer, & Krosnick, 2006).

For this reason, the communication should convey information that is difficult to contradict or falsify, be based on objective facts and observations rather than subjective beliefs, and take advantage of source and context features that may enhance message impact (Crano, 2012). The goal of the message developer is to anticipate the counterarguments likely to be raised and to build in rebuttals to these arguments in the persuasive message. With attitude outcomes that are involving or vested, messages are more likely to persuade if they are based on valid information, and facts rather than opinions (Gorenflo & Crano, 1989). Their internalization involves acquisition and acceptance of new knowledge, a necessary feature if there is to be consistency between attitudes and actions (Wood, Rhodes, & Biek, 1995). In contexts involving outcomes of low vested interest or weakly held attitudes, the effects of ads that do not share these features may not be differentiable from those that do. However, when poorly designed communications meet well-established attitudes, the attitudes usually prevail.

The call for careful consideration of arguments in developing antidrug campaigns may seem obvious, but common practice appears to belie this perception. In fact, easily rebutted messages seem a relatively consistent feature of many mass mediated antidrug campaigns, if we base our definition on the Hovland's requirements. This is not to say that much of the available antidrug media content is not intense or extreme; but it is important to distinguish persuasive messages from extreme ones. Extreme messages, exemplified by those used in the classic *Reefer Madness* and the ongoing *Montana Meth* campaigns, for example, satisfy few, if any, of Hovland's requirements, and as such have been shown to be easily resisted (Anderson, 2010; Erceg-Hurn, 2008). Their very extremity gives rise to rejection by audience members who either have used the illicit substance (or who know those who did) and did not suffer the many and varied slings and arrows promised in the message. Given the earlier discussion of iatrogenesis, it is reasonable to suggest that campaigns using extreme, easily rejected messages such as those that characterized these efforts probably did more harm than good.

Unsuccessful mass mediated drug prevention campaigns can fail in many ways, which are not exhausted by failure to adhere to the first two of Hovland's criteria for a successful persuasive messaging. The final prerequisite of Hovland's model requires that reinforcement be attached to the counterattitudinal position advocated in the persuasive message. This reinforcement need not be palpable; symbolic rewards are more commonly employed, and probably work as well as more tangible ones. The requirement is important because it forces the persuader to

consider possible reasons why a target would forego an established belief and adopt the recommended alternative.

It also leads to a deeper understanding of the kinds of appeals that are most likely to supply the sought-for effects, and those that will prove considerably less likely to deliver. Symbolic reinforcements can come in many guises, and have been studied for many years, although they are not always discussed in behaviorist terms. For example, consider the relatively well-established finding that source credibility can play an important role in boosting the persuasive power of a communication (Crano & Prislin, 2006; Tormala, Briñol, & Petty, 2006). There are many explanations for this regularity, but one of the most persuasive suggests that aligning oneself with an expert or credible or attractive communication source is desirable, or reinforcing. Accepting a well-crafted, data-based message attributed to a recognized and respected information source is reinforcing for those seeking to be right, a motivation commonly recognized as widespread (Festinger, 1954). The specific form of the reinforcement may vary among contexts and persons, but the general rule is clear, and its utility has been demonstrated repeatedly over the years.

Does One Size Fit All?

Research on the DRM indicates that the same norm-based message is not likely to be maximally effective with respondents who hold widely different normative perceptions of use, the validity of those perceptions notwithstanding. Fitting the appropriate normative appeal to the audience's normative beliefs has important persuasive implications. We can expand Blanton's insight into a more general consideration of fitting the message to targets' features. For example, it seems self-evident that a persuasive drug prevention message delivered to resolutely abstinent nonusers should be different from one designed to persuade long-term substance abusers to quit. Historically, most antidrug mass media campaigns have adopted a universalist (or nontargeted) orientation, in which messages are developed for, and aimed at, the population at large. A limiting factor of this approach is that it is based on the improbable assumption that the *same* persuasive strategy can be used effectively to change attitudes and behaviors of a diverse group, from *different* backgrounds, with *different* perspectives, *different* norms, and *different* drug-relevant experiences.

Abundant evidence suggests this assumption is unfounded.[1] For example, Fishbein and colleagues (2002) showed that message receivers' drug use status strongly affected their susceptibility to persuasive appeals; however, they argued that merely distinguishing users from nonusers was unduly insensitive. In addition to the typical user/nonuser distinction, they demonstrated the utility of separating abstinent "intenders" from resolute nonusers to distinguish those adamantly opposed to drug use from those who, although nonusers, might be receptive to use in the future. A similar differentiation is seen in Crano and colleagues' (2008b) distinction between youth they operationally defined as either resolute or vulnerable nonusers (see also Siegel, Alvaro, & Burgoon, 2003). This research showed that both groups of adolescents, neither of whom had ever used marijuana, differed appreciably in terms of future usage as a function of the intensity of their rejection: Marijuana "never users" who would not rule out future initiation (vulnerable nonusers) were significantly more likely to begin usage (37%) the next year than resolute nonusers who *definitely* abjured use (10%), and this discrepancy in lifetime use grew over time. In the fourth year of a nationally representative panel study, about one quarter of the nonusers defined as "resolute" in the first year had used marijuana, compared with nearly two-thirds of those nonusers considered at risk (vulnerable nonusers) at the first year's measurement.

Consistent with these results was a study of adolescents' reactions to different instantiations of anti-inhalant persuasive messages, which showed significant differences in message response among youth who were current users, vulnerable nonusers, or resolute nonusers (Crano et al., 2007). *Users* resisted communications that emphasized inhalants' physical harms, whereas *vulnerable nonusers* were more likely to reject threats to social standing. Users and vulnerable nonusers responded differently when messages were targeted indirectly (i.e., the messages were addressed to parents rather than participants themselves); this variable did not differentially influence resolute nonusers. Vulnerable nonusers were receptive to peer sources, whereas users preferred adult sources. Resolute nonusers were not differentially attuned to peer or adult message sources: the messages were equally effective for this group. These differences suggest that usage status plays a significant role in determining targets' susceptibility to persuasive antidrug messages. Further examining the three-part distinction between users, vulnerable nonusers, and resolute nonusers in preventing illicit substance misuse may hold considerable promise for future campaigns. Traditional mass mediated communication campaigns, however, seem uniquely unprepared to target messages on the basis of receiver features, much less tailor messages to targets. With the advent of new technologies, social networking, and the like, fitting message to receiver may not be farfetched, but for the moment, let us stick with the standard mass mediated approaches.

Some Applications of the Messaging Model

The insights derivable from an application of the general messaging model apply to more than the selection of variables to be used in a message-based persuasion campaign. Hovland's orientation alerts researchers to fundamental obstacles to be overcome. It does not specify the variables that must be used in the persuasion task, but rather the functions they must fulfill if the attempt is to succeed. In this sense, the model is a general framework that informs the construction of messages. It is conceivable that there are additional benefits to be gained in an adopting this general framework for persuasive communication. Disseminating a host of well-received messages could be expected to enhance the effect of every new addition to the persuasive message repertoire of a campaign.

This build-up could be explained in a number of ways—framing, stimulus generalization (Hovland's choice), openness, positive expectations regarding the utility of antidrug messages, and so on, but whatever the chosen mechanism, the point remains that the effect would grow the effectiveness of a campaign. With each addition to the message mix, an accretion of positive effects could be expected. An open mindset fostered by a positive attitude toward the prior messages that constituted the campaign would enhance the likelihood of success of any subsequent message associated with the campaign. Arguably, positive effects found in frequency of exposure research may succeed for this reason, but the effect would be the result of a campaign that has successfully cultivated a positive response (or openness) to its earlier offerings.

Emotion Arousing Communications

From the 1950s onward, study of emotional or fear-arousing messages has been a feature of scientific research in psychology and communication science (Janis & Feshbach, 1953, 1954; Maloney, Lapinski, & Witte, 2011; Witte, 1998). The outlines of the effect of fear arousal on message persuasiveness are now well-known. Communications that augment already high levels of anxiety are likely to be shunned or discounted, and consequently are not effective means of evoking attitude change. This is especially true if the source of the message is not credible or if the means of avoiding the dire outcomes promised in the message are not provided. Emotion arousing communications *can* be persuasive, especially with receivers whose initial emotional involvement in the proscribed activity is minimal. This difference in audience features renders use

of emotion arousing communications in mass media campaigns problematic, if the target sample includes individuals from both extremes of the anxiety spectrum.

The general messaging model anticipates this problem. It holds that those already participating, or inching toward the targeted injurious behavior are not likely to process strongly threatening information, as it is punishing and hence will be avoided or counterargued. If the mass mediated campaign is developed for purposes of cessation, fear arousing messages probably are ill advised. Those who have categorically rejected the disparaged activity (smoking marijuana, getting high on inhalants or methamphetamines, and so on) might be affected by a fear arousing message, as it is unlikely that they would counterargue it, but they are likely to be persuaded by almost any other message form. On the negative side, a media blitz involving an illicit substance, as in the Montana Meth campaign (http://www.montanameth.org.), might produce iatrogenic results (Erceg-Hurn, 2008), as it could suggest to naive targets that meth use was normative, or stimulate curiosity, reactions considered in our discussion of iatrogenic effects.

Over all, then, one must wonder whether the loss of credibility generated in the user community, and the possibility of iatrogenic effects, is worth the effect that may be found in audiences of resolute nonusers who might have been influenced by most other ad formats, many of which would not have immediately scared off or pushed users to greater resistance or higher usage. Preaching to the choir is easy; converting the fallen is considerably more difficult. To maximize rare mass media prevention opportunities, it is well to understand that one size probably does not fit all, though some sizes may fit all better than others.

Overpromising

Conceptually related to the (over-) use of emotion arousing messages is the common practice of overpromising the (dire or sometimes positive) consequences that will ensue if the recommendations contained in mass media communications are, or are not heeded. Our research suggests that creating negative drug-relevant expectations that subsequently are demolished through counter-communication or simple life experiences is a recipe for disaster. Skenderian, Siegel, Crano, Alvaro, and Lac (2008) showed that changes from one year to the next in subjects' expectancies regarding the effects of marijuana use predicted their immediate marijuana intentions and subsequent usage behavior. A positive change in nonusers' expectations concerning the outcome of marijuana usage (that is, change in a pro-marijuana direction), was followed by a statistically significant uptake in marijuana usage relative to that of nonusers whose expectations remained constant or changed in a negative direction. The guidance to be absorbed from this result is that overpromising the dire consequences of drug usage is a risky game, because if the receiver at some point decides that the warning was not truthful, the rebound effect may be severe. Promises about negative effects can be effective in the short run, but the long-term price to be paid for this short-term gain might exceed the costs of having done nothing at all. Avoid overpromising: the tactic will fail, and when it does, it will produce outcomes even more extreme than if it had never been used. In this case, the cure is worse than the disease.

(Socio-personal) Expectancies

An expectancy is a perceived relationship between a behavior and its anticipated outcome (Tolman, 1932). Expectancies may be considered if/then statements: "If I watch this PSA, I will learn accurate information about drugs," or "If I smoke marijuana, I will lose (gain) friends." Expectancies have strong predictive validity for a host of socially problematic behaviors (Siegel, 2011; Siegel et al., 2012). For example, expectations regarding positive or negative outcomes of alcohol use significantly predict drinking behavior over and above demographic factors, alcohol-related attitudes,

and prior drinking (Carey, 1995; Stacy, 1997). Siegel and colleagues (2008) emphasized the importance of socio-personal expectations (SPEs: expectations concerning the relation between specific behaviors and desired social outcomes) in an adolescent sample (also see Siegel, Alvaro, Patel, & Crano, 2009). Their research disclosed that a brief media intervention could affect SPEs, which were significantly predictive of inhalant use.

Research on SPEs suggests that antidrug messages that focus on physical harms of drugs may produce suboptimal results. Such ads, especially those targeting adolescents, are based on the premise that users will cease and nonusers will never initiate if they are made aware of the physical harms of substance misuse. Milam and colleagues' (2000) finding that tobacco smokers perceived smoking as more harmful than nonsmokers calls this assumption into question (see also Crano et al., 2007). Given the importance of social outcomes for most adolescents, SPEs appear to provide a more optimal means of influencing potential drug misuse. Studies that have compared threats of social versus physical harms (Schoenbachler & Whittlerm, 1996; Siegel et al., 2008) consistently reveal that SPEs associated with drug use are susceptible to social influence, predictive of drug use, and can affect drug use attitudes and intentions. As social goals become prominent during adolescence (Erikson, 1968; Hogg, Siegel, & Hohman, 2011), it is reasonable to infer that SPEs should play a greater role in adolescent mass mediated drug prevention (see Blanton et al., 2001, 2008). A media focus on messages that satisfy the general message criteria laid out earlier, and focused on readjusting the socio-personal expectations associated with drug use, offers good prospects for success.

Siegel and J. Burgoon (2002) examined the importance of adolescents' expectations of antidrug media in a wide ranging integrative discussion of expectancy states theory (EST; Berger, Conner, & Fiske, 1974), expectancy violation theory (EVT; J. Burgoon, 1993), and language expectancy theory (Burgoon & Miller, 1985; Burgoon & Siegel, 2003). They detailed the importance of prior anti-drug messaging efforts on newly encountered anti-drug messages, and supplied a framework for understanding how the negative impact of earlier antidrug ad failures could be overcome. Siegel and J. Burgoon (2002) held that creators of antidrug PSAs had to overcome the shortcomings of past campaigns, which resulted in negative expectations for antidrug PSAs. The stronger the resisted counterattitudinal message, the more likely is resistance to subsequent change efforts. Combining the insights of the expectancy approaches leads to the conclusion that prior experiences can create expectations that strongly affect resistance. The more frequently people encounter ineffective antidrug messages, the more confident they become that future messages will offer little benefit. Thus, future messages will be ignored or encoded with a negative bias.

Misdirection and Indirect Influence Effects

"It seems plausible to suppose that an attempt to persuade a person to change his opinion on some issue would be more effective if the persuasive communication were unexpected than if the person anticipated the influence attempt" (Allyn & Festinger, 1961, p. 35). This supposition is compatible with that of Hovland and his colleagues (1953, p. 23), who theorized that a persuasive communication would be particularly effective when the "unintended" receiver believed that the communicator had "no intention to persuade."[2] Obviously, receivers unaware that they are the targets of a persuasive attack are not likely to defend themselves against it. For this reason, indirect change effects have proved intriguing to many researchers involved in minority group influence, whose results support the counterargument explanation (Martin & Hewstone, 2008). With reasonable consistency, minority influence researchers have produced highly unusual but replicable results in which persuasive messages on one topic appear to have failed miserably, but

on examination are shown to have powerful, systematic, and predicted effects on attitude objects that were never mentioned in the persuasive communication (e.g., Crano & Seyranian, 2009; Perez & Mugny, 1987).

Alvaro and Crano (1997) for example, showed that counterattitudinal communications attributed to an in-group minority usually produced little direct influence; however, these messages predictably affected receivers' attitudes on (indirect) issues that had been established in advance as related to the focus of the persuasive message, even though this association was not accessible to the receivers themselves. The researchers established that research participants' attitudes on *gays in the military* and *gun control* were strongly associated, but the participants themselves seriously underestimated the strength of this connection. Consistent with their leniency contract model, analysis disclosed that when attributed to an in-group minority, a persuasive message arguing against gays in the military had no apparent effect; however, subjects receiving this source-message combination became significantly more conservative in their attitudes toward gun control.

A second study that reversing the focal and indirect attitude objects supported the original results: A strong anti-gun control message attributed to an in-group minority resulted in less favorable attitudes toward gays in the military. Relevant for present purposes was Alvaro and Crano (1996) findings that counterargumentation in response to an in-group minority's communication, operationalized as the proportion of negative thoughts assessed in a post-message thought-listing task, was significantly attenuated relative to that observed in the majority or out-group minority message conditions. If conditions motivate receivers not to counter a persuasive message, there is a good chance an associated attitude will change, even if the original message appears to have failed to impart any influence whatsoever.

Crano and Chen (1998) replicated and extended these results in a study that made use of different attitude objects (tuition increase and a proposal that students donate 10 hours of their time, weekly, to university needs). The research replicated the in-group minority effect on associated attitudes, and also demonstrated that large scale changes on the indirect attitude were associated with changes on the focal belief after a delay of one to two weeks. These results suggest persistence when measuring effects of mediated persuasion. Although recommended changes might not occur immediately in response to a persuasive communication, they may arise with the passage of time. This is not conceptualized as a passive process. We hypothesize that information, once introduced successfully, with little counterargumentation or source derogation, may have a long-term effect, even in the absence of immediate changes in the recommended direction. If messages can be delivered in a way that they arouse little counterargumentation and source disparagement, there is a good chance they will come to have the intended effect, even if the circumstances at the time of message delivery render immediate acceptance unlikely.

These results help explain why Crano and colleagues' (2007) adolescent viewers were particularly susceptible to ads that apparently were intended for their parents. Recall the persuasive message was embedded in an antibullying video, and presented as an advertisement. Middle school participants who saw a message that began with "Are you in the sixth, seventh, or eighth grade?" were significantly less persuaded than those who saw the nearly identical ad that began, "Parents, do you have a young teen at home?" Apparently, youth in the parent communication condition did not feel the need to counterargue the message, and this observation held regardless of their drug use status. Importantly, the message delivered in the communication satisfied Hovland's three central requirements for persuasive messages.

Epilogue

Neglect of fundamental principles of messaging may be at least partially responsible for the less than outstanding record of mass media

effectiveness in drug prevention trials. To be sure, some campaigns have performed admirably, but they are rare, and probably could have produced better results with greater attention to principles of persuasion that have been part of the common language of social psychology and communication science for the past 60 years. This review has focused on campaigns that did not live up to their initial promise, not out of a sense of smug self-satisfaction, but rather to encourage future campaign planners to seek out hard won knowledge based on strict adherence to strong social science. Openness on the part of mass media campaign directors to the lessons of research is essential if we are to make progress, but it cannot be taken for granted. Voices of concern about the "direction and execution" of the Campaign (DeJong & Wallach, 2000, p. 77), for example, which has featured heavily in this review, were raised in sufficient time to alter the course of the work. Further, during the campaign itself, unease with the messages being delivered and their lack of connection to established theories of messaging or persuasion were voiced repeatedly (Crano, 2010), but to no avail. A hallmark of the good scientist *and* the responsible science administrator is recognition that one does not know everything and that established knowledge must be considered seriously. Throwing lots of money at a mass media campaign devoid of a reasonable idea of how persuasion works is unwise at best.

In the abstract, the advice provided here is relatively straightforward: Pay attention to established theory, realize that intuition does not trump the insights drawn from years of intense research, ensure campaign messages are based on theory and congruent empirical results, maintain the integrity of the research design, consider the beliefs, norms, and behaviors of the respondents to be studied, attend to the possibility of iatrogenic effects, respond accordingly, and assess the outcome of the effort in a scientifically credible manner. This is not an esoteric formula, but judging from past practice, it is not one that is easy to follow. The guidelines laid out are designed to improve mass communication outcomes. They are offered in a constructive voice to answer the simple question, "Can the mass media play a role in prevention of drug misuse?" In our view, there is no doubt that they can, and have. Can the record of accomplishment be improved? As before, there is no doubt that it can, and that it must. Openness on the part of campaign directors is essential, as is a continued and unrelenting insistence by scholars of communication and persuasion that publicly funded campaigns adhere to well-established, empirically based models in the design and delivery of persuasive messages. Nothing short of unremitting perseverance will work, but when lives hang in the balance, such dedication is worth the effort.

Acknowledgments

Our students in the Health Psychology and Prevention Science Institute at Claremont Graduate University were of incalculable value in their willing support of this work, giving freely and unstintingly of their time in facilitating our review of the massive literature concerned with the use of mass media in drug prevention. We could not have done it without you. Preparation of this research was supported by a grant from the U.S. National Institute on Drug Abuse (R01 DA030490), which we gratefully acknowledge. The contents of this chapter are solely the responsibility of the authors and do not necessarily reflect the views of the Institute.

Notes

1. A choice of audience features is required to maximize outcomes. At the most basic level, we must decide if the goal is prevention or cessation. And, the possibility that targeting one group may disadvantage other groups should be recognized. Until technology progresses to the point that messages can be tailored to each individual's specific proclivities, the mass media approach will be faced with these alternatives.

2. The effect was thought to work through a reduction in counterargumentation, though this possibility was not tested.

References

Allyn, J., & Festinger, L. (1961). The effectiveness of unanticipated persuasive communications. *Journal of Abnormal and Social Psychology, 62*, 35–40.

Alvaro, E. M., & Crano, W. D. (1996). Cognitive responses to minority- or majority-based communications: Factors that underlie minority influence. *British Journal of Social Psychology, 35*, 105–121.

Alvaro, E. M., & Crano, W. D. (1997). Indirect minority influence: Evidence for leniency in source evaluation and counterargumentation. *Journal of Personality and Social Psychology, 72*, 949–964.

Anderson, D. M. (2010). Does information matter? The effect of the Meth Project on meth use among youths. *Journal of Health Economics, 29*, 732–742.

Atkin, C. (2002). Promising strategies for media health campaigns. In W. D. Crano & M. Burgoon (Eds.), *Mass media and drug prevention* (pp. 35–64). Mahwah, NJ: Erlbaum.

Atkin, C., & Wallack, L. (Eds.). (1990). *Mass communication and public health: Complexities and conflict.* Newbury Park, CA: Sage.

Berger, J., Conner, T. L., & Fiske, M. H. (1974). *Expectation states theory: A theoretical research program.* Cambridge, MA: Winthrop.

Berkowitz, A. D. (1997). From reactive to proactive prevention: Promoting an ecology of health on campus. In P. C. Rivers & R. E. Shore (Eds.), *Substance abuse on campus: A handbook for college and university personnel* (pp. 119–139). Westport, CT: Greenwood.

Blanton, H., & Burkley, M. (2008). Deviance regulation theory: Applications to adolescent social influence. In M. J. Prinstein & K. A. Dodge (Eds.), *Understanding peer influence in children and adolescents* (pp. 94–121). New York, NY: Guilford.

Blanton, H., & Christie, C. (2003). Deviance regulation: A theory of action and identity. *Review of General Psychology, 7*, 115–149.

Blanton, H., Stuart A. E., & VandenEijnden R. J. J. M. (2001). An introduction to deviance-regulation theory: The effect of behavioral norms on message framing. *Personality and Social Psychology Bulletin, 2*, 848–858.

Brehm, J. W. (1966). *A theory of psychological reactance.* New York, NY: Academic Press.

Brehm, J. W., & Brehm, S. S. (1981). *Psychological reactance: A theory of freedom and control.* San Diego, CA: Academic Press.

Brock, T. C., & Becker, L. A. (1965). Ineffectiveness of 'overheard' counterpropaganda. *Journal of Personality and Social Psychology, 2*, 654–660.

Burgoon, J. K. (1993). Interpersonal expectations, expectancy violations, and interpersonal communication. *Journal of Language and Social Psychology, 12*, 30–48.

Burgoon, M., Alvaro, E. M., Grandpre, J., & Voloudakis, M. (2003). Revisiting the theory of psychological reactance: Communicating threats to attitudinal freedom. In J. Dillard & M. Pfau (Eds.), *The handbook of persuasion* (pp. 213–232). Thousand Oaks, CA: Sage.

Burgoon, M., & Miller, G. R. (1985). An expectancy interpretation of language and persuasion. In H. Giles & R. N. St. Clair (Eds.), *Language, communication, and social psychology* (pp. 199–229). London, UK: Erlbaum.

Burgoon, M., & Siegel, J. T. (2003). Language expectancy theory: Insight and application. In J. Seiter, & R. Gass (Eds.), *Readings in persuasion, social influence, and compliance gaining* (pp. 149–164). Needham Heights, MA: Allyn & Bacon.

Carey, K. B. (1995). Alcohol-related expectancies predict quantity and frequency of heavy drinking among college students. *Psychology of Addictive Behaviors, 9*, 236–241.

Cho, H., & Boster, F. J. (2002). Effects of gain versus loss frame antidrug ads on adolescents. *Journal of Communication, 58*, 428–446.

Cho, H., & Salmon, C. T. (2007). Unintended effects of health communication campaigns. *Journal of Communication, 57*, 293–317.

Comello, M. L. G., & Slater, M. D. (2011). The effects of drug-prevention messages on the accessibility of identity-related constructs. *Journal of Health Communication, 16*, 458–469.

Commission of Inquiry. (1970). *Interim report of the Commission of Inquiry into the non-medical use of drugs.* Ottawa, CA: Queen's Printer.

Crano, W. D. (1997). Vested interest, symbolic politics, and attitude-behavior consistency. *Journal of Personality and Social Psychology, 72*, 485–491.

Crano, W. D. (2010). Experiments as reforms: Persuasion in the nation's service. In J. P. Forgas, J. Cooper, & W. D. Crano (Eds.), *The psychology of attitudes and attitude change* (pp. 231–248). New York, NY: Psychology Press.

Crano, W. D. (2012). *The rules of influence.* New York, NY: St. Martin's Press.

Crano, W. D., & Chen, X. (1998). The leniency contract and persistence of majority and minority influence. *Journal of Personality and Social Psychology, 74*, 1437–1450.

Crano, W. D., Gilbert, C., Alvaro, E. M., & Siegel, J. T. (2008a). Enhancing prediction of inhalant abuse risk in samples of early adolescents: A secondary analysis. *Addictive Behaviors, 33*, 895–905.

Crano, W. D., & Prislin, R. (2006). Attitudes and persuasion. *Annual Review of Psychology, 57*, 345–374.

Crano, W. D., & Seyranian, V. (2009). How minorities prevail: The context/comparison-leniency contract model. *Journal of Social Issues, 65*, 335–363.

Crano, W. D., Siegel, J. T., Alvaro, E. M., Lac, A., & Hemovich, V. (2008b). The at-risk adolescent marijuana nonuser: Expanding the standard distinction. *Prevention Science, 9*, 129–137.

Crano, W. D., Siegel, J. T., Alvaro, E. M., & Patel, N. (2007). Overcoming adolescents' resistance to anti-inhalant appeals. *Psychology of Addictive Behaviors, 21*, 516–524.

DeJong, W., & Wallack, L. (2000). The Drug Czar's anti-drug media campaign: Continuing concerns. *Journal of Health Communication, 5*, 77–82.

Dillard, J. P., & Shen, L. (2005). On the nature of reactance and its role in persuasive health communication. *Communication Monographs, 72*, 144–168.

Doise, W. (1986). *Levels of explanation in social psychology.* New York, NY: Cambridge University Press.

Donahew, L. (2006). Media, sensation seeking, and prevention. In M. E. Vollrath (Ed.), *Handbook of personality and health* (pp. 299–313). New York, NY: Wiley.

Erceg-Hurn, D. M. (2008). Drugs, money, and graphic ads: A critical review of the Montana Meth Project. *Prevention Science, 9*, 256–263.

Erikson, E. (1968). *Identity youth and crisis.* New York, NY: W. W. Norton.

Farrelly, M. C., Davis, K. C., Haviland, M. L., Messeri, P., & Healton, C. G. (2005). Evidence of a dose response relationship between "truth" anti-smoking ads and youth smoking prevalence. American Journal of Public Health, 95, 425–431.

Feingold, P. C., & Knapp, M. L. (1977). Anti-drug abuse commercials. *Journal of Communication, 27*, 20–28.

Festinger, L. (1954). A theory of social comparison processes. *Human Relations, 7*, 117–140.

Fishbein, M., & Ajzen, I. (2010). *Predicting and changing behavior: The reasoned action approach.* New York, NY: Psychology Press.

Fishbein, M., Cappella, J., Hornik, R., Sayeed, S., Yzer, M., & Ahern, R. K. (2002). The role of theory in developing effective anti-drug public service announcements. In W. D. Crano & M. Burgoon (Eds.), *Mass media and drug prevention: Classic and contemporary theories and research* (pp. 89–117). Mahwah, NJ: Erlbaum.

Gorenflo, D. W., & Crano, W. D. (1989). Judgmental subjectivity/objectivity and locus of choice in social comparison. *Journal of Personality and Social Psychology, 57*, 605–614.

Grandpre, J., Alvaro, E. M., Burgoon, M., Miller, C., & Hall, J. R. (2003). Adolescent reactance and anti-smoking campaigns: A theoretical approach. *Health Communication, 15*, 349–366.

Hanson, A. (1985). Will the government's mass media campaign on drugs work? *British Medical Journal, 290*, 1054–1055.

Heilman, M. E., & Toffler, B. L. (1976). Reacting to reactance: An interpersonal interpretation of the need for freedom. *Journal of Experimental Social Psychology, 12*, 519–529.

Hogg, M. A., Siegel, J. T., & Hohman, Z. (2011). Groups can jeopardize your health: Identifying with un-healthy groups to reduce self-uncertainty. *Self and Identity, 10*, 326–335.

Home Office. (1984). *Prevention: Report of the advisory council on the misuse of drugs.* London: HMSO.

Hornik, R, Jacobsohn, L., Orwin, R., Piesse, A., & Kalton, G. (2008). Effects of the National Anti-drug Media Campaign on youths. *American Journal of Public Health, 98*, 2229–2236.

Hovland, C. I. (1954). Effects of the mass media of communication. In G. Lindzey (Ed.), *Handbook of Social Psychology, Vol. 2* (pp. 1062–1103). Cambridge, MA: Addison-Wesley.

Hovland, C. I., Janis, I. L., & Kelley, H .H. (1953). *Communication and persuasion: Psychological studies of opinion change.* New Haven, CT: Yale University Press.

Hovland, C. I., Lumsdaine, A. A., & Sheffield, F. D. (1949). *Experiments on mass communication.* Princeton, NJ: Princeton University Press.

Jacobsohn, L. (2005). *The mediating role of youth perceptions of marijuana use prevalence in explaining boomerang effects of the national youth anti-drug media campaign.* Paper presented at the annual meeting of the International Communication Association, New York, NY.

Janis, I. L., & Feshbach, S. (1953). Effects of fear-arousing communications. *The Journal of Abnormal and Social Psychology, 48*, 78–92.

Janis, I. L., & Feshbach, S. (1954). Personality differences associated with responsiveness to fear-arousing communications. *Journal of Personality, 23*, 154–166.

Johnson, B. T., & Eagly, A. H. (1990). Involvement and persuasion: Types, traditions, and the evidence. *Psychological Bulletin, 107*, 375–384.

Lancaster, A. R. (2004). What does curiosity really do to the cat? A look at how message exposure can lead to illicit drug trial among college students. *Mass Communication and Society, 7*, 77–95.

Lehman, B., & Crano, W. D. (2002). The pervasive effects of vested interest on attitude-criterion consistency in political judgment. *Journal of Experimental Social Psychology, 38*, 101–112.

Maloney, E. K., Lapinski, M. K., & Witte, K. (2011). Fear appeals and persuasion: A review and update of the Extended Parallel Process Model. *Social and Personality Psychology Compass, 5*, 206–219.

Martin, R., & Hewstone, M. (2008). Majority versus minority influence, message processing and attitude change: The source-context-elaboration model. *Advances in Experimental Social Psychology, 40*, 237–326.

McGuire, W. J. (1991). Using guiding-idea theories of the person to develop educational campaigns against drug abuse and other health threatening behavior. *Health Education Research, 6*, 173–184.

McGuire, W. J. (1996). The Yale communication and attitude-change program in the 1950s. In E. E. Dennis & E. Wartella (Eds.), *American communication research: The remembered history* (pp. 39–59). Hillsdale, NJ: Erlbaum.

McGuire, W. J. (2000). Standing on the shoulders of ancients: Consumer research, persuasion, and figurative language. *Journal of Consumer Research, 27,* 109–122.

McGuire, W. J. (2003). The morphing of attitude-change into social-cognition research. In G. V. Bodenhausen & A. J. Lambert (Eds.), *Foundations of social cognition: A festschrift in honor of Robert S. Wyer, Jr.* (pp. 7–24). Mahwah, NJ: Erlbaum.

Milam, J. E., Sussman, S., Ritt-Olson, A. R., & Dent, C. W. (2000). Perceived invulnerablility and cigarette smoking among adolescents. *Addictive Behaviors, 25,* 71–80.

Miller, C. H., Burgoon, M., Grandpre, J. R., & Alvaro, E. M. (2006). Identifying principal risk factors for the initiation of adolescent smoking behaviors: The significance of psychological reactance. *Health Communication, 19,* 241–252.

Orwin R, Cadell, D., Chu, A., Kalton, G., Maklan, D., Morin, C., et al. (2006). *Evaluation of the National youth anti-drug media campaign 2004 report of findings.* Retrieved May 12, 2012, from https://www.ncjrs.gov/App/publications/Abstract .aspx?id=236869

Palmgreen, P., & Donohew, L. (2010). Impact of SEN-TAR on prevention campaign policy and practice. *Health Communication, 25,* 609–610.

Palmgreen, P., Stephenson, M. T., Everett, M. W., Baseheart, J. R., & Francies, R. (2002). Perceived message sensation value (PMSV) and the dimensions and validation of a PMSV scale. *Health Communication, 14,* 403–428.

Payne, E. G. (1931). *The menace of narcotic drugs.* New York, NY: Prentice-Hall.

Perez, J. A., & Mugny, G. (1987). Paradoxical effects of categorization in minority influence: When being an out-group is an advantage. *European Journal of Social Psychology, 17,* 157–169.

Perkins, H. W., & Berkowitz, A. D. (1986). Perceiving the community norms of alcohol use among students: Some research implications for campus alcohol education programming. *International Journal of the Addictions, 21,* 961–976.

Petty, R. E., & Krosnick, J. A. (1995). *Attitude strength: Antecedents and consequences.* Hillsdale, NJ: Erlbaum.

Quick, B. L., & Stephenson, M. T. (2007). The Reactance Restoration Scale (RRS): A measure of direct and indirect restoration. *Communication Research Reports, 24,* 131–138.

Salmon, C., & Atkin, C. (2003). Using media campaigns for health promotion. In T. L. Thompson, A. M. Dorsey, K. I. Miller, & R. Parrott (Eds.), *Handbook of health communication* (pp. 449–472). Mahwah, NJ: Erlbaum.

Schoenbachler, D. D., & Whittler, T. E. (1996). Adolescent processing of social and physical threat communication. *Journal of Advertising, 25,* 37–54.

Sheppard, M. A., Goodstadt, S. M., & Willett, M. M. (1987). The drug education-drug use dilemma. *Journal of Drug Education, 17,* 197–200.

Sherif, M., & Hovland, C. I. (1961). *Social judgment theory: Assimilation and contrast effects in communication and attitude change.* New Haven, CT: Yale University Press.

Siegel, J. T. (2011). Dying for romance: Risk taking as purposive behavior. *Psychology, Health and Medicine, 16,* 719–726. Retrieved May 9, 2012, from http://www.ncbi.nlm.nih.gov/pubmed/21745031

Siegel, J. T., Alvaro, E. M., & Burgoon, M. (2003). Perceptions of the at-risk nonsmoker: Are potential intervention topics being overlooked? *Journal of Adolescent Health, 33,* 458–461.

Siegel, J. T., Alvaro, E. M., Crano, W. D., Skenderian, J. J., Lac, A., & Patel, N. (2008). Influencing inhalant intentions by changing socio-personal expectations. *Prevention Science, 9,* 153–165.

Siegel, J. T., Alvaro, E. M., Patel, N., & Crano, W. D. (2009). "...you would probably want to do it. Cause that's what made them popular": Exploring perceptions of inhalant utility among young adolescent non-users and occasional users. *Substance Use and Misuse, 44,* 597–615.

Siegel, J. T., & Burgoon, J. K. (2002). Expectancy theory approaches to prevention: Violating adolescent expectations to increase the effectiveness of public service announcements. In W. D. Crano & M. Burgoon (Eds.), *Mass media and drug prevention: Classic and contemporary theories and research* (pp. 163–186). Mahwah, NJ: Erlbaum.

Siegel, J. T., Crano, W. D., Alvaro, E. A., Lac, A., Rast, D., & Kettering, V. (2012). Dying to be popular: Why do adolescents go to extremes? In M. A. Hogg & D. Blaylock (Eds.), *Extremism and the psychology of uncertainty* (pp. 163–186). Malden, MA: Wiley-Blackwell.

Skenderian, J. J., Siegel, J. T., Crano, W. D., Alvaro, E. E., & Lac, A. (2008). Expectancy change and adolescents' intentions to use marijuana. *Psychology of Addictive Behaviors, 22,* 563–569.

Stacy, A. W. (1997). Memory activation and expectancy as prospective predictors of alcohol and marihuana use. *Journal of Abnormal Psychology, 106,* 61–73.

Stephenson, M. T., & Palmgreen, P. (2001). Sensation seeking, perceived message sensation value, personal involvement and processing of anti-marijuana PSAs. *Communication Monographs, 68,* 49–71.

Tolman, E. C. (1932). *Purposive behavior in animals and men.* London, UK: Century/Random House.

Tormala, Z. L. (2008). A new framework for resistance to persuasion: The resistance appraisals hypothesis. In W. D. Crano & R. Prislin (Eds.), *Attitudes and attitude change* (pp. 213–234). New York, NY: Psychology Press.

Tormala, Z. L., Briñol, P., & Petty, R. E. (2006). When credibility attacks: The reverse impact of source credibility on persuasion. *Journal of Experimental Social Psychology, 42,* 684–691.

Tormala, Z. L., & Petty R. E. (2002). What doesn't kill me makes me stronger: The effects of resisting persuasion on attitude certainty. *Journal of Personality and Social Psychology, 83,* 1298–1313.

Tormala, Z. L., & Petty R. E. (2004). Resistance to persuasion and attitude certainty: The moderating role of elaboration. *Personality and Social Psychology Bulletin, 30,* 1446–1457.

Visser, P. S., Bizer, G. Y., & Krosnick, J. A. (2006). Exploring the latent structure of strength-related attitude attributes. In M. P. Zanna (Ed.), *Advances in experimental social psychology,* (Vol. 38, pp. 1–67). San Diego, CA: Elsevier Academic.

Walster, E., & Fetsinger, L. (1962). The effectiveness of "overheard" persuasive communication. *Journal of Abnormal and Social Psychology. 65,* 395–402.

Witte, K. (1998). Fear as motivator, fear as inhibitor: Using the extended parallel process model to explain fear appeal successes and failures. In P. A. Andersen & L. K. Guerrero (Eds.), *Handbook of communication and emotion: Research, theory, applications, and contexts* (pp. 423–450). San Diego, CA: Academic Press.

Wolfson, S. (2000). Students' estimates of the prevalence of drug use: Evidence for a false consensus effect. *Psychology of Addictive Behaviors, 14,* 295–298.

Wood, W., & Quinn, J. M. (2003). Forewarned and forearmed? Two meta-analytic syntheses of forewarnings of influence appeals. *Psychological Bulletin, 129,* 119–138.

Wood, W., Rhodes, N., & Biek, M. (1995). Working knowledge and attitude strength: An information-processing analysis. In R. E. Petty & J. A. Krosnick (Eds.), *Attitude strength: Antecedents and consequences* (pp. 283–313). Hillsdale, NJ: Erlbaum.

CHAPTER 19

Persuasion in the Marketplace

How Theories of Persuasion Apply to Marketing and Advertising

L. J. Shrum, Min Liu, Mark Nespoli, and Tina M. Lowrey

Persuasion runs indelibly through all aspects of our lives. Some instances are subtle (e.g., effects of entertainment media), others can be in-your-face annoying (e.g., political communications). If asked, and given sufficient time, most people can come up with a long list of everyday persuasion attempts and practices. However, we suspect that at the top of pretty much everyone's list would be advertising. Whether it is the result of constant exposure to ads, their often entertaining nature, or simply because of our (American) hyperconsumer culture, there are few things that more quintessentially capture the notion of persuasion than advertising. We love the ads (at least, we watch a lot of them), we hate them (at least, we often devise elaborate schemes to avoid watching them), and we may even fear them (mind control). In fact, the early fears about the persuasive power of propaganda on citizens in the 1930s and 1940s soon morphed into worries about the persuasive power of advertising, particularly the worry about subliminal persuasion through advertising (cf. Bargh, 2002; Brannon & Brock, 1994; Packard, 1957).

Given advertising's prominence in the domain of persuasion, it is not surprising that theories of persuasion have played a central role in scholarly research on effects of advertising (and marketing communications more generally). In this chapter, we provide a review of scholarly work on persuasion in the marketplace. However, we hasten to admit that a thorough coverage of all of the applicable persuasion theories and their tests is beyond the scope of this chapter. There are numerous theories of persuasion that have implications for advertising and marketing, many of which are covered in this volume. Rather, we have chosen to highlight the persuasion theories that have been most influential in advertising, marketing, and consumer behavior research over the last 30 years. Some of these theories will be familiar to communication researchers (e.g., theory of reasoned action; elaboration likelihood model), others less so (e.g., persuasion knowledge model). We provide a brief presentation and discussion of each theory, and then review the research that applied these theories to marketing questions. Finally, in the last section, we discuss some new directions in consumer research that pertain to concepts related to persuasion (e.g., preference construction and choice, perceptions, liking).

Persuasion Theories in Marketing, Advertising, and Consumer Behavior Contexts

Theory of Reasoned Action

Although perhaps not a strict persuasion theory, the theory of reasoned action is a model of behavioral intentions developed by Fishbein and Ajzen (1975; also see chapter 8 in this volume). The model incorporates both attitudes and subjective norms that people hold in predicting their future behavior. Formally, the theory of reasoned action is:

$$B \sim BI = A_{act}(w_1) + SN(w_2)$$

where

B = a particular behavior

BI = intention to engage in the particular behavior

A_{act} = attitude toward engaging in the behavior

SN = subjective norm pertaining to what others think.

The theory posits that the most proximal input into a behavior is a person's intention to engage in that behavior. (Although seemingly obvious, this assumption is important because it implies that behavior is intentional.) In turn, behavioral intentions are determined by one's attitude toward performing the behavior or act (A_{act}) and one's beliefs about what important others think about one performing the behavior (SN). The weights for each component (w_1, w_2) indicate that the relative weights for each component of behavioral

intention will vary across people and situations. For example, some behavioral intentions may be overly influenced by subjective norms (wearing a particular brand of clothing), whereas other intentions are more heavily influenced by personal attitudes (choice of chewing gum).

Fishbein and Ajzen further specified that each component of intention, attitudes, and subjective norms were themselves determined by specific beliefs about each. Using an expectancy-value approach, they quantified attitude toward the behavior as a cross-product of the subjective likelihood that performing a particular behavior (b) would lead to a specified outcome (i) and their evaluation of that outcome (e):

$$A_{act} = \sum_{i=1}^{n} b_i e_i$$

where n represents the number of different consequences that come to mind. Similarly, Fishbein and Azjen quantified the subjective norm component as the cross-product of the belief that an important other (j) thinks one should perform a particular behavior (b) and one's own motivation to comply with that important other (m):

$$SN = \sum_{j=1}^{n} b_j e_j \; .$$

Tests of the Model

Given that marketers are particularly keen on being able to predict the behavior of their customers, the theory of reasoned action was put to the test in a number of consumer situations, and formed the basis of a number of doctoral dissertations (cf. Lutz, 1973b; Ryan, 1975). For example, the Fishbein model (or variations of it) has been shown to be predictive of the purchase of a specific brand of grape drink (Bonfield, 1974), toothpaste (Wilson, Mathews, & Harvey, 1975), generic prescription drugs (Brinberg & Cummings, 1984), football tickets (Lutz, 1973a), model of automobile (Raju, Bhagat, & Sheth, 1975), and even the purchase of term papers (Weddle & Bettman, 1973). In a comprehensive meta-analysis, Sheppard, Hartwick, and Warshaw (1988) found very strong evidence of the predictive validity of both the relation between intentions and behavior and between the combination of attitudes and subjective norms and behavioral intentions. Interestingly, and of particular interest to marketers, the meta-analysis found that the predictive validity of intentions on behavior was substantially stronger when the criterion variable represented a choice among alternatives ($r = .77$) than when it did not ($r = .47$).

More recent studies have shown that the Fishbein and Ajzen model is predictive of consumer behavior across cultures. For example, Bagozzi, Wong, Abe, and Bergami (2000) found that the theory of reasoned action predicted fast food restaurant patronage in samples from the U.S., Italy, Japan, and the People's Republic of China. However, they also found that the effects were generally stronger in the U.S. sample, and that the relative influence of attitudes and subjective norms differed across samples. Specifically, those in Western cultures, which are more individualistic (independent) and emphasize internal aspects of the self in decision-making (e.g., be oneself), showed much stronger correlations between attitudes and intentions than those in Eastern cultures. In contrast, those in Eastern cultures, which are more collectivistic (dependent) and emphasize how personal actions influence the group, showed much stronger correlations between subjective norms and intentions than those in Western cultures.

In general, the theory of reasoned action model is attractive to marketers because it affords them the ability to determine what components of intentions to target. For example, because the theory is quantifiable, it is relatively easy for marketers to determine all of the components of the model through surveys. This allows them to determine which beliefs about the consequences of a purchase decision are salient, how these beliefs are evaluated, which others' opinions about the behavior are most salient, and how motivated consumers are to comply with what those others think. Just as important, for any particular product or service, regression analyses can reveal the relative weights that the attitudes and subjective norms represent. Consequently, each variable in the entire equation represents a marketing opportunity. Advertisements and collateral marketing can be created to change the belief about the behavior (a Volvo results in greater safety), the evaluation of the belief (how important safety is), what important others (e.g., parents, spouse) would want you to do, and how much you care about what they think.

In sum, the theory of reasoned action has had substantial impact on marketing research, both academic and in marketing practice. It was one of the first models that provided a clear articulation and quantification of the inputs into behavioral intentions, and did so in a way that was easily measurable, and thus easy for marketers to implement. However, one limitation of the model is that it restricts itself to volitional behaviors. Thus, the model has little to say about behaviors performed outside of awareness and specific intention. In fact, the model specifies that thoughts must mediate actions, and thus does not easily allow for the possibility of spontaneous, impulsive types of behaviors or other influences outside of conscious volition (mood, anger, etc., Eagly & Chaiken, 1993; for a spirited debate of these issues, see Fishbein & Middlestadt, 1995, 1997; Haugtvedt & The Consumer Psychology Seminar, 1997; Herr, 1995; Miniard & Barone, 1997; Schwarz, 1997).

To address the possibility that there may be multiple routes to persuasion (and the formation of attitudes) in general (for a review, see Chaiken & Trope, 1999), dual process models of attitude formation and cognitive processing were developed. In the next section, we review the elaboration likelihood model (ELM) of persuasion (Petty & Cacioppo, 1986), which has been the dominant persuasion model in consumer research over the last three decades.

Elaboration Likelihood Model

The ELM is a model of persuasion that proposes two distinct routes to persuasion, the central route and the peripheral route (for a more in-depth discussion of the ELM, see chapter 9 of this volume), which refer to attitude changes that occur through different levels of evaluative processing. In the central route, attitudes are formed through an extensive, effortful process that scrutinizes a message for the quality of its arguments. In many respects, this highly effortful central route to persuasion resembles the highly effortful process of attitude formation described by the theory of reasoned action. In contrast, the peripheral route refers to attitude formation that is based on nonargument cues, such as mood, source attractiveness (when not relevant to the argument quality), and heuristics (e.g., number of arguments, source expertise, message length).

The ELM provides an integrative model that addresses some of the perplexing inconsistencies in earlier attitude research. As Petty and Wegener (1999) note, attitude research in the late 1970s was in a remarkable state of disarray. Commonly accepted variables of attitude change, such as the mood of the receiver and the credibility of the message source, often produced conflicting effects (cf. Kelman & Hovland, 1953; Sternthal, Dholakia, & Leavitt, 1978; Zanna, Kiesler, & Pilkonis, 1970). The ELM was intended to provide a unifying framework that could explain how the classic inputs into persuasion (source, message, recipient, context) could have different impacts, depending on the particular route to persuasion. Thus, either the central route or the peripheral route can be evoked in various situations involving different message types, individual differences among receivers, and environmental (or situational) factors. Persuasion can be effective in both routes, although the strength, durability, and resistance of attitudes formed via the two routes may differ (Haugtvedt & Kasmer, 2008; Petty & Wegener, 1998).

The underlying mechanism of the ELM is indicated in its name: elaboration likelihood.

The model posits that when people have both the motivation and the ability to process the information presented in a persuasive communication, the likelihood of message elaboration is high, and people will take the central route. In contrast, when the likelihood of message elaboration is low as a result of either lack of motivation or ability to process information, people tend to take the peripheral route to persuasion. Which route is taken has a number of important implications. First, it determines which components of a persuasive communication will be the most effective, either central cues (message quality) or peripheral cues (mood, expertise, source attractiveness). This helps explain the rather counterintuitive finding that quality of the message may have little effect on persuasion in some situations, such as when motivation or ability to process the arguments is low, but other seemingly comparatively trivial variables (liking for background music in an ad) may have strong effects.

A second important implication of which route to persuasion is taken pertains to the qualities of the attitudes formed. The two routes may yield attitudes that are of equal valence and extremity. However, other important qualities of the attitudes will differ as a function of the two routes. Attitudes formed through the central route tend to be more highly accessible, held with more confidence, more predictive of behavior, more resistant to change, and persist longer over time, compared to attitudes formed through the peripheral route (Petty & Krosnick, 1995). Attitudes formed through the central route result from active information processing and a well-integrated cognitive structure, whereas attitudes formed through the peripheral route are led by passive acceptance or rejection of simple cues and are weaker, particularly over the long term.

Tests of the Model

Given that the classic persuasion inputs (source, message, recipient, context) that the ELM addresses are all critical components of advertising, the ELM has had substantial influence on persuasion research in marketing and advertising. One of the first studies in consumer behavior to employ the ELM investigated the role of product involvement (Petty, Cacioppo, & Schumann, 1983). Petty et al. manipulated three factors: motivation to process the information in the ad, central cues, and peripheral cues. Motivation was manipulated through product involvement (personally relevant or irrelevant), the central cue was manipulated through argument quality (strong or weak arguments), and the peripheral cue was manipulated via the source (celebrity or noncelebrity endorser). Supporting the ELM, argument quality had a greater effect on attitudes under high than low involvement conditions, whereas the celebrity endorser had a greater effect under low than high involvement conditions.

As noted, even though attitudes formed via both the central and peripheral routes may produce apparently equivalent attitudes (reflected by attitude scores), the two routes produce attitudes that differ on other important qualities. In a series of studies, Haugtvedt and colleagues tested the elaboration-persistence and elaboration-resistance hypotheses, which state that the more extensive elaboration that occurs through the central route produces more persistent attitudes and attitudes more resistant to change (Haugtvedt & Petty, 1992; Haugtvedt, Schumann, Schneier, & Warren, 1994; Haugtvedt & Wegener, 1994). These studies showed that whether degree of elaboration was operationalized via individual differences variables (e.g., need for cognition, Cacioppo & Petty, 1982) or situational manipulations of personal relevance, central route attitudes persisted longer over time and changed less after exposure to an opposing message than did peripheral route attitudes.

One aspect of the ELM that has caused some confusion is precisely what makes a cue central or peripheral. Consider the example of source attractiveness. This variable is typically referred to as a peripheral cue, which it often is. Examples might include automobile and beer ads, which often employ attractive endorsers. Clearly, the attractiveness of the endorser has little relation to the message in these instances. However, that is not always the case. In some instances, endorser attractiveness may be perceived to be very relevant to the message. For example, the attractiveness of endorsers or models may be considered particularly relevant for certain products but not others. Consistent with this notion, research shows that an endorser's physical attractiveness serves as a central cue for beauty products, such as shampoo (Petty & Cacioppo, 1980) and razors (Kahle & Homer, 1985), yet other aspects of the source, such as their celebrity status (with attractiveness held constant) serve as a peripheral cue for the same product (razors; Petty et al., 1983; see also Kang & Herr, 2006).

Shavitt, Swan, Lowrey, and Wänke (1994) directly examined the relevance hypothesis by testing the proposition that the influence of endorser attractiveness as a peripheral or central cue depends on the message processing goals that receivers have at the time of exposure. Participants were exposed to ads for a fictitious restaurant that was ostensibly supposed to open soon. Processing route was manipulated through personal involvement (to open in a local or distant area), and endorser attractiveness was also varied. The third factor, motive for processing, was manipulated via a priming task intended to make either sensory or image attributes salient. Participants were primed with either a sensory cue, in which they rated 20 sensory experiences (e.g., smelling fresh air, feeling sore muscles) on how good or bad they made them feel), or an image cue in which they rated 20 image events (wearing a Rolex, losing a job) on how much they would make an impression on others. The results from both attitude ratings and cognitive responses showed that under image prime conditions, endorser attractiveness served as a central cue (influenced attitudes under high but not low involvement conditions), but under sensory prime conditions, the opposite effects occurred.

Extensions of the Model

The general notion of dual routes to persuasion has led to advances in other aspects of attitudes and persuasion research that have had a strong input on marketing and advertising research (Haugtvedt & Kasmer, 2008). One example is the notion of metacognitive processing, or "thinking about thinking." This line of research looks at the extent to which thoughts about thought processes involved in attitude formation affect attitudes, particularly for attitude qualities such as attitude confidence, resistance, and certainty (for a review, see Petty, 2006). For example, attitude certainty tends to increase when people perceive themselves as resisting a persuasive communication (Tormala & Petty, 2002). In a follow-up to that set of studies, Tormala and Petty (2004) demonstrated that this effect depends on source credibility. Participants' product attitudes were more certain and predicted behavior better when they perceived themselves to be resisting the persuasive communication than when they did not, but only when the communication came from an expert source.

In sum, the ELM has proved to be a robust model for predicting the effects of advertising and marketing messages on consumer attitudes and behavior. It provides a clear theoretical framework for understanding the conditions under which typical executional variables will have an effect, thereby providing both a guide for how marketers can maximize the persuasiveness of their ads and how consumers can maximize their resistance to those ads. More recently, other models of persuasion have been developed that provide a somewhat different focus on how consumers process persuasive communications, and in particular the thoughts consumers have about motives underlying messages. In the next section, we analyze the persuasion knowledge model.

Persuasion Knowledge Model

Unlike the theory of reasoned action and elaboration likelihood model, both of which originated in the field of social psychology, the persuasion knowledge model (Friestad & Wright, 1994) is uniquely marketing-focused. Although the model could likely be applied to persuasion in other contexts, to date its focus has been on the interaction between marketers and consumers. Because the model is relatively new and has had little exposure outside of the marketing literature, we begin with a more thorough description of the model compared to the previous ones we discussed, and then proceed to discuss recent tests of the model.

The persuasion knowledge model was formally introduced in 1994 as the first model to explain how knowledge of marketers' persuasion tactics affects consumers' responses to such tactics (Friestad & Wright, 1994). The model asserts that over time, consumers develop knowledge of marketers' persuasion tactics and, in doing so, become better able to adapt and respond to such attempts in order to achieve their own personal goals. Figure 19.1. provides a depiction of the model and its components (for a review, see Campbell & Kirmani, 2008).

Friestad and Wright (1994) decompose the persuasion process into two primary elements: the target and the agent. The target refers to the intended recipient of the persuasion attempt (the consumer), whereas the agent represents whomever the target identifies as the creator of the persuasion attempt (the marketer). The persuasion attempt encompasses not only the message of the agent, which itself is influenced by the agent's knowledge of the topic, target, and the effectiveness and applicability of different persuasion tactics, but also the target's perception of the agent's persuasion strategy.

The persuasion knowledge model presumes that consumers formulate coping strategies in order to decide how to respond to marketers' persuasion attempts in a way that optimally aligns with their own goals. When creating such strategies, consumer targets are said to be motivated to utilize and allocate cognitive resources between three different knowledge structures: knowledge of persuasion, knowledge of the agent, and knowledge of the persuasion topic(s). A target's knowledge of persuasion typically depends on three factors: experience, cognitive ability, and motivation. Experience and cognitive ability are straightforward; however, motivation can be influenced in a number of ways.

Figure 19.1   The Persuasion Knowledge Model

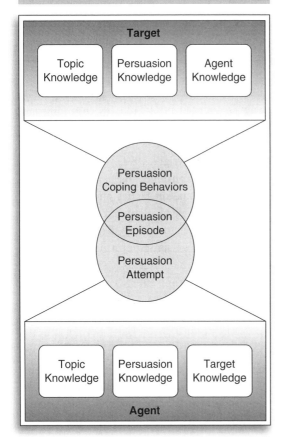

Source: "The Persuasion Knowledge Model: How people cope with persuasion attempts," by M. Friestad and P. Wright, 1994, *Journal of Consumer Research, 21,* p. 1–31. Copyright 1994 by University of Chicago Press. Used with permission.

It can be enhanced by factors such as unfamiliarity with the agent, similar persuasion behaviors having been observed in a different context, use of an uncharacteristic persuasion tactic, or belief that knowledge of the agent is outdated. It can also be deterred by factors such as difficulty in the identification of the agent, perceived leeway of a salesperson, or perceived irrelevance of the agent in the target's personal, professional, and marketplace relationships. Cultural differences may also play a role in motivation. For example, individuals in independent self-construal (e.g., Western)

cultures may interpret persuasion attempts predominantly in terms of a personal attitude on the persuasion topic, whereas individuals in interdependent self-construal cultures (e.g., Eastern) may interpret such attempts in terms of a personal attitude on the social relationship with the agent. Such different interpretations may lead to different persuasion responses.

The interaction of the target's coping behaviors and the agent's persuasion attempt forms what Friestad and Wright (1994) refer to as the persuasion episode. The persuasion episode may include one encounter, such as a sales presentation, or multiple episodes, such as a series of television advertisements presented over time. Furthermore, consumers and marketers may switch roles, with the consumer becoming the agent and the marketer becoming the target when, for example, a consumer attempts to negotiate or bargain, or otherwise influence a firm's selling tactics in any way. Regardless of who occupies which role, the model assumes that both agents and targets want to maximize the effectiveness of their persuasion production and persuasion coping behavior respectively.

The persuasion knowledge model also asserts that consumers utilize persuasion knowledge to evaluate marketers' persuasion behavior on two primary dimensions: perceived effectiveness and perceived appropriateness. Consumers judge persuasion behavior to be effective when it seems to have produced psychological effects that strongly influence purchase decisions. Consumers deem persuasion behavior appropriate to the extent it appears to be ethical or normatively acceptable (i.e., within the rules of the game), especially with regard to consumers' relationship expectations. For example, if a marketer's persuasion attempts are perceived as disrespectful or unexpectedly careless, it will likely lead to a negative consumer evaluation, potentially damaging brand equity and the reputation of the firm overall.

The model also rests on the fundamental assumption that people are "moving targets." In other words, the validity of a consumer's knowledge about the marketer, the marketer's persuasion tactics, and the persuasion topic will ebb and flow over time. A similar thing can be said for marketers, as their knowledge of consumers' interests, preferences, and expectations is also likely to fluctuate over time. As a result, causal relationships between firm behavior and consumer responses are prone to changing over time as well, and, as such, must be reexamined every so often to ensure that they are still valid.

Tests of the Model

A number of studies have provided support for key components of the model. For example, one key component is the notion that consumers have well-developed knowledge structures about persuasion tactics and that people generally understand the motives of persuasion tactics. Consistent with this proposition, research suggests that lay people do have clear knowledge of persuasion tactics of advertising, and the beliefs of lay people about how advertising works are actually quite similar to those of academic marketing scholars (Friestad & Wright, 1995). Moreover, these persuasion knowledge structures are evident in middle school children. Children's knowledge of advertising tactics tends to increase with age, and knowledge about these tactics is positively correlated with skepticism toward advertising (Boush, Friestad, & Rose, 1994; for a review, see Wright, Friestad, & Boush, 2005).

Another aspect of the model that has received support is that consumers make spontaneous, active inferences about agent tactics when consumers encounter persuasive appeals. People use simple cues such as perceived effort a company puts into an appeal as a signal of the company's belief in their product (Kirmani & Wright, 1989) and that these inferences can result from cues as simple as the size of an ad (Kirmani, 1990). Consumers also have schemas (and thus expectations) of tactics used for various product categories and that these schemas guide processing of the persuasion attempts

(Hardesty, Bearden, & Carlson, 2007). Moreover, consumers use their knowledge of persuasion tactics and underlying motives to form strategies to cope with marketers' persuasion attempts, and aspects of the consumer (their relationship with the marketer and their experience with persuasive tactics) guide which strategy is employed (Kirmani & Campbell, 2004).

The general notion that consumers understand the motives of companies as well as salespeople, and that consumers have schemas and expectations about persuasion tactics, has important and sometimes counterintuitive implications about the effectiveness of persuasion attempts. We know from the elaboration likelihood model and other similar persuasion models that consumers often do not pay close attention to persuasion attempts. In persuasion knowledge terms, in these instances, consumers may not have a persuasion knowledge schema fully activated. Thus, one would expect that when knowledge of persuasion tactics is low, persuasion would likely proceed through the peripheral route to persuasion. However, the process of activating persuasion knowledge may lead to central route processing, which in some cases may lead to decreased persuasion. Consistent with this reasoning, DeCarlo (2005) showed that when persuasion knowledge was activated by increasing the salience of ulterior motives, attitudes towards a salesperson were actually more favorable, and purchase intentions were lower when the strength of the sales message arguments were weaker (mildly positive) than when they were stronger, but the reverse was true when salience of ulterior motives was low.

Other research also supports the notion that the activation of persuasion knowledge can have a detrimental effect. For example, take the case of flattery in personal selling. A substantial amount of research has shown that flattery can have positive effects on attitudes toward the flatterer in a variety of domains (Gordon, 1996). However, the persuasion knowledge model suggests that if this flattery comes from a salesperson, and persuasion knowledge (e.g., ulterior motives) is activated, then flattery may actually backfire. In fact, research suggests that this is indeed the case. Flattery by salespeople can spontaneously activate suspicions of ulterior motives, oftentimes even more than a situation warrants (sinister attribution error; Kramer, 1994), and thus decrease rather than increase persuasion (Campbell & Kirmani, 2000).

Although the findings regarding detrimental effects of salesperson flattery fit nicely within the persuasion knowledge model, other research suggests that the process may not be that simple. In a provocative set of studies, Chan and Sengupta (2010) showed that flattery by marketers actually produces two attitudes, one explicit (of which one is aware and can control) and one implicit (outside a person's awareness), which coexist with each other in memory. The explicit attitude, which is what most prior research has assessed, did indeed appear to be corrected for, or discounted. Explicit attitudes were always more negative than implicit ones. More importantly, implicit attitudes were much stronger predictors of behavioral intention than were explicit attitudes. These results suggest that even though consumers are knowledgeable of persuasive tactics and attempt to correct for them, they may not always be successful, even though their responses on attitude scales suggest they are.

As the research reviewed clearly shows, persuasion knowledge can be easily activated by environmental cues. One implication of the model, and a challenge for marketers, is to understand how to navigate consumers' propensities to activate persuasion knowledge. For example, one marketing persuasion tactic that has seen a large increase in usage is product placement (Shrum, 2004, 2012), which is the practice of inserting branded products into films, television, programs, and other media (McCarty, 2004; McCarty & Lowrey, 2012). One question that has worried advertisers is which placements are most effective. Placements can vary greatly, from simple, subtle background placements to more overt placements that include a shot of the brand name or even a mention in the dialogue. Although effectiveness may depend on how it is measured (e.g., via recall, attitudes, etc., Law & Braun-LaTour, 2004), the persuasion knowledge model makes some predictions about this process. If prominence of a placement in film is sufficient to cause viewers to notice the placement, it may activate persuasion knowledge and thus reduce brand attitudes. Consistent with this reasoning, Cowley and Barron (2008) found that prominent placements produced more negative attitudes for those who were high in program involvement (and thus more likely to notice the placement) than for those who were low in program involvement. Thus, not properly managing consumers' persuasion knowledge activation can be detrimental to the goals of particular marketing tactics.

In sum, the key contribution of Friestad and Wright's persuasion knowledge model is that consumers are active and often knowledgeable participants in marketers' persuasion efforts, and that their persuasion knowledge, motivation, cognitive ability, and goals are all factors that should be taken into account when examining the effectiveness of any marketing attempt at persuasion. Furthermore, the interaction between marketers' persuasion efforts and consumers' strategies for coping with those efforts is one that is constantly changing, as the persuasion knowledge of both consumers and marketers varies over time. Finally, the model is useful for both the targets and the agents. It provides agents (marketers) with an understanding of how consumers react to persuasion attempts and guidance on how to minimize persuasion knowledge activation. For targets (consumers), it provides a model for how they may actively discount or correct for persuasion attempts, how they may actually overcorrect in some situations, but also how their corrections may ultimately not be sufficient (Chan & Sengupta, 2010).

Nonconscious Processing and Persuasion

The three theories just reviewed represent the primary theoretical models that have impacted marketing, advertising, and consumer behavior research over the last few decades. These models continue to be tested and refined, particularly the elaboration likelihood model and persuasion knowledge model. However, in the most recent years, the area of research that has had perhaps the most provocative impact is the role of non-conscious processing in consumer judgment and decision making (Bargh, 2002; Dijksterhuis, Smith, van Baaren, & Wigboldus, 2005). As a number of scholars of nonconscious processing have noted, there are different aspects of aware-ness that may play a role in how environmental features may influence consumer outcomes out-side of consumer awareness, and lack of awareness of any one of these may lead to nonconscious effects (Chartrand, 2005). Three particular aspects are important: awareness of an environ-mental stimuli, awareness of the automatic pro-cesses that influence behavior, and awareness of the actual outcome.

A good example of lack of awareness of envi-ronmental stimuli is through subliminal presen-tation. The notion of subliminal persuasion is one with which most students and scholars of persuasion are very familiar, and the potential use of the concept has long been a fear of many lay people. Interestingly, the reason for this fear is captured by the persuasion knowledge model: people worry that they will not know they are being persuaded, and thus their persuasion knowledge will not be activated, leaving them vulnerable to the persuasive communication.

Although there have been quite a number of scholarly writings dismissing the notion of sub-liminal effects in general and subliminal persua-sion in particular (Pratkanis & Aronson, 1992), we now know that subliminal effects are actually fairly easy to produce, at least in the lab (for a review, see Dijksterhuis, Aarts, & Smith, 2005). Examples include the mere exposure effect, in which sub-liminal exposure to various stimuli increased liking for those stimuli in a linear function of frequency of exposure (Zajonc, 1968), subliminal exposure to positive versus negative symbols prior to a supra-liminal presentation of an image that influenced liking for the image (Murphy & Zajonc, 1993), subliminal exposure to stereotypical information

that influenced behavior in the direction of the stereotype (Bargh, Chen, & Burrows, 1996), sub-liminal presentation of threatening stimuli that induced anxiety (Robles, Smith, Carver, & Wellens, 1987), and subliminal conditioning of attitudes (Krosnick, Betz, Jussim, & Linn, 1992), among a host of others.

Some recent research has actually demon-strated subliminal persuasion in a setting concep-tually similar to the lay notion of subliminal advertising. Strahan, Spencer, and Zanna (2002) primed thirst by subliminally exposing partici-pants to either thirst- related or non-thirst-related words. Although they did not find any differences in self-reported thirst, those subliminally primed with thirst drank more of a liquid whose brand name suggested a thirst-quenching attribute (Super Quencher) than of a liquid whose brand name suggested a non-thirst-related attribute (PowerPro). A second study replicated the same general effect by showing that subliminally primed mood (via sad faces) caused participants to prefer a music choice that was described as mood lifting to music described as powerful. Thus, these stud-ies suggest that although subliminal priming may not create needs (i.e., make someone thirsty), priming the goal (quench thirst) can influence choices that can help achieve the goal.

Although the specter of nonconscious persua-sion has always been held in fear and fascination by consumers, nonconscious influences on beha-vior do not require subliminal presentation of the primes. As Bargh has pointed out a number of times (cf. Bargh, 1992, 1999; see also Chartrand, 2005), if people are unaware of how the prime may affect them, they are just as likely to be influ-enced. For example, when people walk into a store, they may be aware of music being played (supraliminal presentation). What they may not know, however, is that the tempo of music can affect the speed with which consumers shop. Slow music causes people to go slower in their shopping, fast music causes them to shop faster (Milliman, 1982).

Thus, consumers may not know that depart-ment stores are playing slower music to get them to shop longer (and thus spend more money), whereas fast food stores are playing faster music to decrease customer dining time and increase customer turnover. As another example, when consumers go into a grocery store to buy some fruit, they are clearly aware of the sign that advertises two lemons for $1. What they are unlikely to be aware of, however, is that the number chosen in the advertisement influences their buying behavior independent of need. Thus, consumers will tend to buy more items when those items are advertised as four lemons for $2 than when they are advertised as two lemons for $1 (Wansink, Kent, & Hoch, 1998). This effect results from an anchoring and adjustment process (Tversky & Kahneman, 1974), in which the applications of the primes are conscious, but because consumers are unaware of the primes' effects, consumers have no more ability to combat the primes' effects than they do when primes are presented outside their awareness.

Another example of how conscious environmental primes may influence nonconscious, goal-directed behavior can be seen in a set of experiments by Chartrand, Huber, Shiv, and Tanner (2008). Chartrand et al. primed groups of participants with different goals (value vs. image) via a scrambled sentence task. Later, participants were given a fictional scenario in which they had to choose between a pair of socks that represented a good value (Hanes socks at $6 for two pairs) or a good image (Nike socks at $5.25 for one pair). When participants were primed with the image goal, they were much more likely to choose the Nikes (48%) than when they were primed with the value goal (18%).

Finally, conscious environmental primes can exert an influence on consumer behavior if consumers are unaware of the actual outcomes of their behavior. Brian Wansink and colleagues have developed an extensive program of research that looks at how simple environmental cues influence eating habits despite conflicting goals (Wansink, 2010). For example, people tend to eat more when the same portions are served on larger plates or bowls than when they are served on smaller ones. The larger plates make the amount of food on the plate look smaller relative to the size of the plate, and thus people underestimate how much they are actually consuming (Wansink & van Ittersum, 2006).

New Directions in Persuasion in the Marketing Place: The Next Big Thing(s)

So what's next in commercial persuasion? From our vantage point, we see the field progressing in three different areas that have some degree of overlap and synergy. These are a continued intensive investigation of nonconscious processing and persuasion, a renewed focus on the role of mood in persuasion (and consumer decision-making in general), and the incorporation of social cognitive neuroscience into the study of persuasion and decision-making processes.

Nonconscious Processing and Persuasion

In our opinion, the previous review of nonconscious processing and persuasion barely touches the surface of research currently being conducted. As we noted in the previous section, what makes consumers so fearful of subliminal advertising is the notion that they may not be able to defend against an unwanted persuasion attempt. However, stimuli need not be outside of conscious awareness to persuade: Supraliminal primes may also influence attitudes and behavior without consumers' awareness if they are not aware of the influence of the prime on their attitudes and behaviors.

Consequently, we believe that marketing and consumer research will increasingly focus how supraliminal stimuli can influence consumer behavior outside of consumers' awareness. One example we touched on earlier is nonconscious goal pursuit. As Morsella and Bargh (2011) note, material objects can prime goals. For example, scents such as cleaning fluid can prime goals of cleanliness (Holland, Hendriks, & Aarts, 2005), seeing dollar bills can prime greed motives (Vohs, Mead, & Goode, 2006), and briefcases can prime competitiveness but backpacks cooperation (Kay, Wheeler, Bargh, & Ross, 2004). It is not too difficult to imagine that the marketing environment can be manipulated to influence goal activation. Indeed, North, Hargreaves, and McKendrick (1999) demonstrated that manipulating the type of in-store music (French vs. German) increased sales of French and German wines, respectively.

Mood and Emotion

The effects of mood and emotions on consumer behavior are well-documented. Much of marketing efforts are designed to put consumers in a more positive mood, and most of the extant marketing research has focused on the effect of mood valence. However, more recent theoretical models of emotion have expanded the inquiry to look at how different moods of the same valence (e.g., sadness vs. anger) may produce qualitatively different decisions, depending on the context. For example, Lerner and colleagues have proposed the Appraisal-Tendency Framework as a model to distinguish the effects of different types of emotions on decision-making (Han, Lerner, & Keltner, 2007; Lerner & Keltner, 2000).

They detail in particular how two similarly valenced emotions—fear and anger—produce different perceptions of risk. Fear, which is associated with low certainly, was associated with increased perceptions of risk, whereas anger, which is associated with high certainty, decreased risk perceptions. In another demonstration using different emotions having similar valences (sadness and disgust), they showed that sadness, which is associated with an appraisal theme of loss, increased choice prices, whereas disgust, which is associated with wanting to expel, reduced choice prices. In contrast, both sadness and disgust reduced selling prices (Lerner, Small, & Lowenstein, 2004). Thus, disgust eliminated the well-documented endowment effect (Kahneman, Knetsch, & Thaler, 1990),

whereas sadness actually reversed it. It is important to note here that the emotions that influenced those decisions were incidental (primed by a prior irrelevant situation).

Other models of affect have also been introduced in the consumer behavior literature. For example, what is referred to as the Affect-based Evaluation and Regulation Model (Andrade & Cohen, 2007; see also Shiv, 2007), integrates both goal-directed (affect regulation) and informational (affect evaluation) properties of affect. The key contribution of this research is its focus on the underlying mediators of each component: The link between affective evaluation and behavior is mediated by cognitive appraisals, whereas the link between affective regulation and behavior is mediated by motivational appraisals. The general framework has been used to make predictions in a variety of disparate domains, including risk taking, eating, and helping behavior. Although this work and that of Lerner and colleagues has primarily focused on decision making more generally, and not persuasion in particular, the next generation of persuasion research will likely focus on applying these concepts to persuasion situations.

Social Cognitive Neuroscience

The third area we see becoming a focal area of research in the coming years is the application of social cognitive neuroscience to persuasion. Advances in neuroscience techniques now allow social and cognitive scientists to determine neural correlates of many of the mental processes that are integral parts of persuasion theories (e.g., emotions, memory, thought activation, etc.). Integrating neuroscience with persuasion theories allows for more direct tests of existing theory, potential refinements of theory, and tests of new theories (Shiv, 2007). Consider the debate around the theory of reasoned action, and its stipulation that thoughts mediate action. The use of neuroscience techniques may allow for the resolution of this debate by tracing neural outputs during persuasion situations. Similarly, the notion that certain types of cues (e.g., attractive models) may function as peripheral ones in some situations but central in others have the potential for direct tests using neuroscience techniques.

Some neuroscience research on persuasion has already begun to test aspects of the persuasion process and existing persuasion theory. For example, results from fMRI scans have been shown to predict behavior change over and above self-reports (Falk, Berkman, Mann, Harrison, & Lieberman, 2010). In tests associated with the elaboration likelihood model, fMRI scans were used to investigate the neural processes that predict effects of source expertise on attitude development and change (Klucharev, Smidts, & Fernandez, 2008). Neuroscience techniques have been used to document actual changes in perceptions of pain resulting from placebos (Wager et al., 2004), to show that cognitive dissonance occurs automatically independent of explicit memory (Lieberman, Ochsner, Gilbert, & Schacter, 2001; see also Shiv, 2007), and that the "pain of paying" is more than a metaphor by showing that spending money activates an area of the brain that is also active during the experience of physical pain (Knutson, Rick, Wimmer, Prelec, & Lowenstein, 2007).

Conclusion

As noted in the introduction, persuasion is all around us, and even more so in a consumer society such as the U.S., where marketing and persuasion are virtually synonymous. Thus, where better to understand persuasion principles, develop new research questions, and test new persuasion models than the marketplace? The different streams of research reviewed here just touch on the many different theories of persuasion that have application to marketing contexts. Rather than take a comprehensive approach to reviewing persuasion theories and applications in marketing, we have attempted to highlight the theories that have had

the most recent impact. Across those theories, there are important overlaps as well as differences. Many of the differences were developed as researchers noted that current models had difficulty accounting for certain patterns of data. That will surely continue, and so new discoveries should be welcome but not surprising.

One type of new discovery that we highlighted at the end of this chapter pertains to nonconscious processing. This represents one of the exciting new frontiers in persuasion research, as researchers attempt to determine just what types of judgments are conscious and which ones are driven by more automatic (nonconscious) responses to stimuli. As researchers attempt to answer the question of what consciousness is actually good for (Bargh & Chartrand, 1999; Baumeister, Mele, & Vohs, 2010), the more we learn about what types of consumer judgments are actually driven by nonconscious processes. Although it is perhaps uncomfortable to realize how little control we actually have over daily decisions, the more we learn about how these persuasion processes work, the better we should be at making good decisions.

References

Andrade, E. B., & Cohen, J. B. (2007). Affect-based evaluation and regulation as mediators of behavior. The role of affect in risk taking, helping and eating patterns. In K. D. Vohs, R. F. Baumeister, & G. Loewenstein. *Do emotions help or hurt decision making? A hedgefoxian perspective* (pp. 35–68). New York, NY: Russell Sage.

Bagozzi, R. P., Wong, N., Abe, S., & Bergami M. (2000). Cultural and situational contingencies and the theory of reasoned action: Application to fast food restaurant consumption. *Journal of Consumer Psychology, 9,* 97–106.

Bargh, J. A. (1992). Why subliminality does not matter to social psychology: Awareness of the stimulus versus awareness of its influence. In R. F. Boorstein & T. F. Pitman (Eds.), *Perception without awareness: Cognitive, clinical, and social perspectives* (pp. 236–255). New York, NY: Guilford Press.

Bargh, J. A. (1999). The cognitive monster: The case against controllability of automatic stereotype effects. In S. Chaiken & Y. Trope (Eds.), *Dual-process theories in social psychology* (pp. 361–382). New York, NY: Guilford Press.

Bargh, J. A. (2002). Losing consciousness: Automatic influences on consumer judgment, behavior, and motivation. *Journal of Consumer Research, 29,* 280–285.

Bargh, J. A. (2005). Bypassing the will: Toward demystifying the nonconscious control of social behavior. In R. R. Hassin, J. S. Uleman, & J. A. Bargh (Eds.), *The new unconscious* (pp. 37–58). New York, NY: Oxford University Press.

Bargh, J. A., & Chartrand, T. L. (1999). The unbearable automaticity of being. *American Psychologist, 54,* 462–479.

Bargh, J. A., Chen, M., & Burrows, L. (1996). Automaticity of social behavior: Direct effects of trait construct and stereotype activation on action. *Journal of Personality and Social Psychology, 71,* 230–244.

Baumeister, R. F., Mele, A. R., & Vohs, K. D. (Eds.) (2010). *Free will and consciousness: How might they work?* New York, NY: Oxford University Press.

Bonfield, E. H. (1974). Attitude, social influence, personal norm, and intention interactions as related to brand purchase behavior. *Journal of Marketing Research, 11,* 379–389.

Boush, D. M., Friestad, M., & Rose, G. M. (1994). Adolescent skepticism toward TV advertising and knowledge of advertiser tactics. *Journal of Consumer Research, 21,* 165–175.

Brannon, L. A., & Brock, T. C. (1994). The subliminal persuasion controversy: Reality, enduring fable, and Polonius's wheel. In S. Shavitt & T. C. Brock (Eds.), *Persuasion: Psychological insights and perspectives* (pp. 279–293). Boston, MA: Allyn and Bacon.

Brinberg, D., & Cummings, V. (1984). Purchasing generic prescription drugs: An analysis using two behavioral intention models. In T. Kinnear (Ed.), *Advances in consumer research* (Vol. 11, pp. 229–234). Provo, UT: Association for Consumer Research.

Cacioppo, J. T., & Petty, R. E. (1982). The need for cognition. *Journal of Personality and Social Psychology, 42,* 116–131.

Campbell, M. C., & Kirmani, A. (2000). Consumers' use of persuasion knowledge: The effects of accessibility and cognitive capacity on perceptions of an influence agent. *Journal of Consumer Research, 27,* 69–83.

Campbell, M. C., & Kirmani, A. (2008). I know what you're doing and why you're doing it: The use of persuasion knowledge model in consumer research. In C. P. Haugtvedt, P. Herr, & F. R. Kardes (Eds.), *Handbook of consumer psychology* (pp. 449–573). New York, NY: Erlbaum.

Chaiken, S., & Trope, Y. (Eds.). (1999). *Dual process theories in social psychology.* New York, NY: Guilford Press.

Chan, E., & Sengupta, J. (2010). Insincere flattery actually works: A dual attitudes perspective. *Journal of Marketing Research, 47,* 122–133.

Chartrand, T. L. (2005). The role of conscious awareness in consumer behavior. *Journal of Consumer Psychology, 15,* 203–210.

Chartrand, T. L., Huber, J., Shiv, B., & Tanner, R. J. (2008). Nonconscious goals and consumer choice. *Journal of Consumer Research, 35,* 189–201.

Cowley, E., & Barron, C. (2008). When product placement goes wrong: The effects of program liking and placement prominence. *Journal of Advertising, 37*(1), 89–98.

DeCarlo, T. E. (2005). The effects of sales message and suspicion of ulterior motives on salesperson evaluation. *Journal of Consumer Psychology, 15,* 238–249.

Dijksterhuis, A., Aarts, H., & Smith, P. K. (2005). The power of the subliminal: On subliminal persuasion and other potential applications. In R. R. Hassin, J. S. Uleman, & J. A. Bargh (Eds.), *The New Unconscious* (pp. 77–106). New York, NY: Oxford University Press.

Dijksterhuis, A., Smith, P. K., van Baaren, R. B., & Wigboldus, D. H. (2005). The unconscious consumer: Effects of environment on consumer behavior. *Journal of Consumer Psychology, 15,* 193–202.

Eagly, A. H., & Chaiken, S. (Eds.). (1993). *The psychology of attitudes* (2nd ed.). Orlando, FL: Harcourt Brace.

Falk, E. B., Berkman, E. T., Mann, T., Harrison, B., & Lieberman, M. D. (2010). Predicting persuasion-induced behavior change from the brain. *The Journal of Neuroscience, 30*(25): 8421–8424. doi: 10.1523/JNEUROSCI.0063-10.2010

Fazio, R. H. (1986). How do attitudes guide behavior? In R. M. Sorrentino & E. T. Higgins (Eds.),

The handbook of motivation and cognition: Foundations of social behavior (pp. 204–243). New York, NY: Guilford Press.

Fishbein, M., & Ajzen, I. (1975). *Beliefs, attitudes, intentions, and behavior: An introduction to theory and research.* Reading, MA: Addison-Wesley.

Fishbein, M., & Ajzen, I. (2010). *Predicting and changing behavior: The reasoned action approach.* New York, NY: Psychology Press.

Fishbein, M., & Middlestadt, S. (1995). Noncognitive effects on attitude formation and change: Fact or artifact? *Journal of Consumer Psychology, 4,* 181–202.

Fishbein, M., & Middlestadt, S. (1997). A striking lack of evidence for nonbelief-based attitude formation and change: A response to five commentaries. *Journal of Consumer Psychology, 6,* 107–115.

Friestad, M., & Wright, P. (1994). The persuasion knowledge model: How people cope with persuasion attempts. *Journal of Consumer Research, 21,* 1–31.

Friestad, M., & Wright, P. (1995). Persuasion knowledge: Lay people's and researchers' beliefs about the psychology of advertising. *Journal of Consumer Research, 22,* 62–74.

Gordon, R. A. (1996). Impact of ingratiation on judgments and evaluations: A meta-analytic investigation. *Journal of Personality and Social Psychology, 71,* 54–70.

Han, S., Lerner, J. S., & Keltner, D. (2007). Feelings and consumer decision making: The Appraisal-Tendency Framework. *Journal of Consumer Psychology, 17,* 158–168.

Hardesty, D. M., Bearden, W. O., & Carlson, J. P. (2007). Persuasion knowledge and consumer reactions to pricing tactics. *Journal of Retailing, 83,* 199–210.

Haugtvedt, C. P., & The Consumer Psychology Seminar. (1997). Beyond fact or artifact: An assessment of Fishbein and Middlestadt's perspectives on attitude change processes. *Journal of Consumer Psychology, 6,* 99–106.

Haugtvedt, C. P., & Kasmer, J. A. (2008). Attitude change and persuasion. In C. P. Haugtvedt, P. Herr, F. R. Kardes (Eds.), *Handbook of consumer psychology* (pp. 419–436). New York, NY: Erlbaum.

Haugtvedt, C. P., & Petty, R. E. (1992). Personality and persuasion: Need for cognition moderates the persistence and resistance of attitude changes. *Journal of Personality and Social Psychology, 63,* 308–319.

Haugtvedt, C. P., Schumann, D. W., Schneier, W. L., & Warren, W. L. (1994). Advertising repetition and variation strategies: Implications for understanding attitude strength. *Journal of Consumer Research, 21,* 176–189.

Haugtvedt, C. P., & Wegener, D. T. (1994). Message order effects in persuasion: An attitude strength perspective. *Journal of Consumer Research, 21,* 205–218.

Herr, P. M. (1995). Whither fact, artifact, and attitude: Reflections on the theory of reasoned action. *Journal of Consumer Psychology, 4,* 371–380.

Holland, R. W., Hendriks, M., & Aarts, H. A. G. (2005). Smells like clean spirit: Nonconscious effects of scent on cognition and behavior. *Psychological Science, 16,* 689–693.

Kahle, L. R., & Homer, P. M. (1985). Physical attractiveness of the celebrity endorser: A social adaptation perspective. *Journal of Consumer Research, 11,* 954–961.

Kahneman, D., Knetsch, J. L., & Thaler, R. H. (1990). Experimental tests of the endowment effect and the Coase Theorem. *The Journal of Political Economy, 98,* 1325–1348.

Kang, Y. S., & Herr, P. M. (2006). Beauty and the beholder: Toward an integrative model of communication source effects. *Journal of Consumer Research, 33,* 123.

Kay, A. C., Wheeler, S. C., Bargh, J. A., & Ross, L. (2004). Material priming: The influence of mundane physical objects on situational construal and competitive behavioral choice. *Organizational Behavior and Human Decision Processes, 95,* 83–96.

Kelman, H. C., & Hovland, C. I. (1953). "Reinstatement" of the communicator in delayed measurement of opinion change. *The Journal of Abnormal and Social Psychology, 48,* 327–335.

Kirmani, A. (1990). The effect of perceived advertising costs on brand perceptions. *Journal of Consumer Research, 17,* 160–171.

Kirmani, A., & Campbell, M. C. (2004). Goal seeker and persuasion sentry: How consumer targets respond to interpersonal marketing persuasion. *Journal of Consumer Research, 31,* 573–582.

Kirmani, A., & Wright, P. (1989). Money talks: Perceived advertising expense and expected product quality. *Journal of Consumer Research, 16,* 344–353.

Klucharev, V., Smidts, A., & Fernandez, G. (2008). Brain mechanisms of persuasion: How 'expert power' modulates memory and attitudes. *Social Cognitive and Affective Neuroscience, 3,* 353–366. doi: 10.1093/scan/nsn022

Knutson, B., Rick, S., Wimmer, E., Prelec, D., & Loewenstein, G. (2007). Neural predictors of purchases. *Neuron, 53,* 147–156.

Kramer, R. M. (1994). The sinister attribution error: Paranoid cognition and collective distrust in organizations. *Motivation and Emotion, 18,* 199–230.

Krosnick, J. A., Betz, A. L., Jussim, L. J., & Lynn, A. R. (1992). Subliminal conditioning of attitudes. *Personality and Social Psychology Bulletin, 18,* 152–162.

Law, S., & Braun-LaTour, K. (2004). Product placements: How to measure their impact. In L. J. Shrum (Ed.), *The psychology of entertainment media: Blurring the lines between entertainment and persuasion* (pp. 63–78). Mahwah, NJ: Erlbaum.

Lerner, J. S., & Keltner, D. (2000). Beyond valence: Toward a model of emotion-specific influences on judgment and choice. *Cognition and Emotion, 14,* 473–493.

Lerner, J. S., Small, D. A., & Loewenstein, G. (2004). Heart strings and purse strings: Effects of emotions on economic transactions. *Psychological Science, 15,* 327–341.

Lieberman, M. D., Ochsner, K. N., Gilbert, D. T., & Schacter, D. L. (2001). Do amnesics exhibit cognitive dissonance reduction? The role of explicit memory and attention in attitude change. *Psychological Science, 12,* 135–140.

Lutz, R. J. (1973a). *Comparison of two alternative models of the attitude-behavior relationship.* Paper presented at the meeting of the American Psychological Association meeting, Montreal, Canada.

Lutz, R. J. (1973b). Cognitive change and attitude change: A validation study (Doctoral dissertation, University of Illinois, 1973). *ProQuest Dissertations and Theses, 0090,* 285.

McCarty, J. A. (2004). Product placement: The nature of the practice and potential avenues of inquiry. In L. J. Shrum (Ed.), *The psychology of entertainment media: Blurring the lines between entertainment and persuasion* (pp. 45–61). Mahwah, NJ: Erlbaum.

McCarty, J. A., & Lowrey, T. M. (2012). Product integration: Current practices and new directions. In L. J. Shrum (Ed.), *The psychology of entertainment media: Blurring the lines between entertainment and persuasion* (2nd ed., pp. 45–61). Mahwah, NJ: Erlbaum.

Milliman, R. E. (1982). Using background music to affect the behavior of supermarket shoppers. *Journal of Marketing, 46*(3), 86–91.

Miniard, P. W., & Barone, M. J. (1997). The case for noncognitive determinants of attitude: A critique of Fishbein and Middlestadt. *Journal of Consumer Psychology, 6,* 77–91.

Morsella, E., & Bargh, J. A. (2011). Unconscious action tendencies: Sources of 'un-integrated' action. In J. Decety & J. T. Cacioppo (Eds.), *The Oxford handbook of social neuroscience.* New York, NY: Oxford University Press.

Murphy, S. T., & Zajonc, R. B. (1993). Affect, cognition, and awareness: Affective priming with optimal and suboptimal stimulus exposures. *Journal of Personality and Social Psychology, 64,* 723–739.

North, A. C., Hargreaves, D. J., & McKendrick, J. (1999). The influence of in-store music on wine selections. *Journal of Applied Psychology, 84,* 271-276.

Packard, V. (1957). *The hidden persuaders.* New York, NY: David McKay.

Petty, R. E. (2006). A metacognitive model of attitudes. *Journal of Consumer Research, 33,* 22.

Petty, R. E., & Cacioppo, J. T. (1980). Effects of issue involvement on attitudes in an advertising context. In G. G. Gorn & M. E. Goldberg (Eds.), *Proceedings of the Division 23 Program,* (pp. 75–79). Montreal, Canada: American Psychological Association.

Petty, R. E., & Cacioppo, J. T. (1986). *Communication and persuasion: Central and peripheral routes to attitude change.* New York, NY: Springer/Verlag.

Petty, R. E., Cacioppo, J. T., & Schumann, D. (1983). Central and peripheral routes to advertising effectiveness: The moderating role of involvement. *Journal of Consumer Research, 10,* 135–146.

Petty, R. E., & Krosnick, J. A. (Eds.). (1995). *Attitude strength: Antecedents and consequences.* Hillsdale, NJ: Erlbaum.

Petty, R. E., & Wegener, D. T. (1998) Attitude change: Multiple roles for persuasion variables. In D. Gilbert, S. Fiske, & G. Lindzey (Eds.), *The handbook of social psychology* (4th ed., Vol. 1, pp. 323–390). New York, NY: McGraw-Hill.

Petty, R. E., & Wegener, D. T. (1999). The elaboration likelihood model: Current status and controversies. In S. Chaiken & Y. Trope (Eds.), *Dual process theories in social psychology* (pp. 41–72). New York, NY: Guilford Press.

Pratkanis, A. R., & Aronson, E. (1992). *Age of propaganda: The everyday use and abuse of persuasion.* New York, NY: W. H. Freeman.

Raju, P., Bhagat, R., & Sheth, J. (1975). Predictive validation and cross-validation of the Fishbein, Rosenberg and Sheth Models of attitudes. In M. J. Schlinger (Ed.), *Advances in consumer research* (Vol. 2, pp. 405–426). Chicago, IL: Association for Consumer Research.

Robles, R., Smith, R., Carver, C. S., & Wellens, A. R. (1987). Influence of subliminal visual images on the experience of anxiety. *Personality and Social Psychology Bulletin, 13,* 399–410.

Ryan, M. J. (1974). An empirical test of a predictive model and causal chain derived from Fishbein's behavioral intention model and applied to a purchase intention situation (Doctoral dissertation, University of Kentucky, 1974). *ProQuest Dissertations and Theses, 0102,* 297.

Schwarz, N. (1997). Moods and attitude judgments: A comment on Fishbein and Middlestadt. *Journal of Consumer Psychology, 6,* 93–98.

Shavitt, S., Swan, S., Lowrey, T. M., & Wänke, M. (1994). The interaction of endorser attractiveness and involvement in persuasion depends on the goal that guides message processing. *Journal of Consumer Psychology, 3,* 137–162.

Sheppard, B. H., Hartwick, J., & Warshaw, P. (1988). The theory of reasoned action: A meta-analysis of past research with recommendations for modifications and future research. *Journal of Consumer Research, 15,* 325–343.

Shiv, B. (2007). Emotions, decisions, and the brain. *Journal of Consumer Psychology, 17,* 174–178.

Shrum, L. J. (Ed.). (2004). *The psychology of entertainment media: Blurring the lines between entertainment and persuasion.* Mahwah, NJ: Erlbaum.

Shrum, L. J. (Ed.). (2012). *The psychology of entertainment media: Blurring the lines between entertainment and persuasion* (2nd ed.). New York, NY: Routledge.

Sternthal, B., Dholakia, R., & Leavitt, C. (1978). The persuasive effect of source credibility: Tests of cognitive response. *Journal of Consumer Research, 4,* 252–260.

Strahan, E. J., Spencer, S. J., & Zanna, M. P. (2002). Subliminal priming and persuasion: Striking while the iron is hot. *Journal of Experimental Social Psychology, 38,* 556–568.

Tormala, Z. L., & Petty, R. E. (2002). What doesn't kill me makes me stronger: The effects of resisting persuasion on attitude certainty. *Journal of Personality and Social Psychology, 83,* 1298–1313.

Tormala, Z. L., & Petty, R. E. (2004). Source credibility and attitude certainty: A metacognitive analysis of resistance to persuasion. *Journal of Consumer Psychology, 14,* 427–442.

Tversky, A., & Kahneman, D. (1974). Judgment under uncertainty: Heuristics and biases. *Science, 185*(4157), 1124–1131.

Vohs, K. D., Mead, N. L., & Goode, M. R. (2006). The psychological consequences of money. *Science, 314,* 1154–1156.

Wager, T. D., Rilling, J. K, Smith, E. E., Sokolik, A., Case, K. L., Davidson, R. J., et al. (2004). Placebo-induced changes in fMRI in the anticipation and experience of pain. *Science, 303,* 1162–1167.

Wansink, B. (2010). From mindless eating to mindlessly eating better. *Physiology and Behavior, 100*(5), 454–463.

Wansink, B., & van Ittersum, K. (2006). The visual illusions of food: Why plates, bowls and spoons can bias consumption volume. *The Journal of the Federation of American Societies of Experimental Biology, 20*(4), A618.

Wansink, B., Kent, R. J., & Hoch, S. J. (1998). An anchoring and adjustment model of purchase quantity decisions. *Journal of Marketing Research, 35,* 71–81.

Weddle, D. E., & Bettman, J. R. (1973). Marketing underground: An investigation of Fishbein's behavioral intention model. In S. Ward & P. Wright (Eds.), *Advances in consumer research* (Vol. 1, pp. 310–318). Urbana, IL: Association for Consumer Research.

Wilson, D. T., Mathews, H. L., & Harvey, J. W. (1975). An empirical test of the Fishbein behavioral intention model: Introduction and theory. *Journal of Consumer Research, 1*(4), 39–48.

Wright, P., Friestad, M., & Boush, D. M. (2005). The development of marketplace persuasion knowledge in children, adolescents, and young adults. *Journal of Public Policy & Marketing, 24*(2), 222–233.

Zajonc, R. B. (1968). Attitudinal effects of mere exposure. *Journal of Personality and Social Psychology, 9,* 1–27.

Zanna, M. P., Kiesler, C. A., & Pilkonis, P. A. (1970). Positive and negative attitudinal affect established by classical conditioning. *Journal of Personality and Social Psychology, 14*(4), 321–328.

CHAPTER 20

Persuasion in the Legal Setting

John C. Reinard

The study of persuasion in the courts has a lengthy history among scholars of communication. Aristotle (trans. 1941) identified the forensic exchange as a major division of oratory (1358^b6) and explained the close link:

> Since rhetoric exists to affect the giving of decisions—the hearers decide between one political speaker and another, and a legal verdict *is* a decision—the orator must not only try to make the argument of his speech demonstrative and worthy of belief; he must also make his own character look right and put his hearers, who are to decide, into the right frame of mind. ($1377^b21–1377^b24$)

With the founding of European universities during the Middle Ages, the study of rhetoric (expanded to include law) was at the center of the core curriculum. Despite a few breaks in the chain along the way, this close linkage has endured as a standard part of both communication studies and the practice of law. Today, the study of communication and the law has grown from a cottage industry to a major part of the communication field. Each professional organization in the field

has an interest group, division, or commission dedicated to legal communication. The American Society of Trial Consultants has nearly 500 members (up over 40% since the first edition of this chapter was written in 2002). There is little doubt that legal persuasion is a major part of the field. Indeed, it has grown to such an extent that an exhaustive overview is nearly impossible. Accordingly, this chapter reviews elements of persuasion in the legal setting with a close focus on social scientific research on message form.[1] The next section presents a brief summary of events and media coverage that occur prior to the trial itself. The following section, and the bulk of this chapter, offers a close examination of persuasive communication as it occurs during the trial. The final section considers issues for future research.

The Pretrial Phase

The possible impact of pretrial publicity remains a concern among constitutional scholars as well as persuasion researchers. The American Bar Association reported that pretrial publicity descriptions of 27% of criminal suspects were "problematic" (Imrich, Mullin, & Linz, 1995). Furthermore, between 1994 and 2004, over 7,000 defendants claimed that pretrial publicity made it impossible for them to receive fair trials (Chrzanowski, 2006). Not surprisingly, most research has indicated that pretrial publicity influences jurors (e.g., Daftary-Kapur, Dumas, & Penrod, 2010; Kovera & Greathouse, 2008). This appears to be true regardless of whether the trial is short or long (Kramer & Kerr, 1989) or whether measures are taken before or after evidence is presented (Studebaker & Penrod, 2005). Importantly, jurors exposed to pretrial publicity confused the information in the publicity with evidence actually presented in the trial (Ruva & McEvoy, 2008; Ruva, McEvoy, & Bryant, 2007). Although most pretrial publicity was inimical to defendants (Imrich et al., 1995), sometimes it benefited defendants, as when (1) the pretrial publicity reports also included the suggestion that there were racist intentions behind spreading the publicity (Fein, Morgan, Norton, & Sommers, 1997), (2) the publicity involved stories of mistaken identification of an innocent man (Greene & Loftus, 1984), (3) the publicity was generally hostile to the prosecution (Daftary-Kapur, 2010), or (4) the publicity involved trials similar to the defendant's (Greene & Wade, 1988).

Not all pretrial publicity is equal. Hvistendahl (1979) found that information about a prior criminal record led to significantly increased numbers of guilty verdicts especially when compared to publicity about the defendant's use of a fictitious address, information regarding the defendant's race, or the defendant's gang membership. Prejudicial effects were also potent when the publicity involved eyewitness identifications (Devenport, Studebaker, & Penrod, 1999), character evidence (Otto, Penrod, & Dexter, 1994), and reports of physical evidence (Shaw & Skolnick, 2004).

Naturally, pretrial publicity affects jurors differently. Mock jurors with high ego-involvement become less confident in their verdicts (Freundlich, 1985). One study (Hoiberg & Stires, 1973) found that relatively less intelligent women presented with strongly biased pretrial publicity of a heinous rape were most influenced by it, although men and highly intelligent women were not. Even among men, the publicity sometimes can backfire. Men presented with pretrial publicity portraying perpetrators of acquaintance rape as predators responded with increased pro-defendant judgments in an acquaintance rape case (Mullin, 1997; Mullin, Imrich, & Linz, 1996). Butler (2007) found that death-qualified jurors tended to believe that pretrial publicity had minimal effect on the defendant's right to due process. Kovera (2002) found that jurors' attitudes toward rape affected how much pretrial publicity affected juror decisions.

Attorneys and judges seem assured that intensive *voir dire* examinations to select jurors can protect against pretrial publicity bias (Hans & Vidmar, 1986, pp. 63–78). Attorneys rarely present change of venue motions, and 88% of judges have never ruled on one (Siebert, Wilcox, & Hough, 1970, pp. 4–6). Yet, research does not suggest that active *voir dire* actually reduces pretrial publicity effects (Dexter, Cutler, & Moran, 1992; Kerr, Kramer, Carroll, & Alfini, 1991; Kerr, Niedermeier, & Kaplan, 1999; Sue, Smith, & Pedroza, 1975; but see Padawer-Singer, Singer, & Singer, 1974). Even when a judge admonished jurors to disregard any pretrial publicity, jurors still were influenced by the damaging publicity (Sue, Smith, & Gilbert, 1974). Another method of control, a continuance or delay for a couple of days, appeared to help partially overcome the effects of pretrial publicity bias (Kramer, Kerr, & Carroll, 1990).

Messages In the Courtroom

Charges

The charge itself is a proposition that may sensitize some jurors. For instance, in criminal trials, as the severity of the charges and penalties increase, juries become less and less willing to convict, even if the defendants are viewed as guilty

(Grofman, 1985). Increasing the number of options to return reduced charges seems to enhance the chances that jurors will convict on one (Larntz, 1975). Jurors given the option of returning "guilty but mentally ill" rendered that verdict two thirds of the time instead of using the options of "guilty" and "not guilty by reason of insanity" (Poulson, 1990). To convict on a case involving severe penalties, jurors seemed to demand increased amounts of evidence (Thomas & Hogue, 1976), and they usually reduced their overall rates of conviction (Kerr, 1978). Sometimes trials involve multiple counts of crimes alleged against defendants. Experiments using both actual jurors and student jurors and controlling for similarity of the charges, evidence, and judges' instructions found that defendants charged with three crimes were most likely to be convicted (Tanford, 1985; Tanford & Penrod, 1984).

Burden of Proof

Verdicts are also affected by the burden of proof shouldered by prosecutors and plaintiffs. The standard of proof required for a decision against the defendant may be proof "beyond a reasonable doubt," "by a preponderance of the evidence," or "clear and convincing evidence." As the standard of proof increases, rates of guilty verdicts decline (see Kagehiro, 1990). Yet, when the judge defined "beyond a reasonable doubt" as one's being firmly convinced of guilt, rates of guilty verdicts for murder increased (Koch & Devine, 1999). When the judge explained that the standard did not mean that one had to be "absolutely certain of guilt" rates of guilty verdicts of mock jurors increased (Wright & Hall, 2007).

Formal presumptions on the interpretation of evidence are meaningful elements of jurors' decision making when jurors are made aware of them. Three types of presumptions (conclusive, mandatory, and permissive) were presented to student jurors as part of criminal trials in which the defendant blameworthiness was manipulated (Schmolesky, Cutler, & Penrod, 1988). The conclusive presumption used to suggest defendant guilt increased the numbers of guilty verdicts, although other presumptions did not. Even so, when ratings of defendant culpability were high, jurors were willing to discount presumptions that tended to benefit the defendant.

In civil cases, the higher the damages plaintiffs request, the more money they seem to receive. Of course, judging whether this pattern is causal requires experimental work holding the trial evidence constant. Such work with mock jurors supported these expectations (Hastie, Schkade, & Payne, 1999; Raitz, Greene, Goodman, & Loftus, 1990) across types of personal injury cases, regardless of victim sex and race (Malouff & Schutte, 1989). When the defense made an award recommendation, jurors were increasingly likely to return verdicts for the plaintiff (Ellis, 2002).

Persuasion During Jury Selection

Voir dire, or the questioning of potential jurors to select a jury, may be a persuasive process in which attorneys build rapport, obtain commitments, preview the case, introduce the client in a favorable light, begin arguing the case, guide the jury in its methods of deliberating, commence the process of image-building, humanize the defendant, and familiarize the jury with relevant factual and legal concepts. In practice, statements and questions from judges and attorneys accounted for approximately 60% of the sentences uttered during the *voir dire* "questioning" of potential jurors (Johnson & Haney, 1994). Defense attorneys used *voir dire* more aggressively than did prosecutors (Johnson & Haney, 1994), and attorney-led questioning stimulated more candid self-disclosure than did judge questioning (Jones, 1987).

Ironically, in California, where substantial restrictions have been placed on attorney questioning, judges were pleased with their own abilities to conduct *voir dire* examinations, though they believed that attorneys took too much time with juror questioning (Smith, 1995). When *voir dire* questions were completed individually rather than *en masse,* attorneys raised increased numbers of objections to jurors for cause (Nietzel & Dillehay, 1982). Yet this aggressive questioning still often failed to exclude jurors who were opposed to basic foundations of the U.S. legal system (Johnson & Haney, 1994). Sometimes jurors admit biases but are asked by judges whether they believe that they could set aside their biases and be fair. If jurors answer affirmatively, the jurors are considered "rehabilitated" and may be accepted in the empanelled jury. Rehabilitated jurors' verdicts have not been found to differ from those of unrehabilitated jurors when participating in murder trials involving an insanity defense (Crocker & Kovera, 2010).

Voir dire can influence verdicts. Jurors exposed to extensive *voir dire* examination perceived the defendant as less culpable than did other jurors (Dexter et al., 1992). Indeed, lawyers were least effective in securing desired verdicts when they avoided the use of *voir dire* questions strategically designed to influence jurors (Arsenault & Reinard, 1997; Reinard & Arsenault, 2000). Such strategic questions functioned by altering perceptions of the defendant's character that, in turn, affected verdicts (Reinard, Arsenault, & Geck, 1998). On the other hand, the attorney's use of strategic questions asking jurors to overlook the defendant's undesirable past reduced verdicts of guilt (Reinard & Arsenault, 2000).

Extending this work into contrasts of strategic questions attempting to promote a sense of juror rapport or empathy with the defense, Reinard, Khalid, and Liso (2001) found that verdicts for the defense were enhanced by the use of questions that requested jurors to reciprocate positively to the defense expressions of trust in them. Yet, verdicts for the defense were not enhanced by questions that previewed the case or that attempted to create rapport through similarity appeals. Reinard (2009) found that verdicts were positively affected by the use of *voir dire* questions that attempted to promote positive attitudes toward the defendant by showing empathy. In follow-up work, it was discovered that the interaction of the use of all three *voir dire* question forms actually produced their effects by promoting positive changes in the character assessments of the defendant and the defense attorney and a negative shift in the perception of the prosecuting attorney's competence (Reinard, 2010).

Voir dire questions have been examined as a deterrent to racial bias against defendants from ethnic minority groups. The U.S. Supreme Court ruling in *Batson v. Kentucky,* 476 U.S. 79 (1986) forbade lawyers from using preemptory challenges to eliminate potential jurors because of race. Yet, enforcement of the ruling has been difficult. In experimental work with lawyers, law students, and other college students, mock jurors showed a strong disposition to exclude jurors based on race, though they usually explained the challenge in race-neutral terms (Sommers & Norton, 2008). Another study found that when *voir dire* questioning involved questions about racism, mock jurors deliberating in a trial involving an African American defendant compensated by producing increasingly lenient verdicts (Sommers, 2006). In a review of the literature, two authors (Sommers & Norton, 2008) lamented that lawyers' continued exclusion of ethnic minorities from juries (all the while denying any racial decision making) may make it impossible to rely on *voir dire* processes as a solution to racial prejudice in the courtroom.

Opening Statements

Attorneys' opening statements are supposed to provide a case preview rather than extended argument. Nevertheless, one should not be surprised that opening statements can have powerful argumentative functions (see Perrin, 1999, esp. pp. 110–132), even though such strategies as fanciful name calling (*People v. Johnston,* 1994), directly refuting the opposition's case (e.g., *State v. Bell,* 1972), and interpreting upcoming evidence (Strong, 1992, pp. 17–19) have been ruled argumentative. Indeed, an examination of 19 opening statements found that all were subject to some objection from the opposition, the plurality of which involved "various types of circumstantial evidence—using a theme, drawing inferences for the jury, characterizing a person or event in some argumentative way, or discussing the mental condition of a person" (Perrin, 1999, p. 140).

Opening statements also are believed to be influential since jurors are believed to make decisions early in the trial process (e.g., Freundlich, 1985; but see Weld & Danzig, 1940).[2] Yet, a review of 50 trials revealed that juries thought defense opening statements were less well prepared than prosecutors' statements, even though, of course, defense attorneys did not perceive any inferiority in themselves (Linz, Penrod, & McDonald, 1986). Even so, the influence of the prosecution's opening statement was reduced when the following defense argument was strong (Wallace & Wilson, 1969). Yet, the first opening statement juries hear seems to be particularly important in a couple of ways. First, the first opening statement serves a strong agenda-setting function and appears to "prime the pump" such that jurors' assessments of witnesses and evidence tend to follow its organization (Bayly, 1989). Second, the length of the first opening statement appears to affect reactions to others that follow. The defense gained an advantage if it followed a brief opening statement with an extensive one (Pyszczynski & Wrightsman, 1981).

Opening statement structure has been examined. Evidence is mixed regarding whether a story format is superior to a legal comparison-expository structure (e.g., McCullough, 2007). If the defense attorney's opening statement promised evidence exonerating the defendant and then failed to introduce such proof, the prosecution's reminder to the jury (in this case, presentation of an alibi witness) reduced the defense attorney's influence on the verdict (Pyszczynski, Greenberg, Mack, & Wrightsman, 1981). Yet if the prosecution failed to remind jurors of the broken promise, the defense opening statement increased the likelihood of an acquittal. In fact, if a promised witness were absent, the mere mention of that fact by the

judge or by the attorney affected jury decision making against the side that was expected to produce the witness (Johnstone, 1994).

Many times opening statements include inoculation of jurors against counterpersuasion (cf., chapter 14 in this volume). Researchers found that such a strategy was effective when the defense inoculated mock jurors against damaging evidence by mentioning it early in the trial, unless the prosecuting attorney explained "to the mock jurors that the stealing thunder tactic had been used" (Dolnik, Case, & Williams, 2003, p. 267). Bucolo and Cohn (2010) found that when attorneys included comments in the opening and closing statements to make race of the African American defendant a salient matter (in other words, playing the "race card"), jurors rendered significantly fewer guilty verdicts than when the materials were deleted.

Language can play a role in this process. In adapting to jurors, African American attorneys speaking to predominantly African American juries often used African American vernacular English (Hobbs, 2003). When plaintiffs' lawyers' opening and closing statements used "personal language" and a preemptive attack that the defense had a weak case, the strategy stimulated judgments for the plaintiffs unless the jurors had low need for cognition (Payne, 2007).

Defense Case Strategies

Defendants may deny charges, or they may present affirmative defenses that offer outside explanations as excuses. When simply denying the charges, exonerating and incriminating facts about the defendant were most influential on intensifying jurors' verdict dispositions when the attorney presented the information in a heterogeneous, rather than a homogeneous order (Kaplan & Miller, 1977).

Affirmative defenses seem difficult to argue. For instance, when defendants gave affirmative defenses for retracting confessions, they were more likely to be convicted of murder than when pleas included appeals to the Fifth Amendment or denial of the charges by reference to an alibi (Fischer & Fehr, 1985). Even so, an affirmative defense including testimony to prove mitigating circumstances was effective in reducing mock jurors' recommended sentence (Suggs & Berman, 1979). Mock jurors were least likely to recommend the death penalty when mitigating evidence showed "The defendant was (i) diagnosed with schizophrenia, not medicated, and suffered from severe delusions and hallucinations, (ii) drug addicted and high at the time of the murder, (iii) diagnosed as borderline mentally retarded during childhood, or (iv) severely physically and verbally abused by his parents during childhood" (Barnett, Brodsky, & Davis, 2004).

When defendants invoked the Fifth Amendment by itself, simulated jurors increased rates of guilty verdicts (Shaffer, Case, & Brannen, 1979). In one experiment, mock jurors placed approximately the same proof obligations on both sides in a murder case, regardless of the defense strategy (simple denial or self-defense) and despite the judge's instruction about the location of the burden of proof (Posey, 1996). Consistent with the law, in a medical malpractice lawsuit, damage awards were cut in half when the plaintiff was shown to be partially negligent (Zickafoose & Bornstein, 1999). Not surprisingly, an eccentric defense seemed to be rejected by jurors.

An attempt to create juror empathy with the defendant was tested in a patricide trial in which a child defendant claimed self-defense due to sexual abuse by the victim (Haegerich & Bottoms, 2000). When student jurors were asked to take the perspective of the defendant and to consider how they would feel under the circumstances of the trial, jurors were most likely to decide not guilty. When a landlord defendant treated tenants coldly and as objects, the plaintiff awards increased (Holt, O'Connor, Smith, Gessner, Clifton, & Mumford, 1997). On the other hand, when criminal defendants already had suffered greatly, the severity of jury decisions was reduced (Shaffer, Plummer, & Hammock, 1986).

Insanity Defenses

Arguing the insanity defense is particularly challenging. It appears to succeed slightly less than 1% of the time (Cirincione, Steadman, & McGreevy, 1995) and only when defendants suffer from the most severe mental disorders (Lymburner & Roesch, 1999). Yet, these statistics somewhat overstate things. In reality, mental health examiners agree on insanity decisions 81% of the time, and fully 86% of insanity defense cases are not contested by the prosecutors (Rogers, Bloom, & Manson, 1984).

There are many reasons insanity defenses are risky. In the first place, the insanity defense is often misperceived and unpopular with the public (Borum & Fulero, 1999). In the second place, defining "insanity" has proven to be quite nettlesome, and lawyers and psychiatrists sometimes bewilder each other (Gutheil, 1999). Because *insanity* is not a medical term describing a particular malady, complicated rules such as the M'Naghten, the Durham, the Brawner, Michigan's Guilty But Mentally Ill statute, and the American Law Institute's Model Penal Code have formed various notions of insanity. When jurors have been tested on their understanding of the various rules on which they have been instructed, comprehension has averaged between 40% (Arens, Granfield, & Susman, 1965) and slightly more than 50% accuracy (Ogloff, 1993).

Recovered Memory Cases

In some cases, counselors and hypnotists have encouraged children and adult witnesses—often believed to be victims of sexual abuse—to testify about "events" they had "forgotten" or "repressed." Although this controversial approach has been attacked as little more than the power of suggestion, in a criminal case, repressed testimony was only slightly less influential on convictions (58%) than was nonrepressed testimony (67%; Key, Warren, & Ross, 1996). Whether jurors believed in such evidence depended on the perceived strength of evidence, their belief in the repression of memory, and the kinds of mass media news stories they had heard about the credibility of recovered memories (Rosen, 1997). In child abuse cases featuring repressed memory evidence, victims who were either 3 or 13 years old at the time were not as believable as 8-year-old victims (Key et al., 1996). In a case involving delayed charges of child sexual abuse, evidence of threats and evidence of a relationship between the defendant and the victim influenced jury verdicts (Read, Connolly, & Welsh, 2006). Yet, in nonjury trials, verdicts were predicted by the length of the delayed memory of abuse, the severity of the offence, claims of repression of memory generally, a past relationship between defense and the victim, and the presence of evidence of an expert witness testifying to the credibility of delayed memory of sexual abuse.

Use of the Entrapment Defense

One way to respond to criminal charges is by claiming that defendants were induced to engage in illegal behavior by law enforcement officials. Because such a strategy admits the illegal behavior itself, it requires subtle argument, and jurors have had difficulty in understanding judges' instructions on the defense (Borgida & Park, 1988). As a result, juries have relied predominately on evidence of the defendants' past criminal conduct to reach verdicts. Lewis (1997) found that jurors in a drug case carefully tracked information about the number of times that the defendant refused enticements from law enforcement officers. If the defendant initially turned down suggestions from law enforcement officials, the jury grew increasingly receptive to the entrapment defense.

The Battered Woman Defense

The defense has been made that a "battered woman's" homicide is a form of preemptive self-defense against her chronic beating by an abusive spouse. Research is mixed on whether expert testimony has great (Kasian, Spanos, Terrance, &

Peebles, 1993) or limited influence on jurors' decisions (Mechanic, 1997). The battered woman syndrome defense seemed increasingly persuasive for the defense when an expert witness was added to the defense case evidence (Schuller, McKimmie, & Janz, 2004).

Case Evidence

Survey research has shown that case evidence is the most potent single influence on verdicts (e.g., Poulson, Braithwaite, Brondino, & Wuensch, 1997).[3] But, what makes evidence strong or weak is an open issue. One explanation was offered by Pettus (1990): "The clear and well told story is considered effective evidence, whereas the unclear, nonsensical story is considered ineffective evidence" (p. 92). The tone set by key witnesses can make a difference. When testimony against a defendant in a murder case was introduced in an opinionated manner, judgments of guilt increased. But when the testimony was presented in an unopinionated way, student jurors were likely to find the defendant guilty of the lesser charge of manslaughter (Ludwig & Fontaine, 1978). Beyond verdicts alone, jurors' overall interpretations were affected by the placement of judges' instructions to jurors (Elwork, Sales, & Alfini, 1977). When the judge explained the burden of proof before the presentation of evidence, conviction rates declined (Kerr, Atkin, Stasser, Meek, Holt, & Davis, 1976). Furthermore, when an active judge commented on testimony from a doubtful eyewitness by issuing limiting instructions, summarizing relevant testimony, and explaining the role of eyewitness testimony, the jury disregarded the troubled material during its deliberations (Katzev & Wishart, 1985).

The impact of emotional evidence has attracted increased interest among researchers. For mock jurors looking at a transcript of the testimony, credibility was reduced when witnesses used neutral or incongruent emotions to deliver emotional material (Kaufmann, Drevland, Wessel, Overskeid,

& Magnussen, 2003). One study found that although individual mock jurors tended to be influenced by emotional testimony from a rape victim (in contrast to a neutral emotional presentation), but these effects disappeared when the jurors deliberated (Dahl, Enemo, Drevland, Wessel, Eilertsen, & Magnussen, 2007). Furthermore, the impact of emotional testimony from a female rape victim also was reduced when the judge instructed jurors that such emotional material did not indicate believable reactions (Bollingmo, Wessel, Sandvold, Eilertsen, & Magnussen, 2009).

Confession evidence often is used by prosecutors in criminal cases and it tends to be persuasive, often more persuasive than eyewitness identifications or character testimony (Kassin & Neumann, 1997). Although student jurors rejected confessions that were the result of threats of punishment against the defendants, they were strongly influenced when confessions were either freely given or the products of offers of leniency (Kassin & Wrightsman, 1980). Evidence that the police used interrogation strategies to trick or deceive defendants by claiming that they had evidence against the defendant that they did not, resulted in reduced guilty verdicts (Woody & Forrest, 2009; but Henkel, 2008). When the defense added expert testimony from psychologists explaining how false-evidence methods and other common police interrogation strategies produced false confessions, jurors responded with enhanced rejection of evidence from police. When the camera angle in a video recording of a confession included only the defendant, mock jurors returned more guilty verdicts than when the recording was framed to show both the defendant and the police interrogators (Lassiter et al., 2005). If the recanted confession were claimed to have been influenced by the defendant's medical condition or the defendant's mental illness, conviction ratings increased in frequency (Henkel, 2008). When confession evidence was introduced from an accomplice, a jailhouse informant, or a member of the community, the material was persuasive, despite evidence produced to show that the witness may

have received a reward for offering such testimony (Neuschatz, Lawson, Swanner, Meissner, & Neuschatz, 2008).

Alibi Evidence

One of the most obvious ways to defend against a criminal charge is to argue that a defendant could not have committed a crime because she or he was at another location at the time. In recent years this topic has become an established area for research (see Burke & Turtle, 2003). Since strong alibis appear to have great influence on juries (Allison & Brimacombe, 2010; Olson & Wells, 2004b), the dominant issue involves identifying what makes a strong alibi strong. On one hand, alibi evidence usually is made most believable when corroborated by other evidence (Olson & Wells, 2004a). On the other hand, under some circumstances, corroboration can decrease an alibi's impact (Burke & Turtle, 2004; Culhane & Hosch, 2004b). A weak alibi actually may increase the possibility of false convictions (Olson & Wells, 2004a). When an alibi was supplied by a defendant's girlfriend, it was not as persuasive as when the witness was a neighbor, even when the girlfriend offered an unambiguous alibi (Culhane & Hosch, 2004a). Yet, others found that unambiguous alibi evidence from a close significant other reduced guilty verdicts more than when alibi evidence was completely absent (Olson & Wells, 2004a). Some research has found that alibi evidence presented during a police investigation is more persuasive when corroborated by other witnesses than when presented at trial (Sommers & Douglass, 2007). This curious finding was explained by "the fact that a case has proceeded to trial implies to perceivers that the alibi is relatively weak" (p. 41).

Witness Evidence

Research on the presentation of evidence by witnesses involves the study of testimony from defendants, eyewitness testimony, expert testimony, and scientific evidence. In addition, the impact of inadmissible evidence has been investigated.

Defendant testimony—or the absence thereof—may play a dramatic role in the trial setting. In one of the few controlled experiments on the subject, three stereotypical signals of lying (fidgeting, avoiding eye contact, and disfluencies) were used in a deposition by an African American defendant accused of breaking and entering (Pryor & Buchanan, 1984). Not surprisingly, student jurors rated the defendant as least guilty when the signs of nervousness were minimized. A defendant tended to receive more lenient verdicts when they appeared distressed (Savitsky, Czyzewski, Dubord, & Kaminsky, 1976) or remorseful (Bornstein, Rung, & Miller, 2002), especially when compared to a defendant who appeared angry (MacLin, Downs, MacLin, & Caspers, 2009).

Eyewitness testimony can be quite influential with jurors (Lindsay, 1994), with as many as 83% of mock jurors influenced by such evidence (Brigham & Bouthwell, 1983). Yet, the fallibility of eyewitness testimony is well established. For example, Lindsay, Lim, Marando, and Cully (1986) exposed mock jurors to various numbers of eyewitnesses testifying for the prosecution and defense in a purse-snatching case. Although unopposed witnesses were most effective, internally inconsistent testimony (including alibi testimony) also was persuasive for the defense. Whether the eyewitness identified or failed to identify the suspect made a difference. Student jurors were presented with two types of non-identification information (eyewitness testimony and fingerprint evidence) in situations where there were one or two eyewitnesses or contradictory evidence (McAllister & Bregman, 1986). Regardless of evidence type, identifications influenced decisions more than did non-identifications (i.e., statements that a person was not at a location).

In other inquiry, when eyewitness evidence and fingerprint evidence were contrasted, positive examples of each were most influential on verdicts, and the absence of interactions indicated that the effects were independent of each other (Bregman & McAllister, 1987). Similarly, when an alibi eyewitness claimed that the defendant either was or was not at another location when a crime was committed, mock jurors tended to discount nonidentification information if it failed to meet their expectations (McAllister & Bregman, 1989). Jurors treated "earwitness testimony" (identification made on the basis of overheard voices) with the same credibility as eyewitness testimony, despite warnings that earwitness identifications were highly fallible (Laub, 2010).

Expert witnesses tend to be influential, especially when the testimony was presented early in the trial, when it was specifically linked to the case under consideration (Brekke & Borgida, 1988), and when there was no opposing expert witness (Levett & Kovera, 2009). In contrasts of expert witness varieties (e.g., physicians, psychiatrists, psychologists, chemists, document examiners, polygraph examiners, police, eyewitnesses, firearms experts, accountants, appraisers), members of the professions were most persuasive with actual jurors, although other experts could be influential when the relevance of their testimony could be established (Saks & Wissler, 1984). Jurors were strongly influenced by testimony from psychiatrists (McMahon, 1974).

In related inquiry, judges and lawyers considered forensic evidence on mental health to be most useful when it dealt with clinical diagnoses and analyses of whether legal thresholds had been met (Redding, Floyd, & Hawk, 2001). In another study, jurors were persuaded by expert presentation of data about groups of people most likely to commit rape (Brekke & Borgida, 1988). In a civil case, expert economic testimony of the plaintiff's loss of wages and benefits seemed influential to juries (Greene, Downey, & Goodman-Delahunty, 1999), whereas juries tended to discount the lawyer's recommendations about "pain and suffering" awards. When judges admitted expert testimony into evidence, mock jurors were more persuaded by it than when the same evidence was presented in speeches outside the courtroom (Schweitzer & Saks, 2009). In other work (McKimmie, Newton, Terry, & Schuller, 2004), mock jurors responded most positively to expert testimony when the sex of the expert was compatible with the case gender orientation.

Scientific evidence is often presented to jurors, and they often have a difficult time understanding it (Daftary-Kapur, Dumas, & Penrod, 2010). When mock jurors were presented with ambiguous technical evidence in a civil case, information processing was hindered (Horowitz, Bordens, Victor, Bourgeois, & Forster-Lee, 2001), but when the technical evidence was clear, the credibility of witness introducing it was increased. In one study involving DNA evidence, jurors separated or combined probabilities incorrectly and gave such probabilistic evidence less influence than it should have received (Schklar & Diamond, 1999). Juries sometimes do not know what to do with statistics.

For instance, Thompson and Schumann (1987) examined a case in which blood typing evidence showed that only 1 person in 100 shared the actual perpetrator's blood type. Fully 60% of the jurors decided for the defendant when the defense responded by arguing that such numbers meant that in the city of 100,000 people, 1,000 people had the same blood type. Using tortured statistical sophistry, the defense attorney opined that because the defendant was only 1 of the 1,000 people in the city with the culprit's blood type, that fact meant that there was only 1 chance in 1,000 that the defendant committed the crime. The problem of dealing with statistical evidence has been vexing, and proper interpretation of statistics presented by expert witnesses remains at an unsatisfactory level (see Fienberg, 1989, esp. pp. 149–189). *Inadmissible evidence* sometimes is presented to jurors. Although few claim that jurors can "unlisten" to what they have heard, the most common remedy is for judges to instruct jurors to disregard the questionable material.[4] Yet, such instructions are not always effective. In their literature review of inadmissible testimony research, Daftary-Kapur, Dumas, and Penrod (2010) observed that additional attention to forgetting inadmissible material usually anchored it further. In the first place, few jurors seem able to remember the instructions

to disregard the testimony (Henkel, 2008). In the second place, jurors seem able to disregard only mundane information (Hirsch, Reinard, & Reynolds, 1976). In fact, jurors who heard unusual evidence (in language or in form) damaging to a defendant, rendered more guilty verdicts when the evidence was ruled inadmissible than when it was ruled admissible (Pickel, Karam, & Warner, 2009). Evidence of a past criminal record (Greene & Dodge, 1995) especially if the past record involved crimes similar to the trial subject (Allison & Brimacombe, 2010), and emotional materials remained influential and were amplified by judges' instructions (Edwards & Bryan, 1997). Similar effects also were found on perceptions of witness credibility (Horn, 1976). Disturbingly, the little research on the subject indicates that judges are not superior to juries in ignoring biasing or inadmissible material (Wistrich, Guthrie, & Rachlinski, 2005).

If there is a pattern to the matter, it seems that jurors use inadmissible materials along with other case arguments and evidence when they believe such information is true and relevant (Mosmann, 1998). In a meta-analysis of 48 studies, it was discovered that the instruction to disregard inadmissible material amplified the impact of the evidence (especially when attorneys were heard arguing over inadmissibility), except when judges offered a rationale for the inadmissibility ruling (Steblay, Hosch, Culhane, & McWethy, 2006).

Even judges' instructions to disregard the inadmissible material are not always effective. As far back as 1977, Wolf and Montgomery exposed mock jurors to inadmissible testimony in which the questionable evidence was ruled either admissible, inadmissible, or inadmissible accompanied by the judge's instruction to disregard the evidence. Biasing effects were eliminated when the judge ruled the material inadmissible, whereas the testimony was amplified when the judge ordered jurors to disregard it. Reinard and Reynolds (1978) found that raising an objection to inadmissible testimony in a criminal trial amplified it despite the judge's ruling, and when a defense objection was overruled, the bias was greatest.

Yet research also shows that jurors were most likely to reject inadmissible materials: when the judge gave detailed explanations as to why coerced confessions were both unreliable and unjust (Kassin & Wrightsman, 1981); when jurors with a highly developed sense of justice received reminders of their mortality (Cook, Arndt, & Lieberman, 2004); when wiretap evidence in a murder trial was explained to be unreliable (as opposed to reasoning that it violated due process protections; Kassin & Sommers, 1997; Mallard & Perkins, 2005); when jurors were given reason to be suspicious about the motives of the advocates and witnesses who introduced the inadmissible evidence (Fein, McCloskey, & Tomlinson, 1997); when an official source (Reinard, 1989), especially a police officer (Reinard, 1981) or a county government fingerprint expert (Reinard, 1985), introduced the inadmissible materials; when the jurors had negative attitudes toward the criminal justice system and the police (Casper & Benedict, 1993); and when inadmissible testimony involved a "mild" violation of due process guarantees (Fleming, Wegener, & Petty, 1999).

In civil cases (Cox & Tanford, 1989), inadmissible testimony by itself was most persuasive when favoring the defendant instead of the victim or others in the trial. Adult jurors presented with inadmissible evidence were unable to disregard inadmissible evidence when objections to it were sustained unless the judge also gave a specific instruction on the matter (Shaffer, 1985). How inadmissible testimony produces its effects has been investigated. In two separate efforts (one with single cases and one across two case types) to develop causal models of the impact of inadmissible testimony, inadmissible testimony was found to affect sentence recommendations as a function of the verdict and the character perceptions of the defendant (Geck & Reinard, 2009; Reinard, 1989) found that the nature of

the inadmissible testimony, the type of witness introducing it (official or nonofficial source), and the perceived character of the defendant influenced verdicts.

Manner of Evidence Presentation

Not surprisingly, sensational visual materials possessed by prosecutors may influence decisions if judges permit their introduction. As a rule, when jurors are presented gruesome photographs, they tend to show increased anger toward the defendant (Bright & Goodman-Delahunty, 2006), which biases jury decision making (Semmler & Brewer, 2002). Other work has found that being shown photos of victim injuries in vandalism, arson, child abuse, child molestation, or homicide cases led mock jurors to increase recommendations of sentence lengths (Ahola, Hellstrom, & Christianson, 2010). Juries easily discount recreations, as in the case of video reenactments in a wrongful death civil case (Fishfader, Howells, Katz, & Teresi, 1996).

The language and manner of trial participants can influence jurors. In particular, disfluent witnesses, witnesses with poor grammar, and witnesses who used lower-class language styles were viewed as less credible than those whose speech approximated Standard English (Conley, O'Barr, & Lind, 1978). The phrasings of defendants also affected jurors. A defendant who loudly denied the charges and intemperately protested against them was likely to be perceived as guiltier than a defendant who testified with a tone of moderation (Yandell, 1979). Yet, a study of 13 trials showed no changes in credibility or believability when the witness made repeated use of disclaimers in reaction to assertions from the questioning attorneys (Stutman, 1986b).

Witnesses occasionally appear in some form of disguise or identity masking, such as when government agents or organized crime informants present evidence. One study attempted to check the effect of electronic masking of videotaped testimony (Towell, Kemp, & Pike, 1996).

None of the methods (placing a gray circle over the witness's face, using pixilation masking, using negation of the witness's face, repeating out of synchrony video images of the courtroom, or placing a static image of a witness's face before jurors as the audio portion of the testimony was played to them) affected witness credibility ratings, but all methods except the negation and out of synchrony conditions impaired jurors' ability to remember the testimony.

Direct Examination and Cross-Examination

Direct examination is the chance for one side to introduce evidence to support essential claims. One might imagine that the opposition would have its own plan for undermining this set of claims through cross-examination. But in a study of rape trials, whatever the direct examination covered tended to be reviewed in the same order in all subsequent questioning (Sanford, 1987). The agenda-setting function of the direct examination is quite strong. Although attorneys might wish to read a physician's deposition into the record, controlled experimentation in an industrial accident case revealed that direct testimony was more influential on the awards granted (Jacoubovitch, Bermant, Crockett, McKinley, & Sanstad, 1977). Based on observations of actual trials, Antieau (1999) found that attorneys using indirect language in direct examination enhanced jurors' favorable impressions of witnesses. The phrasing of questions made a significant difference in the answers secured and, as a consequence, in the potential influence produced.

In one study, simply asking a car crash eyewitness, "About how fast were the cars going when they *smashed into* each other?," increased mock jurors' perceptions of the speed of the cars more than when the collision was described as cars that "hit" or "contacted" each other (Loftus & Palmer, 1974). Similar work involving car crashes revealed that attorneys who used unmarked adverbs ("How fast was the car going?") during witness

questioning induced more extreme perceptions of speed and damage (Lipscomb, McAllister, & Bregman, 1985). Jurors also seemed to pay attention to the practical implications of witness answers. If the witness made a statement with indirect language (e.g., "After I heard the shot, I went to the telephone"), jurors completed the implication in their own minds (e.g., inferring that the witness made a phone call, probably to the police; Harris, Teske, & Ginns, 1978).

Cross-examination can be very influential, sometimes even reversing juror decisions. In the case of eyewitnesses, defense attorney cross-examination that exposed inconsistencies in testimony reduced rates of conviction among mock jurors (Berman & Cutler, 1996). These effects were great even when the inconsistencies dealt with peripheral rather than central case facts (Berman, Narby, & Cutler, 1995). Even among highly credible witnesses, exposing inconsistencies in testimony resulted in discounting the evidence (Devine & Ostrom, 1985). The phrasing of cross-examination questions can influence jurors. A lawyer's asking for very brief responses to specific questions stimulated the impression that witnesses were not as competent, intelligent, or assertive as those whose answers were not so constricted by the cross-examiner (Conley, O'Barr, & Lind, 1978).

Cross-examining attorneys often use leading questions that suggest desired answer and some research has revealed that defense attorneys using them decrease the frequency of guilty verdicts (Gibbs, Sigel, Adams, & Grossman, 1989). In one study of 42 cross-examination sessions, student jurors exposed to extensive use of leading questions during cross-examination were more likely to believe accurate than inaccurate witnesses, whereas nonleading questions were most likely to stimulate belief in inaccurate witnesses (Wells, Lindsay, & Ferguson, 1979). Even so, the use of leading questions and questions designed to increase control over the witness resulted in decreased amounts of the witness's testimony (Stutman, 1986a). Other work has found that the prosecuting attorneys' attempts to attack the experts by asking personally intrusive cross-examination questions (e.g., "has your own husband/wife ever cheated on you?" "do you often encourage your clients to talk about their sexuality and sexual concerns with you?") backfired and actually led higher witness credibility ratings than when nonintrusive questions were asked (Larson & Brodsky, 2010).

Closing Statements

Much lore and some research have been dedicated to the closing statement. Jurors reported believing that the closing argument was vital, some rating it as second only to the presentation of evidence (Matlon, Davis, Catchings, Derr, & Waldron, 1985). Furthermore, 75% of lawyers believed that the closing arguments could have decisive effects in close cases (Walter-Goldberg, 1985). Disturbingly, in death penalty cases, improper statements made by prosecuting attorneys in the closing statements increased the rates at which jurors voted for the death penalty (Platania, 1996). Significant relationships existed among actual jurors' favoring the prosecutor's closing argument and juror recall, belief, and interestingness. Yet no relationship was found among these elements and juror verdicts. Some studies noted a general recency effect favoring the influence of closing arguments over opening statements (e.g., Wood, Sicafuse, Miller, & Chomos, 2011). During argument in the sentencing portion of a trial, the prosecution (which speaks first in that portion of the trial) has an advantage over the defense because the defense must respond to the prosecution demands and, hence, the prosecution gets to structure the flow of the argument (Englich, Mussweiler, & Strack, 2005).

Judges' Instructions

Judges are considered the captains of the court. Although lawyers' lore probably exaggerates this effect, there is little doubt that judges' comments affect jurors. Jurors have been found to return verdicts that please the judge (O'Mara,

1972). In one experiment with jury-eligible adults, even when admonished to disregard the judge's behavior and form their own opinions, jurors returned verdicts in accordance with the judge's dispositions (Hart, 1995).

The judge's instructions are designed to influence jurors to promote the cause of justice, but they have often featured jargon, passive voice, and odd syntax (Buchanan, Pryor, Taylor, & Strawn, 1978). By one estimate, 45% of judges' instructions may be misunderstood (Charrow & Charrow, 1979). Even in capital cases, where courts have paid great attention to refining instructions, jurors tend not to understand them, and closing arguments by attorneys have seemed impotent to overcome the defect (Haney & Lynch, 1997).

The Status of Legal Persuasion Research

Since the first edition of this volume, much has changed, but many of the concerns expressed in 2002 still remain. Because many studies of legal persuasion have reflected variable-by-variable inquiry, advances in the study of persuasion in the law have suffered by the failure to guide much research by relevant theories or conceptualizations. To be sure, the story model has focused much research, but the failure to provide consistent support for this theory may be taken as a general sign that the search for theoretic alternatives still is required. Some have thought of enlisting the contributions of other theories designed for the general study of persuasion, and there is little question that such an approach may be of some benefit. Yet, it also must be recognized that the legal setting is a genre of communication (the forensic setting) that also is typified by distinct forms of language, lines of argument, and case construction forms. Thus, it would make sense for legal persuasion theorists to search for new analogies to guide research or, at least, to adapt existing theories to the unique influences of the legal setting.

Such projects require movement beyond simple appropriation of influence theories to the full development of new applications. In short, *there is a pressing need for new theory that is purpose-built for the study of persuasion in the legal setting.*

Despite the contributions of research in legal persuasion, considerable criticism—often from practitioners—has been directed at the entire domain of study. Though recognizing the benefit of laboratory research, DeMatteo and Anumba (2009) urged caution in generalizing about demographic variables in jury research. The primary charges involve issues of research using mock jurors and the realism of laboratory research in legal persuasion. *Future research on legal communication should utilize samples that show close correspondence with jury pools and methods that accurately capture and control the real-world exigencies of the domain.*

Most research in legal persuasion has involved the trial setting, and though it is justifiably the focus of this chapter, one may wonder if the most important legal persuasion is ignored by this approach. In reality, "Only about 5 to 15 percent of felony cases actually go to trial" (Kressel & Kressel, 2002, p. 6). Thus, most persuasion takes place in negotiations settings other than the court. Yet, this form of persuasion is difficult to study and, hence, it rarely is the object of inquiry. *Without discounting the value of trial research, scholarly inquiry in legal communication would be wise to broaden the scope of investigation to include alternative locations for persuasive legal argument.*

Summary

The role of legal persuasion as a branch of communication studies has grown dramatically over the recent years. The study of persuasion in the courtroom has shown great contributions to the research and theory in the areas of pretrial publicity messages, courtroom messages (including the impact of trial charges, juror assessment of

issue surrounding the burden of proof, persuasion during *voir dire* proceedings, the impact of opening statements, defense case strategies including insanity defenses, recovered memory cases, use of the entrapment defense, the battered woman defense), case evidence (confession evidence, alibi evidence), witness evidence (defendant testimony, eyewitness testimony, expert witnesses, scientific evidence, inadmissible evidence), the manner of evidence presentation, direct and cross-examination, closing statements, and judges' instructions. This chapter makes a selective review of each of these topics and concludes with a discussion of the general status of work in legal persuasion research as it enters the first year of the 21st century.

Notes

1. It should be mentioned that this chapter is limited to trial-related persuasion although, of course, lawyers often have to persuade their clients during interviews. Furthermore, negotiation and alternative dispute resolution issues are excluded from this discussion largely for practical reasons of space limitations. Similarly, parole board decisions, juvenile justice hearings, and family court hearings are excluded. In addition, unlike the previous version of this chapter, sections on theoretic orientations, source characteristics (including race), and juror dispositions have been excluded, though they are available from the author on request.

2. A popular claim has been the assertion that 80% of jurors make up their minds during the opening statement (see Perrin, 1999, p. 124). Apparently, this often cited statistic was based on a misreading of the American Jury Project of Kalven and Zeisel (1966, esp. p. 488). These authors found that in nearly 90% of the cases, the jurors' initial opinions on entering the jury rooms did not change. In addition, because more than 80% of the criminal cases were decided in favor of the prosecution, there was opportunity for the statistic to take on a life of its own as it was retold as trial lore. In 1988, Zeisel responded to users of the misrepresented statistic and encouraged them to use caution (Zeisel, 1988).

3. Indeed, both race and juror dispositions often are vital influences. Quite the contrary is the case. In their summary of the literature on race in trial persuasion, Sommers (2007) explained, "Though the extant literature is not always consistent and has devoted too little attention to the psychological mechanisms underlying the influence of race, this body of research clearly demonstrates that race has the potential to impact trial outcomes" (p. 171). Jury dispositions similarly are known to have a strong influence on the reception of attempts at attorney persuasion.

4. Some studies claimed to investigate inadmissible testimony but really did not. For instance, Carretta and Moreland (1983), J. Johnson (1994), Sue, Smith, and Caldwell (1973), and Werner, Kagehiro, and Strube (1982) presented participants with newspaper-style summaries of trials in which inadmissible testimony was included. Participants did not actually hear or read trials in which the evidence was or was not presented.

References

Ahola, A. S., Hellstrom, A, & Christianson, S. A. (2010). Is justice really blind? Effects of crime descriptions, defendant gender and appearance, and legal practitioner gender on sentences and defendant evaluations in a mock trial. *Psychiatry, Psychology and Law, 17*, 304–324.

Allison, M., & Brimacombe, C. (2010). Alibi believability: The effect of prior convictions and judicial instructions. *Journal of Applied Social Psychology, 40*, 1054–1084.

Antieau, L. D. (1999). Indirectness in the courtroom: A question of politeness or control? *Masters Abstracts International, 37*, 0430.

Arens, R., Granfield, D. D., & Susman, J. (1965). Jurors, jury charges, and insanity. *Catholic University Law Review, 14*, 1–29.

Aristotle. (1941). *Rhetorica.* In W. R. Roberts (Trans.), *The works of Aristotle* (Vol. 11). Oxford UK: Clarendon Press.

Arsenault, D. J., & Reinard, J. C. (1997, April). *The effect of attorney-directed question types in* voir dire *upon jury deliberation, defendant culpability, and attorney sociability.* Paper presented at the meeting of the Western Psychological Association, Seattle, WA.

Barnett, M., Brodsky, S., & Davis, C. (2004). When mitigation evidence makes a difference: Effects of psychological mitigating evidence on sentencing decisions in capital trials. *Behavioral Sciences & the Law, 22*, 751–770.

Bayly, M. J. (1989). The impact of opening statement presentation order and trial information content on jurors' evaluations of the trial and defendant. *Dissertation Abstracts International: Section B: The Sciences and Engineering, 50*(5), 2203B.

Berman, G. L., & Cutler, B. L. (1996). Effects of inconsistencies in eyewitness testimony on mock juror decision making. *Journal of Applied Psychology, 81*, 170–177.

Berman, G. L., Narby, D. J., & Cutler, B. L. (1995). Effects of inconsistent eyewitness statements on mock-jurors' evaluations of the eyewitness, perceptions of defendant culpability, and verdicts. *Law and Human Behavior, 19*, 79–88.

Bollingmo, G., Wessel, E., Sandvold, Y., Eilertsen, D., & Magnussen, S. (2009). The effect of biased and non-biased information on judgments of witness credibility. *Psychology Crime & Law, 15*, 61–71.

Borgida, E., & Park, R. (1988). The entrapment defense: Juror comprehension and decision making. *Law and Human Behavior, 12*, 19–40.

Bornstein, B. H., Rung, L. M., & Miller, M. K. (2002). The effects of defendant remorse on mock juror decisions in a malpractice case. *Behavioral Sciences & the Law, 20*, 393–409.

Bregman, N. J., & McAllister, H. A. (1987). Perceived innocence or guilt: Role of eyewitness identification and fingerprints. *Southern Psychologist, 3*, 49–52.

Brekke, N., & Borgida, E. (1988). Expert psychological testimony in rape trials: A social-cognitive analysis. *Journal of Personality and Social Psychology, 55*, 372–386.

Brigham, J. C., & Bouthwell, R. K. (1983). The ability of prospective jurors to estimate the accuracy of eyewitness identifications. *Law and Human Behavior, 7*, 19–30.

Bright, D. A., & Goodman-Delahunty, J. (2006). Gruesome evidence and emotion: Anger, blame, and jury decision-making. *Law and Human Behavior, 30*, 183–202.

Buchanan, R. W., Pryor, A., Taylor, K. P., & Strawn, D. (1978). Legal communication: An investigation of juror comprehension of pattern instructions. *Communication Quarterly, 26*, 31–35.

Bucolo, D., & Cohn, E. (2010). Playing the race card: Making race salient in defence opening and closing statements. *Legal and Criminological Psychology, 15,* 293–303.

Burke, T. M., & Turtle, J. W. (2003). Alibi evidence in criminal investigations and trials: Psychological and legal factors. *Canadian Journal of Police and Security Services, 1,* 286–294.

Burke, T., & Turtle, J. (2004, March). *Can you back me up? How the perception of an alibi is affected by the characteristics of the corroborator.* Paper presented at the annual meeting of the American Psychology-Law Society, Scottsdale, AZ.

Butler, B. (2007). The role of death qualification in jurors' susceptibility to pretrial publicity. *Journal of Applied Social Psychology, 37,* 115–123.

Casper, J. D., & Benedict, K. M. (1993). The influence of outcome information and attitudes on juror decision making in search and seizure cases. In R. Hastie (Ed.), *Inside the juror: The psychology of juror decision making* (pp. 65–83). New York, NY: Cambridge University Press.

Charrow, R. P., & Charrow, V. R. (1979). Making legal language understandable: A psycholinguistic study of jury instructions. *Columbia Law Review, 79,* 208–218.

Chrzanowski, L. (2006). Rape? Truth? And the media: Laboratory and field assessments of pretrial publicity in a real case. *Dissertation Abstracts International: Section B: The Sciences and Engineering, 67*(1), 580B.

Cirincione, C., Steadman, H. J., & McGreevy, M. A. (1995). Rates of insanity acquittals and the factors associated with successful insanity pleas. *Bulletin of the American Academy of Psychiatry and the Law, 23,* 399–409.

Conley, J. M., O'Barr, W. M., & Lind, E. A. (1978). The power of language: Presentation style in the courtroom. *Duke Law Journal, 6,* 1375–1399.

Cook, A., Arndt, J., & Lieberman, J. (2004). Firing back at the backfire effect: The influence of mortality salience and nullification beliefs on reactions to inadmissible evidence. *Law and Human Behavior, 28,* 389–410.

Cox, M., & Tanford, S. (1989). Effects of evidence and instructions in civil trials: An experimental investigation of rules of admissibility. *Social Behavior, 4,* 31–55.

Crocker, C., & Kovera, M. (2010). The effects of rehabilitative *voir dire* on juror bias and decision making.

Law and Human Behavior, 34, 212–226. doi: 10.1007/s10979-009-9193-9

Daftary-Kapur, T. (2010). The effects of pre- and post-venire publicity on juror decision-making. *Dissertation Abstracts International: Section B: The Sciences and Engineering, 70*(10), 6605B.

Daftary-Kapur, T., Dumas, R., & Penrod, S. (2010). Jury decision-making biases and methods to counter them. *Legal and Criminological Psychology, 15,* 133–154.

Dahl, J., Enemo, I., Drevland, G., Wessel, E., Eilertsen, D., & Magnussen, S. (2007). Displayed emotions and witness credibility: A comparison of judgements by individuals and mock juries. *Applied Cognitive Psychology, 21,* 1145–1155.

DeMatteo, D., & Anumba, N. (2009). The validity of jury decision-making research. In J. D. Lieberman & D. A. Krauss (Eds.), *Jury psychology: Social aspects of trial processes: Psychology in the courtroom* (Vol. 1, pp. 1–23). Burlington, VT: Ashgate.

Devenport, J. L., Cutler, B. L., & Penrod, S. D. (1998, March). *The impact of opposing expert testimony in cases involving eyewitness identification evidence.* Paper presented at the biannual meeting of the American Psychology-Law Society, Redondo Beach, CA.

Devenport, J. L., Studebaker, C. A., & Penrod, S. D. (1999). Perspectives on jury decision making: Cases with pretrial publicity and cases based on eyewitness identifications. In F. T. Durso, R. Nickerson, S. Dumais, R. Schvaneveldt, M. Chu, & S. Lindsay (Eds.), *Handbook of applied cognition* (pp. 819–845). New York, NY: Wiley.

Devine, P. G., & Ostrom, T. M. (1985). Cognitive mediation of inconsistency discounting. *Journal of Personality and Social Psychology, 49,* 5–21.

Dexter, H. R., Cutler, B. L., & Moran, G. (1992). A test of *voir dire* as a remedy for the prejudicial effects of pretrial publicity. *Journal of Applied Social Psychology, 22,* 819–832.

Dolnik, L., Case, T., & Williams, K. (2003). Stealing thunder as a courtroom tactic revisited: Processes and boundaries. *Law and Human Behavior, 27,* 267–287.

Edwards, K., & Bryan, T. S. (1997). Judgmental biases produced by instructions to disregard: The (paradoxical) case of emotional information. *Personality and Social Psychology Bulletin, 23,* 849–864.

Ellis, L. (2002). Don't find my client liable, but if you do . . . Defense recommendations, liability verdicts, and general damage awards. *Dissertation Abstracts International: Section B: The Sciences and Engineering, 63*(3-B), 1608.

Elwork, A., Sales, B. D., & Alfini, J. J. (1977). Juridic decisions: In ignorance of the law or in light of it? *Law and Human Behavior, 1,* 163–169.

Englich, B., Mussweiler, T., & Strack, F. (2005). The last word in court: A hidden disadvantage for the defense. *Law and Human Behavior, 29,* 705–722.

Fein, S., McCloskey, A. L., & Tomlinson, T. M. (1997). Can the jury disregard that information? The use of suspicion to reduce the prejudicial effects of pretrial publicity and inadmissible testimony. *Personality and Social Psychology Bulletin, 23,* 1215–1226.

Fein, S., Morgan, S. J., Norton, M. I., & Sommers, S. R. (1997). Hype and suspicion: The effects of pretrial publicity, race, and suspicion of jurors' verdicts. *Journal of Social Issues, 53,* 487–502.

Fienberg, S. E. (Ed.). (1989). *The evolving role of statistical assessments as evidence in the courts.* New York, NY: Springer-Verlag.

Fischer, S. M., & Fehr, L. A. (1985). The effect of defendant's plea on mock juror decisions. *Journal of Social Psychology, 125,* 531–533.

Fishfader, V. L., Howells, G. N., Katz, R. C., & Teresi, P. S. (1996). Evidential and extralegal factors in juror decisions: Presentation mode, retention, and level of emotionality. *Law and Human Behavior, 20,* 565–572.

Fleming, M. A., Wegener, D. T., & Petty, R. E. (1999). Procedural and legal motivations to correct for perceived judicial biases. *Journal of Experimental Social Psychology, 35,* 186–203.

Freundlich, K. F. (1985). Effects of pretrial publicity and ego level on verdict and jury deliberation styles. *Dissertation Abstracts International: Section B: The Sciences and Engineering, 45,* 3055B–3056B.

Geck, S., & Reinard, J. C. (2009, February). *A model of the biasing effects of inadmissible testimony on jury decisions.* Paper presented at the Western States Communication Association Convention, Phoenix-Mesa, AZ.

Gibbs, M. S., Sigal, J., Adams, B., & Grossman, B. (1989). Cross-examination of the expert witness: Do hostile tactics affect impressions of a simulated jury? *Behavioral Sciences & Law, 7,* 275–281.

Greene, E., & Dodge, M. (1995). The influence of prior record evidence on juror decision making. *Law and Human Behavior, 19,* 67–78.

Greene, E., Downey, C., & Goodman-Delahunty, J. (1999). Juror decisions about damages in employment discrimination cases. *Behavioral Sciences & the Law, 17,* 107–121.

Greene, E., & Loftus, E. F. (1984). What's new in the news? The influence of well-publicized news events on psychological research and courtroom trials. *Basic and Applied Social Psychology, 5,* 211–221.

Greene, E., & Wade, R. (1988). Of private talk and public print: General pre-trial publicity and juror decision-making. *Applied Cognitive Psychology, 2,* 123–135.

Grofman, B. (1985). The effect of restricted and unrestricted verdict options on juror choice. *Social Science Research, 14,* 195–204.

Gutheil, T. G. (1999). A confusion of tongues: Competence, insanity, psychiatry, and the law. *Psychiatric Services, 50,* 767–773.

Haegerich, T., & Bottoms, B. L. (2000). Empathy and jurors' decisions in patricide trials involving child sexual assault allegations. *Law and Human Behavior, 24,* 421–448.

Haney, C. (1984). On the selection of capital juries: The biasing effects of the death-qualification process. *Law and Human Behavior, 8,* 121–132.

Haney, C., & Lynch, M. (1997). Clarifying life and death matters: An analysis of instructional comprehension and penalty phase closing arguments. *Law and Human Behavior, 21,* 575–595.

Hans, V. P., & Vidmar, N. (1986). *Judging the jury.* New York, NY: Plenum Press.

Harris, R. J., Teske, R. R., & Ginns, M. J. (1978). Memory for pragmatic implications from courtroom testimony. *Bulletin of the Psychonomic Society, 6,* 494–496.

Hart, A. J. (1995). Naturally occurring expectation effects. *Journal of Personality and Social Psychology, 68,* 109–115.

Hastie, R., Schkade, D. A., & Payne, J. W. (1999). Juror judgments in civil cases: Effects of plaintiff's requests and plaintiff's identity on punitive damage awards. *Law and Human Behavior, 23,* 445–470.

Henkel, L. (2008). Jurors' reactions to recanted confessions: Do the defendant's personal and dispositional characteristics play a role? *Psychology, Crime & Law, 14,* 565–578.

Hirsch, R. O., Reinard, J. C., & Reynolds, R. A. (1976, May). *The influence of objection to mundane and sensational testimony on attorney credibility.* Paper presented at the meeting of the Rocky Mountain Psychological Association, Phoenix, AZ.

Hobbs, P. (2003). 'Is that what we're here about?': A lawyer's use of impression management in a closing argument at trial. *Discourse & Society, 14,* 273–290.

Hoffman, H. M., & Brodley, J. (1952). Jurors on trial. *Missouri Law Review, 17,* 235–251.

Hoiberg, B. C., & Stires, L. K. (1973). The effect of several types of pretrial publicity on the guilt attributions of simulated jurors. *Journal of Applied Social Psychology, 3,* 267–275.

Holt, R. W., O'Connor, J. A., Smith, J. L., Gessner, T. L., Clifton, T. C., & Mumford, M. D. (1997). Influences of destructive personality information on decision making. *Journal of Applied Social Psychology, 27,* 781–799.

Horn, E. R. (1976). The effects of a prior conviction and kind of conflicting evidence on the attribution of credibility to a witness by a juror. *Dissertation Abstracts International: Section B: The Sciences and Engineering, 37,* 2570B.

Horowitz, I. A., Bordens, K. S., Victor, E., Bourgeois, M. J., & ForsterLee, L. (2001). The effects of complexity on jurors' verdicts and construction of evidence. *Journal of Applied Psychology, 86,* 641–652.

Hvistendahl, J. (1979). The effect of placement of biasing information. *Journalism Quarterly, 56,* 863–865.

Imrich, D. J., Mullin, C., & Linz, D. (1995). Measuring the extent of prejudicial pretrial publicity in major American newspapers: A content analysis. *Journal of Communication, 45*(3), 94–117.

Jacoubovitch, M. D., Bermant, G., Crockett, G. T., McKinley, W., & Sanstad, A. (1977). Juror responses to direct and mediated presentations of expert testimony. *Journal of Applied Social Psychology, 7,* 227–238.

Johnson, C., & Haney, C. (1994). Felony *voir dire:* An exploratory study of its content and effect. *Law and Human Behavior, 18,* 487–506.

Johnstone, R. (1994). The empty chair doctrine revisited: An examination of the relative influences of attorneys and judges. (Master's thesis, San Jose State University, 1993). Masters Abstracts International, 32, 0734.

Jones, S. E. (1987). Judge- versus attorney conducted *voir dire:* An empirical investigation of juror candor. *Law and Human Behavior, 11,* 131–146.

Kagehiro, D. K. (1990). Defining the standard of proof in jury instructions. *Psychological Science, 1,* 194–200.

Kaplan, M. F., & Kemmerick, G. D. (1974). Juror judgment as information integration: Combining evidential and nonevidential information. *Journal of Personality and Social Psychology, 30,* 493–499.

Kaplan, M. F., & Miller, C. E. (1977). Judgments and group discussion: Effect of presentation and memory factors on polarization. *Social Psychology Quarterly, 40,* 337–343.

Kasin, M., Spanos, N. P., Terrance, C. A., & Peebles, S. (1993). Battered women who kill: Jury simulation and legal defenses. *Law and Human Behavior, 17,* 289–312.

Kassin, S. M., & Neumann, K. (1997). On the power of confession evidence: An experimental test of the fundamental difference hypothesis. *Law and Human Behavior, 21,* 469–484.

Kassin, S. M., & Sommers, S. R. (1997). Inadmissible testimony, instructions to disregard, and the jury: Substantive versus procedural considerations. *Personality and Social Psychology Bulletin, 23,* 1046–1054.

Kassin, S. M., & Wrightsman, L. S. (1980). Prior confessions and mock juror verdicts. *Journal of Applied Social Psychology, 10,* 133–146.

Kassin, S. M., & Wrightsman, L. S. (1981). Coerced confessions, judicial instructions, and mock juror verdicts. *Journal of Applied Social* Psychology, *11,* 489–506.

Katzev, R. D., & Wishart, S. S. (1985). The impact of judicial commentary concerning eyewitness identifications on jury decision making. *Journal of Criminal Law and Criminology, 76,* 733–745.

Kaufmann, G., Drevland, G. C. B., Wessel, E., Overskeid, G., & Magnussen, S. (2003). The importance of being earnest: Displayed emotions and witness credibility. *Applied Cognitive Psychology, 17,* 21–34.

Kerr, N. L. (1978). Severity of prescribed penalty and mock jurors' verdicts. *Journal of Personality and Social Psychology, 36,* 1431–1442.

Kerr, N. L., Atkin, R. S., Stasser, G., Meek, D., Holt, R.W., & Davis, J. H. (1976). Guilt beyond a reasonable doubt: Effects of concept definition and assigned decisional rule on the judgments of mock jurors. *Journal of Personality and Social Psychology, 34,* 282–294.

Kerr, N. L., Kramer, G. R., Carroll, J. S., & Alfini, J. J. (1991). On the effectiveness of *voir dire* in criminal cases with prejudicial pretrial publicity: An empirical study. *American University Law Review, 40,* 665–701.

Kerr, N. L., Niedermeier, K. E., & Kaplan, M. F. (1999). Bias in jurors vs. bias in juries: New evidence from the SDS perspective. *Organizational Behavior and Human Decision Processes, 80,* 70–86.

Key, H. G., Warren, A. R., & Ross, D. F. (1996). Perceptions of repressed memories: A reappraisal. *Law and Human Behavior, 20,* 555–563.

Koch, C. M., & Devine, D. J. (1999). Effects of reasonable doubt definition and inclusion of a lesser charge on jury verdicts. *Law and Human Behavior, 23,* 653–674.

Kovera, M. B. (2002). The effects of general pretrial publicity on juror decisions: An examination of moderators and mediating mechanisms. *Law and Human Behavior, 26,* 43–72.

Kovera, M. B., & Greathouse, S. M. (2008). Pretrial publicity: Effects, remedies, and judicial knowledge. In E. Borgida & S. T. Fiske (eds.), *Beyond common sense: Psychological science in the courtroom* (pp. 261–279). Malden, MA: Blackwell Publishing.

Kramer, G. P., & Kerr, N. L. (1989). Laboratory simulation and bias in the study of juror behavior: A methodological note. *Law and Human Behavior, 13,* 89–99.

Kramer, G. P., Kerr, N. L., & Carroll, J. S. (1990). Pretrial publicity, judicial remedies, and jury bias. *Law and Human Behavior, 14,* 409–438.

Kressel, N. J., & D. F. Kressel. (2002). *Stack and sway: The new science of jury consulting.* Boulder, CO: Westview Press.

Larntz, K. (1975). Reanalysis of Vidmar's data on the effects of decision alternatives on verdicts of simulated jurors. *Journal of Personality and Social Psychology, 31,* 123–125.

Larson, B. A., & Brodsky. S. L. (2010). When cross-examination offends: How men and women assess intrusive questioning of male and female expert witnesses. *Journal of Applied Social Psychology, 40,* 811–830.

Laub, C. (2010). Can earwitness limitations be overcome by the court system? Strategies to help mock jurors appreciate the limitations of earwitness testimony. *Dissertation Abstracts International: Section B: The Sciences and Engineering, 71*(4), 2712.

Lewis, E. W. (1997). A social psychological investigation of legal entrapment. *Dissertation Abstracts International: Section B: The Sciences and Engineering, 58,* 458B.

Levett, L. M., & Kovera, M. B. (2009). Psychological mediators of the effects of opposing expert testimony on juror decisions. *Psychology, Public Policy, and Law, 15,* 124–148.

Lindsay, R. C. L. (1994). Expectations of eyewitness performance: Jurors' verdicts do not follow from their beliefs. In D. F. Ross, J. D. Read, & M. P. Toglia (Eds.), *Adult eyewitness testimony: Current trends and developments* (pp. 362–384). New York, NY: Cambridge University Press.

Lindsay, R. C. L., Lim, R., Marando, L., & Cully, D. (1986). Mock-juror evaluations of eyewitness testimony: A test of metamemory hypotheses. *Journal of Applied Social Psychology, 16,* 447–459.

Linz, D., Penrod, S., & McDonald, E. (1986). Attorney communication and impression making in the courtroom: Views from off the bench. *Law and Behavior, 10,* 281–302.

Lipscomb, T. J., McAllister, H. A., & Bregman, N. J. (1985). Bias in eyewitness accounts: The effects of question format, delay interval, and stimulus presentation. *Journal of Psychology, 119,* 207–212.

Loftus, E. F., & Palmer, J. P. (1974). Reconstruction of automobile destruction: An example of the interaction between language and memory. *Journal of Verbal Learning and Behavior, 13,* 585–589.

Ludwig, K., & Fontaine, G. (1978). Effect of witnesses' expertness and manner of delivery of testimony on verdicts on simulated jurors. *Psychological Reports, 42,* 955–961.

Lymburner, J. A., & Roesch, R. (1999). The insanity defense: Five years of research (1993–1997). *International Journal of Law and Psychiatry, 22,* 213–240.

MacLin, M., Downs, C., MacLin, O., & Caspers, H. (2009). The effect of defendant facial expression on mock juror decision-making: The power of remorse. *North American Journal of Psychology, 11,* 323–332.

Mallard, D., & Perkins, D. (2005). Disentangling the evidence: Mock jurors, inadmissible testimony and integrative encoding. *Psychiatry, Psychology and Law, 12,* 289–297.

Malouff, J., & Schutte, N. S. (1989). Shaping juror attitudes: Effects of requesting different damage amounts in personal injury trials. *Journal of Social Psychology, 129,* 491–497.

Matlon, R. J., Davis, J. W., Catchings, B. W., Derr, W. R., & Waldron, V. R. (1985, November). *Factors affecting jury decision-making.* Paper presented at the meeting of the Speech Communication Association, Denver, CO.

McAllister, H. A., & Bregman, N. J. (1986). Juror underutilization of eyewitness nonidentifications: Theoretical and practical implications. *Journal of Applied Psychology, 71,* 168–170.

McCullough, G. W. (2007). Function of text structure in jurors' comprehension and decision making. *Psychological Reports, 101,* 723–730.

McKimmie, B. M., Newton, C. J., Terry, D. J., & Schuller, R. A. (2004). Jurors' responses to expert witness testimony: The effects of gender stereotypes. *Group Processes and Intergroup Relations, 7,* 131–143.

McMahon, E. A. (1974). A study of the relationship of psychiatric testimony and juror variables to the decision process. (Doctoral dissertation, University of Florida). *Dissertation Abstracts International, 35,* 3025B.

Mosmann, A. L. (1998). Nothing but the truth: Mock jurors' use of stricken evidence in decision-making. *Dissertation Abstracts International: Section B: The Sciences and Engineering, 59,* 893B.

Mullin, C. R. (1997). The impact of acquaintance rape scripts and case-specific pretrial publicity on juror decision-making. *Dissertation Abstracts International: Section B: The Sciences and Engineering, 57,* 3733B.

Mullin, C. R., Imrich, D. J., & Linz, D. (1996). The impact of acquaintance rape stories and case specific pretrial publicity on juror decision making. *Communication Research, 23,* 100–135.

Neuschatz, J., Lawson, D., Swanner, J., Meissner, C., & Neuschatz, J. (2008). The effects of accomplice witnesses and jailhouse informants on jury decision making. *Law and Human Behavior, 32,* 137–149.

Nietzel, M. T., & Dillehay, R. C. (1982). The effects of variations in *voir dire* procedures in capital murder trials. *Law and Human Behavior, 6,* 1–13.

Ogloff, J. R. P. (1993). Jury decision making and the insanity defense. In N. J. Castellan Jr. (Ed.), *Individual and group decision making: Current issues* (pp. 167–201). Hillsdale, NJ: Erlbaum.

Olson, E. A., & Wells, G. L. (2004a, March). *Not as easy as it looks: Alibi generation influences alibi evaluation.* Paper presented at the American Psychology-Law Society Annual Conference, Scottsdale, AZ.

Olson, E., & Wells, G. (2004b). What makes a good alibi? A proposed taxonomy. *Law and Human Behavior, 28,* 157–176.

O'Mara, J. J. (1972). The courts, standard jury charges: Findings of a pilot project. *Pennsylvania Law Review, 120,* 166–175.

Otto, A. L., Penrod, S. D., & Dexter, H. R. (1994). The biasing impact of pretrial publicity on juror judgments. *Law and Human Behavior, 18,* 453–469.

Otto, A. L., Penrod, S. D., & Hirt, E. (1990). *The influence of pretrial publicity on juror judgments in civil case.* Unpublished manuscript.

Padawer-Singer, A. M., Singer, A., & Singer, R. (1974). *Voir dire* by two lawyers: An essential safeguard. *Judicature, 57,* 386–391.

Payne, C. R. (2007). The elaboration likelihood model of persuasion: Implications for trial advocacy. *The International Journal of Speech, Language and the Law, 14,* 309–312.

Perrin, L. T. (1999). From O. J. to McVeigh: The use of argument in the opening statement. *Emory Law Journal, 48,* 107–167.

Pettus, A. B. (1990). The verdict is in: A study of jury decision making factors, moment of personal decision, and jury deliberations—From the jurors' point of view. *Communication Quarterly, 38,* 83–97.

Pickel, K. L., Karam, T. J., & Warner, T. C. (2009). Jurors' responses to unusual inadmissible evidence. *Criminal Justice and Behavior, 36,* 466–480.

Platania, J. (1996). Prosecutorial misconduct promotes wrongful death sentences. (Doctoral dissertation, Florida International University, 1995). *Dissertation Abstracts International, 56,* 5226B.

Posey, A. J. (1996). Blame assignment in affirmative defense cases: Who has the burden of proof? *Dissertation Abstracts International: Section B: The Sciences and Engineering, 56,* 7098B.

Poulson, R. L. (1990). Mock juror attribution of criminal responsibility: Effects of race and the guilty but mentally ill (GBMI) verdict option. *Journal of Applied Social Psychology, 20,* 1596–1611.

Poulson, R. L., Braithwaite, R. L., Brondino, M. J., & Wuensch, K. L. (1997). Mock jurors' insanity defense verdict selections: The role of evidence, attitudes, and verdict options. *Journal of Social Behavior and Personality, 12,* 743–758.

Poulson, R. L., Brondino, M. J., Brown, H., & Braithwaite, R. L. (1998). Relations among mock jurors' attitudes, trial evidence, and their selections of an insanity defense verdict: A path analytic approach. *Psychological Reports, 82,* 3–16.

Poulson, R. L., Wuensch, K. L., Brown, M. B., & Braithwaite, R. L. (1997). Mock jurors' evaluations of insanity defense verdict selection: The role of death penalty attitudes. *Journal of Social Behavior and Personality, 12,* 1065–1078.

Pryor, B., & Buchanan, R. W. (1984). The effects of a defendant's demeanor on juror perceptions of credibility and guilt. *Journal of Communication, 34*(3), 92–99.

Pyszczynski, T. A., Greenberg, J., Mack, D., & Wrightsman, L. S. (1981). Opening statements in a jury trial: The effect of promising more than the evidence can show. *Journal of Applied Social Psychology, 11,* 434–444.

Pyszczynski, T. A., & Wrightsman, L. S. (1981). The effects of opening statements on mock jurors' verdicts in a simulated criminal trial. *Journal of Applied Social Psychology, 11,* 301–313.

Rahaim, G. L., & Brodsky, S. L. (1982). Empirical evidence versus common sense: Juror and lawyer knowledge of eyewitness accuracy. *Law and Psychology Review, 7,* 1–11.

Raimo, A. M. (1987). Psychological challenges to eyewitness testimony. *American Journal of Forensic Psychology, 5,* 23–36.

Raitz, A., Greene, E., Goodman, J., & Loftus, E. F. (1990). Determining damages: The influence of expert testimony on jurors' decision making. *Law and Human Behavior, 14,* 385–395.

Read, J., Connolly, D., & Welsh, A. (2006). An archival analysis of actual cases of historic child sexual abuse: A comparison of jury and bench trials. *Law and Human Behavior, 30,* 259–285.

Redding, R. E., Floyd, M. Y., & Hawk, G. L. (2001). What judges and lawyers think about the testimony of mental health experts: A survey of the courts and bar. *Behavioral Sciences & the Law, 19,* 583–594.

Reinard, J. C. (1981, February). *Effects of inadmissible evidence from law enforcement officers on jury decisions.* Paper presented at the meeting of the Western Speech Communication Association, San Jose, CA.

Reinard, J. C. (1985, February). *The effects of witness inadmissible testimony on jury decisions: A comparison of four sources.* Paper presented at the meeting of the Western Speech Communication Association, Fresno, CA.

Reinard, J. C. (1989, February). Explaining inadmissible testimony effects on jurors: Crucial experimental tests of a model of the influence of inadmissible material. Paper presented at the meeting of the Western Speech Communication Association, Spokane, WA.

Reinard, J. C. (1993, February). *A model of the effects of inadmissible testimony on civil case decisions.* Paper presented at the meeting of the Western States Communication Association, Albuquerque, NM.

Reinard, J. C. (2009, November). *An experimental study of the use of* voir dire *questions to preview case elements and promote positive attitudes toward defendants.* Paper presented at the meeting of the National Communication Association, Chicago, IL.

Reinard, J. C. (2010, February). *Study of* voir dire *questions previewing cases advancing positive assessment of defendants: A causal model.* Paper presented at the meeting of the Western States Communication Association, Anchorage, AK.

Reinard, J. C., & Arsenault, D. J. (2000). The impact of forms of strategic and non-strategic *voir dire* questions on jury verdicts. *Communication Monographs, 67,* 159–177.

Reinard, J. C., Arsenault, D. J., & Geck, S. (1998, February). *Models of the influence of strategic* voir dire *questions on jury decision making.* Paper presented at the meeting of the Western States Communication Association, Denver, CO.

Reinard, J. C., Khalid, O., & Liso, J. (2001, February). *Persuading the jury through* voir dire *questioning designed to establish rapport and empathy.* Paper presented at the meeting of the Western States Communication Association, Coeur d'Alene, ID.

Reinard, J. C., & Reynolds, R. A. (1978). The effects of inadmissible testimony objections and rulings on jury decisions. *Journal of the American Forensic Association, 15,* 91–109.

Rogers, J., Bloom, J., & Manson, S. (1984). Insanity defenses: Contested or conceded? *The American Journal of Psychiatry, 141,* 885–888.

Rosen, A. P. (1997). Factors affecting juror decision-making in repressed-memory cases. *Dissertation Abstracts International: Section B: The Sciences and Engineering, 58,* 0447B.

Ruva, C. L., & McEvoy, C. (2008). Negative and positive pretrial publicity affect juror memory and decision making. *Journal of Experimental Psychology: Applied, 14,* 226–235.

Ruva, C., McEvoy, C., & Bryant, J. (2007). Effects of pre-trial publicity and jury deliberation on juror bias and source memory errors. *Applied Cognitive Psychology, 21,* 45–67. doi: 10.1002/acp.1254

Saks, M. J., & Wissler, R. L. (1984). Legal and psychological bases of expert testimony: Surveys of the law and of jurors. *Behavioral Sciences & the Law, 2,* 435–449.

Sanford, S. (1987). The nature of discourse in the courtroom: The complete rape trial. *Dissertation Abstracts International, A: The Humanities and Social Sciences, 48,* 2460A.

Savitsky, J., Czyzewski, D., Dubord, D., & Kaminisky, S. (1976). Age and emotion of an offender as determinants of adult punitive reactions. *Journal of Personality, 44,* 311–320.

Savitsky, J., & Sim, M. (1974). Trading emotions: Equity theory of reward and punishment. *Journal of Communication, 24*(1), 140–147.

Schaffer, S. J. (1985). Can jurors disregard inadmissible evidence? (Doctoral dissertation, American University, 1984). *Dissertation Abstracts International, 45,* 1595B.

Schklar, J., & Diamond, S. S. (1999). Juror reactions to DNA evidence: Errors and expectancies. *Law and Human Behavior, 23,* 159–184.

Schmolesky, J. M., Cutler, B. L., & Penrod, S. D. (1988). Presumption instructions and juror decision making. *Forensic Reports, 1,* 165–192.

Schuller, R., McKimmie, B., & Janz, T. (2004). The impact of expert testimony in trials of battered women who kill. *Psychiatry, Psychology and Law, 11,* 1–12.

Schweitzer, N. J., & Saks, M. J. (2009). The gatekeeper effect: The impact of judges' admissibility decisions on the persuasiveness of expert testimony. *Psychology, Public Policy, and Law, 15,* 1–18.

Semmler, C., & Brewer, N. (2002). Effects of mood and emotion on juror processing and judgments. *Behavioral Sciences & the Law, 20,* 423–436.

Shaffer, D. R., Case, T., & Brannen, L. (1979). Effects of withheld evidence on juridic decisions: Amount of evidence withheld and its relevance to the case. *Representative Research in Social Psychology, 10,* 2–15.

Shaffer, D. R., Plummer, D., & Hammock, G. (1986). Hath he suffered enough? Effects of jury dogmatism, defendant similarity, and defendant's pretrial suffering on juridic decisions. *Journal of Personality and Social Psychology, 50,* 1059–1067.

Shaw, J. I., & Skolnick, P. (2004). Effects of prejudicial pretrial publicity from physical and witness evidence on mock juror's decision making. *Journal of Applied Social Psychology, 34,* 2132–2148.

Siebert, F., Wilcox, W., & Hough, G., III. (C. R. Bush, Ed.). (1970). *Free press and fair trial: Some dimensions of the problem.* Athens: University of Georgia Press.

Smith, M. (1995). Evaluation of the effects of Proposition 115 on *voir dire* practices in the criminal justice system. *Masters Abstracts International, 33,* 769.

Sommers, S. R. (2006). On racial diversity and group decision making: Identifying multiple effects of racial composition on jury deliberations. *Journal of Personality and Social Psychology, 90,* 597–612.

Sommers, S. R., & Douglass, A. (2007). Context matters: Alibi strength varies according to evaluator perspective. *Legal and Criminological Psychology, 12,* 41–54.

Sommers, S. R., & Norton, M. (2008). Race and jury selection: Psychological perspectives on the peremptory challenge debate. *American Psychologist, 63,* 527–539.

Sporer, S., Penrod, S., Read, D., & Cutler, B. L. (1995). Choosing, confidence, and accuracy: A meta-analysis of the confidence-accuracy relation in eyewitness identification studies. *Psychological Bulletin, 118,* 315–327.

Steadman, J. J., Keitner, L., Braff, J., & Arvanites, T. M. (1983). Factors associated with a successful insanity plea. *American Journal of Psychiatry, 140,* 401–405.

Steblay, N., Hosch, H. M., Culhane, S. E., & McWethy, A. (2006). The impact on juror verdicts of judicial instruction to disregard inadmissible evidence: A meta-analysis. *Law Human Behavior, 30,* 469–492.

Strong, J. W. (Ed.). (1992). *McCormick on evidence* (4th ed.). New York, NY: John Wiley.

Studebaker, C. A., & Penrod, S. D. (1997). Pretrial publicity: The media, the law, and common sense. *Psychology, Public Policy, and Law, 3,* 428–460.

Studebaker, C. A., & Penrod, S. D. (2005). Pretrial publicity and its influence on juror decision making. In N. Brewer & K. D. Williams (Eds.), *Psychology and law: An empirical perspective* (pp. 254–275). New York, NY: Guilford Press.

Stutman, R. K. (1986a, February). *Testimony control and witness narration during courtroom examination.* Paper presented at the meeting of the Western Speech Communication Association, Tucson, AZ.

Stutman, R. K. (1986b). Witness disclaiming during examination. *Journal of the American Forensic Association, 23,* 96–101.

Sue, S., Smith, R. E., & Gilbert, R. (1974). Biasing effects of pretrial publicity on judicial decisions. *Journal of Criminal Justice, 2,* 163–171.

Sue, S., Smith, R. E., & Pedroza, G. (1975). Authoritarianism, pretrial publicity, and awareness of bias in simulated jurors. *Psychological Reports, 37,* 1299–1302.

Suggs, D., & Berman, J. J. (1979). Factors affecting testimony about mitigating circumstances and the fixing of punishment. *Law and Human Behavior, 3,* 251–260.

Tanford, S. (1985). Decision-making processes in joined criminal trials. *Criminal Justice and Behavior, 12,* 367–385.

Tanford, S., & Penrod, S. (1984). Social inference processes in juror judgments of multiple-offense trials. *Journal of Personality and Social Psychology, 47,* 749–765.

Thomas, E. A., & Hogue, A. (1976). Apparent weight of evidence, decision criteria, and confidence ratings in juror decision making. *Psychological Review, 83,* 442–465.

Thompson, W. C., Fong, G., & Rosenhan, D. (1981). Inadmissible evidence and juror verdicts. *Journal of Personality and Social Psychology, 40,* 453–463.

Thompson, W. C., & Schumann, E. L. (1987). Interpretation of statistical evidence in criminal trials. *Law and Human Behavior, 11,* 167–187.

Towell, N. A., Kemp, R. I., & Pike, G. E. (1996). The effects of witness identity masking on memory and person perception. *Psychology, Crime, and Law, 2,* 333–346.

Wallace, W., & Wilson, W. (1969). Reliable recency effects. *Psychological Reports, 25,* 311–317.

Walter-Goldberg, B. (1985). The jury summation as speech genre: An ethnographic study of what it means to those who use it (language/lawyer). *Dissertation Abstracts International, A: The Humanities and Social Sciences, 46,* 3710A.

Weld, H. P., & Danzig, E. R. (1940). A study of the way in which a verdict is reached by a jury. *American Journal of Psychology, 53,* 518–536.

Wells, G. L., Lindsay, R. C., & Ferguson, T. J. (1979). Accuracy, confidence, and juror perceptions in eyewitness identification. *Journal of Applied Psychology, 64,* 440–448.

Whitley, B. E., Jr. (1987). The effects of discredited eyewitness testimony: A meta-analysis. *Journal of Social Psychology, 127,* 209–214.

Wistrich, A. J., Guthrie, C., & Rachlinski, J. J. (2005). Can judges ignore inadmissable[sic] information: The difficulty of deliberately disregarding. *University of Pennsylvania Law Review, 153,* 1251–1345.

Wolf, S., & Montgomery, D. A. (1977). Effects of inadmissible evidence and level of judicial admonishment to disregard on the judgments of mock jurors. *Journal of Applied Social Psychology, 7,* 205–219.

Wood, S. M., Sicafuse, L. L., Miller, M. K., & Chomos, J. C. (2011). The influence of jurors' perceptions of attorneys and their performance on verdict. *The Jury Expert, 23*(1), 23–34. Retrieved from http://www.thejuryexpert.com/2011/01/the-influence-of-jurors-perceptions-of-attorneys-and-their-performance-on-verdict/

Woody, W., & Forrest, K. (2009). Effects of false-evidence ploys and expert testimony on jurors' verdicts, recommended sentences, and perceptions of confession evidence. *Behavioral Sciences & the Law, 27,* 333–360.

Wright, D., & Hall, M. (2007). How a "reasonable doubt" instruction affects decisions of guilt. *Basic and Applied Social Psychology, 29,* 91–98.

Yandell, B. (1979). Those who protest too much are seen as guilty. *Personality and Social Psychology Bulletin, 5,* 44–47.

Zeisel, H. (1988, Summer). A jury hoax: The superpower of the opening statement. *The Litigator,* pp. 17–18.

Zickafoose, D. J., & Bornstein, B. H. (1999). Double discounting: The effects of comparative negligence on mock juror decision making. *Law and Human Behavior, 23,* 577–596.

Ziemke, M. (2010). To flatter the jury: Ingratiation effects during closing arguments. *Masters Abstracts International, 48*(1), 0630.

CHAPTER 21

Persuading in the Small Group Context

Kyle R. Andrews, Franklin J. Boster, and Christopher J. Carpenter

n 1935, Muzafer Sherif brought subjects into a dark room with a pinpoint of light shining on the wall. The task of the subjects was to estimate the distance that pinpoint of light was moving. The light was actually stationary, but because of the autokinetic effect, it appears otherwise to the human eye. Making judgments alone, subjects' distance estimates varied substantially. Sherif then had the same subjects make distance estimates in groups. Across a series of trials the variance in the judgments decreased until the group members converged on a value approximating closely the mean of the initial individual group member estimates. This resulting estimate was proffered by the subjects even when they were asked to make estimates privately on subsequent trials, indicating that the group influence that occurred was not merely an external acquiescence to the group, but rather involved private acceptance as well.

In another study of perceptual acuity, Solomon Asch (1951, 1955) had subjects report which of three lines matched a fourth reference line. The answer was obvious—so obvious that virtually none of the subjects (<1%) provided the wrong answer when making the decision alone. Because of the environment in which they made their decision, however, subjects were not nearly as accurate when responding in a group context. Of the group members participating in the experiment, only one was an actual subject. The remainder were confederates trained to give a uniform, incorrect answer, all delivered save one prior to the subject's turn. In this situation Asch found that subjects gave the wrong answer 36.8% of the time. Post-experimental interviews indicated that although some of the subjects thought they could have been wrong in their judgments, the majority knew they were correct, but instead conformed with their fellow group members.

These two studies are often cited as early experimental demonstrations of two types of influence: influence that results in public conformity and private acceptance (Sherif), and influence that results in public conformity but not private acceptance (Asch). Subsequently, theorists have offered a variety of alternative terms for these two concepts, such as Festinger's (1953) public conformity with private acceptance versus public conformity without private acceptance, Deutsch and Gerard's (1955) informational influence versus normative influence, and Kelman's (1961) internalization versus compliance. Pertinent to this chapter, this conceptual distinction facilitates defining persuasion by identifying it with public conformity with private acceptance, and serves to distinguish it from other forms of social influence. Consistent with Bettinghaus (1981), a persuasion attempt will be construed as any effort to alter, reinforce, or shape the attitude of another via verbal or nonverbal communication. If the communication attempt is successful and private acceptance results, then persuasion will be said to have occurred. This chapter focuses solely on persuasion that occurs in the group context, to the exclusion of other forms on influence that are known to occur in groups.

The term "group" is harder to define. In the main, scholars agree that three or more individuals are necessary to term the collective a group, with some disagreement on whether dyadic interactions should be considered group interactions. Groups must meet requirements in addition to a lower limit of members, however. Shaw (1981) suggests that groups are collections of people who are interdependent, interact often, have a collective identity, share common goals, have organizational structure, and in some way(s) satisfy the needs of fellow group members. If "groupness" is viewed as a quantitative, not qualitative, distinction, then a collection of people that fulfill these criteria to a greater extent can be considered more of a group than other collections of people.

Complexities in the Study of Group Persuasion

Although valuable, distinctions such as persuasion versus compliance present an overly simple view of group influence. One reason is that there are empirical relationships between these constructs. So, for example, in cognitive dissonance and self-perception experiments, scholars have demonstrated that obtaining compliance can lead to attitude change (see Festinger & Carlsmith, 1959; and Bem, 1965, for seminal examples). A second reason is that in natural settings in which it is clear that social influence has occurred (e.g., Jonestown) it is difficult, perhaps impossible, to parse the forms that influence takes. And, even if this task could be managed, it would be yet more challenging to quantify the amount of influence due to each of the parsed sources of influence.

Nevertheless, in certain domains considerable strides in delineating the process by which groups can persuade each other have been made. The remainder of this chapter focuses on three of these areas: the ways in which group members persuade each other, the ways in which group members are persuaded by nongroup members, and the ways in which nongroup members are persuaded by group members.

Persuasion Within Groups

The Choice Shift

A choice shift occurs when a group's post-discussion decision is more extreme than the mean of the group members' pre-discussion decisions. Initially, evidence of group decisions that were more risky than the pre-discussion average was uncovered (Stoner, 1961), and thus the phenomena was termed originally the risky shift. Evidence of a cautious shift soon emerged, however, resulting in the more generic phrase, group polarization, and later the choice shift.

In a typical choice shift experiment, subjects read choice dilemmas (CD), scenarios in which they must choose between two alternative courses of action. One of these alternatives, Option A is said to result in a relatively modest return, but with a high probability of occurring. The other alternative, Option B, is said to have the potential to result in a very high return, but with a low probability of occurring. Subjects are then presented with a range of probabilities that Option B would succeed, and their task is to rate the probability of Option B succeeding necessary for them to choose instead of Option A. One example used by Wallach, Kogan, and Bem (1962) is that of a college student who has to choose between going to medical school and becoming a doctor (an option that has a high probability of success for this student), or attempting to become a concert pianist (the preferred profession, but one at which the student is said to be less likely to succeed). The response items provided to the subject offer a range of probabilities that the college student will succeed as a concert pianist (10% chance of success, 20% chance of success, etc.), and the subjects must decide the lowest probability of success they would be able to tolerate for them to recommend that the college student attempt to become a concert pianist. After making these decisions individually, subjects then discuss the scenario in groups, and come to a collective decision. It is these group decisions that are typically more extreme (either more cautious or more risky) than the mean of the individual group members' prediscussion position.

A number of theories have been proposed to explain this effect, and to use Deutsch and Gerard's (1955) distinction, they can generally be categorized into theories based in normative influence and theories based in informational influence. Social comparison theory (SCT) is the dominant normative explanation (see Laughlin & Early, 1982). In a clear summary of SCT, Pruitt (1971) argues that mere exposure to the views of other group members is both necessary and sufficient to obtain the choice shift. He asserts that group members are motivated to equal or exceed their fellow group members of certain valued dimensions, such as risk or caution. Moreover, although they may be incorrect, prior to discussion, group members believe that they do so. Subsequent exposure to the opinions of others serves to indicate to many group members that they were incorrect. These group members then adjust their opinions accordingly so that they equal or exceed the group norm that they underestimated (see also Boster & Hale, 1989, p. 534).

Recently, alternative normative explanations have been proposed. According to the self-categorization explanation, group members naturally contrast their in-group to out-groups, especially when group salience is high. When this contrast process occurs, in-group members shift their opinions in such a way as to make their group more differentiated from an out-group, thus resulting in a more polarized group decision (Abrams, Wetherell, Cochrane, Hogg, & Turner, 1990, but see Krizan & Baron, 2007). Complementary findings have emerged from research on group polarization in the computer-mediated context. A number of studies (Lee, 2007; Sia, Tan, & Wei, 2002; Spears, Lea, & Lee, 1990) have found that when group members are deindividuated via the process of computer-mediated communication, group identity increases and group polarization is enhanced. Lee (2008) found evidence that individuated groups were more adept at distinguishing strong versus weak arguments than deindividuated groups, and were also more likely to make decisions based on message content. Deindividuated groups, on the other hand, processed less systematically, and incorporated normative considerations in making judgments.

A second more recent normative explanation is Henningsen & Henningsen's (2004) moderation-elasticity theory. Building on the work of Cialdini and colleagues (Cialdini, Levy, Herman, & Evenbeck, 1973; Cialdini, Levy, Herman, Kozlowski, & Petty, 1976; Cialdini & Petty, 1981), the moderation-elasticity explanation proposes that group members choose more moderate positions before an anticipated interaction because they do not know the positions of others, and moderate positions present the possibility for more social rewards than extreme positions. Once the position of group members is known, the hedging benefits of a moderate position disappear, and it behooves the group member to move in the direction of the group position (either as a result of normative or informational pressures), resulting in the choice shift.

More relevant to this chapter are the explanations of group polarization rooted in informational influence. The foremost informational influence explanation is persuasive arguments theory (PAT). PAT postulates that a pool of arguments favoring both risky and cautious alternatives exists. For CD items that produce a risky shift, the pool of risky arguments exceeds in both number and persuasiveness the pool of cautious arguments, the reverse being the case for CD items that produce a cautious shift. The complete pool of arguments is unknown to each group member, and the set of known arguments varies from group member to group member. Discussion results in sharing arguments so that each group member is exposed to novel arguments. Because of the skewed distribution of arguments in the argument pool, discussion results in each group member learning of more reasons and more extreme reasons to embrace the risky (cautious) alternative. Consequently, group members change their opinions and embrace more extreme positions.

Isenberg's (1986) review found evidence consistent with the PAT explanation of the choice shift. The first type of evidence comes from studies that have coded the arguments presented in group discussion, and then examined whether the number of risky (cautious) arguments correlates positively with the riskiness (cautiousness) of the final decision. Studies of this type generally find that there is a correlation between the number of risky (cautious) arguments presented during discussion, and the extent of a risky (cautious) shift. Of course, strong evidence for causality cannot be provided by correlational data, as a third factor could be the cause of both the type of arguments presented in discussion and the type of risky shift observed.

More robust evidence for PAT comes from studies that measure individual posttest positions and compare them to the final group position. If persuasion did occur and is the mechanism that explains the shift, then the final group position is expected to equal the mean of the individual group members' posttest positions.

Studies that have examined both variables (Boster, Fryrear, Mongeau, & Hunter, 1982; Boster, Mayer, Hunter, & Hale, 1980) have found that there is a very high correlation between them (exceeding .80.)

Another type of evidence discussed by Isenberg (1986) involves experiments that control the number of risky versus cautious arguments received by group members. When subjects receive more risky (cautious) arguments than cautious (risky) arguments, a risky (cautious) shift typically emerges, which is the expected outcome if the choice shift is the result of persuasion, not normative pressures.

Although the data indicate that process of persuasion explains choice shifts accurately, there is disagreement as to how that processes is manifested (Meyers & Seibold, 1990). A number of alternative explanations of the persuasion process have been proposed, including Hoffman's (1961) group valence model (GVM; see also Hoffman & Kleinman, 1994), McPhee, Poole, and Seibold's (1982) distribution of valence model (DVM; see also McPhee, 1994), and Boster and colleagues' (1980, 1982) linear discrepancy model (LDM).

GVM proposes that the most important factor in determining the adoption of a decision choice is not the attitudes of individual group members toward each decision choice, but the group's perception of a decision choice's valence. A study testing the GVM would code the arguments provided in group discussion for each decision option, and calculate a valence score for each option by subtracting the number of negatively valenced comments from the number of positively valenced comments. The decision option the theory predicts the group will choose is the option that has the largest positive differential score.

The DVM proposes, on the other hand, that individual judgments do matter in determining the group outcome. The group decision choice predicted by the DVM is the choice that has the highest valence for the most group members. An experiment testing the DVM would assess the valence of comments made by individual group members during discussion, and calculate which option was described more positively by each group member. A decision criterion, such as majority rule, is then applied, such that the decision option that was most positive for the most group members would be the decision option predicted to be chosen by the group.

In many cases both models make the same predictions, but there are cases where the models differ. An example would be when a minority makes a number of strong arguments for a given position, and a majority argues less strongly for a different position. The GVM would predict that the minority position would prevail, as its decision option would have had the highest differential between positive and negative arguments presented. Alternatively, DVM would predict that the majority position would prevail, as the largest number of group members would have spoke in favor of the majority position during discussion. Meyers and Brashers (1998) is one of the few studies to test competing predictions from the two models, and found the data to be more consistent with the DVM than the GVM for cases in which the models made competing predictions.

Although both the GVM and DVM attend carefully to the types or arguments offered in discussion, they specify neither the operative form of social influence nor the process used by group members to influence each other. A model that attempts to address this issue is the LDM (Boster et al., 1980, 1982, 1991), a version of French's (1956) theory of communication discrepancy. The LDM proposes that all group members are persuaded by the arguments advanced by their fellow group members throughout the group discussion process until a consensual position is reached. Individual group members hear the arguments of other group members, compare the argument position to their own attitude position, and adjust their attitude in the direction of the position advocated in the argument. If each group member were to speak with equal frequency, LDM would predict that the final group decision would be equal to the mean of individual group members' attitudes

before discussion. If group members do not speak with equal frequency, the final position reached by the group will be a weighted mean of individual prediscussion attitudes, with frequency of speech being the weighting variable.

Tests of the LDM have provided data consistent with the model (Boster et al., 1980, 1982, 1991). When group members with risky initial attitudes talk more than group members with cautious initial attitudes, a risky shift is observed; the opposite occurs when group members with cautious initial attitudes dominate discussion. For choice decision items that consistently produce a risky (cautious) shift, LDM posits (as does PAT) that there exists more risky (cautious) arguments available and accessible to group members on these topics and that they are expressed during discussion.

The LDM does not propose that extreme members are disproportionately influential unless they speak more frequently than other group members. Research on extreme group members has generally found they are not more influential than more moderate group members (Myers & Murdoch, 1972). Nevertheless, there is some evidence that extreme group members play a disproportionate role in group discussions. Van Swol (2009) found evidence of extreme group members talking more, both in terms of the proportion of total words spoken and the proportion of conversational turns. But, although groups were polarized after discussion, groups with an extreme member did not polarize to a greater extent than groups without extreme members.

Van Swol (2009) suggests that an explanation for why the presence of extreme members does not lead to increased polarization is that the conversational dominance of extreme group members prevents others group members from hearing the positions that might be espoused by all of their fellow group members, as well as from having the opportunity to be polarized by the repetition of their own positions. Brauer, Judd, and Gliner (1995) found that the repeated expression of one's opinion (and defense of that opinion) in group discussion leads to believing that opinion more strongly. Employing an experimental design that induced independently the number of times subjects repeated their position and the number of times each subject heard another subject's position (Study 1), they found that the number of times subjects repeated their position was a substantial predictor of group polarization. Thus, informational influence's role in the group polarization effect might be due not just to group members persuading each other to be more extreme, but group members persuading themselves as well.

Both the normative and informational influence camps can point to a large body of research consistent with their position. In an extensive literature review Isenberg (1986) speculated that both normative and informational influence have independent effects on the choice shift. Other alternatives are possible, of course, such as one form of influence leading to the other, or normative and informational influence combining nonadditively to affect group decisions.

An experiment by Boster and Mayer (1984) was done to test such an alternative possibility. They designed an experiment that varied majority position and argument strength, to test the effects of normative and informational influence, respectively. The majority position induction worked correctly, in that subjects were aware of the position held by a majority of group members. The argument strength induction did not work, however. Instead, the authors' report that participants perceived the arguments of the majority to be more persuasive than those of the minority. Causal analysis found that the perception of argument strength mediated the relationship between majority position and choice shift. Put differently, normative and informational influences did not operate independently to affect group decisions, but instead were linked in a causal sequence in which the perceived quality of arguments was determined by the number of persons advocating them.

Other studies report evidence of a more sophisticated relationship. Lee (2008) found that in a computer-mediated context, deindividuated subjects failed to distinguish between strong and weak arguments, whereas individuated subjects did. Additionally, individuated subjects were more persuaded by strong arguments than weak arguments, whereas deindividuated subjects were not. Examining individuated and deindividuated subjects separately across two decision tasks, Lee found that for individuated subjects, perceived argument quality, and not group identity, was an important predictor of conformity. Alternatively, for deindividuated subjects both perceived argument quality and group identity were statistically significant predictors of conformity for the first decision task, and only group identity for the second task.

Thus, deindividuation and group identity inductions influenced whether normative or informational cues affected decisions. Similar results were found by Boster and Hale (1989), who tested whether varying the ambiguity of the experimental materials affected whether normative or informational influence would dominate. When the experimental materials were ambiguous, SCT (but not PAT) predicted the choice shift; when the experimental materials were not ambiguous, PAT (but not SCT) predicted the choice shift. These findings point to a more nuanced picture of normative and informational influence in choice shifts, and are consistent with previous research on the ability of contextual features to alter the meaning of a persuasive message (Asch, 1948).

The Influence of Minorities

A large body of research has emerged on the ability of minority group members to influence majority group members, beginning with the seminal work of Moscovici, Lage, and Naffrechoux (1969). The Moscovici et al. experiment was motivated by the fact that a substantial corpus existed on the processes and effects of majority influence; whereas little research had been done examining whether and how minorities can influence majorities. In the Moscovici et al.

(1969) experiment subjects were shown blue slides and in the presence of others had to report what color they saw. Of the six people in the group, four were subjects and two were confederates instructed to answer "green" instead of "blue." In one condition, the confederates reported the slide as green on all 36 trials; in a second condition, the confederates reported the slide as green on 24 trials and blue on the other 12 trials. In a control condition, subjects answered without hearing the minority group members' judgments. The consistent minority condition resulted in subjects giving an answer of green 8.42%. The influence of the minority decreased dramatically when it behaved inconsistently, resulting in wrong answers only 1.25% of the time. In the control condition only 0.25% of the subjects judged the slides to be green. Although the size of the effect certainly was not large in comparison to research on majority influence, it was still sizable, and especially so given that correct answer was obvious.

A variety of theories with divergent experimental procedures has emerged to explain the effect. One of the earliest was Moscovici's (1980, 1985) dual process model, which posits that minorities influence majorities using informational influence, whereas majorities influence minorities via normative influence. More precisely, majorities encourage a comparison process in minorities, whereby minorities compare their position to the majority and focus on the relationships they have (and want to maintain) with the majority. The result is superficial processing that, if it results in a change in position, will produce compliance without internal acceptance. In contrast, minorities encourage the majority to engage in a validation process, whereby majority members try to understand the minority position. This process is thought to entail deeper processing, and thus result in more attitude change (if not public acceptance). Other dual process models (e.g., Nemeth, 1986) that have been proposed focus instead on how the relative positions of each group encourage convergent thinking (minorities focus on the majority position) or divergent thinking (majorities exposed to minority positions focus not just on the minority position, but other related ideas as well). Other attempts at explaining the phenomena include single process models (Latané & Wolf, 1981; Tanford & Penrod, 1984), as well as more general theories (Turner, 1991).

Given the variety of theories proposed on the topic, as well as the different ways in which tests of the various models have been conducted, it is difficult to draw firm, specific conclusions (Wood et al., 1994). Nonetheless, some broad conclusions can be drawn. The first is that although there is evidence that minority influence occurs, and this evidence is consistent with the dual process model (Wood et al., 1994), majority influence is both more powerful and more prevalent.

Second, minority members are more likely to influence majority members if they are consistent, both in terms of comments made throughout the course of the discussion, and in terms of consistency with other minority group members (Wood et al., 1994; for an example, see Meyers, Brashers, & Hanner, 2000). Note that the confederates in Moscovici et al. (1969) experiment met both of these behavioral criteria—in the condition in which the highest rate of influence was obtained, both confederates claimed that the slides were green on all 36 trials. Recent research has uncovered an additional way in which minorities can demonstrate consistency and increase their ability to influence—via the use of abstract language (Sigall, Mucchi-Faina, & Mosso, 2006). Linguists have found that when action is described abstractly, it tends to convey permanence and immutability to situational context, whereas concrete language conveys the opposite. Sigall et al. found that minorities using abstract language versus concrete language in group discussion were viewed as more consistent, and also had more success in exerting indirect influence. The influence of majorities, however, was not affected by whether they used abstract or concrete language.

Other behavioral characteristics of minority group members increase their persuasiveness as well. Persuasiveness of minorities is increased if the minority has agreed with the majority previously (Hollander, 1958), or has convinced majority members to defect (Clark, 1998). Whether the minority is an active versus a passive minority is another contributing factor (Kerr, 2002). An active minority is one that is aware that they are in the minority, is interdependent with others, and expects to interact with group members in the future. Kerr (2002) found that for low-relevance topics, passive minorities were not persuasive, regardless of whether they proffered strong or weak arguments. Active minorities, however, were more persuasive when presenting strong arguments compared to weak arguments, indicating that only active minorities instigate systematic processing among majority group members. Similar to the notion of an active minority, Baron and Bellman (2007) found data consistent with a "courage hypothesis;" minorities harassed by the majority in group discussions were more persuasive on multiple persuasion measures than minorities who were not harassed. These data indicate that minorities who defy majorities despite potential negative social sanctions are more likely to influence.

Another factor that affects the extent to which minority influence is likely to occur is the discussion task. Intellective tasks, or tasks that have demonstrably correct answers, result in more minority influence than judgmental tasks, or tasks without demonstrably correct answers. As Crutchfield (1955) demonstrated, normative influence increases when ambiguity increases, and it is possible that the reduction in normative influence on intellective tasks minority persuasion to occur. Intellective tasks likely also allow for stronger arguments to be made, and given that minority influence occurs primarily through informational influence, intellective tasks present a more fertile setting for minority influence to take root.

When attitude change does occur as a result of minority influence, investigators have also found that the nature of that attitude change differs from the attitude change observed as a result of majority influence. Martin, Hewstone, and Martin (2003, 2008) found that minority messages employing strong arguments were more resistant to counterpersuasion than majority messages, an effect found to result from the minority message instigating systematic processing. Consequently, the attitudes changed via minority influence were more highly correlated with behavioral intentions than attitudes changed via majority influence, again suggesting minorities instigate systematic processing (Martin, Martin, Smith, & Hewstone, 2007). Even when minority influence is unsuccessful immediately, it can have the effect of reducing the certainty with which majority members hold their opinion, when those majority members recognize that, they rejected the persuasive message because it was delivered by the minority, and when they recognize that this reason for rejecting these arguments is illegitimate. Additionally, those who viewed the reason as illegitimate (versus those who did not) were more likely to be persuaded by a subsequent message (Tormala, DeSensi, & Petty, 2007).

The research on minority influence points to a number of conclusions. First, if minorities are to influence majorities, they do so by persuading majority group members. Second, minorities are more persuasive when they act consistently, both in their expressed position and in their agreement with each other. And, third, tasks for which there are demonstrably correct answers present a better opportunity for minority influence than those that do not have a demonstrably correct answer. The mechanism by which minority influence occurs, that is, the factor(s) that mediate the relationship, has not been addressed frequently or definitively. Many minority group experiments are conducted on ad hoc groups, do not code the messages delivered during discussion, or both. Exceptions exist. Meyers, Brashers, and Hanner (2000) examined the argument patterns used by successful and unsuccessful minority and majority subgroups, and found that minority and majority groups' patterns of argument differed, as did successful and unsuccessful minority factions. Van Swol and Seinfeld (2006) examined the types of information provided by minority and majority group members in discussion, finding that successful minorities discussed more common information than successful majorities. Future research would benefit from examining these minority communication processes in greater depth.

Individual Differences

There is considerable research on individual differences that can lead to a person being an influential minority member, although it is not usually referred to as minority influence. Instead, it is generally termed opinion leadership. The study of opinion leadership has a long history in the social sciences, beginning with early studies on the role of influential network members (Katz & Lazerfeld, 1955; Lazerfeld, Berelson, & Gaudet, 1948) and continuing through modern diffusion scholarship (Rogers, 2003). Harnessing the power of opinion leaders is an effective means of affecting behavior change within a population, with examples ranging from campaigns to increase safe sex practices (Kelly et al., 1992; Miller, Klotz, & Eckholdt, 1998) and mammogram testing (Earp et al., 2002) to encouraging the implementation of different treatment practices among physicians (Soumerai et al., 1998).

Because of conceptually amorphous definitions of what constitutes opinion leadership, and because many of the most effective means to identify influential network members require an arduous and expensive data collection process (see Valente & Pumpuang, 2007, for a review), the usual methods by which campaign designers go about trying to identify opinion leaders is varied and inefficient. In response to these problems, Boster, Kotowski, Andrews, and Serota (2011) developed self-report measures to assess three dimensions of opinion leadership: the extent to which someone is highly connected within their social network, the extent to which someone possesses unusual persuasive abilities,

and the extent to which someone is a subject matter expert on healthy lifestyle issues.

A person high on all three measures (usually designated as being above the 75th percentile) is termed a superdiffuser. Boster et al. (2011) report considerable evidence consistent with the construct validity of these measures (see also Carpenter et al., 2009). Moreover, research has demonstrated that they can be adapted to areas outside of the health domain, such as politics (Serota, Carpenter, Andrews, & Boster, 2009). Finally, a campaign conducted using superdiffusers to diffuse multivitamin usage in a college population provided some preliminary evidence that superdiffusers can be effective diffusing health information, with more students at the experimental campus reporting having heard about people taking multivitamins, and fewer students ceasing to take multivitamins, compared to the control campus (Boster, Carpenter, Andrews, & Mongeau, 2012). Future research would benefit from examining the utility of employing superdiffusers to induce change and the extent to which the use of superdiffusers combines additively or nonadditively with the implementation of a traditional mass media campaign.

Of course, influential members of a network cannot always be relied on to pursue the same goals as the campaign designer. A health superdiffuser's opinion on a health topic could differ from the stance advocated in the campaign, and such a person could work assiduously to prevent adoption of the campaign recommendations. Evidence of this type of effect has been found in other programs of research. David, Cappella, and Fishbein (2006) conducted an experiment in which adolescents engaged in a chat room discussion regarding an antidrug public service advertisement, hypothesizing that those who were high sensation seekers (and hence more likely to have tried marijuana and have pro-marijuana attitudes) would engage in biased processing, counterargue more, and dominate discussion in a manner that persuades other group members not to accept the campaign message. They found data consistent with their predictions: high sensation seekers spoke more than middle or low sensation seekers, contributed more pro-drug than anti-drug comments, and made more negative comments about people in the discussion group. Furthermore, this behavior resulted in subjects in the chat condition reporting more pro-marijuana beliefs and attitudes, more pro-marijuana normative pressure, and being more likely to believe that they would be ostracized socially if they refused marijuana, compared to the no-chat condition.

Outsiders Versus Insiders

The question of whether in-group members are persuaded more effectively by a fellow in-group member versus an outsider has been investigated in one form or another for some years. Lewin (1947) found that women who were part of decision groups were substantially more likely to serve organ meats than those who heard a lecture urging them to do so (32% v. 3%). Mackie and colleagues (Mackie, Gastardo-Conaco, & Skelly, 1992; Mackie, Worth, & Asuncion, 1990) have also found evidence that in-group members are more persuasive than out-group members, but the effects of message source combined nonadditively with argument quality. Subjects were persuaded more by a relevant, strong message from an in-group source than a relevant, weak message (and not persuaded at all by messages from an out-group source). When the message topic was irrelevant to the group, however, there was a main effect only for group status.

Additional evidence for the persuasiveness of in-group members comes from studies building on self-categorization theory (Turner, 1987, 1991). Haslam, Jetten, O'Brien, and Jacobs (2004) found evidence that information provided by in-group members affected how subjects anticipated a potentially stressful upcoming event (a mental arithmetic task), although information from out-group members did not. When

an out-group member described the task as either stressful or challenging, subjects reported equal levels of stress. When an in-group member was the source, however, subjects reported feeling substantially less stress when the source said the task was challenging compared to when they described it as stressful.

Drawing on social comparison theory and self-categorization theory, Haslam et al. proposed that information from in-group sources was viewed as more valid than information provided by out-group members, as the in-group member was more qualified to provide information regarding social reality. In a conceptually similar experiment, Platow et al. (2005) found evidence that social proof in the form of canned laughter was more influential on subject behavior when it was attributed to in-group members versus out-group members. Subjects listening to a stand-up routine were more likely to laugh, smile, laugh for a longer duration, and rate the audio recording more positively if they were led to believe that the people on the prerecorded laugh track were in-group members compared to out-group members. Platow et al. (2006) extended the effect to a physiological dependent variable in a pain tolerance experiment that required subjects to hold their hands in ice water. Subjects who had received assurance from an in-group member (vs. out-group member) that the second experimental trial was easier than the first demonstrated significantly lower physiological arousal during the second trial (as measured by galvanic skin response).

Out-group members are not always ineffective persuaders, however. Wilder (1990) found evidence that differentiating out-group members, such as by providing information to subjects about out-group members' hometowns, majors, and names, increases their persuasive impact to the same levels as in-group members. So, although in-group members are usually more persuasive than out-group members, there are conditions under which in-group members will be relatively ineffective, and out-group members will be relatively effective.

Groups Persuading Non-group Members

Whether or not groups persuade non-group members is a question that first entails making a conceptual distinction, albeit one that is very difficult to make in practice. A group member can persuade a non-group member, independent of group affiliation—indeed, without the target even knowing the group membership of the source. Conversely, a group member could also persuade a non-group member, but with the source's group affiliation highly salient to the target (recognizing that salient target group affiliation is not necessarily the cause of persuasion, if persuasion does occur). Finally, the collective messages or actions of a group can persuade a target (recognizing that the members of the source group can vary in the extent to which they are differentiated as individuals to the target).

It is on this last area that the remainder of this section focuses. A good example is the research on the intra-audience effect, conducted by Hocking, Margreiter, and Hylton (1977) as a test of an idea proposed by Hylton (1971). Students were asked to attend a bar on one of two nights as part of a bogus experiment. Thirty confederates attended the bar on both nights. On the first night, the confederates exhibited little reaction to the band that was playing. The confederates talked among themselves, and did not seem to pay any attention to the band, nor react in one way or another to the songs that were played. The following night the same confederates acted very differently to a performance by the same band—they danced, applauded loudly, and cheered for an encore. The students asked to go to the bar were queried during the next class meeting for their evaluation of the band. As hypothesized, those students who had attended on the night when confederates exhibited positive reactions to the band rated the band far more positively than those students who had attended the bar on the night that the confederates exhibited indifference to the band.

Although the mediator(s) of the effect could not be specified, Hocking et al. (1977) proposed that the nonverbal messages of the confederates led to the differences in band evaluations. Notably, Festinger's social comparison theory (1950, 1954) could be applied to the case of intra-audience effects as well. Festinger theorized that when people are unsure of the accuracy of their beliefs, they are motivated to bolster them by consulting physical reality or by comparing themselves to others. The latter is more likely to occur when an objective, nonsocial means of comparison is not available. Other people are viewed as an accurate source of information, and informational influence can occur as a result of this comparison process. (It should be noted that research since Festinger's original formulation has uncovered a variety of other motivations for engaging in social comparison.) In the case of the Hocking et al. (1977) experiment, subjects were asked to form an attitude for a stimulus (a band) for which nonsocial, objective means of determining quality did not exist. Thus, the subjects looked to the opinions of others, and surmised from the enthusiastic nonverbal messages of the confederates that the "correct" belief was a positive endorsement. It is also possible to view the results of Hocking et al. in light of the research by Haslam et al. (2004) and Platow et al. (2005, 2006) discussed previously. Perhaps the students in the bar viewed themselves as being in the same in-group as the other bar goers, making them more likely to be influenced by intra-audience effects due to self-categorization and social comparison.

Directions for the Future

Four aspects of persuasion involving groups have been examined in the previous sections. Two dealt with persuasion within groups (choice shift, minority influence), one with the relative persuasive impact of minority versus majority members, and one with the ability of groups to influence individuals not affiliated with the group (intra-audience effects). This final section summarizes these corpuses and provides suggestions for future avenues of research.

The Choice Shift

The choice shift is a robust phenomenon, replicated frequently. The effect is consistent as well; certain experimental materials produce risky shifts and others produce cautious shifts across experiments. Thus, the focus of scholarship has been on theoretical frameworks to explain the findings. Numerous explanations have emerged over the last 50 years; some grounded in normative influence and some in informational influence. There has been little effort to integrate them, however, despite their pronounced similarities.

An integrated theory would have to address the relationship between informational and normative influence. Both normative and informational influences operate in choice shift experiments, and future theories must recognize this fact to advancement knowledge in this area. Evidence thus far suggests that informational and normative influence combining additively might be inadequate. Furthermore, testing such a model would be contingent on the ability to distinguish clearly between informational and normative influence, a task that has proven elusive to date.

Finally, the external and ecological validity of traditional choice shift experiments must be addressed if the claims of applicability proposed in many of the discussions of the phenomena are to be justified. Most experiments on the topic are conducted using students who are of the same status, have similar backgrounds, are not highly involved in the topic, and are making decisions in the absence of stress and time pressures. The contexts in which the choice shift is often offered as an explanation—the Cuban Missile Crisis, the Bay of Pigs invasion, the escalation of the Vietnam War—did involve those potentially important moderators. If, or how, those factors affect group decision making will not be understood until experiments are conducted that can approximate them convincingly.

The Influence of Minorities

Much like the choice shift, research on the influence of minorities would benefit from theoretical integration. Such a theory would have to account for the balance of normative and informational influence used, with majorities using the former more often than the later and minorities using the later more often than the former. The specific mechanisms by which the majority and minority exert normative and informational influence also remain unclear. Finally, an integrative theory would also have to account for the variety of persuasive outcomes unearthed in minority and majority research, such as direct influence, indirect influence, and delayed influence.

Similar to the choice shift, minority influence studies have many of the same external or ecological validity challenges. For instance, in natural groups, minorities have characteristics that are not always modeled in experimental situations. For example, minorities might know the majority's position better than the majority knows the minority position (Robinson & Keltner, 1996), giving them an initial persuasive advantage. Similarly, many experimental settings may occur too quickly to let nuances of minority influence unfold. Although majorities have the initial advantage when it comes to normative influence, minorities may be able to increase their ability to influence via normative means by silencing some members of the majority (Noelle-Neumann, 1993), thereby decreasing the majority's primary advantage.

Other factors change during discussion as well. Minorities espousing consistent positions throughout discussion are more persuasive than those who do not, a result that emerges from majorities viewing minorities' consistency positively. Because it takes time to demonstrate consistency of opinion, a majority's understanding of a minority position may be seen as less radical after the majority hears the complete minority explanation. This point is particularly applicable when the majority has preconceived notions of the minority position. In a study examining preferences of English faculty in selecting works for an introductory course syllabus, Robinson and Keltner (1996) found that traditionalists overestimated the amount of change advocated by revisionists, who in fact selected many works from the traditional literary canon. In a discussion format if the majority impression of the minority changed over time, it would affect the majority's view of the reasonableness of the minority.

In-Group Versus Out-Group Sources

Research on in-group and out-group sources has generated interesting findings about when either group will be influential. Disparities between experiments in how group identity is induced, however, complicate matters. Many experiments adopt Turner's (1982) definition of in-groups as "two or more individuals who share a common identification" (p. 15), and what constitutes an induction of common identification varies considerably across experiments. Many experiments use relatively trivial common identifications, such as university affiliation (Mackie et al., 1990, 1992; Wilder, 1990). Although typically effective at inducing perceptions of group identity, such inductions are not isomorphic with the level of in-group identity one would feel with one's immediate family or a long-standing work group, and the extent to which these differences affect results is not entirely clear. Finally, as with the previously discussed research streams, the area would benefit from theoretical developments that specify when one would expect in-groups to be persuasive and when we would expect out-groups to be persuasive.

Intra-audience Effects

Little research has been conducted on intra-audience effects since the work of Hylton (1971) and Hocking et al. (1977). In addition to the need for more research in the area, such experiments would be aided by a clearer conceptual development of the term "intra-audience effect." One question stemming from this ambiguity involves the difference between intra-audience effects and emotional contagion (Hatfield, Cacioppo, & Rapson, 1992). One distinction between the two might be the extent to which intra-audience effects are characterized as verbal and nonverbal signals that are interpreted cognitively by the receiver as information about the social environment. Conversely, the emotional contagion explanations focus on imitation, below conscious awareness, and the involvement of uncontrollable processes such as mirror neuron activation (see Iacoboni, 2009, for a review). Another distinction contrasts intra-audience effects based in informational influence versus the normative influence a group might have on a person's evaluation of an attitude object, perhaps because of a desire to be perceived as a good group member. As with other steams of research discussed in this chapter, whether these distinctions could be measured accurately is just as important to advancement as whether the distinction can be made conceptually.

References

Abrams, D., Wetherell, M., Cochrane, S., Hogg, M. A., & Turner, J. C. (1990). Knowing what to think by knowing who you are: Self-categorization and the nature of norm formation, conformity and group polarization. *British Journal of Social Psychology, 29,* 97–119.

Asch, S. E. (1948). The doctrine of suggestion, prestige, and imitation in social psychology. *Psychological Review, 55,* 250–276.

Asch, S. E. (1951). Effects of group pressure upon the modification and distortion of judgments.

In H. Guetzhow (Ed.), *Groups, leadership, and men* (pp. 177–190). Pittsburg, PA: Carnegie Press.

Asch, S. E. (1955). Opinions and social pressure. *Scientific American, 193*, 31–35.

Baron R. S., & Bellman S. B. (2007). No guts, no glory: Courage, harassment and minority influence. *European Journal of Social Psychology, 37*, 101–124.

Bem, D. J. (1965). An experimental analysis of self persuasion. *Journal of Experimental Social Psychology, 1*, 199–218.

Bettinghaus, E. P. (1981). *Persuasive communication.* New York, NY: Holt, Rinehart & Winston.

Boster, F. J., Carpenter, C. J., Andrews, K. R., & Mongeau, P. A. (2012). Employing interpersonal influence to promote multivitamin use. *Health Communication, 27*, 399–407.

Boster, F. J., Fryrear, J. E., Mongeau, P. A., & Hunter, J. E. (1982). An unequal speaking linear discrepancy model: Implications for the polarity shift. In M. Burgoon (Ed.), *Communication Yearbook 6* (pp. 395–418). Beverly Hills, CA: Sage.

Boster, F. J., & Hale, J. L. (1989). Response scale ambiguity as a moderator of the choice shift. *Communication Research, 16*, 532–551.

Boster, F. J., Hunter, J. E., & Hale, J. L. (1991). An information-processing model of jury decision making. *Communication Research, 18*, 524–547.

Boster, F. J., Kotowski, M. R., Andrews, K. R., & Serota, K. (2011). Identifying influence: Development and validation of the connectivity, persuasiveness, and maven scales. *Journal of Communication, 61*, 178–196.

Boster, F. J., & Mayer, M. E. (1984). Choice shifts: Argument qualities or social comparisons. In R. N. Bostrom (Ed.), *Communication Yearbook 8* (pp. 393–410). Beverly Hills, CA: Sage.

Boster, F. J., Mayer, M. E., Hunter, J. E., & Hale, J. L. (1980). Expanding the persuasive arguments explanation of the polarity shift: A linear discrepancy model. In D. Nimmo (Ed.), *Communication Yearbook 4* (pp. 165–176). New Brunswick, NJ: Transaction Books.

Brauer, M., Judd, C. M., & Gliner, M. D. (1995). The effects of repeated expressions on attitude polarization during group discussions. *Journal of Personality and Social Psychology, 68*, 1014–1029.

Carpenter, C. J., Kotowski, M. R., Boster, F. J., Andrews, K. R., Serota, K. S., & Shaw. A. S. (2009). Do superdiffusers argue differently? An analysis of argumentation style as a function of diffusion ability. *Argumentation and Advocacy, 45,* 151–170.

Cialdini, R., Levy, A., Herman, P., & Evenbeck, S. (1973). Attitudinal politics: The strategy of moderation. *Journal of Personality and Social Psychology, 25,* 100–108.

Cialdini, R., Levy, A., Herman, C., Kozlowski, L., & Petty, R. (1976). Elastic shifts of opinion: Determinants of direction and durability. *Journal of Personality and Social Psychology, 34,* 663–672.

Cialdini, R., & Petty, R. (1981). Anticipatory opinion effects. In R. Petty, T. Ostrom, & T. Brock (Eds.), *Cognitive responses in persuasion.* Hillsdale, NJ: Erlbaum.

Clark, R. D., III. (1998). Minority influence: The role of the rate of majority defection and persuasive arguments. *European Journal of Social Psychology, 28,* 787–796.

Crutchfield, R. S. (1955). Conformity and character. *American Psychologist, 10,* 191–198.

David, C., Cappella, J. N., & Fishbein, M. (2006). The social diffusion of influence among adolescents: Group interaction in a chat room environment about antidrug advertisements. *Communication Theory, 16,* 118–140.

Deutsch, M., & Gerard, H. G. (1955). A study of normative and informational social influence upon individual judgment. *Journal of Abnormal and Social Psychology, 51,* 629–636.

Earp, J. L., Eng, E., O'Malley, M. S., Altpeter, M., Rauscher, G., Mayne, L., et al. (2002). Increasing use of mammography among older, rural African American women: Results from a community trial. *American Journal of Public Health, 82,* 646–654.

Festinger, L. (1950). Informal social communication. *Psychological Review, 57,* 271–282.

Festinger, L. (1953). An analysis of compliant behavior. In M. Sherif & M. O. Wilson (Eds.), *Group relations at the crossroads* (pp. 323–256). New York, NY: Harper.

Festinger, L. (1954). A theory of social comparison processes. *Human Relations, 7,* 117–140.

Festinger, L., &Carlsmith, J. M. (1959). Cognitive consequences of forced compliance. *Journal of Abnormal and Social Psychology, 58,* 203–210.

French, J. R. P., Jr. (1956). A formal theory of social power. *Psychological Review, 63,* 181–194.

Haslam, S. A., Jetten, J., O'Brien, A., & Jacobs, E. (2004). Social identity, social influence, and reactions to potentially stressful tasks: Support for the self-categorization model of stress. *Stress and Health, 20,* 3–9.

Hatfield, E., Caccioppo, J. T., & Rapson, R. L. (1992) Primitive emotional contagion. *Review of Personal and Social Psychology, 14,* 151–177.

Henningsen, D. D., & Henningsen, M. L. M. (2004). Predeliberation moderation on choice dilemmas: Proposing a moderation-elasticity theory of choice shift. *Communication Monographs, 71,* 148–160.

Hocking, J. E., Margreiter, D. G., & Hylton, C. (1977). Intra-audience effects: A field test. *Human Communication Research, 3,* 243–249.

Hoffman, L. R. (1961). Conditions for creative problem-solving. *Journal of Psychology, 52,* 429–444.

Hoffman, L. R., & Kleinman, G. B. (1994). Individual and group in group problem solving: The valence model redressed. *Human Communication Research, 21,* 36–59.

Hollander, E. P. (1958). Conformity, status, and idiosyncrasy credit. *Psychological Review, 65,* 117–127.

Hylton, C. (1971). Intra-audience effects: Observable audience response. *Journal of Communication, 21,* 253–265.

Iacoboni, M. (2009). Imitation, empathy, and mirror neurons. *Annual Review of Psychology, 60,* 653–670.

Isenberg, D. J. (1986). Group polarization: A critical review and meta-analysis. *Journal of Personality and Social Psychology, 50,* 1141–1151.

Katz, E., & Lazarsfeld, P. F. (1955). *Personal influence.* New York, NY: Free Press.

Kelly, J. A., St. Lawrence, J. S., Stevenson, L. Y., Hauth, A. C., Kalichman, S. C., Diaz, Y. E., et al. (1992). Community AIDS/HIV risk reduction: The effects of endorsements of popular people in three cities. *American Journal of Public Health, 82,* 1483–1489.

Kelman, H. (1961). Processes of opinion change. *Public Opinion Quarterly, 25,* 57–78.

Kerr, N. L. (2002). When is a minority a minority? Active versus passive minority advocacy and social influence. *European Journal of Social Psychology, 32,* 471–483.

Krizan, Z., & Baron, R. S. (2007). Group polarization and choice-dilemmas: How important is self-categorization? *European Journal of Social Psychology, 37,* 191–201.

Latane, B., & Wolf, S. (1981). The social impact of minorities and majorities. *Psychological Review, 88,* 438–453.

Laughlin, P. R., & Early, P. C. (1982). Social combination models, persuasive arguments theory, social comparison theory, and the choice shift. *Journal of Personality and Social Psychology, 42,* 273–280.

Lazarsfeld, P., Berelson, B., & Gaudet, H. (1948). *The people's choice.* New York, NY: Columbia University Press.

Lee, E.-J. (2007). Deindividuation effects on group polarization in computer-mediated communication: The role of group identification, public-self-awareness, and perceived argument quality. *Journal of Communication, 57,* 385–403.

Lee, E.-J. (2008). When are strong arguments stronger than weak arguments? Deindividuation effects on message elaboration in computer-mediated communication. *Communication Research, 35,* 646–665.

Lewin, K. (1947). Group decision and social change. In T. M. Newcomb & E. L. Hartley (Eds.), *Readings in social psychology* (pp. 330–344). New York, NY: Holt.

Mackie, D. M., Gastardo-Conaco, M. C., & Skelly, J. J. (1992). Knowledge of the advocated position and the processing of in-group and outgroup persuasive messages. *Personality and Social Psychology Bulletin, 18,* 145–151.

Mackie, D. M., Worth, L. T., & Asuncion, A. G. (1990). Processing of persuasive in-group messages. *Journal of Personality and Social Psychology, 58,* 812–822.

Martin, R., Hewstone, M., & Martin, P. Y. (2003). Resistance to persuasive messages as function of majority and minority source status. *Journal of Experimental Social Psychology, 39,* 585–593.

Martin, R., Hewstone, M., & Martin, P. Y. (2008). Majority versus minority influence: The role of message processing in determining resistance to counter-persuasion. *European Journal of Social Psychology, 38,* 16–34.

Martin, R., Martin, P. Y., Smith, J. R., & Hewstone, M. (2007). Majority versus minority influence and prediction of behavioral intentions and behavior. *Journal of Experimental Social Psychology, 43,* 763–771.

McPhee, R. D., Poole, M. S., & Seibold, D. R. (1982). The valence model unveiled: A critique and reformulation. In M. Burgoon (Ed.), *Communication Yearbook 5* (pp. 259–278). New Brunswick, NJ: Transaction Books.

Meyers, R. A., & Brashers, D. E. (1998). Argument in group decision making: Explicating a process model and investigating the argument-outcome link. *Communication Monographs, 65,* 261–281.

Meyers, R. A., Brashers, D. E., & Hanner, J. (2000). Majority-minority influence: Identifying argumentative patterns and predicting argument-outcome links. *Journal of Communication, 50,* 3–30.

Meyers, R. A., & Seibold, D. R. (1990). Perspectives on group argument: A critical review of persuasive arguments theory and an alternative structurational view. In J. A. Anderson (Ed.), *Communication Yearbook 13* (pp. 268–302). Newbury Park, CA: Sage.

Miller, R., Klotz, D., & Eckholdt, H. (1998). HIV prevention with male prostitutes and patrons of hustler bars: Replication of an HIV preventive intervention. *American Journal of Community Psychology, 26,* 97–131.

Moscovici, S. (1980). Toward a theory of conversion behavior. *Advances in Experimental Social Psychology, 13,* 209–239.

Moscovici, S. (1985). Social influence and conformity. In G. Lindzey & E. Aronson (Eds.), *Handbook of social psychology* (3rd ed., Vol. 2, pp. 347–412). New York, NY: Random House.

Moscovici, S., Lage, E., & Naffrechoux, M. (1969). Influence of a consistent minority on the responses of a majority in a color perception task. *Sociometry, 32,* 365–380.

Myers, D. G., & Murdoch, P. J. (1972). Is risky shift due to disproportionate influence by extreme group members? *British Journal of Social and Clinical Psychology, 11,* 109–114.

Nemeth, C. (1986). Differential contributions of majority and minority influence. *Psychological Review, 93,* 23–32.

Noelle-Neumann, E. (1993). *The spiral of silence.* Chicago, IL: University of Chicago Press.

Platow, M. J., Haslam, S. A., Both, A., Chew, I., Cuddon, M., Goharpey, N., et al. (2005). "It's not funny when they're laughing": A self-categorization social-influence analysis of canned laughter. *The Journal of Experimental Social Psychology, 41,* 542–550.

Platow, M. J., Voudouris, N. J., Coulson, M., Gilford, N., Jamieson, R., Najdovski, L., et al. (2007). In-group reassurance in a pain setting produces lower levels of physiological arousal: Direct support for a self-categorization analysis of social influence. *European Journal of Social Psychology, 37,* 649–660.

Pruitt, D. G. (1971). Choice shifts in group discussion: An introductory review. *Journal of Personality and Social Psychology, 20,* 339–360.

Robinson, R. J., & Keltner, D. (1996). Much ado about nothing? Revisionists and traditionalists choose an introductory English syllabus. *Psychological Science, 7,* 18–24.

Rogers, E. (2003). *Diffusion of Innovation* (5th ed.). New York, NY: Simon & Schuster.

Serota, K. B., Carpenter, C. J., Andrews, K. R., & Boster, F. J. (2009). *Influentials in America: Identifying political superdiffusers.* Paper presented at the annual meeting of the National Communication Association, Chicago, Illinois.

Shaw, M. E. (1981). *Group dynamics.* New York, NY: McGraw-Hill.

Sherif, M. (1935). A study of some social factors in perception. *Archives of Psychology, 27,* 1–60.

Sia, C.-L., Tan, B. C. Y., & Wei, K.-K. (2002). Group polarization and computer-mediated communication: Effects of communication cues, social presence, and anonymity. *Information Systems Research, 13,* 70–90.

Sigall, H., Mucchi-Faina, A., & Mosso, C. (2006). Minority influence is facilitated when communication employs linguistic abstractness. *Group Processes and Intergroup Relations, 9,* 443–451.

Soumerai, S. B., McLauglin, T. J., Gurwitz, J. H., Guadagnoli, E., Hauptman, P. J., Borbas, C., et al. (1998). Effect of local medical opinion leaders on quality of care of acute myocardial infarction. *Journal of the American Medical Association, 279,* 1358–1363.

Spears, R., Lea, M., & Lee, S. (1990). De-individuation and group polarization in computer-mediated communication. *British Journal of Social Psychology, 29,* 121–134.

Stoner, J. A. F. (1961). *A comparison of individual and group decision involving risk.* Unpublished master's thesis, Cambridge, Massachusetts Institute of Technology.

Tanford, S. E., & Penrod, S. (1984). Social influence model: A formal integration of research on majority and minority influence processes. *Psychological Bulletin, 95,* 189–225.

Tormala, Z. L., DeSensi, V. L., & Petty, R. E. (2007). Resisting persuasion by illegitimate means: A metacognitive perspective on minority influence. *Personality and Social Psychology Bulletin, 33,* 354–367.

Turner, J. C. (1982). Toward a cognitive redefinition of the social group. In H. Tajfel (Ed.), *Social identity and intergroup behavior* (pp. 15–40). Cambridge, UK: Cambridge University Press.

Turner, J. C. (1987). The analysis of social influence. In J. C. Turner, M. A. Hogg, P. J. Oakes, S. D. Reicher, & M. S. Wetherell (Eds.), *Rediscovering the social group: A self-categorization theory* (pp. 68–88). Oxford, UK: Blackwell.

Turner, J. C. (1991). *Social influence.* Pacific Grove, CA: Brooks/Cole.

Valente, T. W., & Pumpuang, P. (2007). Identifying opinion leaders to promote behavior change. *Health Education and Behavior, 34,* 881–896.

Van Swol, L. M. (2009). Extreme members and group polarization. *Social Influence, 4,* 185–199.

Van Swol, L. M., & Seinfeld, E. (2006). Differences between minority, majority, and unanimous group members in the communication of information. *Human Communication Research, 32,* 178–197.

Wallach, M. A., Kogan, N., & Bem, D. J. (1962). Group influence on individual risk-taking: *Journal of Abnormal and Social Psychology, 65,* 75–86.

Wilder, D. A. (1990). Some determinants of the persuasive power of in-groups and out-groups: Organization of information and attribution of independence. *Journal of Personality and Social Psychology, 59,* 1202–1213.

Wood, W., Lundgren, S., Ouellette, J. A., Busceme, S., & Blackstone, T. (1994). Minority influence: A meta-analytic review of social influence processes. *Psychological Bulletin, 115,* 323–345.

CHAPTER 22

When Presumed Influence Turns Real

An Indirect Route of Media Influence

Ye Sun

ow do messages shape one's attitudes and behaviors? Various theoretical lenses have been offered in this volume to understand the workings of persuasive communications through eliciting intended cognitive or emotional responses in the target audience. Media messages, however, can also inadvertently "cause" behaviors. Penn State University students, following the firing of the football coach Joe Paterno in a recent scandal, stormed into the downtown streets and overturned a television news van, a symbol of the news media, as they believed news reports had exaggerated Mr. Paterno's role in the scandal and misled the public (Schweber, 2011). Or earlier in 2011, in the wake of the nuclear plant crisis in Japan, a great "salt rush" hit the east coast of China after messages were spread on the Internet that the iodine contained in the salt would help prevent sickness from radiation exposure. Whereas salt purchase itself could be a direct effect of those messages, purchasing in bulk and hoarding was a preemptive response fueled by fear of "competing" others who must have been persuaded by the messages. In both cases, individuals

displayed such behaviors not primarily because the messages in question directly convinced them to do so, but because they thought that such messages must have influenced other people.

Such scenarios depict an image of message recipients that is eclipsed in traditional persuasion research: Message recipients, like us persuasion and media effects scholars, also ponder over the persuasive effects of messages. They have their own lay theories about the power of messages on other audience members, such as the belief that the news reports about Joe Paterno had skewed the public's perception about him, or the messages about the iodine in salt would lead others to hoard salt. Such presumptions about media effect, when transformed into actual behaviors, become the real effect of the media messages (Gunther, Perloff, & Tsfati, 2008).

This indirect route from message to attitudinal or behavioral outcomes via speculations about other audience members is succinctly characterized as "the influence of presumed influence" (IPI, hereafter; Gunther & Storey, 2003). Different from traditional persuasion perspectives focusing on direct, intended effects of persuasive messages, it shifts analytical attention to how recipients' subjective perceptions about message effects shape their personal or social behaviors. This chapter is organized as follows. First, I will sketch out the larger theoretical background from which IPI originated, with a focus on the third-person effect framework (TPE, hereafter; Davison, 1983). Then I will take a look at IPI as a process model and review the empirical findings from the extant literature. Following that I will engage in a substantive analysis of the key components of IPI, mapping out some underlying conceptual dimensions and bringing forth a few conceptual issues. Finally, based on the previously mentioned review and analysis, I will discuss problems with current IPI research in terms of empirical rigor, theoretical vigor, and practical significance, and call for more efforts from future research to tackle these challenges.

Theoretical Background

Theoretical Origin: The Third-Person Effect (TPE)

Influence of presumed influence is an outgrowth of the third-person effect, an influential framework in the past three decades that has rerouted theoretical thinking about media effects. The idea of TPE is quite simple: Individuals tend to perceive a persuasive communication to have a greater impact on other people—the "third persons"—than on themselves (the perceptual component); and such beliefs may lead to real actions (the behavioral component; Davison, 1983). On the perceptual component, findings from a wide array of media contexts have attested to the robustness of the perceptual bias. A recent meta-analysis (Sun, Pan, & Shen, 2008) yields an average effect size of $d = .646$ ($r = .307$) based on 372 effect sizes from 106 studies, falling between the "medium" ($d = .50$) and "large" effect ($d = .80$; Cohen, 1988), and

not subject to variations in methodological factors, such as study setting, population, and design.

Theoretical explanations of such perceptual disparity have been proposed and examined. There is some, but inconclusive, evidence for both *motivational* accounts, which theorize the perceptual difference as a "bias" resulting from individuals' inherent drive to protect or enhance their ego (e.g., "self-serving bias," Gunther & Mundy, 1993; or "self-enhancement bias," Perloff, 2002), and *cognitive* accounts, which treat the perceptual difference as an "error" in cognitive processing and judgment-making due to differential cognitive schema or information structure related to self and other (e.g., fundamental attribution error, Gunther, 1991; the self-categorization explanation, Reid & Hogg, 2005). So far the existing evidence suggests that the self-other perceptual difference is probably determined by multiple factors (Perloff, 2009), and TPE scholars are working toward developing an integrated theoretical framework that can "differentiate, incorporate, and explain" both cognitive and motivational factors (Shen, Pan, & Sun, 2010, p. 51).

The empirical research surrounding the behavioral component has yielded a less clear picture. Whether and how the self-other perceptual disparity leads to behavioral consequences remains an open question. Though Xu and Gonzenbach's (2008) meta-analysis of studies on the TPE behavioral hypothesis reports an overall effect size of $r = .13$, which the authors claim is "not that trivial" for mass communication research (p. 382), the pool is worryingly small (10 studies with 26 effect sizes) with almost all the studies with inconsistent findings excluded through screening procedures (e.g., Atwood, 1994; Salwen, 1998; Salwen & Driscoll, 1997; Tewksbury, Moy, & Wei, 2004). Understanding of the behavioral component is also limited by a strong bias in empirical research in favor of investigating media regulation or censorship behaviors in negative contexts.

For example, 17 out of the 26 effect sizes in Xu and Gonzenbach's (2008) meta-analysis are related to censorship behaviors. A rough count of the journal articles published recently (from 2008 till September 2011) on the TPE behavioral component (counted only when self-other perceptual gap is used as a predictor) reveals a sustaining trend: 13 out of the 21 articles have examined support for censorship or media regulation as the outcome variable. When other behavioral contexts are examined, the evidence is often null or counterhypothetical (e.g., Chia, 2007, Choi, Leshner, & Choi, 2008, on ideal body image and dieting behaviors or body dissatisfaction; Eisend, 2008, on scarcity appeal in advertising and purchasing intentions). Given the lack of consistent empirical evidence, the constraint to censorship behaviors, and theoretical under-explication, what we know about the behavioral component of TPE remains quite limited.

Influence of Presumed Influence

Rooted in TPE, IPI grows out of the interest in explaining behavioral reactions as enacted perceptions about media influences. Compared to TPE, IPI posits a similar process: "People perceive some influence of a message on *others* (italics added) and then react to that perception of influence" (p. 201, Gunther & Storey, 2003). The critical difference between IPI and TPE is that the posited causal antecedent of behaviors in IPI is perceived effects on others, instead of self-other perceptual difference as in TPE. In other words, the presumed influence on *others* alone, regardless of perceived effect on self, is postulated to be a basis for attitudinal or behavioral decisions.

This theoretical move, as Gunther and Storey (2003) claim, makes IPI a "more general" model "with broader application" (p. 201). According to them, as perceived message influence on others in either positive or negative directions may lead to behavioral consequences, IPI is freed from constraints to negative message contexts and regulation behaviors. As a more general model, they argue, IPI allows for a wider range of attitudinal or behavior consequences to be examined. Indeed, as

the empirical review shows in the next section, a much more diverse catalogue of behavioral contexts have been examined under the umbrella of IPI (though it should be noted that this difference is more an outcome of researchers' choices and does not necessarily reflect the different theoretical scopes of the two frameworks).

Though Gunther and Storey (2003) go as far as to declare that "the third-person effect is just a special case of this broader general model" (p. 201), this claim is somewhat premature. As IPI and TPE propose different causal antecedents (i.e., presumed influence on others vs. self-other perceptual differences), the two are virtually competing hypotheses for the message perception-behavior process. The viability and/or contingency of these two frameworks require further theoretical and empirical investigations. This chapter's focus on IPI, rather than suggesting that IPI supersedes or transplants TPE, stems from the very recognition that the two literatures need separate scrutiny and synthesis. IPI is chosen as the focus of this chapter for two reasons. First, a few extensive reviews focusing on TPE are already available for interested readers, such as Perloff (2009), Gunther et al. (2008), and Tal-Or, Tsfati, and Gunther (2009), to name a few recent ones. Second, IPI tackles behavioral consequences in a more direct and focused way, and thus is more pertinent to the study of persuasion processes. The wider range of behaviors examined in extant IPI literature also renders the review and discussion more interesting to persuasion scholars.

Current Findings on IPI: A Process View

IPI as a Multistep Process

Drawing on the previous work on "persuasive press inference" (Gunther, 1998), Gunther and Storey (2003) delineate a few consecutive steps to describe the indirect route from message to behavioral outcomes. First, individuals form basic impressions about the media content upon exposure (*self-exposure*). Second, through "presumed reach" (Gunther, Bolt, Borzekowski, Liebhart, & Dillard, 2006), individuals assume that the media content they are exposed to reaches a broader audience. Based on their own exposure to the media content, they infer other audience members' level of exposure (*self-exposure* → *other-exposure*). Third, individuals further assume that others, who presumably have viewed or will view the media content, have been or will be influenced by it accordingly (*other-exposure* → *presumed influence*). Finally, the presumed reactions by others to the media content serve as guidance for individuals' own attitudinal or behavioral decisions (*presumed influence on others* → *influence on self*). Figure 22.1. depicts this entire process.

This process has been tested in an array of behavioral contexts, with variations at times in terms of what elements are included or how they are measured. The overarching goal guiding these studies is to verify the mediating role of presumed influence on others between message exposure and attitudinal/behavioral manifestations. Empirical findings from different contexts are reviewed next.

Health-Related Attitudes and Behaviors

Smoking

Using data collected from sixth through eighth graders from the spring and fall terms of 2003, Gunther and colleagues examined how smoking-related messages may indirectly influence teenagers' smoking attitudes and intentions. Testing the IPI process with regard to both pro-smoking and anti-smoking messages with the data from the spring, Gunther et al. (2006) ascertained that the indirect pathways were significant and in the expected directions. More specifically, teenagers' exposure to both pro-smoking and anti-smoking messages, via increased estimates of peer exposure to such messages, influenced their perceptions of smoking prevalence among their peers, which then affected their smoking attitudes and susceptibility.

Paek and Gunther (2007), focusing on anti-smoking messages using the data from the fall, analyzed non-smokers and smokers separately, and for each group, investigated the potentially differential roles of proximal peers ("your close friends") versus distal others ("other students your age in your school"). The expected IPI process, for smokers and nonsmokers alike, was confirmed when close friends were the referent others. When distal others were considered, presumed influence had no significant relationship with attitude toward smoking. Consistent with these findings, Paek's (2009) study on nonsmoking college students found that presumed influence of cigarette advertising on close peers, but not on distant others, mediated the relationship between self-reported exposure to such advertisements and smoking intention. Taking advantage of the two-wave panel data, Paek, Gunther, McLeod, and Hove (2011) examined how the IPI

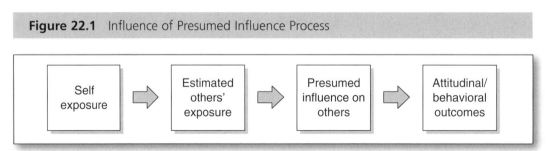

Figure 22.1   Influence of Presumed Influence Process

| Self exposure | → | Estimated others' exposure | → | Presumed influence on others | → | Attitudinal/ behavioral outcomes |

Source: "The Influence of Presumed Influence," by A.C. Gunther and J.D. Storey, 2003, *Journal of Communication, 53,* p. 199-215. Copyright 2003 by Wiley.

process might unfold over time. Presumed influence of anti-smoking messages on close peers at Time 1 had no direct impact on smoking attitudes or susceptibility at Time 2, though its indirect effect was significant, mediated by presumed influence at Time 2.

Ideal Body Images on the Media and Body Dissatisfaction

Teenagers who consume media representations of ideal body images can be impressionable to the portrayed media norm and perceived peer judgment. Through an in-depth interview, Milkie (1999) uncovered prevalent perceptions held by high-school girls that they were judged by their peers in accordance with the norms portrayed on the media. Gentles and Harrison (2006) showed that African American adolescent girls were not immune to this process either: Increased consumption of media body images led to heightened perceptions of peer expectations using the media images as the standard. More specifically, girls with larger body size tended to think that their peers expected them to be smaller, and those with smaller body size felt the opposite.

Park's (2005) study, formally testing the IPI process using structural equation modeling (SEM hereafter), showed that exposure to beauty and fashion magazines was associated with perceived prevalence of the thin-ideal images, which then led to greater presumed influence of such images on others. The presumed influence had an indirect impact on one's desire to be thin, mediated by the presumed influence on self. Direct association between presumed influence and behavioral intentions, however, was either negative, opposing the hypothesis (when other women were considered), or nonsignificant (when other men were considered). In their study of male college students in Singapore, Chia and Wen (2010) found that perceived effects of media portrayals of ideal body images on male friends and female friends were unrelated to body dissatisfaction, intention of going on a diet or going to a gym regularly, but negatively related to intention of going through cosmetic surgery (for "male friends") and taking diet pills (for "female friends") respectively.

Sexual Attitudes and Behaviors

Studies that applied the IPI framework to adolescents' sexual attitudes and behaviors have revealed a rather complicated picture. On one hand, there was supportive evidence suggesting that greater exposure to sex-related media content, positively predicting perceived peers' exposure to these contents (Chia, 2006; Chia & Lee, 2008), led to adolescents' perceptions of increasingly permissive peer norms (Chia, 2006; Chia & Gunther, 2006), which then fed into their own sexual attitude and their intentions to engage in sexual activities (Chia, 2006). On the other hand, across these three studies, there was equally strong evidence for the "projection effect" as an alternative explanation (which posits that perceptions of peer norms are a result of one's projecting their own attitudes onto others). Chia and Gunther (2006) concluded that college students' misperceptions of peer sexual norms could be a function of both presumed influence of sexual media content and projection of their own attitudes.

Advertising

Advertising and Materialism

Chia and her colleagues adopted the IPI framework to examine how the expanding advertising landscape in Asian countries may contribute to increased materialistic values. Studies of Chinese college students (Jiang & Chia, 2009) and adolescents in Singapore (Chia, 2010) supported the indirect effect of self-exposure to advertising on materialistic attitudes, mediated by perceived peer exposure, and presumed influence on peers. Perceived parents' viewing of advertisements, however, did not predict perceived level of materialism of the parents (Chia, 2010).

Direct-to-Consumer Advertising

Huh and Langteau's (2007) study examined how physicians' perceptions of the influence of DTC advertising on patients may affect their support for government regulations of DTC ads and their own prescription decisions. Support for regulation was explained mainly by physicians' attitude toward DTC advertising, not by presumed influence on patients. Among a host of prescription-related decisions that were examined in the study, only the refusal to prescribe requested drugs was predicted by the perceived detrimental influence of DTC advertising.

Political Communication

In political realms, IPI has been used as a tool to understand individuals' decisions on political issues and politicians. Tsfati and Cohen, in their studies of minority groups in Israel (such as Arabs in Israel, Tsfati, 2007; peripheral developmental towns, Tsfati & Cohen, 2003; and Gaza settlers, Tsfati & Cohen, 2005), showed that members of a minority group, perceiving the media coverage of their group to have influenced the general audience, believed that such coverage created or reinforced the negative, stigmatized image of their group in the mind of the public. Such perceptions culminated in a stronger sense of political and social alienation (Tsfati, 2007), greater political inefficacy (Tsfati & Cohen, 2005), and a stronger inclination toward relocation (Tsfati & Cohen, 2003; Tsfati & Cohen, 2005).

Cohen and Tsfati (2009) applied IPI to the study of strategic voting—shifting one's vote away from a personally preferred party in order not to waste the vote—in Israel, where the multiparty system makes strategic voting more important. They measured strategic voting both using self-report survey data from the years 2003 and 2006, and by identifying actual shifts in votes after the election. Their findings showed that above and beyond the perceived effect of media

coverage on self and a host of other relevant factors, the presumed influence of media coverage of the elections on others consistently predicted strategic voting. Sophisticated voters, as shown by their studies, seem to indeed assess the trend of public opinion by gauging the possible media effect on other voters and then make voting decisions on that basis.

Cohen, Tsfati, and Sheafer (2008) turned their attention to political elites and examined how political elites' belief in media power may play a role in their use of media for achieving political goals. Surveying 56 members from the Israeli Knesset, the authors showed that political elites' perceptions of media influence on the public, via increasing media motivation and effort, were associated with the increased media coverage they received as well as their parliamentary activities. In other words, the belief in media power on the public was shown to lead politicians to more actively use media to promote their political agenda.

Conceptual Underpinnings: A Component View of IPI

Explicating "Influence"

The *influence* of presumed influence, the endpoint of the process that anchors the importance of the model, refers to an individual's attitudinal and/or behavioral responses resulting from considerations about how relevant social others may react to certain media messages. Taken as a "process concept" (McLeod & Pan, 2005, p. 17), it implies changes as a result of preceding causes. Taken as a "variable concept" or a "mega-concept" (p. 17), it denotes a collection of responses—attitudinal or behavioral—that come about in various message contexts of interest.

In IPI studies, the construct of "*influence*" has been operationalized in diverse ways. Based on existing studies and a few previous categorizations (i.e., Gunther et al., 2008; Tal-Or et al., 2009), we can delineate two conceptual dimensions undergirding the behavioral responses.

One dimension concerns the *direction* of response, that is, where an individual shifts his or her actions in relation to the presumed trend of others' responses. One can decide to act either largely *with* (converge with) or *against* (diverge from) the perceived trend. The second dimension concerns the *mechanism* of response (i.e., the nature of considerations and motives that primarily drive the behavioral decision). Behaviors can be driven primarily by considerations of others' expectations, interpersonal or social pressures (i.e., normative influence), or by considerations of potential consequences or implications of others' behaviors (i.e., ecological influence).

Crossing these two dimensions, four categories of behaviors can be derived (Table 22.1). Compliance versus defiance characterizes the bifurcation of behavior responses resulting from *normative* considerations (also see Tal-or et al., 2009). *Compliance* behaviors refer to instances where individuals bring their behaviors closer to the perceived expectations of the referent group. Such compliance can be in the form of initiation or reinforcement of attitudes/behaviors perceived to be prevalent in and/or sanctified by the referent

group, for example, teenagers starting to smoke to be part of the peer group (Gunther et al., 2006). Compliance can also be changes from the other end of the behavioral spectrum (i.e., giving up behaviors or positions perceived to be "unacceptable" or "undesirable" to the referent group). Peripheral developmental town residents' consideration of relocating away from a town that they believed was disliked by the majority others is a case that illustrates such behaviors (Tsfati & Cohen, 2003). Or the heightened sense of alienation and political inefficacy (Tsfati, 2007; Tsfati & Cohen, 2005) as a result of perceived normative expectations is also a subtle form of being co-opted by the "mainstream view" (Gunther et al., 2008, refer to such responses as "withdrawal" behaviors).

Defiance behaviors, in contrast, refer to those that run counter to the perceived norms. These behaviors are not researched as much in extant IPI research. One example is from the Tsfati and Cohen's (2005) study, which showed that Gaza settlers who perceived greater negative media influence on the public opinion about their group felt more resistant against evacuation and more justified to resort to violence. Chia and

Table 22.1 Typology of Behavioral Outcomes Along Two Dimensions

		Direction	
		Convergent	Divergent
Nature of Influence	Normative	Compliance	Defiance
	Ecological	Coordination	Rectification

Wen's (2010) finding that the more influence college male students perceived of media portrayals of ideal bodies on other friends, the *less* likely they were to indicate an intention of going to a gym regularly may also be suggestive of resistance against or "defiance" of perceived norms.

Under *ecological* considerations, coordination and rectification are two possible types of behavioral responses. *Coordination* reactions (see also Cohen & Tsfati, 2009) refer to *adaptive* behaviors based on calculations of how others' possible behaviors may affect the chances to achieve their own goals. For example, Cohen and Tsfati (2009) showed that sophisticated voters switched their vote from their preferred, smaller party to a bigger one that appeared to be more favored by the media and therefore more influential on other voters (Study 2). In an experimental study conducted by Tal-Or, Cohen, Tsfati, and Gunther (2010), they showed that when respondents believed that the article they read on a sugar shortage had more influence on others, they indicated a stronger intention to rush to the stores to purchase sugar.

On the other hand, there are situations where perceived behavioral reactions by others are regarded to inflict harm or sustain some less-than-optimal conditions. Under such circumstances, individuals may be motivated to take up actions to fix the problems or deficiencies and improve their surroundings. Sun, Shen, and Pan (2008) use the term "*rectification*" to designate such behaviors. It includes, but is not confined to, restrictive or regulatory reactions toward media messages (labeled as "prevention behaviors," Gunther et al., 2006, Tal-Or et al., 2009). Rectifying behaviors can also include other actions designed to redress situations deemed problematic. Lim and Golan (2011) showed that respondents were more likely to participate in "social media activism" behaviors, including posting comments or their own countering video online, when they believed that a YouTube parody video on Al Gore and global warming negatively influenced others. Such "corrective" behaviors (also see Rojas, 2010) are aimed at dispelling potential misperceptions or correcting biases that may be propagated by the media. Even in the context of media content with positive influences such as public service announcements, Sun et al. (2008) argued, "rectification" could take the form of promotional behaviors to further disseminate the messages and amplify their influence. All of these behaviors, restrictive, corrective, or promotional, share the goal of improving the less-than-desirable social conditions due to perceived excessive or insufficient media influences on others.

Unpacking "Presumed Influence"

"Presumed influence" (PI in short) denotes one's subjective perceptions of the exerted or potential impact of the given media content on some referent others. Though seldom explicitly explicated, PI entails two connected aspects. The primary aspect is the subjective estimate of the extent or likelihood of message influence on the referent others. Operational measures are typically variants of this more general formula: "How much influence do you think [the media message] has on [the referent others]?" The second, ensuing aspect is the presumed collective responses from others (deemed either potentially possible or already actualized) resulting from such influence. For instance, Gunther and colleagues' (2006) study employed the perceived smoking prevalence among peers as a proxy measure of presumed influence of smoking-related messages. The first aspect is an estimate of message influence in terms of its extent and magnitude, whereas the second aspect captures speculations of the substantive effects of the message on others, that is, how it may have made others (re)act in certain ways.

Both aspects are important to the construct validity of PI. Without including the first aspect, the notion of *media as a source of perceived norms* would be missing. Perceptions of peer smoking prevalence, for example, can be a result of direct observation or communication, instead of an inference based on presumed media influence.

On the other hand, not measuring the second aspect, the presumed responses from others, can also be inadequate. Sheer perception of the magnitude of influence does not necessarily prompt behavioral responses. Rather, "how one responds to a message depends largely on *what the message is thought to do* to [others] (italics added)" (Tewksbury et al., 2004, p. 140). Jensen and Hurley's (2005) study included what they called "presumed behavior" to explicitly capture the likelihood that others were thought to do something (such as talking about the issue or acting on the issue), and found that such presumed behaviors associated with different referent others had varied roles in motivating respondents to engage in behavioral responses.

Emphasizing the second aspect is also to highlight that inherent to PI is a media-referent relationship that is context-bound and referent-specific. The presumed message influence is a relational assessment, not a context-free evaluation of the message content or other message properties alone. This difference distinguishes PI from other related notions, such as perceived effectiveness/argument quality of a message, or perceived utility/gains of a message system/tool, the focal assessment of which is the properties of the evaluated object (though such evaluation inevitably evokes some referents in the mind of the respondents, Dillard & Sun, 2008).

Delimiting borderlines between PI and these other notions serves to maintain the theoretical identity of IPI. Take as an illustration Tsfati, Cohen, and Gunther's (2011) study, where "presumed media influence" was measured in terms of how "published research featured in the mass media" is believed to give scholars more publicity, help their academic careers, get research funding, and so on (pp. 152–153). Strictly speaking, these items capture individuals' beliefs about the benefit or utility of publicizing research on the media outlets, an assessment not bound to specific referents or contexts. As such, they can very well be measures of the "*belief*" component in the Theory of Attitude (Attitude= $\Sigma b_i e_i$; Fishbein & Ajzen, 1975) in predicting attitude toward the behavior in question. The study could be regarded as a test of the direct linkage between beliefs (about media as a tool to advance some relevant goals) and attitudes (toward using media as such a tool), instead of an indirect route between media messages and behaviors via reasoning about referent others as postulated in IPI.

Self, Others, and Messages

Self and Referent Others

Though the perceived influence on self is no longer a critical element in the theoretical formulation of IPI (Gunther & Storey, 2003), the construal of self-other relationship is nonetheless intrinsic to the perception-behavior process. The self-other relationship in IPI studies can be broadly put in two categories. One type is nested, where self (the respondent) is part of the referent group on the dimension evaluated, such as friends or other college students (Gunther et al., 2006), or other voters in the country (Cohen & Tsfati, 2009). The other type of self-other relationship is juxtaposed, where the referent others belong to an out-group on the characteristics defined by the context of the study. Such in-group and out-group distinction can be based on demographic characteristics, such as gender (e.g., female respondents vs. "other men in general," Park, 2005), race (e.g., Israeli Arabs vs. Israeli Jews, Tsfati, 2007), or party affiliation (e.g., Democrats, Independents, and Republicans, Hoffner & Rehkoff, 2011). Groups can be sociologically or institutionally defined as occupants of different positions in a specific social system (i.e., physicians vs. clients in the DTC advertising context, Huh & Langteau, 2007; or congressmen vs. the public, Cohen et al., 2008). Perceptions of group boundaries can also be created through media portrayal, such as the "featured group" of media reports on some issues vs. the rest (for example, the Gaza settlers vs. other audience members in Tsfati & Cohen, 2005).

Do all the referent others weigh the same on one's decision-making? The existing evidence suggests not. Presumed influence of anti-smoking messages on distant peers was not related to one's own smoking attitudes or intention, but that on close friends was (Paek, 2009; Paek & Gunther, 2007). The indirect effect of advertising on materialism was mediated by teenagers' perception regarding their friends, but not that regarding their parents (Chia, 2010). These findings have shown that "Not all others are equal." The literature to date, though, does not yet offer compelling arguments as to why they are not equal. Although the relevance of the referent group seems to be an easy explanation to evoke, the ad hoc usage of such an explanation borders on tautology if self-other relationships are not theoretically explicated *a priori* and examined as an empirical question on its own. A combination of individual, interpersonal, and contextual factors may be responsible for differential judgment processes involving different referent others.

Message

Message tends to be the "backgrounded" element in IPI research. In most IPI studies, researchers usually provided the respondents with a general description of media messages in a broad topic area, such as "news media coverage of the elections" (Cohen & Tsfati, 2009), "anti-smoking messages on TV" (and magazines, billboards, etc.; Gunther et al., 2006), or "media content that includes talk about sex, sexual behavior, and sexual relationship" (Chia & Lee, 2008). Respondents were asked to recall their own exposure to these messages before estimating others' exposure to such messages and the presumed influence on others. Message characteristics and individuals' own perceptions and interpretations of such messages are rarely measured.

Such operational practice can marshal some defense. That is, when the goal of the study is to explain the formation, reinforcement, or change in one's attitudes or behavior in a given message environment resulting from a cumulative process involving constant exposure to such messages, a vague, broad measure has face validity in terms of capturing the immersion of the individual in the message environment. In a theoretical light, however, such self-report exposure measures without attention to message characteristics are problematic in at least two ways. First, using exposure as the antecedent factor presupposes that individuals use the "exposure is effect" heuristic to make judgments about influence on others. This assumption does not necessarily hold. Lim and Golan's (2011) experimental study just demonstrated the opposite: The perceived likelihood of exposure, manipulated as high versus low numbers of views on YouTube, had no significant effect on presumed influence on others, whereas perceived persuasive intent of the message (manipulated through source intent) did. Broken linkages between exposure variables and presumed influence were also shown in a few other studies, especially when the referent others were regarded as distant (e.g., distal peers in Paek & Gunther, 2007; Paek, 2009) or different (i.e., parents, Chia, 2010; male others, Park, 2005) from self.

Second, without examining conceptual characteristics of messages, the theoretical processes between message construal and judgment-making remain opaque. The problem of the lack of specific message explication looms large when unexpected results turn up and require further explanations. As Paek et al. (2011) lamented, "our global measure of exposure ... does not allow further explication of the reasons for the unintended association" (referring to the positive association between exposure to anti-smoking messages and smoking outcomes; p. 141). Though ad hoc explanations could be summoned up, they remain uncompelling speculations.

Directions for Future Research

Based on the review of empirical evidence and the conceptual analysis, I will make three critical observations of problems or challenges that face IPI research.

(I) Despite a sizable body of research studies on the process of IPI, its empirical credence is not yet quite established due to inconsistencies in extant findings and a general lack of causal evidence.

Inconsistencies in Empirical Findings

Though most studies show satisfying model fit indices, inconsistencies in specific findings should not be overlooked. For example, in the context of anti-smoking messages, the direct effect of self-exposure to anti-smoking messages on smoking susceptibility was shown to be nonsignificant in Gunther et al. (2006), but counterintuitively, positive in other analyses (Paek & Gunther, 2007; Paek et al., 2011). In Paek et al. (2011), the overall indirect effect from anti-smoking message exposure to smoking susceptibility at Time 1 was negative (−.02, $p < .05$), but positive at Time 2 (.04, n.s.). Such results, both internally inconsistent and in contradiction with some external literature (i.e., meta-analytic findings on the effectiveness of anti-smoking campaigns, Sussman, Sun, & Dent, 2006), call for more investigations in this context, especially as the findings reported in these three studies were all based on the same data source.

Some other inconsistencies include Gunther and Storey (2003), where the predicted process received support from the self-report data, but not when actual measures of observed interactions were used as an outcome variable, or Park (2005), which showed positive indirect effect but negative direct effect of presumed influence on other women on one's desire to be thin. Though the authors made ad hoc explanations for these inconsistencies, more empirical investigations are needed in future research to replicate or explain such findings.

The Lack of Causal Evidence

As extant studies rely heavily on cross-sectional self-report survey data (Tal-Or et al., 2009), a prominent concern with IPI research is that the evidence does not translate to causal interpretations. Studies that use SEM analysis seldom test out alternative models. When reversed causal links did get tested, the evidence tended to be equally favorable for the alternative models. For example, reversing the causal path between self-exposure and smoking attitudes/susceptibility produced a model fit as good as (Paek & Gunther, 2007), or even a slightly better fit than (Gunther et al., 2006), the original model. Chia and her colleagues' research on sexual norm perceptions also showed equivalent support for the alternative explanation, the projection effect.

Simply acknowledging the lack of causal evidence as a weakness in discussion sections, which most research papers do, is not enough. How to parse out causal processes poses methodological as well as theoretical challenges that should be taken up by future IPI research. Randomized experimental studies and longitudinal studies, as effective ways to establish causal evidence, should be conducted more often. So far, only two experimental studies (Lim & Golan, 2011; Tal-Or et al., 2010) and one longitudinal study (Paek et al., 2011) bespeak such efforts.

A Cautionary Note About SEM

As SEM has been a popular technique used in IPI studies, a note of caution should be made emphatic. One common misuse of SEM, as SEM scholars have alerted us to, is to prioritize "adjudging" fit over theory-testing (Hayduk, Cummings, Boadu, Pazderka-Robinson, & Boulianne, 2007). A symptom of such misuse in IPI studies is that variables are sometimes added to or removed from the originally posited IPI process without theoretical justifications. For example, in Park (2005) presumed influence on self was inserted between presumed influence on others and attitudinal outcome, a modification of the original IPI model without sufficient theoretical justification. In Paek et al. (2011), peer exposure was removed from the model solely based on model trimming procedures without any discussion of the theoretical reasons and implications.

Moreover, another problem of overemphasis on model fitness indices (FI) is that the conventionally used FIs have less *bona fides* than usually credited with. Saris, Satorra, and Van Der Veld (2009) showed with simple examples that the conventional FIs could lead "substantively relevant misspecification" (e.g., imposing wrong restrictions on certain parameters) to be retained and "substantively irrelevant misspecification" (e.g., good enough for practical purposes though not exactly the same as the "true" model) to be rejected. FIs are also unable to detect common perils to SEM analysis (such as common method variance and simultaneity, to which IPI studies are particularly vulnerable) that can inconsistently bias path coefficients and invalidate causal inferences (Antonakis, Bendahan, Jacquart, & Lalive, 2010; Cole, Ciesla, & Steiger, 2007). IPI scholars should use SEM with more discretion, prioritize theory-testing, and interpret the results with great care.

(II) The lack of conceptual explication and theoretical explanation can jeopardize the development of the IPI framework. More theory-building efforts are needed to move IPI from a descriptive model to an explanatory and predictive theoretical framework.

IPI, in its current formulation, is a depiction of "regular succession" (Psillos, 2002). It describes, but does not explain. Using Dubin's (1978) terms, it involves the "*what*" and "*how*" elements, but not "*why*." Though the process formulation of IPI contains causal propositions (e.g., presumed influence causes attitudinal/behavioral change; or exposure of others leads to presumed influence on them), it has yet to offer cogent causal explanations. Without answering the "why" questions, IPI will remain an interesting descriptive framework, but not a theory.

Theory-building is a long-term project. One starting point is conceptual explication. The "component" analysis section of this chapter engages a little bit with this task. Delineating formal conceptual typologies, like the one for behavioral consequences discussed earlier, is an important task in constructing theories (Hage, 1972). Such conceptual categories have heuristic functions in generating theoretical questions that build up for theory-development.

For example, with the conceptual categories of behavioral outcomes, questions can be raised about the contingent conditions and different mechanisms responsible for different types of behaviors. Does IPI have the same explanatory or predictive power across the subdimensions? How may different types of involvement be related to normative or instrumental behaviors? What are the factors that may determine the tipping point toward "convergent" versus "divergent" reactions? Such inquiries will help IPI scholars deductively derive a set of testable propositions and shed light on the underlying causal mechanisms.

Conceptual characteristics of the self-other relationship should also be more carefully analyzed to understand how construal of others (in relation to self and message context) influences one's own attitudinal/behavioral outcomes. Though extant literature has examined different kinds of referents, conceptual characteristics of the self-other relationship have not been directly explicated or examined yet. A more fundamental question that faces IPI research is what are the situations in which the thought of referent others arises and matters in the first place. In other words, when referent others are specified to the respondents in the surveys in current IPI research, the assumption is that the real-world decision-making process involves these others. Are there conditions under which such an assumption simply does not hold? Do we risk reifying the notion of presumed influence if we leave that assumption unchecked? Since "there are many different grounds that could lead one actor to treat a subset of other actors as a comparison point" (Marsden & Friedkin, 1993), which referent others are called for by different message contexts and behavioral domains? Some qualitative, exploratory research is needed to establish a more solid foundation to justify the referent other measures and explicate the conceptual dimensions.

(III) Finally, a bigger question for IPI scholars to ponder over is what theoretical space and practical grounds IPI can carve out for itself in the landscape of media effects and persuasion research.

IPI Versus TPE

As briefly argued earlier, though Gunther and Storey (2003) suggest that IPI is a broader model under which TPE is a special case, we should not rush to that conclusion without adequate theoretical and empirical investigations. The two frameworks posit different causal antecedents (i.e., perceived effects on others vs. self-other perceptual gap), and therefore imply different theoretical explanations for behavioral responses. For example, IPI, by uncoupling perceived effect on others and that on self and placing sole emphasis on the former, implies that individuals' assessment of the normative or ecological environment is used as a separate piece of social information in behavioral decisions. In TPE, on the other hand, using the self-other perceptual difference as a predictor highlights a social comparison process, where the latitude of difference between perceived self-position and other-position generates motivation for actions. Perceptions of *how differently* others are affected by messages than self account for variance in behavioral inclinations, instead of considerations of others' reactions alone. Given that both frameworks have garnered some empirical support (for example, Rojas, 2010, and Lim & Golan, 2011, respectively supported TPE and IPI hypotheses regarding "corrective actions") and both are theoretically underexplicated, we need more theorizing as well as more carefully crafted and purposeful research designs to identify the conditions for the viability (or nonviability) of each framework.

IPI versus TRA

The Theory of Reasoned Action (TRA) also includes the thought of others in the equation to predict behavioral outcomes. The primary difference between IPI and TRA is that IPI connects the dots between messages and others, explicitly specifying the relationship between the two. In TRA, the "others" usually refer to close individuals, such as family members or partners, and the perceptions of their thoughts are presumably based more on intimate knowledge or experiences. In IPI, referent others are usually a broader group, and presumptions about them are inferences made based on media messages. In addition, in terms of the mechanism of influence, the subjective norm component in TRA is mostly about the normative influence, whereas in IPI, as discussed earlier, other types of mental calculations can be encompassed.

Practical Implications? Message, Message, Message!

Generally speaking, a major practical contribution of IPI is the very knowledge that media messages have indirect, unintended effects that can also be consequential. If nothing else, this at least reminds campaign practitioners that they need to pretest indirect effects in addition to the direct, intended effects of messages.

What about implications of IPI for intervention strategies and message design? Though IPI scholars have suggested that a social-norm approach be used in media campaigns to correct erroneous perceptions (e.g., Chia & Gunther, 2006; Paek et al., 2011), this is not a unique contribution of IPI. Research on peer norm and peer influence has long found that the misperceptions of norms contributed to risk behaviors and correction of such norm perceptions can be another venue for behavioral change (Clapp & McDonell, 2000; Prentice & Miller, 1993). Furthermore, social-norm campaigns have already been widely implemented and so far produced rather mixed results (i.e., Clapp, Lange, Russell, Shillington, & Voas, 2003; Wechsler et al., 2003), casting doubt on their effectiveness.

So far IPI research has yielded few practical insights regarding message design and strategies in the context of persuasion campaigns. As discussed before, unlike in other persuasion perspectives, the message element in IPI is rather neglected. Lim and Golan's (2011) study showed that explicating message content can and should be a new direction for IPI research, and can potentially open up a fruitful area where IPI meets traditional persuasion theories to generate interesting questions. Their experimental finding that the perceived persuasive intent of the message led to greater presumed influence has clear practical implications for message design. It also suggests the feasibility for IPI scholars to move away from exposure as the exogenous explanatory factor and switch to message factors as the theoretical anchor of the process. Such a switch has practical value in addition to theoretical importance. More specifically, knowledge about the effect of exposure itself does not have much practical utility, as limiting or increasing individuals' exposure to the media content would be a rather constrained or ineffective intervention strategy in real life. A lot can be done, however, if we have a solid stock of knowledge about how message characteristics directly or indirectly influence message processing and relate to attitudinal or behavioral consequences. Such knowledge will help practitioners design more effective persuasion messages and intervention programs.

Summary

This chapter presents a review and an analytical discussion of the research on influence of presumed influence. Representing an indirect model of media effects, IPI complements traditional persuasion perspectives with its central idea that a message can indirectly influence individuals' attitudes or behaviors by shaping their presumptions about the message influence on other audience members. A review of extant findings from a wide range of health, advertising, and political contexts largely shows support for the postulated IPI process, though the inconsistencies in extant findings and the lack of causal evidence require that future investigations pay attention to such problems and make efforts to resolve them.

The component view of IPI attempts some conceptual explication of the key components of IPI through which some underlying conceptual dimensions are clarified and a few conceptual issues are raised. Future research should engage in more in-depth conceptual and theoretical explications and investigate causal explanations for the posited relationships. IPI should move from the "descriptive" stage to the "explanatory" stage of theory development, where *theory construction, theory testing*, and *theory reformulation* are focal tasks (Reynolds, 1971, p.155). Theoretical explications, combined with experimental studies or longitudinal studies, are necessary to make that move.

References

Antonakis, J., Bendahan, S., Jacquart P., & Lalive, R. (2010). On making causal claims: A review and recommendations. *The Leadership Quarterly, 21*, 1086–1120.

Atwood, E. L. (1994). Illusions of media power: The third-person effect. *Journalism Quarterly, 71*(2), 269–282.

Chia, S. C. (2006). How peers mediate media influence on adolescents' sexual attitudes and sexual behavior. *Journal of Communication, 56*, 585–606.

Chia, S. C. (2007). Third-person perceptions about idealized body image and weight-loss behavior. *Journalism & Mass Communication Quarterly, 84*(4), 677–694.

Chia, S. C. (2010). How social influence mediates media effects on adolescents' materialism. *Communication Research, 37*, 400–419.

Chia, S. C., & Gunther, A. C. (2006). How media contribute to misperceptions of social norms about sex. *Mass Communication & Society, 9*, 301–320.

Chia, S. C., & Lee, W. (2008). Pluralistic ignorance about sex: The direct and the indirect effects of media consumption on college students' misperception of sex-related peer norms. *International Journal of Public Opinion Research, 20*(1), 52–73.

Chia, S. C., & Wen, N. (2010). College men's third-person perceptions about idealized body image and consequent behavior. *Sex Roles, 63*(7/8), 542–555.

Choi, Y., Leshner, G., & Choi, J. (2008). Third-person effects of idealized body image in magazine advertisements. *American Behavioral Scientist, 52*(2), 147–164.

Clapp, J. D., Lange, J. E., Russell, C., Shillington, A., & Voas, R. (2003). A failed norms social marketing campaign. *Journal of Studies on Alcohol, 64,* 409–414.

Clapp, J. D., & McDonnell, A. (2000). The relationship of perceptions of alcohol promotion and peer drinking norms to alcohol problems reported by college students. *Journal of College Student Development, 41,* 19–26.

Cohen, J. (1988). *Statistical power analysis for the behavioral sciences* (2nd ed.). Hillsdale, NJ: Erlbaum.

Cohen, J., & Tsfati, Y. (2009). The influence of presumed media influence on strategic voting. *Communication Research, 36*(3), 359–378.

Cohen, J., Tsfati, Y., & Sheafer, T. (2008). The influence of presumed media influence in politics: Do politicians' perceptions of media power matter? *Public Opinion Quarterly, 72*(2), 331–344.

Cole, D. A., Ciesla, J. A., & Steiger, J. H. (2007). The insidious effects of failing to include design-driven correlated residuals in latent-variable covariance structure analysis. *Psychological Methods, 12*(4), 381–398.

Davison, W. P. (1983). The third-person effect in communication. *Public Opinion Quarterly, 47,* 1–15.

Dillard, J. P., & Sun, Y. (2008). Questions about structure, referent, and bias in judgments of the effectiveness of persuasive messages. *Journal of Health Communication, 13*(2), 149–168.

Dubin, R. (1978). *Theory development.* New York, NY: Free Press

Eisend, M. (2008). Explaining the impact of scarcity appeals in advertising. *Journal of Advertising, 37*(3), 33–40.

Fishbein, M., & Ajzen, I. (1975). *Belief, attitude, intention, and behavior: An introduction to theory and research.* Reading, MA: Addison-Wesley.

Gentles, K., & Harrison, K. (2006). Television and perceived peer expectations of body size among African American adolescent girls. *Howard Journal of Communications, 17,* 39–55.

Gunther, A. C. (1991). What we think others think: Cause and consequences in third-person effect. *Communication Research, 18,* 355–372.

Gunther, A. C. (1998). The persuasive press inference: Effects of mass media on perceived public opinion. *Communication Research, 25* (2), 486–504.

Gunther, A. C., Bolt, D., Borzekowski, D. L. G., Liebhart, J. L., & Dillard J. P. (2006). Presumed influence on peer norms: How mass media indirectly affect adolescent smoking. *Journal of Communication, 56,* 52–68.

Gunther, A. C., & Mundy, P. (1993). Biased optimism and the third-person effect. *Journalism Quarterly, 70,* 58–67.

Gunther, A. C., Perloff, R. M., & Tsfati, Y. (2008). Public opinion and the third-person effect. In W. Donsbach & M. Traugott (Eds.), *Handbook of public opinion.* Thousand Oaks, CA: Sage.

Gunther, A. C., & Storey, J. D. (2003). The influence of presumed influence. *Journal of Communication, 53,* 199–215.

Hage, J. (1972). *Techniques and problems of theory construction in sociology.* New York, NY: Wiley.

Hayduk, L., Cummings, G., Boadu, K., Pazderka-Robinson, H., & Boulianne, S. (2007). Testing! Testing! One, two, three-testing the theory in Structure Equation Models. *Personality and Individual Differences, 42,* 841–850.

Hoffner, C., & Rehkoff, R. A. (2011). Young voters' responses to the 2004 U.S. presidential election: Social identity, perceived media influence, and behavioral outcomes. *Journal of Communication, 61*(4), 732–757.

Huh, J., & Langteau, R. (2007). Presumed influence of DTC prescription drug advertising: Do experts and novices think differently? *Communication Research, 34*(1), 25–52.

Jensen, J. D., & Hurley, R. J. (2005). Third-person effects and the environment: Social distance, social desirability, and presumed behavior. *Journal of Communication, 55,* 242–256.

Jiang, R., & Chia, S. C. (2009). The direct and indirect effects of advertising on materialism of college students in China. *Asian Journal of Communication, 19*(3), 319–336.

Lim, J. S., & Golan, G. J. (2011). Social media activism in response to the influence of political parody videos on YouTube. *Communication Research, 38,* 710–727.

Marsden, P. V., & Friedkin, N. E. (1993). Network studies of social influence. *Sociological Methods and Research, 22,* 125–149.

McLeod, J. M., & Pan, Z. (2005). Concept explication and theory construction. In S. Dunwoody, L. B. Becker, D. M. McLeod, & G. M. Kosicki (Eds.), *The evolution of key mass communication concepts: Honoring Jack M. McLeod* (pp. 14–76). Cresskill, NJ: Hampton Press.

Milkie, M. A. (1999). Social Comparisons, reflected appraisals, and mass media: The impact of pervasive beauty images on black and white girls' self-concepts. *Social Psychology Quarterly, 62,* 190–210.

Paek, H. (2009). Differential effects of different peers: Further evidence of the peer proximity thesis in perceived peer influence on college students' smoking. *Journal of Communication, 59,* 434–455.

Paek, H., & Gunther, A. C. (2007). How peer proximity moderates indirect media influence on adolescent smoking. *Communication Research, 34,* 407–432.

Paek, H., Gunther, A. C., McLeod, D. M., & Hove, T. (2011). How adolescents' perceived media influence on peers affects smoking decisions. *Journal of Consumer Affairs, 45*(1), 123–146.

Park, S. (2005). The influence of presumed media influence on women's desire to be thin. *Communication Research, 32,* 594–614.

Perloff, R. M. (2002). The third-person effect. In J. Bryant & D. Zillmann (Eds.), *Media effects: Advances in theory and research* (2nd ed., pp. 489–506). Mahwah, NJ: Erlbaum.

Perloff, R. M. (2009). Mass media, social perception, and the third-person effect. In M. B. Oliver & J. Bryant (Eds.) *Media effects: Advances in theory and research.* (pp. 252–268). Mahwah, NJ: Erlbaum.

Prentice, D. A., & Miller, D. T. (1993). Pluralistic ignorance and alcohol use on campus: Some consequences of misperceiving the social norm. *Journal of Personality and Social Psychology, 64,* 243–256.

Psillos, S. (2002). *Causation and explanation.* Chesham, UK: Acumen.

Reid, S. A., & Hogg, M. A. (2005). A self-categorization explanation for the third-person effect. *Human Communication Research, 31,* 129–161.

Reynolds, P. D. (1971). *A primer in theory construction.* Indianapolis, IN: Bobbs-Merrill.

Rojas, H. (2010). "Corrective" actions in the public sphere: How perceptions of media and media effects shape political behaviors. *International Journal of Public Opinion Research, 22*(3), 343–363.

Salwen, M. B. (1998). Perceptions of media influence and support for censorship: The third-person effect in the 1996 presidential election. *Communication Research, 25,* 259–285.

Salwen, M. B., & Driscoll, P. D. (1997). Consequences of third-person perception in support of press restrictions in the O. J. Simpson trial. *Journal of Communication, 47(2),* 60–75.

Saris, W. E., Satorra, A., & van der Veld, W. (2009). Testing structural equation models or detections of misspecifications? *Structural Equation Modeling, 16*(4), 561–582.

Schweber, N. (2011, November 10). Penn state students clash with police in unrest after announcement. *The New York Times.* Retrieved November 12, 2011, from http://www.nytimes.com

Shen, L., Pan, Z., & Sun, Y. (2010). A test of motivational vs. cognitive explanations for third-person perception. *American Journal of Media Psychology, 3,* 32–53.

Sun, Y., Pan, Z., & Shen, L. (2008). Understanding the third-person perception: Evidence from a meta-analysis. *Journal of Communication, 58,* 280–300.

Sun, Y., Shen, L., & Pan, Z. (2008). On the behavioral component of the third-person effect. *Communication Research, 35,* 257–278.

Sussman, S., Sun, P., & Dent, C. W. (2006). A meta-analysis of teen cigarette smoking cessation. *Health Psychology, 25,* 549–557.

Tal-Or, N., Cohen, J., Tsfati, Y., & Gunther, A. C. (2010). Testing causal direction in the influence of presumed media influence. *Communication Research, 37*(6), 801–824.

Tal-Or, N., Tsfati, Y., & Gunther, A. C. (2009). *The influence of presumed media influence: Origins and implications of the third-person perception.* In R. L. Nabi & M. B. Oliver (Eds.), *The Sage handbook of media processes and effects* (pp. 99–112). Thousand Oaks, CA: Sage.

Tewksbury, D., Moy, P., Weis, D. S. (2004). Preparations for Y2K: Revisiting the behavioral component of the third-person effect. *Journal of Communication, 54,* 138–155.

Tsfati, Y. (2007). Hostile media perceptions, presumed media influence, and minority alienation: The case of Arabs in Israel. *Journal of Communication,* *57,* 632–651.

Tsfati, Y., & Cohen, J. (2003). On the effect of the "third-person effect": Perceived influence of media coverage and residential mobility intentions. *Journal of Communication, 53*(4), 711–727.

Tsfati, Y., & Cohen, J. (2005). The influence of presumed media influence on democratic legitimacy: The case of Gaza settlers. *Communication Research, 32,* 794–821.

Tsfati, Y., Cohen, J., & Gunther, A. C. (2011). The influence of presumed media influence on news

about science and scientists. *Science Communication, 33*(2), 143–166.

Wechsler, H., Nelson, T., Lee, J. E., Seiberg, M., Lewis, C., & Keeling, R. (2003). Perception and reality: A national evaluation of social norms marketing interventions to reduce college students' heavy alcohol use. *Quarterly Journal of Studies on Alcohol, 64,* 484–494.

Xu, J., & Gonzenbach, W. (2008). Does a perceptual discrepancy lead to action? A meta-analysis of the behavioral component of the third-person effect. *International Journal of Public Opinion Research, 20*(3), 375–385.

CHAPTER 23

How Does Technology Persuade?

Theoretical Mechanisms for Persuasive Technologies

S. Shyam Sundar, Jeeyun Oh,
Hyunjin Kang, and Akshaya Sreenivasan

istorically, media and communication technologies have been seen as amplifiers of persuasive communications. From microphones to smartphones, communication technologies have served to boost the signal strength of persuasive messages. Mass-media technologies, such as the printing press, radio, and television, have boosted reception strength by expanding the reach and frequency of these messages. In fact, rich areas of persuasion research, such as propaganda, are premised on harnessing the vast dissemination potential of media and communication technologies.

Yet, theoretical attention to the role played by technology in persuasion is surprisingly scarce. The general tendency has been to view technology either as a channel for conveying persuasive messages (Fogg, Lee, & Marshall, 2002) or as a bundled environment with inherent and immutable constraints (Holbert, 2002). In assuming that a given media technology is a constant, both these approaches call for adapting message and psychological variables to suit the exigencies of the medium.

This is probably because classic definitions of "persuasion" (Miller, 1980, see chapter 5) focus on message and psychological variables by emphasizing (1) the use of symbols and (2) the social nature of the phenomenon. Highlighting the importance of communication, Dillard (2010) defines persuasion as one social actor using symbols to change the opinion or behavior of another social actor. However, the label of "social actor" need not be restricted to humans, but can indeed be extended to technologies, as demonstrated by numerous studies in the CASA (Computers as Social Actors) literature, which show that individuals tend to apply social rules of human-human interaction when interacting with technologies, even though they agree that computers do not have intentions (Reeves & Nass, 1996).

Likewise, the notion of "symbols" need not be restricted to the message content of communication. With the arrival of digital media, there is a growing realization that even nonlinguistic technological features can serve as symbols with persuasive appeal (Sundar, 2008a). In fact, the traditional separation of source and/or message from the technology that delivers the message is no longer conceptually defensible given that new media technologies are erasing the boundaries between source and receiver, as well as those between message and medium. For example, customization technologies make the receiver the source of messages, and interactive interfaces transform the nature of the message so significantly that the sheer existence of interactive features can serve as a persuasive message.

It must be noted, however, that technological features such as customization and interactivity are anything but fixed. They have become highly variable, given the "app culture" of modern media such as websites and tablets. The variable use and deployment of applications on websites makes it less useful for us to think and theorize about the Web as a whole media form or as a uniform "symbol system" (Salomon, 1979). Even specific genres of websites, such as social networking sites, cannot be treated as distinct, coherent media because they have several applications that afford dynamic changes in form and functionality. Therefore, no two examples of online social-networking platforms are the same. Not only are new applications developed all the time and continually change the technology of a medium, they are also increasingly available across media (e.g., same app available for tablets as well as smartphones), thereby diminishing the differences between media forms.

Given this lack of distinctiveness and the absence of uniformity within any given medium, the role of technology in persuasion cannot be meaningfully assessed by comparing different media (e.g., computers vs. robots), but by investigating the contribution made by specific features (e.g., morphology) or affordances (e.g., interactivity) of media technologies. Toward this

end, we adopt a "variable-centered," rather than "object-centered," approach to the study of technology (Nass & Mason, 1990) and examine structural features that underlie interface design, characteristics that facilitate specific actions and thereby affect both the nature and effects of communication (Sundar, 2009).

Studies in the persuasive computing literature do not specify which aspects of a computer (e.g., Fogg, 2002), game (Bang, Torstensson, & Katzeff, 2006), or a household appliance (McCalley, Kaiser, Midden, Keser, & Teunissen, 2006) affect credibility and other user attitudes. We still do not know how and why persuasive technologies work. In the sections that follow, we attempt to provide some answers by viewing persuasive technologies not as specific tools or objects, but as variables related to technological affordances, such as interactivity and navigability, that may influence persuasion via five theoretical mechanisms.

How Technology Persuades

Theory and research suggest that technology can persuade individuals by (1) triggering cognitive heuristics about the nature of content, (2) enabling the receiver to be the source, (3) creating greater user engagement, (4) constructing alternative realities with enhanced vividness, self-representation, self-presence, spatial presence, and transportation, and (5) affording easier access to information.

Cognitive Heuristics

While cognitive heuristics triggered by message content are well-documented in the dual-process literature, those stimulated by interface affordances are only now beginning to be studied. Even if users do not actively engage interactive tools on an interface, the mere presence of interactivity can sometimes cue a series of cognitive heuristics that dictate their evaluation of the interface as well as its content (Sundar, 2008a). For instance, a website with a plethora of interactive tools can give users an impression that this is a participatory forum, open and democratic in nature, with visitors afforded a voice. The MAIN model (Sundar, 2008a) proposes that affordances related to modality, agency, interactivity, and navigability manifest themselves in the form of interface cues that trigger mental shortcuts (i.e., cognitive heuristics) for judging the quality and credibility of the content delivered via the interface. Sundar, Xu, and Dou (2012) identify 20 such heuristics that could play a role in shaping consumers' attitudes and behaviors in the context of online advertising and marketing.

Interface affordances do not exist as structural or ontological characteristics alone, but also possess cues that trigger perceptions in the form of quick evaluations (i.e., heuristics) about the perceived consequences of their use (Sundar & Bellur, 2010). In other words, the perception of a certain action possibility in the interface can directly contribute to positive or negative judgments of the credibility of content conveyed by the interface even without using it. For instance, the appearance of dialogue boxes during the course of browsing a website can enhance the feeling of constant interaction with the system, and thereby invoke the *interaction heuristic*. Similarly, *control heuristic* can be triggered by a device highlighting its ability to afford user control over the nature and flow of information (Sundar & Bellur, 2010). In fact, Sundar and Bellur (2010) offer a detailed list of heuristics for each type of interactivity: interaction and responsiveness heuristics for modality interactivity; activity, control, choice and ownness heuristics for source interactivity; and contingency, telepresence, and flow heuristics for message interactivity.

These heuristics are suggestive of theoretical mechanisms by which interactivity affordances influence the perceived value of the information and the medium, and thereby affect credibility, but they do not always have to occur via heuristic processing. In fact, the rules of thumb invoked by

affordances could serve as important analytical tools for aiding systematic processing of underlying information. If the user is willfully applying the heuristic to arrive at credibility judgments of content, the processing is said to be conscious or controlled, rather than automatic. Therefore, interactivity can affect persuasion via both heuristic and systematic processes. The following three heuristics are quite reflective of this theoretical approach to understanding the effects of persuasive technologies.

Old Media Heuristic

Given the multimodal nature of modern media interfaces, the use of modalities resembling those used in older media can trigger mental shortcuts that lead to credibility judgments of content. Sundar (2000) found that providing audio downloads significantly lowered the perceived journalistic quality of news stories, especially when pictures were included in the stories. In contrast, text-only and text-plus-picture modalities elicited more positive evaluations. Newspapers have been traditionally seen as more credible sources of information, associated with stringent gatekeeping standards, whereas broadcast media outlets that use audio and/or video modalities tend to be perceived as less credible sources.

Thus, a website resembling a newspaper can serve to invoke a "newspaper schema," leading to positive credibility evaluations. This rule-of-thumb is labeled *old media heuristic* by the MAIN model (Sundar, 2008a). As a result, the same message could be seen as more persuasive when presented via text rather than via audio and pictures. Depending on how the invoked heuristic is processed, this effect could follow one of two possible mechanisms, as would be predicted by dual-process models in social cognition: If it is processed heuristically, then the mere old-media look of the site can directly boost positive ratings. But, if it is processed systematically, the old-media look will prompt users to engage in controlled processing of the information, as opposed to the more automatic and passive processing of news content typically associated with electronic media. And, assuming that the content is strong, this effortful route is also likely to promote persuasiveness.

Machine Heuristic

When technology is the attributed source of communication, it can be quite persuasive. Sundar and Nass (2001) found that participants rated identical news stories as being higher in quality when they thought that the computer terminal, rather than news editors, chose them. This may be due to the operation of the *machine heuristic*—if a machine chose the news story, then it must be objective in its selection and free from ideological bias (Sundar, 2008a). A good example is our tendency to trust the order of search results by an automated engine, such as Google, and automatically assign higher importance to those results that appear at the top without critically assessing the intentionality behind the rank-ordering of the output (Pan et al., 2007). Therefore, persuasion is likely to be higher and less subject to counterargumentation when the message is delivered by an interface that is machine-like in its appearance as well as operation.

Bandwagon Heuristic

Aside from imbuing agency to the machine, modern communication technologies provide agency to receivers themselves, both collectively and individually. Social media have made it possible for users, as a collective, to weigh in on virtually everything online, from voting on top news stories to fact-checking on health information in a bulletin-board to reviewing products on e-commerce sites. Even without actively opining, users can send a collective message by simply visiting certain online venues. Their actions are compiled by any number of algorithms and applications to produce metrics such as number of hits, number of visitors, and so on. The number of Diggs on a social-bookmarking site and the list of most viewed news stories are just two

examples of *audience-as-source*, which may ultimately influence what users choose to read or believe online.

Psychologically, audience-as-source activates the *bandwagon heuristic,* which has been shown to positively influence intention to purchase products from an e-commerce site (Sundar, Oeldorf-Hirsch, & Xu, 2008). This heuristic is triggered by any interface cue that signifies the popularity of certain content (e.g., the number of views of a YouTube video clip) or products (e.g., product review and star-ratings of a product listed in Amazon.com) and is shown to be stronger than the authority heuristic triggered by the presence of expert opinion (Sundar, Xu, & Oeldorf-Hirsch, 2009). Users seem to believe that if many other people think that something is good, then they must too. Elements of consensus (Chaiken, 1987) and/or endorsement (Metzger, Flanagin, & Medders, 2010) constitute this bandwagon effect, with important implications for persuasion using tools of social media.

Bandwagon, machine, and old-media heuristics are three examples of a wide range of mental shortcuts identified by the MAIN Model (Sundar, 2008a) as being triggered by interface features rather than content attributes. Yet, these heuristics can play an important role in determining the outcomes of persuasive communications (Sundar et al., 2012), both by their sheer presence and by offering unique functionality that was absent in older media.

User as Source

Self-agency is a powerful contributor of persuasive outcomes, as evidenced by the rise and success of technologies that afford customization by individual users. By enabling users to influence the nature and process of an interaction, these affordances make each individual user feel like they are a relevant actor in the interaction, and thereby aid persuasion. For instance, in marketing studies, products designed by the consumers generate significantly higher acceptance (Franke, Schreier, & Kaiser, 2009), and consumers in financial portals show higher willingness to provide personal information when they are provided with customizable web interfaces (Coner, 2003).

The agency model of customization (Sundar, 2008b) posits that "*self-as-source*" is the fulcrum of psychological benefits derived from customization. According to this model, technological affordances imbue a higher sense of agency by allowing the user to serve as a source of his or her information, and thereby become the center of his or her interaction universe. This translates to positive cognitive, affective, and behavioral responses toward both the interface and content of customizable media. Theoretically, two classes of mechanisms govern these persuasive effects. One pertains to the sheer affordance of the user acting as a source (e.g., the user's ability to perform the tailoring on their own or digitally publish content that they create, as in social media). The other pertains to the content that results from the process of the user acting as a source.

Self-determination theory (Ryan & Deci, 2000) belongs in the former category, given its emphasis on user autonomy. Easy-to-use tools of customization and social media not only provide autonomy, but also a sense of competence or self-efficacy (Bandura, 1997) to operate them. In addition, they afford endorsement of content by others, which can nurture psychological bonding with both the process and components of communication, and thereby have a positive impact on content perception. Studies in community psychology (McMillan, 1996; McMillan & Chavis, 1986) have shown that feelings of membership, sense of belonging, and trust enhance sense of community, which can generate positive persuasive outcomes. For instance, Richardson et al. (2010) found that adding virtual community features to an online walking program helped participants stay engaged in the program. Another study showed that online spaces that foster a sense of community positively affected attitudes and behaviors toward the community (Firpo, Kasemvilas, Ractham, & Zhang, 2009).

Kim and Sundar (2011) found that sense of community is indeed a significant mediator of the relationship between the perceived number of times a thread is shared in a discussion board and users' attitudes toward posting. Together, these factors of autonomy, competence, and relatedness serve to enhance the degree of self-determination (Ryan & Deci, 2000) and thereby the intrinsic motivation to engage with the interface and its contents.

A related construct is that of perceived *control* afforded by the self acting as the source (Sundar, 2008b). Power users of technology are especially likely to feel a higher sense of control when using customizable features, in part because they seek personal control over their privacy (Sundar & Marathe, 2010), and a greater sense of empowerment (Weissman, 1988). When they customize, users are also known to feel a higher sense of accomplishment (Norton, Mochon, & Ariely, 2011) and ownership (Pierce, Kostova, & Dirks, 2003), both of which positively predict user attitudes toward the object of customization.

Recent research shows that a sense of *identity* could be a stronger motivation than sense of control for users to customize their web portals (Marathe & Sundar, 2011). In addition to improving the functionality of the interface to suit one's needs, customization lets us project our identity onto the interfaces and devices that we own. Sundar (2008b) asserts that individuals' motivation to express their identity on media interfaces stems from the general human tendency of egocentricity. As a consequence, they will be able to perceive some aspect of their self in the interfaces. As Petty, Wheeler, and Bizer (2000) suggest, the real psychological appeal of a personalized message is that the message is oriented to some aspect of one's self and implies a connection between one's personality and message tone. In general, personalization of both messages and interface features (such as cell-phone faceplates) serve to make the user feel unique and distinct from others, thereby promoting positive attitudes toward the interface.

When it comes to evaluating the outcomes of customization, perceived *relevance* of the resulting content is considered a key mediator of the persuasive effect of interactive technologies (Kalyanaraman & Sundar, 2006). Whether the user performs the tailoring (customization) or the system does it based on the user's prior behavior (personalization), the resulting content is likely to closely match the user's interests and be perceived higher in utility (Sundar & Marathe, 2010), thereby leading to positive attitudes toward the interface as well as the content. The effectiveness of tailored health messages relies quite heavily on this mechanism. Tailored health messages have positive effects on health behaviors, including healthy dietary behaviors (e.g., Campbell et al., 1994; Oenema, Brug, Dijkstra, de Weerdt, & de Vries, 2008), physical activities (e.g., Marcus et al., 2007; Oenema et al., 2008), cancer screening (e.g., Jerant et al., 2007), and smoking cessation (e.g., Oenema et al., 2008; Strecher et al., 2008). These studies suggest that personal relevance enhances cognitive preconditions toward message processing and thereby increases message impact by providing individualized information on behavioral factors for achieving well-being goals (Hawkins, Kreuter, Resnicow, Fishbein, & Dijkstra, 2008).

Another variable that is closely associated with relevance is *involvement*. When the self is the source, both the process of customization and the ensuing content are of great personal interest to the user, thereby increasing his or her involvement with the interface (Kalyanaraman & Sundar, 2006; Zaichkowsky, 1985). Therefore, the user is likely to engage more deeply with the interface and its content, as predicted by ELM and other dual-process models. This kind of processing is known to result in attitudes that are strong, durable, and more predictive of behaviors (Petty & Cacioppo, 1986). However, not all users have the same appetite for involvement, especially with the interface. While power users show more positive attitudes toward the content and website when they are allowed to customize, nonpower users show more positive attitudes

when the site personalizes the content for them—a complex phenomenon involving a trade-off between convenience and concern for privacy (Sundar & Marathe, 2010).

In sum, technological features that enable users to serve as sources of information can influence persuasion not only by increasing users' agency, identity, and self-determination, but also by ensuring that the content is more relevant and involving.

User Engagement

The concept of user involvement discussed earlier is particularly important for understanding the role of interactive media in persuasion. By calling for heightened user activity, interactivity is assumed to breed greater involvement in the interaction, leading some scholars to propose that it stimulates central processing of mediated information. For example, Sundar and Kim (2005) showed that interactively rendered advertisements promoted purchase intentions by increasing product knowledge and product involvement.

Sundar, Kalyanaraman, and Brown (2003) created three versions of a political candidate's website that were identical in content, but differed in the extent to which they permitted contingent interaction. High-interactivity had multiple layers of hyperlinks and medium-interactivity featured two layers, whereas the low-interactivity version had one scrollable page without any hyperlinks. Participants liked the candidate more and agreed more with his policy positions when the website had a medium level of interactivity versus low or high levels of interactivity.

Surprisingly, participants' prior level of interest in politics did not interact with interactivity to influence their attitudes, implying that interactivity has the ability to make even apathetic users get involved in the content offered by the site. However, this advantage is negated when the site is very high in interactivity. Thus, to the extent interactivity calls for greater user activity without imposing too much of a navigational load, it can encourage both apathetic and interested users to process the content centrally, rather than peripherally.

When interactivity is high though, there is some evidence to suggest that frequency of Internet use (indicative perhaps of the ability of users) makes a difference to the moderating role of involvement. Liu and Shrum (2009) showed that heavy Internet users (> 7.5 hours per week) were more likely than light users to explore the full potential of high interactivity. This difference does not matter under conditions of low involvement, because interactivity is simply treated as a peripheral cue on the interface, leading directly to positive attitudes without actually engaging the affordance.

Therefore, in theoretically inferring the effects of interactivity on persuasion using dual-process models, such as ELM (Petty & Cacioppo, 1986) and HSM (Chaiken, 1987), we have to keep in mind that the construct of involvement has two different loci—prior user involvement with content and the degree of involvement generated by interactivity features on the interface. Given that interactivity is an affordance, that is, subject to user's interpretation and use, the former would lead to the latter, but not always. The technology of interactivity can serve to directly boost the latter through a number of mechanisms.

Sundar (2007) refers to the latter as user engagement, which is said to be affected by three different species of interactivity—modality interactivity, source interactivity, and message interactivity—in theoretically distinct ways. *Modality interactivity* refers to the different tools available on the interface for accessing the embedded information, tools such as hyperlinks, mouse-overs, sliders, and drag and zoom features. Together, these functional features serve to enhance the mapping ability of our sensory channels, or perceptual bandwidth (Reeves & Nass, 2000), resulting in a richer mental representation of the underlying content.

Modality-interactivity features are often seen as "bells and whistles" and can lead directly to positive attitudes toward the interface and its content, as shown in a recent study comparing interaction modalities, such as slide and 3-D carousel with plain scrolling (Sundar, Xu, Bellur, Jia, Oh, & Khoo, 2010). Another study (Sundar, Bellur, Oh, Xu, & Jia, 2011) comparing different combinations of modality-interactivity tools on a website found that users' perceptual assessment of the interface (perceived natural mapping, intuitiveness, and ease of use of the site) predicted their degree of absorption in the site, which in turn influenced user attitudes toward the website, as well as the content in it. Therefore, the persuasive effect of interactivity as a feature of the medium rests on the degree to which it enhances perceptual representation of the information.

Source interactivity influences the level of user engagement by affording greater agency to the user. A recent field experiment (Sundar, Oh, Bellur, Jia, & Kim, 2011) showed that participants who were able to change themes of a portal site and engage in active blogging through it became more absorbed in their activities on the site and showed more positive attitudes toward it than participants who were not able to cosmetically customize the site or generate new content, but only filter existing content. When users are the prime agents of the interaction, their level of engagement with the content is significantly enhanced. The primary theoretical mechanism is based on customization leading to higher engagement, as discussed earlier in the context of self-agency.

Message interactivity, the degree to which the system engages users in reciprocal communication, serves to emphasize the conceptualization of interactivity in the processual sense (Burgoon, Bonito, Ramirez, Dunbar, Kam, & Fischer, 2002) with the key underlying mechanism of "contingency" in message exchange (Rafaeli, 1988). Studies have shown that users tend to pay more attention (Sundar & Constantin, 2004), process information more centrally (Sundar et al., 2003), and feel more motivated to participate in online forums (Wise, Hamman, & Thorson, 2006) when the system allows them to have a threaded interaction.

In fact, higher degree of contingency has been found to mediate the relationship between message interactivity and other psychological outcomes, including user engagement. In a recent study with a movie recommendation site (Sundar, Bellur, Oh, Jia, & Kim, 2012), higher message interactivity in the form of footprints of user actions, responsive suggestions in a search box, and live-chatting with an online agent led to greater perceived contingency and engagement with the site, which ultimately created more positive attitudes toward it and higher intention to recommend the site to others. At the level of messages, mediators such as connectedness, reciprocity, responsiveness, and specificity of responses could explain some of the reasons why users demonstrate such iterative and prolonged forms of involvement and engagement with new media.

Whether conceptualized as a modality feature, source feature, or message feature, the primary role of interactivity in the interactivity effects model (Sundar, 2007) is to create greater engagement with content via mechanisms related to perceptual bandwidth, customization, and contingency respectively. These effects are moderated by user factors, such as their expertise in using the interface and prior involvement in the content of the interaction.

Realistic Alternative Realities

Media technologies can also aid persuasion by creating alternative realities for users. Constructs such as vividness, self-representation, self-presence, spatial presence, and transportation are important for the effectiveness of persuasive technologies in that they create more realistic experiences for users, thereby affecting persuasion outcomes.

Vividness

Richer modalities create higher levels of vividness, which can change users' perception of a source and/or message. Vividness has been defined as the representational richness of a mediated environment shaped by its formal features (Steuer, 1992). The number of different senses engaged in the interaction (*breadth*) and the level of resolution within each of the perceptual channels (*depth*) together constitute the vividness of a medium. Given that individuals use all five senses in the real world, vivid representations using multiple modalities can increase the level of telepresence, or the sense of being present in the mediated environment (Lombard & Ditton, 1997; Steuer, 1992), thereby enhancing the perceived directness of the mediated experience. Jin (2010) found that when technology offers haptic stimuli with force feedback, such as terrain effects, acceleration and lateral forces in an online advertising context, it successfully induces desired perceptions of brand personality, such as "masculine" and "rugged." As Fazio and Zanna (1981) pointed out in their seminal article on attitude formation, direct experience leads to stronger, more persistent, and more accessible attitudes than indirect experience.

Consistent with this, Coyle and Thorson (2001) found that a more vivid website (with audio and animation) is able to maintain positive attitudes toward the website even after 2 weeks. Klein (2003) found that a product website evoked greater telepresence when it had full-motion video and audio (compared to only text and still pictures), leading to stronger acceptance of claims made on the site. In the context of computer-mediated communication, Bente, Rüggenberg, Krämer, and Eschenburg (2008) found that real-time audio and video enhance emotional closeness and interpersonal trust of the interaction partner.

Self-Representation

In addition to vivid audiovisual and haptic modalities, an increasingly common modality for experiencing games and other virtual environments is through an avatar. While text allows you to read about an event, audio to hear it, and video to see it, avatars let you experience the event through a proxy. An avatar is a computer-generated visual representation of a user that can be customized to fit any desired appearance (Holzwarth, Janiszewski, & Neumann, 2006; Jin, 2009) and possess human-like characteristics, such as speech. This can have profound implications for persuasion. By offering a representation of our own selves, avatars have been known to change both our online and offline behaviors.

In communication research, the persuasive effect of avatars has been studied from the lens of behavioral confirmation theory (Snyder, Tanke, & Berscheid, 1977), which posits that mediated human interaction is guided by one's perception of the other, with the latter's behaviors being affected by this perception to the point of reaffirming the former's expectations of the latter. In any given interaction among people—comprised of a perceiver and a target—the target tends to behave in a manner that confirms the perceiver's expectation of the target.

By extension, in a virtual environment, the image of an avatar can dictate the avatar user's behavior in the virtual world in accordance with the user's assumption about how the avatar is perceived by other users. Yee and Bailenson (2007) coined the term *"Proteus Effect"* to signify the tendency among individuals to model their online behavior after their digital self-representation. In their study, participants who were assigned attractive avatars showed greater intimacy with confederates compared to participants assigned unattractive avatars. Likewise, they tended to be more dominant when their digital representation was a tall, rather than short, avatar.

Perhaps the more important contribution of using avatars is that they enhance our ability to vicariously experience the mediated environment. Social cognitive theory (Bandura, 2001) has long documented the human tendency to enact observed action performed by a model, based on vicarious learning of the consequences of the action. In traditional media, the model is typically another human being. But, in virtual environments, avatars can serve as models. Given

that they are self-representations, the vicarious experience is likely to be even stronger. Fox and Bailenson (2009) found that those who observed their avatars gaining or losing weight in accordance with their physical exercise performed significantly more exercise in the real world than those without such vicarious reinforcement.

Self-Presence

While avatars allow users to experience mediated environments through a proxy, virtual reality (VR) goes a step further by affording self-presence of the user in those environments. Self-presence is defined as the user's mental model of their own body being present in the virtual world (Biocca, 1997). VR is by far the richest modality in terms of heightening the sense of self-presence in mediated reality, so much so that simulated behaviors in a VR setting have become efficient therapy for curing a traumatic experience from the same behavior in the real world.

A study on the treatment of driving phobias in patients following an accident showed that those who underwent a VR simulation recorded a significant reduction in travel distress, travel avoidance, and maladaptive driving strategies compared to those who were administered a game version of the treatment (Walshe, Lewis, Kim, O'Sullivan, & Wiederhold, 2003). In a study with arachnophobes, Garcia-Palacios, Hoffman, Carlin, Furness, and Botella (2002) found that 83% of the patients in the VR treatment group (holding a virtual spider with tactile feedback), showed clinically significant improvement in their disorder compared to 0% in the control group without any treatment.

Spatial Presence

A related construct is spatial presence, which can be enhanced by navigability affordances that aid user motion within a virtual environment. Wirth and colleagues (2007) proposed that gamers use available spatial cues in the mediated universe to mentally construct a spatial situation model (SSM), which serves to shift their primary ego-reference frame (PERF) from the physical world to the mediated one. Spatial presence can be induced by the interior design of virtual environments, but a key element is user navigation through the mediated space. Game designers are careful to plot out various navigational pathways in order to design several absorbing experiences for the user.

The very act of navigating through a game world can constitute a compelling narrative—a primary consideration for designers of serious games for health—that is designed with the persuasive intent of exposing individuals to information in a certain sequence. Balakrishnan and Sundar (2011) found that the traversibility afforded by steering motion increased spatial presence in a virtual space, whereas a guidance tool negatively affected spatial presence. They attributed this somewhat counterintuitive result to the real-world resemblance of the steering motion and perceived complexity of the guidance tool employed on a tablet PC dashboard. The study suggests that in order to promote spatial presence among users in a mediated environment, navigability tools should be carefully designed to signify easy access to individual goals.

Transportation

By encompassing and capturing the user's full attention, richer modalities simulate the object, story, and context of persuasion as if they were occurring in the physical world. Such immersion (Murray, 1997) in the mediated world is likely to aid the seamless integration of simulated behaviors into the behavioral script in users' minds. In other words, the resulting mental imagery of the situations portrayed in the fictional world is so vivid that they seem to directly apply to their corresponding real-world situations. Also called transportation (Green & Brock, 2000), this heightened level of immersion experienced by individuals in virtual narrative worlds can explain the persuasive effects of rich modalities, such as interactive virtual environments and video games.

Chapter 13 in this volume on narrative persuasion identifies four mechanisms: narrative makes readers or viewers less likely to counterargue the persuasive message, more likely to elaborate on it, provide imagery to help process the message, and lead them to vicariously experience the characters' fates. Empirical findings from previous research suggest that richer modalities can facilitate this process of narrative persuasion by inducing greater degree of transportation to the mediated world. An interactive virtual environment with a narrative has been shown to reduce risky behaviors among men who have sex with men compared to face-to-face counseling alone (Read et al., 2006). Likewise, Wang and Calder (2006) found that transporting individuals in a narrative setting helps create better product recall and leads to subsequent purchase.

In sum, modalities in newer media have aided the persuasion process by rendering content more vivid, transporting users to an alternate reality, and affording them greater self-representation, self-presence, and spatial presence.

Access to Information

Modern media technologies do not simply provide information, but situate them in particular spatial configurations for users to access, using a variety of online tools, such as toolbars and offline tools such as joysticks. Information of importance can sometimes appear in layered form for users to explore. Interface features can be deeply suggestive of the ways in which users can move from one location to another in mediated environments, in keeping with spatial metaphors such as "site" and "cyberspace." Navigability affordances on the interface that determine how users move in a mediated environment can therefore serve the critical role of improving user access to persuasive messages. They facilitate easier access to pertinent information, and in doing so, reduce search costs and cognitive burden for users. A growing body of literature in marketing also indicates that navigational tools for sorting and comparing product information have positive effects on consumers' attitudes toward shopping, as well as toward specific products. A simple reduction of search cost can positively affect users' attitudes. For example, Lynch and Ariely (2000) found that search cost reductions accruing from navigational ease in comparison shopping decreased price sensitivity among users, increased their liking for the products that they selected, and maintained their retention probability when they were contacted two months later.

Navigability affordances can also provide useful cues to focus user attention toward relevant information and minimize effort in locating it. Information foraging theory (e.g., Pirolli, 2007; Pirolli & Card, 1999) suggests that online users' behavior patterns related to information consumption are influenced by the information scent emitted by cues on the interface, which provide hints about content in distal locations. When the interface is navigable and accessible in this way, it produces positive outcomes for persuasion. For instance, users of a comprehensive health system with navigation support and decision analysis tools perceived better quality of life, higher health care competence, and greater social support compared to those with only simple Internet access (Gustafson et al., 2008). Likewise, adding a search option for personal stories related to breast cancer significantly influenced users' attitudes toward coping with cancer (Overberg et al., 2010).

While navigation tools afford information at the right place, pervasive and ubiquitous computing technologies make information available at the right time. Systems that enable just-in-time messaging (Intille, 2002) have been known to change people's behaviors. Examples include a mobile phone application for helping people lose weight by tracking their calorie intake, and a mobile system for helping people quit smoking by suggesting decreasing frequency of daily smoking.

In an environment of information overload, search and navigational tools serve to provide much-needed scaffolding to users, helping them access relevant information with ease and reducing the burden of searching, thereby enhancing user experience of the mediated environment and contributing to persuasion outcomes.

Persuasive Potential of Technologies

The discussion thus far covers a variety of theoretical mechanisms via which communication technologies aid the process of persuasion. Even though some of the work reviewed in previous sections was not intended to inform persuasion theory, they hold key insights for theory and design of persuasive technologies.

First, it is quite clear that technology is an alternative source of persuasive messages. The source need not always be human. Even websites, robots, avatars, and virtual agents can persuade people. Such attributes of technological sources as expertise (e.g., Hu & Sundar, 2010), specialization (e.g., Koh & Sundar, 2010a; 2010b), attractiveness (e.g. Yee, Bailenson, & Ducheneaut, 2009), similarity (e.g., Fox & Bailenson, 2009), anthropomorphism (Zanbaka, Goolkasian, & Hodges, 2006) and perceived realism (e.g. Guadagno, Blascovich, Bailenson, & McCall, 2007) can affect how individuals evaluate their credibility.

Technology is also shown to affect perceptions of content credibility and level of user engagement. As detailed in previous sections, affordances related to modality, agency, interactivity, and navigability of communication technologies not only affect how individuals perceive message content, but also their level of engagement with it (e.g., Sundar, Xu, Bellur, Oh, & Jia, 2011) and subsequent evaluations (e.g. Sundar, 2000; Sundar & Marathe, 2010).

Perhaps most important, our review reveals that technological factors affect the process of persuasion by changing user attitudes and behaviors. Attitudinal outcomes include brand or product evaluation (e.g., Fransen, Fennis, & Pruyn, 2010; Schlosser, 2003), willingness to pay (e.g., Franke et al., 2009), attitudes toward website (e.g., Liu & Shrum, 2009), attitudes toward political candidates featured on websites (Sundar et al., 2003), and attitudes about messages advocated by virtual agents (Guadagno, Blascovich, Bailenson, & McCall, 2007). Behavioral outcomes include browsing activity (Kalyanaraman & Sundar, 2006), reducing undesirable behaviors (e.g., Noar, Pierce, & Black, 2010), increasing desirable behaviors (e.g., Baranowski, Buday, Thompson, & Baranowski, 2008), and pursuing a healthy lifestyle (e.g., Campbell et al., 1994; Marcus et al., 2007).

Conclusion

This chapter represents a move away from treating persuasive technologies as mere vessels for holding and carrying persuasive messages. By now, it should be clear even to the casual reader that aspects of these technologies themselves contribute to persuasion outcomes in significant ways. This is not simply a matter of explaining additional variance, however. Instead, it is a matter of assessing how different aspects of the technology can contribute to persuasion in different ways. While this chapter has attempted to delineate the theoretical mechanisms by which technological factors influence the persuasion process, much work remains to be done in developing and testing specific theoretical questions.

For example, under the first mechanism described in this chapter, it is important for us to investigate both the nature of interface cues that trigger cognitive heuristics and ways in which the heuristics result in persuasion outcomes. Sometimes, the sheer presence of an affordance on an interface can serve as a cue (e.g., a fancy modality such as 3-D carousel leading to the "bells and whistles" heuristic). At other times, cues appear in the form of metrics (e.g., bandwagon indicators) that are an outcome of affordances seeking user input. It is unclear if both these types of cues operate in a similar fashion in influencing persuasion, or whether they trigger heuristics in distinct ways. Further, a methodological challenge is to

accurately track when a user invokes a given heuristic during their interaction with a technology (Bellur & Sundar, 2010).

Considerable conceptual, theoretical, and methodological work remains to be done with the other mechanisms as well. Allowing the user to be the source is one of the hallmarks of web 2.0, with social media applications being deployed daily to produce persuasive outcomes. Users seem to be seduced by the ability to act as sources, given that it increases their sense of agency, identity, and self-determination. While this speaks to the stickiness of the persuasive technologies themselves (i.e., it may guarantee repeat usage of the interface), the translation into outcomes of persuasion (such as positive attitudes and behaviors) is yet to be mapped out. Likewise, the relationship between engagement with the tool and engagement with the persuasive content needs further theoretical as well as empirical exploration.

Considerable investments in persuasive communications have already been made in the domain of games and other virtual environments, but most rely on simple exposure, and tend to treat alternate realities as just additional media for mass communications. While navigational tools have been deployed effectively by sites and apps, empirically verified mechanisms related to self-representation, self-presence, and spatial presence are yet to be systematically translated into practice.

A particular challenge for both theoreticians and practitioners is the integration of the effects of persuasive technologies with those of persuasive messages. The future lies in proposing interaction hypotheses that predict combined effects of specific technological variables and specific source, message and user variables identified by traditional persuasion research. Technological affordances related to modality, agency, interactivity, and navigability could amplify, neutralize, or negate long-held persuasion findings by serving as cues on the interface, modifying the manifestation of persuasive content, and changing the nature of user engagement in the process of persuasion. Together, persuasive messages and persuasive technologies will serve to shape the meaning and outcomes of persuasive communications.

Acknowledgment

This research was supported by the National Science Foundation (NSF) via Standard Grant No. IIS-09l6944 and by the Korea Science and Engineering Foundation under the WCU (World Class University) program at the Department of Interaction Science, Sungkyunkwan University, Seoul, South Korea (Grant No. R31-2008-000-10062-0).

References

Balakrishnan, B., & Sundar, S. S. (2011). Where am I? How can I get there? Impact of navigability and narrative transportation on spatial presence. *Human Computer Interaction, 26,* 161–204.

Bandura, A. (1997). *Self-efficacy: The exercise of control.* New York, NY: W. H. Freeman.

Bandura, A. (2001). Social cognitive theory of mass communication. *Media Psychology, 3,* 265–299.

Bang, M., Torstensson, C., & Katzeff, C. (2006). The power house: A persuasive computer game designed to raise awareness of domestic energy consumption. In W. A. IJsselsteijn, Y. A. W. De Kort, C. J. H. Midden, J. H. Eggen & E. A. W. H. Van den Hoven (Eds.), *Persuasive 2006* (pp. 123–132). Berlin, Germany: Springer.

Baranowski, T., Buday, R., Thompson, D., & Baranowski, J. (2008). Playing for real: Video games and stories for health-related behavior change. *American Journal of Preventive Medicine, 34,* 74–82.

Bellur, S., & Sundar, S. S. (2010, June). *How can we tell when a heuristic has been used? Models for measurement of heuristics.* Paper presented at the 60th annual conference of the International Communication Association, Singapore.

Bente, G., Rüggenberg, S., Krämer, N. C., & Eschenburg, F. (2008). Avatar-mediated networking: Increasing social presence and interpersonal trust in Net-based collaborations. *Human Communication Research, 34,* 287–318.

Biocca, F. (1997). The cyborg's dilemma: Progressive embodiment in virtual environments. *Journal of Computer-Mediated Communication, 3,* 1–29.

Burgoon, J. K., Bonito, J. A., Ramirez, A. Jr., Dunbar, N. E., Kam, K., & Fischer, J. (2002). Testing the interactivity principle: Effects of mediation, propinquity, and verbal and nonverbal modalities in interpersonal interaction. *Journal of Communication, 52,* 657–677.

Campbell, M. K., Devellis, B. M., Strecher, V. J., Ammerman, A. S., Devellis, R. F., & Sandler, R. S. (1994). Improving dietary behavior: The effectiveness of tailored messages in primary-care settings. *American Journal of Public Health, 84,* 783–787.

Chaiken, S. (1987). The heuristic model of persuasion. In M. P. Zanna, J. M. Olson, & C. P. Herman (Eds.), *Social influence: The Ontario Symposium* (Vol. 5, pp. 3–39). Hillsdale, NJ: Erlbaum.

Coner, A. (2003). Personalization and customization in financial portals. *Journal of American Academy of Business, 2,* 498–504.

Coyle, J. R., & Thorson, E. (2001). The effects of progressive levels of interactivity and vividness in web marketing sites. *Journal of Advertising, 30,* 65–77.

Dillard, J. P. (2010). Persuasion. In C. R. Berger, M. E. Roloff, & D. R. Roskos-Ewoldsen (Eds.), *The handbook of communication science* (pp. 203–218). Thousand Oaks, CA: Sage.

Fazio, R. H., & Zanna, M. P. (1981). Direct experience and attitude-behavior consistency. In L. Berkowitz (Eds.), *Advances in experimental social psychology* (Vol. 14, pp. 161–202). New York, NY: Academic Press.

Firpo, D., Kasemvilas, S., Ractham, P., & Zhang, X. (2009). Generating a sense of community in a graduate educational setting through persuasive technology. *Proceedings of the 4th International Conference on Persuasive Technology (Persuasive 2009).* New York, NY: ACM Press.

Fogg, B. J. (2002). *Persuasive technologies: Using computer power to change attitudes and behaviors.* San Francisco, CA: Morgan Kaufmann.

Fogg, B. J., Lee, E., & Marshall, J. (2002). Interactive technology and persuasion. In J. P. Dillard and M. Pfau (Eds.), *The persuasion handbook: Developments in theory and practice* (pp. 765–788). Thousand Oaks, CA: Sage.

Fox, J., & Bailenson, J. N. (2009). Virtual self-modeling: The effects of vicarious reinforcement and identification on exercise behaviors. *Media Psychology, 12,* 1–25.

Franke, N., Schreier, M., & Kaiser, U. (2009). The "I designed it myself" effect in mass customization. *Management Science, 56,* 125–140.

Fransen, M. L., Fennis, B. M., & Pruyn, A. H. (2010). Matching Communication modalities: The effects of modality congruence and processing style on brand evaluation and brand choice. *Communication Research, 37,* 576–598.

Garcia-Palaciosa, A., Hoffman, H., Carlin, A., Furness, T. A., III, & Botella, C. (2002). Virtual reality in the treatment of spider phobia: A controlled study. *Behavior Research and Therapy, 40,* 983–993.

Green, M. C., & Brock, T. C. (2000). The role of transportation in the persuasiveness of public narratives. *Journal of Personality and Social Psychology, 79,* 701–721.

Guadagno, R., Blascovich, J., Bailenson, J., & McCall, C. (2007). Virtual humans and persuasion: The effects of agency and behavioral realism. *Media Psychology, 10,* 1–22.

Gustafson, D. H., Hawkins, R., McTavish, F., Pingree, S., Chen, W. C., Volrathongchai, K., et al. (2008). Internet-based interactive support for cancer patients: Are integrated systems better? *Journal of Communication, 58,* 238–257.

Hawkins, R. P., Kreuter, M., Resnicow, K., Fishbein, M., & Dijkstra, A. (2008). Understanding tailoring in communicating about health. *Health Education Research, 23,* 454–466.

Holbert, R. L. (2002). The embodied meaning of media forms. In J. P. Dillard and M. Pfau (Eds.), *The persuasion handbook: Developments in theory and practice* (pp. 749–764). Thousand Oaks, CA: Sage.

Holzwarth, M., Janiszewski, C., & Neumann, M. M. (2006). The influence of avatars on online consumer shopping behavior. *Journal of Marketing, 70,* 19–36.

Hu, Y., & Sundar, S. S. (2010). Effects of online health sources on credibility and behavioral intentions. *Communication Research, 37*(1), 105–132.

Intille, S. S. (2002). Designing a home of the future. *IEEE Pervasive Computing, 1,* 80–86.

Jerant, A., Kravitz, R. L., Rooney, M., Arnerson, S., Kreuter, M., & Franks, P. (2007). Effects of a tailored interactive multimedia computer program on determinants of colorectal cancer screening: A randomized controlled pilot study in physician offices. *Patient Education and Counseling, 66,* 67–74.

Jin , S.-A. A. (2009). Modality effects in second life: The mediating role of social presence and the moderating role of product involvement. *Cyber Psychology and Behavior, 12,* 717–721.

Jin, S.-A. A. (2010). Effects of 3D virtual haptics force feedback on brand personality perception: The mediating role of physical presence in advergames. *Cyber Psychology, Behavior, and Social Networking, 13,* 307–311.

Kalyanaraman, S., & Sundar, S. S. (2006). The psychological appeal of personalized content in web portals: Does customization affect attitudes and behavior? *Journal of Communication, 56,* 110–132.

Kim, H. S., & Sundar, S. S. (2011). Using interface cues in online health community boards to change impressions and encourage user contribution. *Proceedings of the 2011 Annual Conference on Human Factors in Computing Systems (CHI'11),* 599–608.

Klein, L. R. (2003). Creating virtual product experiences: The role of telepresence. *Journal of Interactive Marketing, 17,* 41–55. doi: 10.1002/dir.10046

Koh, Y. J., & Sundar, S. S. (2010a). Effects of specialization in computers, web sites and web agents on e-commerce trust. *International Journal of Human-Computer Studies, 68,* 899–912.

Koh, Y. J., & Sundar, S. S. (2010b). Heuristic versus systematic processing of specialist versus generalist sources in online media. *Human Communication Research, 36,* 103–124.

Liu, Y., & Shrum, L. J. (2009). A dual-process model of interactivity effects. *Journal of Advertising, 38,* 53–68.

Lombard, M., & Ditton, T. (1997). At the heart of it all: The concept of presence. *Journal of Computer-Mediated Communication, 3.* doi: 10.1111/j.1083-6101.1997.tb00072.x

Lynch, J. G., & Ariely, D. (2000). Wine online: Search costs affect competition on price, quality and distribution. *Marketing Science, 19,* 83–103.

Marathe, S., & Sundar, S. S. (2011). What drives customization? Control or identity? *Proceedings of the 2011 Annual Conference on Human Factors in Computing Systems (CHI'11),* 781–790.

Marcus, B. H., Lewis, B. A, Williams, D. M., Dunsiger, S., Jakicic, J. M., Whiteley, J. A., et al. (2007). A comparison of Internet and print-based physical activity interventions. *Archives of internal medicine, 167*, 944–949.

McCalley, T., Kaiser, F., Midden, C. J. H., Keser, M., & Teunissen, M. (2006). Persuasive appliances: Goal priming and behavioral response to product-integrated energy feedback. In W. A. IJsselsteijn, Y. A. W. De Kort, C. J. H. Midden, J. H. Eggen, & E. A. W. H Van den Hoven (Eds.), *Persuasive 2006* (pp. 45–49). Berlin, Germany: Springer.

McMillan, D. W. (1996). Sense of community. *Journal of Community Psychology, 24*, 315–325.

McMillan, D. W., & Chavis, D. M. (1986). Sense of community: A definition and theory. *Journal of Community Psychology, 14*, 6–23.

Metzger, M. J., Flanagin, A. J., & Medders, R. B. (2010). Social and heuristic approaches to credibility evaluation online. *Journal of Communication, 60*, 413–439.

Miller, G. R. (1980). On being persuaded. In M. Roloff & G. R. Miller (Eds.), *Persuasion: New directions in theory and research* (pp. 11–28). Beverly Hills, CA: Sage.

Murray, J. (1997). *Hamlet on the holodeck: The future of narrative in cyberspace.* Cambridge, MA: MIT Press.

Nass, C., & Mason, L. (1990). On the study of technology and task: A variable-based approach. In J. Fulk & C. Steinfeld (Eds.), *Organizations and communication technology* (pp. 46–67). Newbury Park, CA: Sage.

Noar, S. M., Pierce, L. B., & Black, H. G. (2010). Can computer-mediated interventions change theoretical mediators of safer sex? A meta-analysis. *Human Communication Research, 36*, 261–297.

Norton, M. I., Mochon, D., & Ariely, D. (2011). The 'IKEA Effect': When labor leads to love. Harvard Business School Marketing Unit Working Paper No. 11-091. Retrieved from SSRN, May 11, 2012: http://ssrn.com/abstract=1777100

Oenema, A., Brug, J., Dijkstra, A., de Weerdt, I., & de Vries, H. (2008). Efficacy and use of an internet-delivered computer-tailored lifestyle intervention, targeting saturated fat intake, physical activity and smoking cessation: A randomized controlled trial. *Annals of Behavioral Medicine, 35*, 125–135.

Overberg, R., Otten, W., de Man, A., Toussaint, P., Westenbrink, J., & Zwetsloot-Schonk, B. (2010). How breast cancer patients want to search for and retrieve information from stories of other patients on the Internet: An online randomized controlled experiment. *Journal of Medical Internet Research, 12*(1). doi:10.2196/jmir.1215

Pan, B., Hembrooke, H., Joachims, T., Lorigo, L., Gay, G., & Granka, L. (2007). In Google we trust: Users' decisions on rank, position, and relevance. *Journal of Computer-Mediated Communication, 12.* Retrieved May 11, 2012, from http://jcmc.indiana.edu/vol12/issue3/pan.html

Petty, R. E., & Cacioppo, J. T. (1986). *Communication and persuasion: Central and peripheral routes to attitude change.* New York, NY: Springer-Verlag.

Petty, R. E., Wheeler, S. C., & Bizer, G. Y. (2000). Attitude functions and persuasion: An elaboration likelihood approach to matched versus mismatched messages. In J. M. Olson (Eds.), *Why we evaluate: Functions of attitudes* (pp. 133–162). Mahwah, NJ: Erlbaum.

Pierce, J. L., Kostova, T., & Dirks, K. T. (2003). The state of psychological ownership: Integrating and extending a century of research. *Review of General Psychology, 7*, 84–107.

Pirolli, P. (2007). *Information foraging theory: Adaptive interaction with information.* Cambridge, UK: Oxford University Press.

Pirolli, P., & Card, S. K. (1999). Information foraging. *Psychological Review, 106*, 643–675.

Rafaeli, S. (1988). Interactivity: From new media to communication. In R. Hawkins, J. Weimann, & S. Pingree (Eds.), *Advancing communication science: Merging mass and interpersonal processes* (pp. 124–181). Newbury Park, CA: Sage.

Read S. J., Miller, L. C., Appleby, P. R., Nwosu, M. E., Reynaldo, S., Lauren, A., et al. (2006). Socially optimized learning in a virtual environment: Reducing risky sexual behavior among men who have sex with men. *Human Communication Research, 3*, 1–34.

Reeves, B., & Nass, C. (1996). *The media equation.* Stanford, CA: CSLI.

Reeves, B., & Nass, C. (2000). Perceptual user interfaces: Perceptual bandwidth. *Communications of the ACM, 4*, 65–70.

Richardson, C. R., Buis, L. R., Janney, A. W., Goodrich, D. E., Sen, A., Hess, M. L., et al. (2010). An online community improves adherence in an internet-mediated walking program. part 1: Results of a randomized controlled trial. *Journal of Medical Internet Research, 24.* doi: 10.2196/jmr.1338

Ryan, R. M., & Deci, E. L. (2000). Self-determination theory and the facilitation of intrinsic motivation, social development, and well-being. *American Psychologist, 55,* 68–78.

Salomon, G. (1979). Media and symbol systems as related to cognition and learning. *Journal of Educational Psychology, 71*(2), 131–148.

Schlosser, A. E. (2003). Experiencing products in the virtual world: The rule of goal and imagery in influencing attitudes versus purchase intentions. *Journal of Consumer Research, 30,* 184–198.

Snyder, M., Tanke, E. D., & Berscheid, E. (1977). Social perception and interpersonal behavior: On the self-fulfilling nature of social stereotypes. *Journal of Personality and Social Psychology, 35,* 656–666.

Steuer, J. (1992). Defining virtual reality: Dimensions determining telepresence. *Journal of Communication, 42,* 73–93.

Strecher, V. J., McClure, J., Alexander, G., Chakraborty, B., Nair, V., Konkel, J., et al. (2008). The role of engagement in a tailored web-based smoking cessation program: Randomized controlled trial. *Journal of Medical Internet Research, 10*(5). doi:10.2196/jmir.1002

Sundar, S. S. (2000). Multimedia effects on processing and perception of online news: A study of picture, audio, and video downloads. *Journalism and Mass Communication Quarterly, 77,* 480–499.

Sundar, S. S. (2007). Social psychology of interactivity in human-website interaction. In A. N. Joinson, K. Y. A. McKenna, T. Postmes, & U. D. Reips (Eds.), *The Oxford handbook of internet psychology* (pp. 89–104). Oxford, UK: Oxford University Press.

Sundar, S. S. (2008a). The MAIN model: A heuristic approach to understanding technology effects on credibility. In M. J. Metzger & A. J. Flanagin (Eds.), *Digital media, youth, and credibility* (pp. 72–100). Cambridge, MA: MIT Press.

Sundar, S. S. (2008b). Self as source: Agency and customization in interactive media. In E. Konijn, S. Utz, M. Tanis, & S. Barnes (Eds.), *Mediated interpersonal communication* (pp. 58–74). New York, NY: Routledge.

Sundar, S. S. (2009). Media effects 2.0: Social and psychological effects of communication technologies. In R. L. Nabi & M. B. Oliver (Eds.), *The SAGE handbook of media processes and effects* (pp. 545–560). Thousand Oaks, CA: Sage.

Sundar, S. S., & Bellur, S. (2010). Concept explication in the internet age: The case of interactivity. In E. P. Bucy & R. L. Holbert (Eds.), *Sourcebook for political communication research: Methods, measures, and analytical techniques* (pp. 485–500). New York, NY: Routledge.

Sundar, S. S., Bellur, S., Oh, J., Jia, H., & Kim, H. S. (2012, May). *The importance of message contingency: An experimental investigation of interactivity in an online search site.* Paper presented at the 62nd annual conference of the International Communication Association, Phoenix, AZ.

Sundar, S. S., Bellur, S. Oh, J., Xu, Q., & Jia, H. (2011). *User experience of on-screen interaction techniques: An experimental investigation of clicking, sliding, zooming, hovering, dragging and flipping.* Manuscript submitted for publication.

Sundar, S. S., & Constantin, C. (2004). *Does interacting with media enhance news memory? Automatic vs. controlled processing of interactive news features.* Paper presented at the 54th annual conference of the International Communication Association, New Orleans, LA.

Sundar, S. S., Kalyanaraman, S., & Brown, J. (2003). Explicating website interactivity: Impression-formation effects in political campaign sites. *Communication Research, 30,* 30–59.

Sundar, S. S., & Kim, J. (2005). Interactivity and persuasion: Influencing attitudes with information and involvement. *Journal of Interactive Advertising, 5,* 6–29. Retrieved May 11, 2012, from http://www.jiad.org/article59

Sundar, S. S., & Marathe, S. S. (2010). Personalization versus customization: The importance of agency, privacy, and power usage. *Human Communication Research, 36,* 298–322.

Sundar, S. S., & Nass, C. (2001). Conceptualizing sources in online news. *Journal of Communication, 51,* 52–72.

Sundar, S. S., Oeldorf-Hirsch, A., & Xu, Q. (2008). The bandwagon effect of collaborative filtering technology. *Proceedings of CHI'08 Extended Abstracts on Human Factors in Computing Systems, 26,* 3453–3458.

Sundar, S. S., Oh, J., Bellur, S., Jia, H., & Kim, H. S. (2012). Interactivity as self-expression: A field experiment with customization and blogging. *Proceedings of the 2012 Annual Conference on Human Factors in Computing Systems (CHI'12),* 395–404.

Sundar, S. S., Xu, Q., Bellur, S., Jia, H., Oh, J., & Khoo, G-S. (2010, June). *Click, drag, flip, and mouse-over: Effects of modality interactivity on user engagement with web content.* Paper presented at the 60th annual conference of the International Communication Association, Singapore.

Sundar, S. S., Xu, Q., Bellur, S., Oh, J., & Jia, H. (2011). Beyond pointing and clicking: How do newer interaction modalities affect user engagement? *Proceedings of the 2011 Annual Conference Extended Abstracts on Human Factors in Computing Systems (CHI EA'11),* 1477–1482.

Sundar, S. S., Xu, Q., & Dou, X. (2012). Role of technology in online persuasion: A MAIN Model perspective. In S. Rodgers & E. Thorson (Eds.), *Advertising theory* (pp. 355–372). New York, NY: Routledge.

Sundar, S. S., Xu, Q., & Oeldorf-Hirsch, A. (2009). Authority vs. peer: How interface cues influence users. *Proceedings of the 27th International Conference Extended Abstracts on Human Factors in Computing Systems (CHI'09),* 27, 4231–4236.

Walshe, D. G., Lewis, E. J., Kim, S. I., O'Sullivan, K., & Wiederhold, B. K. (2003). Exploring the use of computer games and virtual reality in exposure therapy for fear of driving following a motor vehicle accident. *Cyber Psychology & Behavior, 6,* 329–334.

Wang, J., & Calder, B. J. (2006), Media transportation and advertising. *Journal of Consumer Research, 33*(2), 151–162.

Weissman, J. R. (1988). Have it your way: What happens when users control the interface. In M. A. Siegel (Eds.), *Design and evaluation of computer/human interfaces: Issues for librarians and information scientists* (pp. 95–104). Urbana, IL: Graduate School of Library and Information Science, University of Illinois at Urbana-Champaign.

Wirth, W., Hartmann, T., Böcking, S., Vorderer, P., Klimmt, C., Schramm, H., et al. (2007). A process model of the formation of spatial presence experiences. *Media Psychology, 9,* 493–525.

Wise, K., Hamman, B., & Thorson, K. (2006). Moderation, response rate, and message interactivity: Features of online communities and their effects on intent to participate. *Journal of Computer-Mediated Communication, 12,* 24–41.

Yee, N., & Bailenson, J. N. (2007). The Proteus effect: The effect of transformed self-representation on behavior. *Human Communication Research, 33,* 271–290.

Yee, N., Bailenson, J. N., & Duchenaut, N. (2009). The Proteus effect: Implications of transformed digital self-representation on online and offline behavior. *Communication Research, 36,* 285–312.

Zaichkowsky, J. L. (1985). Measuring the involvement construct. *Journal of Consumer Research, 12,* 341–352.

Zanbaka, C., Goolkasian, P., & Hodges, L. F. (2006). Can a virtual cat persuade you? The role of gender and realism in speaker persuasiveness. *Proceedings of CHI 2006,* 1153–1162.

Author Index

Subject Index

About the Authors

Eusebio M. Alvaro (PhD, University of Arizona, 2000) is a Research Associate Professor in the School of Behavioral and Organizational Sciences at Claremont Graduate University where he also co-directs the Health Psychology and Prevention Science Institute. His basic research addresses social influence processes with an emphasis on biased message processing, resistance to persuasion, indirect effects of persuasive messages, and mechanisms by which minorities achieve change. His applied research and evaluation activities involve persuasion in the context of health promotion, disease prevention, and medicine with a focus on messages targeting health behavior change (i.e., drug use and organ donation).

Kyle Andrews (PhD, Michigan State University, 2009) is an Assistant Professor in the Department of Communication at Northern Illinois University, where he teaches courses in persuasion, compliance gaining, and campaigns. His current research focuses on decision making in social dilemma situations, social influence in health and environmental contexts, and information diffusion within social networks.

Charles Atkin (PhD, University of Wisconsin, 1971) is the Chair of the Department of Communication and University Distinguished Professor at Michigan State University. He has published seven books and many articles and chapters relating to mass media effects and health. He is co-editor of *Mass Communication and Public Health* and *Public Communication Campaigns*. Atkin has frequently presented testimony to federal hearings of the U.S. Congress and regulatory agencies. He's served as campaign design consultant or evaluation researcher on numerous public information programs in the health arena, and received the "Outstanding Health Communication Scholar" award from the Health Communication divisions of ICA and NCA.

Elisabeth Bigsby (PhD, University of Georgia, 2010) is an Assistant Professor in the Department of Communication Studies at Northeastern University in Boston, MA. Her current research focuses on the impact and role of message features and message perceptions in persuasive health communication. Prior to her Northeastern University appointment, she worked as a Research Director for the Center of Excellence in Cancer Communication at the Annenberg School for Communication at the University of Pennsylvania.

Helena Bilandzic (Dr. Phil., Ludwig-Maximilians-Universität in Munich, 2003; Habilitation degree, University of Erfurt, 2009) is a Professor at the University of

Augsburg in Germany, where she teaches media effects, media psychology, and empirical methods. She has also taught at universities in Munich, Erfurt, Ilmenau, Berlin, Hamburg, and Friedrichshafen. Her current research interests include narrative experience and persuasion, cultivation, media use, and methodology.

Graham Bodie (PhD, Purdue University) invests his scholarly energy as Assistant Professor at The Louisiana State University (LSU) investigating listening and other forms of supportive communication. He has authored over 40 articles and book chapters and continually seeks ways to use research toward the betterment of others. His endeavors have been recognized by formal awards including the *International Listening Association Research Award* and funded by the Louisiana Board of Regents and LSU's Council on Research.

Franklin J. Boster (PhD, 1978) is a Professor of Communication at Michigan State University, adjunct professor of Law at Michigan State University, and adjunct professor of Community and Behavioral Health at the University of Iowa. He has published on social influence and group dynamics in communication, psychology, law, health, and business journals. Presently he is studying methods of accelerating the diffusion of health information. He is a recipient of the Golden Anniversary Award (NCA), the Charles H. Woolbert Award (NCA), and the John E. Hunter Meta-Analysis Award (ICA), as well as the Distinguished Faculty Award and the Faculty Impact Award, both from Michigan State University.

Rick Busselle (PhD Michigan State, 1997) is an Associate Professor in The Murrow College of Communication at Washington State University. His research focuses on the perceived realism of stories and the role of perceived realism in narrative processing, persuasion, and social constructions related to crime, poverty, mental illness, and audience members' perceptions of victims. He teaches communication theory, quantitative research methods, and courses related to narrative processing, media processes and effects, and stereotypes.

Deborah A. Cai is a Professor and Chair of Strategic Communication at Temple University (Philadelphia).

Christopher J. Carpenter (PhD, Michigan State University, 2010) is an Assistant Professor in the Department of Communication at Western Illinois University. He researches cognitive processing theories of persuasion, compliance-gaining techniques, employing opinion leaders in behavior change campaigns, close relationships, and online social networking. He has published in a variety of journals, including *Health Communication, Communication Monographs, Communication Research Methods and Measures, Argumentation and Advocacy, Psychology of Women Quarterly,* and *Personality and Individual Differences.* His work appeared on four top paper panels and he was invited to participate in a debate at The University of Oxford concerning online social networking.

Josh Compton (PhD, University of Oklahoma, 2004) is a Senior Lecturer in Speech in the Institute for Writing and Rhetoric at Dartmouth College. His research explores resistance to persuasion, image repair, and speech pedagogy. He has received the Outstanding Professor Award from the National Speakers Association, the Bob R. Derryberry New Forensics Educator Award, and the L. E. Norton Award for Outstanding Scholarship. His recent work appears in *The Colbert/Stewart Effect: Essays on the Real Impacts of Fake News; The Daily Show and Rhetoric: Arguments, Issues and Strategies; and Teaching, Learning,* and the *Net Generation: Concepts and Tools for Reaching Digital Learners.*

William D. Crano (PhD, Northwestern University) is the Oskamp Professor of Psychology at Claremont Graduate University's School of Behavioral and Organizational Sciences. His research focuses on persuasion and social influence, with emphasis on the use of media to prevent drug misuse in youth. He is a Fellow of the American Psychological Association and the Association for Psychological Science, and was former Chair of the Society for Experimental Social Psychology. His previous books include *Principles and Methods of Social Research* and *Social Psychology* (both with Marilynn Brewer), *Mass Media and Drug Prevention* (with Michael Burgoon, co-editor), and *The Rules of Influence.*

James Price Dillard (PhD, Michigan State University, 1983) is a Liberal Arts Research Professor in the Department of Communication Arts at The Pennsylvania State University. His research emphasizes theory and empirical research on the role of emotion in persuasion. He has received the John E. Hunter Award for Meta-Analysis and is a Fellow of the International Communication Association. His previous edited books include *Seeking Compliance: The Production of Interpersonal Influence Messages* and (with Michael Pfau) the first edition of *The Persuasion Handbook.*

David R. Ewoldsen (PhD, Indiana University, 1990) is a Professor at The Ohio State University with a joint appointment in the School of Communication and the Department of Psychology. His primary research interests involve theories of persuasion and attitude change and media psychology. He was the founding co-editor of the journal *Media Psychology* and founding editor of *Communication Methods & Measures.* He has co-edited three volumes, including the *Handbook of Communication Science, Communication and Social Cognition,* and *Communication and Emotion.*

Edward L. Fink is a Professor of Communication, Affiliate Professor of Sociology, Affiliate Professor of Psychology, Affiliate Professor of the PhD Program in Second Language Acquisition, and Distinguished Scholar-Teacher at the University of Maryland, College Park.

J. Michael Hogan (PhD, University of Wisconsin, 1983) is a Liberal Arts Research Professor and Director of the Center for Democratic Deliberation at Penn State. He is the author, co-author, or editor of seven books and more than 50 essays and book chapters on political campaigns and social movements, foreign policy debates, presidential rhetoric, and public opinion. He is a recipient of the NCA Distinguished Scholar Award and a scholarly advisor to the National Constitution Center. He also co-directs *Voices of Democracy,* an NEH-funded online curriculum resource. Before moving to Penn State, Hogan taught at Indiana University and at the University of Virginia.

R. Lance Holbert (PhD, University of Wisconsin, 2000) is an Associate Professor in the School of Communication at The Ohio State University. His research interests focus on a mix of political communication, entertainment media, and persuasion. He recently co-edited (with Erik Bucy) *The Sourcebook of Political Communication Research* and co-authored (with Max McCombs) *The News and Public Opinion: Media Effects on Civic Life.*

Hyunjin Kang (MA, Michigan State University) is a PhD candidate in the College of Communications at The Pennsylvania State University. Her research explores psychological effects of new media technologies. She is especially interested in exploring the positive and negative effects of customization in interactive media. Her studies also investigate potential role of new media technologies in persuasion.

Min Liu is a PhD candidate in Marketing at the University of Texas at San Antonio. Her research interests include judgment and decision making, and cross-cultural research. She focuses on how consumers make decisions in marketing contexts, how their preferences are formed, and how different cultural backgrounds may influence consumers' perceptions and choices. Prior to her doctoral study, Ms. Liu worked in a marketing research company as well as a university, which inspired her to pursue an academic career in marketing.

Tina M. Lowrey (PhD, University of Illinois) is a Professor at the University of Texas at San Antonio. Her research interests include the application of psycholinguistic concepts to understanding marketing communications phenomena, children's acquisition of consumption knowledge, and gift-giving and ritual. Her two most recent edited books include *Brick and Mortar Shopping in the 21st Century*, and *Psycholinguistic Phenomena in Marketing Communications.*

Paul A. Mongeau (PhD, Michigan State University, 1988) is a Professor in the Hugh Downs School of Human Communication at Arizona State University in Tempe. His research interests focus on cognitive processing of influence messages as well as communication in the earliest stages of relationships. His most recent work has focused on modern sociosexual norms on college campuses, specifically focusing on diversity within friends with benefits relationships. He is co-author (with James B. Stiff) of the second edition of *Persuasive Communication* and past editor of *Communication Studies* and the *Journal of Social and Personal Relationships.*

Mark Nespoli is a doctoral student in Marketing at the University of Texas at San Antonio. His current research interests include the impact of time perception on consumer behavior, cross-cultural consumer behavior, and consumer ethics. He earned his MBA and BA (*Summa cum Laude*) from The University of Arizona.

Jeeyun Oh (MA, Seoul National University) is a PhD candidate in the College of Communications at The Pennsylvania State University. As part of the Media Effects Research Lab at Penn State, her research focuses on psychological effects of technological affordances unique to Web-based mass communication. Her studies experimentally investigate the effects of interactivity and multimodality in Web interfaces on online users' cognition, perceptions, and attitudes. Her research interests also include the effect of video game interfaces and human-robot interaction.

Daniel J. O'Keefe (PhD, University of Illinois at Urbana-Champaign, 1976) is the Owen L. Coon Professor in the Department of Communication Studies at Northwestern University. His work focuses on research synthesis concerning persuasive message effects. He has received the National Communication Association's Golden Anniversary Monograph Award, the International Communication Association's Best Article Award, and the International Society for the Study of Argumentation's Distinguished Research Award. He is the author of *Persuasion: Theory and Research* (Sage).

Richard M. Perloff (PhD, University of Wisconsin–Madison, 1978; Postdoctoral Fellow, The Ohio State University, Social Psychology, Journalism, and Communication, 1979) is a Professor of Communication at Cleveland State University. He is nationally known for his work on the third-person effect and his book on persuasion. He co-edited a book on political information-processing with Sidney Kraus and is the author of *Political Communication: Politics, Press, and Public in America* and *The Dynamics of Persuasion: Communication and Attitudes in the 21st century* (4th edition). His work on the third-person effect and political persuasion have appeared in edited volumes, including *Media Effects: Advances in Theory and Research* (3rd edition), *Handbook of Political Marketing*, and *Handbook of Political Communication* (with Bruce Newman, 2nd edition). Perloff received a Distinguished Faculty Research Award from Cleveland State University in 1999 and is a Fellow of the Midwest Association for Public Opinion Research. Combining his political communication work with university-related governing, he served as chair of the Department of Communication and director of the School of Communication at Cleveland State from 2003–2011.

Brian L. Quick (PhD, Texas A&M University, 2005) is an Associate Professor in the Department of Communication at the University of Illinois at Urbana-Champaign. His work examines the role of cognition and emotion in processing persuasive health ads as well as analyzing media portrayals of health issues to understand how these messages create, change, and reinforce belief structures. His research has published in the *American Journal of Transplantation, Communication Research, Health Communication, Human Communication Research;* the *Journal of Applied Communication Research;* the *Journal of Broadcasting and Electronic Media;* the *Journal of Health Communication*, and other outlets.

John C. Reinard (PhD, University of Southern California, 1975) is a Professor and Chair of Communication Studies at California State University, Fullerton. His research has focused on persuasion, communication and the law, communication and stress, and argumentation. The Communication Institute for Online Scholarship has listed him as one of the top 50 scholars in persuasion and in the study of communication and the law. He is the author of *Introduction to Communication Research* (now in its fourth edition, in addition to an international and Chinese language version), *Communication Research Statistics*, and *Foundations of Argument: Effective Communication for Critical Thinking.*

Nancy Rhodes (PhD, Texas A&M University, 1991) is an Associate Professor of Communication Studies at Indiana University–Purdue University Indianapolis (IUPUI).

Her research interests are at the intersection of Communication and Psychology; she is particularly interested the study of persuasion and social influence in the context of health-risk behaviors such as cigarette smoking, underage drinking, and teen risky driving. She also has research interests in gender roles as they relate to healthy and unhealthy behavior.

Charles T. Salmon (PhD, University of Minnesota, 1985) is a Professor and Director of Graduate Research Programmes in the Wee Kim Wee School of Communication and Information at Nanyang Technological University in Singapore. His current research focuses on communication and public will, unintended effects of communication campaigns, and health and environmental communication. He has been a Rockefeller Foundation Scholar in Bellagio, Italy, a Fulbright Scholar at Tel Aviv University, Israel, and a Visiting Scientist at the U.S. Centers for Disease Control and Prevention.

Kiwon Seo is a PhD candidate in the Department of Communication Arts and Sciences at The Pennsylvania State University. His research interests include effects of visual image, emotion, and message framing on persuasion.

Lijiang Shen (PhD, University of Wisconsin–Madison, 2005) is an Associate Professor in the Department of Communication Studies at the University of Georgia. His primary area of research considers the impact of message features and audience characteristics in persuasive health communication, cognition, and affect in message processing and the process of persuasion/resistance to persuasion; and quantitative research methods in communication.

L. J. Shrum (PhD, University of Illinois) is a Professor and Chair of Marketing at the University of Texas at San Antonio. His research applies social cognition concepts to understand the determinants of consumer judgments. He has written extensively on the psychological processes underlying the effects of media on judgments. His most recent research is on the multiple roles of the self in consumer judgment, particularly with respect to self-threat and its influence on conspicuous consumption and materialism. His most recent edited book is the second edition of *The Psychology of Entertainment Media: Blurring the Lines between Entertainment and Persuasion*.

Jason T. Siegel (PhD, University of Arizona, 2004) is a Research Associate Professor of Psychology at Claremont Graduate University's School of Behavioral and Organizational Sciences. His research typically involves the application of social psychological theories to the health domain. Organ donation and substance abuse have been a central focus of Dr. Siegel's research. Most recently, Jason has been exploring means of persuading people with depression.

Akshaya Sreenivasan is a PhD candidate in the College of Communications at The Pennsylvania State University. Her research interests include the psychological aspects of communications technology and the use of information and communication technologies for development (ICT4D). She is currently working on a project that investigates the impact of augmented reality in health communications campaigns. Additionally, she is also part of the technology for development forum at Penn State University.

Ye Sun (PhD, University of Madison–Wisconsin, 2008) is an Assistant Professor in the Department of Communication at the University of Utah. Her research focuses on individuals' perceptions of media messages and the indirect effects of persuasion. Her research on the third-person effect has appeared in the *Journal of Communication* and *Communication Research.* She is a recipient of the John E. Hunter Award for Meta-Analysis.

S. Shyam Sundar (PhD, Stanford) is a Distinguished Professor and founding Director of the Media Effects Research Laboratory at Penn State University. He also holds a visiting appointment as World Class University (WCU) Professor of Interaction Science at Sungkyunkwan University in Seoul, Korea. His research investigates social and psychological effects of technological elements unique to online communication, ranging from web sites to social media. Sundar has been identified as the most published author of Internet-related research in the field during the medium's first decade. He was elected chair of the Communication and Technology division and Vice-President of the International Communication Association, 2008–2010.

John M. Tchernev (BS, Northwestern University, 2001) is a doctoral student in the School of Communication at The Ohio State University who formerly worked as a professional television writer. His research involves persuasion in media entertainment contexts, with particular focus given to narrative influence and political satire. Some of his recent peer-reviewed works have appeared in *Journal of Communication* and *Mass Communication and Society.*

Marco Yzer (PhD, University of Groningen, 1999) is an Associate Professor in the School of Journalism and Mass Communication at the University of Minnesota, and adjunct Associate Professor in the University of Minnesota's School of Public Health. His research focuses on motivational processes that explain how mass-mediated and interpersonal communication facilitate or inhibit health behavior. His work has appeared in communication, psychology, and public health journals, and has been supported by the National Institutes of Health.

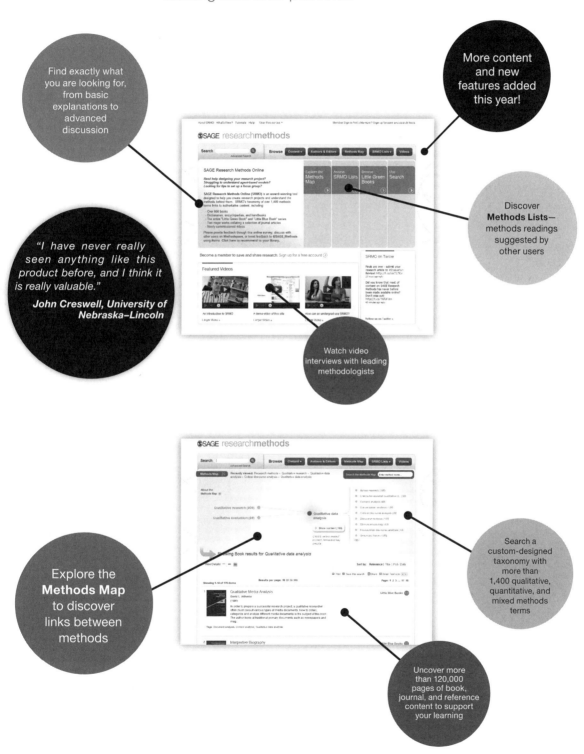

⑤SAGE research**methods**

The essential online tool for researchers from the world's leading methods publisher

Find exactly what you are looking for, from basic explanations to advanced discussion

More content and new features added this year!

Discover **Methods Lists**— methods readings suggested by other users

"I have never really seen anything like this product before, and I think it is really valuable."

John Creswell, University of Nebraska–Lincoln

Watch video interviews with leading methodologists

Explore the **Methods Map** to discover links between methods

Search a custom-designed taxonomy with more than 1,400 qualitative, quantitative, and mixed methods terms

Uncover more than 120,000 pages of book, journal, and reference content to support your learning

Find out more at
www.sageresearchmethods.com